MOUNT CARMEL S			
STUDENT		YEAR	
Kathryn Stamp	208	93/4	
Chris Fowler	Period 2	Fall 94	
HOFFMANN JEFF CARON	205	95	V. GOOD
Chrissy Frohlich	205	96	Very Good

MATH IN CONTEXT 9

AUTHORS

Frank Ebos, Senior Author
Faculty of Education
University of Toronto

David W. McKillop
Nova Scotia Teacher's College
Truro, Nova Scotia

Elizabeth Milne
Cowichan Secondary School
Duncan, British Columbia

Barbara J. Morrison
Calgary Separate School Board
Calgary, Alberta

Kay Whelan
Labrador City Collegiate
Labrador City, Newfoundland

CONTRIBUTING WRITERS

Bill J. Walters
Oshawa, Ontario

Wally Webster
London, Ontario

NATIONAL REVIEWERS/CONSULTANTS

Jean Crawford
Calgary, Alberta

Albert J. Dalton
St. John's, Newfoundland

Katie Pallos-Haden
Edmonton, Alberta

Ron Woo
Coquitlam, British Columbia

ONTARIO REVIEWERS/CONSULTANTS

Karen A. Allan
Whitby, Ontario

K. Appleby
London, Ontario

John Battaglia
Windsor, Ontario

Doug Benton
Uxbridge, Ontario

Frank Di Pietro
Windsor, Ontario

Mary Donaghy
Orleans, Ontario

William C. Farmer
Thunder Bay, Ontario

Don Gray
Windsor, Ontario

Ron Lancaster
Oakville, Ontario

Jeri Lunney
Ottawa, Ontario

Gerry MacMillan
Port Dover, Ontario

E. Mandzuk
St. Catharines, Ontario

Ann Pearce
Oxford, Ontario

H.E.M. Sandblom
Onaping, Ontario

Rick White
Pickering, Ontario

Rod Yeager
Orangeville, Ontario

Nelson Canada wishes to thank the following schools and students for their contribution during classroom testing: Pine Ridge Secondary School, Pickering; Gloucester High School, Ottawa; Medway High School, London; St. Mildred's-Lightbourn School, Oakville; Orangeville District Secondary School, Orangeville.

Nelson Canada

© Nelson Canada
A Division of Thomson Canada Ltd., 1993

Published in 1993 by
Nelson Canada,
A Division of Thomson Canada, Ltd.
1120 Birchmount Road
Scarborough, Ontario
M1K 5G4

ISBN 0-17-603069-7

Canadian Cataloguing in Publication Data

Ebos. Frank, 1939–
    Math in context 9

Includes index.
ISBN 0-17-603069-7

1. Mathematics.   I. Title.

QA107.E36   1993   510   C93–093867–4

The symbol for year is a. For the sake of clarity,
the word year has been used, in full, in place of a.

Printed and bound in Canada

23456789 / FP / 9876543

Project Manager   Colin Garnham
Project Editor   Tony Rodrigues
Editorial Consultant   Joe Banel
Mathematics Consultant   David Hamilton
Editorial Manager   Susan Green
Senior Production Editor   Sandra Manley
Art Director   Bruce Bond
Series Design   Rob McPhail
Cover Design   Liz Nyman
Designers   John Robb, Hania Fil, Julia Hall
Photo Research and Permissions   Vicki Hunter,
    Ann Ludbrook
Associate Editors   Diane Brassolotto, Stephen Cowie,
    Deborah Davies, David Gargaro, Anna-Maria
    Garnham

The authors wish to express their thanks to
Rose Mary Ebos, Andrew Clowes, Lesley Ebos,
Lori Ebos, Michael Ebos, Bill Allan, and Sharon Kerr.

Illustration

Creative Art
Kathryn Adams: 294; Deborah Crowle: 399, 420; Don
Gauthier: 257, 285, 180, 185 (top), 230 (top), 241 (top),
491; Scott Gwilliams: 332, 205, 241 (bottom), 136; Chris
Hayes: 423; Ron Job: 70, 71, 96, 138, 185 (centre), 189,
191, 192, 193, 207, 230 (bottom), 236, 324, 331, 401, 411
(top), 429; Robert Johannsen: 57, 62, 86, 232; Don Kilby:
215; Stuart Knox: 339; Susan Leopold: 145, 201; Pierre-
Paul Pariseau: 83, 291, 311; Maureen Paxton: 108, 120,
310, 426; Margo Stahl: 105; Marion Stuck: 153; Bart
Vallecoccia: 250; Paul Zwolak: 204

Technical Art
Frank Zsigo, Julia Hall

TABLE OF CONTENTS

CHAPTER 1 SENSE OF MATHEMATICS

CHAPTER 2 BUILDING GEOMETRY

CHAPTER 9 WORKING WITH ALGEBRA

CHAPTER 10 PROBLEM SOLVING WITH ALGEBRA

CHAPTER 11 WORKING BACKWARDS

CHAPTER 12 RELATIONS AND FUNCTIONS

CHAPTER 13   GEOMETRY

CHAPTER 14   DATA MANAGEMENT

CHAPTER 15   WORKING WITH TRANSFORMATIONS

Here are some features you will find in your book.

Math in a Real Context
Your book will help you see how math relates to everyday situations.

Problem Solving
There are many opportunities for you to learn and apply problem solving skills.

- Activities in all chapters help you develop problem solving skills and strategies.

- Skills and strategies for working with mathematics are organized using your *Problem Solving Plan.*

Manipulatives
Many activities use various materials to help you explore new concepts and develop new skills.

Working Together
Activities throughout the book give you the chance to learn mathematics with a partner or in a small group.

Making Connections
Your book continually encourages you to apply the skills you have learned and involves you in research to extend your learning.

Math Journal
Keeping a journal can help you express your insights about mathematics. Keeping a journal also encourages you to summarize what you learn, using examples of your own.

You Already Know...
These remind you of skills and strategies you have worked with earlier.

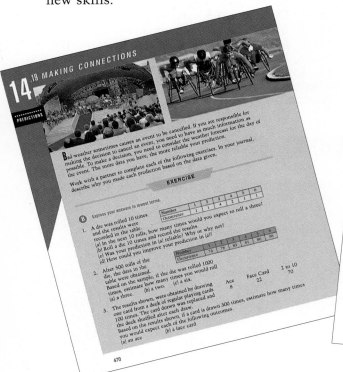

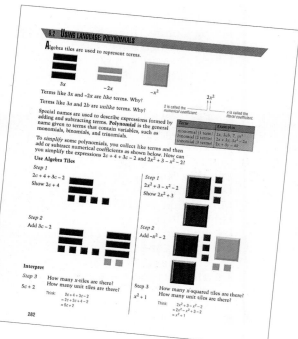

Technology

The "Technology Insight" pages extend your understanding of the impact of technology on everyday activities. These pages also include features of scientific and graphics calculators, as well as provide insight into computers.

Calculators

Watch for calculator key sequences suggested throughout the book. These sequences show how you can use a calculator more effectively.

Explorations

Exploration activities help you to develop mathematical concepts for yourself.

Across the Curriculum

Look for thematic pages that extend the relevance of mathematics in the study of other disciplines.

Projects

Look for projects that you can try throughout the book. The projects show you how your mathematics is applied in different fields of study.

Calculation Sense

These activities extend your ability to select appropriate calculation strategies.

Self Evaluation

Your book provides you with many opportunities to check your knowledge and to think about the strategies you use when working with mathematics.

Review

Chapter reviews and cumulative reviews offer you a chance to look back and practise the mathematics you have learned and the problem solving skills and strategies you have used.

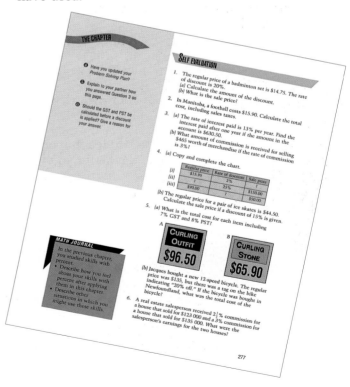

PROBLEM SOLVING

In previous years, you started developing your skills for solving problems. You were asked to solve two kinds of problems.

The skill or strategy you need to solve a problem is immediately evident.

Since you recognize the skill or strategy to use, you plan your solution and solve the problem.

The skill or strategy you need to solve a problem is not immediately evident.

Since you do not immediately recognize the solution, you need a plan that allows you to look for clues, to ask yourself key questions, and so on.

To solve any problem successfully, you need to decide what the answers are to these two questions:

What information does the problem ask me to find?

What information is given to me in the problem?

Once you clearly understand the answers to these questions, you can develop your plan of attack. Sometimes, to solve a problem, you can use a systematic approach. Other times, you need to be more inventive and creative. Page 41 of Chapter 1 shows a plan that will help you develop the best approach.

As you seek solutions to problems and acquire skills and strategies, you begin to accumulate a list of key questions to ask yourself in order to help you decide upon a strategy.

ACTIVITY 1
(a) Make a list of key questions you have asked yourself in order to help you solve a problem.
(b) Create a problem of your own that can be solved by asking the questions in part (a).

There is no simple approach to learn in order to solve problems. However, the more practice and experience you have, the better you will become at solving problems. By building a framework of key questions, strategies, and experiences, you better equip yourself to solve problems.

Try the problems on the next page. Keep a list in your journal of key questions and strategies you use.

ACTIVITY 2
Your math book will introduce you to other problem solving strategies.
(a) Look through this math book and list some of the problem solving strategies used.
(b) Compare your list in (a) with the problem solving strategies you use to solve the problems on the next page. What new strategies did you find in (a) that might have helped you solve the problems on the next page?

1. Michael and Yoshio were supposed to be at school by 8:30. Michael's watch was 7 min fast and Yoshio's watch was 6 min slow. They both thought they had arrived 5 min late.
   (a) What time did they each actually arrive at school?
   (b) What was the difference in time between their watches?

2. Sometimes, when trying to solve a problem, you might be "stumped" because you do not know the meaning of all the words.
   (a) Read the problem shown carefully. Do you understand all the words?
   (b) Solve the problem.
   (c) Create and solve a similar problem of your own. Compare your problem to others.

   > In how many ways can you serve seven different courses of a meal?

3. To solve some problems, you can begin by listing possible answers and deciding which ones are correct.
   (a) Write the most recent year that reads the same backwards, forwards, and upside down.
   (b) Write the first year after Confederation that reads the same backwards, forwards, and upside down.

4. The knight in chess makes a move by moving two squares in one direction and then one square in the perpendicular direction as shown.
   (a) Can the knight move to every square of the grid shown without landing on the same square twice?
   (b) Create a similar problem of your own. Solve the problem. Compare your problem to others in the class.

   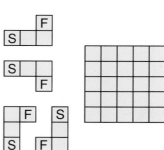

5. A chart is often helpful to sort out information in a problem. Use a chart for each of the following.
   (a) Samuel, James, and Malivai are married to Jennifer, Samantha, and Christine but not necessarily in that order. Who is married to whom?

   - Samantha's sister is married to Malivai.
   - Samuel has never met Christine.
   - Christine is an only child.

   (b) Peter, Steven, and Pitman are brothers who exercise regularly. One lifts weights, another cycles, and the third swims. Use the following clues to find out how each brother exercises.

   - Peter cannot swim.
   - Steven does not own a bike.
   - Pitman does not like the outdoors.

6. (a) Diophantus was a Greek mathematician. When he died, his epitaph offered a challenge as shown. Based on the information, how long did Diophantus live?
   (b) In your library, find out more about Diophantus and his contributions to the study of mathematics.

   > Diophantus
   > passed $\frac{1}{6}$ of his life in childhood, $\frac{1}{12}$ in youth and $\frac{1}{7}$ as a bachelor. His son was born 5 years after his marriage, but died 4 years before his father did, and only lived to $\frac{1}{2}$ of his father's age.

MATHEMATICS AS COMMUNICATION

Regularly listening, speaking, reading, and writing about mathematics will help your understanding grow. Working together with others in your class, either in pairs or in groups, gives you good opportunities to discuss mathematical ideas.

ACTIVITY 1

(a) Select one of the following topics with which you are familiar.
  (i)   Adding numbers on your calculator.
  (ii) Subtracting numbers on your calculator.
  (iii) Multiplying numbers on your calculator.
  (iv) Dividing numbers on your calculator.
(b) Explain to others in the class how you can use your calculator to add, subtract, multiply, or divide numbers on your calculator.
(c) Be prepared to answer any questions about your explanation.

ACTIVITY 2

Locate the glossary and indexes at the back of this book.

(a) What do you think is the purpose of the glossary? the indexes?

(b) In your journal, write a brief paragraph explaining how you can use the glossary and the indexes to help you learn mathematics.

ACTIVITY 3

In your journal, list some everyday words (like sum and probability) that you also use in mathematics.

(a) Compare the ordinary way you use each word to the way you use each word mathematically. How are the uses alike? How are they different?

(b) As you learn new mathematical words throughout the year, write them in your journal. Compare the way you use each word in everyday language to the way you use each word mathematically. How are the uses alike? How are they different?

LINKS TO REAL LIFE

Did you know that mathematics is used constantly by everyone, both in the world of work and in everyday life? Mathematics is always shaping and changing the way we live.

LOOKING AHEAD 1

Refer to the "Making Connections" section on page 48 of Chapter 1.
(a) How can your skills with fractions help you to complete the exercise?
(b) Look through the rest of the book to find the sections that have "Making Connections" as part of their title. Make a list of the different careers in which mathematics is applied. In your journal, describe whether you would wish to pursue any of these careers. Give reasons for your answer.

LINKS TO OTHER SUBJECTS

LOOKING AHEAD 2

Refer to the sections you found in the previous "Looking Ahead" activity.
(a) How do these sections relate to other subjects you study in school?
(b) How can mathematics help you in other subject areas? Give an example.

LINKS WITHIN MATHEMATICS

Knowing how one area of mathematics affects another can help you solve problems.

LOOKING AHEAD 3

Refer to Section 1.2 of this book.
(a) List some of the skills you need to complete the section.
(b) Describe how your skills in (a) can be used as you complete Section 1.2.
(c) In what other parts of mathematics can these skills also be helpful?
(d) Pick your own math topic. Repeat parts (a), (b), and (c) for your topic.

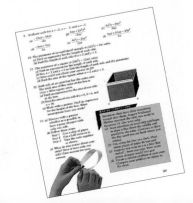

You can often discover relationships by organizing information and looking for a pattern.

LOOKING AHEAD

(a) Complete the explorations below. Decide on the best way to organize your work.
(b) In your journal, describe any patterns and relationships you notice.
(c) Describe how your organization in (a) can help you complete other explorations.

EXPLORATION ① *Work Together*

1. Use a rectangular piece of paper.
   (a) Fold a piece of paper in half. Then open it. How many times have you folded the paper? Into how many equal parts is the paper divided?
   (b) Fold the piece of paper in half again. How many times have you folded the piece of paper? Into how many equal parts is the paper divided?

2. Keep using the piece of paper in Question 1.
   (a) Fold the piece of paper in half again. How many times have you folded the paper?
   (b) Into how many equal parts is the paper divided?

3. (a) Use another piece of paper. Fold it in half as many times as you like.
   (b) Have others in the group predict the number of equal parts into which the paper will be divided. Open up the paper to verify the prediction.

EXPLORATION ② *Work Together*

In the previous exploration, you folded a single piece of paper in half to obtain 2 equal parts. When you folded the paper in half again, you obtained 4 equal parts. If this process were continued 3 more times, the number of equal parts would be found as $2 \times 2 \times 2 \times 2 \times 2 = 32$.

4. Expressions like the one above can be written in a more compact form.
   (a) Describe any patterns you see in the completed part of the chart.
   (b) Copy and complete the chart. Refer to your patterns in (a).
   (c) Refer to Exploration 1. Write, in exponent form, the numerals used.

Factor Form	Exponent Form	
$2 \times 2 \times 2 \times 2 \times 2$	2^5	Five is the number of times 2 is repeated. It is read as "two to the exponent five."
$(+3) \times (+3) \times (+3)$	$(+3)^3$	
$(-5) \times (-5) \times (-5) \times (-5)$	$(-5)^4$	
$3 \times 3 \times 3 \times 3 \times 3 \times 3$		
$(-2) \times (-2)$		

5. Look ahead to the work with exponents on page 24.
   (a) How can the skills on page 24 help you?
   (b) What other skills did you learn on page 24?

During the year, you will work with partners and in small groups to develop your mathematical skills and strategies.

LOOKING AHEAD 1

Here are some ideas that can help you work and learn cooperatively with others.
- Give praise for a job well done.
- Provide help *and* ask for help.
- Value other opinions.
- Make sure everyone has a chance to participate.
- Use a quiet voice. Your voice should carry only far enough so that all members of the group can hear you.

(a) In your journal, add to the list above by writing ways that you have found helpful when working with others.

(b) In your journal, make a list of ways that you feel will help you contribute more to the success of a group through this year.

LOOKING AHEAD 2

Look through your book for activities that involve working in pairs or in groups.

(a) How do you think working with others will help you learn mathematics? Write your answers in your journal.

(b) How can you contribute even more to the group?

(c) How can you encourage others to participate more in the group?

LOOKING AHEAD 3

(a) Try the explorations with fractions and exponents that follow on pages 20–21 and 25–27. What will you explore?

(b) How do you think working with others will help you learn the mathematics in the explorations?

TECHNOLOGY IN MATHEMATICS

Technology and mathematics strongly support and serve each other.

- Technology can help you solve mathematical problems.
- A knowledge of mathematics is often needed in the development of new technology.

LOOKING AHEAD 1

Look through the book for the "Technology Insight" pages.
(a) What kinds of technology do you see?
(b) What careers that involve technology can you list?
(c) How do you think working with technology can help you learn mathematics?

LOOKING AHEAD 2

Look through the book for calculator key sequences.
(a) Which key sequences would you use on a scientific calculator? on a graphics calculator?
(b) In your journal, describe when you think it is most appropriate to use a calculator. When is it less appropriate to use a calculator?
(c) Make a list of the keys on your calculator that you use most often. Describe the function of each key.
(d) Make a list of all other keys. Refer to the manual for your calculator. What is the function of each key?

SELF EVALUATION

Your book offers many opportunities to check your progress in mathematics. You will find a page at the end of each chapter, as well as features throughout each chapter, devoted to self evaluation.

LOOKING AHEAD 1

As you solve problems throughout the year, ask yourself questions like the following to help you evaluate your progress.

- Am I applying the strategies I have learned?
- Can I reword the problem in a simpler form?
- Can I summarize my observations verbally and in writing?
- Are my answers reasonable? How do I know?
- Have I made any assumptions? What are they?

Add to this list throughout the year. Keep your list of questions in your journal.

LOOKING AHEAD 2

Refer to the explorations of fractions on pages 20–21 and explorations of exponents on pages 25–27.
(a) List any new words that you learn in the explorations.
(b) How can you summarize the skills you learn in the explorations?
(c) How do you think keeping neat notes will help you in the future?
(d) Flip through the rest of your math book. How can these skills help you as you learn other mathematics?

LOOKING AHEAD 3

(a) Begin the year by copying the *Self-help Checklist* into your journal.
(b) Keep tests and exams to show your progress. How can you use them to help you learn?

Self-Help Checklist	
– What do I already know about this topic that can help me?	– Is there a pattern here that will help?
– What do I need to know before I continue?	– What assumptions am I making? Are they right?
– Which words are most important?	– Does this problem remind me of anything else?
– Did I follow the instructions logically?	– Who can I ask for help?

When developing skills to solve problems, manipulatives can often help.

EXPLORATION ①

1. (a) Use a sheet of paper. Fold the paper into eight equal parts.

   (b) Shade $\frac{1}{2}$ of the paper. How many parts have been shaded in all?

   (c) Shade a further $\frac{1}{8}$ of the sheet. What fraction of the paper has been shaded in all? What is $\frac{1}{2} + \frac{1}{8}$?

2. (a) Use another sheet of paper. Fold the paper into ten equal parts.

   (b) Shade $\frac{1}{2}$ of the paper. How many parts have been shaded in all?

   (c) Shade a further $\frac{1}{5}$ of the paper. What fraction of the paper has been shaded in all? What is $\frac{1}{2} + \frac{1}{5}$?

EXPLORATION ②

3. (a) Use a sheet of paper. Fold the paper into eight equal parts.

   (b) Cut out $\frac{1}{2}$ of the paper. How many folded parts have you cut out?

   (c) Use the piece of the paper from (b). Cut out three folded parts. What fraction of the original sheet have you cut out?

   (d) How much of the original sheet do you have left? What is $\frac{4}{8} - \frac{3}{8}$?

   (e) What is the value of $\frac{1}{2} - \frac{3}{8}$?

4. (a) Use another sheet of paper. Fold the paper into six equal parts.

   (b) Cut out $\frac{2}{3}$ of the paper. How many folded parts have you cut out?

   (c) Use the piece from (b). Cut out three folded parts. What fraction of the original sheet have you cut out?

   (d) How much of the original sheet do you have left? What is $\frac{4}{6} - \frac{3}{6}$?

   (e) What is the value of $\frac{2}{3} - \frac{1}{2}$?

5. (a) Write addition and subtraction expressions of your own using fractions.
   (b) Find the difference of your fractions in (a).

EXPLORING FRACTIONS

Fractions occur frequently in your everyday activities. **Fractions** are used to describe part of a whole.

In the explorations, sheets of paper are used to show you ways to communicate with fractions. Work with others in the class to complete each exploration. You can also use other manipulatives. Look at page 44 of Chapter 1 to see other manipulatives you can use.

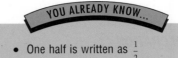

YOU ALREADY KNOW...

- One half is written as $\frac{1}{2}$
- One quarter is written $\frac{1}{4}$

EXPLORATION ① *Work Together*

1. Use a sheet of paper.
   (a) Fold the sheet of paper to show three equal parts.
   (b) Now fold the paper in half.
   (c) Unfold the sheet of paper. How many equal parts are there?
   (d) Write a fraction to describe each equal part in (c).

2. Use another sheet of paper.
   (a) Fold the paper in half, then in half again, and then in half again.
   (b) Unfold the sheet of paper. How many equal parts are there?
   (c) Write a fraction to describe each equal part in (b).

3. Use another sheet of paper.
   (a) Fold the paper into as many equal parts as you wish.
   (b) Have others in your group write a fraction to describe each equal part in (a).

EXPLORATION ② *Work Together*

4. (a) Fold a sheet of paper in half.
   (b) Fold another sheet of paper in half and then in half again.

   (c) Compare the equal parts in each piece of paper. How is $\frac{1}{2}$ related to $\frac{2}{4}$?

   (d) Fold another sheet of paper into eight equal parts.

   (e) Compare your sheets of paper. How is $\frac{1}{2}$ related to $\frac{4}{8}$?

   (f) How is $\frac{2}{4}$ related to $\frac{4}{8}$?

5. Refer to your results in Question 4.

   (a) Write three other fractions that are related to $\frac{1}{2}$ in a similar way.

   (b) Explain to the other members of your group any patterns and relationships you used to write the fractions.

   (c) Write fractions of your own. Use your patterns and relationships in (b) to write three other fractions that are *equivalent* to your fractions.

6. (a) Use a piece of paper. Fold the paper into four equal parts.
   (b) What fraction of the paper is in each equal part? What is $\frac{1}{4}$ of one?

   (c) Interpret your result in (b). What is $\frac{1}{4} \times 1$?

7. Use ten counters like those shown.
   (a) Separate the counters into two equal parts.
   (b) How many counters are in each part?

   What is $\frac{1}{2}$ of ten?

   (c) Interpret your result in (b). What is $\frac{1}{2} \times 10$?

8. Use the counters in Question 7.
   (a) Separate the counters into five equal parts.
   (b) How many counters are in each part? What is $\frac{1}{5}$ of ten?

   (c) Interpret your result in (b). What is $\frac{1}{5} \times 10$?

9. (a) Use a piece of paper. Fold the paper into two equal parts.
   (b) How much of the paper is in each part?
   (c) Take one part and fold it into four equal parts. How much of the original piece of paper

   is in each part? What is $\frac{1}{4}$ of $\frac{1}{2}$?

   (d) Interpret your result in (c). What is $\frac{1}{4} \times \frac{1}{2}$?

10. Use a piece of paper to illustrate each of the following.

   (a) $\frac{1}{2}$ of $\frac{1}{3}$ (b) $\frac{3}{4}$ of $\frac{1}{2}$ (c) $\frac{1}{4}$ of $\frac{2}{3}$ (d) $\frac{3}{4}$ of $\frac{1}{6}$ (e) $\frac{1}{2}$ of $\frac{1}{6}$

   (f) $\frac{2}{3} \times \frac{1}{8}$ (g) $\frac{2}{3} \times \frac{1}{5}$ (h) $\frac{4}{5} \times \frac{2}{3}$ (i) $\frac{3}{4} \times \frac{2}{3}$ (j) $\frac{1}{3} \times \frac{1}{6}$

11. (a) Use three pieces of paper. Fold each piece into two equal parts.
    (b) Refer to your paper in (a). How many equal parts are there?

    (c) Interpret your result in (b). What is $3 \div \frac{1}{2}$?

12. (a) Use two pieces of paper. Fold each piece into four equal parts.
    (b) Refer to your paper in (a). How many equal parts are there?

    (c) Interpret your result in (b). What is $2 \div \frac{1}{4}$?

LOOKING AHEAD

Four mathematical skills are shown on these pages.
(a) Do each of the following calculations.
(b) Describe how you used the skills in the explorations to do each calculation.
(c) Look through the rest of the book. What math skills will you explore?

Adding Fractions

To add fractions, you need to find equivalent fractions with a common denominator.

$$\frac{2}{3} + \frac{1}{4} = \frac{8}{12} + \frac{3}{12}$$

$$= \frac{11}{12}$$

Think: $\frac{2}{3} = \frac{2 \times 4}{3 \times 4}$

$= \frac{8}{12}$

1. Find each sum.

    (a) $\frac{1}{10} + \frac{1}{10}$ (b) $\frac{1}{4} + \frac{3}{4}$ (c) $\frac{3}{5} + \frac{1}{5}$

2. Add.

    (a) $\frac{3}{4} + \frac{1}{2}$ (b) $\frac{5}{6} + \frac{1}{3}$ (c) $\frac{3}{10} + \frac{2}{5}$

3. Calculate.

    (a) $\frac{1}{2} + \frac{1}{3}$ (b) $\frac{2}{3} + \frac{1}{4}$ (c) $\frac{3}{5} + \frac{1}{3}$

    (d) $\frac{3}{8} + \frac{1}{3}$ (e) $\frac{3}{4} + \frac{1}{6}$ (f) $\frac{2}{3} + \frac{1}{10}$

The skills you learn for adding fractions extend to mixed numbers.

4. Find the sum of mixed fractions.

    (a) $3\frac{1}{4} + 2\frac{1}{4}$ (b) $3\frac{1}{5} + 2\frac{3}{5}$ (c) $2\frac{1}{3} + 3\frac{2}{3}$

5. Find the sum.

    (a) $1\frac{1}{2} + 3\frac{1}{4}$ (b) $2\frac{1}{3} + 2\frac{1}{6}$ (c) $3\frac{1}{4} + 1\frac{3}{8}$

Subtracting Fractions

To subtract fractions, you need to find equivalent fractions with a common denominator.

$$\frac{2}{3} - \frac{1}{4} = \frac{8}{12} - \frac{3}{12}$$

$$= \frac{5}{12}$$

Think: $\frac{1}{4}$ and $\frac{3}{12}$ are **equivalent fractions.**

1. Find the difference.

    (a) $\frac{4}{5} - \frac{1}{5}$ (b) $\frac{3}{4} - \frac{1}{4}$ (c) $\frac{7}{10} - \frac{1}{10}$

2. Subtract.

    (a) $\frac{3}{4} - \frac{1}{2}$ (b) $\frac{4}{5} - \frac{1}{10}$ (c) $\frac{5}{6} - \frac{1}{3}$

3. Calculate.

    (a) $\frac{1}{2} - \frac{1}{3}$ (b) $\frac{2}{3} - \frac{1}{4}$ (c) $\frac{3}{5} - \frac{1}{3}$

    (d) $\frac{3}{8} - \frac{1}{3}$ (e) $\frac{3}{4} - \frac{1}{6}$ (f) $\frac{2}{3} - \frac{1}{10}$

The skills you learn for subtracting fractions extend to mixed numbers.

4. Find the difference.

    (a) $3\frac{1}{4} - 2\frac{1}{4}$ (b) $3\frac{3}{5} - 2\frac{1}{5}$ (c) $4\frac{2}{3} - 2\frac{1}{3}$

5. Subtract.

    (a) $3\frac{2}{3} - 1\frac{1}{2}$ (b) $6\frac{5}{6} - 3\frac{1}{4}$ (c) $8\frac{1}{3} - 2\frac{1}{5}$

    (d) $5\frac{1}{2} - 3\frac{3}{5}$ (e) $6\frac{2}{5} - 2\frac{3}{4}$ (f) $5\frac{1}{4} - 3\frac{2}{3}$

Multiplying Fractions

You multiply fractions as shown below.

$$\frac{1}{2} \times \frac{3}{5} = \frac{1 \times 3}{2 \times 5}$$
$$= \frac{3}{10}$$

1. Find each product.

   (a) $\frac{1}{2} \times \frac{1}{3}$ (b) $\frac{1}{2} \times \frac{1}{4}$ (c) $\frac{1}{2} \times \frac{1}{5}$

   (d) $\frac{1}{3} \times \frac{2}{3}$ (e) $\frac{2}{3} \times \frac{1}{5}$ (f) $\frac{3}{8} \times \frac{1}{2}$

2. Find each product.

   (a) $3 \times \frac{1}{3}$ (b) $8 \times \frac{1}{8}$ (c) $\frac{3}{4} \times \frac{4}{3}$

   (d) $\frac{5}{4} \times \frac{4}{5}$ (e) $\frac{3}{8} \times \frac{8}{3}$ (f) $\frac{9}{5} \times \frac{5}{9}$

   What do you notice about each of the above answers?

3. A product may be written as shown.

   $$\frac{2}{3} \times \frac{4}{5} = \left(\frac{2}{3}\right)\left(\frac{4}{5}\right)$$

   Find each product.

   (a) $\left(\frac{2}{3}\right)\left(\frac{1}{4}\right)$ (b) $\left(\frac{1}{6}\right)\left(\frac{3}{4}\right)$ (c) $\left(\frac{10}{3}\right)\left(\frac{3}{4}\right)$

   (d) $\left(\frac{3}{4}\right)\left(\frac{4}{5}\right)$ (e) $\left(\frac{7}{8}\right)\left(\frac{4}{5}\right)$ (f) $\left(\frac{3}{10}\right)\left(\frac{5}{6}\right)$

4. Multiply.

   (a) $\frac{2}{3} \times 2\frac{1}{3}$ (b) $\frac{1}{4} \times 3\frac{1}{8}$ (c) $\frac{3}{5} \times 1\frac{2}{3}$

   (d) $\frac{2}{3} \times 3\frac{1}{4}$ (e) $3\frac{1}{2} \times \frac{4}{5}$ (f) $3\frac{1}{8} \times \frac{4}{3}$

5. Calculate.

   (a) $1\frac{1}{8} \times \frac{8}{9}$ (b) $\frac{3}{4} \times 1\frac{1}{3}$ (c) $\frac{2}{5} \times 2\frac{1}{2}$

   (d) $1\frac{1}{5} \times \frac{5}{6}$ (e) $\frac{3}{8} \times 2\frac{2}{3}$ (f) $\frac{4}{5} \times 1\frac{1}{4}$

   What do you notice about each of the above answers?

Dividing Fractions

To divide a fraction, you invert and multiply as shown below.

$$\frac{3}{4} \div \frac{2}{3} = \frac{3}{4} \times \frac{3}{2}$$
$$= \frac{9}{8}$$

1. Calculate.

   (a) $\frac{3}{4} \div \frac{1}{4}$ (b) $\frac{3}{5} \div \frac{1}{5}$ (c) $\frac{5}{9} \div \frac{1}{3}$

2. Simplify.

   (a) $\frac{3}{8} \div \frac{1}{2}$ (b) $\frac{5}{6} \div \frac{2}{3}$ (c) $\frac{4}{9} \div \frac{3}{4}$

   (d) $\frac{3}{8} \div \frac{3}{4}$ (e) $\frac{8}{9} \div \frac{8}{12}$ (f) $\frac{4}{7} \div \frac{7}{8}$

3. Simplify.

   (a) $\frac{5}{6} \div 5$ (b) $\frac{3}{4} \div 9$ (c) $\frac{7}{9} \div 7$

   (d) $\frac{9}{10} \div 6$ (e) $3 \div \frac{3}{5}$ (f) $9 \div \frac{3}{4}$

4. Simplify each of the following. Be sure you read carefully!

   (a) $14 \div \frac{7}{10}$ (b) $9 \div \frac{4}{3}$ (c) $12 \div \frac{2}{3}$

   (d) $24 \div \frac{3}{4}$ (e) $56 \div \frac{8}{7}$ (f) $15 \div \frac{3}{2}$

   (g) $36 \div \frac{1}{4}$ (h) $48 \div \frac{8}{5}$ (i) $32 \div \frac{1}{4}$

5. Simplify.

   (a) $5\frac{1}{2} \div 18$ (b) $3 \div 1\frac{1}{2}$ (c) $6\frac{2}{3} \div \frac{4}{5}$

   (d) $63 \div 1\frac{1}{8}$ (e) $9\frac{1}{3} \div 2\frac{1}{3}$ (f) $7\frac{3}{5} \div 3\frac{4}{5}$

6. Calculate each of the following.

   (a) $64 \div \frac{1}{2}$ (b) $\frac{6}{5} \times \frac{3}{2}$ (c) $12 \div \frac{15}{16}$

COMMUNICATING WITH EXPONENTS

In mathematics, words are often used to describe relationships. The number shown to the right is written in *exponent* form. Each part has a special name as shown.

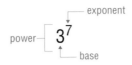

When communicating with exponents, you can use special words.

You can read 3^2 as "three squared."

Think: You can visually think of 3^2 using this square.

Remember: $3^2 = 9$

You can read 3^3 as "three cubed."

Think: You can visually think of 3^3 using this cube.

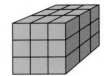

Remember: $3^3 = 27$

EXERCISE

1. Find the missing exponent.
   (a) $5^? = 25$ (b) $10^? = 1000$ (c) $2^? = 32$ (d) $4^? = 256$
   (e) $3^? = 243$ (f) $7^? = 49$ (g) $9^? = 729$ (h) $6^? = 216$

2. Evaluate.
   (a) $3^4 + 3$ (b) $3^5 \div 3^2$ (c) $3^4 - 3^3$ (d) $3^5 \times 3^4$
   (e) $4^5 + 4^2$ (f) $6^2 \div 6$ (g) $5^6 - 5^2$ (h) $4^3 - 4$

3. Evaluate each expression. Communicate each expression to your partner.
   (a) $4^3 + 4^2$ (b) $5^3 - 3^3$ (c) $9^2 - 5^2$ (d) $3^3 + 3^2$
   (e) $3^5 + 2^4$ (f) $7^3 - 4^3$ (g) $8^2 - 9$ (h) $4^4 - 3^3$

4. Calculate.
   (a) $3^5 - 4^2$ (b) $2^8 - 3^2$ (c) $5^2 + 3^4$ (d) $6^3 + 3^5$
   (e) $6^3 - 7^2$ (f) $5^5 - 3^5$ (g) $2^4 - 7$ (h) $4^5 - 4^2$

5. Evaluate.
   (a) $3^5 \times 3$ (b) $2^7 \times 2^3$ (c) $4^2 \times 4^3$ (d) $5^3 \times 5^2$
   (e) $4^4 \div 4^2$ (f) $3^6 \div 3^4$ (g) $7^3 \div 7^2$ (h) $5^5 \div 5^4$

6. Which is greater,
   (a) the sum of four cubed and three squared?
   (b) the difference of eight cubed and 75?
   (c) the product of three cubed and three cubed?
   (d) the quotient of seven cubed and fourteen?

7. Which expression has the greater value?
   (a) $3^3 + 2, 2^3 + 3$ (b) $4^4 \div 2^4, 4^4 - 2^4$ (c) $1^1 + 1^5, 1^1 + 15$

8. A solution has a paramecium cell and an amoeba cell. Over a period of time, the amoeba cell doubles four times and the paramecium cell doubles seven times. How many cells are now in the solution?

EXPLORING EXPONENTS

There are many patterns and relationships you can use to help you work with exponents.

EXPLORATION **Work Together**

1. Copy and complete the chart.

Expression	Expanded Form	Exponent Form
$4^3 \times 4^4$ $5^3 \times 5^2$ $3^2 \times 3^3$ $15^3 \times 15^3$	$(4 \times 4 \times 4) \times (4 \times 4 \times 4 \times 4)$ $(5 \times 5 \times 5) \times (5 \times 5)$ $(3 \times 3) \times (\square \times \square \times \square)$	$4^7 = 4^{4+3}$ $5^5 = 5^{3+2}$ $3^5 = 3^{\square}$

2. Refer to the chart in the previous question.
   (a) What patterns do you notice?
   (b) Communicate to the rest of your group how you can multiply powers with the same base.
   (c) Refer to your answers in (a) and (b). Write each of the following as a single power.
      (i) $4^3 \times 4^2$ (ii) $5^5 \times 5^8$ (iii) $11^4 \times 11^9$ (iv) $8^9 \times 8^3$
   (d) Create similar expressions of your own to those in (c). Evaluate each expression and have others in the group evaluate each expression.

3. Copy and complete the chart.

Expression	Expanded Form	Exponent Form
$4^3 \div 4^2$ $5^4 \div 5^2$ $3^4 \div 3^2$ $15^3 \div 15^3$	$(4 \times 4 \times 4) \div (4 \times 4)$ $(5 \times 5 \times 5 \times 5) \div (5 \times 5)$ $(3 \times 3 \times 3 \times 3) \div (\square \times \square)$	$4^1 = 4^{3-2}$ $5^2 = 5^{4-2}$ $3^2 = 3^{\square}$

4. Refer to the chart shown in the previous question.
   (a) What patterns do you notice?
   (b) Communicate to the rest of your group how you can **divide** powers with the same base.
   (c) Refer to your results in (a) and (b). Write each of the following as a single power.
      (i) $5^3 \div 5^2$ (ii) $9^9 \div 9^8$ (iii) $11^{14} \div 11^9$ (iv) $8^9 \div 8^3$
   (d) Create expressions of your own similar to those in (c). Evaluate each expression and have others in the group evaluate each expression.

EXPLORING OTHER EXPONENTS

In mathematics, you often explore patterns to simplify calculations.

EXPLORATION ① **Work Together**

1. Copy and complete the chart.

Expression	Expanded Form	Exponent Form
$(4^3)^2$	$(4^3) \times (4^3)$	$4^6 = 4^{3 \times 2}$
$(5^4)^2$	$(5^4) \times (5^4)$	$5^8 = 5^{4 \times 2}$
$(3^3)^4$	$(3^3) \times (3^3) \times (3^3) \times (3^3)$	$3^{12} = 3^{3 \times 4}$
$(15^3)^3$		

2. Refer to the chart in the previous question.
   (a) What patterns do you notice?
   (b) Communicate to the rest of your group how you can calculate the *power of a power*.
   (c) Refer to your results in (a) and (b). Write each of the following as a single power.

   (i) $(5^3)^2$ (ii) $(9^9)^8$ (iii) $(11^{14})^9$ (iv) $(8^9)^3$

   (d) Create expressions of your own similar to those in (c). Evaluate each expression and have others in the group evaluate each expression.

3. Copy and complete the chart.

Expression	Expanded Form	Exponent Form
$(4 \times 3)^2$	$(4 \times 3) \times (4 \times 3)$	$4^2 \times 3^2$
$(5 \times 3)^3$	$(5 \times 3) \times (5 \times 3) \times (5 \times 3)$	$5^3 \times 3^3$
$(7 \div 3)^3$	$(7 \div 3) \times (7 \div 3) \times (7 \div 3)$	$7^3 \div 3^3$
$\left(\dfrac{5}{3}\right)^3$	$\left(\dfrac{5}{3}\right) \times \left(\dfrac{5}{3}\right) \times \left(\dfrac{5}{3}\right)$	$\left(\dfrac{5^3}{3^3}\right)$

4. Refer to the chart shown in the previous question.
   (a) What patterns do you notice?
   (b) Communicate to the rest of your group how you can calculate the *power of a quotient*.
   (c) Refer to your results in (a) and (b). Write each in exponent form.

   (i) $(4 \times 7)^2$ (ii) $(12 \div 5)^8$ (iii) $(11 \times 4)^9$ (iv) $\left(\dfrac{3}{5}\right)^3$

   (d) Create expressions of your own similar to those in (c). Evaluate each expression and have others in the group evaluate each expression.

5. (a) Copy and complete. Use your patterns for multiplying powers.
    (i) $3^4 \times 3^0 = 3^?$ (ii) $4^5 \times 4^0 = 4^?$ (iii) $6^3 \times 6^0 = 6^?$
    (iv) $4^0 \times 4^7 = 4^?$ (v) $6^0 \times 6^3 = 6^?$ (vi) $5^0 \times 5^7 = 5^?$
   (b) Copy and complete. Use your patterns for dividing powers.
    (i) $3^4 \div 3^0 = 3^?$ (ii) $4^5 \div 4^0 = 4^?$ (iii) $6^3 \div 6^0 = 6^?$
    (iv) $7^6 \div 7^0 = 7^?$ (v) $11^{17} \div 11^0 = 11^?$ (vi) $8^9 \div 8^0 = 8^?$
   (c) Use your results from (a) and (b). Suggest a value for any base with an exponent of zero.

6. (a) What is the value of each of the following?
    (i) 4^0 (ii) 3^0 (iii) 6^0 (iv) $(-11)^0$ (v) $(-6)^0$
   (b) Evaluate each of the following.
    (i) $(3 + 6)^0$ (ii) $(-7 + 6)^0$ (iii) $(2.6 - 1.8)^0$ (iv) $(3.2 - 1.9)^0$
   (c) Create similar expressions of your own. Evaluate your expressions. Have others in your group evaluate your expressions.

7. (a) Copy and complete. Use your patterns for multiplying powers.
    (i) $3^4 \times 3^{-1} = 3^?$ (ii) $4^5 \times 4^{-1} = 4^?$ (iii) $6^{-1} \times 6^0 = 6^?$
    (iv) $4^{-1} \times 4^7 = 4^?$ (v) $6^{-1} \times 6^3 = 6^?$ (vi) $5^{-1} \times 5^7 = 5^?$
   (b) Use your results from (a). Suggest a value for any base with a negative exponent.

8. (a) What is the value of each of the following?
    (i) 4^{-1} (ii) 3^{-1} (iii) 6^{-1} (iv) $(-11)^{-1}$ (v) $(-6)^{-1}$
   (b) Create similar expressions of your own. Evaluate your expressions. Have others in your group evaluate your expressions.

9. After you complete an exploration in mathematics, you should summarize it.
   (a) Refer to your work in the previous explorations. Copy and complete each of the following to summarize patterns and relationships for working with exponents.

- Multiplying Powers: $4^4 \times 4^2 = 4^{\boxed{}}$ Think: Keep the base the same
                                $= 4^{\boxed{}}$ and $\boxed{}$ the exponents.

- Dividing Powers: $4^4 \div 4^2 = 4^{\boxed{}}$ Think: Keep the base the same
                             $= 4^{\boxed{}}$ and $\boxed{}$ the exponents.

- Power of a Power: $(3^3)^5 = \boxed{}$ Think: Keep the base the same
                            $= 3^{15}$ and $\boxed{}$ the exponents.

- Negative Exponents: $7^{-3} = \dfrac{1}{7^3}, 3^{-5} = \dfrac{1}{3^5}, 4^{-9} = \boxed{}$

- Zero Exponents: $8^0 = 1, 12^0 = 1, 14^0 = \boxed{}$

   (b) Create expressions of your own to show how the patterns in (a) can be used.

Four mathematical skills that you explored on the previous pages are summarized below.

- Do each of the calculations shown.
- Use the patterns and relationships you explored to help you.

Multiplying Powers
To multiply powers with the same base, keep the base the same and add the exponents.

1. Write each of the following as a power.
   (a) $3^5 \times 3^3$ (b) $4^5 \times 4^3$ (c) $3^2 \times 3$
   (d) $12^4 \times 12^3$ (e) $8^5 \times 8^3$ (f) $4^4 \times 4^4$

2. Write each as a power.
   (a) $2^5 \times 2^3$ (b) $7^5 \times 7^3$ (c) $13^2 \times 13$
   (d) $12^4 \times 12$ (e) $6^5 \times 6^3$ (f) $7^4 \times 7^4$

3. Evaluate each of the following.
   (a) $2^3 \times 2^5 \times 2^2$ (b) $7^4 \times 7 \times 7^2$
   (c) $5^4 \times 5^2 \times 5^3$ (d) $3^2 \times 3^4 \times 3^6$
   (e) $1^5 \times 1^6 \times 1^9$ (f) $4^2 \times 2^4 \times 4^2$

4. Write each of the following as a power.
   (a) $7^{-5} \times 7^3$ (b) $4^5 \times 4^{-3}$
   (c) $3^{-2} \times 3^6$ (d) $12^{-4} \times 12^3$
   (e) $8^5 \times 8^{-3}$ (f) $5^4 \times 5^{-4}$
   (g) $15^4 \times 15^{-3}$ (h) $6^5 \times 6^{-7}$

5. Write each of the following as a power with positive exponents only.
   (a) $2^{-3} \times 2^{-5}$ (b) $3^{-2} \times 3^{-5}$
   (c) $11^{-3} \times 11^{-5}$ (d) $8^{-2} \times 8^{-4}$
   (e) $7^{-5} \times 7^{-2}$ (f) $6^{-3} \times 6^{-6}$
   (g) $11^{-1} \times 11^{-1}$ (h) $4^{-5} \times 4^{-1}$

6. Evaluate each of the following.
   (a) $3^{-2} \times 3^3 \times 3^0$
   (b) $5^2 \times 5^{-3} \times 4^0$
   (c) $6^2 \times 6^3 \times 6^{-1} \times 6^0 \times 5^0$
   (d) $(5^3 \times 5^3 \times 5^3 \times 6^3 \times 7^3)^0$
   (e) $(4^3 \times 4^{-2} \times 4^0 \times 4^{-1})^{-1}$

Dividing Powers
To divide powers with the same base, keep the base the same and subtract the exponents.

1. Write each of the following as a power.
   (a) $2^7 \div 2^3$ (b) $3^6 \div 3^3$ (c) $3^4 \div 3^3$
   (d) $11^3 \div 11$ (e) $1^{46} \div 1^5$ (f) $10^6 \div 10^4$

2. Write each as a power.
   (a) $5^7 \div 5^3$ (b) $9^6 \div 9^3$ (c) $13^4 \div 13^3$
   (d) $7^3 \div 7^2$ (e) $8^6 \div 8^5$ (f) $2^6 \div 2^4$

3. Evaluate each of the following.
   (a) $10^5 \div 10^3 \div 10$ (b) $9^8 \div 9^2 \div 9^3$
   (c) $4^6 \div 4^3 \div 4^3$ (d) $6^5 \div 6 \div 6$
   (e) $1^9 \div 1^4 \div 1^5$ (f) $2^3 \div 2^2 \div 2$

4. Write each of the following as a power.
   (a) $8^{-5} \div 8^3$ (b) $6^6 \div 6^{-4}$
   (c) $3^{-4} \div 3^5$ (d) $8^{-4} \div 8^5$
   (e) $9^6 \div 9^{-4}$ (f) $5^4 \div 5^{-4}$
   (g) $5^5 \div 5^{-3}$ (h) $7^5 \div 7^{-2}$

5. Write each of the following as a power with positive exponents only.
   (a) $2^{-4} \div 2^{-3}$ (b) $5^{-2} \div 5^{-5}$
   (c) $11^{-4} \div 11^{-2}$ (d) $7^{-3} \div 7^{-4}$
   (e) $9^{-5} \div 9^{-5}$ (f) $6^{-3} \div 6^{-6}$
   (g) $10^{-1} \div 10^{-1}$ (h) $14^{-4} \div 14^{-4}$

6. Evaluate each of the following.
   (a) $3^{-2} \times 3^3 \div 3^0$
   (b) $7^5 \div 7^{-5} \div 3^0$
   (c) $7^{-3} \times 7^2 \div 7^{-1} \times 4^0 \times 3^0$
   (d) $(4^3 \div 4^{-3})^{-1}$
   (e) $(5^3 \times 5^{-3})^0$

Power of a Power

1. Simplify. Write in exponent form.
   (a) $(2^2)^3$ (b) $(3^3)^2$ (c) $(10^4)^3$
   (d) $(3^2)^4$ (e) $(7^2)^4$ (f) $(9^2)^2$

2. Simplify. Explain to your partner which relationship with exponents you used.
   (a) $(2^3)^2$ (b) $(3^2)^4$ (c) $(8^2)^4$
   (d) $(5^3)^1$ (e) $(7^1)^5$ (f) $(11^2)^2$

3. Simplify.
   (a) $(2^3)^{-2}$ (b) $(3^2)^{-4}$ (c) $(8^2)^{-4}$
   (d) $(5^3)^{-1}$ (e) $(7^1)^{-5}$ (f) $(11^2)^{-2}$

4. Compare your answers in Questions 2 and 3. How are the answers alike? How are they different?

5. Simplify.
   (a) $2^3 \times 2^5 \times (2^2)^2$
   (b) $3^5 \times (3^2)^2 \div 3^4$
   (c) $(4^2)^3 \times (4^4)^2 \div 4^2$
   (d) $(3^3)^3 \div (3^2)^3 \times (3^0)^{13}$
   (e) $(5^5)^0 \times (2^5)^{-1} \times 2^5$
   (f) $(7^2)^2 \div 7^3 \times 7^{-1} \times 7^0$
   (g) $(2^3)^4 \div (2^3)^2 \times (2^3)^0 \times (2^3)^{-1}$

6. Simplify.
   (a) $(4^5)^2 \div 4^{-1} \div 4^0 \times (4^3)^2$
   (b) $(6^2)^2 \times (6^3)^3 \times (6^4)^4 \times (6^5)^5$
   (c) $5^2 \div 5 \times (5^3)^2 \div (5^2)^3 \times 5^0$
   (d) $3^4 \times 3^2 \div (3^2)^3 \div (3^4)^{-1} \times 3^0$
   (e) $2^3 \times (2^2)^7 \times (2^2)^{-7} \times 4^0$
   (f) $(5^2)^3 \div 25 \times 5^2 \div 75^0 \times 5^{-1}$

Power of a Product or Quotient

1. Simplify. Write in exponent form.
   (a) $(4 \times 3)^5$ (b) $(2 \times 3)^5$
   (c) $(6 \times 2)^6$ (d) $(5 \times 4)^2$

2. Simplify. Explain to your partner which relationship with exponents you used.
   (a) $(5 \times 2)^4$ (b) $(7 \times 1)^4$
   (c) $(3 \times 3)^3$ (d) $(1 \times 8)^5$

3. Simplify.
   (a) $(5 \times 2)^{-4}$ (b) $(7 \times 1)^{-4}$
   (c) $(3 \times 3)^{-3}$ (d) $(1 \times 8)^{-5}$

4. Compare your answers in Questions 2 and 3. How are the answers alike? How are they different?

5. Simplify.
   (a) $\left(\dfrac{2}{3}\right)^3$ (b) $\left(\dfrac{1}{4}\right)^4$ (c) $\left(\dfrac{1}{2}\right)^6$

   (d) $\left(\dfrac{2}{5}\right)^2$ (e) $\left(\dfrac{4}{7}\right)^5$ (f) $\left(\dfrac{1}{5}\right)^2$

6. Simplify.
   (a) $\left(\dfrac{2}{3}\right)^{-3}$ (b) $\left(\dfrac{1}{4}\right)^{-4}$ (c) $\left(\dfrac{1}{2}\right)^{-6}$

   (d) $\left(\dfrac{2}{5}\right)^{-2}$ (e) $\left(\dfrac{4}{7}\right)^{-5}$ (f) $\left(\dfrac{1}{5}\right)^{-2}$

7. Compare your answers in Questions 5 and 6. How are your answers alike? How are they different?

8. Evaluate.

   (a) $\left(\dfrac{1}{2}\right)^2 \times \left(\dfrac{1}{2}\right)^3 \times \dfrac{1}{2}$

   (b) $\left(\dfrac{2}{3}\right)^{-4} \times \left(\dfrac{2}{3}\right)^5 \times \left(\dfrac{2}{3}\right)^2 \div \dfrac{2}{3}$

   (c) $\dfrac{3}{4} \div \dfrac{3}{4} \times \left(\dfrac{3}{4} \times \dfrac{3}{4}\right)^{-2}$

INVESTIGATE PERCENT

Suppose that 20% of the books checked out of your library last week were fiction. The percent symbol, %, is a concise way of writing "out of 100." You can write the percent as a fraction and a decimal number as shown below.

As a Percent	As a Fraction	As a Decimal Number
20%	$20\% = \dfrac{20}{100} = \dfrac{1}{5}$	$20\% = \dfrac{20}{100} = 0.20$

To solve some problems with percent, you need to change the percent to a decimal number.

EXAMPLE

Suppose Tamu harvested 316 kg of tomatoes. Of these, 15% were still green. How many kilograms of tomatoes are still green?

SOLUTION

$$15\% \text{ of } 316 = 15\% \times 316$$
$$= 0.15 \times 316$$
$$= 47.4$$

Think: To solve this problem, you need to find 15% of 316 kg.

Thus, 47.4 kg of the tomatoes are still green.

ACTIVITY 1

Refer to the example above. How can it help you calculate each of the following?
(a) 69% of 1850
(b) 33% of 562
(c) 7% of 10
(d) 15% of 465
(e) 23% of 296
(f) 33% of 496
(g) 4.2% of 20
(h) 9.8% of 40
(i) 24.6% of 512

ACTIVITY 2

Refer to the example above. Use the solution to help you solve each problem.

(a) If 2% of milk is butterfat, how much butterfat is there in 60 L of milk?

(b) Rhonda bought a bicycle for $119.50. She sold it after one year at a loss of 15%. By how much money did the bicycle depreciate?

(c) One year Canadians spent $250 million going to the movies. If at least 80% of that was spent on U.S. feature movies, how much money was spent on seeing U.S. features?

(d) One year 31.6 million U.S. visitors came to Canada. If 64.2% of those visitors stayed a day, how many visitors stayed a day?

the skills on this page, and the provincial sales taxes from page 257, to help you in ter 1.

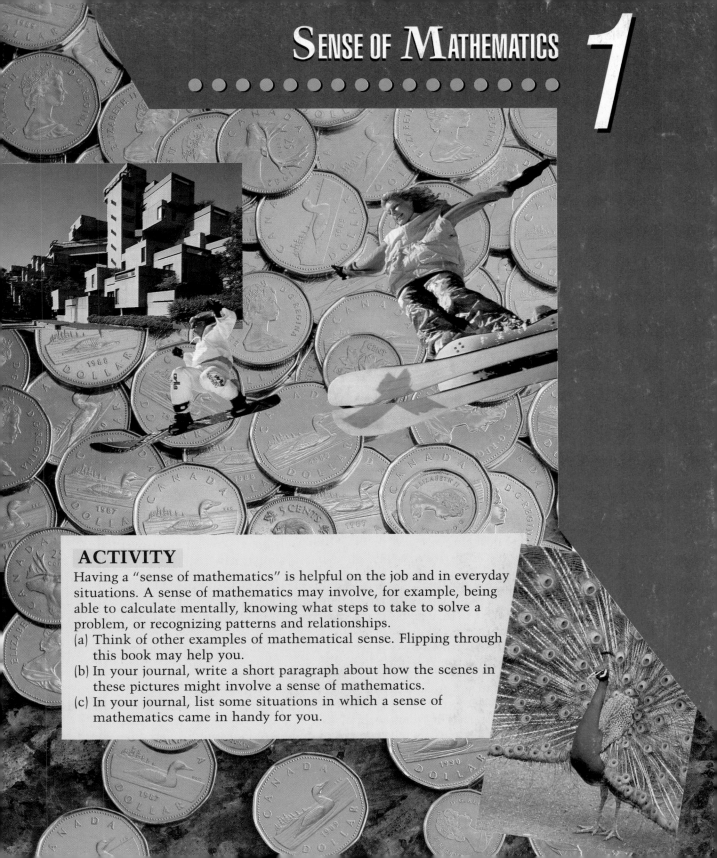

ACTIVITY

Having a "sense of mathematics" is helpful on the job and in everyday situations. A sense of mathematics may involve, for example, being able to calculate mentally, knowing what steps to take to solve a problem, or recognizing patterns and relationships.

(a) Think of other examples of mathematical sense. Flipping through this book may help you.

(b) In your journal, write a short paragraph about how the scenes in these pictures might involve a sense of mathematics.

(c) In your journal, list some situations in which a sense of mathematics came in handy for you.

1.1 EXPLORING PATTERN SENSE

Exploring and predicting patterns can contribute to a sense of mathematics. Many of these patterns can help you simplify your work and solve more problems.

EXPLORATION ① Look for Patterns

1. Refer to the quilt shown.
   (a) What shapes are used to construct the quilt? Why do you think this is so?
   (b) Using the same shapes, how might you design a different quilt?
   (c) Choose shapes of your own. Design a different quilt.

2. (a) Find other pictures in this book that show how shapes can be used.
   (b) Why were these particular shapes used?
   (c) Use the shapes to design a pattern of your own.

EXPLORATION ② Prediction Sense

3. (a) Examine the following: A $1 \times 8 + 1$ B $12 \times 8 + 2$ C $123 \times 8 + 3$
   Evaluate the expressions. What do you notice about your answers?
   (b) Write the next three expressions for the pattern in (a). Predict an answer for each expression. Check your predictions using a calculator.

4. (a) Examine the following: A 3×37 B 6×37 C 9×37
   Evaluate the expressions. What do you notice about your answers?
   (b) Write the next three expressions for the pattern in (a). Predict an answer for each expression. Check your predictions using a calculator.

5. (a) Examine the following: A 1×1 B 11×11 C 111×111
   Evaluate the expressions. What do you notice about your answers?
   (b) Write the next three expressions for the pattern in (a). Predict an answer for each expression.
   (c) Decide with a partner how you can use your calculator to check your predictions in (b). Check your predictions.

6. Work with a partner. A calculator may help you.
   (a) Create expressions of your own that are similar to those in Questions 3 and 4 and that lead to a pattern when evaluated.
   (b) Have others in the class repeat parts (a) and (b) of Questions 3 and 4 for your expressions.

EXPLORATION ③ *Graph Sense*

In some cases, you can make better sense of data using a graph. Graphs are a compact way to show different pieces of data.

CFCs are chlorofluorocarbons that used to be employed as the propellant in aerosol cans. Where else are they found?

7. Refer to the graph shown to the right. It shows the cumulative effects of different gases towards global warming.
   (a) From the graph, what temperature increase is due to each gas?
   (b) If you were to remove CFCs and methane, by how much would the temperature rise be reduced?

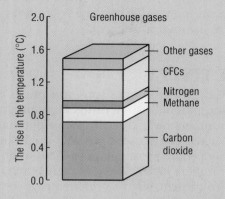

8. (a) Create problems of your own that are based on the graph above. Solve your problem and compare it to others in the class.
   (b) How are numbers communicated in your problem?

9. (a) Discuss with a partner how CFCs get into the earth's atmosphere. How can you reduce the amount of CFCs entering the atmosphere?
   (b) What do you think is meant by the term "global warming"?
   (c) What else do you think causes global warming?
   (d) Make a list of other global concerns. Pick one of the concerns from your list. In your journal, write a short paragraph on how you can help reduce the problem.

10. (a) Create a problem of your own based on each graph below.
    (b) Solve your problem and compare it to others in the class. Solve the other problems.
    (c) Find other graphs of your own, like those shown below, that relate to environmental concerns. Start a class collage of the graphs. For each graph, show how numbers are communicated.

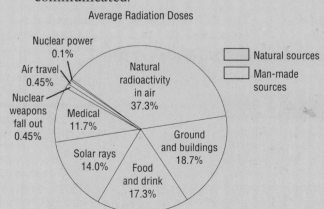

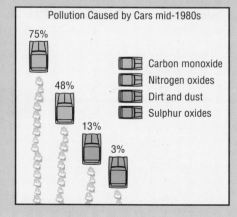

33

As a consumer, you need to make decisions about how you spend money. To do this, you often need to make sense of decimal numbers.

ACTIVITY

(a) Make a list of questions you might ask when you purchase something. How might decimal numbers be involved in your purchase?

(b) Make a list of questions that might be asked by the people in the picture. How might decimal numbers be involved in their purchase? (You might want to refer to page 14.)

(c) How is GST calculated? PST calculated? Refer to page 257.

Often, information is given about a product that can help you decide if it is the best value.

When you purchase an item, you should ask yourself:
- What is the total cost?
- Do I have enough money?
- Have I shopped around?
- How much am I saving?
- Can I get a discount if I buy more?
- How much will taxes add to the cost?

EXAMPLE

Shamir was given a gift of $140.00 to buy items for his guitar.
- A case cost $69.98.
- GST was 7%. PST was 10%.
- Extra strings cost $29.98.
- A music stand cost $14.48.

(a) What is Shamir's total cost, including tax, for the items?

(b) How much money is left from the $140.00?

SOLUTION

(a) Total of items is $114.44. | The GST is 7% of $114.44 or $8.01. | The PST is 10% of $114.44 or $11.44. | The total is $133.89.

(b) The amount of money spent is calculated as shown. There is $6.11 left.

EXERCISE

A

1. Find the following values.
   (a) $6.29 + $16.29 + $4.28
   (b) $469.28 – $123.39
   (c) $869 – $337.51 + $68.74
   (d) $12.46 + $32.45 – $8.98
   (e) $17.44 – $9.35 + $6.35
   (f) $116.08 – $97.19 – $1.84
   (g) $76.34 – $15.28 + $88.63
   (h) $63.22 + $109.68 – $74.00
   (i) $12.44 – $9.92 + $74.22

2. Find the missing amounts for these sales receipts.

```
 *
 *       19.95
 ST      10.99
 GST     30.94
 PST      2.17
 TOTL     2.48
```

```
0125    5.78
0178   18.01
0591   32.89
ST     ▨▨▨
TX      3.97
TTL    60.65
```

```
         1.59
         2.99
        24.35
ST      28.93
TX1      2.03
TX2     ▨▨▨
CA      34.06
```

B Estimate first. Does your answer make sense? Did you use a calculator?

3. A camp counsellor was in charge of buying hamburgers for the campers. Thirteen people wanted hamburgers with cheese and 17 wanted them without cheese. How much will the counsellor have to spend?

With Cheese $1.65

Plain $1.45

4. An apartment building was being renovated. It needed 240 fluorescent lights at $3.98 each. How much will the lights cost in total, to the nearest $10?

5. The regular price of a hairsetter is $33.58. How much is saved by buying it on sale at 20% off?

6. The regular price of a CD player is $339.95. How much will you save if you buy it now at 15% off?

7. Sara bought a CD for $12.95 at A and B Records. When she was at another record store, she saw the same CD for $11.49.
   (a) How much cheaper was the CD at the second store?
   (b) If you were Sara, what would you do now?

8. Raghib paid $54.85 for each of four new radial tires. After one month, a crack developed on one of the tires and he returned it for a replacement.
   (a) If the tire company gave him a refund of $35.95 for the tire, how much would he need to buy a new tire?
   (b) Is the refund from the company reasonable? Give reasons.

9. Dina saved $20 to go to a hockey game. Her transportation cost $6.35, the ticket, $8.00, a program, $2.50, and food, $1.55. How much money did she have left?

10. It costs $9.94 for two pairs of shorts. Yan bought four pairs of shorts and the tax was $1.39. How much change will Yan get from $25.00?

PARTNER PROJECT

Refer to a newspaper.
(a) Find different stores that are advertising the same items. Which store has the better price?
(b) Suppose you wanted to buy the items in (a). Make a list of questions you might ask yourself before going to one store or the other.

1.3 MAKING CONNECTIONS

To get a sense of a career, you might wish to collect as much information about that career as you can.

ACTIVITY 1

In your journal, write a short paragraph to describe a typical day in a career that interests you. Make a list of the math skills you would use during that day.

ACTIVITY 2

(a) List some of the careers you could pursue in the airline industry.
(b) Write a short report on the math skills you might use in one of the careers you listed in (a).
(c) Does your report make connections to real life? to another subject area? You might need to revise your report to include these.

Do you think you would enjoy working at an airport? Why?

EXERCISE

B Review your skills with fractions.

1. The seating capacity of a Douglas DC-10 aircraft is large enough to hold a small town. If a Douglas DC-10 has 250 passengers, then
   (a) what fraction of the jet is filled?
   (b) what fraction of the jet is not filled?

DC10 Specifications	
Wing span	50.4 m
Length	55.6 m
Width of fuselage	6.0 m
Tail height	17.7 m
Passenger capacity	300

2. How many DC-10 plane-loads would be needed to take all the residents of Caledonia (population 3540) on a Caribbean holiday?

3. (a) A three-storey building is about 12.5 m high. How much higher is the tail of a Douglas DC-10?
   (b) Is the tail of the DC-10 higher than the tallest part of your school?

4. For each of the following, write a fraction to show approximately what fraction of the plane was full.
    (a) The de Havilland Dash 8-100 has a capacity of 37 passengers. For a trip from Montréal to Fredericton, the plane had 20 passengers.
    (b) The Boeing 767-233ER has a capacity of 229 passengers. On a trip from Vancouver to Paris, there were 174 passengers.
    (c) The Boeing 737-210 has a capacity of 72 passengers. The students in your class flew to Halifax.

5. Suppose you manage an airline that operates a Boeing 767. Would you cancel a flight if it had only 20 passengers? Give reasons for your answer.

6. A seating diagram for the British Aerospace 146-200 is shown below.

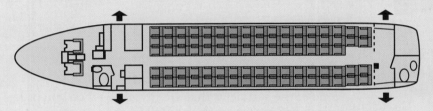

    (a) How many passenger seats does the plane have?
    (b) About what fraction of the plane would your class fill?
    (c) Create a problem of your own about this plane. Solve your problem. Compare your problem to others in the class.

7. Let's assume that the actual plane in Question 6 is about 260 times bigger than the diagram shown. What are the approximate dimensions of the actual plane?

8. The Boeing 747-133 jet has 16 executive-class seats and 466 economy-class seats.
    (a) What is the passenger capacity of this jet?
    (b) On a flight from St. John's to Vancouver, there were nine executive-class passengers and 188 economy-class passengers. About what fraction of the plane was full?
    (c) On a flight from Halifax to London, there were seven executive-class passengers and 274 economy-class passengers. About what fraction of the plane was full?
    (d) Find a seating diagram for another airplane. Create a problem of your own using the diagram. Solve your problem and compare your problem to others in the class.

MATH JOURNAL

Suppose there is a space shuttle flight between the earth and the moon. You have been hired as a pilot on the shuttle.
(a) What math skills would you use as a pilot of such a shuttle?
(b) In your journal, write a short paragraph to describe what the take-off, flight, and landing would be like, going from Canada to the moon.

1.4 MAKING SENSE

Do you have a sense of how much mathematics is involved in getting a pizza? With the ingredients available as shown below, you could order thousands of different types of pizzas.

INGREDIENTS			
PEPPERONI, MUSHROOMS, BACON, TOMATOES	GREEN OLIVES, GREEN PEPPERS, ONIONS, SALAMI	ANCHOVIES, HOT PEPPERS, PINEAPPLE, HAM	
Prices	Small	Med.	Large	Ex. Large
Basic: Sauce and Cheese	5.25	7.25	8.50	9.75
With 1 ingredient	5.75	8.00	9.50	11.00
With 2 ingredients	6.25	8.75	10.50	12.25
With 3 ingredients	6.75	9.50	11.50	13.50
Each additional ingredient	0.50	0.75	1.00	1.25

ACTIVITY *Work with a Partner*

Some of the activities that are involved when you order a pizza are shown in the photos to the left.
(a) List the activities shown in the order they occur.
(b) What math skills do you think might be used in each activity?
(c) What other activities, not shown in the pictures, might happen when you order a pizza?

EXERCISE

A Refer to the pizza price list above.

1. What is the cost for each of the following pizzas?
   (a) a small pizza with pepperoni and bacon
   (b) a medium pizza with bacon, olives, and tomatoes
   (c) an extra large pizza with salami, mushrooms, and hot peppers

2. What was the average cost per person for each of the following pizza orders?
   (a) Three people ordered a medium pepperoni pizza.
   (b) Five people ordered an extra large pepperoni pizza with mushrooms.
   (c) Eight people split two medium pizzas with pepperoni, mushrooms, and onions.

Estimate an answer first.

3. Refer to the list of ingredients on the previous page. Calculate the cost of pizza per person for each of the following orders.
   (a) The Yearbook Committee (15 people) orders:
   - 3 extra large pizzas with onions, pepperoni, and mushrooms
   - 4 medium pizzas with mushrooms, bacon, tomatoes, and hot peppers
   (b) A class of 28 students orders:
   - 4 extra large pizzas with pepperoni, bacon, olives, and ham
   - 2 extra large pizzas with peppers and bacon
   - 4 medium pizzas with salami, hot peppers, and pepperoni
   (c) The school swim team (40 members) places an order for the following pizzas:
   - 4 extra large pizzas with ham, bacon, olives, and onions
   - 4 extra large pizzas with peppers, salami, and tomatoes
   - 5 medium pizzas with hot peppers, pepperoni, and pineapple

4. Suppose you ordered your favourite pizza for everyone in your class.
   (a) How many pizzas would you order?
   (b) How much would you pay for the pizzas?

5. How many different types of pizzas can you order if you use the following ingredients?
   (a) pepperoni and peppers
   (b) pepperoni, mushrooms, and tomatoes
   (c) Use your results in (a) and (b). Predict how many types of pizza you can make with the following items:
       salami, green peppers, olives, bacon
   (d) Based on your results in (a), (b), and (c), predict how many types of pizza you can make with the following items:
       pepperoni, mushrooms, bacon, tomatoes, green peppers

6. (a) Suppose you have just purchased four medium round pizzas. Each pizza has a diameter of 30 cm. What would be the dimensions of a square pizza with the same area?
   (b) Suppose a small pizza has a diameter of 22 cm. How many small pizzas would you need to buy to have the same area of pizza as in (a)?
   (c) List any assumptions you have made in (a) and (b).
   (d) Create a similar problem of your own using pizzas. Solve your problem and compare it to others in the class.
   (e) In your journal, write a short paragraph about the person who first invented pizza. Use your library to find in what country the person was born, and describe what you think the first pizza looked like.

MAKING CONNECTIONS
(a) Survey others in your class to determine what people like on their pizza.
(b) What is the most common ingredient on the pizza?
(c) What is the most common number of ingredients on the pizza?
(d) Some pizza outlets will charge more money for the second ingredient ordered than any other ingredient. Give reasons why you think an outlet might do this.

One of the main reasons you study mathematics is to develop the ability to solve problems, not only in mathematics but in everyday situations.

Problems fall into two main categories.

   I   The path to the solution is immediately clear.
   II The path to the solution is not immediately clear.

For a problem of the second type, using different strategies can help you think about a strategy to solve the problem. By exploring the problem with one of your previously-developed skills, you might be able to find a solution. The more strategies you learn, the better able you will be to solve a problem. Try the following activity.

ACTIVITY 1

(a) Copy the *Problem Solving Plan* on the next page into your Math Journal. Leave space after each part to record additional strategies, skills, and key questions as you solve problems throughout the year. Thus, you will create your own personal *Problem Solving Plan*.

(b) In the section "Think About the Problem," these questions can be asked. Discuss with your partner what you think they mean. Provide examples.
- Do I understand the given information?
- Which words are most important in the problem?
- Can I identify information that is not needed?
- Is there any information missing?
- Can I draw a diagram to summarize information?

(c) In the section "Think About a Strategy," these questions can be asked. Discuss with your partner what you think they mean. Provide examples.
- Can I use a pattern?
- Can I act out the problem?
- Can I draw a diagram?
- Can I solve a simpler problem?
- Can I work backwards?
- Can I use manipulatives?

(d) In the section "Work it Out," these questions can be asked. Discuss with your partner what you think they mean. Provide examples.
- Will the strategy lead to the solution easily?
- Are my assumptions valid?
- Are my calculations correct?
- Are there any other strategies that can make the solution easier?
- Do I understand each step of the solution?

(e) In the section "Think About Your Solution," these questions can be asked. Discuss with your partner what you think they mean. Provide examples.
- Does the solution make sense?
- Can I explain the solution to my partner?
- Can I verify the solution?
- Did I answer the question that was originally posed?
- Did I make a final statement?

Your Problem Solving Plan

1. Think About the Problem.

As you start any problem, ask yourself these two questions.

   I   What am I asked to find?   II What am I given?

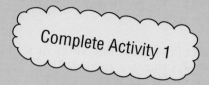

2. Think About a Strategy.

Look for a skill or strategy that will help you solve the problem.

Remember: Ask yourself, "What do I know *already* that can help me solve the problem?"

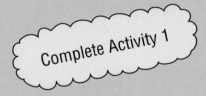

3. Work it Out.

In this stage, you will actually solve the problem.

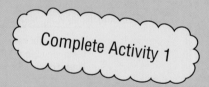

4. Think About Your Solution.

Look back at your solution.

ACTIVITY 2

The problems that follow can be solved using different problem solving strategies.
(a) As you solve the problems, list the different strategies you used and place them in your chart.
(b) Write examples of your own to show how the strategies you have listed in (a) are applied.

1. (a) A digit is represented by the letter S. What is one value of S if S6SS6 is divisible by four? Are there any other values of S that are suitable?
    (b) A digit is represented by the letter A. What is the value of A if A1AA1 is divisible by 19?

2. Three views of a cube are shown.
    (a) What is opposite the black circle?
    (b) Construct the cube showing all six sides.

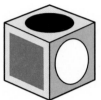 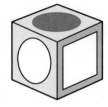 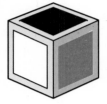

3. Mitch, Dawna, and Fernando are President, Treasurer, and Secretary of their class. Fernando likes Mitch's sister. He also enjoys meeting with the President and the rest of the council. The Treasurer never attends any meetings and has no brothers or sisters. Which positions do Fernando, Dawna, and Mitch hold?
    (a) How can the chart shown help you organize the information given?
    (b) How can the chart be used to help you solve the problem?
    (c) Solve the problem. What position does each person hold?

	President	Secretary	Treasurer
Mitch			
Dawna			
Fernando	X		

↑
The treasurer never attends any meetings.
Fernando likes meeting with the President.
Thus, Fernando is not the President (X).

4. Sometimes, to solve a problem, you need to read each word carefully.
    During a severe storm on Lake Erie, a sightseeing boat sank, killing 23 of the 48 passengers. The accident occurred along the 49th parallel (the international boundary between Canada and the United States). Where were the survivors buried?
    (a) Do you understand each word in the problem above?
    (b) What is the answer to the problem?
    (c) Create and solve a similar problem of your own.

5. The design shown is made from line segments.
    (a) How many line segments are there in all?
    (b) Explain to your partner the strategy you used to solve the problem.

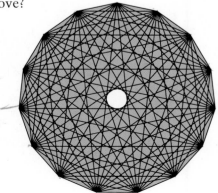

6. (a) Which of the following does not belong in the list? Why?

         DEED   BED   HOOD   COULD

   (b) Create a similar problem of your own. Solve your problem and compare your problem to others in the class.

7. Each letter in the following expressions represents one digit. No digit is used more than once. What does each expression represent?

(a)
$$\begin{array}{r} ON \\ + \ YOUR \\ \hline MARK \end{array}$$

(b)
$$\begin{array}{r} BRUSH \\ - \ YOUR \\ \hline TEETH \end{array}$$

(c)
$$\begin{array}{r} SEND \\ + \ MORE \\ \hline MONEY \end{array}$$

(d)
$$\begin{array}{r} HOW \\ + \ ARE \\ \hline YOU \end{array}$$

   (e) Create a similar expression of your own. Have others in the class decide what your expression is.

8. Refer to the shape shown.
It is constructed from 27 smaller cubes.

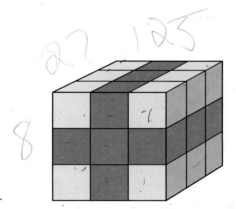

   (a) A stripe is painted onto the shape as shown. Suppose the shape is taken apart to show the individual cubes. What fraction of these cubes would have at least one side painted?

   (b) What fraction of the cubes would have no sides painted?

   (c) Find the sum of the fractions in (a) and (b). What do you notice about the sum?

9. A field mouse is very small. It generally has a mass between 4 g and 10 g and needs to eat about $\frac{1}{2}$ of its body mass in food each day. Working with a partner, answer the following questions in a report and present your report to the class.

   (a) Why does a field mouse need to eat such a great fraction of its body mass?

   (b) What math skills can be used to help you estimate about what fraction of body mass a mammal needs to eat each day?

   (c) Estimate about what fraction of your body mass you eat each day. How did you make this estimate?

   (d) Why do you think a newborn baby needs to be wrapped warmly immediately after birth?

ACTIVITY 3

In your earlier work with mathematics, you solved a variety of problems and recorded your strategies in your journal.

(a) Make sure there is an example for each strategy used.

(b) This book will introduce you to other problem solving strategies. Look through the book and list some problem solving strategies used.

(c) Compare your list with the strategies you have in your journal from last year. Which strategies do you recognize?

There are many ways to get a sense of mathematics. Explorations can help you discover mathematical concepts and develop mathematics for yourself. At other times, manipulatives can help you solve problems by letting you "see" the solution more clearly.

ACTIVITY 1   *Work with a Partner*

1. Refer to the manipulatives shown on this page.
   (a) How might some of these materials be used to solve a problem?
   (b) Create a problem and show how you might solve it.
   (c) Suggest a math problem that can be solved using some of these materials.

ACTIVITY 2   *Work in a Small Group*

2. (a) Flip through this book. Make a list of the materials that are used. What kinds of problems are solved using the materials?
   (b) How might these manipulatives be used in the activities on the next page?

ACTIVITY 3

3. (a) Numbers are represented by the number of squares on the grid paper below. What are the four numbers?

   (b) Based on the pattern, what is the tenth number in this pattern?
   (c) What is the sum of the first ten numbers in this pattern? Can you explain how you found the sum?

4. The squares shown on the grid paper of Question 3 can be represented as tiles.

   The first number shows a sum of 1. The second number shows the sum of 1 + 3. The third number shows the sum of 1 + 3 + 5 and the fourth number shows the sum of 1 + 3 + 5 + 7.
   (a) What is the sum shown in the fifth number?
   (b) What is the sum shown in the tenth number?
   (c) What is the sum shown in the thousandth number?

ACTIVITY 4

5. (a) Use 4 × 4 dot paper. What is the triangle you can construct that has the greatest perimeter possible?
   (b) Give reasons why you think your triangle in (a) has the greatest perimeter.

6. (a) Use 4 × 4 dot paper. What is the triangle you can construct that has the greatest area possible?
   (b) Give reasons why you think your triangle in (a) has the greatest area.

7. (a) Create an activity of your own that uses 5 × 5 dot paper. Complete your activity.
   (b) Have others in the class complete your activity.

ACTIVITY 5 *Work in a Group*

8. (a) Based on your work in Activities 3 and 4, create a similar pattern of your own.
   (b) Create a problem of your own based on the pattern in (a). Solve your problem. Compare your problem to others in the class.

Often, you want to have a sense of the cost of a purchase before you pay for it. Suppose you are considering purchasing five cassette tapes at $8.99 each. An estimated cost for five tapes can be found as

$$5 \times \$9 = \$45.$$

To make an estimate, first round off the numbers. Then calculate. Often, these calculations can be done mentally.

$38.4 + 63.8 = 102.2$
$38.4 + 63.8$
$\doteq 40 + 60$
$= 100$

Does the answer make sense?
Are these approximately equal?

The answer makes sense.

Thus, the answer is reasonable.

$0.937 - 0.486 = 0.451$
$0.937 - 0.486$
$\doteq 1 - 0.5$
$= 0.5$

Does the answer make sense?
Are these approximately equal?

The answer makes sense.

Thus, the answer is reasonable.

Knowing if your answer is reasonable is important when you work with a calculator. Answer the following in your journal.
(a) Why is it important to check that your result on a calculator is reasonable?
(b) List situations in which knowing if an answer is reasonable is important.

EXERCISE

B Review how to round numbers.

1. Match each statement with an estimate.

Statement	Estimate
(a) 21 tickets at $5.10 each	A $125 + 10$
(b) sale special: $19.99 off the price of a jacket which regularly sells for $58.99	B 20×5
(c) skates for $123.98 and a stick for $9.99	C $1.50 \div 5$
(d) one felt pen at $1.49 for 5	D $60 - 20$

2. For each of the following, estimate which answer makes sense. For those that do not make sense, find a more reasonable answer.

You Buy	You Pay
(a) 4 cassette tapes for $7.99 each	$31.96
(b) 12 kg of sugar for $0.69/kg	$8.28
(c) 8 loaves of bread for $0.79 each	$7.76
(d) 25 light bulbs at $1.98 for 4	$10.88
(e) a 7-kg roast for $8.80/kg	$25.43

1.8 CALCULATOR SENSE

Sometimes, when obtaining decimals for
fractions, you can see patterns. These
patterns can help you determine whether an
answer makes sense when you convert a
fraction to a decimal number.

$$\frac{1}{11} = 0.09090909\ldots = 0.\overline{09}$$ ☐ C 1 ÷ 11 =

$$\frac{2}{11} = 0.18181818\ldots = 0.\overline{18}$$ ☐ C 2 ÷ 11 =

ACTIVITY 1

(a) Based on the above pattern, predict the decimal equivalents for $\frac{3}{11}$, $\frac{4}{11}$, and $\frac{5}{11}$.
(b) Use your calculator to verify your predictions.
(c) Choose other fractions and find the decimal equivalents on your calculator. Check that your decimal equivalents makes sense.

ACTIVITY 2

(a) When you use your calculator, you need to ensure your answer makes sense. Make a list of questions that you can ask to ensure the answer on your calculator makes sense.
(b) Ask yourself the questions in (a) as you complete the following exercise.

EXERCISE

B   Use your calculator. Refer to your manual if necessary.

1. (a) Find the decimal equivalents for $\frac{1}{9}$, $\frac{2}{9}$, and $\frac{3}{9}$.
   (b) Predict the decimal equivalents for $\frac{4}{9}$, $\frac{5}{9}$, and $\frac{6}{9}$. Verify your predictions.
   (c) Calculate other decimal equivalents for fractions of your own. What patterns do you notice?

2. A calculator was used to evaluate each expression. Which of the answers are reasonable?
   (a) $755 + 324 - 519 = 560$ (b) $23 + 68 \times 99 = 9009$
   (c) $524 \div 4 \times 33 = 4323$ (d) $77 - 36 + 44 \div 22 = 42.5$

3. A calculator was used to evaluate each expression. Which of the answers are reasonable?
   (a) $59.7 - 33.8 \div 22.4 \times 36.4 = 42.0875$ (b) $33.6 \times 44.71 - 55.3 \times 22 = 285.656$
   (c) $42.6 + 21.4 - 56.7 \times 21.4 = 156.22$ (d) $23.7 \div 13.5 + 445.67 = 457.3$

Often, managers of sports teams have to make sense of data that have been collected during games. Patterns can help coaches during a game. To find these patterns, they need to use skills with decimal numbers.

Suppose you are the coach of a local hockey team. For a crucial face-off, you have the chart shown to help you decide which player should take the face-off.

	Federko	Goodenough
Number of face-offs tried	109	126
Number of face-offs won	53	65
$\dfrac{\text{Number of face-offs won}}{\text{Number of face-offs tried}}$	$\dfrac{53}{109}$	$\dfrac{65}{126}$

To find who has the better record, calculate the decimal equivalent.

$$\frac{53}{109} \doteq 0.486 \qquad \frac{65}{126} \doteq 0.516$$

Since 0.516 > 0.486, the coach might select Goodenough to take the face-off. However, there are other considerations. Try the following activity.

ACTIVITY
In your journal:
(a) Describe other factors that might affect your decision regarding which player should take the face-off.
(b) Write a short paragraph describing a similar situation in a hockey game and how you, as the coach, were able to make your decision quickly.

EXERCISE

 A Use a calculator.

1. Convert each fraction to an equivalent decimal number.

(a) $\dfrac{1}{4}$ (b) $\dfrac{3}{5}$ (c) $\dfrac{2}{3}$ (d) $\dfrac{3}{8}$ (e) $\dfrac{3}{10}$ (f) $\dfrac{5}{7}$ (g) $\dfrac{4}{9}$ (h) $\dfrac{13}{55}$ (i) $\dfrac{44}{57}$

2. Use a calculator to help you decide which fraction is greater.

(a) $\dfrac{55}{98}, \dfrac{75}{122}$ (b) $\dfrac{54}{74}, \dfrac{48}{91}$ (c) $\dfrac{206}{607}, \dfrac{309}{808}$ (d) $\dfrac{561}{1005}, \dfrac{310}{876}$

3. (a) What is the first step in deciding which player should take an important face-off?
   (b) Which of the two players shown in the chart would you use for an important face-off? Why?

	Harris	Butler
Number of face-offs won	96	48
Number of face-offs tried	138	91

4. The fraction $\dfrac{\text{Shots on goal}}{\text{Number of games played}}$ is used to calculate a player's record for *shots on goal*. Which player has the best record?

	Davise	Bourne
Shots on goal	23	36
Number of games played	49	78

5. (a) Which player has the best record for shots on goal?
   (b) Suppose you are the coach of the team. Which player would you have on the ice in the final minutes to try and win the game?

	Williams	Schultz	Moxey
Shots on goal	32	48	59
Number of games played	42	58	69

6. (a) From the newspaper clipping, who has the best record for Goals (G) ÷ Games Played (GP)?
   (b) Arrange the players in order of the best record to the worst record for G ÷ GP.
   (c) Which two players with good records for G ÷ GP and the greatest number of points would you send into a final playoff game?
   (d) Find similar standings of your own in the newspaper. Repeat (a), (b), and (c) for your standings.

SCORING

	GP	G	A	PTS
Weir	78	24	17	41
Young	41	21	16	37
Pirus	66	15	30	45
Larose	80	22	57	79
Irvine	76	14	31	45
Wilson	76	19	23	42
Dupont	80	18	18	36
Jarvis	77	30	20	50

Games Played

Goals

GROUP PROJECT

(a) Describe how fractions or decimal numbers might be used to compare performances of players in different sports.
(b) Make a list of various players in one of the sports in (a) along with their performances.
(c) Use fractions or decimal numbers to compare the performances.
(d) Write a short paragraph to describe a possible situation in a sporting event where a comparison is necessary. Describe how you, as the coach, would select the best player(s) to be used in the situation.

1.10 JOURNAL SENSE

"Trying it out" by making notes, jotting ideas, or keeping track of attempts can help you make sense of a problem. You can use your journal to record your ideas and information in a similar way involving mathematics.

Begin your journal, if you have not done so already, by trying the following activities.

ACTIVITY 1

The photograph shows a police officer making notes in a journal.
(a) Why do you think a police officer records information?
(b) In what situations is it useful for people in other occupations to record information? Use examples to illustrate your answer.

ACTIVITY 2

Think of situations in which writing notes, jotting ideas, or keeping track of attempts have helped you. List them in your journal.

Your journal is also a place where you can record your ideas and feelings about mathematics. By keeping notes, you will be able to see how your ideas change over time.

ACTIVITY 3

In your journal, complete each of the following statements.
(a) Some things I do really well are
(b) Some things I do really well in math are
(c) Some things I want to be better at
(d) Today, I would describe how I feel about math as

ACTIVITY 4

The following words have occurred in your earlier work in mathematics.

| right angle | symmetry | similar | area | integer | ratio |
| hypotenuse | congruent | simplify | rate | equation | factor |

(a) Write your own meaning for each word.
(b) Use an example of your own to illustrate the meaning of each word.
(c) Now try the vocabulary sense section on the next page.

Shown below are new words that you will encounter in this book. Complete the following activity to get a sense of how to communicate these words clearly.

ACTIVITY

Refer to the words shown below.

(a) In your journal, list each word you have seen before. Write a meaning for each word you know. Give an example to help explain your meaning.

(b) Flip through the book to see if you can find some of these words. How can this book help you find the definition of a word that you do not know?

(c) Keep adding to the list in (a) as you complete each section. In your journal, describe how doing this could help you develop your vocabulary.

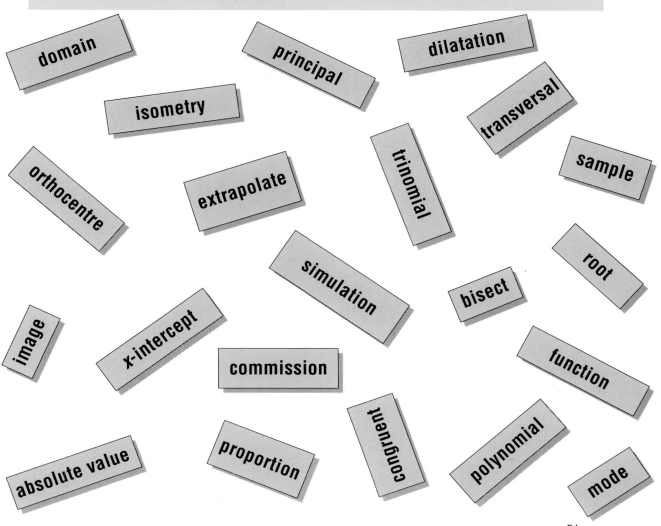

Did you know that the strategies you use when playing games or doing magic tricks can improve your sense of mathematics?

The activities that follow will set up magic tricks that you can try and games that you can play. As you complete each activity, write in your journal:

- the mathematical skills and strategies that were used.
- any strategies that were used to complete the magic trick or win the game.
- any patterns and relationships you found.

ACTIVITY 1 *Coin-Tac-Toe*

To play this game, you will need:
- four pennies
- four nickels
- a grid like the one shown

Rules

1. One player uses four pennies, the other uses four nickels. Both players use a board like the one shown.
2. Each player places coins on the board, one at a time, trying to obtain three of the same coins in a row, column, or diagonal.
3. Once all coins are placed on the board, each player moves coins one at a time to an available space.
4. The winner is the first player to obtain three of the same coins in a row, column, or diagonal.

(a) What strategy did you use to try and win the game?
(b) What math skills were involved in successfully carrying out your strategy?
(c) Create a similar game of your own. Play the game with your partner.

ACTIVITY 2   *Twenty-One*

To play this game, you will need 21 counters.

Rules
1. Randomly place 21 counters in between you and the other player.
2. Decide who goes first.
3. Alternate turns and remove between one and four counters.
4. The player who removes the last counter(s) is the winner.

(a) What strategy can you use to ensure you always win?
(b) What math skills are involved in successfully carrying out your strategy?
(c) Create a similar game of your own and develop a strategy to always win your game. Repeat (a) and (b) for your game.

ACTIVITY 3   *Tumbler Teaser Trick*

1. A magician arranges three cups as shown below. Turning over two cups at a time, the magician can get all three right side up. How many times do the cups need to be turned over, two at a time, so that all the cups are standing right side up?

2. The magician then turns the cups back over so that they appear as shown below. The magician asks for volunteers from the audience to try turning them over, two at a time, so that they all stand right side up.
   (a) Will the volunteers be able to do so?
   (b) Why can the magician perform the trick successfully but the volunteers cannot?
   (c) Suppose you are the manager of a magician who performs this trick. In your journal, describe how you would coach your magician to perform the trick effectively in front of a live audience.

1. Estimate the cost for each of the following.
   (a) 62 hockey pucks at $2.09 each
   (b) 305 spark plugs at $3.89 each
   (c) 197 soccer uniforms at $19.80 each
   (d) 1984 ceramic tiles at $1.12 each

2. (a) Refer to the following expressions. How are they alike? How are they different?
   (i) 15×25 (ii) 25×35 (iii) 35×45
   (b) Evaluate the expressions in (a). What do you notice?
   (c) Write the next five expressions that will continue the pattern. Predict the value of each expression.
   (d) Check your prediction in (c). How reasonable was your answer?

3. Alicja wants to buy five blouses. Each blouse costs $17.89. The total sales tax is $13.42. Alicja has $100.00.
   (a) Can she purchase the blouses?
   (b) How much more money does she need?

4. In a badminton tournament, when a player loses, that player is eliminated. Suppose there are 27 players in the tournament.
   (a) What is the minimum number of games you need to play to determine a winner?
   (b) List any assumptions you made.

5. Use your calculator. Work with a partner.
   (a) Add 49.6, 9.6, 100.3, and 121.
   (b) Subtract 6.96 from the sum of 14.38 and 22.4.
   (c) Divide the sum of 49.3 and 126.6 by the product of 9.6 and 12.
   (d) Explain to your partner how you used your calculator in (a), (b), and (c).

6. An octahedron has eight faces. On each face, a shape is drawn. Different views of the octahedron are shown.
   (a) Which face is opposite △?   (b) Which face is opposite O?

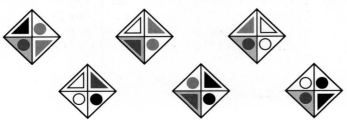

❶ List two careers that you think might involve the skills in this chapter. Give reasons for your answer.

❷ What entries have you made in your journal? What other entries could you make related to this chapter?

❸ What questions can you now add to your *Problem Solving Plan*? Have you added them?

MAKING CONNECTIONS

Refer to the opening page of this chapter.
(a) Create a problem of your own using the pictures. Solve your problem.
(b) Compare your problem to others in the class. Solve the other problems.

④ Choose a question on this page. Discuss with your partner whether a calculator is the most efficient way to solve the problem.

⑤ How might you develop your mental math skills in this chapter? What else can you do to improve them?

⑥ Write an example of how you might use the skills in this chapter on your way home from school.

MATH JOURNAL

(a) Make a list of all the new skills and terms you learned in this chapter.
(b) Write an example to illustrate any you might be unsure about.

SELF EVALUATION

1. (a) Develop a plan to estimate the number of letters on this page. Explain your plan to your partner.
   (b) Use your plan to estimate the number of letters on this page. Compare your estimate with those of others in the class.

2. (a) Refer to the following expressions. How are they alike? How are they different?
   (i) 9×9 (ii) 99×99 (iii) 999×999
   (b) Evaluate the expressions in (a). What do you notice?
   (c) Write the next five expressions that will continue the pattern. Predict the value of each expression.
   (d) Check your prediction in (c). How reasonable was your answer?
   (e) Create a similar pattern of your own. Repeat (a), (b), and (c) using your pattern.

3. Refer to the list of ingredients for pizzas shown in Section 1.4. Suppose you and nine friends have $45 to spend on pizza.
   (a) How many pizzas would you buy?
   (b) What toppings would you put on your pizzas?
   (c) Are there any other costs you are not considering when you buy the pizzas?

4. Suppose you have a piece of plywood that measures 40 cm by 60 cm.
   (a) Find the minimum number of cuts you need to make to construct a piece that measures 30 cm × 80 cm.
   (b) Create a similar problem of your own. Solve your problem. Compare your problem to others in the class.

5. Follow these instructions using your calculator and its memory key.
   A: Subtract the sum of 963 and 481 from 1500.
   B: Divide the product of 82 and 45 by 18.
   C: Multiply the sum of 481 and 293 by 28.
   D: Divide the sum of 983 and 460 by 39.
   E: Find the quotient when the sum of 939 and 486 is divided by 75.
   Now add your answers in A, B, C, D, and E.

Some calculators have the ability to work with fractions. The following key sequences apply to the CASIO fx-7700G graphics calculator. The key sequences for your calculator may vary. Check your manual.

Converting Fractions into Decimal Numbers

You can input a fraction, like $\frac{15}{16}$ on your calculator using the following key sequence.

The display screen on your calculator appears as shown.

$$15\lrcorner16$$
$$0.9375$$

AC 15 $a\frac{b}{c}$ 16

By pressing EXE $a\frac{b}{c}$, the calculator will convert the fraction to a decimal number.

By pressing $a\frac{b}{c}$ again, you will once again have the fraction.

Operations with Fractions

The following key sequence will show you how to add $1\frac{5}{6} + \frac{22}{9}$. The screen of the calculator is shown to the right.

$$1\lrcorner5\lrcorner6+22\lrcorner9$$
$$4\lrcorner5\lrcorner18\lrcorner$$

AC 1 $a\frac{b}{c}$ 5 $a\frac{b}{c}$ 6 + 22 $a\frac{b}{c}$ 9 EXE

The screen shows the sum as a mixed number. In this case, the answer is $4\frac{5}{18}$.

By pressing the key $a\frac{b}{c}$, you can see the answer as a decimal number.

By now pressing SHIFT $a\frac{b}{c}$, you will see your answer as an improper fraction.

ACTIVITY   *Work in a Group*

You may need to refer to the manual of your graphics calculator.
(a) How are the key sequences for converting fractions and decimal numbers like those above? How are they different?
(b) How are the key sequences for the operations with fractions alike? How are they different?
(c) Use your calculator to answer some questions you worked on earlier in this chapter. Check your notebook to ensure the answers on your calculator are reasonable.

BUILDING GEOMETRY

2

2.1 EXPLORING GEOMETRY

EXPLORATION ① *Discuss with a Partner*

1. Refer to the illustration on the previous page. In your journal, record your observations.
   (a) Identify the different geometric shapes you find in the buildings.
   (b) Make a list of the properties of each shape. Discuss the properties with your partner.

2. (a) Why do you think the designer chose the particular shapes on the previous page? Give reasons for your answer.
   (b) Suppose you were asked to design a shape of your own. Which shapes would you choose? How would you use them?

EXPLORATION ② *Write with a Partner*

3. Use a dictionary to help you.
   (a) What do you think is meant by the word "octagon"?
   (b) List other words that start with "oct." Give a meaning for each word. How are these meanings like the meaning of "octagon"?
   (c) Write other words that end with the letters "agon." Write a meaning for each word.

4. (a) What do you think the words "eccentric" and "concentric" mean?
   (b) How are your meanings in (a) alike? How are they different?
   (c) The following prefixes are used in this chapter: equi, bi, tri, poly, hex. Write words you know that use these prefixes.
   (d) Write a meaning for each word in (c). How can the prefixes be used to help you remember each word?

EXPLORATION ③ *Work with a Partner*

5. (a) Copy each of the shapes shown below. With your partner, devise a plan to find the "centre" of each shape. Where do you think the "centre" of the shape is? Find the centre.
   (b) Repeat your plan in (a) for other similar shapes of your own. Give reasons why you think finding the centre would be a useful skill.

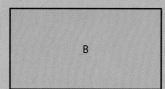

6. Suppose you are a fabric designer. You might want to
    develop a design like the one to the right.
    (a) How do you think finding the centre of a circle
        would help you create this design?
    (b) Create a design of your own that uses the centre of a
        shape. Describe any other math skills you used to
        create the design.
    (c) Compare your design with others in your group.
        How are the math skills used to create each design
        alike? How are they different?

7. (a) Use toothpicks and marshmallows to
        construct one of each shape. How are
        the shapes alike? How are they
        different?
    (b) Predict which shape(s) can be used to
        support a book if the shape is placed at
        each corner of the book.

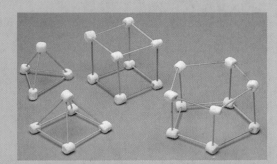

8. Play the following game with a partner.
    A Copy and cut out the cards.
    B Shuffle the cards thoroughly and deal
       them to each player. The cards are
       stacked in front of each player.
    C Each player will turn over the top card
       at the same time. The first player to
       notice a match and correctly identify
       the match takes the opponent's card.
    D The player with the most cards when
       all cards are out wins.

59

Angles play an important role in your everyday life.

- How are angles important in the pictures above?
- Find other examples where angles are important.

As you complete the following activities, summarize in your journal any patterns and relationships you see to help you copy angles. Once you have completed the activities, make a list of how the methods for copying angles are alike and how they are different.

ACTIVITY 1

(a) You can use a protractor to make a copy of the angle shown. Describe how you might do so.
(b) Use your method in (a) to make a copy of the angle. How can you show that the angles are equal?
(c) Repeat (a) and (b) for other angles.

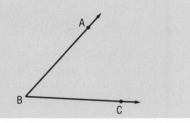

ACTIVITY 2   *Work with a Partner*

The steps below are used to copy an angle.
(a) Describe each of the steps.
(b) Draw your own angle. Label it ∠ABC.
(c) Use the steps above to make a copy of ∠ABC. Label it ∠DEF.
(d) Check your work. Is ∠ABC = ∠DEF?

Step 1

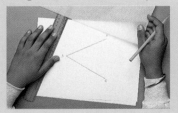

Step 2

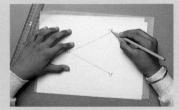

Step 3

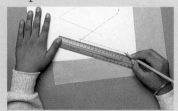

ACTIVITY 3

(a) The following steps are used to copy an angle. In your own words, describe each of the steps.

Step 1

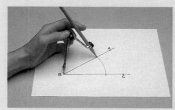

Step 2

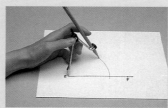

Step 3

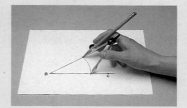

Step 4

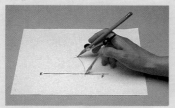

Step 5

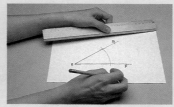

(b) Draw your own angle. Label it ∠ABC.
(c) Use the steps above to make a copy of ∠ABC. Label it ∠DEF.
(d) Check your work. Is ∠ABC = ∠DEF?

ACTIVITY 4

The steps below are used to copy an angle.
(a) Describe each of the steps given to copy the angle.
(b) Draw your own angle. Label it ∠ABC.
(c) Use the steps below to make a copy of ∠ABC. Label it ∠DEF.
(d) Check your work. Is ∠ABC = ∠DEF?

Step 1

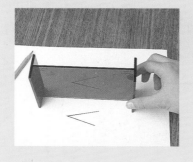

Step 2

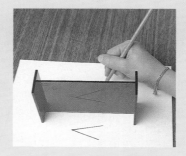

Step 3

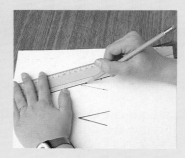

Have you ever seen a speed skier in action? A speed skier can travel at speeds that exceed 200 km/h. The speed reached depends upon the angle of the ski slope.

To estimate the measure of the angle of the ski slope, you can relate the angle to known measures.

acute: an angle between 0° and 90°

right: a 90° angle

obtuse: an angle between 90° and 180°

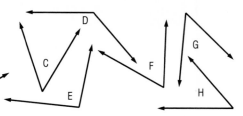

ACTIVITY *Work with a Partner*

1. (a) Estimate the angle of the ski slope above.
   (b) Make a list of the questions you asked to estimate the angle in (a).
   (c) Compare your questions in (b) to those of your partner. Does your partner have any questions that you could add to your list?

2. (a) You and your partner each draw a different ski slope. Measure the angle of your slope.
   (b) Trade your ski slope with your partner and estimate the measure of the slope. How reasonable was your estimate?

EXERCISE

A Review the special names given to angles.

1. (a) Estimate the size of each angle. Then measure.
   (b) How reasonable was your estimate?

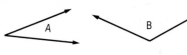

2. (a) Sketch angles you think have the measures shown.
   (i) 90°   (ii) 120°   (iii) 60°   (iv) 30°
   (b) Measure each angle. How reasonable were your sketches?

3. (a) Estimate the measure of the angles shown in the photos. Then measure the angles. How reasonable were your estimates?
   (b) Find other angles around your classroom. Estimate the size of the angles. Then measure. How reasonable were your estimates?

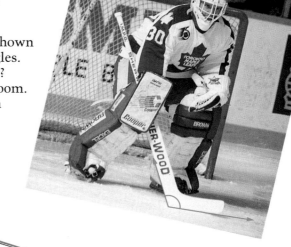

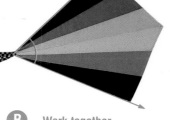

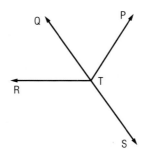

B Work together.

4. Use the diagram.
   Copy and complete the chart.

	Name of angle	Estimate	Measure
(a)	∠PTS	?	?
(b)	∠PTQ	?	?
(c)	∠QTR	?	?
(d)	∠RTS	?	?
(e)	sum of angles above	?	?

5. (a) Fold paper to create angles like those shown below.
   (b) Estimate the measure of each angle.
   (c) Measure each angle. How reasonable were your estimates?

2.4 INVESTIGATING TRIANGLES

Triangles play an important role in this structure.

ACTIVITY

(a) What is the important role played by the
    triangles in the picture?
(b) In what other structures do triangles play
    an important role?

Triangles are often classified according to their
special properties. For each investigation, describe
why the name used is suitable.

INVESTIGATION 1

1. (a) An *equilateral* triangle is shown. Construct the triangle.
   (b) Measure the sides and angles of the triangle.
       What do you notice about the measures?
   (c) Describe how you can use the information
       in (b) to construct an equilateral triangle.
   (d) Construct any equilateral triangle.

2. (a) What properties of equilateral triangles were
       used in Question 1?
   (b) Use the properties in (a) to construct
       equilateral triangles of your own.

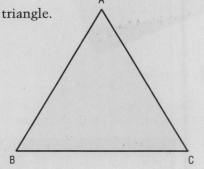

INVESTIGATION 2

3. (a) An *isosceles* triangle is shown. Construct the triangle.
   (b) Measure the sides and angles of the triangle.
       What do you notice about the measures?
   (c) Describe how you can use the information
       in (b) to construct an isosceles
       triangle.
   (d) Construct any isosceles triangle.

4. (a) What properties of isosceles triangles were
       used in Question 3?
   (b) Use the properties in (a) to construct
       isosceles triangles of your own.

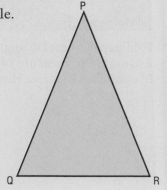

INVESTIGATION 3

5. (a) A *scalene* triangle is shown. Construct the triangle.
   (b) Measure the sides and angles of the triangle. What do you notice about the measures?
   (c) Describe how you can use the information to construct a scalene triangle.
   (d) Construct any scalene triangle.

6. (a) What properties of scalene triangles were used in Question 5?
   (b) Use the properties in (a) to construct scalene triangles of your own.

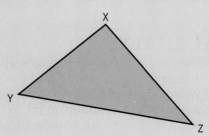

INVESTIGATION 4

You can also classify a triangle as follows:
- A *right* triangle has one angle that is 90°.
- An *acute* triangle has no angles greater than or equal to 90°.
- An *obtuse* triangle has one angle that is greater than 90°.

7. (a) Measure the sides and angles of each triangle below. Record your results in a chart.
   (b) How would you name each of the triangles shown below using the names above?
   (c) How else can you name each triangle using the names shown in the previous investigations?

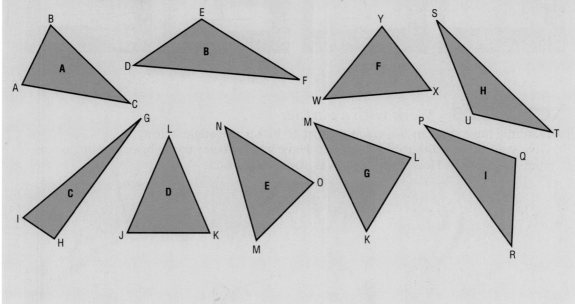

Mathematical words and words in everyday language are often connected.

ACTIVITY 1

(a) How are the following words alike? How are they different?

bicycle   bilingual   bicentennial   bilateral   biweekly

(b) What is the meaning of each word in (a)?
(c) Refer to the meanings in (b). What do you think the prefix "bi" means?
(d) What do you think is meant by the term "bisect"?

To **bisect** a figure means that you divide the figure into two equal parts. To bisect an angle means to divide the angle into two equal parts. The following activities show how to bisect an angle.

ACTIVITY 2   *Work with a Partner*

The diagrams show the steps used to bisect an angle using a pair of compasses and a straightedge. Describe each of the steps and use them to bisect an angle of your own.

Step 1

Step 2

Step 3

Step 4

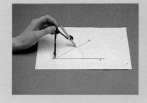  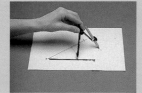 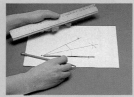

ACTIVITY 3   *Work with a Partner*

(a) Describe how you can use tracing paper to bisect the angle below.
(b) Give your description to your partner. Have your partner try to bisect an angle using your description. How reasonable was your description?

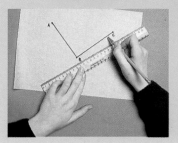  

A   Review how to bisect angles.

1. (a) Draw an angle of 70°.
   (b) Estimate where you might draw the bisector.
   (c) Construct the bisector of the angle.
   (d) What is the measure of each part? Check by measuring.

2. (a) Draw an angle of 45°.
   (b) Estimate where you might draw the bisector.
   (c) Construct the bisector of the angle.
   (d) What is the measure of each part? Check by measuring.

3. (a) Draw any acute angle and measure it.
   (b) Estimate where you might draw the bisector.
   (c) Construct the bisector of the angle.
   (d) What is the measure of each part? Check by measuring.

B   Be sure to use a sharp pencil.

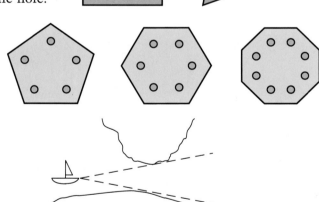

4. A hole for a bolt is to be drilled at the
   centre of the figures.
   (a) Copy each figure onto a piece of paper.
   (b) Bisect the angles. The intersection of
   the bisectors is the location of the hole.

5. Bolts are to be placed at these
   locations on the face plates.
   (a) Copy the diagram onto a
   separate piece of paper.
   (b) Bisect each angle to find the
   location of the bolts.

6. Copy the diagram. Find the path
   the ship is required to take to pass
   through the opening.

PARTNER PROJECT

Have you ever cut a circular pizza into slices? To do so, you use your skills with
estimation.
(a) Describe how estimation is involved.
(b) What are some other ways you could use your skills with estimation?
(c) In your journal, describe some other situations in which this skill could be used.

Companies design logos so that people can immediately identify and remember their products. Many logos, like the one shown, are based on a design that uses the bisectors of angles.

Using bisectors of angles, you can make up your own original designs and logos.

1. (a) Construct a copy of this design.
   (b) Use your own shading for the design.

2. For the design, ∠BAC is bisected. Construct a copy of the design.

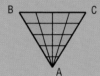

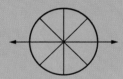

3. To construct the design, a line is drawn through the centre of the circle. The straight angle is then bisected, and so on. Construct a copy of the design.

4. Make a copy of the design.

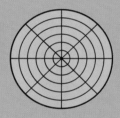

5. For each logo below:
   (a) Examine how the bisector of an angle might be used.
   (b) Construct a copy of the logo.
   (c) Find other logos and repeat parts (a) and (b).
   (d) Construct a design or logo of your own using bisectors of angles. In your journal, describe a company that might want to use your logo.

Your skills with bisecting can be applied in construction and design.

ACTIVITY 1 *Work with a Partner*

(a) Sketch a road in your notebook.
(b) Suppose you are a surveyor. You need to show where the lines are to be painted. What skills do you need to construct a white line exactly down the middle of the road?
(c) Add the white line to the road you sketched in (a).

To paint the white line down the middle of a road, you need to construct the right bisector of a line. Work with a partner to complete these activities.

ACTIVITY 2 *Work with a Partner*

The steps below are used to construct a perpendicular bisector. Describe each of the steps. Use them to construct your own perpendicular bisector.

Step 1   *Step 2*   *Step 3*

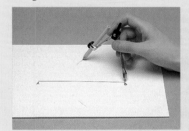  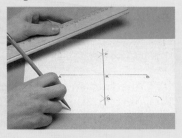

ACTIVITY 3 *Work with a Partner*

The steps below are used to construct a perpendicular to a line from a point not on the line. Describe each of the steps. Use your steps to construct a perpendicular to a line from a point not on the line.

Step 1   *Step 2*   *Step 3*   *Step 4*

   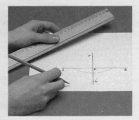

A Review your skills with constructions.

1. (a) Draw a line segment 8 cm in length.
    (b) Construct the right bisector of the line segment.
    (c) What is the measure of each part? Check by measuring.

2. (a) Draw a line segment 10 cm in length.
    (b) Describe to your partner how you can find the perpendicular bisector of the line by folding the paper.
    (c) Construct the perpendicular bisector by folding the paper.
    (d) What is the measure of each part? Check by measuring.

3. (a) Copy the line segments and the points shown below.
    (b) Describe to your partner how you can construct a perpendicular to AB through point C.
    (c) Use your plan in (b). Construct a perpendicular to AB that passes through C.
    (i)   (ii)

B Work Together.

4. (a) Construct an obtuse triangle as shown.
    (b) Construct the right bisector of the base CD.

5. (a) Construct any equilateral triangle.
    (b) Construct the right bisector of each of its sides.

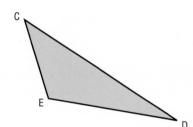

6. (a) Draw a line segment, AB, 4 cm in length.
    (b) Divide AB into four equal parts.

7. (a) Draw a line, PQ, 5 cm in length.
    (b) Divide PQ into eight equal parts.

8. A support is to be placed under the wood at its centre. Copy the diagram and construct the support.

9. A bridge is built as shown. A perpendicular support is placed on the rock, R, in the river.
   (a) Copy the diagram.
   (b) Construct the support.

10. To calculate the distance from the boat to the shore, a perpendicular is drawn. How far is the boat from the shore if 1 cm represents 2.75 km?

11. The pieces shown below can be used to form the letter "X."
    (a) Copy and cut out the pieces.
    (b) Fit the pieces together to form the "X."
    (c) How are the skills of bisecting lines and angles used to construct the pieces of the "X"?
    (d) Construct a letter of your own and use your skills with bisecting to cut the letter into different parts. Have others in the class find the letter you used.

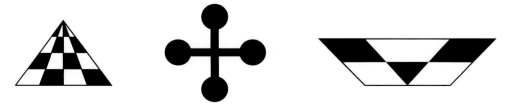

12. Right bisectors of line segments have been used to construct these designs. Make a copy of the designs.

BISECTORS

ACTIVITY 1   *Work in a Small Group*

1. (a) Copy the triangle shown to the right.
   (b) Bisect each of the angles. Extend the bisectors to intersect. What do you notice?
   (c) Place a pin at the point where the bisectors intersect. Can you balance the triangle at that point?
   (d) Repeat the above steps for other triangles of your own. What do you notice?

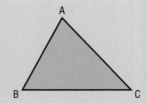

2. (a) Based on your work in Question 1, can you draw a circle inside each of the triangles so that the circle touches each side of the triangle exactly once?
   (b) Describe how you can find the centre of each circle. (The centre of such a circle is called an **incentre**.)

ACTIVITY 2   *Work in a Small Group*

3. (a) Copy the triangle shown to the right.
   (b) Find the perpendicular bisectors of each of the sides. Extend the perpendicular bisectors. What do you notice?
   (c) Draw a circle that passes through the three vertices of the triangle. What do you notice about the centre of the circle?
   (d) Repeat the above steps for other triangles of your own. What do you notice?
   (e) Based on your work above, can you draw a circle that passes through the vertices of a triangle? (The centre of the circle is called the **circumcentre**.)

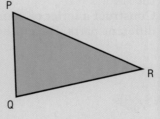

ACTIVITY 3   *Work in a Small Group*

4. (a) Copy the triangle shown to the right.
   (b) Construct the perpendicular from each vertex to the opposite side. What do you notice?
   (c) Repeat the above steps for other triangles of your own. What do you notice? (The point of intersection of the perpendiculars is called the **orthocentre**.)

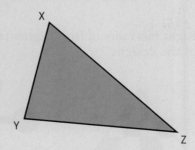

2.9 MAKING CONNECTIONS

ART

There are many well-known Canadian artists and some, such as Alex Colville, Hortense Gordon, and Harold Klunder, have had their work sold world-wide. Like many artists, Colville, Gordon, and Klunder have used geometric skills in their work.

ACTIVITY   *Work with a Partner*

1. Shown below are some pieces of art by Colville, Gordon, and Klunder.
   (a) What geometric skills do you think were used to create each piece?
   (b) What math skills do you think were used to create each piece?

2. Find paintings of your own.
   (a) What math skills do you think were used in the paintings?
   (b) In your journal, describe whether or not you like the paintings. Give reasons for your answer.

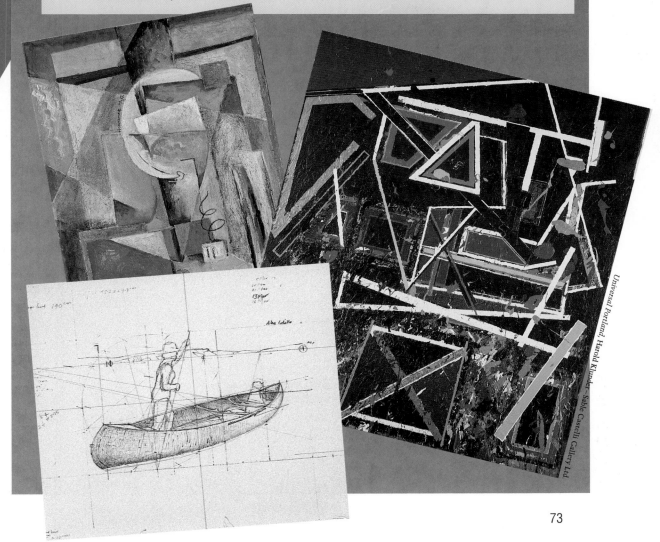

Universal Portland, Harold Klunder—Sable Castelli Gallery Ltd.

There are many similarities between playing sports and doing math.

ACTIVITY

(a) In your journal, list some of the special vocabulary associated with each sport shown in the photos.

(b) Describe how playing sports and doing math can be similar.

Just as each sport uses special vocabulary, each branch of mathematics uses special vocabulary.

You need to know the special vocabulary to work with circles.

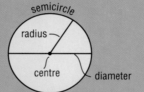

Concentric circles have the same centre.

You also need to know the names of the line segments and angles related to circles.

AB is a chord.
CD is an arc.

∠CPD is an inscribed angle on arc CD.

∠COD is a central angle on arc CD.

Work in groups to complete each of the following explorations. In your journal, summarize the properties and relationships of circles that you find.

1. (a) Construct a circle with a radius of 4 cm. Mark the centre of the circle.
   (b) Draw a chord. Construct its right bisector. Through what point does the right bisector pass?
   (c) Draw another chord and construct its right bisector. Through what point does it pass?

2. (a) Draw a circle of your own. Repeat the steps in Question 1.
   (b) What do you notice in (a)? Compare your results to others in the class. What do you notice?

3. (a) Summarize the relationships you have found in Questions 1 and 2.
   (b) What type of problem are you now able to solve? Create and solve one such problem.

4. (a) In the diagram, ΔABC is inscribed on the diameter BC.
   (b) Measure ∠BAC. What do you notice?

5. (a) Draw a circle of your own. Mark the centre. Construct the triangle on the diameter.
   (b) Measure the angle inscribed on BC. What do you notice?
   (c) Repeat the steps above for other circles of your own.
   (d) Compare your observations with others in the class. What do you notice?

6. (a) Summarize the relationships you have found in Questions 4 and 5.
   (b) What type of problem are you now able to solve? Create and solve one such problem.

7. (a) In the diagram, two angles are inscribed on DC. Name the inscribed angles.
   (b) Measure the inscribed angles. What do you notice?

8. (a) Draw a circle of your own. Mark any arc. Inscribe two angles on your arc.
   (b) Measure the inscribed angles. What do you notice?

9. (a) Summarize the relationships you have found in Questions 7 and 8.
   (b) What type of problem are you now able to solve? Create and solve one such problem.

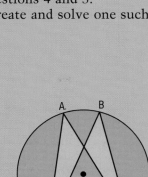

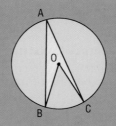

10. (a) In the diagram, an inscribed angle and a
       central angle are shown. Name the inscribed
       angle and the central angle.
    (b) Measure the inscribed angle and the central
       angle. What do you notice?

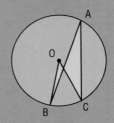

11. (a) In the diagram, an inscribed angle and a central
       angle are shown. Name the inscribed angle and
       the central angle.
    (b) Measure the inscribed angle and the central
       angle. What do you notice?

12. (a) Draw a circle of your own. Mark any arc. Draw
       an inscribed angle and a central angle.
    (b) Measure the inscribed angle and the central angle. What do you notice?

13. (a) Summarize the relationships you have found in Questions 10, 11, and 12.
    (b) What type of problem are you now able to solve? Create and solve one
       such problem.

MAKING CONNECTIONS

(a) Refer to the diagram. The points form a circle. What special
    properties do you think this nine-point circle has?
(b) Follow these steps to construct a nine-point circle.
    Step 1 Construct a large triangle on a piece of paper.
    Step 2 Perform a construction to find the midpoint of each side of the
             triangle. Label each point A, B, and C.
    Step 3 Construct a perpendicular line from each angle
             to the opposite side. Label the point of
             intersection on the sides as D, E, and F. The
             line you have constructed is called an *altitude*.
             What do you notice about the point of
             intersection of the altitudes?
    Step 4 Find the midpoint of the line that
             joins each vertex and the point of
             intersection of the altitudes.
             Label the points G, H, and I.
    Step 5 Draw the circle that passes through
             all the points in Steps 2, 3, and 4.
             Shade your circle. The circle is
             called the *nine-point circle*.

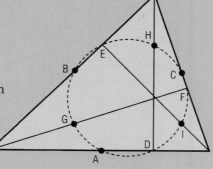

(c) In your journal, describe why the
    circle is appropriately named.

A good way to summarize relationships in mathematics is to represent the relationships using diagrams. Diagrams can be easier to remember than words alone.

ACTIVITY

In each diagram below, the centre of the circle is O.
(a) Describe the relationship that is being shown in each diagram.

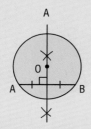

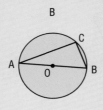

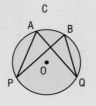

(b) Describe what type of problem can be solved using the relationships.
(c) Check your conclusions in (a) at the bottom of the page once you have finished this activity.

Once you have summarized the properties, you can use them to solve problems.

EXAMPLE
Find the centre of the base of a circular can.

SOLUTION

Step 1
Trace the bottom of the can.

Step 2
Draw a chord AB. Construct its right bisector. (The right bisector passes through the centre of the circle.)

Step 3
Draw another chord PQ. Contruct its right bisector. (The right bisector passes through the centre of the circle.)

Step 4
Mark the intersection point C. The centre of the circle is C.

Now find the centre of a can.

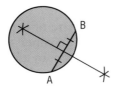

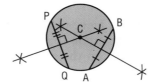

A The right bisector of any chord passes through the centre of the circle.

B The angle inscribed in a semicircle is 90°.

C Angles inscribed in a circle on the same arc are equal.

D The measure of a central angle is twice the measure of the inscribed angle on the same arc.

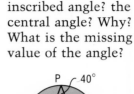

EXERCISE

A Review the properties of a circle.

1. (a) Which angle is drawn on the diameter? What is the missing value?

(b) Which angles appear to be equal? What is the value of ∠P?

(c) Which angle is the inscribed angle? the central angle? Why? What is the missing value of the angle?

B Work with a partner.

2. (a) Draw a large circle on a piece of paper.
   (b) Fold the paper so that a chord appears on the circle.
   (c) Fold the paper to find the right bisector of the chord.
   (d) Repeat (b) and (c) for a different chord.
   (e) Through what point will each of the right bisectors pass?

3. (a) Draw a large circle on a piece of paper.
   (b) Fold the paper to form a diameter.
   (c) Fold the paper again so that a triangle is formed with two vertices as the end points of the diameter and a third on a semicircle.
   (d) Measure the angle that touches the semicircle. What do you notice?

4. (a) Draw a large circle on a piece of paper.
   (b) Mark two points on the circle to form an arc.
   (c) Fold the paper so that the two end points, and a third point on the circle, are used to form an angle.
   (d) Repeat (c) to form a different angle.
   (e) Measure the two angles. What do you notice?

5. (a) Draw a large circle on a piece of paper. Mark the centre of the circle.
   (b) Mark two points on the circle to form an arc. Fold the paper so that the two end points, and a third point on the circle, are used to form an angle.
   (c) Fold the paper so that the two end points and the centre of the circle form an angle.
   (d) Measure the angles in (b) and (c). What do you notice?

6. Find the missing measures. All linear measures are in centimetres.

(a)

(b)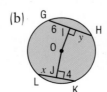

(c)

78

7. Find the
   missing measures.

(a)

(b)

(c)

8. Find the
   missing measures.

(a)

(b)

(c)

9. The corner of a piece of
   paper is a 90° angle and is
   placed on a circle as shown.
   (a) Why is BC the diameter?
   (b) How can the above corner be used
       to find the centre of the circle?

10. Three towns, Akron, Bellows, and Camden
    are shown. A water reservoir is to be built
    the same distance from the three towns.
    (a) Copy the diagram.
        Construct the right
        bisector of AB.
    (b) Construct the right bisector
        of CB to intersect the other
        right bisector at R.
    (c) Why is R the same distance from Akron, Bellows, and Camden?

11. (a) Make a list of all the ways you can find the centre of a circle.
    (b) In your journal, show when each method can be used.

12. (a) How can you find the centre of a circle by folding paper? Try it!
    (b) What properties of the circle did you use to find the centre of the circle?
    (c) What other properties of circles can you find by folding paper?

SELF EVALUATION

Test yourself. Refer to your notes and your journal.
(a) Write down all the new skills and terms that you learned and recorded.
(b) Now compare what you have written in (a) with the skills and terms used in this
    chapter. Is there anything that you missed?
(c) How can you improve the way in which you take notes so that you do not miss
    any skills taught? Try these ideas in the next chapter.

1. Estimate, then measure each angle. What type of angle is each?

(a) 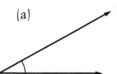 (b)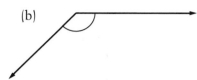

2. The measures of sides and angles are shown for triangles. What type of triangle is each?
   (a) 5 cm, 8 cm, 5 cm (b) 44°, 90°, 46°

3. (a) Draw any angle.
   (b) Have your partner estimate the measure of the angle.
   (c) Have your partner bisect the angle.

4. (a) Draw any line AB and a point C on the line.
   (b) Have your partner construct a perpendicular to AB through C.

5. A triangle is shown. Make suitable measures. Construct a copy of the triangle. What type of triangle is it?

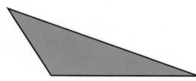

6. How are the angles A and B related in each diagram? O is the centre of the circle.

(a)   (b)   (c)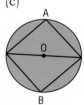

7. (a) Construct circles that have radii measuring 2 cm, 3 cm, 4 cm, 5 cm, 6 cm.
   (b) Use the circles in (a) to draw a design.

8. Use only a straightedge and a pair of compasses to construct an angle that measures $22\frac{1}{2}°$.

THINKING ABOUT

❶ How did you use patterns and relationships to help you discover relationships in geometry?

❷ What did you learn about geometry that you did not know before?

❸ In what career(s) do you think the skills in this chapter would be useful?

MAKING CONNECTIONS

Refer to the opening page of this chapter.
(a) Create a problem of your own using the picture. Solve your problem.
(b) Compare your problem with others in your class. Solve the other problems.

❹ What new skills have you learned in geometry?

❺ Describe how you solved Question 1(b) on this page. Explain to your partner why you solved it as you did.

❻ Refer to section 2.1. Modify the game to include all words and terms from this chapter. Play the game with your partner.

MATH JOURNAL

Geometric shapes occur often in design.

(a) List three geometric shapes that appear in the design of your school.

(b) Why do you think these shapes are used in the design?

SELF EVALUATION

1. (a) Complete the chart for each angle.

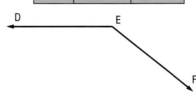

	Estimate	Measure
∠ACB	?	?
∠DEF	?	?

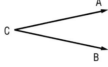

(b) Construct an angle that is equal to the sum of the angles above.

2. Construct a design that uses bisectors of line segments and angles.

3. (a) Construct an equilateral triangle with sides 6.5 cm in length.
   (b) Find its incentre, orthocentre, and circumcentre.

4. (a) Construct a diagram(s) to illustrate the meaning of each of the following.
   A central angle on a chord
   B inscribed angle on a chord
   C inscribed angle on a diameter
   (b) How are the diagrams in A, B, and C the same? How are they different?

5. What is the value of each missing angle?

(a)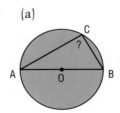

(b)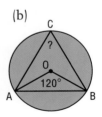

6. Take a piece of paper. Mark a point P and a line segment AB. Construct a perpendicular from P to the line segment AB.

7. (a) Draw any three points, P, Q, and R, on a piece of paper.
   (b) Construct the right bisector of QR to intersect the right bisector of PQ at O.
   (c) Draw a circle, with centre O, through the points P, Q, and R.

Increasingly novel uses are being found for the computer. In fact, computers are now used in many ways to help people live more efficiently.

Refer to the photographs:
- Describe how each person's life would be different without the computer.
- Describe how you think math skills can be used to develop each piece of technology.

A student works at a computer that gives a printout in Braille.

A computer-controlled robot equipped with sensors can be used to hold fragile objects.

An in-vehicle computer helps a driver plan a trip, and provides step-by-step instructions on how to get to the desired destination.

A speech therapist uses a terminal with voice-recognition facility.

- **R**efer to the picture. Identify opposite ideas.
- In your journal, describe the opposites represented.
- Find other pictures that represent opposite ideas.
- Create a class display.

3.1 EXPLORING INTEGERS

In mathematics, integers can be used to represent opposite ideas. You can use red and black unit tiles to help you interpret integers ... $-2, -1, 0, +1, +2, ...$

 represents -1 represents $+1$

EXPLORATION ① Work in a Small Group

1. You can use unit tiles to represent the following.
   (a) Use red tiles to represent 5 km west.
   (b) Use black tiles to represent the opposite integer in (a). Write the opposite integer.
   (c) Write the integer used to represent each of the following. Write its opposite.
      (i) 4 km east   (ii) 2 km west   (iii) 7 steps up
      (iv) $9 less   (v) $12 more   (vi) 8 km north

EXPLORATION ② Work in a Small Group

2. The expression $(+5) + (+3)$ is represented by unit tiles.

   (a) What is the net result of adding 5 black unit tiles and 3 black unit tiles?
   (b) Use your work in (a). What is the answer for $(+5) + (+3)$?

3. (a) Use unit tiles to represent $(-5) + (-3)$. What is the net result?
   (b) Use your work in (a). What is the answer for $(-5) + (-3)$?

4. The expression $(-5) + (+3)$ is represented using unit tiles.
   1 black unit tile together with
   1 red unit tile gives a net result
   of zero.

   (a) What is the net result of adding 5 red unit tiles and 3 black unit tiles?
   (b) Use your work in (a). What is the answer for $(-5) + (+3)$?

5. (a) Use unit tiles to represent $(+5) + (-3)$. What is the net result?
   (b) Use your work in (a). What is the answer for $(+5) + (-3)$?
   (c) Use unit tiles to represent each of the following. Find the answer.
      (i) $(-4) + (+2)$ (ii) $(-4) + (-2)$ (iii) $(+4) + (-2)$ (iv) $(+4) + (+2)$
      (v) $(+8) + (+6)$ (vi) $(+8) + (-6)$ (vii) $(-8) + (+6)$ (viii) $(-8) + (-6)$

6. (a) Use unit tiles to represent an addition expression of your own.
   (b) Write your expression in (a) and the answer.

7. (a) Represent the integer +5 using unit tiles.
   (b) What is the net result of taking two unit tiles from (a)?
   (c) Use your work in (b). What is the answer for (+5) – (+2)?

8. (a) Use unit tiles to represent –5.
   (b) What is the net result of taking two red unit tiles from (a)?
   (c) Use your work in (b). What is the answer for (–5) – (–2)?

9. Use unit tiles to represent each expression. Write the answer.
   (a) (+6) – (+3) 　(b) (+7) – (+4) 　(c) (+2) – (+1) 　(d) (+8) – (+5)
   (e) (–7) – (–3) 　(f) (–5) – (–4) 　(g) (–8) – (–6) 　(h) (–9) – (–1)

10. (a) Write subtraction expressions of your own similar to those in the previous question.
    (b) Use unit tiles to represent each expression. Write the answer.

EXPLORATION ④　*Work with a Partner*

11. To find the answer to (+4) – (–3), Jacqueline uses unit tiles.

Step 1　　　　　　*Step 2*　　　　　　　　　　*Step 3*

She realizes that she can't subtract red unit tiles from black unit tiles.

Jacqueline decides to represent +4 in another way.

She removes 3 red unit tiles. What is the net result?

12. (a) Describe how you could use unit tiles to find (–5) – (+7).
    (b) Use your work in (a). What is the answer for (–5) – (+7)?

13. (a) Use unit tiles to answer each of the following.
    (i) (–7) – (+5) 　　(ii) (+9) – (–6) 　　(iii) (+11) – (–7)
    (b) Use unit tiles to represent your own expressions involving integers. What are the answers? Have your partner evaluate your expressions.
    (c) Then, compare your results with those of others in the class.

In your journal, describe what math skills you think voyageurs would have used. Give examples.

A group of voyageurs travelled due east from camp for 10 km. When they came to the falls, they turned around, and had to travel 3 km due west to try another route. At that point, what was their position from camp?

You can use integers to translate and solve the problem above.

Use $+10$ to show 10 km due east.

Use -3 to show 3 km due west.

To find the final position, you add the integers.

Use unit tiles.

$$(+10) + (-3) = +7$$

Think:
Make a sketch to visualize the problem.

Thus, their final position was 7 km due east of the camp.

A calculator can also be used to help you add integers.

EXAMPLE
Add.
(a) $(+6) + (-2)$ (b) $(-8) + (+5)$

SOLUTION
(a) $\boxed{6} + \boxed{2} \boxed{+/-} \boxed{=} \ 4$ (b) $\boxed{c} \ \boxed{8} \boxed{+/-} \boxed{+} \boxed{5} \boxed{=} -3$

STRATEGIES TO HELP

- Write integers like +3 as 3 and +5 as 5.
- Negative integers like −3 must *always* be written with the negative sign.

A Use tiles to help you. Work with a partner.

1. The tiles show a gain of 8 and a loss of 3.
   (a) Write an addition expression to represent a gain of 8 and a loss of 3.
   (b) Evaluate the expression in (a).

2. What is the sum in each statement? Use integers to show your work.
   (a) a gain of 3 and a gain of 5
   (b) a gain of 8 and a gain of 12
   (c) a loss of 2 and a loss of 7
   (d) a loss of 9 and a loss of 4

3. What is the sum of the following?
   (a) a gain of 8, a loss of 4
   (b) a loss of 6, a gain of 3
   (c) a gain of 6, a loss of 8
   (d) a loss of 12, a gain of 12

4. Find the following sums.
   (a) $(+6) + (+3)$ (b) $(+4) + (-3)$ (c) $(-7) + (-2)$ (d) $(+4) + (+2)$
   (e) $(-6) + (+3)$ (f) $(-6) + (+5)$ (g) $(-6) + (+6)$ (h) $(-4) + (-4)$

5. Use integers to show how to find the final position of each of the following.
   (a) Canoeing 15 km west of camp and then returning 12 km east towards camp.
   (b) Lowering a diver 10 m and then raising her 8 m.
   (c) Raising a flag 11 m and then lowering it 2 m.

B Use a calculator to help you. Estimate first.

6. Find the sum of the integers.
   (a) $3, -2$ (b) $-3, 2$ (c) $-3, -2$ (d) $5, -4$ (e) $6, -9$

7. Find the sum.
   (a) $6 + (-4)$ (b) $-8 + 4$ (c) $8 + (-2)$ (d) $-7 + (-7)$ (e) $(-8) + (-8)$

8. Evaluate.
   (a) $-5 + 7$ (b) $3 + (-4)$ (c) $-2 + (-1)$ (d) $-8 + 8$ (e) $0 + (-8)$
   (f) $-9 + (-6)$ (g) $4 + (-1)$ (h) $6 + (-8)$ (i) $-3 + (-2)$ (j) $-30 + (-20)$

9. Find the sum.
   (a) $3 + (-2) + 5$ (b) $-4 + (-6) + 1$ (c) $-2 + 8 + (-5)$
   (d) $-3 + (-6) + (-1)$ (e) $-4 + 8 + (-2)$ (f) $(-2) + (-1) + 3$

10. Find the sum.
    (a) $19 + (-3) + (-2) + (-1) + 6 + (-5)$ (b) $19 + (-9) + 20 + (-40) + (-30)$

11. Last Monday, Jessica had $264 in her bank account. On Tuesday, she wrote cheques for $60 and $92. On Thursday, she deposited $21.
    (a) Use integers to create an expression to show how much money is in Jessica's account.
    (b) What is the final amount in her account?

12. In a recent four-round golf tournament, Dawn Coe had the following scores:
    $-2, +1, -1, -2$.
    (a) What was her final score?
    (b) Suppose the winner of the tournament had a score two less than Dawn's. What was the winning score?

> On a golf course with a par of 72, a score of 71 can be written as -1. A score of 74 can be written as $+2$.

13. In a five-round golf tournament, the following scores were recorded. The winner of the tournament had the lowest score. Who won the tournament?
    (a) Jennifer $-3, +2, -1, -2, +1$
    (b) Yuval $-3, +2, +1, 0, -2$
    (c) Ying $-2, -1, 0, +1, +2$
    (d) José $+2, +3, -1, -5, -2$

14. To qualify for a golf tour, a player's total score must be less than $+5$.
    (a) Estimate which of the following players qualified for the tour.
    (b) Calculate each total score. Which players qualified? How reasonable was your estimate?
    A Samir $+1, -2, +4, -3, +2, 0, +1, -2, -2$
    B Story $-1, -2, +3, +2, 0, +1, -2, +2, +1$
    C Vince $-2, +1, 0, +3, +2, +1, -1, +2, 0$

15. Find the February 21 temperature (°C) in each city in the table.

	Victoria	Edmonton	Calgary	Yellowknife	Saskatoon	Regina	Winnipeg	Fort Erie	Ottawa	Montréal	Québec City	Charlottetown	Fredericton	Saint John	Moncton	Halifax	Gander
Temp. (°C) on Feb 20	8	−8	−7	−18	−6	−16	−22	6	2	3	−1	−3	2	2	0	3	−9
Change in temp. from Feb 20 to Feb 21	−3	2	−9	4	−4	−3	−7	3	−2	6	−3	1	−2	6	−3	−3	−2

16. (a) Write different integers on 12 cards and place them in a box. Have the first player reach in and remove a card. The player records the integer as the score.
    (b) The next player reaches in and removes a card. The integer on the card is added to the previous score. The player receives that score.
    (c) The next player reaches in and removes a card. The integer is added to the score in (b).
    (d) Repeat (c) until all the cards are gone. The winner is the player who has the greatest total. Keep the cards for later use.

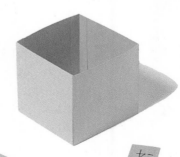

3.3 SUBTRACTING INTEGERS

Wildlife in Canada's high Arctic has adapted to extremes in climate. The Arctic hare, for example, endures a temperature range from −47°C in winter to +24°C in summer.

Suppose the high temperature was +3°C yesterday. The temperature then dropped by +5°C to reach the low. What low temperature would the Arctic hare be exposed to for this day?

To find the low temperature, you need to evaluate (+3) − (+5).

To help you subtract, you can think of using unit tiles as follows.

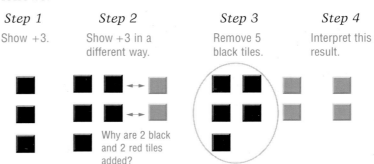

Step 1	*Step 2*	*Step 3*	*Step 4*
Show +3.	Show +3 in a different way.	Remove 5 black tiles.	Interpret this result.

Why are 2 black and 2 red tiles added?

There are two red unit tiles left. Thus, (+3) − (+5) = −2.

Therefore, the low temperature was −2°C.

Ellesmere Island, Northwest Territories
• in winter (top) • in summer (bottom)

ACTIVITY

• What are some other parts of the world that have extremes in climate?
• List places and their temperature ranges.
• Create and solve a problem using these numbers.

EXERCISE

A   Remember: Think of unit tiles to help you subtract integers.

1. Evaluate. Use unit tiles to help you.
   (a) (+7) − (+5)   (b) (−8) − (+7)   (c) (+3) − (+1)
   (d) (+9) − (+7)   (e) (−4) − (+3)   (f) (−1) − (+6)

2. Evaluate. Use unit tiles to help you.
   (a) (+7) − (−8)   (b) 0 − (−5)   (c) (+9) − 0
   (d) (+7) − (−7)   (e) (−8) − (−4)   (f) (−3) − (−8)

3. What are the values of ■?

A	B	C
$(6) - (3) = $ ■	$(4) - (2) = $ ■	$(9) - (2) = $ ■
$(6) - (2) = $ ■	$(4) - (1) = $ ■	$(9) - (1) = $ ■
$(6) - (1) = $ ■	$(4) - (0) = $ ■	$(9) - (0) = $ ■
$(6) - (0) = $ ■	$(4) - (-1) = $ ■	$(9) - (-1) = $ ■
$(6) - (-1) = $ ■	$(4) - (-2) = $ ■	$(9) - (-2) = $ ■
$(6) - (-2) = $ ■	$(4) - (-3) = $ ■	$(9) - (-3) = $ ■
$(6) - (-3) = $ ■	$(4) - (-4) = $ ■	$(9) - (-4) = $ ■

4. Complete each of the following by subtracting. In your journal, write any patterns you see.

(a)

4	4	4	4
1	0	-1	-2
3	4	■	■

(b)

-2	-2	-2	-2
2	1	0	-1
-4	-3	■	■

(c)

-1	-1	-1	-1
2	3	4	5
-3	-4	■	■

5. Refer to the unit tiles shown.
   (a) What subtraction expression can be represented using the tiles?
   (b) Evaluate the expression.
   (c) Compare your expression to others in the class. What do you notice?

6. Find the missing values of ■. Write the next three rows for each pattern.
   (a) $(+2) - (-6) = +8$
   $(+1) - (-6) = +7$
   $0 - (-6) = $ ■
   $(-1) - (-6) = $ ■

   (b) $(-8) - (-9) = +1$
   $(-8) - (-8) = 0$
   $(-8) - (-7) = $ ■
   $(-8) - (-6) = $ ■

   (c) Create your own pattern.

B   Your *Problem Solving Plan* may help with these problems.

7. Calculate.
   (a) $(+5) - (-3)$
   (b) $(+11) - (-8)$
   (c) $(+15) - (+12)$
   (d) $(-9) - (-3)$
   (e) $(-5) - (-4)$
   (f) $(-13) - (-8)$
   (g) $0 - (-4)$
   (h) $(-9) - 0$

8. Subtract.
   (a) 5 from 12
   (b) 8 from -3
   (c) -1 from 2
   (d) 6 from -13
   (e) -8 from -7
   (f) 14 from -2
   (g) -5 from 0
   (h) 0 from -5

9. Find each difference.
   (a) $6 - 3$
   (b) $-2 - 1$
   (c) $-5 - 4$
   (d) $2 - 6$
   (e) $3 - 5$
   (f) $-4 - 8$
   (g) $-2 - 2$
   (h) $3 - 3$
   (i) $10 - (-5)$
   (j) $-8 - (-10)$
   (k) $40 - (-24)$
   (l) $-16 - (-6)$
   (m) $9 - (-1)$
   (n) $-10 - 13$
   (o) $17 - 21$
   (p) $-12 - (-3)$

10. Subtract.
   (a) $15 - (-25)$
   (b) $-15 - (-25)$
   (c) $-20 + 32$
   (d) $7 - (-43)$
   (e) $-7 + 43$
   (f) $92 - (-21)$
   (g) $63 - (-4)$
   (h) $-27 + 43$
   (i) $56 - (-8)$
   (j) $-65 - (-103)$
   (k) $225 - (-410) - 36$

11. A store's temperature was 18°C. Its walk-in freezer had a temperature of – 16°C.
    (a) Write an expression to find how much warmer the store was than the freezer. Estimate an answer.
    (b) Evaluate your expression in (a). How much warmer was the store?

12. Refer to the information in the previous question.
    (a) Suppose the question asked how much colder the freezer room was than the store. How would your expression change?
    (b) Evaluate your expression in (a). How much colder is the freezer room than the store?
    (c) How are your answers in (b) and Question 11 alike? How are they different?

13. (a) The temperature in a tent is 6°C. The temperature outside the tent is – 18°C. What change in temperature would you experience if you went outside?
    (b) Create a problem of your own similar to (a). Solve your problem and have others in the class solve the problem.

14. Refer to the example of the Arctic hare on page 89.
    (a) How much greater is the summer temperature than the winter temperature?
    (b) How much lower is the winter temperature than the summer temperature?
    (c) What do you notice about your answers in (a) and (b)?

15. Work with a partner.
    (a) Write 12 consecutive integers on separate cards.
    (b) Arrange the cards to form the shape shown so that no two consecutive integers share the same side.
    (c) Create a problem of your own using the cards. Solve your problem and have others in the class solve your problem.

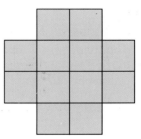

16. Evaluate.
    (a) $7 - (-1) + (-3)$ (b) $(-10) - (-5) + 6$ (c) $(-7) - (-5) - (-3)$
    (d) $(-12) - (-4) - (-4) - 5 - (-3) + 6$ (e) $16 - 4 - (-2) + 10 - (-4) - (-1) + 8$
    (f) $-15 - (-1) + 8 - 2 - (-3) - 9 + 4$ (g) $-12 - (-3) + 5 - 7 + (-2) - 8 - (-4)$

17. Find the missing integer in each.
    (a) $+7 - a = 2$ (b) $-4 - b = 5$ (c) $c - (-3) = -8$
    (d) $d - (+7) = -10$ (e) $-9 - e = 0$ (f) $f - (+2) = 14$

CALCULATION SENSE

You can decide whether the answer to a question will be positive or negative.

$(+3) + (-5)$ Think: The answer will be negative. Why?
$(+6) - (+8)$ Think: The answer will be negative. Why?

For each of the following, decide first whether the answer is positive or negative. Then, find the answer.
(a) $(-4) + (-2)$ (b) $(+6) - (+3)$ (c) $(+10) + (-17)$ (d) $(-8) - (-9)$
(e) $(-12) + (-9)$ (f) $(+11) - (+6)$ (g) $(+7) + (-8)$ (h) $(-2) - (+6)$

3.4 SUBTRACTING INTEGERS: USING PATTERNS

Work with a partner to complete the following activities. In your journal, record your findings.

ACTIVITY 1

1. How are the expressions below alike? How are they different?

Subtraction	Related Addition
$(+6) - (+4) = +2$	$(+6) + (-4) = +2$
$(-6) - (+4) = -10$	$(-6) + (-4) = -10$
$(-6) - (-4) = -2$	$(-6) + (+4) = -2$

2. What pattern is suggested that can be used to help you subtract integers?

ACTIVITY 2

Continue working with a partner to complete the following exercises. In your journal, summarize any patterns that you think can help you subtract integers. As you obtain new information, include it in your summary.

3. Find the value of each ■. What do you notice about your answers?

A	B
$(+8) - (+1) = ■$	$(+8) + (-1) = ■$
$(+8) - (-1) = ■$	$(+8) + (+1) = ■$

4. Copy and complete.
   - Compare your answers in each column. How are they alike? How are they different?
   - Do you notice any patterns?

	Subtraction	Related Addition
(a)	$(+6) - (+3) = ■$	$(+6) + (-3) = ■$
(b)	$(-5) - (+2) = ■$	$(-5) + (-2) = ■$
(c)	$(-4) - (-3) = ■$	$(-4) + (+3) = ■$

5. (a) Create expressions of your own to subtract integers.
   (b) Have your partner write the related addition for each expression in (a). Then evaluate each expression.

ACTIVITY 3

6. Use your results from Activity 1 and Activity 2. Write a pattern that can be used to subtract integers. Use the pattern to subtract the following.
   (a) $(-7) - (+9)$ (b) $(+10) - (-9)$ (c) $(+10) - (+12)$ (d) $(-7) - (-5)$

3.5 LOOKING BACK: SUBTRACTION

Here is a summary of the different methods to subtract integers. You can evaluate $(-3) - (-2)$ in the following ways.

Use Tiles	Represent -3.	Remove 2 red tiles.	Interpret your answer. Thus, $(-3) - (-2) = -1$.

Use a Related Addition

$(-3) - (-2) = (-3) + (+2)$
$\qquad\qquad\quad = -1$

Use a Calculator

c 3 +/- − 2 +/- = −1

In your journal, choose examples to illustrate each method. Solve your example.

EXERCISE

A Think about how to subtract integers.

1. Calculate.
   (a) $(+8) - (+9)$
   (b) $(+10) - (+7)$
   (c) $(+8) - (+10)$
   (d) $(-3) - (-4)$
   (e) $(-4) - (-3)$
   (f) $(+6) - (-9)$

2. Evaluate.
   (a) $(-10) - (+7)$
   (b) $(+11) - (-8)$
   (c) $(-3) - (-8)$
   (d) $(+7) - (-9)$
   (e) $(+6) - (-3)$
   (f) $(-5) - (-7)$

3. Calculate.
   (a) $-3 + (-5) - (-4)$
   (b) $-11 + 3 - (-7)$
   (c) $14 - (-8) + (-6)$
   (d) $-5 + (-7) - 11$
   (e) $26 - 17 - (-19)$
   (f) $-7 - (-6) + (-8)$

B Estimate your answer and tell your partner what you think each answer is before calculating.

4. Replace ■ with either > or <. In your journal, describe how you could determine the appropriate symbol mentally.
   (a) $13 - (-3)$ ■ $-12 - 24$
   (b) $9 + (-3)$ ■ $-3 + (-4)$
   (c) $5 - (-3)$ ■ $-4 - (+5)$

5. During a golf tournament, Wanda had a score of -3 on the first day. Her total score after the second day was $+4$. What was her score on the second day?

6. Janine was playing the video game, *Super Collision*. Her score in the first game was 87 points. Her total score for two games was -136 points. What was Janine's score in the second game?

During hockey games, players are given plus/minus scores to compare performances (refer to the clipping below photo). For each of three games, Ayako earned the following plus/minus scores.

Game 1: -2 Game 2: -2 Game 3: -2

Her total standing for the three games can be written as a product: $(+3) \times (-2) = ?$

ACTIVITY 1

Unit tiles and patterns can be used to help you find an answer. Work with a partner to complete the following activity.

1. Six red tiles are shown.
   (a) How would you use these unit tiles to give meaning to $(+3) \times (-2)$?
   (b) What is the answer for $(+3) \times (-2)$?

2. Use unit tiles to represent each product. Find the answer.
   (a) $(+6) \times (-2)$ (b) $(+5) \times (-2)$
   (c) $(+4) \times (-3)$ (d) $(+7) \times (-3)$
   (e) $(+8) \times (-2)$ (f) $(+3) \times (-5)$

3. How can the tiles above be used to represent $2 \times (-3)$?

In hockey, you calculate a player's plus/minus standing as follows:
- If a player is on the ice and a goal is scored by the player's team, the player receives +1.
- If a player is on the ice and the opposing team scores, the player receives -1.

ACTIVITY 2

A	B
$(+3) \times (+1) = +3$	$(+1) \times (+3) = +3$
$(+3) \times (0) = 0$	$(0) \times (+3) = 0$
$(+3) \times (-1) = -3$	$(-1) \times (+3) = -3$
$(+3) \times (-2) = -6$	$(-2) \times (+3) = -6$

4. (a) What do you notice about the expressions and answers in both columns? Test what you see using examples of your own.
   (b) Use the patterns in (a) to find the following products.
      (i) $(+5) \times (-2)$ (ii) $(+7) \times (-3)$ (iii) $(-3) \times (+4)$ (iv) $(-8) \times (+7)$
   (c) Based on your observations, suggest how you might multiply integers. Use examples of your own to illustrate your suggestions.

A Work with a partner.

1. (a) What multiplication
   expressions are suggested
   by the tiles shown?
   (b) What is the answer for each
   multiplication above?

A  B

2. Use tiles to represent each of the following expressions. Find the answers.
   (a) $(+4) \times (-3)$ (b) $(+3) \times (+6)$ (c) $(+5) \times (-2)$ (d) $(+3) \times (+3)$
   (e) $(+5) \times (+2)$ (f) $(+4) \times (-6)$ (g) $(+3) \times (-5)$ (h) $(+8) \times (+1)$

3. Use tiles or a pattern to find each answer. Then, describe how these expressions are like
   the ones in the previous question and how they are different.
   (a) $(-3) \times (+4)$ (b) $(+6) \times (+3)$ (c) $(-2) \times (+5)$ (d) $(+3) \times (+3)$
   (e) $(+2) \times (+5)$ (f) $(-6) \times (+4)$ (g) $(-5) \times (+3)$ (h) $(+1) \times (+8)$
   (i) $(+3) \times (-4)$ (j) $(-2) \times (+4)$ (k) $(+4) \times (-1)$ (l) $(+3) \times (-3)$

B Look for patterns. Record them in your journal.

4. Find each product. Use a calculator.
   (a) $(+5) \times (+6)$ (b) $(-3) \times (+7)$ (c) $(-11) \times (+8)$ (d) $(+9) \times (-1)$
   (e) $(+6) \times (-4)$ (f) $(-3) \times (+10)$ (g) $(+10) \times (+11)$ (h) $(-5) \times (+2)$
   (i) $(+4) \times (+11)$ (j) $(-4) \times (+12)$ (k) $(-8) \times (+3)$ (l) $(-2) \times (+17)$
   (m) $(-5) \times (+9)$ (n) $(+6) \times (-11)$ (o) $(-11) \times (+12)$ (p) $(-5) \times (+5)$

5. Calculate. Then check your work with a calculator.
   (a) $(+4) \times (-3)$ (b) $(-2) \times (+6)$ (c) $(+3) \times (-8)$ (d) $(-4) \times (+5)$
   (e) $(-7) \times (+2)$ (f) $(-3) \times (+5)$ (g) $(-8) \times (+4)$ (h) $(+7) \times (+9)$
   (i) $(+8) \times (-2)$ (j) $(+5) \times (-3)$ (k) $(+2) \times (-11)$ (l) $(-4) \times (+1)$
   (m) $(-7) \times (+8)$ (n) $(+10) \times (-4)$ (o) $(+12) \times (-13)$ (p) $(+9) \times (-15)$

6. Refer to the example on the previous page.
   (a) Suppose Ayako had a plus/minus score of -3 for each of 4 games. Write a product to
       find her total standing.
   (b) Solve the problem in (a).
   (c) Create and solve problems of your own using plus/minus scores.

MATH JOURNAL

In your journal, summarize patterns for multiplying integers. Write examples of your
own to illustrate your summary. Include answers to
(a) "What is the sign of the product of a positive integer and a positive integer?"
(b) "What is the sign of the product of a positive integer and a negative integer?"
(c) "What is the sign of the product of a negative integer and a positive integer?"

3.7 SUMMARIZING MULTIPLICATION

In the previous section, you explored patterns and relationships to help you multiply integers. You found that the product of a
- *positive* integer and a *positive* integer is a *positive* integer.
- *positive* integer and a *negative* integer is a *negative* integer.
- *negative* integer and a *positive* integer is a *negative* integer.

ACTIVITY *Work in a Small Group*

1. (a) How can you use the following to verify the statements above?
   (b) What other patterns can help you multiply integers?

$(+3) \times (-2) = -6$ Think: $(-2) \times (+3) = -6$ Think:
$(+2) \times (-2) = -4$ The products $(-2) \times (+2) = -4$ The products
$(+1) \times (-2) = -2$ increase by 2. $(-2) \times (+1) = -2$ increase by 2.
$(0) \times (-2) = 0$ $(-2) \times (0) = 0$
$(-1) \times (-2) = +2$ $(-2) \times (-1) = +2$
$(-2) \times (-2) = +4$ $(-2) \times (-2) = +4$

2. Use your results in Question 1. What do you notice about the product of a negative integer and a negative integer?

The activity above suggests that the product of two negative integers is a positive integer.

You can use your skills with multiplying integers to solve problems.

EXAMPLE

The temperature of a solution in a science experiment was 0°C. Over the next 4 h, the temperature dropped 3°C each hour. Use integers to find the final temperature.

STRATEGIES TO HELP

Ask yourself:
- Do I need to add? subtract? multiply?
- How can I summarize the steps that I need to use?
- Will my *Problem Solving Plan* help?

SOLUTION

Step 1 First find the total number of degrees the temperature dropped.

$(+4) \times (-3) = -12$ ⌐C⌐ 4 ×⌐ 3 ⌐+/-⌐ ⌐=⌐ -12

Step 2 Then, find the change in temperature.

$(0) + (-12) = -12$ ⌐C⌐ 0 ⌐+⌐ 12 ⌐+/-⌐ ⌐=⌐ -12

Step 3 Interpret your answer to write a final statement.

Thus, the final temperature was -12°C.

A In your journal, record any new words and symbols you use.

1. Copy and complete each pattern. Extend each pattern for 3 more rows.
   (a) $(-5) \times (+2) = ?$ (b) $(-7) \times (+3) = ?$ (c) $(+2) \times (-4) = ?$
      $(-5) \times (+1) = ?$ $(-7) \times (+2) = ?$ $(+1) \times (-4) = ?$
      $(-5) \times 0 \quad = ?$ $(-7) \times (+1) = ?$ $0 \times (-4) = ?$
      $(-5) \times (-1) = ?$ $(-7) \times 0 \quad = ?$ $(-1) \times (-4) = ?$
      $(-5) \times (-2) = ?$ $(-7) \times (-1) = ?$ $(-2) \times (-4) = ?$

2. Suggest a pattern to find the product of each. Then find the final product.
   (a) $(-3) \times (-4)$ (b) $(-2) \times (-5)$ (c) $(-7) \times (-1)$ (d) $(-4) \times (-5)$
   (e) $(-8) \times (-5)$ (f) $(-9) \times (-7)$ (g) $(-3) \times (-1)$ (h) $(-6) \times (-6)$
   (i) $(-6) \times (-3)$ (j) $(-9) \times (-2)$ (k) $(-3) \times (-8)$ (l) $(-1) \times (-1)$

3. In your journal, describe how the table to the right might be used to help you multiply integers. Use examples to help your explanation. What labels could you use for the chart?

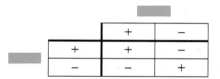

	+	−
+	+	−
−	−	+

B You can use your *Problem Solving Plan* to help organize your solutions.

4. Multiply.
   (a) $(+4) \times (-2)$ (b) $(+2) \times (-2)$ (c) $(0) \times (-2)$ (d) $(-3) \times (+2)$
   (e) $(-3) \times (+3)$ (f) $(-3) \times (+4)$ (g) $(+3) \times (-1)$ (h) $(+3) \times (-2)$
   (i) $(+3) \times (-3)$ (j) $(-3) \times (+5)$ (k) $(-2) \times (+5)$ (l) $(-1) \times (+5)$

5. Find each product.
   (a) $(+4) \times (-4)$ (b) $(+3) \times (-1)$ (c) $(-5) \times (-3)$ (d) $(+5) \times 0$
   (e) $(-2) \times (+2)$ (f) $(-4) \times (-3)$ (g) $(-2) \times (+6)$ (h) $(+3) \times (-6)$
   (i) $0 \times (+1)$ (j) $(-7) \times (-9)$ (k) $(+6) \times (+9)$ (l) $(-9) \times (+4)$

6. Which of the following products have the same value?
   (a) $(+3) \times (-2)$ (b) $(-5) \times 0$ (c) $(-4) \times (+3)$ (d) $(-1) \times (-6)$
   (e) $(-3) \times (+2)$ (f) $(-4) \times (-3)$ (g) $(-2) \times (+6)$ (h) $(+2) \times (+3)$

7. (a) In your journal, explain why $(-3) \times (-4)$ can also be written as $(-3)(-4)$.
   (b) Refer to (a). Evaluate the following.
      (i) $(-3)(-4)$ (ii) $(+5)(-7)$ (iii) $(-9)(+8)$ (iv) $(+6)(+7)$

8. Calculate each expression whose value is less than zero.
   (a) $(-1)(+1)$ (b) $(+3)(-4)$ (c) $(-1)(-4)$ (d) $(+7)(+4)$
   (e) $(-4)(-3)$ (f) $(-9)(-8)$ (g) $(-4)(+6)$ (h) $(0)(-66)$
   (i) $(-7)(-6)$ (j) $(+10)(-6)$ (k) $(+12)(+5)$ (l) $(-1)(+7)$

9. Sometimes you can write expressions in a different form. For example, $(+3)(-3)$ can be written as $3(-3)$. Interpret what each expression below means. Then find the final product.
   (a) $3(-2)$ (b) $4(-3)$ (c) $5(-5)$ (d) $-2(+1)$ (e) $-3(+3)$
   (f) $-4(+2)$ (g) $-3(+3)$ (h) $-2(-3)$ (i) $-4(-4)$ (j) $-6(-6)$

10. At the city pool, the temperature of the water on a cool night drops 2°C each hour.
    (a) Use integers to show how to obtain the temperature drop in 5 h.
    (b) The original temperature of the pool is 25°C. What is the temperature after 5 h?

11. Fran's average golf score is -12. Suppose Fran played 6 rounds of golf.
    (a) Use integers to show how to obtain her score after playing 6 rounds.
    (b) What would you predict Fran's total score to be after playing 6 rounds?

12. The temperature on Mars drops 15°C each hour during the Martian night.
    (a) Use integers to show how to obtain the temperature drop in 5 h.
    (b) What is the temperature drop in 12 h?
    (c) Create a problem of your own based on the above information. Solve your problem and also have others in the class solve it.

13. Use the integer cards you used in Section 3.2. Put the cards into the box.
    (a) Have each player remove two cards at a time.
    (b) Find the product of the cards in (a) and record the product as the score for that round.
    (c) Each player repeats (a) and (b) until all cards have been removed. Find each total score.
    (d) The winner is the player with the greatest score.

14. Find the integer represented by each variable. Once you have completed the next section, try this question again. In your journal, describe other ways you can find the value of the variable.
    (a) $-6 \times a = -30$ (b) $-15 \times b = 75$
    (c) $c \times (-13) = -52$ (d) $9 \times d = -81$

MAKING CONNECTIONS: SCIENCE

(a) Research the various moons in our solar system. How many moons are there?
(b) Find the average high temperature on each moon and the average low temperature on each moon.
(c) Create a problem using the information in (b) whose answer requires you to multiply integers. Compare your problem to others in the class.

3.8 DIVIDING INTEGERS

The skills you learn in one sport often can help you play another sport. Similarly, the skills you learn when multiplying integers can help you divide integers. Work together and complete the following activities. In your journal, summarize any patterns that can help you divide integers.

ACTIVITY 1

1. (a) Describe how the unit tiles are used to represent $(-8) \div (+2)$.
   (b) Use your work in (a). What is the answer to $(-8) \div (+2)$?

2. Use unit tiles to represent the following expressions. Find the answer to each expression.
   (a) $(+6) \div (+3)$ (b) $(-12) \div (+4)$ (c) $(+8) \div (+2)$ (d) $(-16) \div (+8)$
   (e) $(-9) \div (+3)$ (f) $(+10) \div (+5)$ (g) $(-8) \div (+4)$ (h) $(-24) \div (+8)$

ACTIVITY 2

3. (a) Find the product of each of the following.
   (i) $(+2) \times (+5)$ (ii) $(-2) \times (+5)$ (iii) $(+5) \times (-2)$ (iv) $(-5) \times (-2)$

   (b) You already know you can write $2 \times 5 = 10$ as a related division as $\frac{10}{5} = 2$ or $\frac{10}{2} = 5$.

   Use this pattern to write each integer expression in (a) as a related division.
   (c) Evaluate your related division expressions in (b).
   (d) In your journal, describe how you used the product of integers to help you divide integers. Give examples of your own to support your description.

In the activities above, you saw that to divide two integers, you can think of a related multiplication. For example, $(-25) \div (+5) = ?$ suggests $? \times (+5) = -25$. Since $(-5) \times (+5) = -25$, then $(-25) \div (+5) = -5$.

Think: What number
multiplied by $+5$ gives -25?
In this case, -5.

To help you divide integers, you can use a calculator.

EXAMPLE
Use a calculator to find each quotient.
(a) $(+26) \div (+13)$ (b) $(-27) \div (+9)$ (c) $(-35) \div (-7)$

SOLUTION

(a) $\boxed{c}$ 26 $\boxed{\div}$ 13 $\boxed{=}$ 2

(b) $\boxed{c}$ 27 $\boxed{+/-}$ $\boxed{\div}$ 9 $\boxed{=}$ -3

(c) $\boxed{c}$ 35 $\boxed{+/-}$ $\boxed{\div}$ 7 $\boxed{+/-}$ $\boxed{=}$ 5

Thus, $(+26) \div (+13) = +2$.   Thus, $(-27) \div (+9) = -3$.   Thus, $(-35) \div (-7) = +5$.

A Review your skills with integers. Refer to the Self Evaluation feature below.

1. (a) Write a division
   expression suggested
   by the tiles at right.
   (b) Evaluate each expression in (a).

   A  B

2. Use your tiles. Suggest how to divide each of the following.

   (a) $\dfrac{+9}{+3}$ (b) $\dfrac{-8}{+4}$ (c) $\dfrac{-6}{+3}$ (d) $\dfrac{+10}{+5}$ (e) $\dfrac{-8}{+2}$

3. Copy and complete the following to find the value of "?".

   (a) $(-4) \times (-7) = +28$ suggests $\dfrac{+28}{-4} = ?$ and $\dfrac{+28}{-7} = ?$

   (b) $(+3) \times (-4) = -12$ suggests $\dfrac{-12}{+3} = ?$ and $\dfrac{-12}{-4} = ?$

   (c) $(-4) \times (+4) = -16$ suggests $\dfrac{-16}{-4} = ?$ and $\dfrac{-16}{+4} = ?$

   (d) $(-4) \times (-6) = +24$ suggests $\dfrac{+24}{-4} = ?$ and $\dfrac{+24}{-6} = ?$

4. Use your work from Question 3. Find each quotient.

   (a) $\dfrac{+36}{+6}$ (b) $\dfrac{-30}{+6}$ (c) $\dfrac{+30}{-6}$ (d) $\dfrac{-30}{-6}$ (e) $\dfrac{-42}{+7}$

5. In your journal, summarize patterns that can be used to divide integers. Include in your summary answers to the following: What is the sign of the quotient when you
   - divide a positive integer by a positive integer?
   - divide a positive integer by a negative integer?
   - divide a negative integer by a positive integer?
   - divide a negative integer by a negative integer?

SELF EVALUATION

So far, you have learned how to add, subtract, multiply, and divide integers. Answer the following in your journal.
(a) How are the skills of adding and subtracting integers alike? How are they different?
(b) How are the skills of multiplying and dividing integers alike? How are they different?
(c) Use examples from this book to support your explanations in (a) and (b) and to help you study and review your work later.

6. Calculate.

   (a) $\dfrac{+42}{-7}$ (b) $\dfrac{-42}{-7}$ (c) $\dfrac{-36}{-6}$ (d) $\dfrac{+36}{-6}$ (e) $\dfrac{-36}{+6}$

7. For each of the following,
   - decide whether the quotient is positive or negative.
   - estimate an answer; then find the answer.

   (a) $(-24) \div (-6)$ (b) $(-36) \div (+9)$ (c) $(-36) \div (+18)$
   (d) $(+50) \div (+25)$ (e) $(+75) \div (-3)$ (f) $(-90) \div (-2)$

8. Calculate. Answer each question whose value is less than zero.

   (a) $(-36) \div (-12)$ (b) $(+15) \div (-3)$ (c) $0 \div (-10)$
   (d) $(+64) \div (-32)$ (e) $(-72) \div (+72)$ (f) $(+72) \div (-9)$ -8
   (g) $(-121) \div (-11)$ (h) $(+150) \div (-30)$ (i) $(-150) \div (-15)$

9. Evaluate. Check your work with a calculator.

   (a) $48 \div (-6)$ (b) $-48 \div (-8)$ (c) $-48 \div (+6)$ (d) $-72 \div (+9)$
   (e) $72 \div (-8)$ (f) $-72 \div (-9)$ (g) $168 \div (-8)$ (h) $-168 \div (+8)$
   (i) $-168 \div (-8)$ (j) $-360 \div (9)$ (k) $-360 \div (-9)$ (l) $360 \div (-9)$

10. Suppose you are an oil researcher. You discover that there is oil 750 m below the surface of the earth. You can drill 5 m each hour.
    (a) Write an expression using integers to show the length of time it will take you to hit the oil.
    (b) Calculate your expression in (a). How long will it take you?

11. A weather balloon records the temperature at a height of 900 m. Suppose the weather balloon descends 4 m each minute.
    (a) Write an expression using integers to find the length of time the balloon will take to reach the earth.
    (b) Solve your expression in (a). How much time is needed?

12. The freezing point of mercury is about $-38°C$ and for alcohol about $-114°C$. How many times lower is the freezing point of alcohol than mercury?

C

13. (a) Suppose that integers are written on cards and you use these cards, as well as the operations addition, subtraction, multiplication, or division, to write expressions for all the integers from -100 to 0. What is the least number of cards you will need?
    (b) What integers will you write on each of the cards? Try it.

Have you ever seen the decibel (dB) meter on a tape recorder? This meter indicates the level at which the music is being played or recorded. At about 0 dB, the amount of distortion and noise is at a minimum.

While recording a guitar solo at her studio, Mara observed the decibel level at 5 different times as follows:

−11 dB, +6 dB, +1 dB, −3 dB, +2 dB

What was the average decibel level?

For best results, the recording level must be around 0 dB. How would the recording sound if the average decibel level was too high? too low?

ACTIVITY 1

To solve a problem like the one above, you often apply skills you learned earlier. Refer to Mara's problem and work in a group.
(a) Which words do you understand?
(b) Which words don't you understand?
(c) Use a dictionary to help you find the meaning of each word in (b). How can the meanings of the words help you solve the problem?

ACTIVITY 2

The skills you learned with average can help you solve the problem above. Refer to the calculations for average shown below.
(a) How are the calculations alike? different?

$$\frac{6+9+10+15}{4} \qquad \frac{(-6)+(-9)+(+10)+(-15)}{4}$$

$$= \frac{40}{4} \text{ or } 10 \qquad = \frac{-20}{4} \text{ or } -5$$

(b) Describe how you can find the average of any group of numbers.

From the results of your activities, you can solve Mara's problem as follows.

$$\frac{(-11)+(+6)+(+1)+(-3)+(+2)}{5} = \frac{-5}{5} \text{ or } -1$$

Thus, the average decibel level is −1 dB.

A Use a calculator. Estimate first, then check your work.

1. Find the average for each.
   (a) $-12, -8, +5$ (b) $-18, +16, -14, -13, +9$ (c) $-9, -7, +15, +16, +12, -15, +14, -2$

2. Find the average of these decibel levels.
   (a) -3 dB, -5 dB, $+8$ dB, -4 dB   (b) -3 dB, $+4$ dB, $+7$ dB, -8 dB
   (c) $+1$ dB, $+2$ dB, $+3$ dB, -7 dB, $+11$ dB, -8 dB, -9 dB

3. Find the average of these temperatures.
   (a) $-4°C, +8°C, -8°C, 0°C$ (b) $+14°C, -23°C, -11°C, +16°C$
   (c) $-28°C, +45°C, -22°C, +32°C, +44°C, -51°C, -21°C, +33°C$

B Work with a partner.

4. The temperatures for the Mojave Desert at five different times throughout
   the year are $+22°C, +17°C, +16°C, +20°C, +10°C$.
   (a) Find the average of the temperatures above.
   (b) Find out more about the Mojave Desert. What other temperatures could be
       included in the list to keep the average the same?

5. The temperatures for Antarctica at seven different times throughout the year are
   $-16°C, -12°C, -11°C, -31°C, -8°C, -10°C, -17°C$.
   (a) Find the average of the temperatures above.
   (b) Find out more about Antarctica. What other temperatures could be included
       in the list to keep the average the same?

6. (a) Create and solve a problem using these temperatures: $-8°C, +6°C, -5°C, -3°C$.
   (b) In your journal, describe why you think you would ever need to find an
       average temperature. Give examples to support your explanation.

7. The decibel levels when recording a song are the following:
   -9 dB, -12 dB, $+7$ dB, $+4$ dB, $+6$ dB, -3 dB, 0 dB.
   (a) What is the average decibel level?
   (b) How much more is the average decibel level than the lowest level?
   (c) How much less is the average decibel level than the highest level?

C

8. Locate some reference books like those shown below.
   (a) Find some interesting facts that can be expressed using integers.
   (b) Create a problem based on these facts.

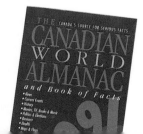

NATURAL RESOURCES

Because there is such a great worldwide demand for valuable metals, prospectors are always trying to find new deposits. One of the newer methods of prospecting for deposits in the earth is airplane or satellite photography.

Once it has been established that an area contains mineral or metal deposits, core samples are taken from the earth to determine the extent of the deposits and at what depths they will be found.

Airplanes with sophisticated equipment can establish whether certain metals can be found in the earth.

The largest open pit mine in Canada is in Labrador City, Nfld. Estimate the depth of the mine.

Find out what metal is mined in Labrador City.

ACTIVITY

A forest manager views forests not only as resources for lumber, but also as natural resources that must be conserved.

(a) Find out more about the occupation of forest manager. In your journal, describe how a forest manager would use mathematics.

(b) Natural resources are also taken from mines. In your journal, describe how you think some of the natural resources of the earth can be conserved. How would integers be involved?

(c) What other occupations make frequent use of integers? In your journal write how integers might be used. Use examples to help your explanation.

B Estimate an answer before you calculate.

1. At the Selkirk Mine, core samples indicated gold at various levels.
   Sept. 23, −274 m   Oct. 1, −284 m   Oct. 15, −301 m   Oct. 31, −325 m
   Find the average depth of the gold.

2. From cores samples taken from a mine site, copper was found at the following levels.
   July 1, −147 m   July 3, −154 m   July 5, −157 m   July 7, −161 m   July 8, −162 m
   What is the average depth of the copper?

3. During a recent expedition, this profile of the bottom of a lake was drawn. What is the average depth of the lake?

4. Four measurements were taken of penetrations into the earth's crust.
   The four measurements are −9432 m, −8992 m, −9785 m, and −10 123 m.
   (a) What is the average of the measurements?
   (b) What is the deepest penetration?

5. The table at the right gives the depths of some of the trenches on the floor of the Pacific Ocean. Find the average depth of these trenches.

Trench	Depth
Mid America Trench	−6669 m
Ryukyu Trench	−7507 m
New Hebrides Trench	−7570 m
Peru Chile Trench	−8064 m
Aleutian Trench	−8100 m
Palau Trench	−8138 m
Japan Trench	−8412 m

6. The needle of a lie detector moves up and down as shown. (Up is positive and down is negative.) The readings appear at 1 s intervals.
   (a) Find the sum of the readings
   (b) Find the average.
   (c) From your answer in (b), would you expect the needle to point more often in the negative part or the positive part in the next 8 s? Why?
   (d) Find out more about lie detectors. When are they used? How are they used? Are they foolproof?

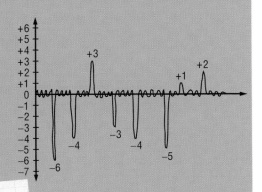

3.11 EXPLORING THE ORDER OF OPERATIONS

What steps do you need to follow if there is more than one operation in an expression? Work together to complete the following explorations. In your journal, record any patterns and relationships you discover.

EXPLORATION ① **Work in a Group**

1. Jenine and Juan used unit tiles to help them evaluate the expression $(+3) + (-2) - (-4)$.
   (a) Interpret the steps shown below. How did the tiles help them evaluate the expression?
   (b) What is the value of the expression?

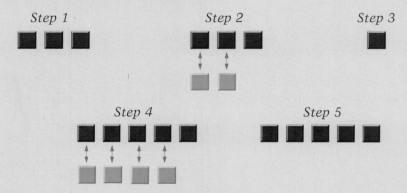

2. Use unit tiles to help you evaluate each of the following. Explain each step to the other members of your group.
   (a) $(+5) - (-2) + (-3)$ (b) $(-4) + (-2) - (+3)$
   (c) $(+2) - (+1) + (+5)$ (d) $(-3) + (-2) - (-5)$

3. Create similar expressions of your own.
   (a) Evaluate your expressions using unit tiles.
   (b) Compare your solutions to those of others in your class.

106

4. Jenine and Juan then used tiles to help them evaluate the expression $(+3) \times (-4) \div (+2)$.
   (a) Interpret the steps shown below. How did they use the tiles to help them evaluate the expression?
   (b) What is the value of the expression?

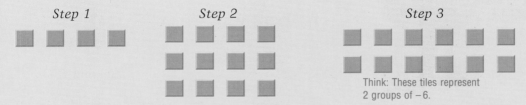

Step 1   Step 2   Step 3

Think: These tiles represent 2 groups of -6.

5. Use the steps above to help you evaluate each of the following.
   (a) $(+6) \div (-2) \times (+4)$ (b) $(-9) \div (+3) \times (+5)$ (c) $(+15) \times (-2) \div (+6)$
   (d) $(-4) \div (+2) \times (+7)$ (e) $(-15) \div (+5) \times (+6)$ (f) $(+3) \times (-8) \div (+12)$

6. (a) Create similar expressions of your own.
   (b) Evaluate your expressions using tiles.
   (c) Compare your solutions to those of others in your class.

EXPLORATION ③ **Mathematical Connections**

7. Use your journal.
   (a) Write the order of operations you used for whole numbers, decimal numbers, and fractions. How are they alike? How are they different?
   (b) Suggest what you think the order of operations will be for integers. Give reasons for your suggestion.

8. Based on your suggestion in Question 7(b), what would be your answer to each of the following?
   (a) $(-8)(-4) \div (+2) - (-3)(-2)$ (b) $(-2)^2 + (-3)^2 - (-4)^2$

MAKING CONNECTIONS: PEOPLE

History is full of examples of creative solutions using manipulatives. *Dido's Problem* was named after Queen Dido of Carthage. She was promised as much land as would lie within the boundaries of a bull's hide. She cut the hide into thin strips, tied them into one long strip and enclosed an area with it.

Work in a group. Make a paper "hide" of your own.
(a) How would you use your paper hide to enclose the greatest area?
(b) Find out what Queen Dido used and what area she actually enclosed.
(c) Select a solution from your work so far this year. Give the solution a name to identify it. Put the solution in your portfolio.

3.12 ORDER OF OPERATIONS

The order in which certain tasks are performed is important. For example, the order in which a magician performs an illusion affects audience impact.

> ## ACTIVITY 1
> Think of an activity you do each day that consists of tasks that occur in a certain order.
> (a) Describe the activity and the order that the tasks are completed.
> (b) What would be the result if the order of the tasks were completely changed?

Similarly, when evaluating expressions, you need to use the correct order of operations.

Order of Operations
- Perform the operations in brackets first.
- Then calculate the powers.
- Then multiply and divide in the order they appear.
- Then add and subtract in the order they appear.

> ## ACTIVITY 2
> Evaluate $(-8)(-4) \div (+2) - (-3)(-2)$. Justify each step.
>
> $(-8)(-4) \div (+2) - (-3)(-2)$ Step 1?
> $= (+32) \div (+2) - (-3)(-2)$ Step 2?
> $= (+16) - (+6)$ Step 3?
> $= +10$ Step 4?

Sometimes, powers are included in expressions.

> ## ACTIVITY 3
> Evaluate $(-2)^2 + (-3)^2 - (-4)^2$. Justify each step.
> Remember: $(-3)^2$ means $(-3)(-3)$.
>
> $(-2)^2 + (-3)^2 - (-4)^2$ Step 1?
> $= 4 + 9 - 16$ Step 2?
> $= 13 - 16$ Step 3?
> $= -3$ Step 4?

The assistant lies down on a platform. The magician "casts the spell."

The magician removes the platform supports to show that his assistant is suspended.

The magician passes a hoop over the assistant to show "no wires attached."

A Remember: Use the order of operations.

1. (a) In your journal, write the order of operations.
   (b) Explain to your partner what each step means, using an example of your own.
   (c) Give reasons to your partner why an order of operations is important when doing calculations. Use an example to help you.

2. Justify each step.

   (a) $(-3) \times (+4) - (+2)^2$
   $= (-3) \times (+4) - (+4)$
   $= (-12) - (+4)$
   $= -16$

   (b) $(-2)^2 + (-12) \div (-3)$
   $= (+4) + (-12) \div (-3)$
   $= (+4) + (+4)$
   $= +8$

3. Calculate. Justify each step in your work.
   (a) $(-3) \times (+4) - (+3)$ (b) $(-8) - (+3) \times (-6)$ (c) $(-8) + (-12) \div (-4)$
   (d) $(-12) \div (-3) + (-3)$ (e) $(-3)^2 - (-2)^2$ (f) $(-5)^2 - (-7) + (-12)$

4. Answer the following in your journal.
   (a) Explain how the following calculator key sequence can be used to calculate $(-3) \times (+5) + (-7)$.

   $\boxed{c}\ 3\ \boxed{+/-}\ \boxed{\times}\ 5\ \boxed{+}\ 7\ \boxed{+/-}\ \boxed{=}\ -22$

   (b) Write the key sequence you would use to calculate $(-7) + (-3) \times (+5)$.
   (c) How are your key sequences in (a) and (b) alike? How are they different?

5. Use a calculator to evaluate each of the following.
   (a) $(-4) + (+16) \div (-4)$ (b) $(-4) + (20) \div (-4)$ (c) $(-6) \times (-9) \times (+15)$
   (d) $(-8) \times (-11) + (+5)$ (e) $(-18) \div (-4) - (+3)$ (f) $(-8) \div (-4) + (+2)$

B Estimate first and use a calculator to check your work.

6. Evaluate.
   (a) $(-8) - (-5) \div (+5)$ (b) $(-9) - (-8) \div (+4)$ (c) $(-11) \times (+2) - (-9)$
   (d) $(-3) + (-3) - (+9)$ (e) $(+14) \div (-7) + (-3)$ (f) $(-2) \times (-3) \div (+6)$
   (g) $(+4) \times (-8) - (-9)$ (h) $(+15) \div (-3) \times (-2)$ (i) $(+20) \div (-10) + (-8)$
   (j) $(-7) - (-3) \times (-2)$ (k) $(+6) + (-9) \times (0)$ (l) $(+15) + (+15) \div (+15)$

7. (a) How are these expressions alike? How are they different?
   (i) $(+4) \times (-7) \div (+4) + (+12)$ (ii) $4 \times (-7) \div 4 + 12$
   (b) Calculate (i) and (ii). Why are the answers the same?

8. Evaluate each of the following.
   (a) $36 \div (-4) - 9$ (b) $(-3)^2 + (-4)^2$ (c) $(-8)^2 - 3^2$
   (d) $-2^2 - (4)(-2)$ (e) $(-3)^2 + (-8) \div (-2)$ (f) $(-8 + 2) \div (-3 + 2)$

9. (a) Explain each step in the
calculations to the right.

$$16 - [3(6 - 3) - 12] = 16 - [3(3) - 12]$$
$$= 16 - [9 - 12] \; ^{-3}$$
$$= 16 + 3$$
$$= 19$$

(b) Calculate each of the following.
   (i) $[-4 + 20] \div (-4)$ (ii) $-3 \times [(-4) + 8^2]$ (iii) $[-6 - (-8)] \div 2$
   (iv) $4 - 3[6 - 5(2 - 3)]$ (v) $2 - 3[4(6 - 3) - 10]$ (vi) $2 - 3[5(4 - 2) - 8]$

10. (a) Explain each step in the
calculations to the right.

$$\frac{(-22 + 2) \div (-5)}{(-8) \div (8 \div 4)} = \frac{(-20) \div (-5)}{(-8) \div 2}$$
$$= \frac{4}{-4}$$
$$= -1$$

(b) Calculate each of the following.
   (i) $\dfrac{-12 - 3}{-3 - 2}$ (ii) $\dfrac{-18 + 6}{(-3)(4)}$ (iii) $\dfrac{(-16 + 4) \div 2}{8 \div (-8) + 4}$

   (iv) $\dfrac{-5 + (-3)(-6)}{(-2)^2 + (-3)^2}$ (v) $\dfrac{20 + (-12) \div (-3)}{(-4 + 12) \div (-2)}$ (vi) $\dfrac{7(-4)(12)}{-64 \div (7 - 3)}$

11. Decide which of the following you can do mentally. Then evaluate each expression.
   (a) $-9 - 3[2(2 - 3)]$ (b) $-4[(-3)(-2) + 4]$
   (c) $160 \div (-4) + 2[3(8 - 4)]$ (d) $(-12) \div (-6) + (-3)(-2)$

12. At noon, the temperature in Yellowknife was 6°C. During the first 6 h after noon, the average change was 0°C/h. For the next 6 h the average change was −2°C/h. Find the temperature at midnight.

13. Find two boxes like the ones shown below. In one box place four cards with the operation symbols +, −, ×, and ÷. In the other box place 21 cards, each with a different integer between −10 and +10. Play this game with a partner.
   (a) Decide which player will go first. That person will select two operation cards and three integer cards.
   (b) Using the cards, create an expression with the greatest value. That is your score for the round. Return the cards to the boxes.
   (c) Take turns reaching into the boxes until both players have completed five turns. Then, find the total score for the five rounds.
   (d) The winner is the one with the greatest total score.

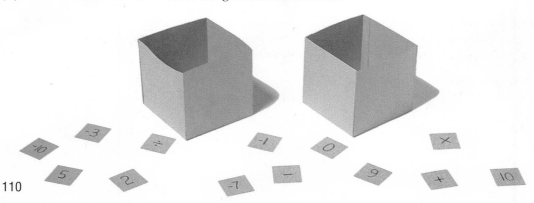

110

Suppose you want to compare the gas consumption of two cars. One car travels 3 km west from the starting point and the other car travels 3 km east.

ACTIVITY

(a) How would you represent the distance travelled by each car in each direction below?

(b) To compare the gas consumption, would you be interested in the direction the cars travelled? Give reasons for your answer.

(c) What factors might affect the gas consumption?

The direction of the cars is not important to the gas consumed, assuming there are no hills or other obstacles. In the activity above, you wrote the direction of the cars as +3 km (3 km east) and –3 km (3 km west).

The distance travelled by both cars is the same. Thus, you can use $|+3| = 3$ and $|-3| = 3$ to represent the distance travelled. Using the symbols $|\ \ |$ shows that you are only interested in the number of kilometres. The symbols represent the **absolute value** of the number.

Thus, $|-3| = 3$ is read as "The absolute value of –3 is 3."

$$|+3| = 3 \qquad |-2| = 2 \qquad \begin{aligned} &|(+3) + (-5)| \\ &= |-2| \\ &= 2 \end{aligned} \qquad \begin{aligned} &|+3| - |-5| \\ &= 3 - 5 \\ &= -2 \end{aligned}$$

EXAMPLE

Calculate.

(a) $+3|(+4) - (+2)|$

(b) $(-3)|(-3) + (-2)|$

SOLUTION

(a)
$$\begin{aligned} +3|(+4) - (+2)| &= +3|+2| \\ &= +3 \times (+2) \\ &= +6 \end{aligned}$$

(b)
$$\begin{aligned} (-3)|(-3) + (-2)| &= (-3)|-5| \\ &= (-3) \times (+5) \\ &= -15 \end{aligned}$$

 **Work together.**

1. Pairs of integers are used to show the distance travelled by two cars. Interpret what is meant by each integer.
   (a) $-5, +5$ (b) $-2, +2$ (c) $+4, -4$ (d) $+11, -11$

2. Find the value of each of the following.
   (a) $|-2|$ (b) $|+3|$ (c) $|-5|$ (d) $|-10|$ (e) $|+8|$

3. Use either $<$, $>$, or $=$ in place of $\bullet$.
   (a) $|-6| \bullet |5|$ (b) $|-3| \bullet |-4|$ (c) $|-6| \bullet |-5|$ (d) $|5| \bullet |-6|$

B   Remember: $3|8 - 3|$ means $3 \times |8 - 3|$.

4. Simplify.
   (a) $3|-2|$ (b) $5|-7|$ (c) $4|-4|$ (d) $5|+6|$
   (e) $4|-2 + 7|$ (f) $-3|5 - 8|$ (g) $2|-3 - (-2)|$ (h) $5|-3 - 6|$

5. Simplify each of the following.
   (a) $|-3| - |4|$ (b) $|-6| - |-3|$ (c) $|-2| + |3|$ (d) $|-6| - |-3|$
   (e) $|6| - 3|-4|$ (f) $|3 - 8|$ (g) $|8 - 3|$ (h) $|4 - 2| + |6 - 3|$

6. Use $<$, $>$, or $=$ to make each of the following true.
   (a) $|-3 + 8|\blacksquare|-8 + 5|$ (b) $|-2 + 6|\blacksquare|-2| + |6|$
   (c) $|-2 - 3|\blacksquare|-2| + |-3|$ (d) $|-5 + 3|\blacksquare|-5| + |3|$

7. Simplify each of the following.
   (a) $-3|2|$ (b) $-6|-2|$ (c) $-3|-3|$
   (d) $-4(-2) + |-3|$ (e) $2(-3) + |-6|$ (f) $-2|-2| - |-3|$
   (g) $-4|-3| - 3|-2|$ (h) $|-6 - (-3)|$ (i) $|-3 - 2| - |-3 - (-2)|$
   (j) $|4 - 8| - 3(4 - |3|)$ (k) $(6 - |3|) - 4(|3| - |2|)$ (l) $4|8 - 11| - 4(|8| - |11|)$

8. Simplify.
   (a) $3|-2| + 2|-6| - 3|8 - 5|$ (b) $3|8 - 3| + 2|4 - 8| - 6|9 - 12|$
   (c) $|4 - 2| + |2 - 6| + |8 - 5|$ (d) $|6 - 9| + 2|3 - 4| + |6 - 1|$

C

9. How many times does the digit 1 or 3 occur when you write the integers between -101 and 0? Give reasons for your answer.

10. (a) Find the values of $|3y|$ and $3|y|$ for each value of y.
        (i) $y = 0$ (ii) $y = -4$ (iii) $y = 4$
    (b) Find the values of $|x^2|$ and x^2 for each value of x.
        (i) $x = 0$ (ii) $x = -4$ (iii) $x = 4$
    (c) Use your answers in (a) and (b) to make conclusions about absolute value.

3.16 MAKING CONNECTIONS

CODED ESSAGES

Sometimes, you might want to give a message to a friend without anyone else understanding what the message says. In such cases, you could use a coded message. Work with a partner on a Cartesian plane to decipher each of the following coded messages. Make up a code of your own and pass a message to your partner or another group in the class.

1. A message is written using a code based on ordered pairs. The symbol ▶ marks the beginning of each new letter. Follow the instructions carefully. Also, the letters of each word are scrambled. You need to unscramble the letters to find the message.

   (a) ▶ Join (−9, 10) to (−8, 9) to (−8, 7) to (−9, 6) to (−11, 6) to (−11, 10) to (−9, 10).
       ▶ Join (−3, 10) to (−6, 10) to (−6, 6) to (−3, 6). Join (−6, 8) to (−4, 8).
       ▶ Join (−1, 6) to (−1, 8) to (2, 6). Join (2, 8) to (2, 10) to (−1, 10) to (−1, 8) to (2, 8).
       ▶ Join (4, 6) to (6, 10) to (8, 6). Join (5, 8) to (7, 8).

   (b) ▶ Join (−12, −1) to (−10, 3) to (−8, −1). Join (−11, 1) to (−9, 1).
       ▶ Join (−5, 1) to (−3, 1) to (−3, −1) to (−6, −1) to (−6, 3) to (−3, 3) to (−3, 2).
       ▶ Join (3, 3) to (0, 3) to (0, −1) to (3, −1). Join (0, 1) to (2, 1).
       ▶ Join (5, −1) to (5, 3) to (8, 3) to (8, 1) to (5, 1).

   (c) ▶ Join (−8, −8) to (−8, −4).
       ▶ Join (−2, −4) to (−2, −6) to (1, −6).
       ▶ Join (−5, −8) to (−5, −4).
       ▶ Join (0, −8) to (0, −4).

2. This code represents one of the oldest English words. What is the word?

   ▶ Join (−10, 6) to (−7, 6) to (−5, 4) to (−5, 1) to (−6, 0) to (−10, 0).
     Join (−6, 0) to (−5, −1) to (−5, −4) to (−7, −6) to (−10, −6) to (−10, 6).
   ▶ Join (−4, −6) to (0, 6) to (4, −6). Join (−2, 0) to (2, 0).
   ▶ Join (5, −6) to (5, 6) to (8, 6) to (10, 4) to (10, −4) to (8, −6) to (5, −6).

3. This may be the most overworked word in the English language. What is the word? Join the following pairs of coordinates.

   ▶ (−5, 4) to (−1, 4)   ▶ (−7, −2) to (−7, 1)   ▶ (3, −2) to (3, 4)
   ▶ (−1, −2) to (−5, −2)   ▶ (−11, 1) to (−11, 4)   ▶ (−11, −2) to (−7, −2)
   ▶ (1, 4) to (5, 4)   ▶ (−5, −2) to (−5, 4)   ▶ (−5, 1) to (−2, 1)
   ▶ (−7, 1) to (−11, 1)   ▶ (−11, 4) to (−7, 4)

4. Half of the longest English palindrome is given in the code. What is the word?

   ▶ Join (−6, 3) to (−5, 3) to (−4, 2) to (−4, 0) to (−5, −1) to (−6, −1) to (−6, 3).
   ▶ Join (−3, 3) to (−3, −1).
   ▶ Join (−12, −1) to (−12, 3) to (−11, 3) to (−10, 2) to (−11, 1) to (−12, 1).
     Join (−11, 1) to (−10, −1).
   ▶ Join (−7, −1) to (−9, −1) to (−9, 3) to (−7, 3). Join (−9, 1) to (−7, 1).
   ▶ Join (−2, 3) to (0, −1) to (2, 3).

1. Calculate.
   (a) $(+7) + (-3)$ (b) $(-5) - (+2)$
   (c) $(+10) + (+7)$ (d) $(-4) - (+2) + (-1)$
   (e) $(-6) + (-3) + (-1)$ (f) $(+3) - (-2) + (+8) - (-9)$

2. (a) Find the missing integers in each pattern.
   (i) $+2, -4, +6, -8, +10, \blacksquare, \blacksquare$
   (ii) $+20, -18, +16, \blacksquare, +12, \blacksquare$
   (iii) $+1, \blacksquare, +7, -10, +13, \blacksquare, \blacksquare$
   (iv) $+1, -2, +4, \blacksquare, +11, -16, \blacksquare, \blacksquare$
   (b) Create a pattern of your own with missing integers. Have others in the class find the value of the missing integers.

3. Find the average of each of the following.
   (a) $-11, +5, +19, -23, +15$
   (b) $+7, +16, +42, -3, -45, -35$

4. Simplify.
   (a) $[(-20) + (+5)] \div (-5)$
   (b) $(-16) \div [(-4) - (+4)]$
   (c) $(+2) \times (-5)^2 - (+3) \times (-2)^2$
   (d) $[(-7) - (+4) + (+5) \times (-3)] \times 0$

5. (a) Find each of the following products.
   (i) $(-3) \times (-3)$ (ii) $(-33) \times (-33)$
   (iii) $(-333) \times (-333)$ (iv) $(-3333) \times (-3333)$
   (b) Use the pattern in (a). Predict the product for $(-33\,333) \times (-33\,333)$. How can you verify your prediction?
   (c) Create a similar pattern of your own. Have others in the class predict an answer based on your pattern.

6. Construct a Cartesian plane.
   (a) Plot the following points.
   $(2, 3), (5, 0), (5, -2), (2, -5), (0, -5), (-3, -2),$
   $(-3, 0), (0, 3)$
   (b) What geometric shape is constructed when each point is joined in order?
   (c) Plot a similar geometric figure having only positive coordinates. Compare your figure with others in the class. How are they the same? How do they differ?

7. The record low temperature for the Mongolian Desert is $-26°C$. Its record high temperature is $42°C$ more. What is the record high temperature?

❶ Geri claims that adding integers always results in an answer greater than zero. Is Geri correct? Give reasons for your answer.

❷ Lise was asked to show zero using unit tiles. She showed nothing and explained, "Zero means nothing, so no tiles are shown." Could Lise have used unit tiles? How?

❸ When Fedore saw $7 - (-3) = 10$, he said, "That can't be correct. The answer is greater than the two numbers being subtracted." Is Fedore correct? Justify your answer.

MAKING CONNECTIONS

Refer to the opening page of this chapter.
(a) Create a problem using the illustration shown.
(b) Solve your problem.
(c) Compare your problem to others in the class. Solve the other problems.

④ In your journal, describe when you might use the skills and strategies of this chapter in a career.

⑤ Refer to one of the questions on these pages. Explain to your partner how you obtained the answer.

⑥ Prepare a one-page summary of all the important ideas you have learned from this chapter.

SELF EVALUATION

1. Calculate.
   (a) $(-3) + (+8)$ (b) $(-6) + (-3)$
   (c) $(+8) - (-3)$ (d) $(+9) + (-6) - (-3)$

2. Refer to the chart. Find the difference between the melting point and boiling point for each substance.

Substance	Melting Point (°C)	Boiling Point (°C)
oxygen	−213	−183
nitrogen	−210	−196
methane (natural gas)	−182	−162
methyl alcohol	−98	65
water	0	100
sulphur	119	444
copper	1083	2595
iron	1535	3000

3. Evaluate each expression. Write the answers in order, from least to greatest.
   (a) $10 + (-5) - 1 \times 8$ (b) $10 \div (-5) \times 1 + 8$
   (c) $10 - (-5) \div 1 + 8$ (d) $10 \div (-5) \times 1 - 8$

4. Calculate.
   (a) $8 \times (-3)$ (b) $-3 \times (-2)$
   (c) $22 \div (-2) \times (-3)$ (d) $-4 \times (-3) \div 6 + (-2) \times 8$

5. (a) Estimate which expression has the greater value.
      (i) $(-6) + 4 - 15 \div 3 + 2 \times (-4)$
      (ii) $\dfrac{(-5)(+6) - (+7)(-3)}{(+7)(-3) - (-3)(6)}$
   (b) Evaluate each expression. How reasonable was your estimate?

6. The depths to which a tree's roots extend are as follows.
   -8 m, -12 m, -9 m, -16 m, -5 m
   What is the average depth of the tree's roots?

7. Simplify.
   (a) $|-3| + |-4|$ (b) $-2|-2|$ (c) $|-4 + (-9)|$
   (d) $4|-3 + 3|$ (e) $-6|2 + 4|$ (f) $6|5 - 9| + |-2|$

8. Follow these instructions.
   (a) Join $(-8, -7)$ to $(-8, 2)$.
   (b) Join $(-8, 2)$ to $(-3, -7)$.
   (c) Join $(-3, -7)$ to $(2, 2)$.
   (d) Join $(2, 2)$ to $(2, -7)$.
   What letter of the alphabet have you made?

MATH JOURNAL

(a) How are the words "positive" and "negative" used in this chapter?
(b) How would you use the words "positive" and "negative" in your life?
(c) How are your answers in (a) and (b) alike? How are they different?

Of the hundreds of inventions developed each year, very few are sold or become popular. In fact, some of the inventions that have appeared over the years could be credited to the "nutty professor." Here are some of them.

Work together and decide
- why you think the invention never sold.
- how mathematics was used in its design.
- what, if anything, you could do to modify the invention to make it more practical today.

Velocipede

The 1897 velocipede was a bicycle and a shower. The cyclist would pedal hard and a pump would carry water from a bath beneath the pump to a shower head over the bicycle seat.

Detective Camera

In the 1890s, there was a craze for detective cameras. People hid these cameras in all sorts of places. One place was inside a hat. The camera was placed inside the hat with the lens sticking through. To take a picture, you needed to take off your hat and press the shutter on the top of the hat.

Cradle Rocker

In the 1870s, a new kind of rocking machine was invented. A person would sit in the chair and gently rock back and forth. This would cause a cradle to rock and a butter churn to operate at the same time.

4.1 EXPLORING CONNECTIONS

Many of the mathematical concepts you study are connected to other math concepts. Seeing these connections will help you understand mathematics better.

ACTIVITY 1 *Work with a Partner*

1. (a) Refer to the pictures on the previous page. Suggest a problem that you think someone might have to solve in each picture.
   (b) Flip through the rest of the chapter. What skills will you explore that can help you solve your problems in (a)?
   (c) Solve each problem in (a) after you finish the chapter.

ACTIVITY 2 *Work with a Partner*

2. Certain symbols have certain meanings for all people.
   (a) What is the meaning of each symbol on the signs?
   (b) What would you do if you saw each sign?
   (c) Find other signs of your own. Repeat (a) and (b) for your signs.

3. Just as symbols on signs have certain meanings, mathematical symbols have certain meanings.
   (a) Make a list of mathematical symbols you have seen.
   (b) What is the meaning of each symbol? How is it used?

ACTIVITY 3

4. Some shapes you have worked with can be made from other shapes. A 4 × 4 shape on a grid can be made from two congruent shapes. Find other congruent shapes that can be used to make the 4 × 4 grid.

4.2 EXPLORING SYMBOLS

Manipulatives are used to explore mathematical ideas. Previously, you worked with black and red *unit tiles* to represent integers.

Red and black strips can also be used to represent different variables. Each strip is called an **x-tile**.

represents x represents $-x$

You can use the x-tiles to create expressions.

represents $2x$ represents $-2x$

The x-tiles can also be used to represent expressions with different variables.

represents $2y$ represents $-2y$

EXPLORATION ① *Work in Pairs*

1. (a) Use x-tiles to represent each of the following expressions.
   (i) $3x$ (ii) $-4x$ (iii) $-2y$ (iv) $4k$
   (b) Set up x-tiles to represent an expression of your own. Have your partner write an expression for the tiles you chose.

EXPLORATION ② *Work in Pairs*

2. Your work with x-tiles is similar to your work with unit tiles. Refer to the tiles shown.
   (a) How are the x-tiles used like unit tiles? How are they different?
   (b) Suggest the net result of the x-tiles.

3. (a) Write the net result of the x-tiles shown below.
   (i)   (ii)   (iii)

   (b) Set up x-tiles to represent an expression of your own. Have your partner write an expression for the tiles you chose.

4. (a) Set up x-tiles to show: (i) $3x$ and $-2x$ (ii) y and $-3y$ (iii) $2a$ and $-4a$.
   (b) Interpret your results in (a). Find the net result of the x-tiles.
   (c) Repeat (a) and (b) using tile arrangements of your own. Have others in the class find the net results.

Skills that you have developed previously can build on one another to extend your knowledge of mathematics. For example, you can use **algebra tiles** (*x*-tiles and unit tiles) to extend your skills with expressions as shown in the following activity.

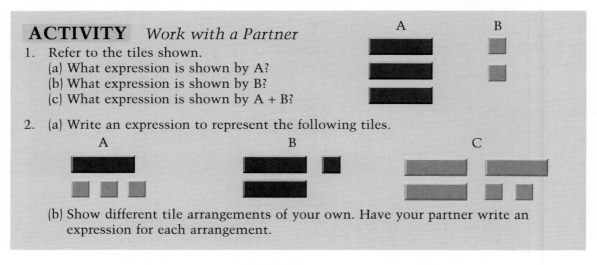

ACTIVITY *Work with a Partner*

1. Refer to the tiles shown.
   (a) What expression is shown by A?
   (b) What expression is shown by B?
   (c) What expression is shown by A + B?

2. (a) Write an expression to represent the following tiles.

   (b) Show different tile arrangements of your own. Have your partner write an expression for each arrangement.

Suppose each variable in Question 2 above has a value of –3. The expressions can be evaluated as follows.

A Use $x = -3$.

$$x - 3 = (-3) - 3$$
$$= -6$$

B Use $x = -3$.

$$2x + 1 = 2(-3) + 1$$
$$= -6 + 1$$
$$= -5$$

C Use $x = -3$.

$$-3x - 2 = -3(-3) - 2$$
$$= 9 - 2$$
$$= 7$$

EXERCISE

A Use algebra tiles to help you.

1. (a) Write an expression for the tiles shown.

   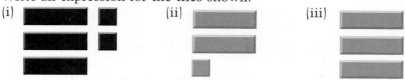

   (i)   (ii)   (iii)

   (b) Suppose the value of the variable is 3. Evaluate each expression in (a).

2. (a) Use your tiles to represent each of the following.
      (i) $-3a + 2$ (ii) $4y - 6$ (iii) $2m + 7$ (iv) $-3k - 4$
   (b) Evaluate each expression in (a) for the value of the variable.
      (i) 2   (ii) –2   (iii) 0

3. Work with a partner.
   (a) Write an expression for each arrangement of tiles.

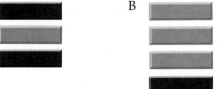

   (b) Find the net result for each arrangement of tiles in (a).
   (c) Interpret the net result of the tiles in (b) using symbols.

B   Any letter of the alphabet can be used to represent a variable.

4. (a) Use algebra tiles to represent each expression.
   (i) $4a$ and $-2a$ (ii) $3x$ and $4x$ (iii) $2k$ and $-k$
   (iv) $5m$ and $-2m$ (v) x and $-2x$ (vi) $3y$ and $2y$
   (b) Find the net result of each expression in (a).
   (c) Evaluate each expression using 2.2 as the value of the variable.

5. Find the net result of each of the following.
   (a) $4a$, $-2a$ (b) $5x$, $2x$ (c) $-3y$, $5y$ (d) $-4a$, $-2a$
   (e) x, $-5x$ (f) $-4k$, $-5k$ (g) $6b$, $4b$ (h) $-m$, $3m$

6. Simplify each expression. Use algebra tiles to help you.
   (a) $3a + 5a$ (b) $4p - 3p$ (c) $-2n + 4n$
   (d) $x - 2x$ (e) $3p - 2p$ (f) $-b + 4b$

7. (a) What might be your first step in evaluating each of the following?
   (i) $5d + 2d$ (ii) $7d - 3d + 6d$ (iii) $5d - 3d + 2d$
   (iv) $4d - 2d + 3d$ (v) $6d - 2d + d + d$ (vi) $4d - 5d + 6d + d$
   (b) Evaluate each expression for $d = 5.5$.

8. Find the net result of each of the following.
   (a) $4a$, $-3b$, $2a$ (b) $3m$, $-6p$, $2m$ (c) p, q, p
   (d) $2a$, $-3b$, $5b$ (e) $2b$, $-3a$, $4b$ (f) $2r$, $-3r$, $5p$

9. Play this game with a partner.
   A Obtain two boxes. Into one put red and black unit tiles. In the other place red and black x-tiles.
   B Take turns reaching into each box and removing some tiles.
   C Create an expression using the tiles.
   D Evaluate the expression for the value of the variable given by your partner.
   E The first player to evaluate ten expressions correctly is the winner.

One important aspect of math is to be able to write expressions to help you solve problems.

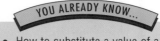

For example, an expression for the consumption of milk in one week can be written as

- How to substitute a value of a variable in an expression.

$C = 2n + n + 3$, where
- C is the consumption in litres.
- n is the number of people in a family.

Suppose there are 4 people in the family. How many litres of milk are consumed each week?

Before you evaluate an expression, it is helpful to simplify it.

$C = 2n + n + 3$
$= 3n + 3$

Think:
To simplify $2n + n$, use your tiles.

$2n$ n

Thus, $2n + n = 3n$.

Then evaluate.

$C = 3n + 3$
$= 3(4) + 3$
$= 15$

The family consumes 15 L of milk in one week.

To solve problems, remember to simplify the expression before you evaluate.

ACTIVITY *Work with a Partner*

Often in mathematics you create words for special expressions. Refer to the example above.

(a) Why do you think the following are called *like* terms?
   (i) $n, 2n$ (ii) $-3m, 4m$ (iii) $-x, -2x$ (iv) $3y, -4y$

(b) Suggest other examples of like terms.

(c) Why do you think the following are called *unlike* terms?
   (i) $3m, 4n$ (ii) $-2k, 4s$ (iii) $-4x, -2y$ (iv) $5a, -2b$

(d) Suggest other examples of unlike terms.

EXERCISE

A   Review your skills with like and unlike terms. Use your algebra tiles.

1. Simplify.
   (a) $2x + 5x - 3x$ (b) $3a - 5a + 6a$ (c) $7n - n + 4n$
   (d) $2m + 3m - 5m$ (e) $5a + 3a + 2a$ (f) $6p - 3p + p$

2. Simplify each of the following expressions.
   (a) $C = 2m + 5m + 3$ (b) $V = 2x - x + 3$ (c) $A = 2l - 1 - 4$
   (d) $M = 5 + 3x - 2x$ (e) $K = 5y - 2 + 3y$ (f) $P = 17 - 3k + 2k$

3. (a) Identify the like terms and the unlike terms.
   (i) $2x, 3x, 4y$ (ii) $5a, -2b, 3a$ (iii) $4m, 5m, 2n$
   (iv) $3v, -4v, 5w$ (v) $-4p, -2q, 5p$ (vi) $-3a, -4b, -2a$
   (b) Find the sum of the terms in each part of (a).

4. Simplify.
   (a) $2m + 3m + n$ (b) $2a + 3b - 4a$ (c) $6x + 2y - y$
   (d) $2p + 3q - 2q$ (e) $5r - 4r - 5q$ (f) $9m - 3n + 4n$

B   Remember: Write a concluding statement for each problem.

5. The cost, C, in dollars, to manufacture cards is given by $C = 125 + n + n$,
   where n is the number of cards. Calculate the cost to make
   (a) 100 cards.   (b) 150 cards.   (c) 200 cards.   (d) 335 cards.

6. The speed, S, in kilometres per hour, of a car that is slowing down is given by
   $S = 80 - 5t - 5t$, where t is the time in seconds. Find the speed of the car after
   (a) 1 s.   (b) 3 s.   (c) 5 s.   (d) 8.5 s.
   (e) Interpret your answer in (d). In your journal, describe what you think the answer
       represents. Give reasons for your answer.

7. The velocity, V, in metres per second, of sound in air is given by $V = 330 - 2t + 2.5t$, where
   t is the air temperature in °C. Find the velocity of sound if the air temperature is
   (a) 20°C.   (b) 10°C.   (c) 32.5°C.   (d) 14.25°C.

8. Refer to the relationship in the previous question.
   (a) Describe whether you think there is a temperature at which sound will not travel.
   (b) Use your library to research more about sound. Is there a temperature at which sound
       waves will not travel?

C

9. The total cost, C, in dollars, of printing a brochure is given by
   $C = 5.25p + 0.08b + 0.02b + 2.80p$, where p is the number of pages in the brochure, and
   b is the number of brochures. By how much does the cost of printing 10 000 copies of an
   eight-page brochure exceed the cost of printing 9000 copies of a ten-page brochure?

10. (a) Arrange five disks as shown to the right.
        Where can you place one straight line
        so that the area covered by the disks is
        divided exactly in half?
    (b) Create a similar problem of your own.
        Compare your problem to others in the class.

127

4.5 WORKING WITH EQUATIONS

The skills you learn in one part of mathematics can help you in your work in other parts of mathematics. The skills you learned with expressions can help you work with equations.

ACTIVITY 1

Which of the following are true?
(a) Mario Lemieux plays professional hockey.
(b) Roberta Bondar plays professional hockey.
(c) ■ plays professional hockey.

In Activity 1, you found the following:
- (a) is true.
- (b) is false.
- (c) may be true depending upon what ■ represents.

Often in mathematics you learn by comparing. Refer to Activity 1 and Activity 2 above. How are the activities alike? How are they different?

When you find the value of a variable that makes an equation true, you are **solving** the equation. One way to solve an equation is by using *systematic trial*.

From the table, the solution to $2x - 4 = 10$ is $x = 7$. You can also call 7 the *root* of the equation. When you solve an equation by systematic trial, you use each trial to refine your estimate.

ACTIVITY 2

Which of the following are true?
(a) $3.3 + 4.4 = 7.7$
(b) $2.2 + 4.5 = 7.7$
(c) $2■ - 4 = 10$

In Activity 2, you found the following:
- (a) is true.
- (b) is false.
- (c) may be true depending upon what ■ represents.

Estimate a value of x.	Evaluate $2x - 4$.	Compare the value to 10.
5	6	too low
10	16	too high
6	8	close
7	10	equals 10

EXERCISE

 A   Review your skills with expressions.

1. For each equation, which value is the solution?
   (a) $x + 8 = 9$ 2, 1   (b) $4 + y = 8$ 4, 3   (c) $m - 3 = 3$ 6, 7

2. (a) Which value, 4, 5, or 8, is the solution to $5h = 25$? Why?

   (b) Which value, 4, 8, or 12 is the solution to $\dfrac{m}{4} = 3$? Why?

3. Solve the following equations using a chart like the one shown.
   (a) $8m = 48$ (b) $3x + 6 = 12$ (c) $\dfrac{m}{3} = 5$

Estimate a value of x.	Evaluate expression.	Compare.

4. Find the root of each equation.
   (a) $4a - 6 = 6$
   (b) $2a - 3 = 1$
   (c) $6 - 3y = 9$
   (d) $2x + 2 = 6$
   (e) $2x - 4 = -6$
   (f) $3m - 9 = -6$

5. Solve. (Remember: To solve an equation means to find the solution.)
   (a) $12n - 3 = 9$
   (b) $8 - 2y = 12$
   (c) $5a - 15 = 10$
   (d) $2x - 5 = 3$
   (e) $4k - 7 = 9$
   (f) $3y - 6 = 12$

6. Find the solution.
   (a) $2m + 5 = 21$
   (b) $3y - 4 = -19$
   (c) $28 - 3r = -8$
   (d) $-3p + 5 = 17$
   (e) $3x - 1 = 8$
   (f) $4y - 20 = 30$

7. For each of the following,
   • what connections do you see?   • solve the equation.

   (a) $\dfrac{m}{3} = 8$
   (b) $\dfrac{p}{2} = 4$
   (c) $\dfrac{q}{3} = -1$
   (d) $\dfrac{t}{4} = 3$

   (e) $\dfrac{m}{3} - 2 = 5$
   (f) $\dfrac{p}{2} + 2 = -1$
   (g) $\dfrac{q}{3} + 1 = -2$
   (h) $\dfrac{t}{4} - 1 = 4$

8. Solve. How are the equations alike? How are they different?

   (a) $\dfrac{p}{2} + 3 = 11$
   (b) $\dfrac{k}{3} + 1 = 3$
   (c) $\dfrac{s}{3} - 1 = -2$
   (d) $\dfrac{x}{3} - 4 = 5$

   (e) $6 + \dfrac{t}{4} = 10$
   (f) $8 - \dfrac{g}{2} = -2$
   (g) $-3 + \dfrac{w}{5} = 4$
   (h) $6 - \dfrac{y}{2} = -3$

9. Equations whose solutions are the same are called **equivalent**. Which of the following are equivalent?

   (a) $3a = -3$
   (b) $\dfrac{t}{4} = -1$
   (c) $4a - 4 = 0$

   (d) $5m + 3 = -2$
   (e) $3x + 6 = 12$
   (f) $4x + 3 = -1$

   (g) $2z - 5 = -7$
   (h) $\dfrac{1}{2}p - 3 = -2$
   (i) $\dfrac{2}{3}k + 6 = 8$

PARTNER PROJECT

Look at this design for a moment.
(a) What illusion do you see?
(b) Suggest a reason why this illusion occurs.
(c) Research illusions in your library. What
    other illusions do you find interesting? How
    is the illusion created?
(d) Try to create an illusion of your own.
    Compare your illusion to others in the class.

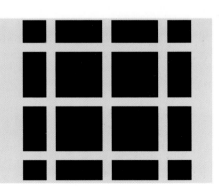

4.6 SOLVING EQUATIONS

You can make connections in math by using previously developed skills in new situations. Earlier you learned how to find equivalent fractions. You can use equivalent fractions to help you solve problems.

Zina tried out for the school hockey team. Two out of every five players who tried out made the team. There are 20 players on the team in all. How many players tried out?

Try this activity to explore how to solve the problem.

ACTIVITY   *Work Together*

(a) Discuss how you can use manipulatives to help you solve the above problem.
(b) Use the method in (a). Solve the problem.
(c) Write a concluding statement. How many players tried out for the team?

To solve the problem above, you can also set up an equation like the following.

Use n to represent the number of players trying out.

$$\frac{\text{number of players on team}}{\text{number of players trying out}} = \frac{2}{5}$$

$$\frac{20}{n} = \frac{2}{5}$$

$$\frac{20}{n} = \frac{2 \times 10}{5 \times 10} \quad \text{Compare.}$$

$$\frac{20}{n} = \frac{20}{50}$$

Thus, 50 players tried out for the team.

EXERCISE

 How are the skills in this section useful to solve equations?

1. Simplify each of the following.

   (a) $\dfrac{6 \times 2}{8 \times 2}$ (b) $\dfrac{15 \times 5}{5 \times 5}$ (c) $\dfrac{12 \times 4}{16 \times 4}$

2. Write two equivalent fractions for each of the following.

(a) $\dfrac{3}{4}$ (b) $\dfrac{2}{3}$ (c) $\dfrac{3}{5}$ (d) $\dfrac{7}{10}$ (e) $\dfrac{18}{20}$

3. For each, write an equivalent fraction with 100 as the denominator.

(a) $\dfrac{1}{2} = \dfrac{\blacksquare}{100}$ (b) $\dfrac{1}{4} = \dfrac{\blacksquare}{100}$ (c) $\dfrac{1}{10} = \dfrac{\blacksquare}{100}$ (d) $\dfrac{1}{5} = \dfrac{\blacksquare}{100}$

4. (a) Find the missing term for the equivalent fractions $\dfrac{\blacksquare}{100} = \dfrac{3}{10}$.

(b) Use equivalent fractions to solve $\dfrac{x}{100} = \dfrac{3}{10}$.

5. Think of equivalent fractions to find the missing terms.

(a) $\dfrac{m}{100} = \dfrac{2}{5}$ (b) $\dfrac{y}{100} = \dfrac{1}{10}$ (c) $\dfrac{x}{100} = \dfrac{1}{4}$ (d) $\dfrac{z}{100} = \dfrac{7}{25}$

6. (a) Find the missing term for the equivalent fractions $\dfrac{25}{100} = \dfrac{\blacksquare}{4}$.

(b) Use equivalent fractions to solve $\dfrac{25}{100} = \dfrac{x}{4}$.

7. Think of equivalent fractions to find the missing terms. Discuss with a partner. Find the missing term in each of the following. In your journal, describe the first step you used.

(a) $\dfrac{10}{100} = \dfrac{x}{10}$ (b) $\dfrac{5}{100} = \dfrac{y}{20}$ (c) $\dfrac{70}{100} = \dfrac{k}{10}$ (d) $\dfrac{60}{100} = \dfrac{m}{5}$

B   Once you learn a skill in math, you use it to solve problems. Use your *Problem Solving Plan* to help you in each of the following.

8. Find each missing term.

(a) $\dfrac{3}{2} = \dfrac{x}{6}$ (b) $\dfrac{15}{y} = \dfrac{3}{2}$ (c) $\dfrac{9}{k} = \dfrac{3}{21}$ (d) $\dfrac{10}{3} = \dfrac{y}{15}$

(e) $\dfrac{12}{15} = \dfrac{4}{w}$ (f) $\dfrac{25}{h} = \dfrac{5}{3}$ (g) $\dfrac{12}{s} = \dfrac{6}{12}$ (h) $\dfrac{4}{8} = \dfrac{y}{80}$

(i) $\dfrac{21}{30} = \dfrac{7}{n}$ (j) $\dfrac{30}{z} = \dfrac{6}{5}$ (k) $\dfrac{75}{12} = \dfrac{s}{4}$ (l) $\dfrac{5}{50} = \dfrac{m}{10}$

9. Solve.

(a) $\dfrac{x}{8} = \dfrac{15}{6}$ (b) $\dfrac{y}{15} = \dfrac{2}{6}$ (c) $\dfrac{9}{k} = \dfrac{7}{21}$ (d) $\dfrac{14}{7} = \dfrac{10}{t}$

(e) $\dfrac{m}{12} = \dfrac{18}{24}$ (f) $\dfrac{10}{15} = \dfrac{8}{s}$ (g) $\dfrac{12}{s} = \dfrac{16}{12}$ (h) $\dfrac{4}{8} = \dfrac{y}{10}$

(i) $\dfrac{n}{20} = \dfrac{9}{15}$ (j) $\dfrac{4}{12} = \dfrac{m}{9}$ (k) $\dfrac{15}{x} = \dfrac{9}{15}$ (l) $\dfrac{3}{21} = \dfrac{7}{y}$

131

10. The runner-up in a school election received 460 votes. For every four votes the runner-up received, the winner received five votes. How many votes did the winner receive?

(a) Interpret the equation $\frac{5}{4} = \frac{w}{460}$ used to solve the above problem.

(b) Solve $\frac{5}{4} = \frac{w}{460}$.

(c) Now answer the original question, "How many votes did the winner receive?"

11. At an international dock, 12 cargo ships arrive for every two luxury liners. Suppose ten luxury liners arrived last month. How many cargo ships arrived last month?

(a) Interpret the equation $\frac{12}{2} = \frac{C}{10}$ used to solve the problem.

(b) Solve $\frac{12}{2} = \frac{C}{10}$.

(c) Write a concluding statement that answers the question "How many cargo ships arrived last month?"

12. An artist can make green paint by mixing blue paint and yellow paint. For every 1 mL of blue paint used, there are 2 mL of yellow paint needed. Suppose Franca has 6 mL of blue paint. How much yellow paint does she need to make green paint?

(a) Interpret the equation $\frac{1}{2} = \frac{6}{P}$ used to solve the problem.

(b) Solve $\frac{1}{2} = \frac{6}{P}$.

(c) Write a concluding statement to answer the question "How much yellow paint is needed?"

C

13. Using a pulley, a person can lift 225 kg with a pull force of 10 kg.
    (a) How many kilograms can be lifted with a pull force of 1 kg?
    (b) Suppose Kinga lifted 450 kg. What pull force was used?
    (c) Find out more about pulleys. Create a problem of your own based on the information you find. Have others in the class solve your problem.

GROUP PROJECT

Create problems of your own using the information in each of the following. Solve your problems and have others in the class solve your problems. List any assumptions that you make.
(a) The record amount of snow that fell in North America in a 24-h period was 1.93 m at Silver Lake, Colorado.
(b) The record snowfall in Canada occurred at Mount Copeland, British Columbia. About 2446 cm fell during the winter of 1971–1972.
(c) The greatest accumulation of snow in Canada, for one day, was 112 cm at Ranger Station, Alberta.

Your skills with fractions can be used to solve a variety of problems. For example, most garbage contains different materials. The chart below lists the following comparison for each type of garbage.

$$\frac{\text{mass of garbage type}}{\text{total mass of garbage}}$$

CONTENT OF GARBAGE		
Paper Products	$\frac{9}{25}$	Think: $\frac{?}{100}$
Yard Waste	$\frac{19}{100}$	
Glass	$\frac{2}{25}$	Think: $\frac{?}{100}$
Metals	$\frac{9}{100}$	
Food	$\frac{9}{100}$	
Plastics	$\frac{2}{25}$	
Wood/Fabric	$\frac{1}{25}$	
Textiles	$\frac{1}{50}$	
Other	$\frac{5}{100}$	

Refer to the table above to answer the following. Work together.

1. Suppose a garbage can contains 25 kg of garbage. What mass of garbage would you expect to be
   (a) paper products?   (b) wood/fabric?   (c) glass?

2. Apartment buildings dispose of garbage in large containers. Suppose a container contains 250 kg of garbage. What mass of garbage would you expect to be
   (a) textiles?   (b) plastics?   (c) metals?

3. If a sample of garbage contains 1 kg of wood/fabric, what mass of garbage would you expect to be plastics? What assumptions have you made to solve the problem?

4. Once garbage has been collected, it needs to be disposed of.
   (a) Find out how garbage is disposed of where you live.
   (b) What problems do you see in disposing of garbage in this way?
   (c) Write a brief report on recycling as a way to dispose of local garbage.
   (d) Write a brief report to suggest why garbage is a global concern.

Have you ever noticed that it is more difficult to walk down some ramps than others?

EXPLORATION ①

1. (a) Which ramp do you think is easier to walk down? Why?

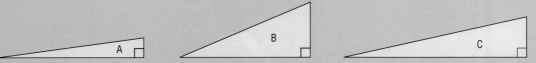

(b) Measure to find the height of each ramp (rise) and the length of each ramp (run).

(c) Calculate $\dfrac{\text{rise}}{\text{run}}$ to find the *slope* of each ramp.

(d) Sketch ramps of your own. Repeat the parts of (a), (b), and (c) for your ramps.

(e) What do you notice about the slope of each ramp? How can the slope help you decide which ramp is easier to walk down?

Inclined planes are shown below. A protractor is used to measure the angle. A block of material is placed on the plane. The slope of the plane, when the material begins to slide, is calculated to the right.

Use slope $= \dfrac{\text{rise}}{\text{run}}$

$= \dfrac{15\ \text{cm}}{30\ \text{cm}}$ or 0.5

Thus, the slope of the inclined plane is 0.5.

EXPLORATION ② *Work with a Partner*

2. Use a block of wood and a board as an inclined plane. Copy the chart shown.

	Attempt 1	Attempt 2	Attempt 3
angle			
slope			

(a) Place a block of wood on the inclined plane and do the following steps.

Step A Incline the plane until the block of wood begins to slide.

Step B Record the angle of the plane at which the sliding begins.

Step C Measure to record the slope of the plane at which sliding begins.

(b) Repeat Steps A, B, and C a number of times. Record your data in the chart. What do you notice about the values of the angles and the slopes?

(c) Repeat parts (a) and (b) using different materials for the inclined plane and for the object on the plane. For example, use a piece of cardboard, an eraser, and so on.

(d) Based on your results for the data you collected, what conclusion can you make?

3. Use a block of wood and a board as an inclined plane. Copy the chart shown.

	Attempt 1	Attempt 2	Attempt 3
Angle at which the block continues to slide			
Slope at which the block continues to slide			

   (a) Place the wood on the plane and incline the plane gently.

   Step A Push the block of wood gently. Continue this procedure until the block slides on its own.

   Step B Record the angle of the inclined plane at which the block continues to slide.

   Step C Find and record the slope of the inclined plane at which the block continues to slide.

   (b) Repeat Steps A, B, and C a number of times. Record the data in the chart. What do you notice about the values of the angles and the slopes?

4. Repeat Question 3 using different materials for the inclined plane and for the object on the plane. For example, use a piece of cardboard and an eraser, and so on.
   (a) What do you notice about the values of the angles and the slope of the planes?
   (b) In your journal, describe industries in which knowing how to calculate the slope of a plane would be necessary.

5. (a) Use the roofs shown below. Which roof do you think is the steepest?

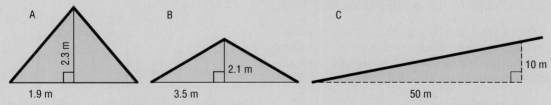

   (b) Calculate the slope for each roof. What do you notice about the slope of the steepest roof?
   (c) Repeat (a) and (b) by calculating some roof slopes of your own. What do you notice about the slopes as the roofs get steeper?

6. Work with a partner and find a number of wheel chair ramps.
   (a) Find the slope of each wheel chair ramp.
   (b) What do you notice about the slopes of the ramps?

7. Suppose you were to design wheel chair ramps for your school.
   (a) Where would you place the ramps?
   (b) What slope would each ramp have?

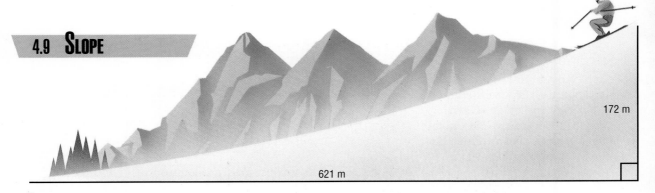

4.9 SLOPE

172 m

621 m

In the previous section, you explored slope and found that the relationship is as follows.

$$\text{Slope} = \frac{\text{rise}}{\text{run}}$$

rise

run

You can use this relationship to find the slope of the ski hill above.

From the ski hill, rise = 172 m and run = 621 m.

Use slope $= \dfrac{\text{rise}}{\text{run}}$

$= \dfrac{172 \text{ m}}{621 \text{ m}}$

$= 0.277$

Thus, the slope of the ski hill is about 0.277.

To extend your skills, you can combine your knowledge of slope and coordinate grids to find the slope of a line on a grid as shown. First, select two points on the line.

Use slope $= \dfrac{\text{rise}}{\text{run}}$

$= \dfrac{+2}{-4}$ or $\dfrac{-1}{2}$

The slope is $-\dfrac{1}{2}$ or -0.5.

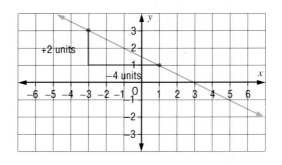

+2 units

−4 units

ACTIVITY

Examine the slope of the line shown above.
(a) In your journal, describe how a line with a positive slope looks and how a line with a negative slope looks.
(b) Provide examples to support your descriptions in (a).

A Review the meanings of rise, run, and slope.

1. For each line, calculate its
   - rise
   - run
   - slope

   (a) 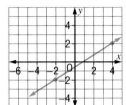   (b) 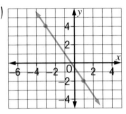   (c)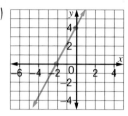

2. (a) The slope of a line segment parallel to the x-axis is zero. Why?
   (b) The slope of a line segment parallel to the y-axis is undefined. Why?

B Be sure to label the axes and the origin properly.

3. (a) If a line has a slope of $\frac{2}{3}$ and passes through the point (1, 3), describe how you would plot a second point to draw the graph.

   (b) If a line has a slope of $-\frac{4}{5}$ and passes through the point (–2, 4), describe how you would plot a second point to draw the graph.

4. A line segment PQ has coordinates P(1, 4) and Q(3, 1). Find the
   (a) run of PQ.   (b) rise of PQ.   (c) slope of PQ.
   (d) run of QP.   (e) rise of QP.   (f) slope of QP.
   (g) What do you notice about the slopes?

5. Each pair of points is on a line. Find the slope of each line.
   (a) A(4, 5), B(3, 7)   (b) C(1, 6), D(3, 9)   (c) E(–3, 4), F(–8, 1)
   (d) G(6, –5), H(9, –3)   (e) J(–5, –7), K(8, –2)   (f) L(9, –1), M(0, 4)

6. Calculate the slope of each line segment.
   (a) AB   (b) BC   (c) CD   (d) AD
   (e) What do you notice about the above slopes?

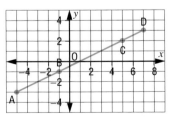

7. Construct each line.

   (a) slope $\frac{2}{3}$, through (4, 5)   (b) slope $\frac{4}{5}$, through (–1, 3)

   (c) slope $-\frac{1}{2}$, through (–3, –4)

137

SAFETY

Suppose you are designing a new building. There are certain safety standards that you need to know. They are summarized below.

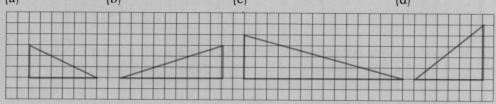

SAFETY STANDARDS

- If you want to push a wheel chair up a ramp, the slope should not exceed 0.125.
- If you want to park your car on a driveway or a street, the slope should not exceed $\frac{2}{9}$.
- If you are building stairs, the slope should not exceed $\frac{5}{6}$.
- If you want to walk up a ramp, the slope should not exceed 0.3.

1. Each ramp is shown on a grid. Which ramps are safe for walking?
   (a)　　　　　(b)　　　　　　　　(c)　　　　　　　　　(d)

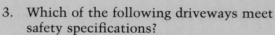

2. A grid is placed on the picture. The ramp is to be used for walking up and down. Does the ramp meet safety specifications?

3. Which of the following driveways meet safety specifications?
   (a) The run of Maggie's driveway is 8 m and the rise is 2.1 m.
   (b) The rise of Plinio's driveway is 1.2 m and the run is 5.5 m.

4. A number of staircases are shown as sketched on a plan. Which of the staircases meet safety specifications?
   (a)　　　　　　　　　　(b)　　　　　　　　(c)

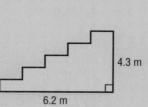
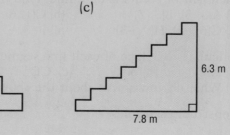

4.3 m　　　3.9 m　　　6.2 m　　　4.6 m　　　6.3 m　　　7.8 m

5. Some streets in San Francisco have a run of 9 m and a rise of 4.2 m.
   (a) Would it be safe to park your car on such streets? Give reasons for your answer.
   (b) In your journal, explain what you can do to park your car safely on one of these streets.

In the previous section, you found the slope of a line on a grid. In this section, you will extend your skills with lines and coordinate grids to explore how to find the midpoint of a line segment.

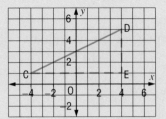

YOU ALREADY KNOW...

- How to plot points on a coordinate grid.
- How to find the slope of a line.

EXPLORATION   **Work with a Partner**

1. (a) Draw the line segment CD, shown to the right, on a coordinate grid.
   (b) Draw a right triangle on your line segment as shown.
   (c) Use a pair of compasses and a straightedge to construct the right bisector of each side of the triangle.
   (d) Extend the bisectors so that they intersect. What are the coordinates of the midpoint of CD?

2. (a) Repeat Question 1 for other line segments that you draw on a coordinate grid.
   (b) What are the coordinates of the midpoint of each line segment?

3. Refer to your constructions in Questions 1 and 2.
   (a) What are the end points of each original line segment?
   (b) What are the coordinates of the midpoint of each line segment?
   (c) Suggest how the coordinates in (a) and (b) are related.

4. Use your results in Question 3.
   (a) Suggest the midpoint of each line segment shown below.

(i) 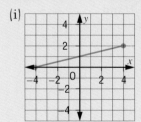   (ii) 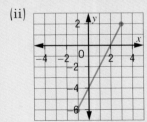   (iii)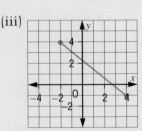

   (b) Use your constructions in Question 1. Check that your coordinates of each midpoint are reasonable.

5. (a) On a coordinate grid, draw different line segments. Identify the end points.
   (b) Have your partner identify the midpoint of each line segment.
   (c) Suggest another method for finding the midpoint of a line segment (for example, folding paper). Use your method to verify that the midpoints you find on your partner's line segments are reasonable.

4.12 MIDPOINT

You can combine your work with coordinate grids, your problem solving skills, and your work with geometry to develop new skills. For example, in the previous section, you explored how to find the midpoint of a line segment drawn on a grid. Your exploration suggested that to find the midpoint, you find the average of the x-coordinates of the end points and the average of the y-coordinates of the end points.

EXAMPLE 1
Find the midpoint of a line with endpoints at P(3, –4) and Q(7, 4).

SOLUTION
Let M represent the coordinates of the midpoint.

Use M $= \left(\dfrac{3+7}{2}, \dfrac{-4+4}{2} \right)$

$= (5, 0)$

The coordinates of the midpoint of PQ are (5, 0).

You can also use the relationship to find one end point when you know the other end point and the midpoint, as shown below.

EXAMPLE 2
One end point of a line is (3, 5). The midpoint is (1, 3). Find the coordinates of the other end point.

SOLUTION
Let x represent the x-coordinate of the end point.   Use E $= \left(\dfrac{3+x}{2}, \dfrac{5+y}{2} \right)$
Let y represent the y-coordinate of the end point.

You already know the midpoint is (1, 3).   Thus, $\dfrac{3+x}{2} = 1$ and $\dfrac{5+y}{2} = 3$.

For $\dfrac{3+x}{2} = 1$ **For** $\dfrac{5+y}{2} = 3$

$3 + x = 2$ Think: $\dfrac{2}{2} = 1$ $5 + y = 6$ Think: $\dfrac{6}{2} = 3$

$x = -1$ $y = 1$

Thus, the other end point has coordinates (–1, 1).

EXERCISE

 A   Review your skills with integers.

1. Find the midpoint of each
   line segment on the coordinate
   grid to the right.

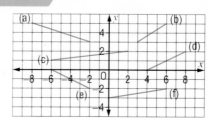

2. Line segment PQ has end points at P(8, 4) and Q(4, 4).
   (a) Sketch the line segment on a coordinate grid.
   (b) Find the coordinates of the midpoint.

3. Find the coordinates of the midpoint of each line segment.
   (a) A(1, 4), B(6, 9)   (b) D(3, −3), G(−3, 9)   (c) P(6, −1), Q(−7, 4)

4. One end point of a line is at (3, 7). Find the other end point if the midpoint is
   (a) (3, 5)   (b) (2, 8)   (c) (−3, 6)   (d) (−5, −5)

 B Remember: Make a final statement when you solve a problem.

5. (a) The diameter of a circle has end points A(−4, 9) and B(−3, 2). Find the coordinates of the centre of the circle.
   (b) The diameter of a circle has end points P(3, 4) and Q(−7, 1). Find the coordinates of the centre of the circle.

6. (a) The diameter of a circle has one end point at M(4, 5). The centre of the circle is at N(2, 3). Find the other end point of the diameter.
   (b) The radius of a circle has end points at O(−1, 3) and P(2, 2). Find a possible end point for the diameter. What assumptions have you made?

7. A beam has end points at W(−2, 4) and X(5, 7). A support post is placed at the midpoint of the beam. At what point does the post touch the beam?

8. One end support of a tennis net is at Y(−5, 8). A support bar is placed in the middle of the net at Z(−1, 1). Find the coordinates of the other end support.

C

9. One end point of a line segment is A(−2, 4). The midpoint is B(−1, 7). Find the coordinates of the other end point.

10. (a) Use 21 disks like those shown below. Follow these rules to play this game with a partner.
    Rule 1 Decide who will go first.
    Rule 2 Each player removes between one and four disks from the board.
    Rule 3 The player who removes the last disk is the winner.
    (b) What strategy can be used so that you will always win the game? What math skills have you used?
    (c) Create a similar game of your own. Develop a strategy so that you will always win the game.

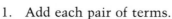
1. Add each pair of terms.
   (a) $3x$, $2x$ (b) $-6y$, $-2y$
   (c) $8a$, $-6a$ (d) $6a$, $-3a$

2. The total cost, T, in thousands of dollars, of digging trenches for underground cables is given by $T = 6.8n + 2.6n - 2$ where n is the length of the trench in kilometres. Find the total cost for $n = 8.6$.

3. Solve.
   (a) $p - 4 = 19$ (b) $-2y = -34$ (c) $w \div 7 = -8$
   (d) $15 = x - 3$ (e) $m \div 2 = -13$ (f) $7 + k = -1$

4. Find the root of each equation.
   (a) $4x = 12$ (b) $\dfrac{y}{3} = 4$ (c) $\dfrac{1}{3} = 2y$

5. Solve.
   (a) $\dfrac{9}{\blacksquare} = \dfrac{12}{36}$ (b) $\dfrac{2}{3} = \dfrac{20}{\blacksquare}$ (c) $\dfrac{10}{15} = \dfrac{8}{\blacksquare}$
   (d) $\dfrac{x}{16} = \dfrac{3}{8}$ (e) $\dfrac{y}{8} = \dfrac{60}{24}$ (f) $\dfrac{40}{65} = \dfrac{80}{z}$

6. On a bottle drive, Marc collected 975 bottles. For every five bottles collected, one was not recyclable. How many bottles were not recyclable?

   (a) Interpret the equation $\dfrac{x}{975} = \dfrac{1}{5}$ used to solve the problem.

   (b) Solve $\dfrac{x}{975} = \dfrac{1}{5}$.

   (c) Write a concluding statement that answers the question "How many bottles were not recyclable?"

7. (a) Calculate the slope of the line segment using these pairs of points.
      (i) A, B (ii) B, C
      What do you notice about the slopes that you found?
   (b) Find the coordinates of the point midway between each pair of points in (a).

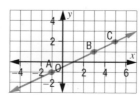

THINKING ABOUT

❶ What have you learned about equations that you did not know before?

❷ What problem solving skills did you use in this chapter to help you learn new skills?

❸ Read this chapter again. List the skills with which you are comfortable. Which skills do you need to study more?

MAKING CONNECTIONS

Refer to Activity 1 on page 122.
(a) Solve the problems you created in the activity.
(b) Have others in the class solve your problems.
(c) Explain to others in the class what skills from this chapter you used to solve each problem.

❹ Refer to Question 3 on this page. Which equations are equivalent? How do you know?

❺ Pick any problem in this chapter. Explain to your group how you solved it.

❻ How would a calculator be useful when solving equations in this chapter? Why?

SELF EVALUATION

1. Simplify each of the following.
   (a) $3a - 2a$
   (b) $6b - 8b$
   (c) $6m - 2m$
   (d) $-4p - 6p$

2. The cost of renting a snowblower, C, in dollars is given by $C = 5 + 5t + 2.25t$ where t is the time in days. Find the cost of renting a snowblower for each time.
   (a) 3 d
   (b) 5 d
   (c) 6 d
   (d) 14 d

3. Find each root.
   (a) $2x + 2 = 10$
   (b) $3x - 1 = 14$
   (c) $7x + 6 = 13$
   (d) $4x + 6 = 10$
   (e) $3x - 9 = -3$
   (f) $5x - 3 = 2$

4. Solve.
   (a) $x + 5 = 9$
   (b) $y - 3 = 7$
   (c) $5 + p = -4$
   (d) $-5 + x = 4$
   (e) $2 = m - 10$
   (f) $2 = 10 + w$

5. Find the missing value.
   (a) $\dfrac{2}{7} = \dfrac{\blacksquare}{21}$
   (b) $\dfrac{4}{8} = \dfrac{\blacksquare}{4}$
   (c) $\dfrac{\blacksquare}{8} = \dfrac{3}{4}$
   (d) $\dfrac{2}{3} = \dfrac{4}{x}$
   (e) $\dfrac{15}{p} = \dfrac{3}{5}$
   (f) $\dfrac{8}{5} = \dfrac{24}{x}$

6. The winner in a school election received 625 votes. For every five votes the winner received, the runner-up received three votes. How many votes did the runner-up receive.

   (a) Interpret the equation $\dfrac{3}{5} = \dfrac{w}{625}$ used to solve the problem.

   (b) Solve $\dfrac{3}{5} = \dfrac{w}{625}$.

   (c) Answer the question "How many votes did the runner-up receive?"

7. Find the midpoint and slope of each line segment.

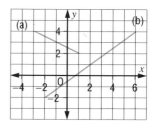

MATH JOURNAL

In this chapter, you have learned to solve some equations.
- Write and solve an equation using the skills in this chapter.
- Describe how you felt when you learned to solve a particular type of equation.

1. Use your calculator.
   (a) Find the sum of 26.5, 9.87, 3.42, and 0.91.
   (b) Subtract 2.47 from the product of 14.8 and 0.56.
   (c) Multiply the difference of 12.34 and 7.8 by the sum of 15.6 and 3.75.

2. Calculate.

   (a) $\dfrac{2}{5} + \dfrac{1}{3} \div \dfrac{4}{15}$ (b) $\left(\dfrac{5}{8} - \dfrac{1}{4}\right) \div \dfrac{2}{3}$ (c) $\dfrac{2}{3} \times \dfrac{5}{8} \div \dfrac{5}{6}$ (d) $\dfrac{3}{4} + \dfrac{1}{2} \times \dfrac{2}{3}$

3. Calculate.

   (a) $6 - [(4 \times 2 + 1) \div 3]$ (b) $\dfrac{46 \times 8 - 8}{16 \div 4 + 4}$ (c) $7.8 \times 19.6 - 18.65$

   (d) $158 \div 2 + 3[6(8 - 5)]$ (e) $\dfrac{28.5 + 7.64 - 3.97}{7.6 \times 2}$ (f) $\dfrac{12^2 - 3 \times 12}{2 + 4 \div 2}$

4. Find the following sums.
   (a) $-3 + (-2) + (-1) + (-4) + (-5) + (-6)$
   (b) $-1 + 6 + (-7) + 8 + (-3) + 3$
   (c) $4 + (-8) + 6 + (-12) + 3 + (-10)$

5. The temperatures recorded for a week were $-8°C$, $-6°C$, $-4°C$, $-3°C$, $0°C$, $2°C$, and $-2°C$.
   (a) Calculate the average daily temperature.
   (b) How much did the temperature change from the start of the week to the end of the week?

6. (a) Draw any obtuse angle.
   (b) Divide the angle in (a) into four equal parts.

7. For each of the following triangles,
   • predict what type of triangle each is.
   • construct the triangle. How accurate was your prediction?
   (a) AC = 7.5 cm, BC = 5.5 cm, $\angle C = 59°$
   (b) AB = 9 cm, $\angle B = 90°$, BC = 12 cm
   (c) BC = 4.75 cm, $\angle B = 44°$, $\angle C = 95°$

8. Two clocks are placed side-by-side. One clock works perfectly, while the other clock loses 5 min each hour. Both clocks started at noon on May 1.
   (a) On what day will the clocks read the same time again? What assumptions have you made?
   (b) Describe to your partner the math skills and the problem solving skills you used to solve the problem in (a).
   (c) Create a similar problem of your own. Solve your problem and compare your problem to others in the class. Discuss the math skills and the problem solving skills needed to solve each problem.

RATIONAL NUMBERS 5

Like many advances throughout history, our number system evolved as needs arose. The first numbers used were the natural or counting numbers.

$$N = \{1, 2, 3, 4, \ldots\}$$

However, the natural numbers lacked a symbol for zero. Centuries later, around the fifteenth century, the first printed use of zero occurred. With zero, whole numbers evolved.

$$W = \{0, 1, 2, 3, 4, \ldots\}$$

Soon, the + and − signs first appeared. The need to represent opposite ideas led to the development of negative numbers, and so integers evolved.

$$I = \{\ldots, -2, -1, 0, +1, +2, \ldots\}$$

Finally, a need arose for numbers between integers. These numbers are called rational numbers. In this chapter, you will learn how rational numbers are used.

Previously, you used integers to express opposite ideas.

5 points gained (+5)	$125 earned (+125)	34 steps up (+34)
5 points lost (–5)	$125 lost (–125)	34 steps down (–34)

The following numbers also show opposite ideas. They are called **rational numbers**. What do you notice about them?

$4.50 earned (+4.50) $12\frac{1}{2}$ points gained $(+12\frac{1}{2})$

$4.50 lost (–4.50) $12\frac{1}{2}$ games behind $(-12\frac{1}{2})$

You can use materials to represent *rational numbers*.

Represents +1   Represents –1

Represents $+\dfrac{1}{2}$ Represents $-\dfrac{1}{2}$

Thus, +4.50 can be represented as

and $-2\dfrac{1}{2}$ can be represented as

Before you begin the explorations on the next page, work with a partner and try the following activity.

ACTIVITY   *Work with a Partner*

1. (a) Write some integers and rational numbers of your own.
   (b) Write the opposite of each integer and rational number in (a).
   (c) What do you notice about your numbers in (a) and (b)?

2. Use the integers –1, +3, –3, and –2.
   (a) Create as many different *rational numbers* as possible using the integers.
   (b) Write four different integers of your own. Repeat (a) using your integers.
   (c) In your journal, write what you think is meant by a rational number. Use (a) and (b) to help you. How are rational numbers like numbers you have seen before? How are they different?

EXPLORATION ①

1. What rational number is represented by each of the following?

   (a)    (b)    (c)

2. Use materials to represent each of the following rational numbers. Sketch the representation in your journal.

   (a) $+2\dfrac{1}{2}$　　　 (b) $-3\dfrac{1}{2}$　　　 (c) -4　　　 (d) $+3$　　　 (e) $+5\dfrac{1}{2}$

3. (a) Suggest how materials may be used to represent these numbers.

   (i) $+4\dfrac{1}{2}$　　 (ii) $-3\dfrac{3}{4}$　　 (iii) $-2\dfrac{3}{4}$　　 (iv) $+4\dfrac{3}{8}$　　 (v) $-3\dfrac{1}{4}$

   (b) Write rational numbers of your own. Use materials to represent each number. Sketch the representation in your journal.

EXPLORATION ②　*Work with a Partner*

4. Serena earned $4.50 for babysitting. She spent $3.50 on lunch.
   (a) How are the materials at the right used to show how much she earned and how much she spent?
   (b) Interpret the materials shown. How much money did she have left?

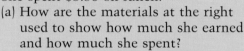

5. Create a problem of your own similar to Question 4 using materials. Solve your problem and compare your solution to that of your partner's.

6. For each, write the net result.

   (a) 　　　 (b) 　　　 (c)

7. (a) In your journal, describe a situation that can be illustrated by each result in Question 6.
   (b) Create a problem of your own similar to Question 4, using the materials in Question 6. Solve your problem and compare your solution to your partner's.

To build rational numbers, you can use integers.

$\dfrac{-2}{3}, \dfrac{3}{-2}, \dfrac{+2}{+3}, \dfrac{4}{-1}, \dfrac{5}{1}$ are rational numbers in fraction form.

Previously, you graphed integers on a number line. You can also graph rationals between the integers as shown. For example, you can mark the point halfway between 0 and –1 as $-\dfrac{1}{2}$.

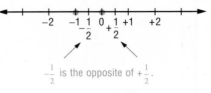

$-\dfrac{1}{2}$ is the opposite of $+\dfrac{1}{2}$.

Your skills with fractions and integers can be combined to write *equivalent* rational numbers as shown.

$$\dfrac{-2}{3} = \dfrac{(-2)(+2)}{(+3)(+2)}$$
$$= \dfrac{-4}{6}$$

$$\dfrac{4}{-5} = \dfrac{(+4)(-1)}{(-5)(-1)}$$
$$= \dfrac{-4}{5}$$

Rational numbers can also be written in *lowest terms* as shown.

$$\dfrac{6}{-9} = \dfrac{6 \div (-3)}{-9 \div (-3)}$$
$$= \dfrac{-2}{3}$$

$$\dfrac{-12}{-8} = \dfrac{-12 \div (-4)}{(-8) \div (-4)}$$
$$= \dfrac{3}{2} \text{ or } 1\dfrac{1}{2}$$

Improper form ⎯⎯⎯⎯ Mixed form

ACTIVITY

(a) How are the rational numbers $\dfrac{2}{-3}$, $\dfrac{-2}{3}$, and $-\dfrac{2}{3}$ alike? How are they different?

(b) Explain to your partner why the rational numbers in (a) might represent the same number. Give reasons for your answer.

To *compare* rational numbers, you follow the same procedure as you did when you compared integers. Refer to the number line shown.

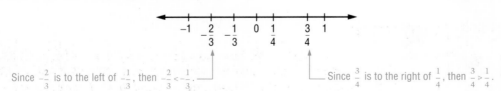

Since $-\dfrac{2}{3}$ is to the left of $-\dfrac{1}{3}$, then $-\dfrac{2}{3} < -\dfrac{1}{3}$.

Since $\dfrac{3}{4}$ is to the right of $\dfrac{1}{4}$, then $\dfrac{3}{4} > \dfrac{1}{4}$.

EXERCISE

A Review your skills with integers.

1. Simplify each of the following rational numbers.

   (a) $\dfrac{-4}{2}$ (b) $\dfrac{-8}{-4}$ (c) $\dfrac{12}{6}$ (d) $\dfrac{-16}{-4}$ (e) $\dfrac{16}{-4}$ (f) $\dfrac{-25}{-5}$

2. Write two equivalent rational numbers for each of the following. (Write your answers with *positive* denominators.)

   (a) $\dfrac{4}{-5}$ (b) $\dfrac{-2}{3}$ (c) $\dfrac{1}{-2}$ (d) $\dfrac{-3}{5}$ (e) $\dfrac{1}{3}$ (f) $\dfrac{3}{-4}$

B Remember: These rational numbers are equivalent: $-\dfrac{1}{2} = \dfrac{-1}{2} = \dfrac{1}{-2}$.

3. Show that   (a) $-\left(\dfrac{-2}{3}\right) = \dfrac{2}{3}$ (b) $-\left(\dfrac{-2}{-3}\right) = \dfrac{-2}{3}$

4. Write these rational numbers in order, from least to greatest.

   (a) $\dfrac{-3}{5}, \dfrac{1}{-3}, -\dfrac{4}{3}$ (b) $\dfrac{-2}{5}, \dfrac{-3}{2}, \dfrac{1}{3}$ (c) $\dfrac{3}{10}, -\dfrac{2}{5}, \dfrac{-1}{2}$

5. Write each of the following in mixed form.

   (a) $\dfrac{-11}{4}$ (b) $\dfrac{-10}{3}$ (c) $\dfrac{12}{-5}$ (d) $\dfrac{15}{4}$ (e) $\dfrac{-20}{7}$ (f) $\dfrac{-18}{4}$

6. Write each of the following in improper form.

   (a) $-3\dfrac{1}{2}$ (b) $-5\dfrac{1}{4}$ (c) $2\dfrac{2}{3}$ (d) $-1\dfrac{7}{10}$ (e) 6   (f) -9

7. Use <, >, or = in place of ● to make each of the following true.

   (a) $-\dfrac{2}{3} ● -\dfrac{5}{6}$ (b) $\dfrac{2}{3} ● \dfrac{3}{4}$ (c) $\dfrac{-2}{5} ● \dfrac{3}{10}$

   (d) $-2\dfrac{1}{2} ● -\dfrac{9}{4}$ (e) $\dfrac{17}{5} ● 3\dfrac{3}{10}$ (f) $\dfrac{-4}{3} ● -3\dfrac{1}{3}$

CALCULATION SENSE

(a) Refer to the manual for your calculator. How can you use your calculator to convert a rational number in fraction form to decimal form?

(b) Convert some rational numbers in this section from fraction form to decimal form.

(c) Write some rational numbers of your own. Write them first in fraction form and then as a decimal number.

Lam scored on 9 of her 12 shots on goal. Marlene scored on 2 of her 3 shots on goal. Use this data in the following activity.

ACTIVITY 1

(a) Write each person's score as a rational number.

(b) To convert each person's score to a decimal number, you can use a calculator key sequence like the following: | c | numerator | ÷ | denominator | = |
Write each score as a decimal number.

(c) Write each as a decimal number.
(i) $\dfrac{3}{5}$ (ii) $-\dfrac{4}{16}$ (iii) $\dfrac{3}{4}$ (iv) $-\dfrac{1}{10}$ (v) $\dfrac{-5}{25}$

(d) Write each as a decimal number.
(i) $\dfrac{1}{3}$ (ii) $\dfrac{-1}{6}$ (iii) $-\dfrac{2}{9}$ (iv) $\dfrac{3}{11}$ (v) $\dfrac{25}{99}$

(e) Compare your decimal numbers in (c) and (d). What do you notice?

In the activity above, you saw two types of decimal numbers used.

This is a **terminating** decimal number.
$$\frac{3}{5} = 0.6$$

This is a **non-terminating** decimal number.
$$\frac{3}{11} = 0.272727\ldots$$

The numerals 2 and 7 are the **period**.

The **length** of the period is 2.

ACTIVITY 2

To show the position of a number on a number line, a decimal number can be written.

(a) Write each as a decimal number. Which rational number is greatest?
(i) $\dfrac{4}{5}$ (ii) $\dfrac{-7}{9}$ (iii) $-8\dfrac{3}{4}$ (iv) $12\dfrac{2}{3}$ (v) $-11\dfrac{1}{6}$

(b) Repeat (a) using rational numbers of your own.

(c) How might you use decimal numbers to show each rational number on a number line?

ACTIVITY 3

You know that $\dfrac{1}{5} = 0.2$ and $\dfrac{1}{4} = 0.25$.

Thus, the decimal number 0.232, or −0.232, occurs as shown. Write each decimal number between two rational numbers.

$$\frac{1}{5} < 0.232 < \frac{1}{4}, \quad -\frac{1}{4} < -0.232 < -\frac{1}{5}$$

(a) 0.434   (b) 0.386   (c) −0.694   (d) 0.121   (e) −0.344

STOCK MARKET

To communicate effectively about a particular subject, you need to be familiar with the vocabulary. The market makes use of many special terms.

ACTIVITY   *Work in a Small Group*

1. (a) What is a stock?
   (b) The following words are associated with buying and selling stocks. What do you think is meant by each?
      • High • Low • Close • Net Change
   (c) Make a list of other words you might use if you are buying stocks or working as a stockbroker. Use the business section in a newspaper to help you.

2. As a stockbroker, you would need to work with rational numbers. What other math skills would a stockbroker need?

---

1. Refer to the stock market chart. Work with a partner.
   (a) Which stock gained the most yesterday?
   (b) Which stock gained the least yesterday?
   (c) Write the stock gains in order from least to greatest. Describe to your partner how you decided which stocks gained the most and which gained the least.

2. Refer to the columns that show the highest price paid per share, the lowest price paid per share, and yesterday's final price per share. Repeat the parts of Question 1 for each column.

Stock Exchange Report   **Date: February 8**

Stock	Sales	High	Low	Close	Net Change
Bridger	3499	$10\frac{3}{4}$	$10\frac{1}{2}$	10	$-\frac{1}{2}$
Brunswick	3900	420	410	410	-2
C.S. Pete	18 110	335	345	345	-2
C. Curtis	1500	44	44	44	$+3$
Comb Met	5000	$17\frac{1}{2}$	$16\frac{3}{4}$	16	$+\frac{7}{8}$
C. Durham	8000	66	63	63	-3
Marcania	3633	13	12	12	$+2$
Merland E.	13 690	278	271	271	-8
Norlex	14 000	$16\frac{1}{4}$	$14\frac{3}{4}$	$15\frac{1}{2}$	$-\frac{1}{2}$
Ponder	500	60	60	60	-2
VanDer	621	360	360	360	$+12$
Westfield	13 800	155	150	155	-8

change from yesterday's final price

name of company

number of shares (stocks) sold

highest price paid per share

lowest price paid per share

yesterday's final price per share

3. (a) How many shares from Brunswick to Ponder had a positive net change?
   (b) How many had a negative net change?

4. Choose a block of stocks from any stock market report or newspaper.
   (a) How many stocks had a positive net change? How many had a negative net change?
   (b) In your journal, write a short paragraph to describe a typical day of a stockbroker. Have the stockbroker explain to a client some reasons why a stock purchased had a negative net change.

Materials, such as black and red squares and parts of squares can help you add rational numbers. As you complete each of the following explorations, summarize in your journal any patterns you observe.

EXPLORATION ①

1. The materials shown represent the expression $\left(+2\frac{1}{2}\right)+\left(+1\frac{1}{2}\right)$.

    (a) What is the net result of adding two black squares and one black square?
    (b) What is the net result of adding a half black square and a half black square?

    (c) Interpret your results to find the answer to $\left(+2\frac{1}{2}\right)+\left(+1\frac{1}{2}\right)$.

    (d) Create similar expressions of your own. Use materials to find the answers.

2. (a) Use materials to represent $\left(-2\frac{1}{2}\right)+\left(-1\frac{1}{2}\right)$. What is the net result?

    (b) Interpret your work in (a). What is the answer to $\left(-2\frac{1}{2}\right)+\left(-1\frac{1}{2}\right)$?

    (c) Create similar expressions of your own. Use materials to find the answers.

EXPLORATION ② *Work with a Partner*

3. The materials shown represent the expression $\left(+2\frac{1}{2}\right)+\left(-1\frac{1}{2}\right)$.

    (a) What is the net result of adding two black squares and one red square?
    (b) What is the net result of adding a half black square and a half red square?

    (c) Interpret your results to find the answer to $\left(+2\frac{1}{2}\right)+\left(-1\frac{1}{2}\right)$.

    (d) Create similar expressions of your own. Use materials to find the answers.

4. (a) Use materials to represent $\left(-2\frac{1}{2}\right)+\left(+1\frac{1}{2}\right)$. What is the net result?

    (b) Interpret your work in (a). What is the answer to $\left(-2\frac{1}{2}\right)+\left(+1\frac{1}{2}\right)$?

    (c) Create similar expressions of your own. Use materials to find the answers.

Mhari adjusted the sight on her bow $2\frac{1}{2}$ cm up and then $1\frac{1}{2}$ cm down.

By how much did she adjust the sight?

Think: Interpret what is given.

- $2\frac{1}{2}$ cm up can be represented by $+2\frac{1}{2}$.

- $1\frac{1}{2}$ cm down can be represented by $-1\frac{1}{2}$ cm.

To solve the problem, Mhari calculated $\left(+2\frac{1}{2}\right)+\left(-1\frac{1}{2}\right)$ using materials as shown below.

 Think: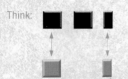

Interpret your result.

The net result is one black square.

Thus, $\left(+2\frac{1}{2}\right)+\left(-1\frac{1}{2}\right)=+1$.

Thus, the net adjustment was 1 cm up.

When you learn new math skills, it helps to compare any new work you do with work you have done previously as shown in the following activity.

ACTIVITY

(a) How are the examples shown below like adding fractions? How are they different?

$$+\frac{1}{2}+\frac{-3}{8} = +\frac{4}{8}+\frac{-3}{8}$$
$$= \frac{+4+(-3)}{8}$$
$$= \frac{+1}{8}$$

$$\frac{2}{-3}+\left(-1\frac{1}{6}\right) = \frac{2}{-3}+\frac{-7}{6}$$
$$= \frac{-4}{6}+\frac{-7}{6}$$
$$= \frac{(-4)+(-7)}{6}$$
$$= \frac{-11}{6} \text{ or } -1\frac{5}{6}$$

Think: $1\frac{1}{6}$ is equivalent to $\frac{7}{6}$.

(b) Create your own examples using work you did before. Rewrite the examples using rational numbers. Find the answers.

You can also add rational numbers written in decimal form as shown.

$$(-5.6)+(+7.8)=+2.2$$

C 5.6 +/− + 7.8 = 2.2

EXERCISE

A   Review your skills with rational numbers.

1. During a competition, Mhari adjusted her sight $1\frac{1}{2}$ cm up and then 1 cm down.
   (a) How can these materials help you find by how much she adjusted her sight?
   (b) Interpret the materials.
   (c) By how much did Mhari adjust her sight in all?

2. Add each of the following.
   (a) $\dfrac{-3}{4} + \dfrac{1}{4}$ (b) $\dfrac{3}{8} + \dfrac{-7}{8}$ (c) $\dfrac{3}{5} + \dfrac{1}{5}$ (d) $-\dfrac{2}{3} + \dfrac{-1}{3}$

3. (a) To find the sum $\dfrac{-1}{2} + \dfrac{-3}{4}$, what is your first step?
   (b) Find the sum in (a).

4. Use equivalent rational numbers to write each pair with a positive common denominator.
   (a) $\dfrac{-1}{2}, \dfrac{1}{-4}$ (b) $\dfrac{3}{-4}, -\dfrac{5}{8}$ (c) $\dfrac{-2}{3}, \dfrac{2}{-5}$ (d) $\dfrac{-1}{3}, \dfrac{2}{-7}$

B   Work together to complete the exercise.

5. Add each of the following.
   (a) $\dfrac{-3}{5} + \dfrac{-7}{10}$ (b) $\dfrac{-1}{5} + \dfrac{3}{10}$ (c) $\dfrac{-2}{5} + \dfrac{-3}{10}$ (d) $\dfrac{7}{8} + \dfrac{-1}{4}$

6. Simplify each of the following.
   (a) $\dfrac{1}{2} + \dfrac{-2}{3}$ (b) $\dfrac{3}{-5} + \dfrac{-3}{4}$ (c) $\dfrac{1}{3} + \dfrac{-1}{8}$ (d) $\dfrac{-1}{3} + \dfrac{1}{4}$

   (e) $\dfrac{1}{-4} + \dfrac{-1}{3}$ (f) $\dfrac{-3}{4} + \dfrac{2}{3}$ (g) $\dfrac{-3}{4} + \dfrac{1}{-4}$ (h) $\dfrac{5}{-12} + \dfrac{-3}{4}$

7. Use < or > in place of ■ to make each of the following true.
   (a) $\dfrac{-3}{4} + \dfrac{-1}{4}$ ■ $\dfrac{-3}{2} + \dfrac{2}{3}$ (b) $-\dfrac{3}{5} + \dfrac{-2}{3}$ ■ $\dfrac{1}{-8} + \dfrac{3}{-4}$

   (c) $\dfrac{-1}{5} + \dfrac{2}{3}$ ■ $\dfrac{-4}{3} + \dfrac{1}{4}$ (d) $-\dfrac{1}{2} + \left(\dfrac{-1}{3}\right)$ ■ $\dfrac{1}{8} + \left(\dfrac{-2}{3}\right)$

8. Add.
   (a) $(+7.3) + (+4.4)$ (b) $(+4.2) + (-5.7)$ (c) $(-4.3) + (+6.8)$
   (d) $(-3.1) + (-7.8)$ (e) $(-4.4) + (+6.2)$ (f) $(-8.1) + (11.4)$

9. Add. Check whether your answer is reasonable.
   (a) $(+7.3) + (+4.4)$
   (b) $(+4.1) + (-7.8)$
   (c) $(-8.3) + (-1.4)$
   (d) $(+5.7) + (-8.9)$
   (e) $(+3.8) + (-4.7)$
   (f) $(+8.5) + (-9.7)$
   (g) $(+11.3) + (-17.8)$
   (h) $(+8.3) + (+1.4)$
   (i) $(-12.4) + (-13.6)$

10. Simplify.
   (a) $-\dfrac{-3}{2} + 1\dfrac{1}{3}$
   (b) $\dfrac{-3}{8} + 2\dfrac{1}{4}$
   (c) $\dfrac{7}{8} + 1\dfrac{1}{2}$
   (d) $\dfrac{-8}{10} + 1\dfrac{5}{10}$

   (e) $-8\dfrac{1}{4} + 9$
   (f) $-2\dfrac{1}{3} + 1\dfrac{2}{3}$
   (g) $\dfrac{-9}{10} + 2\dfrac{2}{5}$
   (h) $8 + 4\dfrac{3}{4}$

11. Maria spent $2\dfrac{1}{4}$ h raking leaves and $\dfrac{3}{4}$ h washing windows. How much time, in total, did she spend on the two tasks?

12. A bus trip is 0.75 h longer than the same trip by train. If the train trip is 2.35 h long, how long is the bus trip?

13. Kim's scores for 5 rounds of a video game were $12\dfrac{1}{2}$, $-5\dfrac{1}{4}$, $-3\dfrac{1}{2}$, $6\dfrac{3}{4}$, and $2\dfrac{1}{4}$.

   Dawna's scores for the same game were $12\dfrac{1}{2}$, $-8\dfrac{1}{4}$, $-7\dfrac{1}{2}$, $14\dfrac{3}{4}$, and $-6\dfrac{1}{4}$.

   (a) What total score did each player receive?
   (b) Who had the greatest score? How do you know?

14. To qualify for a ski vacation in Québec, Yee had to follow these instructions.

   Step A Add $\dfrac{2}{3} + \dfrac{1}{-3}$ to $\dfrac{3}{4} - \dfrac{-2}{3}$.

   Step B Add $\dfrac{2}{-3}$ to your answer in A.

   Step C Add $-\dfrac{3}{4}$ to your answer in B.

   Step D Increase your answer in C by $\dfrac{3}{-8}$.

   What is the final answer?

15. Different views of a cube are shown below.
   (a) Construct the actual cube.
   (b) What is the sum of the opposite faces of the cube?
   (c) Create a problem of your own using the cube. Solve your problem. Compare your problem to others in the class.

155

You can use materials to help you subtract rational numbers as shown in the following exploration. As you complete the exploration, record in your journal any patterns and relationships you can use to subtract rational numbers.

EXPLORATION   *Work with a Partner*

To subtract rational numbers, you need to refer to your earlier skills with integers.

1. The rational number $+3\frac{1}{2}$ is shown using squares.

   (a) What is the result of taking $2\frac{1}{2}$ black squares from $3\frac{1}{2}$ black squares?

   (b) Interpret your results in (a). Find the answer to $\left(+3\frac{1}{2}\right) - \left(+2\frac{1}{2}\right)$.

2. (a) Vanita used the steps shown below to subtract $\left(+2\frac{1}{2}\right) - \left(-1\frac{1}{2}\right)$.

   Step 1

   Step 2

   Step 3

   Think: Vanita realizes she cannot subtract red squares from black squares.

   She decides to represent $\left(+2\frac{1}{2}\right)$ in another way.

   Vanita then removes $\left(-1\frac{1}{2}\right)$ red squares. What is the answer?

   (b) Interpret each step above. In your journal, describe what Vanita is doing in each step and why she is doing it.

   (c) Interpret the steps in (b). What is the answer to $\left(+2\frac{1}{2}\right) - \left(-1\frac{1}{2}\right)$?

   (d) Write similar expressions of your own. Have others in the class use materials to find the answers.

3. Compare how you add and subtract rational numbers. In your journal:
   (a) Describe how the skills are alike and how they are different.
   (b) Use examples of your own to illustrate your answer in (a).

Licia is standing on a diving board $2\frac{1}{2}$ m above the surface of the water. The bottom of the pool is $3\frac{1}{2}$ m below the surface of the water. How far above the bottom of the pool is Licia?

Think: Interpret what is given. The words "How far" are clue words.
- To solve the problem, find $\left(+2\frac{1}{2}\right) - \left(-3\frac{1}{2}\right)$ using materials as shown below.

Step 1

Use $2\frac{1}{2}$ black squares to represent $+2\frac{1}{2}$ m.

Step 2

Represent $+2\frac{1}{2}$ in another way to show red squares.

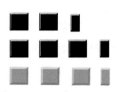

Step 3

Remove $3\frac{1}{2}$ red squares.

Step 4

Interpret your result. Licia is 6 m above the bottom of the pool.

ACTIVITY 1

(a) How are the examples shown below like working with fractions? How are they different?

$$\frac{-2}{3} - \frac{-4}{5} = \frac{-10}{15} - \frac{-12}{15}$$

Think: $\frac{-10}{15}$ is equivalent to $\frac{-2}{3}$

$$= \frac{(-10) - (-12)}{15}$$

$$= \frac{2}{15}$$

$$-14\frac{3}{5} - \left(+5\frac{1}{2}\right) = -14\frac{6}{10} - \left(+5\frac{5}{10}\right)$$

$$= \frac{-146}{10} - \frac{+55}{10}$$

$$= \frac{-201}{10} \text{ or } -20\frac{1}{10}$$

(b) Create your own examples using work you did before. Rewrite the examples using rational numbers. Find the answers.

You can subtract rational numbers using your calculator. $\boxed{\text{c}}$ 5.6 $\boxed{-}$ 8.7 $\boxed{+/-}$ $\boxed{=}$ 14.3 What subtraction is shown?

A Review your skills with fractions.

1. During a diving competition, Licia was 10 m above the surface of the water. The bottom of the pool was $4\frac{1}{2}$ m below the surface of the water.

   (a) How can you use materials to help you find how far Licia is from the bottom of the pool?

   (b) Interpret your materials. How far is Licia from the bottom of the pool?

2. Subtract each of the following.

   (a) $\dfrac{-1}{4} - \dfrac{3}{4}$ (b) $\dfrac{5}{8} - \dfrac{-3}{8}$ (c) $\dfrac{4}{7} - \dfrac{3}{7}$ (d) $-\dfrac{3}{5} - \dfrac{-1}{5}$

3. To find the value of $\dfrac{2}{3} - \dfrac{5}{6}$, what is your first step? Find the value.

B Review all your skills with rational numbers.

4. Simplify each of the following.

   (a) $-\dfrac{4}{5} - \dfrac{1}{10}$ (b) $\dfrac{1}{4} - \dfrac{3}{8}$ (c) $-\dfrac{2}{5} - \dfrac{7}{15}$ (d) $\dfrac{5}{8} - \dfrac{1}{16}$

   (e) $\dfrac{2}{3} - \dfrac{3}{4}$ (f) $\dfrac{-5}{8} - \dfrac{4}{5}$ (g) $\dfrac{-5}{7} - \dfrac{-1}{4}$ (h) $\dfrac{5}{7} - \dfrac{3}{4}$

5. Simplify.

   (a) $-\dfrac{8}{10} - 1\dfrac{5}{10}$ (b) $-8\dfrac{1}{4} - 9$ (c) $-2\dfrac{1}{3} - 1\dfrac{2}{3}$ (d) $\dfrac{-9}{10} - 2\dfrac{2}{5}$

6. Find each difference. Check whether your answer is reasonable.

   (a) $(-6.1) - (+7.6)$ (b) $(-5.2) - (+9.8)$ (c) $(+4.3) - (-5.1)$

   (d) $(+11.3) - (+12.4)$ (e) $(+8.7) - (-2.5)$ (f) $(-12.4) - (-14.3)$

7. In the first computer game, Kalvin scored $12\frac{1}{4}$ points. In the second game, he scored $-5\frac{1}{4}$ points. How many more points is the first game than the second?

8. The temperature of a liquid during the first part of Ellen's experiment averaged $-12.75°C$. During the second part, the average temperature dropped $5.35°C$. What was the average temperature of the liquid during the second part of the experiment?

9. Simplify each of the following expressions.

   (a) $2\dfrac{1}{10} - \dfrac{-1}{5} + 3\dfrac{1}{2}$ (b) $\dfrac{1}{3} + \dfrac{-5}{6} - 1\dfrac{1}{3}$ (c) $-2\dfrac{1}{4} - 1\dfrac{1}{2} - 1\dfrac{2}{3}$

Although rational numbers are often expressed in fraction form, you can express them in decimal form and then use a calculator to help you add or subtract the rational numbers.

ACTIVITY 1   *Work with a Partner*

(a) Use this calculator key sequence to express $-\dfrac{4}{5}$ as a decimal number.

$\boxed{\text{c}}\ 4\ \boxed{+/-}\ \boxed{\div}\ 5\ \boxed{=}$

(b) Use a calculator to express each of the following as a decimal number.

(i) $\dfrac{-3}{4}$ (ii) $+\dfrac{4}{5}$ (iii) $\dfrac{3}{-8}$ (iv) $-\dfrac{7}{10}$ (v) $-\dfrac{9}{8}$

ACTIVITY 2   *Work with a Partner*

Use these steps to find the sum of $\dfrac{-1}{3} + \dfrac{5}{6}$.

(a) Express $\dfrac{-1}{3}$ as a decimal number and place it in the memory of your calculator.

(b) Express $\dfrac{5}{6}$ as a decimal number. Add this decimal number to the memory.

(c) Recall what is now in the memory ($\boxed{\text{MR}}$). What is the answer, as a decimal number?

(d) Use your calculator to find each sum.   (i) $\dfrac{-2}{3} + \dfrac{+4}{+6}$ (ii) $\dfrac{1}{4} + \dfrac{-3}{8}$ (iii) $\dfrac{4}{5} + \dfrac{7}{8}$

ACTIVITY 3   *Work with a Partner*

Use these steps to find the difference of $\dfrac{-2}{5} - \dfrac{1}{-4}$.

(a) Express $\dfrac{-2}{5}$ as a decimal number and place it in the memory of your calculator.

(b) Express $\dfrac{1}{-4}$ as a decimal number. Subtract this decimal number from the number in the memory ($\boxed{\text{M}-}$).

(c) Recall what is now in the memory ($\boxed{\text{MR}}$). What is the answer, as a decimal number?

(d) Use your calculator to find each difference.   (i) $\dfrac{3}{5} - \dfrac{-1}{4}$ (ii) $\dfrac{-3}{8} - \dfrac{-4}{-5}$ (iii) $\dfrac{-2}{3} - \dfrac{4}{5}$

You can use manipulatives to help you multiply rational numbers.

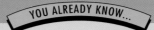
EXPLORATION   *Work Together*

1. (a) How do the materials at the right represent a model to calculate

    $(+3) \times \left(+3\frac{1}{2}\right)$?

    (b) What is the answer to $(+3) \times \left(+3\frac{1}{2}\right)$?

2. (a) How do the materials at the right represent a model to calculate

    $(+3) \times \left(-3\frac{1}{2}\right)$?

    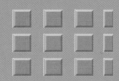

    (b) What is the answer to $(+3) \times \left(-3\frac{1}{2}\right)$?

3. (a) Interpret each group of materials shown below. What do they suggest?
    (b) Write the answer for each product in (a).

    A   B

    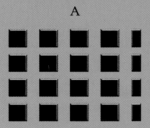

4. (a) Use your materials to represent each product.

    (i) $\left(+5\frac{1}{2}\right) \times (+3)$ (ii) $(+4) \times \left(+2\frac{1}{2}\right)$ (iii) $(+3) \times \left(-4\frac{1}{2}\right)$

    (b) Interpret your answers in (a). Find each product.

5. Work with a partner.
    (a) Set up materials of your own to represent a product.
    (b) Have your partner write the expression and the answer.
    (c) Switch roles with your partner and repeat (a) and (b).

5.11 MULTIPLYING RATIONAL NUMBERS

When taking earth samples, an archaeologist often uses a machine to dig. Suppose Jose uses the machine for 3 d and digs a depth of $3\frac{1}{2}$ m each day. How deep does Jose dig?

Think: Interpret what is given.
The words "dig" and "How deep" are clue words.

- A depth of $3\frac{1}{2}$ m can be represented by $-3\frac{1}{2}$.
- 3 d can be represented by +3.

Step 1
Show $(+3) \times \left(-3\frac{1}{2}\right)$ using materials.

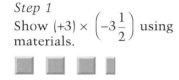

Step 2
Using the materials,

$$(+3) \times \left(-3\frac{1}{2}\right) = -10\frac{1}{2}.$$

Step 3
Thus, Jose digs to a depth of $10\frac{1}{2}$ m.

ACTIVITY

To help you learn new math skills, you can often compare your skills from different parts of mathematics.

(a) How are the examples shown alike? How are they different?

$$\frac{3}{4} \times \frac{5}{7} = \frac{3 \times 5}{4 \times 7}$$
$$= \frac{15}{28}$$

$$\frac{-3}{4} \times \frac{5}{7} = \frac{-3 \times 5}{4 \times 7}$$
$$= \frac{-15}{28}$$

(b) Create your own examples to compare multiplying fractions and rational numbers. How are the examples alike? How are they different?

You can multiply rational numbers using a calculator. What expression is shown?

$\boxed{c}$ 3.65 $\boxed{+/-}$ $\boxed{\times}$ 0.875 $\boxed{=}$ −3.19375

EXERCISE

 Review your skills with multiplying fractions.

1. Refer to the above example. Suppose Jose dug for 4 d.
   (a) How would you use materials to represent how far Jose can dig?
   (b) Set up materials and interpret your result. How far can Jose dig if he digs for 4 d?

2. To find the product of $\left(\dfrac{-3}{4}\right) \times \left(\dfrac{2}{-5}\right)$, what is your first step? Find the answer.

3. Multiply. Write your answer with a positive denominator.

   (a) $\dfrac{1}{2} \times \dfrac{1}{-5}$
   (b) $\left(\dfrac{-1}{3}\right) \times \left(\dfrac{2}{-5}\right)$
   (c) $\dfrac{1}{2} \times \left(-\dfrac{2}{5}\right)$
   (d) $\dfrac{-3}{4} \times \dfrac{1}{3}$

4. For each, decide on the first step to find the product. Then find the product.

   (a) $\left(-\dfrac{3}{4}\right)\left(\dfrac{1}{2}\right)$
   (b) $\left(\dfrac{0}{-2}\right)\left(\dfrac{-3}{8}\right)$
   (c) $\left(-2\dfrac{1}{5}\right)\left(-\dfrac{2}{3}\right)$
   (d) $\left(-3\dfrac{1}{4}\right)\left(\dfrac{-2}{-3}\right)$

   (e) $\left(-\dfrac{4}{5}\right)\left(\dfrac{2}{3}\right)$
   (f) $\left(\dfrac{1}{2}\right)\left(\dfrac{-5}{8}\right)$
   (g) $\left(-3\dfrac{1}{4}\right)\left(\dfrac{4}{7}\right)$
   (h) $\left(-5\dfrac{1}{2}\right)\left(-2\dfrac{1}{4}\right)$

5. Find the following products.

   (a) $\left(\dfrac{-6}{10}\right)\left(\dfrac{1}{-2}\right)$
   (b) $\left(\dfrac{-2}{3}\right)\left(\dfrac{-3}{2}\right)$
   (c) $\left(-\dfrac{2}{3}\right)\left(\dfrac{1}{3}\right)$
   (d) $\left(-\dfrac{2}{3}\right)\left(-\dfrac{1}{3}\right)$

B Write your answers in lowest terms. Use a calculator when needed.

6. Simplify each of the following. Watch the signs.

   (a) $\dfrac{4}{5} \times \dfrac{-20}{25}$
   (b) $\dfrac{3}{-2} \times \dfrac{-1}{3}$
   (c) $-6 \times \dfrac{4}{5}$
   (d) $\dfrac{0}{-10} \times 2\dfrac{1}{4}$

   (e) $10\dfrac{1}{2} \times \dfrac{3}{4}$
   (f) $-7\dfrac{1}{8} \times \dfrac{-2}{3}$
   (g) $\dfrac{-1}{2} \times 2\dfrac{1}{3}$
   (h) $-1\dfrac{1}{10} \times 4\dfrac{1}{5}$

7. Simplify each product.

   (a) $\left(\dfrac{3}{5}\right)\left(\dfrac{1}{-6}\right)\left(\dfrac{-2}{3}\right)$
   (b) $\left(\dfrac{-5}{8}\right)\left(\dfrac{16}{4}\right)\left(\dfrac{-3}{10}\right)$
   (c) $\left(2\dfrac{3}{4}\right)\left(-1\dfrac{1}{4}\right)\left(\dfrac{-3}{8}\right)$

   (d) $\left(\dfrac{-5}{8}\right)\left(\dfrac{4}{10}\right)\left(\dfrac{-6}{8}\right)$
   (e) $\left(\dfrac{2}{-3}\right)\left(\dfrac{6}{-8}\right)\left(\dfrac{-3}{12}\right)$
   (f) $\left(\dfrac{-1}{3}\right)\left(\dfrac{-10}{9}\right)\left(\dfrac{5}{6}\right)$

8. Multiply. Check that your answer is reasonable.
   (a) $(-3.8) \times (+4.5)$
   (b) $(-5.2) \times (-3.8)$
   (c) $(-1.3) \times (+9.9)$
   (d) $(-2.7) \times (-4.4)$
   (e) $(+5.7) \times (+6.7)$
   (f) $(+4.2) \times (0)$
   (g) $(-2.7) \times (-5.3)$
   (h) $(-4.6) \times (-9.8)$
   (i) $(-3.1) \times (-8.8)$

9. Julia feeds her puppies $\dfrac{2}{3}$ of a can of dog food twice a day. How much dog food does she feed them each week?

10. Water evaporates from a storage drum at a rate of $\dfrac{1}{20}$ of the drum's volume each week.

    What fraction of the drum's volume evaporates in $5\dfrac{1}{2}$ weeks?

11. Alain can plant one flat of begonias in 0.75 h. If he plants begonias for his entire 7.5 h shift, how many flats does he plant?

12. If 12.25 bags of seed are needed to plant each hectare of a field, then how many bags are needed to plant a 6.5-ha field?

13. (a) Suppose a stock had a net change of $-\frac{1}{4}$ for three days in a row. What is the total change of the stock?
    (b) Refer to the stock market report on page 151. Create a problem of your own using the report. Solve your problem and have others in the class solve your problem.

14. A music shop sells compact discs and accessories such as blank tapes and carrying cases.
    Half of the space is used for compact discs, $\frac{3}{10}$ for cassette tapes, and $\frac{1}{5}$ for music equipment accessories.

    (a) If $\frac{1}{3}$ of the cassette tape space is used for New Releases, what fraction of the whole store is used for New Release cassettes?

    (b) If $\frac{1}{10}$ of the music equipment accessories space is used for carrying cases, what fraction of the whole store is used for carrying cases?

    (c) If $\frac{1}{4}$ of the compact disc space is used for classical music, what fraction of the whole store is used for classical CDs?

15. Construct two dice, A and B, with the rational numbers as follows:

    A: $+1\frac{1}{2}, +2\frac{1}{2}, +3\frac{1}{2}, +4\frac{1}{2}, +5\frac{1}{2}, +6\frac{1}{2}$

    B: $-1\frac{1}{2}, -2\frac{1}{2}, -3\frac{1}{2}, -4\frac{1}{2}, -5\frac{1}{2}, -6\frac{1}{2}$

    (a) Roll the dice ten times. Find the product of the rational numbers for each roll.
    (b) Find the sum of the products in (a).
    (c) Have your partner roll the dice ten times and repeat (a) and (b).

    The player closest to $-33\frac{1}{4}$ after ten rolls is the winner of the game.

To develop a new skill, try to relate it to something that you already know, as shown in the following activity.

ACTIVITY 1   *Work with a Partner*

(a) Review the vocabulary and skills you used when working with fractions. Make a list of all the vocabulary you used.

(b) How might the vocabulary and skills in (a) be used when working with rational numbers? Give examples to help your explanations.

ACTIVITY 2   *Work with a Partner*

(a) Compare the following. How are they alike? How are they different?

$$\frac{8}{3} \div \frac{4}{5} = \frac{8}{3} \times \frac{5}{4} \qquad \frac{5}{4} \text{ is the reciprocal of } \frac{4}{5} \qquad \frac{-8}{3} \div \frac{-4}{5} = \frac{-8}{3} \times \frac{5}{-4}$$

$$= \frac{2\;\cancel{8}}{3} \times \frac{5}{\cancel{4}\,_1} \qquad\qquad\qquad = \frac{2\;\cancel{-8}}{3} \times \frac{5}{\cancel{-4}\,_1}$$

$$= \frac{10}{3} \qquad\qquad\qquad\qquad\qquad = \frac{10}{3}$$

(b) How can your skills with integers and your skills with fractions be combined to help you divide rational numbers?

When multiplying or dividing rational numbers, they should first be expressed as improper fractions. Then simplify where possible before calculating.

EXAMPLE   Simplify.

(a) $\left(-2\dfrac{1}{2}\right) \div \left(\dfrac{-1}{2}\right)$
 (b) $\left(-\dfrac{2}{3}\right) \div \left(-1\dfrac{1}{5}\right)$

SOLUTION (a) $\left(-2\dfrac{1}{2}\right) \div \left(\dfrac{-1}{2}\right)$
 (b) $\left(-\dfrac{2}{3}\right) \div \left(-1\dfrac{1}{5}\right)$
 Remember: Your first step is to record the expression.

$$= \left(\frac{-5}{2}\right) \div \left(\frac{-1}{2}\right) \qquad\qquad = \frac{2}{3} \div \left(\frac{-6}{5}\right)$$

$$= \frac{-5}{2} \times \frac{2}{-1} \quad\longleftarrow\; \frac{2}{-1} \text{ is the reciprocal of } \frac{-1}{2} \qquad = \frac{1\;\cancel{2}}{3} \times \left(\frac{5}{\cancel{-6}\,_{-3}}\right)$$

$$= \frac{-5}{1} \times \frac{1}{-1} \qquad\qquad\qquad = -\frac{5}{9}$$

$$= \frac{-5}{-1} \text{ or } 5$$

A Express rational numbers with positive denominators.

1. Write the reciprocals of the following. Use a positive denominator.

   (a) $\dfrac{1}{3}$ (b) $\dfrac{-2}{3}$ (c) 3 (d) $-\dfrac{1}{3}$ (e) $2\dfrac{1}{2}$ (f) $-4\dfrac{1}{2}$

2. To simplify each of the following, what is the first step? Find the answer.

   (a) $\dfrac{9}{10} \div \dfrac{3}{-5}$ (b) $\dfrac{4}{3} \div \dfrac{-2}{3}$ (c) $\dfrac{1}{3} \div \dfrac{1}{8}$ (d) $\dfrac{3}{-2} \div \dfrac{-1}{3}$

3. To simplify each of the following, what is the first step? Find the answer.

   (a) $2\dfrac{1}{2} \div \dfrac{-1}{2}$ (b) $\dfrac{-2}{3} \div 4\dfrac{1}{4}$ (c) $\dfrac{-1}{5} \div -2\dfrac{1}{3}$ (d) $-2\dfrac{1}{2} \div -1\dfrac{1}{4}$

B To finish each problem, write a concluding statement.

4. Simplify each of the following.

   (a) $\dfrac{4}{5} \div \dfrac{-20}{25}$ (b) $\dfrac{3}{-2} \div \dfrac{-1}{3}$ (c) $-6 \div \dfrac{4}{5}$ (d) $\dfrac{1}{-10} \div 2\dfrac{1}{4}$

   (e) $10\dfrac{1}{2} \div \dfrac{3}{4}$ (f) $-7\dfrac{1}{8} \div \dfrac{-2}{3}$ (g) $\dfrac{-1}{2} \div 2\dfrac{1}{3}$ (h) $-1\dfrac{1}{10} \div 4\dfrac{1}{5}$

5. It rained for $3\dfrac{1}{2}$ h on Monday and $1\dfrac{3}{4}$ h on Tuesday. How many times longer did it rain on Monday than it did on Tuesday?

6. Zulema ran $2\dfrac{3}{4}$ laps of the track in 9 min. How long did it take her to run one lap?

7. A bus uses $\dfrac{1}{10}$ of a tank of fuel to travel a complete route. If the fuel tank is $\dfrac{7}{8}$ full, how many routes can the bus complete without refuelling?

8. Suppose Zulema scored the following points on a video game.

   $$3\dfrac{1}{2}; \ \dfrac{-7}{8}, \ -4\dfrac{1}{4}, \ 5\dfrac{2}{3}, \ 3\dfrac{3}{4}, \ 11\dfrac{7}{8}, \ -5\dfrac{1}{4}$$

   (a) How many total points did she score?
   (b) What was her average score?

C

9. Simplify each of the following.

   (a) $\dfrac{4}{-5} \times \dfrac{5}{4} \div \dfrac{-3}{8}$ (b) $\dfrac{-5}{3} \times \dfrac{28}{5} \div \dfrac{-8}{6}$ (c) $\dfrac{-5}{8} \div \dfrac{16}{-4} \times \dfrac{-3}{10}$

   (d) $\dfrac{2}{-3} \times \dfrac{6}{-8} \div \dfrac{-3}{12}$ (e) $-1\dfrac{1}{5} \times \dfrac{-2}{3} \div \dfrac{-12}{7}$ (f) $\dfrac{-1}{3} \div \dfrac{-10}{9} \times \dfrac{5}{6}$

In an operating room, the order in which a surgeon performs an operation is crucial. In mathematics, the order in which you perform operations is also crucial.

ACTIVITY 1

The order of operations you have used is shown to the right.

(a) For which numbers have you used the order of operations?

(b) Write an example of your own to show how the order of operations is used for the numbers in (a).

Order of Operations
- Do the calculations in brackets first.
- Then do multiplication and division in the order they appear.
- Then do addition and subtraction in the order they appear.

ACTIVITY 2

The order of operations are applied using rational numbers as shown.

(a) Give reasons why each line is written as it is.

(b) Create a similar expression of your own using rational numbers. Write a solution and have others in the class give reasons for each step in your solution.

$$\left(-2\frac{1}{4}\right) \times \left[\left(-5\frac{1}{2}\right) + \left(+3\frac{1}{4}\right)\right]$$

$$= \left(\frac{-9}{4}\right) \times \left[\left(\frac{-11}{2}\right) + \left(\frac{+13}{4}\right)\right]$$

$$= \left(\frac{-9}{4}\right) \times \left[\left(\frac{(-22) + (+13)}{4}\right)\right]$$

$$= \left(\frac{-9}{4}\right) \times \left(\frac{-9}{4}\right)$$

$$= \frac{81}{16}$$

The order of operations can also be used to solve problems.

EXAMPLE

In Qadry's experiment, the temperature of a gas was checked every minute. Initially, the temperature was +8°C. After 1 min, the temperature was $-2\frac{1}{2}$°C and after 2 min the temperature was $-10\frac{1}{2}$°C. Find the average temperature.

SOLUTION

$$\left[(+8) + \left(-2\frac{1}{2}\right) + \left(-10\frac{1}{2}\right)\right] \div 3$$

$$= \left[\left(\frac{+16}{2}\right) + \left(\frac{-5}{2}\right) + \left(\frac{-21}{2}\right)\right] \div 3$$

$$= \left[\frac{(+16) + (-5) + (-21)}{2}\right] \div 3$$

$$= \frac{-10}{2} \div 3$$

$$= \frac{-5}{3} \text{ or } -1\frac{2}{3}$$

The average temperature was $-1\frac{2}{3}$°C .

A   Use the order of operations.

1. (a) Calculate $\dfrac{3}{4} + \left(\dfrac{1}{2} + \dfrac{3}{8}\right)$ and $\dfrac{3}{4} + \dfrac{1}{2} + \dfrac{3}{8}$.   (b) Why are the answers the same?

2. (a) Calculate $\dfrac{2}{3} - \left(\dfrac{3}{4} - \dfrac{1}{8}\right)$ and $\dfrac{2}{3} - \dfrac{3}{4} - \dfrac{1}{8}$.   (b) Why are the answers different?

B   Review your skills with rational numbers.

3. Calculate. Use the rules for the order of operations.

(a) $\dfrac{1}{3} + \dfrac{2}{3} - \dfrac{1}{2}$ (b) $\dfrac{3}{4} - \dfrac{1}{2} + \dfrac{1}{3}$ (c) $\left(\dfrac{2}{3}\right)\left(-\dfrac{1}{4}\right)\left(-\dfrac{3}{4}\right)$

(d) $\left(\dfrac{3}{4}\right) \div \left(-\dfrac{1}{2}\right) \div \left(\dfrac{2}{3}\right)$ (e) $\left(\dfrac{3}{4}\right)\left(-\dfrac{2}{3}\right) \div \left(-\dfrac{1}{4}\right)$ (f) $\dfrac{5}{8} \div \left(-\dfrac{3}{4}\right) \times \left(\dfrac{2}{3}\right)$

4. Simplify each of the following.

(a) $\dfrac{3}{2} - \left(\dfrac{3}{4} - \dfrac{-1}{4}\right)$ (b) $\dfrac{3}{5} - \dfrac{-1}{10} + \dfrac{-1}{2}$ (c) $\left(\dfrac{-3}{5} + \dfrac{7}{10}\right) \div \dfrac{-1}{2}$

(d) $-\dfrac{4}{5}\left(\dfrac{-3}{4} + \dfrac{-1}{4}\right)$ (e) $\dfrac{-4}{5} - \left(\dfrac{-1}{4} + \dfrac{-4}{5}\right)$ (f) $\dfrac{-3}{5} \div \left(\dfrac{-3}{4} - \dfrac{-9}{10}\right)$

5. Simplify. Which answer is greatest?

(a) $\dfrac{-3}{4} - \left(\dfrac{-3}{4} + \dfrac{4}{-5}\right)$ (b) $\dfrac{-3}{5} - \dfrac{-3}{4} - \dfrac{9}{-10}$ (c) $6 \div \dfrac{-1}{5} - \dfrac{1}{-2}$

6. Shoichi scored these points on a computer game. $-4\dfrac{1}{2}$, $+6\dfrac{1}{2}$, -7, -3, $+8$, $+2\dfrac{1}{2}$, -1, $\dfrac{1}{2}$
What was Shoichi's average score?

7. Mineral deposits were found at these depths.
(a) Find the average of the depths.
(b) Interpret your answer. At what average depth will mineral deposits be found?

$-8\dfrac{1}{2}\,\text{m}, -10\dfrac{1}{4}\,\text{m}, -12\dfrac{1}{2}\,\text{m},$

$-6\dfrac{1}{4}\,\text{m}, -9\dfrac{1}{2}\,\text{m}, -21\dfrac{1}{4}\,\text{m}$

MAKING CONNECTIONS: SCIENCE

1. In Marc's experiment, the temperature in a container dropped every 5 min. Initially, the temperature was –9.25°C. After 10 min, the temperature dropped 0.9°C and after 20 min the temperature was –11.50°C.
(a) Find the average temperature.
(b) Create and solve a similar problem of your own.

2. (a) List situations in science in which knowing the order of events is crucial.
(b) Give reasons why the order of events in each situation is crucial.

5.14 RATIONALS FOR DECIMALS

You have seen that there are two types of decimal equivalents for rational numbers. There is a *terminating* decimal number and a *non-terminating* decimal number.

To find the rational number represented by a terminating decimal number, you can use your skills with place value as shown below.

$$0.55 = \frac{55}{100} \text{ or } \frac{11}{20}$$ Think: Express your answer in lowest terms.

To find a rational number represented by a non-terminating decimal number, follow these steps.

Use x to represent the decimal. $x = 0.222...$
Since the period length is 1, multiply both sides by 10.
$$10x = 10(0.222...)$$

$$10x = 2.222...$$
$$x = 0.222...$$
Subtract. $\overline{10x - x = 2.000...}$

Think:
You can check your work by finding the decimal for $\frac{2}{9}$.

| C | 2 | ÷ | 9 | = | 0.22222222 |

Simplify. $9x = 2$

$$x = \frac{2}{9}$$

Thus $0.\overline{2} = \frac{2}{9}$

EXERCISE

B   Check your answers. Use a calculator to help you.

1.   Find a rational number for each terminating decimal number.
(a) 0.2   (b) −0.25   (c) 0.62   (d) −1.75   (e) 0.3   (f) −0.36

2.   For each of the following, decide whether you would multiply by 10, 100, or 1000 to write the rational number.
(a) $0.\overline{6}$ (b) $-3.\overline{35}$ (c) $0.0\overline{6}$ (d) $-1.\overline{45}$ (e) $0.\overline{5}$ (f) $0.\overline{3}$
(g) Find the rational number for each decimal number above.

3.   Find a rational number for each of the following.
(a) $2.\overline{63}$ (b) $-0.\overline{82}$ (c) $1.\overline{36}$ (d) $0.\overline{315}$ (e) $-1.\overline{157}$
(f) $0.0\overline{46}$ (g) $-2.\overline{3}$ (h) $4.4\overline{5}$ (i) $-0.32\overline{3}$ (j) $0.0\overline{32}$

4.   (a) Use the decimal number $0.4\overline{9}$. Find its rational number.
(b) Compare your number in (a) to the rational number for 0.50. What do you notice? Why do you think this is so?

These *terminating* decimals represent *rational* numbers.

0.3, 0.25, 0.889 998

These *non-terminating* decimals represent *rational* numbers.

0.666..., $2.\overline{234}$

These decimals neither repeat nor terminate.

3.175 017 500 175...
4.223 222 322 223...

Decimal numbers that neither terminate nor repeat represent **irrational numbers**.

Symbols are used to represent rational numbers and irrational numbers as shown below.

Q shows rational numbers $\overline{Q}$ shows irrational numbers

Together, the rational numbers and the irrational numbers form the **real numbers**, R. You cannot list all the real numbers when solving a problem. Thus, a graph is often used to represent the real numbers as shown below.

EXAMPLE 1

Draw the graph of the following.

(a) $\{x \mid x \leq -3, x \in R\}$ (b) $\{x \mid x < 3, x \in R\}$ (c) $\{x \mid x > -2, x \in R\}$

Think: Read as "x is a member of the real numbers."

SOLUTION

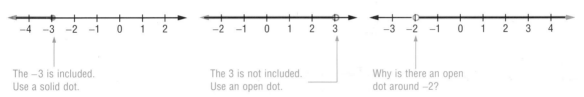

The -3 is included. Use a solid dot.

The 3 is not included. Use an open dot.

Why is there an open dot around -2?

EXAMPLE 2

Draw the graph of $\{x \mid -4 < x \leq 1, x \in R\}$.

SOLUTION

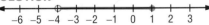

The -4 is not included. Use an open dot.

Think: Draw the graph for $x > -4$.
Then draw the graph for $x \leq 1$.
Check to see if the graphs overlap.

ACTIVITY

(a) Draw the graph of each of the following.

   (i) $\{x \mid -4 < x < 1, x \in R\}$ (ii) $\{x \mid -4 \leq x < 1, x \in R\}$ (iii) $\{x \mid -4 \leq x \leq 1, x \in R\}$

(b) How are the graphs alike? How are they different?

(c) How is each group in (a) like the graph in Example 2? How is it different?

EXERCISE

A   Remember: Irrational numbers have non-terminating and non-repeating decimals.

1. Which of the following represent rational numbers? irrational numbers?
   (a) -4 (b) 6   (c) 2   (d) $-0.555...$ (e) -3
   (f) 1.414 411 441 114...   (g) -6 (h) $-0.221\ 222\ 1\ 22\ 221...$
   (i) $-4.212\ 212\ 222\ 122...$ (j) 0.151 515 151...   (k) 2.121 212 121...

B   Remember the meaning of the inequality symbols <, >, ≤, and ≥ in order to draw the graphs of real numbers.

2. Draw the graph of each of the following.
   (a) $\{x \mid x \geq 3, x \in R\}$ (b) $\{x \mid x \geq 3, x \in I\}$ (c) $\{x \mid x \leq 3, x \in W\}$
   How are the graphs alike? How do they differ?

3. Draw the graph of each.
   (a) $\{x \mid x > 1, x \in I\}$ (b) $\{x \mid x \geq 1, x \in R\}$ (c) $\{x \mid x \leq 6, x \in I\}$
   (d) $\{x \mid x > 1, x \in R\}$ (e) $\{x \mid x \geq 2, x \in R\}$ (f) $\{x \mid -2 < x, x \in R\}$

4. Use symbols to represent each of the following.
   (a)
   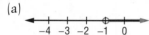
   (b)
   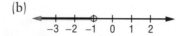
   (c)
   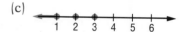

5. Use symbols to describe each of the following.
   (a)
   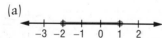
   (b)
   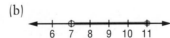
   (c)
   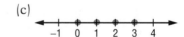

MAKING CONNECTIONS

1. Work with a partner.
   (a) Predict whether you can always write a rational number between pairs of irrational numbers.
   (b) Check your prediction using pairs of irrational numbers of your partner's choosing.

2. An interesting irrational number is π. The decimal number for π is 3.141 592 653 to nine decimal places.

   (a) The number $\frac{355}{113}$ was used by Ch'ung-chih as an approximate value for π. For how many decimal places do the decimals for $\frac{355}{113}$ and π match?

   (b) Use your library. Find other approximations for π that have been used. In your journal, describe why an approximate value for π is often used in calculations.

When you communicate with numbers, you use different words to describe a property. Each property can be illustrated by an example. An example can also help you determine whether the property applies to different numbers.

- Addition of integers is commutative.
$(-8) + (-2) = (-2) + (-8)$

- Subtraction of rationals is not associative.
$$\frac{2}{3} - \left(\frac{1}{2} - \frac{3}{4}\right) \neq \left(\frac{2}{3} - \frac{1}{2}\right) - \frac{3}{4}$$

- When you add two integers, the result is also an integer. The integers are said to be closed with respect to addition.

- When you divide two integers, the result you obtain may not be an integer.
$(-2) \div (+3) = -0.666...$
Thus, integers are not closed with respect to division.

ACTIVITY

The chart below summarizes the properties of the numbers.
✓ shows the property applies.
X shows the property does not apply.
? means you need to decide whether ✓ or X applies.
For each ✓, X, and ?, use an example of your own to justify the decision made.

Property	Sets of numbers	Natural numbers	Whole numbers	Integers	Rationals	Irrationals	Real numbers
Commutative	Addition	✓	✓	✓	✓	✓	✓
	Subtraction	X	?	?	?	?	?
	Multiplication	✓	✓	✓	?	✓	✓
	Division	X	X	X	?	?	?
Associative	Addition	?	✓	✓	✓	✓	✓
	Subtraction	X	?	X	X	X	X
	Multiplication	✓	✓	?	✓	✓	✓
	Division	X	X	X	X	X	X
Distributive	Multiplication over addition	✓	✓	?	✓	✓	?
	Division over addition	X	?	X	?	X	X
	Multiplication over subtraction	✓	?	✓	✓	?	✓
	Division over subtraction	?	X	X	X	X	X
Closed	Addition	✓	?	✓	✓	?	✓
	Subtraction	X	?	✓	✓	X	✓
	Multiplication	✓	✓	✓	?	?	✓
	Division	?	X	X	✓	X	?

Often, to solve a problem, you can draw a diagram to help you plan your solution.

Locate the number $\sqrt{2}$ on the number line.

To solve the problem, you need to remember that $\sqrt{2}$ suggests work you did with right triangles in previous grades. The diagram suggests a method of locating $\sqrt{2}$ on the number line.

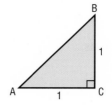

$$AB^2 = 1^2 + 1^2$$
$$AB^2 = 1 + 1$$
$$AB^2 = 2$$
$$AB = \sqrt{2}$$

Step 1 Construct △ABC.

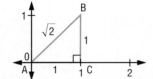

Step 2 Draw an arc. Locate $\sqrt{2}$ on the number line.

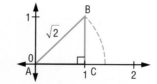

Step 3

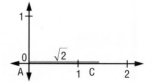

By thinking visually, you can find some other interesting results.

The area of a square is 2 square units.

2 square units

The length of each side is $\sqrt{2}$ units.

$\sqrt{2}$ units

$$\left(\sqrt{2}\right)\left(\sqrt{2}\right) = 2$$

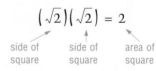

side of square   side of square   area of square

EXERCISE

B Review your skills with exponents.

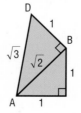

1. To find $\sqrt{2}$ on the number line, a sketch is shown.
    (a) Why is $AD^2 = AB^2 + DB^2$?

    (b) Use the sketch. Locate $\sqrt{3}$ on the number line.

2. Refer to the previous method. Locate each irrational number on the number line.

    (a) $\sqrt{6}$ (b) $\sqrt{7}$ (c) $\sqrt{10}$ (d) $\sqrt{12}$ (e) $\sqrt{13}$

3. (a) Construct a square with sides that measure $\sqrt{5}$ cm.

    (b) Construct a diagram to show $\left(\sqrt{10}\right)\left(\sqrt{10}\right) = 10$.

Can you believe that people actually thought the luxury liner, the *Titanic*, was unsinkable? The body of the ship was divided into 16 watertight compartments. Four of these compartments could be flooded and the *Titanic* would supposedly still float. Unfortunately, on the night of April 15, 1912, on its first voyage, the *Titanic* struck an iceberg and sank off the coast of Newfoundland. More than 1500 people lost their lives on that fateful night. It was over 70 years before the wreck of the *Titanic* was located, lying on the ocean floor at a depth of almost 4000 m. The activities will help you learn more about the *Titanic* and the implications of the technology used to find and explore it.

ACTIVITY 1

1. The *Titanic* was "as long as four city blocks."
   (a) Estimate the length of the *Titanic* in metres.
   (b) The actual length of the *Titanic*, in metres, is given by the following expression. Calculate $32 + (654 - 198) \div 6 + 157$.

2. Find out more about the *Titanic*'s dimensions. Create a problem using the information. Solve the problem.

ACTIVITY 2   *Work with a Partner*

3. The wreck of the *Titanic* was located in August, 1985, using a camera rig called *Argo*. Work with a partner and use your library to answer the following.
   (a) How did *Argo* operate?
   (b) What were some of the obstacles that *Argo* and its operators had to overcome to discover the wreck?

4. Refer to the technology in Question 3.
   (a) What new technology has been used to research the wreck?
   (b) Make a list of other ways this technology could be used.

5. A scale drawing of the depth at which the *Titanic* was found is shown.
   (a) Create a problem using the diagram.
   (b) Solve your problem. Compare your solution to others.

Great Pyramid of Cheops El Gizeh, Egypt

Eiffel Tower Paris, France

Empire State Building New York, U.S.A.

Sears Tower Chicago, U.S.A.

Ostankino Tower Moscow

CN Tower Toronto, Canada

CHAPTER REVIEW

1. Use < or > to replace ● in each of the following.

   (a) $\dfrac{1}{4} \bullet \dfrac{3}{4}$ (b) $-\dfrac{1}{4} \bullet \dfrac{1}{4}$ (c) $\dfrac{-3}{8} \bullet \dfrac{-7}{8}$

2. Write each rational number in lowest terms.

   (a) $\dfrac{-3}{-15}$ (b) $-\dfrac{6}{9}$ (c) $\dfrac{-12}{-9}$

3. Calculate.

   (a) $\dfrac{-3}{5} + \dfrac{1}{5}$ (b) $\dfrac{1}{-6} - \dfrac{-1}{3}$

   (c) $\dfrac{-3}{5} - \dfrac{-1}{-10}$ (d) $\dfrac{-5}{-12} + \dfrac{-1}{-4}$

4. Calculate.

   (a) $\left(\dfrac{-1}{2}\right)\left(\dfrac{1}{-3}\right)$ (b) $\left(-2\dfrac{1}{3}\right)\left(\dfrac{-9}{-14}\right)$

   (c) $\left(\dfrac{2}{3}\right) \div \left(\dfrac{-4}{-9}\right)$ (d) $\left(\dfrac{-2}{3}\right)\left(\dfrac{-2}{3}\right)$

5. Simplify.

   (a) $\dfrac{-3}{5} + \left(\dfrac{2}{3} - \dfrac{1}{-5}\right)$ (b) $\dfrac{-1}{2} \div \left(\dfrac{-1}{3} + \dfrac{-1}{-2}\right)$

6. Draw the graph of each.
   (a) $\{x \mid -3 \leq x < 3, x \in I\}$
   (b) $\{x \mid 8 \geq x \geq -3, x \in R\}$

7. Vito scored the following points on a video game.

   $-3\dfrac{1}{4}, \ +8\dfrac{1}{2}, \ -4\dfrac{1}{2}, \ +6\dfrac{1}{4}, \ +3\dfrac{3}{4}$

   What was his average score?

8. Draw each graph.
   (a) $\{n \mid n \geq -1, n \in R\}$
   (b) $\{k \mid k \leq -3, k \in R\}$

9. Find a rational number for each decimal.

   (a) 0.75   (b) 0.45   (c) $0.\overline{37}$ (d) $1.2\overline{9}$

10. The bottom of a cardboard box is square and has an area of 453.0 cm². Find the length of the sides.

❶ How many of the skills you previously learned did you use when developing your skills with rational numbers?

❷ What properties do rational numbers have in common with integers? Which properties do they not have in common?

❸ Throughout the chapter, you have learned many new words and skills that can be used to solve problems.
(a) List all the new words and skills you have learned.
(b) Write an example to illustrate each word and skill you listed in (a).

MAKING CONNECTIONS

The numbers used on the opening page show some of the number systems that have been used.
(a) Use your library to find other number systems.
(b) Why are the systems in (a) not commonly used today?
(c) What other symbols are used to represent numbers that are different from the symbols in this chapter?

❹ How are rational numbers and irrational numbers alike? How are they different?

❺ How are whole numbers, integers, and rational numbers alike? How are they different?

❻ Have you updated your *Problem Solving Plan* with the skills from this chapter?

1. Use > or < in place of ● for each of the following.

   (a) $-\dfrac{2}{3}$ ● $-\dfrac{5}{6}$ (b) $\dfrac{2}{3}$ ● $\dfrac{3}{4}$ (c) $\dfrac{-2}{5}$ ● $\dfrac{3}{10}$

2. Calculate.

   (a) $\dfrac{1}{-2} + \dfrac{1}{6}$ (b) $\dfrac{-3}{10} - 1\dfrac{1}{5}$ (c) $2\dfrac{1}{3} + \left(-\dfrac{1}{2}\right)$

   (d) $-\dfrac{1}{2} - 2\dfrac{1}{3}$ (e) $\dfrac{-2}{3} + \left(\dfrac{-1}{2} - \dfrac{1}{3}\right)$ (f) $\left(4\dfrac{2}{5} - \dfrac{7}{10}\right) - \dfrac{11}{12}$

3. Calculate.

   (a) $\left(\dfrac{-3}{5}\right)\left(\dfrac{-10}{21}\right)$ (b) $\dfrac{7}{3} \times \left(-3\dfrac{1}{2}\right)$

   (c) $\left(-3\dfrac{1}{4}\right) \div \left(\dfrac{-2}{3}\right)$ (d) $\left(\dfrac{2}{3}\right) \times \left(\dfrac{-4}{3}\right)$

4. Simplify.

   (a) $\dfrac{2}{5} \div \left(\dfrac{-2}{5} + \dfrac{1}{10}\right)$ (b) $\dfrac{-5}{6} + \dfrac{-2}{3} \times \dfrac{3}{4}$

   (c) $\left[\dfrac{1}{8} + \left(\dfrac{-2}{3}\right)\right] \times \dfrac{12}{13}$ (d) $-\dfrac{3}{2} + \dfrac{-1}{-2} - \dfrac{-3}{5}$

5. Ming's scores for five rounds of a game were $3\dfrac{1}{2}$ points, $-1\dfrac{1}{4}$ points, $-2\dfrac{3}{4}$ points, $5\dfrac{1}{4}$ points, and $1\dfrac{1}{4}$ points. What was his total score?

6. Draw each graph.
   (a) $\{a \mid a \le 2, a \in R\}$
   (b) $\{k \mid -3 < k, k \in R\}$

7. Brian's body temperature was $39\dfrac{1}{2}$ °C. It dropped $1\dfrac{3}{4}$ °C. What was Brian's new body temperature?

8. Jena wanted to place a small rectangular table in the corner of a room, as shown. How far is A from the corner, to one decimal place?

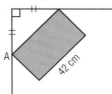

A

42 cm

Various words related to rational numbers are used in the chapter.
(a) What are some of the words?
(b) Which words have you used before?
(c) Use examples to help you remember the words in (a) and (b).

175

1. Refer to the geoboard shown at the right.
   (a) How many isosceles triangles can you make by putting an elastic around the pegs?
   (b) Create a similar problem of your own using a geoboard. Compare your problem to others in the class.

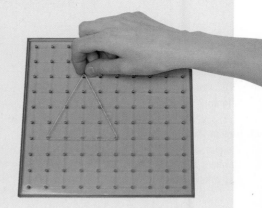

2. Shu plays on a football team. In his league, you can only score three points for a field goal and seven points for a touchdown. Shu claims that the team won the last game 11 to 10. Is Shu's claim correct? Give reasons for your answer.

3. Suppose you build a grid with equal size squares, using toothpicks. Each small square is one toothpick long and one toothpick high.
   (a) If the grid is 11 toothpicks wide and 8 toothpicks high, how many toothpicks are used in all?
   (b) Create a problem of your own based on the toothpicks in (a). Solve your problem and compare your problem to others in the class.

4. Suppose you could count one number every second. In other words, to say "one" would take 1 s, to say "one, two" would take 2 s, and so on.
   (a) Estimate how long it would take you to count to one million.
   (b) How can you verify your estimate in (a)?
   (c) Carry out your plan in (b). How reasonable was your estimate?

5. A number that reads the same either backwards or forwards is called a **palindrome**. How many four-digit palindromes are there? List them.

6. The seven straws shown below are of different lengths. The straws are lined up so that no straw is between two straws that are both longer than itself.
   (a) In how many ways can this be done?
   (b) Suppose the straws were picked up and dropped at random. What is the probability that the straws will land so that no straw is between two straws that are bigger than itself? Explain your answer.

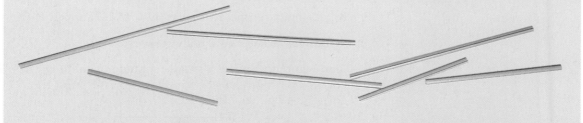

MEASUREMENT 6

Look at the pictures shown. In your journal:

- Describe what questions involving measurement are suggested by the pictures.
- Describe how you might answer the questions.

6.1 EXPLORING AREA

Imagine how your life would be different without accurate measurements. Imagine how buildings would look if construction workers did not use accurate measurements.

The following will explore some ways to measure. Keep a list of the ways in your journal.

EXPLORATION ① *Work Together*

1. Look at your classroom.
   (a) What shape is your classroom?
   (b) What are the least number of measurements that you need to find the distance around your classroom?
   (c) How can you make the measurements in (b) if you have a 40 cm straight edge?
   (d) Use your method in (c). Find the perimeter of your classroom.

2. Suppose you put a ribbon around the perimeter of the door to your classroom.
   (a) Can the method you developed in Question 1 (c) be used? Explain how you would do this.
   (b) Use your method in (a). Find the perimeter of the door.

3. What are other objects in your classroom whose perimeter you can find?
   (a) Develop a method to find the perimeter of each object.
   (b) Use your method to find the perimeter.
   (c) Compare your method with those of others in the class.

EXPLORATION ② *Discuss with a Partner*

4. Sometimes, a measurement is expressed in other terms. For example, the height of a horse is 14 hands.
   (a) What do you think the measurement "hand" means?
   (b) Do you think the measurement is accurate? Can it vary?
   (c) Suppose, in Exploration 1, you used the unit of hand. What would the measurements of the perimeters be?
   (d) Compare your measurements in (c) with those of others in the class. What do you notice?

5. Think of other items you can use to measure objects. For example, a chain, a pole, and so on.
   (a) Make a list of the items.
   (b) Estimate the measure of objects in your class using your items in (a).
   (c) How can you check that your estimates in (b) are reasonable?
   (d) Use your plan in (c). How reasonable were your estimates?
   (e) Suppose, in Exploration 1, you used your items in (a). What would the measurements of the perimeter be?

Work with a Partner

6. (a) Make a list of all the relationships you know to find the perimeter and the area of a shape.
   (b) Which relationships can be used to help you find the perimeter and area of each shape on the grid below?
   (c) Develop a method to find the perimeter and the area of each shape.
   (d) Use your plan in (c). Find the perimeter and the area of each shape.

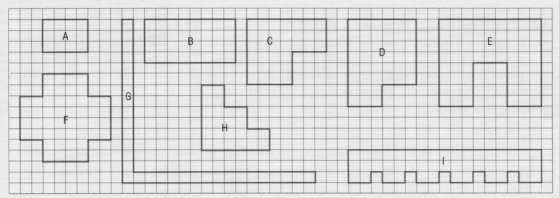

7. (a) Create similar figures of your own and draw them on grid paper.
   (b) Find the perimeter and area of each shape.
   (c) Have others in the class find the perimeter and area of each figure.

EXPLORATION ④ **Work with a Partner**

8. Suppose you want to estimate how many "loonie" coins are needed to represent the height of your school.
   (a) List the data that you need to make a reasonable estimate. What assumptions have you made?
   (b) Find the data needed to estimate the height.

9. Find other places or items around your school whose height you can estimate. For example, the height of a flagpole or the height of a tree.
   (a) List the data you need to make a reasonable estimate. What assumptions have you made?
   (b) Find the pieces of data that you need to estimate each height.
   (c) Compare your estimate with those of others in the class. What do you notice?

MATH JOURNAL

Refer to the explorations in this section.
(a) Make a list of all patterns and relationships that can help you find the perimeter of an object or the area covered by an object.
(b) Use an example of your own to illustrate each relationship in (a).

Before you install a fence around an irrigation pond, you need to know how much fencing you need. Work with a partner to complete the following activity. It will help you find the perimeter of the enclosure and the amount of fencing you need.

ACTIVITY *Work with a Partner*

(a) Calculate $2 \times 40 + 2 \times 25$.
(b) Interpret your result in (a). How much fencing is needed to go around the irrigation pond?
(c) What pattern can help you find the perimeter? Record the pattern.

To find the perimeter of an object, you need to find the distance around it as shown below.

EXAMPLE

(a) Find the perimeter of the recreation area shown below.
(b) Calculate the cost to fence the recreation area if fencing costs $15.25/m.

SOLUTION

(a) To find the perimeter, you need to find the missing measures.

The perimeter can be found as:
$P = 8 + 5 + 14 + 5 + 8 + 10 + 30 + 10$
$= 90$

The perimeter is 90 m.

(b) 1 m of fencing costs $15.25.
Thus, 90 m of fencing cost
$90 \times \$15.25 = \$1372.50$
The cost to fence the recreation area is $1372.50.

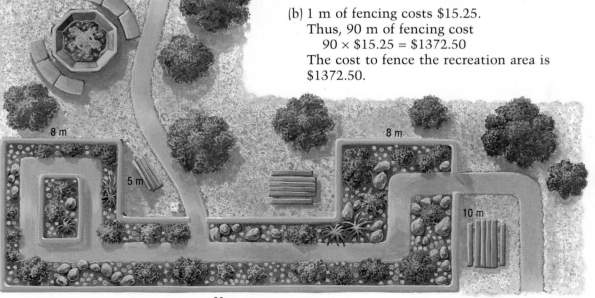

A Look for patterns to help you.

1. Find the perimeter of each figure.

(a)
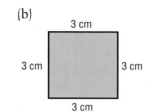
8 m
5 m   5 m
8 m

(b)
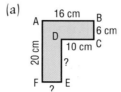
3 cm
3 cm   3 cm
3 cm

(c)
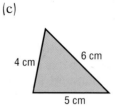
6 cm
4 cm
5 cm

2. For each figure,
   • find the missing sides.
   • find the perimeter.

(a)
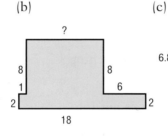
A   16 cm   B
D   6 cm
20 cm   10 cm   C
?
F   ?   E

(b)
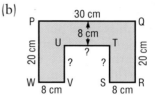
P   30 cm   Q
8 cm
20 cm   U   T   20 cm
?   ?
W   8 cm   V   S   8 cm   R

3. Find each missing side, then calculate the perimeter.
   All sides are measured in centimetres.

(a)
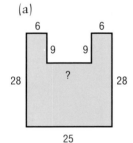
6   6
9   9
28   ?   28
25

(b)
?
8   8
1   6
2   2
18

(c)
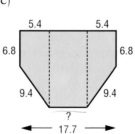
5.4   5.4
6.8   6.8
9.4   9.4
?
← 17.7 →

(d)
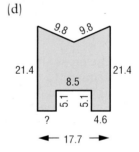
9.8   9.8
21.4   21.4
8.5
5.1   5.1
?   4.6
← 17.7 →

4. (a) Find the perimeter of a rectangular swimming pool if it is 12.4 m long and 5.6 m wide.
   (b) Find the perimeter of a square courtyard if each side measures 16.8 m.

B Use a calculator. Estimate first.

5. A patio is shown in the diagram.
   (a) Calculate the perimeter.
   (b) What is the cost of placing a railing around
       the patio if the cost of railing is $6.29/m?

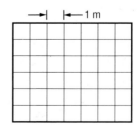
→| |←1 m

6. A rectangular Japanese garden is 27.4 m by 43.5 m.
   (a) Calculate the perimeter.
   (b) Calculate the cost of placing a low decorative fence around the garden if the fencing
       costs $2.69/m.

7. The perimeter of each figure is shown. Find the measure of each missing side.

(a)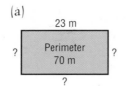

23 m
? Perimeter 70 m ?
?

(b)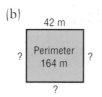

42 m
? Perimeter 164 m ?
?

(c)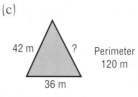

42 m ?
36 m
Perimeter 120 m

8. The amount of fencing needed for a square vegetable garden is 17.6 m. Find the length of one side of the garden.

9. A triangular rose garden has two sides that measure 4.84 m each. The perimeter of the garden measures 14.56 m. Calculate the measure of the remaining side.

10. One side of a rectangle measures 17.1 m. The perimeter is 45.9 m. Calculate the measures of the other three sides.

11. The path walked during a round of golf is shown on the diagram. Each unit represents 75 m.
    (a) Find the distance walked.
    (b) How long did the round take if the players averaged 5 km/h? What assumptions have you made?

12. (a) One side of a rectangular field is 48.6 m. The perimeter is 169.6 m. Calculate the measures of the other sides.
    (b) A triangular vegetable garden has two sides that measure 3.68 m each. The perimeter measures 10.96 m. Calculate the measure of the other side.

13. The cross shown on the grid paper is made by attaching a square to each side of a square.
    (a) Copy and cut out the cross.
    (b) Make two straight cuts so that the cross is cut into four pieces that fit together to form a square.
    (c) What is the perimeter of the square in (b)?
    (d) What relationships can help you predict the perimeter of the square in (b)? Compare your relationships to others in the class.

MAKING CONNECTIONS

Suppose you have a 5 m × 5 m piece of land and wish to plant a vegetable garden.
(a) What type of vegetables would you grow?
(b) How much space is needed for each plant to be healthy?
(c) Draw a diagram of how your garden would look. Put dimensions on your diagram.

6.3 WORKING WITH AREA

Work together to complete the following activity.

ACTIVITY *Work Together*
(a) Look at the pictures. Why would you need to know how to calculate the area in each picture?
(b) What relationship can help you calculate the area in each case?
(c) Find rectangular objects in the classroom. Measure to find the area of each.

EXAMPLE
The dimensions of a square stamp are shown.
(a) Calculate the area of the stamp to one decimal place.
(b) The total area of the stamps used to mail a parcel is 105 cm². About how many stamps were used?

2.4 cm

2.4 cm

SOLUTION
(a) The area of the stamp is given by
$A = l \times w$
$A = 2.4 \times 2.4$
$\quad = 5.76$
The area of the stamp is about 5.8 cm².

(b) The total area of stamps is 105 cm².
The area of one stamp is 5.8 cm².

The number of stamps $= \dfrac{105}{5.8}$ ← total area
← area of 1 stamp
$\quad = 18.1$ ← to 1 decimal place
The number of stamps used is about 18.

Remember, always check whether or not your answer is reasonable.

EXERCISE

A Look for patterns.

1. Calculate the area for each of the figures.

(a)
30 cm
12 cm
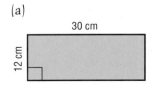

(b)
24 cm
24 cm

(c)
40 cm
32 cm
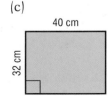

2. Find the area of each piece of land to the nearest square metre.

(a)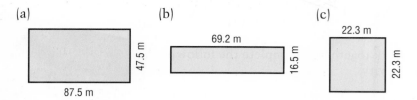

87.5 m × 47.5 m

(b) 69.2 m × 16.5 m

(c) 22.3 m × 22.3 m

3. The dimensions of each stamp are shown. Find the area.

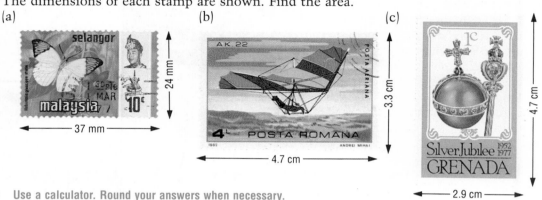

(a) 37 mm × 24 mm

(b) 4.7 cm × 3.3 cm

(c) 2.9 cm × 4.7 cm

B Use a calculator. Round your answers when necessary.

4. (a) Calculate the area of a rectangular floor with sides 5.3 m by 4.6 m.
   (b) Rhonda's square yard has sides of 8.5 m. Calculate the area.

5. The dimensions of a rectangular ice rink are 10.8 m by 24.5 m.
   (a) Find the area of the rink to the nearest tenth of a square metre.
   (b) Calculate the cost of making the ice at $17.92/m².

6. (a) Jim bought some stereo equipment. The base of each of the two speakers is 40 cm long and 35 cm wide. His amplifier measures 53 cm long by 48 cm wide. What total area do the three pieces cover?
   (b) Create a similar problem of your own. Compare your problem to others in the class.

7. A wall is 6.2 m long and 2.7 m high and is to be covered with wallpaper. Each roll of wallpaper is 0.68 m wide.
   (a) How many metres of wallpaper are needed to cover four such walls?
   (b) What assumptions have you made in (a)?
   (c) Visit or phone a store that sells wallpaper. How do they determine how much area a roll of wallpaper will cover?

8. A backyard measures 16.3 m by 14.5 m and is to be sodded with new grass. Each strip of sod is 40.0 cm by 150.0 cm. How many pieces of sod are required?

C

9. (a) A rectangle has an area of 96.0 cm². How many different rectangles can you construct with whole number dimensions?
   (b) Create a similar problem of your own. Compare your problem to others in the class.

In baseball, the pitcher must throw the ball over home plate and between the batter's armpits and knees. This is called the **strike zone** and is shown here as the shaded area ABCD. You can calculate the strike zone area for the player.

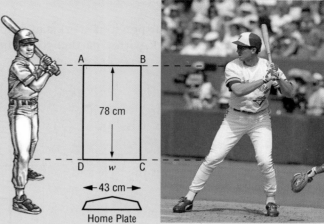

Distance BC is 78 cm.
Distance DC is 43 cm.
Use $A = l \times w$
$ = 78 \times 43$
$ = 3354$

The player's strike zone area is 3354 cm^2.

1. Calculate the strike zone area for each player.

(a) 68cm

(b) 77cm

(c) 96 cm

(d) 85cm

2. Two positions for a baseball player are shown to the right. By how much does the area of the strike zone decrease if the player crouches?

 91cm

 75cm

3. Calculate by how much the area of the strike zone decreases if the player crouches as shown.

(a) 96cm   72cm

(b) 84cm   68cm

4. Work with a partner.
   (a) Position yourself as if you are a batter ready to hit the ball. Have your partner measure you to find the area of your strike zone. Measure your partner the same way. Who has the greater strike zone?
   (b) In your journal, describe under what conditions you should make your strike zone smaller. Would it help a batter to hit the ball if the strike zone were smaller?

6.5 TRIANGLES AND PARALLELOGRAMS

The patterns you obtained in your previous work can help you develop the area of a parallelogram and a triangle. Work with a partner to complete the following activities.

ACTIVITY 1 *Work with a Partner*

1. Count squares to find the area of each rectangle and parallelogram.
   (a) How do the areas of the two figures in A compare? in B? in C?
   (b) What do you notice about the base and height of each figure?

2. Use your results in Question 1.
   (a) Suggest a relationship for finding the area of a parallelogram.
   (b) Use grid paper to draw parallelograms of your own. Use your relationship from (a) to find the area of each parallelogram.
   (c) Compare your parallelograms to others in the class. What do you notice about your relationship?

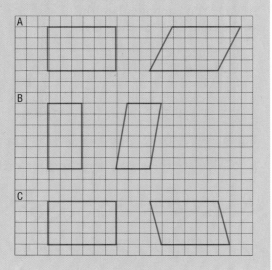

ACTIVITY 2 *Work with a Partner*

3. (a) Find the area of each parallelogram.
   (b) Copy and cut out each parallelogram and then cut each parallelogram along the diagonal. What figures are formed?
   (c) What do you notice about the two figures in (b)?

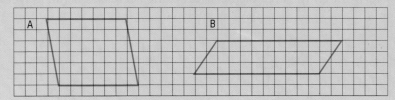

4. Use your results in Question 3.
   (a) Suggest a relationship for finding the area of a triangle.
   (b) Use grid paper to draw triangles of your own. Use your relationship to find the area of each triangle.
   (c) Compare your results to others in the class. What do you notice about your relationship?

A   Round off your answers to one decimal place.

1. Refer to the results in the activities.
    (a) Explain why $A = bh$ can be used as a relationship for the area of a parallelogram.
    (b) Explain why $A = \frac{1}{2}bh$ can be used as a relationship for the area of a triangle.

2. Calculate the area of each parallelogram. Remember: $A = bh$.
    (a)   (b)   (c)   (d)

3. Calculate the area of each parallelogram. Each square represents 1 square unit of area.
    (a)   (b)   (c)   (d)

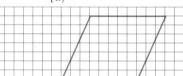

4. Calculate the area of each triangle. Remember: $A = \frac{1}{2}bh$.

    (a)   (b)   (c)

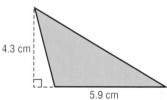
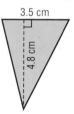

5. Find the area of each of the following triangles.
    (a)   (b)   (c)   (d)

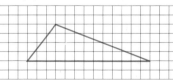
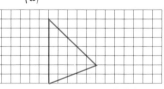

6. Find the area of each of the following.
    (a) parallelogram: base 12 cm, height 8.5 cm   (b) triangle: base 1.8 m, height 5.5 m

7. (a) The height of a parallelogram measures 18 cm and the base is 26 cm. Calculate its area.
   (b) The base of a triangle is 19 cm. The height is 32 cm. Find the area.

8. Find the unknown dimension in each figure.

(a)

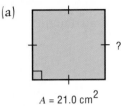

$A = 21.0$ cm^2

(b)

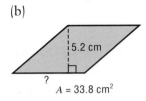

5.2 cm

?

$A = 33.8$ cm^2

(c)

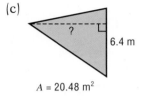

?

6.4 m

$A = 20.48$ m^2

9. (a) The height of a parallelogram measures 16.5 cm and the area is 465.3 cm^2. Calculate its base.
   (b) The tail of an airplane is a triangle with a base of 8.2 m and an area of 35.26 m^2. Calculate the height of the tail.

10. Suppose you own a piece of land shaped like a triangle. It has a base of 150 m and a height of 125 m. A bag of fertilizer covers an area of 30 m^2. How many bags of fertilizer would you need to cover the land?

11. Shawna owns a farm shaped like a parallelogram. The base of her land is 525 m and the height of her land is 750 m.
    (a) Draw a diagram of the farm.
    (b) Suppose one bag of corn seed is required to plant an area of 125 m^2. How many bags of seed does she need to plant her entire farm with corn?

C

12. (a) A triangle has an area of 42 cm^2. How many different triangles can you construct with whole number measures for the base and the height?
    (b) Create a similar problem of your own. Compare your problem to others in the class.

PARTNER PROJECT

(a) Make a list of some products packaged in boxes.
(b) Choose a box from (a). **Estimate the area of each of the surfaces.**
(c) Obtain the box in (b). Measure it to find the actual area of each of the surfaces.
(d) Compare your results in (b) and (c). How reasonable was your estimate?
(e) Manufacturers give a lot of thought to the size and shapes of their packages. Why is this so? Refer to examples in your answer.

SAILING

Most modern sailboats are called sloops. They have two basic sails, the jib and the mainsail. The leading edge of a sail is called the luff. The trailing edge is called the leech. The area of the sail may be calculated from the measures of the luff and the leech.

1. Use the data in the diagram. Calculate the area of
   (a) the mainsail.   (b) the jib.

2. Refer to the diagram of the sailboat.
   (a) Create a problem of your own.
   (b) Solve your problem. Compare your problem to others in the class.

3. Various types of sails are shown below. Calculate the total area of the sails on each sailboat.

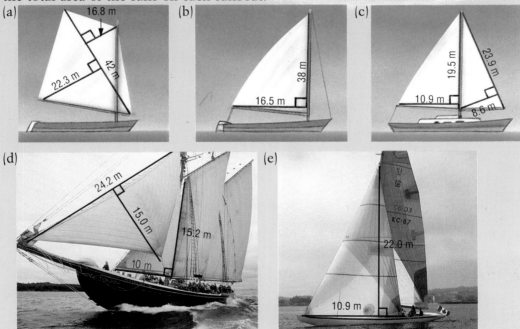

4. Use your library.
   (a) Find the name of each type of sailboat in the previous question.
   (b) Find the names and pictures of other sailboats. Place the dimensions of the sails on each picture. Start a class collage of the sailboats that you find. Beside each picture, calculate the area of each sail.

5. In your journal, write a short paragraph about sailing and how math plays a role in sailing. Describe why sails are made in different shapes and with different areas.

Some shapes, like the one shown to the right, are composed of two simpler shapes. Work with a partner and complete the following activity to help you find the area of this shape.

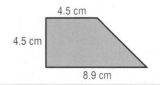

4.5 cm
4.5 cm
8.9 cm

ACTIVITY 1   *Work with a Partner*

(a) Copy and cut out the shape above to the dimensions shown.
(b) What two smaller shapes are used to construct the larger shape?
(c) Cut your shape into the shapes suggested in (b).
(d) Find the dimensions of each smaller shape in (c). Find the area of each shape.
(e) What is the total area of the original shape?

The previous activity suggests that to calculate the total area of shape A below, you need to find the area of shape B and the area of shape C. You then find the sum of the two areas.

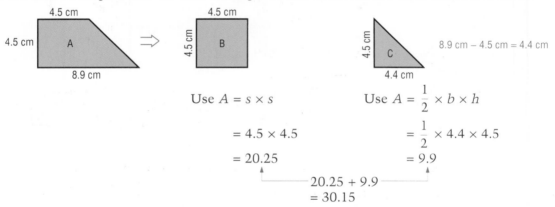

4.5 cm
4.5 cm
A
8.9 cm

4.5 cm
4.5 cm
B

4.5 cm
C
4.4 cm
8.9 cm − 4.5 cm = 4.4 cm

Use $A = s \times s$

$= 4.5 \times 4.5$

$= 20.25$

Use $A = \dfrac{1}{2} \times b \times h$

$= \dfrac{1}{2} \times 4.4 \times 4.5$

$= 9.9$

$20.25 + 9.9$
$= 30.15$

Thus, the area of Shape A is about 30.2 cm^2 (to one decimal place).

ACTIVITY 2   *Work with a Partner*

Regular polygons can also be cut to form other shapes. For example, the regular octagon shown to the right can be cut into eight congruent triangles as shown.

8 sides   8 congruent triangles

(a) What measurements would you need to make to find the area of the regular octagon?
(b) Make the measurements. What is the area of the regular octagon?
(c) Draw a regular polygon of your own. Cut it into smaller parts and suggest a method to find its area. Find its area.

B Review your skills with area.

1. Calculate the area of each shape.

(a)
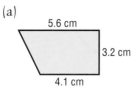
5.6 cm
3.2 cm
4.1 cm

(b)
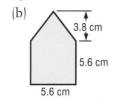
3.8 cm
5.6 cm
5.6 cm

(c)
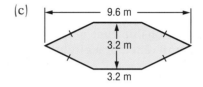
9.6 m
3.2 m
3.2 m

2. Calculate the area of each shape.

(a)
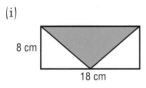
0.9 m
1.3 m
3.9 m

(b)
1.2 cm
1.5 cm
2.8 cm
6.8 cm

(c)
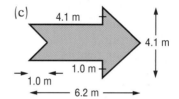
4.1 m
4.1 m
1.0 m
1.0 m
6.2 m

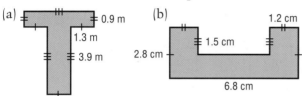

3. (a) Find the area of the shaded part of each diagram.

(i)
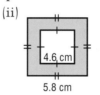
8 cm
18 cm

(ii)
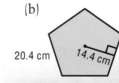
4.6 cm
5.8 cm

(iii)
16.4 m
3.8 m

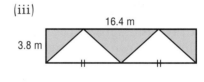

(b) Suggest another way to find each answer in (a). Discuss it with a partner.

4. Calculate the area of each regular polygon.

(a)
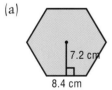
7.2 cm
8.4 cm

(b)

20.4 cm
14.4 cm

(c)
17.4 cm
14.4 cm

5. Calculate the amount of aluminum siding used to cover the side of the house.

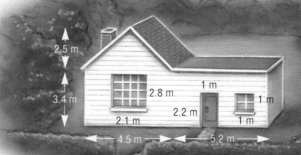

2.5 m
3.4 m
2.8 m
2.1 m
1 m
2.2 m
1 m
1 m
4.5 m
5.2 m

191

The parts of a circle have special names. Some of the parts are shown in the diagram. The distance around the circle is called the **circumference**.

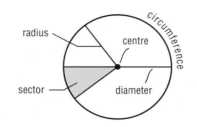

Work together to complete this activity to find a relationship that helps you calculate the circumference of a circle.

ACTIVITY   *Work Together*

Find circular objects like cans and wheels.
(a) Copy and complete the chart.
(b) For each, calculate the
    distance around ÷ distance across.
(c) Based on your results, what
    relationships or patterns do you see?

Object	Distance Around	Distance Across
Wheel	?	?
Can	?	?

The previous activity suggests that for each circular object the value of *circumference (C) ÷ diameter (d)* is about the same. The Ancient Greeks studied this relationship in detail. They used the Greek letter π, pi, to represent the value shown. Based on the results, you can show the relationship as shown to the right.

$$\pi = \frac{C}{d}$$

The relationship can also be written as $C = \pi \times d$

approximate value of π, read as pi,
to two decimal places is 3.14

Knowing this relationship will help you solve problems like the following.

EXAMPLE
A patio umbrella has a diameter of 2.4 m. Find the length of border needed for the edge, to one decimal place.

SOLUTION
Use $C = \pi d$.
$$C = 3.14 \times 2.4$$
$$= 7.5$$
The length of border needed is 7.5 m.

A Review the parts of a circle.

1. Most pizzas have a strip of crust around the edge. Calculate the length of the crusts.

(a)
25 cm

(b)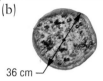
36 cm

(c)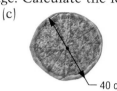
40 cm

(d)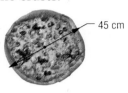
45 cm

2. (a) The diameter of a circle is 14.8 cm. Find its circumference.
    (b) Find the circumference of a circle with a diameter of 23.6 cm.
    (c) The radius of a circle is 32.8 cm. Calculate the circumference.

3. (a) How are the radius and the diameter of a circle related?
    (b) How can you write $C = \pi d$ using radius instead of diameter?
    (c) Use your relationship in (b). Find the circumference of each circle.

(i)
4 cm

(ii)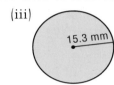
3 m

(iii)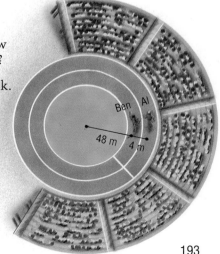
15.3 mm

B Use a calculator. In your manual, find how to use the $\boxed{\pi}$ key.

4. The world's largest solar furnace has a circular mirror with a diameter of 46 m. Find its circumference.

5. One event at the Olympic Games is the discus throw.
    (a) The discus has a diameter of about 10.8 cm. What is the circumference of the discus?
    (b) The discus is thrown by the competitor from within a circle with a diameter of about 1.7 m. Find the circumference of the circle.

6. A famous clock is Big Ben in London, England. The diameter of the face of the clock is about 7.1 m. How far does the tip of the minute hand travel each hour?

7. A circular path is shown. Al runs on the outside track. Ben runs on the inside track.
    (a) How far does each person run?
    (b) How much farther will Al run after
        (i) 5 laps?   (ii) 10 laps?   (iii) 100 laps?
    (c) Find out more about running in a race. Why do competitors often not start in a straight line? When can the competitors all race on the same part of the track? What math skills are used to answer each question?

To solve problems, you will often use the problem solving skill of looking for a pattern. For example, earlier you explored patterns to help you find the area of various figures using the length, width, and height.

In the following exploration, you will explore patterns to find the area of a circle. Work with a partner to complete the exploration. Summarize any patterns and relationships in your journal.

EXPLORATION *Work with a Partner*

1. (a) On a scrap piece of paper, draw a circle with a radius of 10 cm.
   (b) Cut the circle along its diameter to form two semicircles. What is the distance around each circular part?
   (c) Cut each semicircle into equal sectors as shown in Step 2.
   (d) Separate the sectors and fit them together as shown in Step 3. What shape is suggested?
   (e) What is the length of the shape in Step 3? What is the height?
   (f) What is the area of the shape in Step 3?

2. Repeat the parts of Question 1 for other circles. What do you notice?

3. (a) Based on your results above, suggest a relationship to help you find the area of a circle.
   (b) Use your relationship to find the area of the following circles.

Step 1

Step 2

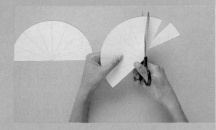

Step 3

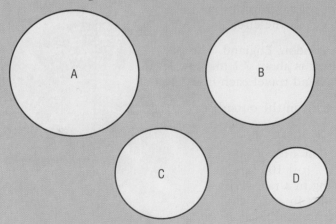

A

B

C

D

6.10 AREA OF A CIRCLE

In the previous exploration, you saw how the area of a parallelogram can be used to help you develop a relationship for the area of a circle. You used steps like the following.

Step 1

Step 2

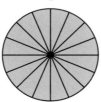

Step 3

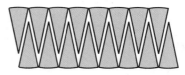

From the steps above,
- the base of the parallelogram is shown by $\pi \times r$.
- the height of the parallelogram is r.

Thus, a relationship to find the area of a circle can be shown as follows.

area of a circle = area of a parallelogram
= base length × height

$$A = \pi \times r \times r$$

This relationship can be written as $A = \pi r^2$ and used to solve problems about circles.

EXERCISE

A Remember: π = 3.14 to two decimal places.

1. Measure to calculate the area of each circle.

2. Calculate the area of a circle with
   (a) a radius of 3 m.   (b) a diameter of 2.4 cm.   (c) a radius of 4.35 mm.

3. By how much does the area of circle A exceed the area of circle B?

4. (a) Calculate the area of a circle with a diameter of 26.2 cm.
   (b) What is the area of a circle with a diameter of 9.5 m?

5. In Olympic events, the diameter of the circle used in the shot put is 2.1 m. Calculate the area of the circle.

6. Juan has a circular lawn with a radius of 13.7 m. The fertilizer he uses covers an area of 50 m². How many bags of fertilizer are needed for his lawn?

7. The circular target for a parachute jump has a diameter of 22.4 m. To make the area more visible, the circle is filled in with chalk. One bag of chalk can cover an area of 15.5 m². How many bags of chalk are needed to cover the circle completely?

Use the table at the right to answer Questions 8, 9, 10, and 11.

8. Calculate the area of
   (a) a small pizza.   (b) a large pizza.

9. Two people equally share a medium pizza. What area of pizza will each person eat?

10. (a) Calculate the cost of a small pizza with two ingredients.
    (b) Calculate the cost per square centimetre of the pizza in (a).
    (c) Create a similar problem of your own using the chart. Solve your problem and compare it to others in the class.

	Small 25 cm	Medium 35 cm	Large 40 cm	Ex Large 45 cm
Basic Tomato Sauce and Cheese	$8.00	$10.00	$10.75	$12.25
One Choice	8.30	10.50	11.25	12.90
Two Choices	8.60	11.00	11.75	13.55
Three Choices	8.90	11.50	12.25	14.20
Four Choices	9.20	12.00	12.75	14.85
Extra or Double Choice	0.30	0.50	0.55	0.65
Double Cheese & Shrimps each count as two choices	0.60	1.00	1.10	1.30
Pepperoni, Mush., Gr. Pepper, Onions	8.90	11.50	12.25	14.20
Each additional ingredient	1.00	1.50	1.75	2.00

11. (a) How many different small pizzas can be made from the combinations shown in the chart if there are six ingredients?
    (b) How many different pizzas can be made from the combinations shown in the chart?
    (c) Create a problem of your own using the data in the chart. Solve your problem and compare it to others in the class.

MAKING CONNECTIONS

In 1912, Max Von Laue passed x-rays through a spherical crystal. Dark points appeared in a symmetrical pattern. He drew circles through the points and a pattern was formed.
(a) Describe how the circles were drawn using the dark points.
(b) What is the least number of measurements needed to find the circumference and area of each circle? Find the circumference and area.

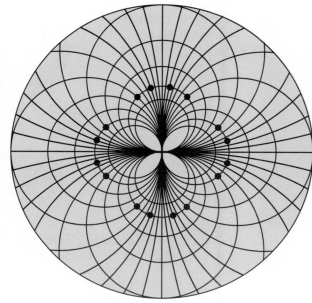

To ensure that packaging is used economically, a manufacturer needs to know the amount of material required for a package. Work together to complete these explorations. Summarize any patterns and relationships you find relating to the *surface area* of a package.

EXPLORATION ① *Work in a Small Group*

1. Use an old cereal box.
   (a) Cut the box along each side and lay it flat on your desk.
   (b) How many equal parts does the box have?
   (c) How can you find the surface area of the box? Find the surface area.

2. Repeat the parts in Question 1 for other boxes that you find. What patterns and relationships can help you find the surface area of any box?

3. Use any box.
   (a) Make measurements and find the surface area without cutting the box.
   (b) Cut out and flatten the box. Calculate the surface area. Were your measurements in (a) reasonable?

EXPLORATION ② *Work in a Small Group*

4. (a) Copy and cut out the net shown.
   (b) Fold the net to construct a shape. What shape have you constructed?
   (c) What measurements do you need to find the surface area of the shape in (b)?
   (d) Measure to find the surface area.

5. (a) Repeat the parts in Question 4 for similar nets of your own.
   (b) What patterns and relationships can help you find the surface area of each shape?

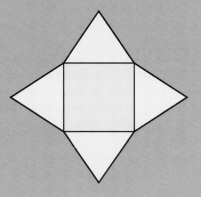

In the previous section, you explored how to find surface area. Work in a small group to complete the following activities.

ACTIVITY 1 *Work in a Small Group*

1. (a) Refer to the shapes shown below. How are they alike? How are they different?
   (b) Based on your previous explorations, suggest a relationship or method to help you find the surface area of each shape.

Prisms

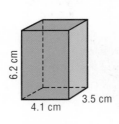

Pyramids

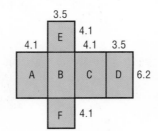

One method for finding the surface area of a shape is to draw the net of the shape. The net of a prism and a pyramid are shown below. The solid can be constructed from the net. Look for faces that are congruent to reduce the number of calculations you need to do.

Rectangular Prism

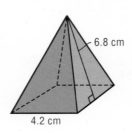

Square-based Pyramid

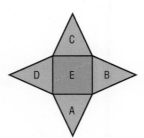

ACTIVITY 2 *Work in a Small Group*

2. (a) For the prism shown above, which faces are congruent? Find the area of each congruent face.
   (b) Use your answer in (a). Find the surface area of the prism.

3. (a) For the pyramid shown above, which faces are congruent? Find the area of each congruent face.
   (b) Use your answer in (a). Find the surface area of the pyramid.

A Work with a partner.

1. The measures of a rectangular prism are shown.
   (a) Draw a net.　　(b) Identify the congruent faces.
   (c) Find the area of the different faces.
   (d) Find the surface area of the prism.

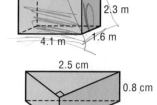

2.3 m

4.1 m　1.6 m

2. The measures of a triangular prism are shown.
   (a) Draw a net.　　(b) Identify the congruent faces.
   (c) Find the area of each face.
   (d) Find the surface area of the prism.

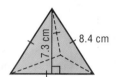

2.5 cm

0.8 cm

1.5 cm　2.0 cm

3. The measures of a triangular pyramid are shown.
   (a) Draw a net.
   (b) How many congruent faces are there?
   (c) Find the area of each face.
   (d) Find the surface area of the pyramid.

7.3 cm　8.4 cm

B Look for a pattern.

4. Find the total surface area.

(a)

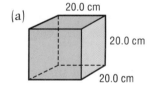

20.0 cm

20.0 cm

20.0 cm

(b)

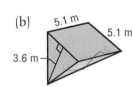

5.1 m

5.1 m

3.6 m

(c)

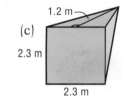

1.2 m

2.3 m

2.3 m

5. The dimensions for a tent are shown.
   (a) How much material is needed to construct the tent?
   (b) What assumption did you make?

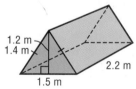

1.2 m
1.4 m

2.2 m

1.5 m

6. Find the total surface area of the wedge of cheese.

8.0 cm

6.5 cm

8.6 cm

7 cm

7. For each shape shown below, estimate the dimensions and find the surface areas.

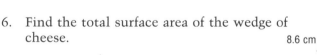

199

6.13 CYLINDERS

You have probably seen many different sizes of cans. You can find the surface area of the metal that is used to make each can. Work with a partner to complete the activity. Summarize any relationships that can help you find the surface area of a can or cylinder.

ACTIVITY *Work with a Partner*

1. (a) Use a can. Cut paper so that it fits snugly around the can. Find the area of the paper.
   (b) Find the area of both ends of the can.
   (c) What is the surface area of the can?

2. (a) Choose a different can. Construct the net of the can.
   (b) Make appropriate measurements and put them on your net.
   (c) Find the surface area of the can.
   (d) In your journal, suggest steps that you can use to find the surface area of any can.

To find the surface area of this can you can follow these steps. Drawing the net of the can will help you.

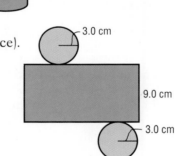

Step 1 Find the area of each end (base).
Use $A = \pi \times r \times r$.
$$A = 3.14 \times 3.0 \times 3.0$$
$$= 28.26$$

Step 2 Find the area of the side.
Use $C = 2\pi r$ to find the length of the side (curved surface).
$$C = 2 \times 3.14 \times 3.0$$
$$= 18.84$$
Use $A = l \times w$ to find the area of the side.
$$A = 18.84 \times 9.0$$
$$= 169.56$$

Step 3 Find the total surface area.
$$28.26 \times 2 + 169.56 = 226.08$$

The surface area of the can (to the nearest 10 cm^2) is about 230 cm^2.

EXERCISE

 Round off your answers to one decimal place.

1. (a) Calculate the area of the base of this can.
   (b) Calculate the area of the curved surface.
   (c) Find the surface area.

4.2 cm

4.0 cm

200

2. Find the total surface area of each can.

(a)

8.4 cm

12.2 cm

(b)

14.6 cm

3.5 cm

(c)

14.3 m

8 m

(d)

1.2 m

1.8 m

B When solving problems, remember to estimate an answer and then calculate. Ask yourself if the answers are reasonable.

3. The height of a can of cat food is 4.5 cm. The diameter is 8.5 cm. Calculate the total surface area of the can.

4. The diameter of a can of tomatoes is 10.1 cm and the height is 11.2 cm. Calculate the total surface area.

5. A can of peaches is 12.5 cm high and has a diameter of 8 cm. Calculate the area of the label that needs to be used.

6. The outside of an oil drum is to be painted with two coats of underwater paint. The diameter of the drum is 0.6 m and it has a height of 1.2 m.
(a) Calculate the surface area of the drum.
(b) There are eight drums in all. How many litres of paint are needed if 1 L covers 6.5 m²?

7. A can of paint has a radius of 8.0 cm and a height of 12.0 cm.
(a) Estimate the surface area of the can.
(b) Calculate the surface area of the can.
(c) Calculate the dimensions of the label needed for the can.

C

8. To construct a closed container, 500 cm² of metal is provided.
(a) Design a cube and a cylinder so that they have the same surface area.
(b) What are the dimensions of the shapes you constructed?

MAKING CONNECTIONS

A thunderstorm is one of nature's most destructive phenomena. After a thunderstorm, the loss to property can be in the millions of dollars.

Did you know that the disturbance created by a thunderstorm is approximately cylindrical in shape? For each storm below, calculate the ground area covered.
(a) The smallest thunderstorm on record measured 2.7 km in diameter and its cloud formation had a height of 8.4 km.
(b) The largest thunderstorm on record measured 43.9 km in diameter. It had a height of 20.3 km.

6.14 INVESTIGATING SPHERES AND CONES

Work with a partner to complete the following activity. Summarize any relationships that will help you find the surface area of a cone and a sphere.

ACTIVITY 1   *Work with a Partner*

1. (a) Make a list of objects that are shaped like spheres and cones.
   (b) In your journal, describe why you might need to find the surface area of the objects you listed in (a).

ACTIVITY 2   *Work with a Partner*

2. (a) Use a piece of paper. Construct a cone.
   (b) Construct the net of your cone in (a). How would you find the area of the curved surface of your cone?
   (c) How would you find the area of the base of your cone?
   (d) Describe how you would find the surface area of your cone.

3. Repeat the above steps for other cones that you construct. What do you notice?

ACTIVITY 3   *Work with a Partner*

4. Use an orange. Peel it.
   (a) Cut the orange in half. Find the area of the cross section of the orange.
   (b) Flatten out the peels that you have. Find the total area of all the peels.
   (c) Describe how you might find the surface area of a sphere.

5. Repeat the steps of Question 4 for other spherical fruits. What do you notice?

ACTIVITY 4   *Work with a Partner*

6. (a) Use any sphere like a tennis ball or a basketball. Find the diameter of the sphere.
   (b) Cut out paper circles that have the diameter in (a). What is the area of each circle?
   (c) Use the circles in (b) to cover the sphere as completely as you can. Cut pieces off the circles if necessary. About how many whole circles are needed to cover a sphere completely?
   (d) What relationship can help you find the surface area of your sphere?

7. Repeat the steps of Question 6 for other balls. What do you notice?

6.15 SPHERES AND CONES

In the previous activities, you explored how to find the surface area of a sphere. You used steps like the following.

Step 1

Step 2

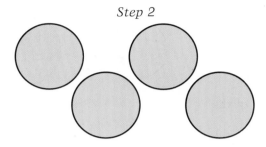

Step 3

Using these steps, you probably found the following relationship to help you find the surface area, *SA*, of a sphere.

$$SA = 4 \times \pi \times r \times r$$

This relationship can help you solve problems. For example, suppose you are a gum ball manufacturer. Each gum ball has a radius of about 0.5 cm. You can find the surface area covered by the candy coating as follows.

Use $SA = 4 \times \pi \times r \times r$
$\doteq 4 \times 3.14 \times 0.5 \times 0.5$
$= 3.14$

Each gum ball will need about 3.14 cm^2 of candy coating.

The amount of canvas used to construct a conical tent can be calculated by finding the sum of step 1 and step 2.

Step 1   Area of curved surface

$A = \pi r s$ ← the slant height as shown in the diagram

area of curved surface

radius of the base of the cone

Step 2   Area of the base of the cone
Use your earlier work to calculate the area of a circle.

$A = \pi r^2$

area of base

radius of the base of the cone

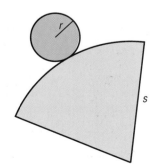

A Review your skills with surface area.

1. Find the surface area of each sphere.

(a)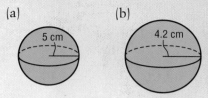
5 cm

(b)
4.2 cm

(c)
10.8 cm

2. (a) Calculate the area of the base of the cone.
(b) Calculate the area of the curved surface.
(c) What is the surface area?

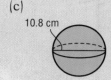
16 cm
6 cm

3. Find the surface area of each of the cones.

(a)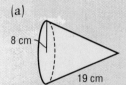
8 cm
19 cm

(b)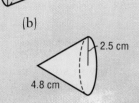
2.5 cm
4.8 cm

(c)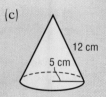
12 cm
5 cm

B Use a calculator.

4. The slant height of a cone is 16.2 cm. Calculate the surface area of the cone if the radius is 7.9 cm.

5. The diameter of the earth is 12 800 km.
   (a) Calculate the surface area of the earth.
   (b) What assumption do you make in obtaining your answer in (a)?

6. Calculate the surface area of the following planets.
   (a) Venus, radius 6050 km
   (b) Mars, diameter 6800 km

7. The radius of a sphere is 15.2 cm. By how much does the surface area of the sphere increase if the radius increases by 2 cm?

8. (a) A tornado is a narrow, funnel-shaped cloud which extends downwards from cumulonimbus clouds. A tract of land 8 km wide and 6.9 km long is destroyed by a tornado. Calculate the area of destruction.
   (b) From the picture, estimate the surface area of the tornado.

In the following exercises, you will use your skills with circles to help you find out more about wheels. Before trying the exercises, work with a partner to complete the following activity.

ACTIVITY *Work with a Partner*
(a) Find different kinds of wheels from newspapers and magazines.
(b) Make a class collage of the pictures that you have found. Describe how you might find the circumference of a wheel.
(c) Find the circumference of each wheel in (b).

1. The wheel of a jet has a diameter of 2.4 m.
   (a) Calculate the circumference of the wheel.
   (b) The runway is 648 m long. Calculate the number of turns the tire will make during take-off. What assumptions have you made?

2. On a racing car, the radius of each front wheel is 42.3 cm and of each rear wheel is 47.9 cm.
   (a) Calculate the distance travelled by the car for one turn of the rear wheels.
   (b) If the front wheels have turned 100 times, how many times have the rear wheels turned?

3. (a) A volleyball for international competition has a diameter of 21.8 cm. What is the circumference of a regulation volleyball?
   (b) Calculate its cross-sectional area.
   (c) Calculate its surface area.

4. (a) An official basketball used in international competition has a diameter of 24.2 cm. What is the circumference of a regulation basketball?
   (b) What is the surface area of the ball?

5. (a) A tennis ball used in international competition has a diameter of 6.8 cm. Calculate the circumference of the tennis ball. What is its surface area?
   (b) The official baseball used in the National and American Leagues has a diameter of 7.4 cm. Calculate the circumference of the baseball. What is its surface area?
   (c) Which ball, the baseball or the tennis ball, has the greater surface area, and by how much is it greater?
   (d) Use a sports ball of your own. Find the surface area of your ball.
   (e) Create a problem of your own using the sports balls in (d). Solve your problem.

6.17 EXPLORING VOLUME

Work in a small group and try the following explorations. In your journal, record any patterns and relationships that can help you calculate the volume of a solid.

EXPLORATION ① Work in a Small Group

1. (a) Use cubes to construct the prism shown.
   (b) How many cubes are needed in (a)?
   (c) Interpret your result in (b). What is the volume of the prism?
   (d) Find the length, width, and height of the prism. How can these measurements be used to find the volume of the prism?

2. Another way to find the volume of a rectangular prism is to think about the area of the base.
   (a) Find the area of the base of the prism.
   (b) How can you use the area of the base to find the volume of the prism?

EXPLORATION ② Work in a Small Group

3. (a) Construct a shape like the one shown.
   (b) How many cubes are needed in (a)?
   (c) Interpret your result in (b). What is the volume of the prism?
   (d) Find the length, width, and height of the prism. How can these measurements be used to find the volume of the prism?

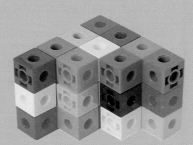

4. Another way to find the volume of a triangular prism is to think about the area of the base.
   (a) Find the area of the base of the prism.
   (b) How can you use the area of the base to find the volume of the prism?

EXPLORATION ③ Work in a Small Group

5. Refer to your work in Explorations 1 and 2. Obtain a cylinder.
   (a) Suggest a method to find the volume of the cylinder.
   (b) Use your method in (a) to estimate the volume.
   (c) Fill up your cylinder with water. Measure its volume.
   (d) How reasonable was your method in (a)?
   (e) Repeat parts (a) to (d) for other cylinders. What relationship will help you find the volume of a cylinder?

To calculate the volume of each petroleum container in the picture, an engineer needs to use relationships for the volume of a prism and the volume of a cylinder.

In the previous section, you explored the volume of prisms and cylinders. The relationships are summarized below.

Prism

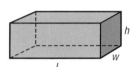

$$V = B \times h$$
$$= l \times w \times h$$

Cylinder

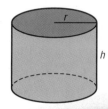

$$V = B \times h$$
$$= \pi \times r \times r \times h$$

The relationships can be used to solve problems like the following.

EXAMPLE 1

A trench is dug with dimensions as shown. Find the volume of dirt removed.

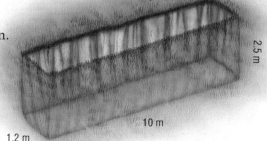

SOLUTION

Use $V = l \times w \times h$.
$$= 10 \times 1.2 \times 2.5$$
$$= 30$$

The volume of dirt removed is 30 m^2.

EXAMPLE 2

Find the volume of the can. Find its capacity to the nearest millilitre.

SOLUTION

Use $V = \pi \times r \times r \times h$.
$$\doteq 3.14 \times 5 \times 5 \times 14.5$$
$$= 1138.25 \text{ cm}^3$$

Since 1 cm^3 = 1 mL, the capacity of the can is 1138 mL.

207

A Round your answers to one decimal place.

1. Find the volume of each solid.

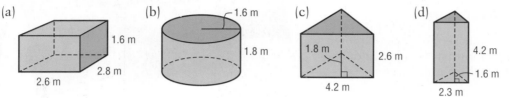

(a)   (b)   (c)   (d)

2. (a) The area of the base of a prism is 84 cm². The height is 24 cm. Find the volume.
   (b) The area of the base of a prism is 37.3 m². The altitude is 8.2 m. Find the volume.

B Check whether your answers are reasonable.

3. A bar of gold is shown.
   (a) Calculate the volume of the gold bar.
   (b) Estimate how much money this bar is worth.

4. (a) A well 28.6 m deep with a radius of 1.3 m is dug.
   Calculate the amount of earth removed.
   (b) What assumption did you make?

5. A circular pool 1.6 m high has a radius of 4.0 m.
   (a) Calculate the volume of water in the pool.
   (b) What assumption did you make?

6. Cement pillars that support bridges are often cylindrical.
   (a) Calculate the volume of a pillar if its height is 12.3 m
   and its radius is 0.5 m.
   (b) Calculate the mass of the pillar if 100.0 cm³ of concrete
   has a mass of 0.51 kg.

7. A large cubical tank whose side measures 4.6 m is filled. How much liquid will be left in
   the tank if it is used to fill a cylindrical tank with a radius of 2.2 m and a height of 4.6 m?

8. An aquarium is 40.3 cm long, 20.1 cm wide, and 14.6 cm deep.
   (a) Calculate the number of litres of water it will hold when full.
   (b) The aquarium is filled so that the water is 3.2 cm from the top. Calculate how much
   water is in it.

9. Work with a partner.
   (a) Create a method for finding the volume of this page.
   (b) Find the volume of this page.
   (c) Suppose you were to tear out this page and fold it in half three times. How would the
   volume change? Give reasons for your answer.

To find the volume of a solid, you can often use relationships developed for other solids. Work together to complete each exploration below. Record any patterns and relationships you find.

EXPLORATION ① Work Together

1. (a) Refer to the solids below. How are they alike? How are they different?

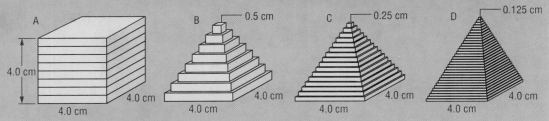

(b) Which solid best approximates the volume of a pyramid?
(c) What measures do you need to find the length and height of each layer?
(d) Write a relationship to help you find the volume of a pyramid.

EXPLORATION ② Work Together

2. (a) Refer to the solids below. How are they alike? How are they different?

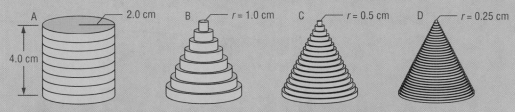

(b) Which solid best approximates the volume of a cone?
(c) What measures do you need to find the radius and height of each layer?
(d) Write a relationship to help you find the volume of a cone.

EXPLORATION ③ Work Together

3. (a) Construct a cube and a pyramid so that each has the same base length and height.
   (b) Fill your pyramid with styrofoam chips and pour them into the cube. How many times will you pour the contents of the pyramid into the cube in order to fill it? What do you notice?

4. (a) Construct a cylinder and a cone so that each has the same base diameter and height.
   (b) Fill your cone with styrofoam chips and pour them into the cylinder. How many times will you pour the contents of the cone into the cylinder in order to fill it? What do you notice?

In the previous sections, you explored relationships to find the volume of solids. A summary of these relationships is shown below.

Volume of a Pyramid

volume of pyramid = $\frac{1}{3}$ volume of prism.

Volume of a Cone

volume of cone = $\frac{1}{3}$ volume of cylinder.

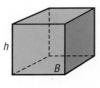

$$V = Bh$$

$$V = \frac{1}{3}Bh$$

height, h

$$V = Bh$$

$$V = \frac{1}{3}Bh$$

Volume of a Sphere

The volume of a sphere can be calculated using this relationship.

$$V = \frac{4}{3}\pi r^3$$

EXERCISE

A Remember: You can use the value of π directly from a calculator with a $\boxed{\pi}$ key.

1. Apply the appropriate formula to find the volume of each solid.

(a)

4.2 m
3.6 m
4.0 m

(b)

4.8 m
5.5 m

(c)

25.0 cm
8.5 cm
12.2 cm

(d)

10.5 m
9.6 m
12.8 m

(e)

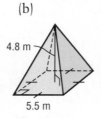

3.9 cm
15.1 cm

(f)

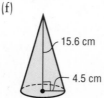

15.6 cm
4.5 cm

(g)

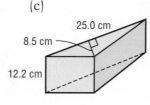

2.2 m

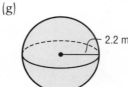

2. (a) Find the volume of a cone with a height of 3.78 cm and with a radius of 1.65 cm.
   (b) Find the volume of a cone 4.2 m in diameter and 6.3 m high.
   (c) Find the volume of a pyramid 11.3 m high with a rectangular base measuring 6.9 m by 2.9 m.

Check whether your answers are reasonable.

3. (a) Find the volume of a spherical tank if the radius is 3.8 m.
   (b) If 1 L = 1000 cm³, find the capacity in litres of the tank in (a).

4. Sulphur is stored in a conical pile. Calculate the volume of the pile, if the height is 14.2 m and the diameter is 34.4 m.

5. A funnel is cone-shaped with a radius of 1.53 cm and a height of 2.26 cm. Calculate how much the funnel will hold if filled.

6. A pile of sand in a bin is shaped like a square-based pyramid. One side of the base is 2.8 m long. The height of the sand is 1.8 m. What is the volume of the sand in the bin?

7. Which container holds more, the hemisphere (half of a sphere) or the cone?

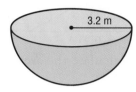
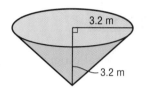

8. (a) A billiard ball has a diameter of 5.25 cm. Calculate the volume of the billiard ball.
   (b) A tennis ball used in international competition has a diameter of 6.75 cm. Calculate its volume.
   (c) Which ball has the greatest cross-sectional area? By how much is it greater?

MAKING CONNECTIONS

Each of the solids below is composed of solids from this section.
(a) What are the solids used?
(b) What is the volume of each solid in (a)?
(c) What is the volume of the original solid?

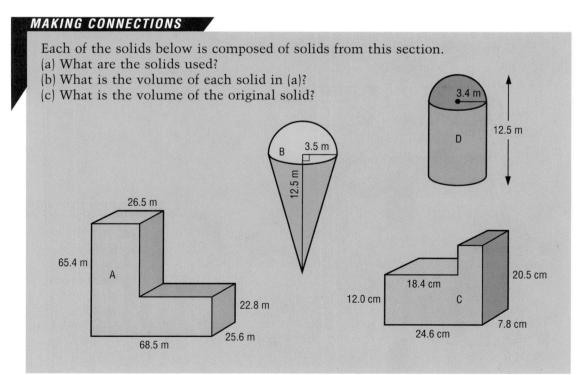

CHAPTER REVIEW

1. Find the perimeter of each.

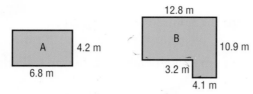

2. (a) Calculate the area of each triangle.

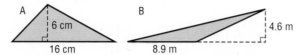

(b) Calculate the area of each parallelogram.

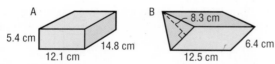

3. (a) Calculate the volume of a prism 10 cm high if it has a
      (i) triangular base area 12.8 m².
      (ii) square base area 123.9 cm².
   (b) Calculate the volume of each of the following prisms.

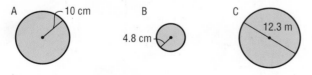

4. Calculate the circumference and area of each circle.

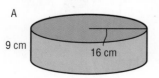

5. Calculate the surface area and volume of each cylinder.

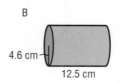

THINKING ABOUT

❶ What patterns helped you to solve problems in this chapter?

❷ Have you updated your *Problem Solving Plan* with new strategies from this chapter?

❸ How can a calculator help you in this chapter? Use examples of your own to support your answer.

MAKING CONNECTIONS

Refer to the opening page of this chapter.
(a) Create a problem based on the pictures.
(b) Solve your problem in (a). Compare your problem to others in the class.

SELF EVALUATION

❹ How are the problems on this page alike? How are they different?

❺ If each dimension in Question 2 were doubled, how would the volume change? Will the volume of a shape always change this much if each dimension is doubled?

❻ Choose a problem on this page. Explain to your partner how you solved it.

1. (a) Calculate the area of each shape.

(b) The base of a triangular garden is 16.2 m and the height is 12.2 m. Calculate its area.

2. (a) Calculate the volume of each of the following.

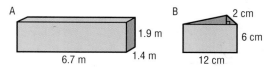

(b) A rectangular trench 1.6 m deep and 1.2 m wide is dug. If the trench is 2.1 m long, calculate the amount of earth removed.

3. (a) Calculate the circumference of each circle.

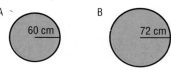

How much further will B go than A if they are each rolled for 800 turns?

(b) The blades of a helicopter form a twirling circle of radius 4.5 m. Calculate the distance a tip travels in 12 min if the blades turn at 300 r/min.

4. Calculate the surface area of each of the following.

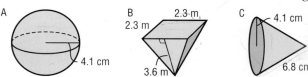

5. Calculate the volume of each of the following.

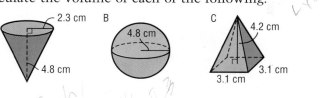

MATH JOURNAL

Suppose you are a sporting goods manufacturer.
(a) Design a new type of ball that can be used in a "baseball" game.
(b) Give reasons why your ball will make "the game" different.

Suppose you are on the school dance committee. Your job is to plan a budget for the dance. Work in a group to complete the following project.

1. In your group, decide what kind of dance you will put on. Will you have a live band, a DJ, or a video dance? Will you serve food? Will you have door prizes? Be very thorough in planning what you do want and what you do not want.

2. Make a complete list of things you will need for your dance. Write these down in a column called Expenses. Then estimate how much money you will need for each expense.

3. Make a complete list of your sources of income. Write these down in a column called Income. Then estimate how much money you will get from each source.

4. If you have access to a spreadsheet, use it to set up a screen similar to the one shown below. Enter in the expenses and income you calculated previously. If you do not have access to a spreadsheet, you will have to perform the calculations manually. Do you think a spreadsheet saves time in this project? Give reasons for your answer.

	A	B	C	D	E
1	Expenses	Amount	Income	Amount	Profit
2	DJ	100	Tickets	345	
3	Posters	25	School Grant	150	
4	Food	80	Draw Tickets	140	
5	Prices	190			
6	Decorations	230			
7					
8	Total	625		635	+10

Note that in this spreadsheet, cell B8 is the total of cells B2 ... B6. Changing any of these values will change the value in B8. Similarly, D8 is the total of D2 ... D4 and E8 is D8 − B8. This feature allows you to change your estimate for any expense or income, and immediately see the change in profit.

5. Use your spreadsheet or spreadsheet simulation to budget for your dance. Compare your group's budget with those of other groups. Do you think the budgets are realistic? In your journal, write how you would use a spreadsheet to help budget another school function. Would a spreadsheet save you time in this project?

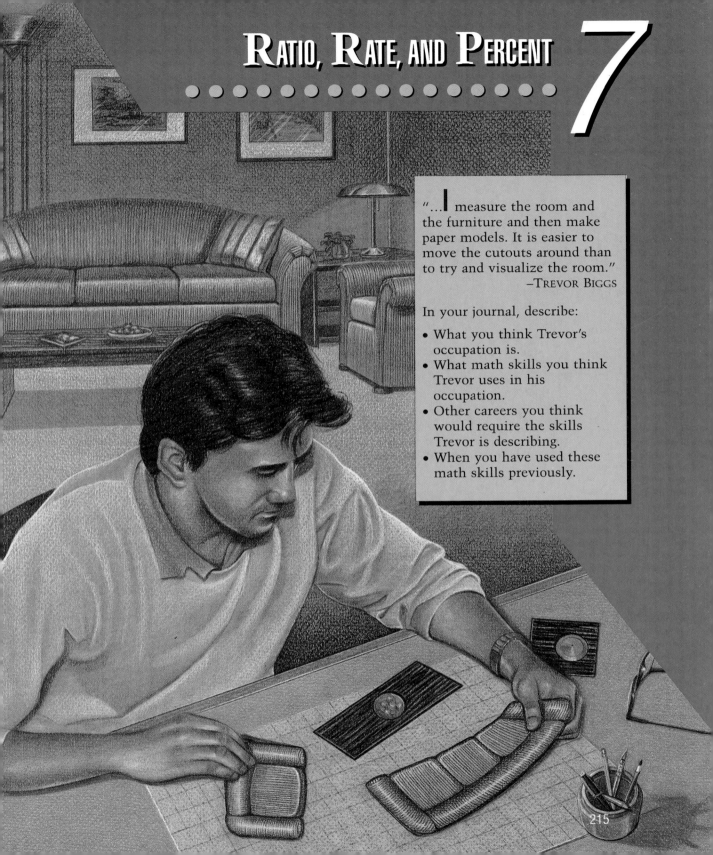

"...I measure the room and the furniture and then make paper models. It is easier to move the cutouts around than to try and visualize the room."

–TREVOR BIGGS

In your journal, describe:

- What you think Trevor's occupation is.
- What math skills you think Trevor uses in his occupation.
- Other careers you think would require the skills Trevor is describing.
- When you have used these math skills previously.

215

7.1 EXPLORING RATIOS

Suppose the garbage in your neighbourhood was analyzed. For every 7 kg thrown away, 3 kg could be recycled. You can compare the mass of garbage collected to the mass of garbage that could be recycled by using a *ratio*.

7 : 3

Mass collected. ⎯⎯⎯⎯⎯⎯ Mass that could be recycled.

The symbol ":" means "is compared to." Thus, you read 7 : 3 as "seven compared to three" or "7 to 3."

EXPLORATION ① *Work Together*

1. (a) Newspaper articles often compare numbers. How would you write ratios for the examples at the right?
   (b) Find other headlines that use ratios. Describe how the ratios are used.
   (c) Refer to the garbage analysis above. Find other environmental ratios. In your journal, interpret each ratio.

ELECTION RESULTS
5 in every 24 persons interviewed are happy about the recent election.

THEY DO IT AGAIN!
Jets beat Flames
No fire left
2 to 1

EXPLORATION ② *Work Together*

2. Write a ratio to compare the number of yellow disks to green disks.
   (a) 3 yellow
       4 green
   (b) 2 yellow
       1 green
   (c) 7 yellow
       5 green

3. The ratio of yellow disks to green disks is given below. Use your counters to show each ratio. What do you notice about each ratio?
   (a) 2 : 5
   (b) 6 : 15
   (c) 4 : 10
   (d) 10 : 25
   (e) 8 : 20

4. Create ratios of your own.
   (a) Represent the ratios using disks.
   (b) Relate your ratios to real-life situations.

EXPLORATION ③   *Work Together to Create Questions*

5. (a) Refer to the newspaper article. Write the information in the article as a ratio.
   (b) If the reporter had interviewed 24 drivers, how many would have been wearing seat belts?
   (c) If 60 drivers were stopped at random, how many drivers would have been wearing seat belts?
   (d) One afternoon, during the survey, 25 drivers were found to be wearing seat belts. How many cars do you think were stopped for the interview?

> **Wear your seat belt. It may save your life.**
> Survey indicates 7 out of 12 drivers don't use them.
>
> Halifax (AP): In a recent study, car drivers were interviewed and it was found that only 5 out of 12 use their seat belts. In the study, researchers found that out of 939 accident reports, 451 people would not have been injured if the appropriate seat belt had been used.

6. (a) Refer to the article shown above. Create similar problems of your own using the information in the article. Solve your problems. Compare your problems to others in the class.
   (b) Repeat part (a) using other newspaper articles. Create a class collage using the articles. Use the collage to create and solve other problems.

EXPLORATION ④   *Work Together*

7. (a) Refer to the Smarties shown below. Estimate the ratio of red Smarties to blue Smarties without counting. How can you check the reasonableness of your estimate?
   (b) Estimate ratios of your own using the Smarties. How reasonable is each estimate?
   (c) Use a different box of Smarties and estimate ratios using the candies.

7.2 WORKING WITH RATIO

Did you know that many crops require about 2000 kg of water to produce 2 kg of food?

To compare the *mass of water* used to the *mass of food* produced, you can use a **ratio**.

mass of water used

2000 : 2

mass of food produced

The numbers 2000 and 2 are the **terms** of the ratio.

The ratio can be written in 2 different forms.

Ratio Form	**Fraction Form**
2000 : 2	$\dfrac{2000}{2}$

Sometimes, you need to write a ratio whose units are not the same. To write the ratio, you need to make the units the same.

For example, you can compare 2 m and 50 cm as shown below.

    You can write 2 m as 200 cm.
    Thus, the ratio is 200 : 50.

ACTIVITY

Did you know that one half of the world's food comes from just 3 types of plants — wheat, rice, and corn?

(a) Write a ratio to compare the amount of the world's food that comes from wheat, rice, and corn to the amount of food that comes from other sources.

(b) Write your ratio from (a) in a different form.

(c) Create problems of your own using your ratios. Solve your problems.

(d) In your journal, describe whether you are surprised by the ratios in this section. Give reasons for your answer.

A   Write each ratio in fraction form and ratio form.

1.   Some compact discs and cassette tapes are shown below.

(a) What is the ratio of compact discs to tapes?
(b) What is the ratio of tapes to compact discs?
(c) How are your ratios above alike? How are they different?
(d) In your journal, explain why the order of the terms is important in a ratio.

2.   A variety of footwear is shown below.

(a) What is the ratio of running shoes to sandals?
(b) What is the ratio of running shoes to boots?
(c) Write a ratio of your own. Interpret your ratio.

3.   Write a ratio to compare the value of each of the following.
(a) a penny to a nickel   (b) a dime to a penny   (c) a dime to a nickel
(d) a quarter to a dime   (e) a dollar to a dime   (f) a nickel to a quarter

B   Remember: The order in which you write the terms is important.

4.   Write the ratio smaller to greater to compare each of the following quantities.
(a) 4 cm, 3 cm   (b) 8 km, 9 km   (c) 19 cm, 20 mm   (d) 250 m, 5 km
(e) 25 m, 40 cm   (f) 400 g, 2 kg   (g) 35 kg, 500 g   (h) 2 t, 250 kg

5. In a class, students had the part-time jobs shown in the chart. Write a ratio to compare
   (a) A to D (b) C to B
   (c) D to C (d) B to D

Job		No. of Students
A	Service Station Attendant	8
B	Pizza Deliverer	5
C	Dishwasher	3
D	Handbill Distributor	3

6. A nut mixture is made up of the nuts shown. Write a ratio to compare
   (a) cashews to Brazil nuts.
   (b) peanuts to filberts.
   (c) filberts to peanuts.
   (d) Brazil nuts to peanuts.

Type of Nuts	Amount
Cashews	40 g
Peanuts	160 g
Filberts	10 g
Brazil nuts	40 g

7. Refer to the data in the previous question. Interpret each ratio.

   (a) $\dfrac{40}{10}$ (b) $\dfrac{160}{40}$ (c) 40 : 40 (d) 10 : 160

8. (a) Refer to rectangles A and B and write ratios to
      (i) compare the perimeter of rectangle A to the perimeter of rectangle B.
      (ii) compare the length of rectangle A to the length of rectangle B.
   (b) Create ratios of your own. Write them in your journal.

9. (a) For the rectangles shown, write a ratio to compare the smaller area to the larger area.
   (b) Write a different ratio of your own. Interpret your ratio.

10. In your journal, describe whether or not the following statement is true: "The ratio of the perimeters of two figures is 1 : 1. The ratio of the areas of the figures is also 1 : 1."

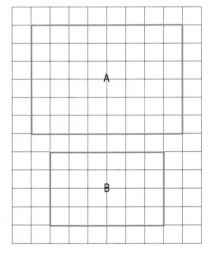

To solve some problems, you often need to obtain more information. For example:
   Four shapes are given. If the sun were the size of a volleyball, which of the following would be size of the earth?

   ▸ a baseball ▸ a pea ▸ a ping-pong ball ▸ a grain of salt

(a) What information do you need in order to solve the problem? From what sources can you find such information?
(b) Solve the problem. Explain to other groups how you and your partner solved the problem.

7.3 ESTIMATING RATIOS

Work with a partner for the following activities.

ACTIVITY 1

1. Use an example to help answer each question.
   (a) What do you think the word "estimate" means?
   (b) What do you think is meant by estimating ratios?

ACTIVITY 2

2. Have your partner place handfuls of black beans and white beans into a bag. Shake the bag to mix them up.
   (a) Reach into the bag and remove some beans. Record the ratio of black beans to white beans. Based on your results, estimate the ratio of black beans to white beans in the bag.
   (b) Put the beans back into the bag, shake them up, and repeat part (a). Modify your estimate if necessary.
   (c) Repeat part (b) 10 times. Use your results to revise your estimate of black beans to white beans.
3. (a) How can you check that your estimate in Question 2 is reasonable?
   (b) What is the actual ratio of black beans to white beans in the bag? How reasonable was your estimate?

ACTIVITY 3

Collect a number of cola, ginger ale, and orange bottle caps.
4. Have your partner place handfuls of cola caps, ginger ale caps, and orange caps into a bag.
   (a) Reach into the bag and remove some caps. Record the ratio of cola caps to ginger ale caps to orange caps. Based on your results, estimate the ratio of cola caps to ginger ale caps to orange caps in the bag.
   (b) Put the caps back into the bag, shake them up, and repeat part (a). Revise your estimate if necessary.
   (c) Repeat part (b) 10 times. Use your results to revise your estimate of cola to ginger ale to orange caps.
5. (a) How can you check that your estimate in Question 4 is reasonable? Check your estimate.
   (b) What is the actual ratio of bottle caps?
   (c) How reasonable was your estimate in Question 4?

Did you know that, for ideal viewing, the ratio of the size of a TV screen to the distance you should sit from it is 4 : 24? How far from your TV should you sit?

Here is how to find how far away you should sit for different screen sizes. First, you need to work with **equivalent ratios**. To write a ratio equivalent to a given ratio, you multiply or divide each term of the ratio by the *same* number. The following ratios are equivalent to 4 : 24.

Given Ratio	Equivalent Ratios

$$4 : 24 \qquad\qquad 4 \div 4 \quad\;\; 24 \div 4 \qquad 4 \times 2 \quad\;\; 24 \times 2$$

$$\underset{\text{Each term is divided by 4.}}{1 : 6} \qquad\qquad \underset{\text{Each term is multiplied by 2.}}{8 : 48}$$

The ratio 1 : 6 is said to be in **lowest terms** or **simplest form** since
- all its terms are whole numbers.
- there is no common factor for its terms.

Suppose a television has a 36 cm screen. For ideal viewing, how far should you sit from the television?

Think: You can use a **proportion**. A proportion shows that two ratios are equivalent. How can you solve the problem mentally?

Let ■ represent the distance you should be from a television, in centimetres.

Thus,

$$\frac{1}{6} = \frac{36}{\blacksquare}$$

$$\frac{1}{6} = \frac{1 \times 36}{6 \times 36} \quad \text{— Compare}$$

$$= \frac{36}{216} \qquad \blacksquare = 216$$

You should be 216 cm or 2.16 m from the TV.

ACTIVITY

At home tonight, check to see if your usual viewing distance is the ideal one. If not, in your journal, describe
(a) how you can make it ideal.
(b) what problems you will face to make it ideal.

Television screens are measured diagonally. Discuss whether or not these students are too close to the TV for best viewing.

A Review your skills with ratios.

1. Use unit tiles.
   (a) Draw another "train" proportional to the one shown.
   (b) Write a ratio to compare the number of tiles in your train to the one shown.
   (c) Write a ratio to compare the number of red tiles in your train to the train shown. What do you notice?

2. By what number was each term of the ratio 4 : 5 multiplied to give each of the following equivalent ratios?
   (a) 8 : 10   (b) 24 : 30   (c) 12 : 15   (d) 28 : 35   (e) 16 : 20   (f) 20 : 25

3. Find the value of ■.

   (a) $\dfrac{3}{5} = \dfrac{■}{10}$ (b) $\dfrac{4}{7} = \dfrac{■}{14}$ (c) $\dfrac{9}{12} = \dfrac{3}{■}$ (d) $\dfrac{10}{15} = \dfrac{■}{3}$

   (e) 10 : 30 = ■ : 3   (f) ■ : 12 = 6 : 24   (g) 2 : 5 = ■ : 10   (h) 25 : ■ = 5 : 5

4. Suppose you are watching a 50 cm television.

   (a) How can you use the proportion $\dfrac{1}{6} = \dfrac{50}{■}$ to find the best viewing distance?

   (b) Solve the proportion. What is the best viewing distance for a 50 cm television?

5. Manon can fix 2 of every 3 broken computers that she gets. She got 15 computers last week.

   (a) How can you use the proportion $\dfrac{2}{3} = \dfrac{x}{15}$ to find the number of computers she can repair?

   (b) Solve the proportion. How many computers can she repair?
   (c) In your journal, suggest how Manon might get her computers.

B Remember: Write a concluding statement. Work together.

6. In an aquarium, there are 5 angelfish and 3 goldfish.
   • What comparisons are made by each ratio below?
   • Write each ratio as a fraction.
   • How are the ratios and fractions alike? How are they different?
   (a) 5 : 3   (b) 3 : 5   (c) 5 : 8   (d) 8 : 5   (e) 3 : 8   (f) 8 : 3

7. Solve each proportion.

   (a) $\dfrac{9}{■} = \dfrac{12}{36}$ (b) $\dfrac{10}{15} = \dfrac{8}{■}$ (c) $\dfrac{■}{15} = \dfrac{64}{24}$ (d) $\dfrac{40}{65} = \dfrac{16}{■}$

8. (a) Read the information to the right. What is an axle ratio?
   (b) A vehicle has an axle ratio of 5 : 1. Find the number of times the drive shaft turns if the rear wheels turn 200 times.

9. A vehicle has an axle ratio of 8 : 3. If a drive shaft turns 400 times per minute, how many times do the rear wheels turn?

10. George fixes 2 out of every 3 dishwashers received. Last month, he received 45 dishwashers. How many can he expect to fix?

11. Engineers have manipulated 35 atoms to form the letters IBM. Suppose the letters IBM were written 6 times. How many atoms would you need?

12. For 1000 turns of the drive shaft, how many times do the rear wheels turn for each axle ratio?
    (a) 10 : 3   (b) 2.5 : 1

13. (a) How many different rectangles, with a perimeter of 16 units, can you construct on a geoboard?
    (b) Write a ratio to compare the perimeter and area of each rectangle in (a).
    (c) Write other ratios of your own by constructing rectangles on a geoboard.

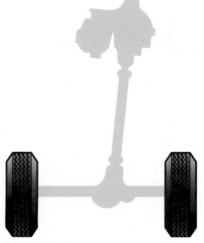

For rear-wheel drive vehicles, the axle ratio expresses the number of revolutions of the drive shaft for every turn of the rear wheels. That is, an axle ratio of 5 : 1 means that the drive shaft turns 5 times for each complete turn of the rear wheels.

MAKING CONNECTIONS

Have you ever been paid for solving problems? A Hungarian mathematician, Paul Erdős, has offered prizes to people who can solve his problems. The least amount he has offered is $25 and the greatest amount he has offered is $10 000.
(a) In your library, find one of the problems.
(b) Work with a partner to try and solve the problem. If you solve the problem, send your solution to the Mathematical Institute of the Hungarian Academy of Science.

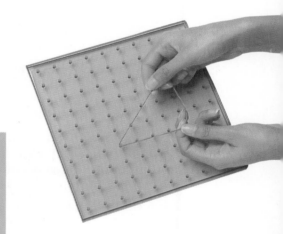

Sometimes, to solve problems, you need to collect data. The following activity will help you collect and record data about ice.

WORKING TOGETHER

Step 1 Fill an ice cube tray with water and freeze it.
Step 2 Remove one of the cubes and place it in a container of water.
Step 3 Estimate the volume of ice that is above the water and the volume of ice that is below the water.
Step 4 Write a ratio to compare the estimates in Step 3.

Repeat the steps of the activity for other containers that you can freeze. Some suggestions are shown below. You may need to line each container with a freezer bag or a plastic wrap so that the ice can be removed easily.

1. (a) Remove the ice from one of the containers and place it in some water. Record estimates of the amount of ice above the water and below the water.
   (b) Suggest a ratio for the volume of ice above the water and the volume of ice below the water. Write the ratio in your journal.
   (c) Repeat parts (a) and (b) for other pieces of ice.

Use your results from this activity in Section 7.7.

2. Suppose you put an ice cube into a glass of water.
   (a) What volume of ice would you expect to be above the water level?
   (b) What volume of ice would you expect to be below the water level?
   (c) Create a problem of your own using ice. Solve your problem and compare your solution to others in the class.

3. In winter, in many parts of Canada, lakes and rivers have a surface of ice.
   (a) In your journal, describe why you think only the surface of lakes and rivers freeze.
   (b) Describe how your life might be different if ice sank instead of floated.

Did you know that apple trees are sprayed to avoid blemishes on the apples?

John did not spray his apple tree. He found that there were 33 apples without blemishes and 69 with blemishes. Thus, the ratio of apples without blemishes to apples with blemishes can be written as $33 : 69$ or $\dfrac{33}{69}$.

When communicating information with ratios, it is often helpful to approximate them.

For example, $\dfrac{33}{69}$ ←—— 33 is about 35
     ←—— 69 is about 70

Since $\dfrac{35}{70}$ can be written as $\dfrac{1}{2}$, you can say that "The ratio of apples without blemishes to apples with blemishes is about $1 : 2$."

Before you begin the exercise, work on the following activity in a group. Record any observations you can.

ACTIVITY

(a) Use the example above. What would the ratio $1 : 1$ mean?

(b) Write other ratios using the example above. Interpret what each ratio means.

B   Write each ratio below in two different forms.

1. For Saturday's tennis match, 765 blue seats and 225 red seats were sold.
    (a) Write the ratio of blue seats to red seats.
    (b) What approximate ratio would you use in everyday conversation to compare the number of blue seats sold to the number of red seats sold?

2. In one day, a fast food outlet sold 332 hot dogs and 765 hamburgers.
    (a) Write the ratio of hot dogs to hamburgers sold.
    (b) What approximate ratio would you use in everyday conversation to compare the number of hot dogs sold to the number of hamburgers sold?

3. Refer to the standings shown.
    (a) Write a ratio of points for and against for both Toronto and Saskatchewan.
    (b) What approximate ratio would you use to compare the points for and against for each team? Why?
    (c) Repeat parts (a) and (b) for other comparisons in the table.

4. Refer to the road signs shown at the bottom of the page.
    (a) Write a ratio to compare
        • signs with an arrow to signs without an arrow.
        • signs using words to signs not using words.
    (b) Locate a book that shows other road signs you will see in Canada. Repeat (a), including these signs.
    (c) Using road signs, create problems of your own that involve ratios. Solve your problems and compare them to others in the class.

CANADIAN LEAGUE

Eastern Conference

	W	L	T	F	A	Pts
Hamilton	8	7	1	332	377	17
Winnipeg	8	8	0	356	375	16
Ottawa	7	9	0	353	383	14
Toronto	6	10	0	334	358	12

Western Conference

	W	L	T	F	A	Pts
Edmonton	13	3	0	505	281	26
Calgary	9	7	0	407	355	18
B.C.	8	7	1	381	361	17
Saskatchewan	4	12	0	291	469	8

227

The experiment with ice cubes you completed in a previous section can be used to help you explore icebergs. The ratios you found for volume of ice above and below the water also apply when you compare mass above and mass below the water level of icebergs.

The part of the iceberg that you see above the water is really the smaller part. The ratio of the mass of the part above the water to the mass of the part below the water is shown below.

Above : Below = 1 : 9

This ratio can be used to solve problems.

EXAMPLE

The mass of the part of the iceberg above the water is estimated to be 36 t.

Estimate the mass of the iceberg below the water.

SOLUTION

Let n represent the mass, in tonnes (t), below the water.

STRATEGIES TO HELP
• Use a proportion. • The mass below the water level is 9 times the mass above.

Thus,

$$\frac{1}{9} = \frac{36}{n}$$

$$\frac{1}{9} = \frac{1 \times 36}{9 \times 36}$$ — Compare.

$$= \frac{36}{324}$$ — Thus, $n = 324$

Thus, the mass of the iceberg below the water is estimated to be 324 t.

A Review your skills with proportions.

1. Find the value of n.

(a) $\dfrac{2}{n} = \dfrac{4}{10}$ (b) $\dfrac{2}{7} = \dfrac{n}{21}$ (c) $\dfrac{n}{15} = \dfrac{3}{5}$ (d) $\dfrac{8}{5} = \dfrac{24}{n}$

2. For each chart, the ratios shown are equal. Find the missing terms.

(a)

	Mickey	Brady
goals scored →	63	s
shots on goal →	168	288

(b)

	Sorenson	Lysiak
goals scored →	p	210
shots on goal →	312	336

B Use your *Problem Solving Plan*. Work with a partner.

3. The tallest iceberg ever sighted reached a height of 167.5 m above the Atlantic Ocean. The height of the great pyramid of Cheops in Egypt is 146.6 m. How much higher is the iceberg?

4. A chunk from an iceberg breaks off and floats away. The mass of the part of the iceberg above the surface of the water is 1113 kg. What is the mass of the part below the surface?

5. The mass of the part of an iceberg showing above the water is 20 t. What mass is below the water?

6. The mass of an iceberg is 560 t. What mass of the iceberg is above the surface of the water?

7. The mass of a good-sized iceberg is 240 000 t.
(a) What mass of the iceberg is under water?
(b) What mass of the iceberg is above water?

8. An ice cube in a drink measures 2.5 cm by 2.5 cm by 2.5 cm. If 1 cm^3 of water has a mass of 1 g, what mass of the ice cube is
(a) below the water?   (b) above the surface?

9. Chunks breaking from Arctic ice form icebergs. Arctic ice is about 60 m thick. The average shoulder height of a person is 1.6 m. How many persons would have to stand, shoulder upon shoulder, to reach the top of the ice?

C

10. At a party, each person used 6 ice cubes. Each bag contained 72 ice cubes. If 8 bags were used, how many people were at the party?

7.8 SCALE DIAGRAMS

Maps, photographs, and blueprints are representations of real objects. A scale diagram also represents a real object. Where have you seen scale drawings used?

For example, an aerial view of a park is shown. To compare the width of the illustration to the actual width of the park, you can write a ratio.

7 : 2100

The number of centimetres in the width of the *picture* of the park.

The number of centimetres in the width of the *actual* park.

The ratio 7 : 2100 tells you how many times a diagram has been increased or reduced in size from the actual object. The ratio 7 : 2100 is called the **scale** or the **scale ratio** of the scale diagram.

To write a ratio comparing the measures on a diagram with the measures on the actual object, the measures can be written using the same units. Scale ratio for the park is often written in lowest terms. In this case, the scale ratio for the park is 1 : 300.

Often, the scale of a diagram can be written in the following form.

   1 cm represents 300 cm   or   1 cm represents 3 m

If you know the scale of a diagram, you can calculate the actual dimensions of the object.

EXAMPLE
A diagram of the flag is drawn using the scale 1 : 17. Measure to find the actual length of the flag.

SOLUTION
The length of the flag in the illustration is 10.8 cm.
Use the scale.
   1 cm represents 17 cm
   10.8 cm on the illustration
   represent 10.8 × 17 cm
   or 183.6 cm
The actual length of the flag is 183.6 cm.

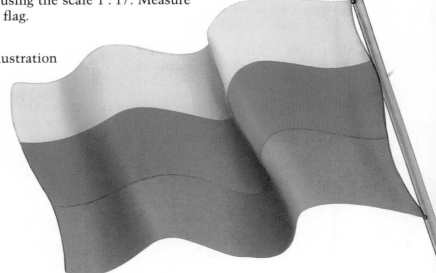

A   Review how to write ratios in lowest terms.

1. What does each of these scales on a diagram mean?
    (a) 1 : 8   (b) 1 : 20   (c) 1 : 25   (d) 1 : 100   (e) 1 : 50   (f) 7 : 30

2. A measurement of 2 cm is made on a diagram. Calculate the corresponding measure on the actual object for each of the following scales.
    (a) 1 : 4   (b) 1 : 5   (c) 1 : 10   (d) 1 : 25   (e) 1 : 50   (f) 1 : 100

B   Remember: Write a concluding statement.

3. A diagram of a boat cruiser is drawn to the scale 1 : 25. What is the length on the diagram of each of these actual measurements?
    (a) 100 cm   (b) 4 m   (c) 2.5 m

4. These scales have not been expressed in lowest terms. How would you rewrite them?
    (a) 3 : 12   (b) 5 : 25   (c) 10 : 40
    (d) 4 cm represent 60 m   (e) 15 m represent 3 cm
    (f) 7 cm represent 63 km   (g) 60 m represent 3 cm

5. The scale on a diagram is 1 cm represents 4 m.
    Calculate the actual length represented by each of the following measures.
    (a) 2 cm   (b) 8 cm   (c) 12 cm
    (d) 12.5 cm   (e) 1.45 cm   (f) 0.4 cm
    (g) 18.25 cm   (h) 50.5 cm   (i) 23.7 cm

6. The scale of a model town used on a movie set is 1 cm represents 1.5 m. The height of one of the model buildings is 30 cm. What is the actual height of the building?

7. A movie company made a large model of a domino to a scale of 1 m represents 2.5 mm. Refer to the dominos below.
    (a) How wide was the model domino?
    (b) What was the length of the model domino?

Sometimes, to help you solve a problem you first need to collect data.

For example, the scale for the acoustic guitar is 1 : 12. To find the actual width of the widest part of the guitar, you need to measure.

The width of the guitar is 3.3 cm.

  1 cm represents 12 cm
  3.3 cm represent 3.3 × 12 cm or 39.6 cm

Thus, the widest part of the guitar is 39.6 cm.

Scale drawing and photos can also be used to represent small objects, as shown below.

ACTIVITY
(a) Measure the widest part of the electric guitar shown. What is the actual width of the electric guitar if the scale is 1 : 12?
(b) Refer to the guitars shown above. Make measurements of your own to find other dimensions for the guitars.
(c) Use newspapers and magazines to find other scale diagrams. Measure to find the actual dimensions of the figure shown.

EXAMPLE

A photo of an integrated circuit in a guitar amp is shown. The scale of the circuit is 20 cm represent 1 cm. Find the actual length of the circuit, to one decimal place.

— length of actual object
— length on photo

SOLUTION

The length of the circuit in the photo is 3.4 cm.

  20 cm represent 1 cm

  1 cm represents $\frac{1}{20}$ cm

  3.4 cm represent $3.4 \times \frac{1}{20}$ cm or 0.17 cm

Thus, the length of the circuit is about 0.2 cm.

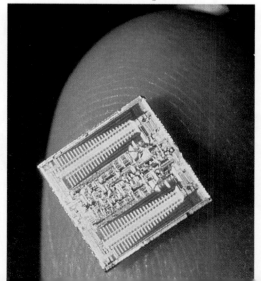

B Use your *Problem Solving Plan.*

1. Mount Everest is the highest mountain peak in the world. It measures 8850 m. How high would a drawing be if the scale used were 1 cm represents 1 km?

2. The scale for the piranha shown is 4 : 5. What is the
   (a) actual length of the head?
   (b) actual diameter of the eye?
   (c) actual width of the mouth?

3. A pet supplies company makes a model of a diver for aquariums. They used an actual height of 1.8 m to make the model. If the scale of the model is 1 cm represents 0.5 m, how tall is the model?

4. The model of a sewer pipe is made to the scale 2 cm represent 1 m. If the width of the model pipe is 6 cm, how wide is the actual pipe?

5. The Channel 8 Sports Team builds a model of a golf course to the scale 1 cm represents 10 m. The model is 75 cm wide. How wide is the actual golf course?

6. (a) The wing span of a jet is 15 m. What scale would you use to draw the wings accurately on this page?
   (b) Choose objects of your own. What scale would you use to draw the objects accurately on this page?

7. A miniature railway is constructed to a scale of 1 : 90. If the model caboose is 15 cm long, what is the actual length, in metres, of the real caboose?

8. A television image of the height of a horse is 21 cm and that of its jockey is 19 cm. If the actual height of the horse is 164 cm, find the height of the jockey.

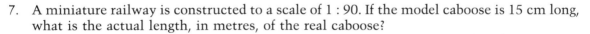

MAKING CONNECTIONS

1. For each of the following objects, the actual measurement is given. What scale would you choose to draw each object so that it could fill a page of your journal?
   (a) The smallest hummingbird has a wing span of 3.8 cm.
   (b) The longest river in Canada is the South Saskatchewan River, measuring about 1380 km in length.
   (c) The smallest moth has a wing span of 3 mm.

2. Refer to the *Guinness Book of World Records*. Pick some "smallest" and "largest" objects of your own and repeat Question 1.

SCIENCE

Ratios are essential in chemistry.

For example, sodium and chlorine combine chemically to form salt. The ratio of the mass of sodium to the mass of chlorine is 46 : 71. Suppose a sample of salt contains 142 g of chlorine. What is the total mass of the salt?

1. Think About the Problem.

(a) Think of what you are to find.
- the mass of salt

(b) Think of what you are given.
- The ratio of sodium to chlorine is 46 : 71.
- There are 142 g of chlorine in the sample.

2. Think About a Strategy.

(a) Think of a strategy you could use.
- Find the mass of sodium in the sample.
- Find the total mass of sodium and chlorine.

(b) Think of a reason for your strategy.
- A proportion can be set up to find the mass of sodium.

"One atom of sodium forms with another atom of chlorine to form salt."

3. Work it Out.

Let d represent the mass, in grams, of sodium.

Think: You can use a proportion.

Thus, $$\frac{46}{71} = \frac{d}{142}$$

Compare

$$\frac{46 \times 2}{71 \times 2} = \frac{92}{142}$$

Thus, $d = 92$.

Therefore, the mass of sodium is 92 g.

4. Think About Your Solution.

The total mass of salt is 142 g + 92 g or 234 g.
- Can you verify your solution?
- Is your solution reasonable?
- Can you solve the problem another way?
- How can a calculator help you solve the problem?
- What other questions should you ask when you think about your solution?

B   Use your *Problem Solving Plan*.

1. The basic substances of sand are silicon and oxygen. The ratio of their masses is $7 : 4$.

   (a) Solve the proportion $\dfrac{7}{11} = \dfrac{y}{550}$.

   (b) Interpret your ratio in (a). What mass of silicon is in 550 kg of sand?

   (c) How can you use the proportion $\dfrac{4}{11} = \dfrac{x}{550}$ to find the mass of oxygen in 550 kg of sand?

2. Nitrous oxide (laughing gas) consists of nitrogen and oxygen. Their masses are in the ratio $7 : 4$. Work with a partner.

   (a) What mass of oxygen is in a container if there are 770 g of nitrogen?

   (b) What is the total mass of laughing gas in a container if there are 770 g of oxygen?

3. Mothballs are made of hydrogen and carbon. The ratio of the mass of hydrogen to the mass of carbon is $1 : 15$. Work with a partner.

   (a) What mass of carbon is there if there are 1200 g of hydrogen?

   (b) Describe how you think you can find the amount of carbon and hydrogen in 1200 g of mothballs.

   (c) Use your process in (b). What mass of hydrogen and oxygen is in 1200 g of mothballs?

4. The metal used for making bells consists of copper and tin mixed in the ratio $4 : 1$. What mass of copper is in a bell that has a mass of 625 kg?

5. Brass is made from copper and zinc mixed in the ratio $17 : 3$. What mass of zinc is in 500 kg of brass?

C

6. Salt consists of sodium and chlorine in the ratio $46 : 71$.

   (a) How much chlorine is in a box of common salt whose mass is 150 g?

   (b) What percent of salt is sodium?

MAKING CONNECTIONS

The following shows some common substances and their molecular structure.
- salt (NaCl)   • water (H_2O)   • dry ice (CO_2)

(a) Draw a diagram you can use to represent each substance.

(b) Create a problem based on the substance. Solve your problem and have others in the class solve your problem.

(c) Choose some common molecules of your own. Find the ratio of atoms in the molecule. Create problems based on your molecules. Solve your problems. Compare your problems with others in the class.

Abasketball court is shown below. The illustration is drawn so that the basketball court has a scale of 1 cm represents 2 m. The players on the court are represented by letters. The players on one team are A, B, C, D, and E. The players on the other team are V, W, X, Y, and Z. Use the illustration to answer the following questions.

1. Calculate the length of
    (a) the basketball court.
    (b) the foul line.
    (c) the distance from the foul line to the outside centre circle.
    (d) the distance from one backboard to the other.

2. A ball is thrown from Rick Fox (W) to Michael Jordan (V). What is the actual distance the ball travels?

3. How far apart are the players?
    (a) A, B   (b) B, E   (c) B, V   (d) C, X

4. For a foul shot, the players line up along each side of the foul area. How far apart are the facing players?

5. Mike Smrek (A) obtains the ball and passes to Jay Triano (B). How far does the ball travel?

6. How far would Jerry (Z) need to go to cover West (E)?

7. (a) In your journal, describe how the basketball game shown in the picture could be proceeding. Describe which team you think has the ball and why you think they have it.
    (b) In your story in (a), also include how you think ratios can be used in the game and some problems that someone else could solve based on your story.

8. How far is each player from his opponent's basket?

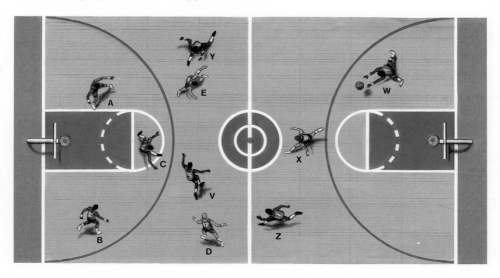

7.12 EXPLORING RATE

You use a **ratio** to compare quantities that are alike. To compare unlike quantities, you will use a **rate**. Work together to complete the following exploration.

EXPLORATION   *Work with a Partner*

Knowing about rates is helpful for understanding data that you see in newspapers, magazines, and other sources of information.

(a) In the pictures below, what is meant by each caption? Discuss with your partner.

(b) In your journal, interpret the rate given in the captions.

(c) Find other pictures of your own. In your journal, write a rate to describe an event in each of your pictures.

The fastest speed reached by a train is 515 km/h.

A horse once reached a speed of 69 km/h.

MOTOCROSS BIKE RENTAL
$25.00/h

J.R. Richard once pitched a baseball over 180 km/h.

...out ratios, you compared quantities expressed in the same units. A **rate** ...e quantities expressed in different units.

...aid $5.90 for each hour worked.

dollar   time

different units

You write this rate as $5.90/h. This rate is called the unit rate because we refer to the amount of pay for each hour worked.

Just as you write ratios in simplest terms, you may write rates in simplest terms. For example, flower seeds are planted at a nursery at the following rate.

400 g of seed for 100 m² of soil
or 4 g of seed for 1 m² of soil

Thus $\dfrac{400}{100} = \dfrac{4}{1}$.

Thus, in simplest terms, the rate is 4 g/m².

The following are other rates with which you are probably familiar.
- 50 m/s reads as "fifty metres per second"
- 60 km/h reads as "sixty kilometres per hour"

ACTIVITY

(a) In your journal, record other similar rates with which you are familiar. Describe how you would read them.
(b) Refer to newspapers and magazines. Find other rates and start a class collage.

Knowing about rate can help you solve problems.

EXAMPLE

A jet can travel a distance of 1395 km in 3 h. What distance would the jet (flying at the same rate) travel in 7 h?

SOLUTION

Let the distance covered be d km.
Write the proportion.

$$\frac{d}{7} = \frac{1395}{3}$$

$$\frac{3d}{21} = \frac{7 \times 1395}{21}$$

Think:
Denominators are equal.
Compare numerators.

$$3d = 9765$$
$$d = 3255$$

Make a final statement.

The distance travelled is 3255 km.

A Review how you can read unit rates.

1. Write each rate.
   (a) Margaret walks 20 m in 10 s.
   (b) The printer produces 1200 sheets in 30 s.

2. At the annual Fun Run in Brandon, the tallies shown to the right were kept for the participants. Write each rate in laps per minute.

   (a)
   (b)
   (c)

Runner	Number of laps around the track	Time taken in minutes
Brenda	28	28
Nancy	30	25
Bernice	20	16

3. A minibike travels 40 km/h.
   (a) How far will it travel in 2 h 15 min?
   (b) How long will it take to travel 800 km?

B Work with a partner. Use a calculator.

4. Your heart beats 75 times in a minute. How many times does your heart beat in one day?

5. The post office sorts 480 letters each minute. How many letters per second are sorted?

6. A short story of 4500 words was typed in 3 h. What was the rate of typing?

7. A section of land, 400 m² in area, is used for trees and costs $20 000. Calculate the total cost per square metre.

8. Joe's compact car consumed 200 L of gasoline to travel 2500 km. Calculate the rate of fuel consumption in litres per 100 km.

9. Do you and your family dry your hair using a hair blower?
   (a) How much does one kilowatt of electricity cost in your home?
   (b) How much do you think it costs to dry your hair each year?

C

10. Jason can type 234 words in 6 min.
    (a) Estimate how long it will take Jason to type the words on this page.
    (b) Explain to your partner how you arrived at your estimate.

11. Water flows from a garden hose at the rate of 20 L/min. How long will it take to fill the tank shown?

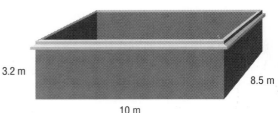

3.2 m

8.5 m

10 m

You often see different advertisements for similar products. To determine which is the better buy, you calculate the unit cost.

When you calculate the unit cost, you are finding the amount of money you would pay for one item, one gram, one litre, and so on. The unit cost for each tube of toothpaste is shown below.

FRESH BRIGHT TOOTHPASTE
75 mL Tube

SMILE BRIGHT TOOTHPASTE
125 mL Tube

Fresh Bright
75 mL costs $0.99.
1 mL costs $\frac{\$0.99}{75}$ or $0.0132/mL.

Smile Bright
125 mL costs $1.49.
1 mL costs $\frac{1.49}{125}$ or $0.01192/mL.

Based on the ads, the Smile Bright is the better buy.

ACTIVITY

The unit price is one consideration. However, there are others.
(a) In your journal describe under what conditions you would travel 15 km to purchase an item that is cheaper than one in your area.
(b) Under what conditions would you not? Give examples to help your explanation.

EXERCISE

 Review your skills with rate.

1. For each of the following, calculate the cost of one item (the unit cost).
   (a) 4 tins of chocolate pudding cost $2.38.
   (b) 5 packages of pizza mix for $5.69.
   (c) A case of 8 one-litre cans of apple juice for $11.95.
   (d) A 4-roll package of paper towels for $1.69.
   (e) A 24-can case of soft drinks for $6.99.

2. For each advertisement at the right, estimate the unit cost. Check your estimate with a calculator.

NECTARINES
6 *for* 55¢

STYROFOAM CUPS
Pkg. of 51
2 *for* $1.00

CHOCOLATE COVERED COOKIES
Package of 30
$1.49

3. Jane and Tony fill their gas tanks with gasoline. The cost for each fill up is shown on the pump.
   (a) Find the cost per litre.
   (b) Which gas costs less?
   (c) In your journal describe whether cost alone is the reason for buying one gasoline instead of another. Give reasons for your answer.

4. Store A sells 6 packages of milk shake mix for $1.75. Store B sells 4 packages of milk shake mix for $1.19.
   (a) Calculate the unit price at Store A.
   (b) Calculate the unit price at Store B.
   (c) Which store has the better buy?
   (d) Store C offers 24 packages for $6.75. Is this price better than the prices at stores A and B? Give reasons for your answer.

5. From the advertisements below, estimate the better buy. How can you check your estimate?
   (a)   (b)

Hilary

3-hole-punched
400 sheets ruled

Refill
$1.99

SCOTT PAPER

Refills 3-Hole
500 sheets ruled

$2¹⁹

6. Find different advertisements for two similar items.
   (a) Find the better buy.
   (b) Create a class collage of the ads. Create problems of your own based on the collage. Solve your problems.
   (c) In your journal, describe why you think stores have sales like these.

7. Copy and cut out the shapes below.
   (a) Construct a square using pieces 1 to 4.
   (b) Construct a square using pieces 1 to 5.

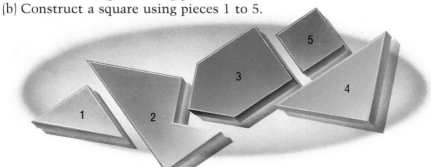

Did you know that certain types of birds have been clocked at speeds in excess of 170 km/h?

There are many more amazing facts from the world of nature which involve the study of rate. The exercise that follows introduces you to a few of them.

EXERCISE

B   Review your skills with rate.

1. The greatest amount of rain to fall in 1 min occurred in Maryland on July 4, 1965, at which time 31 mm fell. If the rain had continued to fall at this rate, how much would have fallen in
    (a) 5 min?   (b) 1 h?

2. Panama recorded the greatest amount of rain to fall in 5 min in 1911. During that time 63 mm fell. How much would the water level have risen in a pool if it had rained at this rate for 1 hr? Express your answer to the nearest tenth of a metre.

3. The greatest rainfall ever recorded in one year was 22 990 mm in India in 1861.
    (a) How many metres is this?
    (b) What was the average monthly rainfall in 1861?

4. Diamonds and pearls are measured in carats. The carat is a unit of mass equal to 0.2 g.
    (a) What is the mass of a 3-carat diamond?
    (b) Find the mass of a 5.5-carat diamond.

5. The cat's heartbeat is recorded at 35 beats in 15 s.
    (a) How many times does the cat's heart beat per minute?
    (b) A dog has a heartbeat rate of 70 beats in 40 s. Which has the faster heartbeat, a dog or a cat?

6. Refer to the chart at the left.
    (a) Calculate the speeds of the animals in metres per second.
    (b) In 4 h, how much further will a lion run than an elephant?
    (c) In 5 h, how much further will a squirrel run than a pig?

Animal	Approximate speed (km/h)
Cat	50
Cheetah	110
Elk	70
Elephant	40
Lion	50
Pig	15
Rabbit	55
Squirrel	20

7.16 WORKING WITH PERCENT

Each day, you see ideas involving percent. You can use your skills with percent to solve problems.

EXAMPLE 1

During a trip down the Amazon, Dana canoed 36 km and portaged 4 km.
(a) Write a decimal number to show the part of the trip taken by canoe.
(b) Write a percent to show the part of the trip taken by canoe.

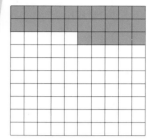

YOU ALREADY KNOW...

- Percent means "per hundred." The symbol "%" is used to show "parts of 100."
- In the diagram, 25% of the squares are shaded. You can compare the number of squares shaded to total squares as 25 : 100.

SOLUTION

(a) **As a Decimal Number**

$$\frac{\text{distance by canoe}}{\text{total distance}} = \frac{36}{40}$$
$$= 0.90$$

$\boxed{\text{c}}$ $\boxed{36}$ $\boxed{\div}$ $\boxed{40}$ $\boxed{=}$ 0.90

Thus, 0.90 of the trip was taken by canoe.

(b) **As a Percent**

$$\frac{\text{distance by canoe}}{\text{total distance}} \times 100 = \frac{36}{40} \times 100$$
$$= 90$$

$\boxed{\text{c}}$ $\boxed{36}$ $\boxed{\div}$ $\boxed{40}$ $\boxed{\%}$ 90

Thus, 90% of the trip was by canoe.

Sometimes, to solve a problem, you need to find the percent of a number.

EXAMPLE 2

Did you know that 2% of the world's rain forests are destroyed each year? There are about 10 000 000 km^2 of rain forests on the earth. How many square kilometres of rain forests are destroyed each year?

SOLUTION

2% of 10 000 000
= 0.02 × 10 000 000
= 200 000

$\boxed{\text{c}}$ $\boxed{0.02}$ $\boxed{\times}$ $\boxed{10000000}$ $\boxed{=}$ 200000

Thus, there are about 200 000 km^2 of rain forests destroyed each year.

ACTIVITY

In your journal:
(a) Describe why you think the rain forests are important.
(b) Decide how many years it will take the rain forests to be destroyed completely.
(c) Discuss why the rain forests are being destroyed. What can be done to save them?

A Round each number to one decimal place.

1. Interpret each of the following. Use a 10×10 grid to help you. Then write a ratio for each percent.

    (a) 2%   (b) 12%   (c) 25%   (d) 2.5%   (e) 12.1%   (f) $13\frac{1}{2}$%

2. Write each percent as a decimal number.
    (a) 25%   (b) 37%   (c) 8%   (d) 63.5%   (e) 75.5%   (f) 3.7%

3. Write each decimal number as a percent.
    (a) 0.39   (b) 0.75   (c) 0.47   (d) 0.8   (e) 0.31   (f) 0.01

4. Write each of the following as a percent.

    (a) $\frac{7}{10}$ (b) $\frac{29}{100}$ (c) $\frac{4}{5}$ (d) $\frac{6}{25}$ (e) $\frac{24}{100}$ (f) $\frac{1}{5}$

5. Find the percentage of each number.
    (a) 4% of 160   (b) 5% of 60   (c) 9% of 80   (d) 69% of 1850

B Refer to the Self Evaluation feature.

6. What percent is each of the following?
    (a) one centimetre of one metre   (b) one milligram of one gram
    (c) one gram of one kilogram   (d) one centilitre of one litre

7. For a trip, 36 km was by canoe and 2 km was by portage.
    (a) What percent was by portage?   (b) What percent was by canoe?

8. (a) In the pulp and paper industry, it has been determined that 100 L of water is used to produce 1 kg of paper. What percent of 500 L of water is used to produce 1 kg of paper?
    (b) Find information of your own about the pulp and paper industry. Create a problem of your own using the data.

9. In Canada, about 77% of the population have telephones. The population of Canada is about 28 000 000. About how many telephones are there in Canada?

10. Of 139 foreign publications, 7 are printed in Portuguese and 15 in Italian.
    (a) What percent are in Portuguese?
    (b) What percent are in Italian?

SELF EVALUATION

In this chapter, you have worked with ratio, rate, and percent.
(a) How are the skills for working with these alike? How are they different?
(b) Give an example of your own to illustrate your answers in (a).
(c) If you have difficulty in (a) or (b), how can you use this book to help you improve your understanding of these skills?

11. The total length of the Trans-Canada Highway is 7871 km.
    (a) If 5.77% of the highway is in Alberta, how many kilometres are in Alberta?
    (b) If 8.3% of the highway is in Saskatchewan, how many kilometres are in Saskatchewan?

12. In the United Kingdom, 38% of the people own telephones, but in Cuba only 3% of the people have them. If Cuba's population is 10 million and there are a total of 55.8 million people in the United Kingdom, how many more telephones are there in the United Kingdom than in Cuba?

13. Suppose 30% of the people in Canada buy books. In Niagara Falls, which has 70 500 people, how many people would buy books?

14. Suppose 20% of Canadians borrow the books they read from a friend. If Alberta has a population of 1 900 000 people, how many Albertans borrow the books they read?

15. Only 15% of Canadians borrow books from the library. If the population of Vancouver is 1 172 200, how many Vancouverites would borrow their books from the library?

16. For a summer camp, 25 people arrived by train, 36 people arrived by bus, 6 people arrived by plane, and 120 people arrived by car.
    (a) What percent came by train?
    (b) What percent came by car?
    (c) What percent did not come by bus?
    (d) Use the information in (a), (b), and (c) to calculate what percent came by plane.

17. The mass of a knife is the same as the mass of 2 spoons. Three spoons have the same mass as a knife and a fork. A plate has the same mass as a knife and a spoon. A fork has a mass of 11 g.
    (a) What percent of the mass of a plate is the mass of a fork?
    (b) Find other percents using the utensils.

MAKING CONNECTIONS

Most of the water your body needs is obtained by drinking it. However, water also makes up much of the food you eat. Refer to the graph.
(a) Estimate the mass of water in 1.5 kg of each item given in the graph.
(b) Calculate the mass of each item that is water.
(c) Find other foods of your own. Find the percent of water in each food. Redraw the bar graph using your foods.

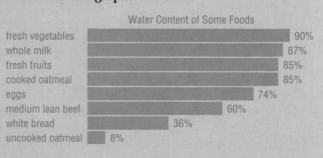

Water Content of Some Foods

fresh vegetables 90%
whole milk 87%
fresh fruits 85%
cooked oatmeal 85%
eggs 74%
medium lean beef 60%
white bread 36%
uncooked oatmeal 8%

7.17 CRITICAL THINKING: MAKING DECISIONS

Suppose a survey showed that 30%, or 165, of those surveyed use public transportation each day. How many people were surveyed?

To solve the problem, you need to find 100% of the number. How is this done?

From the survey,
- 30% of the people surveyed is 165.
- 1% of the people surveyed is $\dfrac{165}{30}$.
- 100% of the people is $100 \times \dfrac{165}{30}$ or 550.

Thus, 550 people were surveyed.

To solve a problem, you need to decide which strategy to use.

ACTIVITY

Work with a partner. For each of the following problems,
- decide how they are alike and how they are different.
- decide on the strategies to solve the problems.
- solve the problems and record all observations in your journal.
(a) What percent of 2000 is 1500?
(b) Find 35% of 840.
(c) If 15% of a number is 30, then find the number.

EXERCISE

A   Check whether your answer is reasonable. Refer to the Calculation Sense feature on the next page.

1. What percent is
   (a) 40 of 200 ?   (b) 75 of 225 ?   (c) 35 of 70 ?

2. Find each percent of each number.
   (a) 15% of 400   (b) 6.2% of 36   (c) 125% of 360
   (d) 12.5% of 150   (e) 13.5% of 260   (f) 29.3% of 280

3. (a) If 12% of a number is 630, find the number.
   (b) If 0.1% of a number is 96, find the number.
   (c) If 130% of a number is 585, find the number.
   (d) If 7.5% of a number is 27, find the number.

B   Decide on the strategy you need to use.

4. (a) How would you interpret each of the following questions? Record your interpretations in your journal.
   (b) Solve each problem.

   (i) A banana is about 76% water. If the amount of water in a banana is 114 g, what is the mass of the banana?

   (ii) Out of a mass of 480 g of cereal, there are 21 g of raisins. What percent of the cereal is raisins?

5. Jennifer earned $325 last month working at the Pizza Boat. She spent $165. What percent did she spend?

6. Jeff bought a tennis racquet for $98. If it decreased in value by 25%, by what amount did it decrease in value?

7. In a survey, 35% of the students said they would prefer live bands at school dances. That response was given by 63 students. How many students were surveyed?

8. One day at the school cafeteria, 62.5% of the 192 hot meals served was the daily special. How many daily specials were served?

9. A test result of 80% is considered an "A." On one test, to get an A, you need to receive 52 marks or more. What was the total number of marks on the test?

10. Out of 600 first-time home buyers, 432 arranged their financing through their builder or real estate broker to pay for their homes. What percent is that?

11. Do you know why ice floats? When water freezes its volume increases by about 12%. Find the volume of ice when these amounts of water freeze.
   (a) 100 mL   (b) 150 mL   (c) 600 mL
   (d) 10.2L   (e) 49.2 L   (f) 5.8 L

CALCULATION SENSE

To estimate an answer with percent, you can use mental math skills.

19% of 203   Think: 46% of 3106   Think:

$\frac{1}{5}$ of 200 = 40   50% of 3000 = 1500

1. Estimate each.
   (a) 22% of 50   (b) 47% of 87
   (c) 33% of 155   (d) 22% of 246

2. Estimate each.
   (a) 18% of 4344   (b) 33% of 2088
   (c) 17% of 4883   (d) 46% of 8645

You have probably seen many examples of percents greater than 100%.

Inflation Running At 200%

Profit This Year 125%

RW

RAY SHEPPARD

Trading card collectors often deal with percents greater than 100%.

In 1983, the catalogue value of a card was $36.50. Ten years later, the catalogue price was $80.00. By what percent had the card increased in price?

$$\frac{\text{Increase in Price}}{\text{Price in 1983}} \times 100\%$$

$$= \frac{80.00 - 36.50}{36.50} \times 100\%$$

$$= \frac{43.50}{36.50} \times 100\%$$

$$= 1.19 \times 100\%$$

 C $\boxed{43.5}$ ÷ $\boxed{36.5}$ % $\boxed{119}$

$$= 119\%$$

The increase in value of the card is 119% of the 1983 catalogue value.

In your journal, describe why you think cards like this one increase in value.

EXERCISE

 A Write your answers to one decimal place.

1. Calculate.
   (a) 120% of 450   (b) 140% of 122   (c) 110% of 236   (d) 109% of 480

2. Find each of the following.
   (a) 115% of $270   (b) 109% of 465 m   (c) 175% of 390 kg   (d) 225% of 450 mg

3. (a) Estimate which is greater.   (b) Calculate which is greater.
      (i) 165% of 265 kg   (ii) 120% of 600 kg

4. Which is greater?
   (a) 100% of 200 or 200% of 100   (b) 300% of 200 or 200% of 300

5. At one time, the height of a fir tree was 2.3 m. Since then it has grown by 123%. Calculate how high it is now.

6. When an inflated balloon was blown up more, it expanded to 130% of its original volume. If the original volume was 120 L, estimate the new volume. Then calculate.

7. Jennifer managed a business and received $29 800 last year. This year, her salary is 112% of last year's. What is her salary this year?

8. Thirty years ago, the average family spent approximately $18.60 a week on groceries. The groceries today are 415% of what they were 30 years ago. How much is an average family spending on groceries?

9. A 1948 silver dollar was worth $260 ten years ago. Since then it has appreciated 330% in price. What is the value today?

10. In 1977, a Bobby Orr rookie hockey card was worth $3.75. Today, the card is worth about $200.00. Estimate by what percent the card has increased in value. Then calculate.

11. In 1967, a Babe Ruth baseball card was worth $5.50. The list price of the card in a catalogue is now $465.55. By what percent has the card increased in value?

12. Recently, Andrea received a 1948 dime that her father had been saving for her. She used the dime to pay her tuition of $750.00. By what percent had the dime increased from its original value?

C

13. Some items that can be found at Canadian antique shows are shown in the illustration. The original selling price and the current catalogue price of each antique is labelled.
   (a) By what percent has each antique increased in value?
   (b) Find antiques of your own in a catalogue. Create and solve similar problems using the antiques.

$68/$1200

$55/$725

$9.25/$200

$1.75/$15

$12/$90

$6.50/$55

This section offers many facts and figures about the human body. Before you begin the exercise, work together to complete the following activity.

ACTIVITY

Refer to the diagram at the right showing the proportion of mineral elements in the body.
(a) Create a problem that can be solved using the information.
(b) Compare your problem to those of others in the class. Solve the other problems.

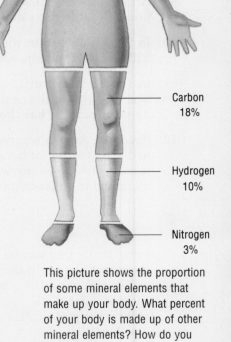

Oxygen 65%

Carbon 18%

Hydrogen 10%

Nitrogen 3%

This picture shows the proportion of some mineral elements that make up your body. What percent of your body is made up of other mineral elements? How do you know?

EXERCISE

B Check that your answers are reasonable.

1. The brain represents about 1.3% of a person's mass. What is the mass of the brain for a human with a body mass of 65 kg?

2. The human body, by mass, is 1.5% calcium.
   (a) If Freddy has a mass of 63 kg, find the amount of calcium in his body.
   (b) Lesley has a mass of 52 kg. Find the amount of calcium in her body.

3. Each minute you are awake, your eye blinks about 25 times. How many times will it blink in
   (a) 1 h?   (b) 1 d?   (c) 1 year?
   (d) Work with a partner. Count the number of times your partner's eyes blink in one minute. Based on this, how reasonable are the answers above?

4. Oxygen is essential for the body to function. About 20.5 cm^3 of oxygen is absorbed in 100 cm^3 of blood. If there are about 6000 cm^3 of blood in your body, about how much oxygen is absorbed?

5. To maintain the health of your body, 750 cm^3 of blood is delivered to your tissues every minute. How much blood is delivered in
   (a) 1 h?   (b) 1 d?   (c) 1 year?

6. Did you know that, by age 2, human beings are 50% of their final height?
   (a) Suppose Bruce, fully grown, is 1.85 m tall. How tall was he at 2 years of age?
   (b) Create a similar problem of your own. Solve your problem. Have others in the class solve your problem.

7. The skin is about 16% of a person's total body mass.
   (a) If Caroline's mass is 40.8 kg, calculate the mass of her skin.
   (b) Gina's mass is 49.2 kg. Calculate the mass of her skin.

8. The surface of the tongue has about 3000 tiny cells called *taste buds*. They tell you if something is sour, sweet, bitter, or salty. The surface area of the tongue is about 38.5 cm^2. How many taste buds are there for every square centimetre?

9. The human body has 206 bones. One quarter of them are in the hands. About how many bones are in the hands?

10. On average, human hair grows at the rate of about 0.35 mm/d.
    (a) How much would you expect hair to grow in 3 weeks?
    (b) If the length of hair is 4.8 cm, how long will it take it to double in length?

11. Blood has 700 times as many red blood cells as white blood cells. In a part of the body, if there are 350 white cells, how many red blood cells would you expect to find?

12. The human circulatory system would stretch 96 000 km if placed end to end.
    (a) If you were to travel 80 km/h, how long would it take you to travel the length of your circulatory system?
    (b) How many days would this trip take you if you travelled non-stop?

13. Are Canadians bony? The bone mass of the average Canadian is 17.5% of the body mass. What is the bone mass for each person with the following body masses?

Grace	96.3 kg	Michelle	87.6 kg
Alicja	62.3 kg	Yuval	103.45 kg

14. For a human being, 43% of the body mass is muscle.
    (a) The mass of muscle that Jolisa has is 25.8 kg. What is her body mass?
    (b) The mass of muscle that Sandra has is 21.5 kg. What is her body mass?

15. Digital numbers are based on straight lines. The number 8 is shown here.
    (a) Use the lines to show how the numerals 0 – 9 are drawn.
    (b) Which line would be used the greatest percent of the time?
    (c) Create and solve a similar problem of your own. Compare your problem to others in the class.

1. Write
   (a) $\frac{3}{4}$ as a percent.
   (b) 70% as a fraction.
   (c) 49% as a decimal.
   (d) $\frac{4}{5}$ as a percent.

2. Write the ratio for each rate in simplest terms.
   (a) Crude oil flows at a rate of 20 L in 15 min.
   (b) 45 hot dogs were sold in 25 min.

3. Write each ratio in lowest terms.
   (a) There are 2 card collectors for every 20 people.
   (b) Out of every 12 flights from Vancouver, 3 go to Montreal.
   (c) Four out of every 16 bales of fibreglass are used for home insulation.

4. (a) At the last card show she attended, Jen sold 45 cards. She had 90 cards. What percent of her collection did she sell?
   (b) Out of 180 school days, Margaret was absent for 5% of them. How many days was she absent?

5. During the year, a school required 15 kg of chalk for 26 classrooms. Portable classrooms have been added and the number of classrooms is now 34. How much chalk should the school order for the coming year?

6. The average Canadian watches 1200 h of television each year. How many hours would the average Canadian watch in one day? in one week? in one month?

7. Of the 38 forest fires started last year, 25 were caused by carelessness. Of the 52 house fires started over the same period, 37 were caused by carelessness. Is the percent of the forest fires started by carelessness greater than the percent of the house fires? Give reasons for your answer.

8. A company's earning for this month increased 16.5% over last month. If the earnings were $980 000 for last month, find this month's earnings.

THINKING ABOUT

❶ Pick three skills from this chapter. Write a problem to be solved that needs these three skills. Solve your problem and have others in the class solve your problem.

❷ Use Question 5 on this page. Explain another way to solve the problem. Compare your method with others in your class. What method do you prefer?

❸ Where did you use ratio, rate, and percent before you began this chapter? Where do you think you will use it in the future?

MAKING CONNECTIONS

Refer to the opening page of this chapter.
(a) Use the picture to help you write a problem that can be solved using the skills in this chapter.
(b) Compare your problem with others in your class. Solve the other problems.

❹ Pick any problem on this page. Explain to your partner how it can be solved.

❺ Which questions on these two pages can you solve mentally?

❻ Use the following terms in a paragraph: ratio, rate, and percent.

MATH JOURNAL

Look back at your journal entries to date.
- Is there anything you need to follow up on?
- How have your feelings about mathematics changed?

SELF EVALUATION

1. Find the missing value in each of the following.
   (a) $\dfrac{m}{8} = \dfrac{30}{12}$ (b) $\dfrac{2}{5} = \dfrac{n}{10}$ (c) $\dfrac{3}{15} = \dfrac{4}{p}$

2. Write each rate in simplest form.
   (a) Jennifer jogs 15 m in 6 s.
   (b) 32 pizzas were delivered in 8 h.

3. Write a percent for each of the following.
   (a) 12 out of 16 fast food outlets serve hamburgers.
   (b) 14 out of 25 service stations have vending machines.

4. (a) What is the value of x if the ratios $12 : 3$ and $x : 30$ are equivalent?
   (b) The number of bales of hay needed is given by the missing term for the equivalent ratios $m : 16$ and $3 : 8$.

5. A Boeing 727 aircraft is drawn using the scale 1 cm represents 5.9 m.
   (a) What is the length of the actual wing span if it measures 5.6 cm on the drawing?
   (b) What is the length of the plane on the diagram if the actual length of the plane is 46.6 m?

6. The world's most powerful rapids are the Nakwakto Rapids, Slingsky Channel, British Columbia. They can flow at a rate of 29.6 km/h. How long would it take you to travel 1 km in these rapids? What assumptions have you made?

7. Jacques bought a new mountain bike. The regular price was $235, but there was a 20% discount offered. How much would Jacques pay in total if he bought the bicycle in your province?

8. Jason studied typing during the first half of the school year. In his first test, he averaged 12 words per minute. At the end of the term, he could type 38 words per minute. By what percent had he increased his typing speed?

9. The staff of the General M Store had its Christmas party at the restaurant. The restaurant adds on a 15% gratuity (tip) to the amount spent. What is the total amount of the bill if $485.25 was spent?

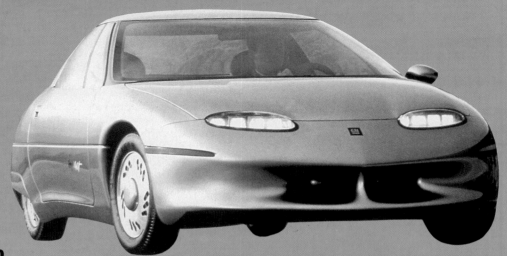

Did you know that a typical car "wastes" about 85% of the gasoline it consumes by converting the gasoline to heat instead of work? The electric car is one way of combatting this problem.

Recently, General Motors unveiled what could be "the car that makes the greatest splash since the 1965 Mustang or the Model T Ford." The Impact is a two-seater car that is equipped with many features, including a stereo system and air-conditioning.

This General Motors Impact (prototype) can:
- Accelerate from 0 to 100 km/h in 7.9 s.
- Reach a top speed of 176 km/h.
- Travel almost 200 km on an 8 h battery charge. The cost to charge the battery will cost about the same as 2 L of fuel.

EXERCISE

1. Suppose you own a car whose gas tank has a capacity of 50 L. How many litres in a full gas tank are converted to heat and not to work?

2. At top speed, how long will it take the Impact to lose its power?

3. (a) Estimate the percent of car trips you think are less than 200 km.
   (b) Refer to your estimate in (a). Do you think an electric car like the Impact will be a good-selling car? Give reasons for your answer.
   (c) Suppose you are president of General Motors. At what price would you sell the car? Why?

4. Find out more about this prototype car. Create problems based on what you find out. Solve your problems and have others in the class solve your problems.

MAKING CONNECTIONS: PERCENT 8

How might you use percent in this part-time job?

What decisions do you need to make when you deposit money?

What percent of your time do you spend on hobbies or other interests?

15% OFF
Reg. $650.00

25% OFF
Reg. $249.99

YOU ALREADY KNOW...

- How to calculate percent.
- How to calculate the percent of a number.

Before doing this exploration, list situations in which you may have used your skills with percent.

EXPLORATION *Work with a Partner*

Suppose you wanted to purchase one of the bicycles shown above.

1. (a) Describe how you could calculate the final prices.
   (b) Use your description in (a). Calculate the final sale price for each bike.

2. When calculating the actual price you pay, what are some of the considerations? Answer the following to help you.
   (a) What is the provincial sales tax for your province?
   (b) What is the Goods and Services tax for Canada?
   (c) How do you calculate the actual cost you pay?

3. Suppose you are the manager of a bicycle store.
   (a) Why would you have a sale on bicycles?
   (b) How would you determine what items to put on sale?
   (c) How would you determine what percent to discount the items?
   (d) Signs such as the following often appear in stores. Why do you think this is so?
       "ALL SALES FINAL"   "NO CHEQUES"

4. Find advertisements in newspapers and magazines where percent is involved.
   (a) Start a class collage of these pictures.
   (b) Create a problem that can be solved using the ads. Solve it. Compare your problem with others in the class.

8.2 SALES TAX

Suppose you own a tropical fish store in British Columbia. A customer wants to buy these items.

Aquarium	$38.75
Light	$19.65
Thermometer	$2.69
Pump	$36.75

To calculate the total cost, you need to add the provincial sales tax (PST) and the Goods and Services tax (GST). Refer to the sales taxes shown. Notice that in British Columbia, the provincial sales tax is 6%. In each province, the Goods and Services tax is 7%.

Total Price	$97.84	Think:
PST:	$5.87	0.06 × 97.84
GST:	$6.85	0.07 × 97.84
TOTAL	$110.56	

Thus, the total cost is $110.56.

EXERCISE

A Refer to the list of sales taxes shown.

1. Estimate which amount, A or B, is the correct amount of PST on each item purchased in Saskatchewan.

			A	B
(a)	cassette tape	$1.89	13¢	90¢
(b)	calculator	$19.90	$1.39	95¢
(c)	ski jacket	$69.00	$3.45	$4.83

2. Calculate the provincial sales tax for each item in Manitoba.
   (a) a camping stove that costs $56.00
   (b) a sleeping bag that sells for $29.50

3. Cash register receipts from all provinces are shown here.
   (a) How can you decide which tax is PST and which tax is GST?
   (b) In which provinces are PST and GST calculated separately?
   (c) In which provinces is PST calculated on top of GST?
   (d) For those provinces that calculate GST and PST separately, how is the PST calculated?

B Round your answers as needed.

4. (a) Calculate the sales taxes on a cassette that costs $7.95 in Manitoba.
   (b) Find the total cost of the cassette.

5. The price of a pair of jeans in Québec is $36.95. Find the total cost of the jeans.

6. (a) What is the total cost of a computer desk that sells for $145.99 in Alberta?
   (b) How much change would you receive if you pay with two $100 bills?

7. A t-shirt costs $27 in British Columbia. Find the amount of change you would receive from a $50 bill.

GROUP PROJECT

Some items have the Goods and Services tax applied, while others do not.
(a) What determines whether or not an item is taxed?
(b) Construct a survey to determine how people feel about the way items are taxed. Do they think some items should not be taxed at all? If so, which items do they think should not be taxed? Why?
(c) Present your results to the rest of the class.

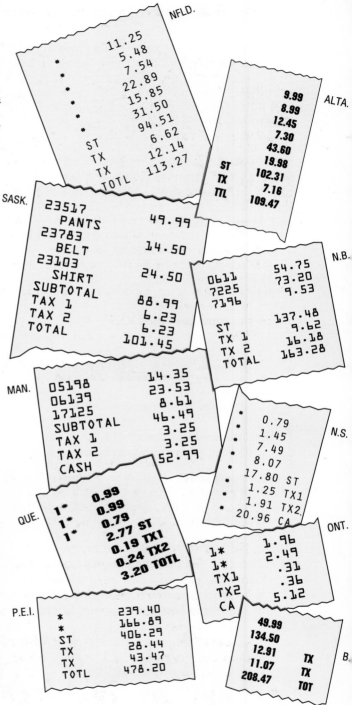

258

8. (a) In which province do you think each item was bought?
   (b) Calculate the total cost of each item, based on your answer above.

9. On a trip to New Brunswick, Joanne bought an aquarium filter for $29.35 including taxes.
   (a) What is the provincial sales tax in New Brunswick?
   (b) How can you calculate the actual cost of the filter?
   (c) Calculate the original cost of the filter.

10. (a) Calculate the total cost in your province of a colour television that has a list price of $495.98.
    (b) In which province will you spend the least for the television?
    (c) How much less will you pay in the province in (b) than in British Columbia?

11. Suppose Joe bought $106.75 worth of taxable items in your store. He returned an item with a list price of $8.75. How much of a refund will Joe receive in all? What assumptions have you made?

C

12. Identify in which province(s) each item was obtained.
    (a) headphones priced at $49.95 for a total cost of $57.45
    (b) a package of blank disks priced at $29.50 for a total cost of $33.34
    (c) two cans of paint priced at $24.50 per can for a total cost of $57.67
    (d) six rolls of wallpaper priced at $12.75 per roll for a total of $87.22

13. (a) Play this game with a partner.
    Rule 1 Line up ten pennies in a row so that the space between each penny is slightly less than a penny's diameter.
    Rule 2 Take turns pushing a penny through the row. Each time you touch a penny in the row, remove it. If you touch two pennies at the same time, remove them both.
    Rule 3 The player who removes the most pennies is the winner.
    (b) Develop a strategy that can be used to win the game.
    (c) How can you use your skills with collecting data and percent to select the strategy?

8.3 PROBLEM SOLVING: USING A TABLE

At a part-time job, you may need to calculate the GST using a table. The chart shows the Goods and Services tax on any amount from $0.00 to $99.99. You read the table as shown.

Find the GST on a purchase of $32.59.

tax on $30 + tax on $2 + tax on 59¢

GST = $2.10 + $0.14 + $0.04
     = $2.28

Goods and Services Tax Table

Amount	Sales Tax	Amount	Sales Tax	Amount	Sales Tax
0.00 – 0.07	0.00	1.00	0.07	10.00	0.70
0.08 – 0.21	0.01	2.00	0.14	20.00	1.40
0.22 – 0.35	0.02	3.00	0.21	30.00	2.10
0.36 – 0.49	0.03	4.00	0.28	40.00	2.80
0.50 – 0.64	0.04	5.00	0.35	50.00	3.50
0.65 – 0.78	0.05	6.00	0.42	60.00	4.20
0.79 – 0.92	0.06	7.00	0.49	70.00	4.90
0.93 – 1.07	0.07	8.00	0.56	80.00	5.60
		9.00	0.63	90.00	6.30

ACTIVITY   Work in a Small Group

(a) Create a table similar to the one above for the provincial sales tax in your province.
(b) Create an example of your own to show how the table works.
(c) In your journal, describe the patterns that can help you create the table.

EXERCISE

B   Use the GST table above and the PST table you created to find the total cost in your province.

1. What is the total tax payable on each item?
   (a) scarf $5.00   (b) comb $0.79   (c) shoes $52.00
   (d) skates $89.95   (e) socks $2.29   (f) tracksuit $42.85

2. Sherri bought a blouse for $25.00.
   (a) Calculate the total tax payable.   (b) Calculate the total cost of the blouse.

3. Chris bought a sweater on sale for $32.95. How much change will he get from $40?

4. A three-ring binder sells for $4.95. A packet of paper costs $0.99. Find the total cost of both items.

5. (a) Each item shown was advertised in the newspaper. Find the total cost of each item.
   (b) Choose items of your own from the newspaper. Find the total cost of each.

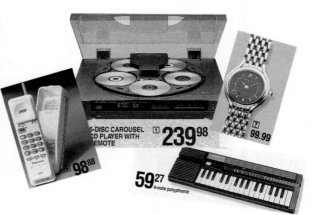

5-DISC CAROUSEL CD PLAYER WITH REMOTE   **239**⁹⁸

99.99

98⁸⁸

59²⁷ 4-note polyphonic

8.4 PERCENT IN PURCHASES

B and B Music has a sale on all cassette tapes. Each cassette tape is being sold for 25% off the regular price.

A sale of 25% off means that you save 25¢ on every dollar of the regular price.

> How much does the Jeff Healey Band cassette, shown, cost?

You can calculate the cost of the tape as follows.

Regular Price	$8.99
Discount 25%	$2.25
Selling Price	$6.74

This is 75% of the regular price.

If you know the selling price and the discount, you can work backwards to find the regular price.

EXAMPLE

The sale price on an all-terrain bike is $129.20. The discount is 20%. What was the regular selling price?

SOLUTION

Rate of Discount   20%   Sale Price = $129.20

Thus, $129.20 is 80% of regular price.

Regular Price $\dfrac{129.20}{0.8} = 161.5$

Think: The denominator in the example above is found as follows:
100% − Rate of Discount

$\boxed{C}$ 129.2 $\boxed{\div}$ 80 $\boxed{\%}$ $\boxed{=}$ 161.5

Thus, the regular price of the all-terrain bike is $161.50.

A Review your skills with percent.

1. What is the amount of discount if each item sells for 20% off?
   (a) backpack $36.80 (b) snorkel $53.95 (c) video tape $16.95

2. For each item, calculate the amount of discount and the sale price.
   (a) Headphones selling for $23.95 are 20% off.
   (b) A tennis racket selling for $136.90 is 35% off.

3. Calculate the sale price for each item.

   (a)
   Save 14%
   Shoes
   Regularly
   $49.98

   (b)
   Save 43%
   Phaser multi-function alarm chronograph
   Regularly
   $59.99

B Use a calculator. Estimate to check whether your answer is reasonable.

4. An $85.00 coat is on sale for $33\frac{1}{3}$% off the regular price.
   (a) What is the amount of discount? (b) What is the sale price of the coat?

5. Lori bought an 18-speed bicycle at a 35%-off sale. The regular price was $295.50. Find the sale price.

6. The regular price of a computer program is $165.00. The discount on the program is $29.70.
   (a) What percent of the selling price is the discount?
   (b) In your journal, describe why you think the manager of a computer store would offer a discount on a program.

7. Refer to the cassettes on the previous page.
   (a) Find the actual cost of all the cassettes.
   (b) Find other discounts from ads in newspapers. Find the actual cost of these items.

MAKING CONNECTIONS: MUSIC STORES

   (a) Refer to newspapers and magazines and find examples of sales for compact discs and cassette tapes. Verify that the final sale prices are correct.
   (b) Suppose you are the manager of a music store. What percent discount would you give on "new arrival" tapes and CDs? Give reasons for your answer.
   (c) By what percent would you expect your business to increase by giving the discount? Give reasons for your answer.
   (d) Create a problem of your own using the above information. Solve the problem.
   (e) Contact a local music store to find out how reasonable your answers are.

A manufacturer of audio-visual equipment might sell a CD player to a retail store for a *cost price* of $215.50. The manufacturer also gives the store a *suggested list selling price* of $350.00.

When a store puts an item on sale, it still needs to make a profit. Thus, the discount is applied to the suggested list price. If the discount is 15%, you can find the selling price and the *profit* the store still makes as follows.

Suggested List Price	$350.00
Discount 15%	$52.50
Selling Price	$297.50

c 350 × 15 % = 52.5

The amount of profit is $297.50 − $215.50 or $82.00.

The percent profit is $\dfrac{82.00}{215.50} \times 100\%$ or about 38%.

1. Copy and complete the chart.

Item	Suggested List Price	Rate of Discount	Cost Price	Selling Price	Profit	Percent Profit
Batteries	$86.50	15%	$50.00	?	?	?
Tires	$52.40	12%	$40.00	?	?	?
Telephone	$129.80	20%	$80.00	?	?	?
Tape Deck	$169.30	23%	$105.00	?	?	?

2. The suggested list price of a boom box is $129.50. The cost price to the retailer is $75.00.
   (a) Suppose the store sells the boom box for 25% off. What is the selling price?
   (b) What profit does the store make?
   (c) Calculate the percent profit.

3. The suggested list price of a computer printer is $230. The cost price to the retailer is $165.
   (a) Suppose the store sells the printer for 15% off. Find the selling price.
   (b) What profit does the store make?

4. The suggested list price of a tennis racquet is $119.80.
   (a) Calculate the rate of discount if the amount of discount is $29.95.
   (b) What is the selling price?
   (c) The cost price is 60% of the suggested list price. What is the profit?
   (d) Calculate the percent profit. What assumptions have you made?

5. Kay's Hardware store buys drills for $25 each and then sells them for $36.99 each.
   (a) What profit does the store make on the sale of each drill?
   (b) If the store wanted to realize a profit of 55%, what should the selling price of each drill be?

In 1985, about 0.776 billion people lived in cities with populations of more than 1 000 000 people. It has been estimated that by the year 2020, these cities will have a total of 2.2 billion people. What is the projected *percent change* in the population of these cities?

Step 1   Find the projected increase.

$$2.200 \text{ billion} - 0.776 \text{ billion} = 1.424 \text{ billion}$$

Step 2   Find the percent change as follows.

$$\frac{\text{projected increase}}{\text{current population}} \times 100\% = \frac{1.424}{0.776} \times 100\%$$

$$= 183.5\%$$

The percent change by the year 2020 is projected to be almost 184%.

ACTIVITY   *Work in Small Groups*

The above problem suggests that large cities will continue to grow. Answer each of the following in your journal.

(a) Make a list of some cities that have more than 1 000 000 people. Do you think each of the cities on your list will continue to grow at the rate projected above? Give reasons for your answer.

(b) Write a short paragraph to describe how you think one of your cities will look in the year 2020. Discuss some of the advantages and disadvantages of this growth as it might affect the environment. Would you like to be mayor of such a city?

EXERCISE

 A   Review your skills with percent.

1. About 4 billion of the world's 5.2 billion people live in less-developed countries. What percent of the world's population lives in less-developed countries?

2. About $\frac{4}{5}$ of the grain produced in North America is fed to animals.
   (a) About what percent of the grain is fed to animals?
   (b) In your journal, describe why you think so much grain is fed to animals.

3. It has been estimated that about four million Canadians lack a proper diet. There are about 26.6 million people in Canada. About what percent of Canadians lack a proper diet?

4. There were approximately 2 000 000 farmers in Canada in 1966. Ten years later, in 1976, there were only about 1 050 000 farmers.
   (a) Calculate the decrease in the number of farmers.
   (b) Calculate the following: $\dfrac{\text{decrease}}{\text{number of farmers in 1966}} \times 100$.
   (c) Interpret your answer in (b).

5. Mexico City had about 3 000 000 people in 1953. By the year 2000, it is projected that the number of people in Mexico City will be 26 000 000.
   (a) Find the projected increase in the population.
   (b) Calculate the following: $\dfrac{\text{projected increase}}{\text{population in 1953}} \times 100$.
   (c) Interpret your answer in (b).

6. In 1969, there were about 330 000 000 km^2 of tropical rain forests in Central America. By 1985, there were only about 204 000 000 km^2.
   (a) Find the percent change in the number of square kilometres of tropical rain forests.
   (b) Predict the number of square kilometres of rain forest that will remain by the time you reach the age of 60.
   (c) In your journal, describe how you think the percent change in the areas of the rain forests will affect the earth. Give reasons for your answer.

7. Shown below are some global issues that affect your world today.
   (a) Discuss the pictures with your partner. What issues do they represent?
   (b) List other global issues that affect the earth today.
   (c) Find out more about each issue in (a). Create and solve a problem based on each issue. Add the problem and solution to your journal.

A bank teller is often the first person to greet customers.

A loans officer determines whether to approve a loan.

A bank manager is responsible for ensuring the bank earns a profit.

8.7 CONSUMERS AND SIMPLE INTEREST

A bank will pay you *interest* at a certain rate to encourage you to deposit money. The amount of money that you deposit is called the **principal**.

One type of investment offered by financial institutions is called a **term deposit**. Term deposits are investments in which you agree to leave your deposited money for a period of time, usually 30 days, 3 months, 6 months, or 1 year. The bank agrees to pay you interest on your deposit.

Suppose you put $1000 into a one-year term deposit that pays 5% *simple interest*. You find that the amount of money earned after one year is as follows:

Principal	$1000	5% of $1000
Interest	$50	$= 0.05 \times \$1000$
Total	$1050	$= \$50$

The money you deposit is *loaned* by the bank to other people.

Suppose $4600 is borrowed from the bank. The bank charges interest at 9% per year. The amount of money owed the bank after one year is found as follows:

Principal	$4600
Interest	$414
Total	$5014

If the money for a loan is paid back in $\frac{1}{2}$ year, then the amount of interest owing is less. For the above example, the interest would be found as follows:

$$\frac{1}{2} \times \$414 \text{ or } \$207.$$

ACTIVITY

Refer to the pictures of careers in a bank. Use your journal.
(a) What skills with percent do you think are needed in each career?
(b) List at least three responsibilities each person would have.

A Write your answers appropriately.

1. Calculate the interest earned for each deposit for one year at the interest rate given.
   (a) $600 at 5% per year   (b) $212 at 6% per year   (c) $1035 at 7% per year

2. Calculate the interest earned for each of the following term deposits.
   (a) $500 at 4% per year for six months
   (b) $800 at 6% per year for six months
   (c) $960 at 5% per year for three months
   (d) $365 at $7\frac{1}{2}$% per year for one month

3. Calculate the interest payable on each loan. The interest rate is calculated yearly.
   (a) $900 at 8% for one year   (b) $1000 at 9% for one year
   (c) $2500 at 10% for three months   (d) $3850 at 7.5% for two months

4. Calculate the total amount owing to the bank at the end of each time period.
   (a) $710 at 10% per year for six months   (b) $710 at 8.5% per year for three months

5. Refer to the chart at the right.
   (a) Calculate the amount of money you would pay the bank at the end of a year for each loan.
   (b) In your journal, describe whether or not it is preferable to pay off a loan as quickly as possible. Give reasons for your answer.

Amount borrowed	Rate of interest
$915.90	7% per year
$675.00	$5\frac{1}{2}$% per year
$889.55	$6\frac{3}{4}$% per year

B Use a calculator. Estimate first.

6. Jack borrowed money to buy a big screen television. The rate of interest on his bank loan was 9.25% per year. Find the interest owed after one year if the loan was $6350.

7. Many financial institutions sell Guaranteed Investment Certificates (GICs) that pay a set rate of interest over a period of time. Leanne invested $3250 in a GIC that earns simple interest at $8\frac{1}{2}$% each year. How much interest will Leanne earn after $3\frac{1}{2}$ years?

PARTNER PROJECT

People withdraw money from bank accounts each day. Thus, a bank needs to keep a reserve of cash.
(a) How do you think a bank estimates how much money to keep on reserve for withdrawals?
(b) Contact a bank near you to help answer the question in (a). How reasonable was your answer?
(c) Find out who is responsible for ensuring that a bank does not run out of money.

8. When you purchase a Canada Savings Bond, it usually pays more interest than if you had deposited the money in a bank account.
   (a) How much money would a $500 bond pay in one year at $7\frac{1}{2}$% per year?
   (b) Find out more about Canada Savings Bonds. What should you consider before deciding if you should buy a Canada Savings Bond?

9. (a) Who earns the greater amount of interest?
     (i) Mr. Bacon, with an investment of $9500 for one year at 9% per year.
     (ii) Mrs. Wong, with an investment of $10 500 for one year at $8\frac{1}{2}$% per year.
   (b) In your journal, describe how you can answer questions like (a) mentally.

10. Colin borrowed $4200 for a family trip. The bank loaned him the money at $10\frac{1}{4}$% per year simple interest.
    (a) How much interest will Colin pay if he repays the loan after $2\frac{1}{2}$ years?
    (b) Do you think Colin should have borrowed money to take the trip? Give reasons for your answer.
    (c) In your journal, make a list of what you feel are valid reasons for borrowing money. What are some things for which you should not borrow money? Give reasons for each choice.

 C

11. Interest rates are continually changing. To see the effect of changing interest rates, find the amount of interest earned in one year, at each annual rate, for a principal of $15 000.

    (a) 5%   (b) $7\frac{1}{4}$%   (c) $8\frac{3}{4}$%   (d) $9\frac{1}{2}$%

    (e) In your journal, describe the type of investment that you think would pay the interest rates above. Give reasons for your answer.

12. Use four tiles like the ones shown.
    (a) How many different shapes can you make using the four tiles, where at least one side of each tile must touch the side of another?
    (b) What percent of the shapes have a perimeter of eight units?
    (c) Repeat (a) and (b) using five tiles.
    (d) Create a problem of your own using the tiles. Compare your problem with others in the class.

In your study of mathematics you will often find similarities, as you will in the following activities.

ACTIVITY 1 *Work in a Small Group*

Start with 100 beans. Suppose the number of beans grows at a rate of 10% each day.
(a) How many beans will you have at the end of the first day?
(b) How many beans will you have at the end of the second day?
(c) How many beans will you have after five days?

ACTIVITY 2 *Work in a Small Group*

Suppose Jennifer deposited $100 in a bank account. She earns interest at a rate of 10% per year.
(a) How much money will Jennifer have at the end of the first year?
(b) How much money will Jennifer have at the end of the second year?
(c) How much money will Jennifer have at the end of the third year?

ACTIVITY 3 *Work in a Small Group*

Compare your results in Activity 1 and Activity 2.
(a) How are your results alike? How are they different?
(b) Look up the word "compound" in the dictionary. How do you think it is related to "compound interest"?

ACTIVITY 4

(a) Visit a bank or trust company and find the percents charged for loans and the percents paid to customers for deposits. What do you notice?
(b) Find out how it is possible for a bank to lose money. What would you do, as a customer, if your bank were losing money? Give reasons for your answer.
(c) Obtain an annual report from a financial institution. Find out how much money the institution earned last year. Are you surprised by the amount?
(d) Look in newspapers and magazines for bank ads that give information about services. Start a class collage of the ads. Create a problem based on one of the ads and add it to the collage. Solve your problem.

Most people want to be financially secure. One way to do this is to begin investing your money early in life. You should look for the interest rate that will earn the most money.

Suppose you have $1000 to invest. Your bank pays interest of 8% per year compounded annually. The following shows you how to calculate the interest compounded after two years.

End of First Year		End of Second Year	
Principal	$1000.00	Principal	$1080.00
Interest	$80.00	Interest	$86.40
Total	$1080.00	Total	$1166.40

Think:
To work with compound interest, add the interest earned after each interest period to the principal.

Loans can be calculated in a similar way.

ACTIVITY

(a) Calculate how much interest you would earn if you invest $1000 at 8% simple interest for two years.
(b) Which is better, investing your money at 8% simple interest or at 8% compound interest?
(c) What other factors would you consider when investing money?

EXERCISE

A Round your answers appropriately.

1. For each of the following investments,
   • write the expression to show the calculation.
   • calculate to find the amount of interest paid at the end of the term.
   (a) $2500 at 8% per year compounded annually for three years
   (b) $675 at 8% per year compounded annually for five years
   (c) $1950 at 8.5% per year compounded annually for seven years

2. For each loan,
   • write the expression to show the calculation.
   • calculate to find the amount to be repaid at the end of the term.
   (a) $5000 at 9% per year compounded annually, to be repaid in two years
   (b) $1780 at 11% per year compounded annually, to be repaid in four years
   (c) $8250 at 10% per year compounded annually, to be repaid in six years

3. Which investment earns more interest, A or B?
   A $1500 at 6.5% per year compounded annually for five years
   B $1250 at 7.5% per year compounded annually for five years

B Use a calculator to solve each of the following problems. Be sure to check that your answers are reasonable.

4. Interest rates are constantly changing. To see the effect of changing interest rates, find the amount of interest $15 000 would earn after 5 years, compounded annually, for each annual rate of interest.

   (a) 6%   (b) $7\frac{1}{2}$%   (c) $8\frac{3}{4}$%   (d) $5\frac{1}{4}$%

5. Zarina invested $2500 at $6\frac{3}{4}$% per annum, compounded annually for five years. She also invested $2000 at $7\frac{1}{2}$% per annum, compounded annually for five years. Which investment earned more interest? How much more?

6. Suppose Arnie invested $1000 at 6% per year, compounded annually.
   (a) Calculate the amount of interest earned after
       (i) 1 year.   (ii) 2 years.   (iii) 5 years.   (iv) 10 years.   (v) 15 years.
   (b) Graph your results in (a).
   (c) Refer to your graph in (b). Estimate how many years it will take for the interest earned to double.
   (d) Estimate how many years it will take for the interest earned to double again.
   (e) Estimate how many years it will take for the interest earned in 1 year to be greater than the original investment.

C

7. (a) Andy invested $1000 at 8% per year for five years. The interest will be compounded semi-annually. (Use 4% compounded every six months.) Calculate the interest Andy will earn.
   (b) Suppose Andy also invested $1450 at $6\frac{1}{2}$% per year, compounded semi-annually for five years. How much interest will he earn altogether?
   (c) If Andy is saving money to buy new furniture for $3995, will he have enough money after five years?

8. If $500 is invested at 8% per year, compounded quarterly (every three months) for one year, explain why the total investment after one year is $500(1.02)^4$.

MAKING CONNECTIONS

1. In the activity on the previous page, your interest after two years could be calculated as 1000(1.08)(1.08).
   (a) What is meant by this calculation?
   (b) How can you use a calculator to calculate compound interest?

2. Use a calculator to answer each of the following.
   (a) Find the amount earned on $500 invested for three years if interest is paid at 9% per year, compounded annually.
   (b) Find the amount you would pay back on a $5000 loan if the money was borrowed at 9.5% per year for a three-year term, compounded annually.

271

Depending on the type of job you have, you can be paid in some of the following ways.

- A **salary** where you receive a fixed amount of money each pay period.
- By the **hour** where you are paid for each hour you work.
- A **commission** where you are paid a percentage of your sales each pay period.
- A **salary and commission** where you receive a fixed amount and a percentage of your sales for each pay period.

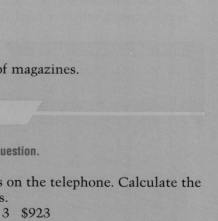

ACTIVITY

In your journal:
(a) Give examples of careers in which employees are paid for each of the four ways shown above.
(b) Describe which method of payment you would prefer. Give reasons for your answer.

If you work on commission, you will use your skills with percent every day.

EXAMPLE

Suppose you sell subscriptions part-time for a magazine and the commission is 12% of your sales. How much will you earn if you sell $128.00 worth of subscriptions?

SOLUTION

Commission rate is 12% of the amount you sell.
12% of $128.00 = 0.12 × $128.00
= $15.36

Thus, you will earn $15.36 for selling $128.00 worth of magazines.

EXERCISE

A Decide how your employer would round your salary in each question.

1. Leah is paid a 10% commission for sales she makes on the telephone. Calculate the amount she is paid each day for the following sales.
   (a) Day 1 $623   (b) Day 2 $465   (c) Day 3 $923

2. Jill is paid 1% for each insurance premium she collects. Calculate the amount of commission she earns for each of these premiums.
   (a) car insurance $780.00   (b) house insurance $585.00   (c) term policy $35 000

3. Calculate the commission received for each of the following sales.
   (a) $465 sale at 3% commission   (b) $690.25 sale at 5% commission
   (c) $30 600 sale at 6% commission   (d) $123 600 sale at 2.5% commission
   (e) Refer to the sales in (a) to (d). What do you think each person is selling?

B   Use a calculator. Estimate to check whether your answer is reasonable.

4. Telly receives 4% commission on all lottery tickets he sells. Calculate the commission if last week he sold $895 worth of tickets.

5. Pat's mother sells homes. Her rate of commission is 3%. Calculate her commission on a house that sold for $129 000.

6. Shirley sells cosmetics. She receives a base salary of $135 each week and a commission of 2% of sales. What did she earn altogether in a week when she sold $1850 worth of cosmetics?

7. Each month, Rose Mary receives commission at the rate of 12% for the first $15 000 worth of paintings she sells and 30% for sales in excess of $15 000. What is her commission on a total of $27 000 in sales?

8. Jackson sells two cars, each priced at $6245.80. His rate of commission is 2.5%. How much commission does he receive?

C

9. Robin sells cars on commission. She receives 2% for new cars and 3% for used cars. How much commission does she earn if she sells two used cars totalling $9125 and one new car at $17 653?

10. Gino receives a commission of 12% on sales up to $8500 per month and 15% on sales over $8500 per month. Calculate the total amount of commission earned for the following sales: March $7600, April $9600, May $11 500, June $12 600.

GROUP PROJECT

Find out more about careers that pay a commission.
(a) List five careers that pay a commission. Which careers interest you? Why?
(b) What math skills do you think you will need to be successful in each career?
(c) Do you think you might be successful in a sales career? Give reasons for your answer.

To solve a problem, you need to make decisions. Ask yourself:
I   "Can I see how to solve the problem?"
II "What can I do if I do not see how to solve the problem?"

To help you organize a problem and its solution, you can use your *Problem Solving Plan*. For example, the following shows how you can use your plan to find how many squares are in the diagram below.

1. Think About the Problem.

(a) Think of what you must find.
  • The number of squares in the diagram.
(b) Think of what you are given.
  • The diagram shown.

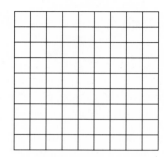

2. Think About a Solution.

(a) Think of a strategy you could use.
  • You could solve a simpler problem.
(b) Think of a reason for your strategy.
  • A simpler problem can lead to a pattern.

3. Work It Out.

Try a
1 × 1 square.

1^2

Total: 1 square

Try a
2 × 2 square.

Think:
4	1 × 1 squares
1	2 × 2 square
5	total squares

$2^2 + 1^2$

Try a
3 × 3 square.

Think:
9	1 × 1 squares
4	2 × 2 squares
1	3 × 3 square
14	total squares

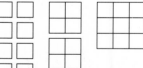

$3^2 + 2^2 + 1^2$

The pattern suggests that, to find the number of squares, you can use the following expression.

$$1^2 + 2^2 + 3^2 + 4^2 + 5^2 + 6^2 + 7^2 + 8^2 + 9^2 = 285$$

4. Think About Your Solution.

There are 285 squares in the diagram.

Think:
• Is the answer reasonable?
• Are there any other ways to solve the problem?
• How can manipulatives be used to solve the problem?

EXERCISE

B Use your *Problem Solving Plan*. Work with a partner.

1. How many equilateral triangles are in the diagram?

2. The first four triangular numbers are shown by the diagram. What is the tenth triangular number?

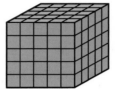

1	3	6	10

3. A cube is constructed from smaller cubes as shown. The outside surface is painted. How many small cubes have the following number of painted faces?
   (a) 1   (b) 2   (c) 0   (d) 3   (e) 4

4. A diagram is used to record the digits from 1 to 9. Each digit is used once. The clues below represent different parts of the diagram. For example, ⌐ represents the top left corner.
   (a) Use the clues below to place all 9 digits in the diagram.

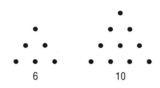

$$\lrcorner + \llcorner = \square \qquad \llcorner - \lrcorner = \ulcorner \qquad \square - \ulcorner = \urcorner$$
$$\sqcap - \sqsubset = \llcorner \qquad \sqcup - \sqsupset = \ulcorner \qquad \llcorner \times \ulcorner = \llcorner$$

   (b) What do you notice about the diagram?

MAKING CONNECTIONS

Claude F. Bradon discovered how magic squares can be used to form artistically pleasing patterns. He found that, by connecting the numbers in order in a magic square, patterns called *magic lines* are formed.

(a) Copy the magic squares. Draw the magic lines.
(b) Shade the shapes formed by the magic lines to form a unique design. Compare your design to others in the class.
(c) Repeat (a) and (b) for magic squares of your own. Compare your squares with others in the class.

6	1	8
7	5	3
2	9	4

8	3	4
1	5	9
6	7	2

16	3	2	13
5	10	11	8
9	6	7	12
4	15	14	1

Read the questions in "Thinking About the Chapter" before beginning the Chapter Review.

1. (a) The price of ski equipment was $382.50, but it was offered at a 25% discount. Find the sale price.
   (b) A profit of 15% was made on boots with a wholesale price of $235. What was the profit? What was the retail selling price?
   (c) Bernice earned 5% commission for selling $12 500 worth of TV sets. How much did she earn?

2. (a) Provincial sales tax of 8% was paid on a pair of running shoes selling for $69.95. What was the PST? What was the GST? What was the total cost of the shoes?
   (b) Joyce bought a coat on sale at $33\frac{1}{3}$% off the regular price of $165.50. What was the sale price? What was the total price?
   (c) PST of $40.06 was paid on an item selling for $312. What percent was the PST? What was the total cost, including GST?

3. Copy and complete the following table.

	Regular price	Rate of discount	Sale price
(a)	$38.60	15%	?
(b)	?	33%	$19.50
(c)	$65.00	?	$60.00

4. The rate of interest for the money in Marta's bank account is 4% per year. The bank states that interest is calculated and compounded monthly.
   (a) Calculate the interest earned after one month on a deposit of $520.
   (b) What is the total amount in Marta's bank account at the end of the month?
   (c) Calculate the total interest earned in the second month.
   (d) What was the total after the second month?
   (e) Use a calculator. Find the total amount in Marta's account at the end of two years.

5. Lance sold subscriptions. He received a commission of 21% of the value of the subscriptions he sold. How much did he earn selling $214.00 worth of subscriptions?

THINKING ABOUT

❶ Refer to Question 1 on this page. Describe to your partner the first decision you made.

❷ Have you got a list of provinces where you calculate the GST before the PST?

❸ Refer to Question 2 on this page. What is the total cost of each item in your province?

MAKING CONNECTIONS

Refer to the pictures on the opening page of this chapter.
(a) Write a short paragraph describing a day working in one of the careers shown.
(b) What math skills are used in the career you described in (a)?

❹ Have you updated your
Problem Solving Plan?

❺ Explain to your partner how
you answered Question 3 on
this page.

❻ Should the GST and PST be
calculated before a discount
is applied? Give a reason for
your answer.

SELF EVALUATION

1. The regular price of a badminton set is $14.75. The rate
of discount is 20%.
(a) Calculate the amount of the discount.
(b) What is the sale price?

2. In Manitoba, a football costs $15.90. Calculate the total
cost, including sales taxes.

3. (a) The rate of interest paid is 13% per year. Find the
interest paid after one year if the amount in the
account is $630.50.
(b) What amount of commission is received for selling
$465 worth of merchandise if the rate of commission
is 3%?

4. (a) Copy and complete the chart.

	Regular price	Rate of discount	Sale price
(i)	$15.95	2%	?
(ii)	?	25%	$150.00
(iii)	$90.00	?	$50.00

(b) The regular price for a pair of ice skates is $44.50.
Calculate the sale price if a discount of 15% is given.

5. (a) What is the total cost for each item including
7% GST and 8% PST?

A  B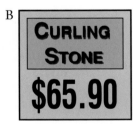

(b) Jacques bought a new 12-speed bicycle. The regular
price was $135, but there was a tag on the bike
indicating "20% off." If the bicycle was bought in
Newfoundland, what was the total cost of the
bicycle?

6. A real estate salesperson received $2\frac{1}{2}$% commission for
a house that sold for $123 000 and a 3% commission for
a house that sold for $135 000. What were the
salesperson's earnings for the two houses?

1. Calculate.

   (a) $\dfrac{2}{5} + \dfrac{1}{4} \div \dfrac{2}{15}$

   (b) $\left(\dfrac{3}{8} - \dfrac{1}{3}\right) \times \dfrac{1}{4}$

   (c) $\dfrac{1}{3} \times \dfrac{4}{7} \div \dfrac{5}{6}$

   (d) $\dfrac{1}{3} \times \left(\dfrac{1}{4} + \dfrac{1}{5}\right)$

2. Calculate each of the following that has an answer greater than 0.

   (a) $\left(\dfrac{-1}{2}\right)\left(\dfrac{1}{-3}\right)$

   (b) $\dfrac{7}{3} \times \left(-3\dfrac{1}{5}\right)$

   (c) $(-1.5)(3.2)$

   (d) $-3.5 \div (2.1 - 4.3)$

   (e) $\dfrac{5}{6} - \dfrac{4}{5} \times \dfrac{-2}{7}$

   (f) $\dfrac{2}{5} \div \left(\dfrac{-2}{5} + \dfrac{1}{10}\right)$

3. Find the root of the following equations.
   (a) $2x + 2 = 10$ (b) $3x - 2 = 16$ (c) $4x - 2 = 2x + 6$

4. Terry and Susan are in a 50-km bike race. Terry's bike has wheels with a diameter of 58.5 cm, while Susan's wheels have a diameter of 61.0 cm. How many more revolutions will Terry's wheels make in the 50-km race?

5. Simplify each of the following.
   (a) $|2| - 5$
   (b) $(6 + 3) + |-8|$
   (c) $-9(-7) - 4(-3 + 1)$
   (d) $|4 - 9| + 2|3 - 4| - 3(6 + 3)$
   (e) $6(4 - 2) - |5(5 - 8)|$
   (f) $|3 - 7| - 5(8 - |-9|)$

6. Estimate which tank has the greatest volume, then calculate. Was your estimate correct?

   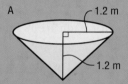   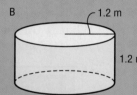   

7. Geoff works in a paint store. His paint mixing machine can prepare 3 L of paint per minute.
   (a) How many litres of paint can Geoff prepare in three hours?
   (b) Geoff is working on a 900-L order. What percent of the order will he have completed after three hours?
   (c) How many more hours will he need to finish the order? What assumption have you made?

8. Solve each problem. Include 7% GST in the total cost calculated on the selling price.
   (a) A sales tax of 8% was paid on an item selling for $69.95. What was the sales tax? What was the total cost?
   (b) A sales tax of 6%, or $6.20, was paid on an item. What was the selling price of the item? What was the total cost?
   (c) A sales tax of $21.84 was paid on an item selling for $312. What percent was the sales tax? What was the total cost?

WORKING WITH ALGEBRA 9

Did you know that algebra is used in movie stunts like this one?

- How do you think algebra might help when planning stunts?
- What other mathematics might be involved?

9.1 EXPLORING ALGEBRA

You have used unit tiles to help you explore integers and algebra tiles (x-tiles and unit tiles) to help you explore expressions and equations. In the following Explorations, you will use algebra tiles to extend your skills.

EXPLORATION ① *Work in a Group*

When working with integers and expressions, you worked with red and black unit tiles and red and black x-tiles.

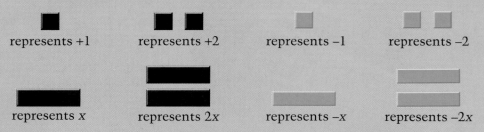

represents +1   represents +2   represents −1   represents −2

represents x   represents 2x   represents −x   represents −2x

1. (a) Write the expression represented by these tiles.

| A | B | C | D |

   (b) Create examples of your own using tiles. Write expressions to represent your examples.

2. (a) Describe why the expression 2x − 5 is represented using the tiles at right.
   (b) Write the expressions represented by the algebra tiles shown below.

| A | B | C |

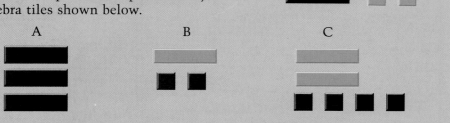

3. Use algebra tiles to illustrate each of the following expressions.
   (a) 5x   (b) −3x   (c) 5x − 2   (d) −3x + 4

4. Algebra tiles can be used to help you simplify expressions like $2(x - 5)$. To **simplify** an expression means to write the expression without brackets. How can the tiles be used to simplify the expression?

Step 1   *Step 2*

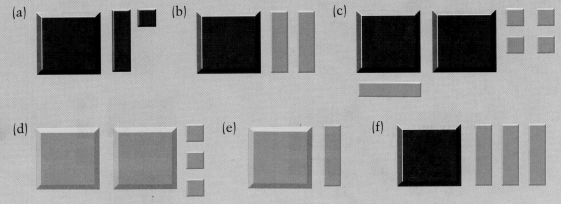

Step 3   Interpret how many x-tiles and how many unit tiles there are. Use your interpretation to find $2(x - 5) = ?$

5. Use your tiles to help you simplify the following.
   (a) $3(x - 2)$ (b) $4(x + 1)$ (c) $5(x + 3)$ (d) $2(x - 6)$
   (e) Suggest expressions of your own. Simplify them.

EXPLORATION ③ **Work in a Small Group**

When working with expressions, you will also work with exponents. The tiles shown to the right are called *x-squared tiles*. Discuss why this term is appropriate.

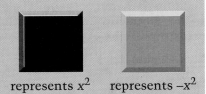

represents x^2 represents $-x^2$

6. What expression is represented by the following tiles?

(a)   (b)   (c)

(d)   (e)   (f)

7. Use algebra tiles to represent each of the following expressions.
   (a) $2x^2 + 3x - 2$ (b) $6x^2 - 7x + 6$ (c) $-x^2 - 2x + 4$
   (d) $4x^2 + 7x - 3$ (e) $-x^2 - 4x - 8$ (f) $-4x^2 + 5x - 6$
   (g) Suggest expressions of your own. Simplify them.

Algebra tiles are used to represent terms.

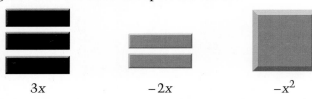

$3x$ $-2x$ $-x^2$

Terms like $3x$ and $-2x$ are *like* terms. Why?

Terms like $3a$ and $2b$ are *unlike* terms. Why?

2 is called the numerical coefficient. x is called the literal coefficient.

Special names are used to describe expressions formed by adding and subtracting terms. **Polynomial** is the general name given to terms that contain variables, such as monomials, binomials, and trinomials.

Term	Examples
*mono*mial (1 term)	$2x$, $3ab$, 7, m^3
*bi*nomial (2 terms)	$2x + 3y$, $3a^2 - 2a$
*tri*nomial (3 terms)	$2x + 3y - 4k$

To *simplify* some polynomials, you collect like terms and then add or subtract numerical coefficients as shown below. How can you simplify the expressions $2c + 4 + 3c - 2$ and $2x^2 + 3 - x^2 - 2$?

Use Algebra Tiles

Step 1

$2c + 4 + 3c - 2$

Show $2c + 4$

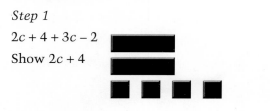

Step 1

$2x^2 + 3 - x^2 - 2$

Show $2x^2 + 3$

Step 2

Add $3c - 2$

Step 2

Add $-x^2 - 2$

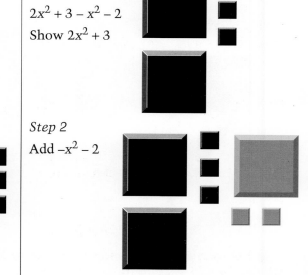

Interpret

Step 3

$5c + 2$

How many x-tiles are there?
How many unit tiles are there?

Think:
$$2c + 4 + 3c - 2$$
$$= 2c + 3c + 4 - 2$$
$$= 5c + 2$$

Step 3

$x^2 + 1$

How many x-squared tiles are there?
How many unit tiles are there?

Think:
$$2x^2 + 3 - x^2 - 2$$
$$= 2x^2 - x^2 + 3 - 2$$
$$= x^2 + 1$$

A Use algebra tiles to help you.

1. Which of the following pairs are like terms? unlike terms?
   (a) $3m, -2m$ (b) $4a, -5b$ (c) $3k, 2m$ (d) $4x, -6x$

   (e) $-2k, \frac{1}{2}k$ (f) $3p, 2pq$ (g) $3ab, -2ab$ (h) $8mn^2, -6m^2n$

2. (a) Use algebra tiles to represent each pair of terms.
   (i) $3x, 2x$ (ii) $-6y, -2y$ (iii) $8a, -6a$ (iv) $-4x^2, -2x^2$
   (b) Find the sum of each pair of terms in (a).

3. Simplify. Remember to use algebra tiles to help you.
   (a) $3a + 2a$ (b) $6b + 8b$ (c) $6m + 2m$ (d) $-4p + 6p$
   (e) $-4a + 3a$ (f) $2q + q$ (g) $3a - 2a$ (h) $-4y + 2y$

4. (a) How would you use algebra tiles to represent $4x^2 + 2x^2$?
   (b) Find the sum in (a).

5. Add. Remember to use algebra tiles to help you.
   (a) $4x^2 + 6x^2$ (b) $3x^2 + 7x^2$ (c) $-2x^2 + 5x^2$ (d) $-4x^2 + 2x^2$

B Work with a partner. Check your work together.

6. Add the following terms.
   (a) $2x, -3x, -4x$ (b) $-2m, 3m, 6m$ (c) $3ab, 2ab, -ab$
   (d) $8mp, -2mp, 6mp$ (e) $2xy, 4xy, -5xy$ (f) $7pq, 4pq, 10pq$

7. Simplify.
   (a) $2x + 5x + 3x$ (b) $4a + 2a - a$ (c) $8n - 5n + n$
   (d) $6pq + 3pq - 2pq$ (e) $9m^2 + 10m^2 - 3m^2$ (f) $7rq^2 + 4rq^2 + 3rq^2$

8. Add the following terms.
   (a) $4a, -3b, 2a$ (b) $3m, -6p, 2m$ (c) $pq, -3pq, 3pq$
   (d) $2a, -3b, 5b$ (e) $2ab, -3ab, 4a$ (f) $2r, -3r, 5p$

9. Simplify.
   (a) $2m + 3m + n$ (b) $2a + 3b + 4a$ (c) $6x - 2y + 3x$
   (d) $8k + 2m - k$ (e) $2p + 3q - p$ (f) $-6g - 3t + 2g$

10. Simplify each of the following by collecting like terms.
    (a) $3a + 2a + 3b - 2b$ (b) $4x + x - y + 3y$ (c) $-x + 2y + 4y - 3y$
    (d) $6a - 4b + 7a - b$ (e) $3y + 2x - y + x$ (f) $3m - n + m - 2m$

11. Refer to your answers on this page. Decide which answers are
    (a) monomials.   (b) binomials.   (c) trinomials.
    (d) Justify your answer to your partner.

12. (a) What expressions are represented by the following tiles?
    (b) Find the sum of the expressions in (a). Show the steps used to find the sum of the two expressions.

A

B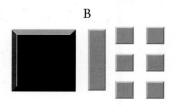

13. Simplify.
    (a) $2x^2 + 3x + 4 + 5x^2 + 6x$
    (b) $4a^2 + 2a + 3 + 3a^2 - 4a$
    (c) $y^2 + 2y + 6 + y - 3y^2$
    (d) $5m^2 - 2m + 6 + 4m^2 + 3m - 2$

14. Simplify.
    (a) $(5x^2 - 9) + (3 - x^2)$
    (b) $(3ab + 4b) + (2b - 5ab)$
    (c) $(6g^2 - g) + (2g - g^2 + 4)$
    (d) $(4m^2 - 2m - 4) + (-3m^2 - 2m + 5)$
    (e) $(7p^2 - 2p + 8) + (3p - 4p^2)$
    (f) $(2x^2y - 3xy + 7) + (xy - 3x^2y - 2)$

15. Simplify each of the following. Which expressions are equivalent?
    (a) $a + 3a - a - b$
    (b) $6x - 8 + 3x$
    (c) $3x - 2x + 4y - 3y$
    (d) $2x^2 + 3x - 2x^2$
    (e) $a + a - 3b + 2b$
    (f) $3a - a + 2b - 3b$
    (g) $4x + 2y - x - 2y$
    (h) $-3y + 3x + 4y - 2x$
    (i) $x^2 + x - x^2 + 2x$
    (j) $2x - y - x + 2y$
    (k) $(6y - 2y) + (3x - 8x)$
    (l) $(8k - 3m) + (2k - 5m)$

16. Each of the following expressions is equivalent to $3x - 5y + z$. Find the value of the missing numerical coefficients.
    (a) $x + 2y - 2z + ?x - 7y + ?z$
    (b) $-x + 2y - 3z + 4x + ?y + ?z$
    (c) Create similar expressions of your own. Compare your expressions to others in the class.

17. The unit tiles shown below form rectangles.
    (a) How many different rectangles are there in A? in B? in C?
    (b) Suppose you continued the pattern using four tiles and five tiles. How many rectangles would be formed by each?
    (c) What relationship can you form to find the number of rectangles formed by any number of tiles in this pattern?

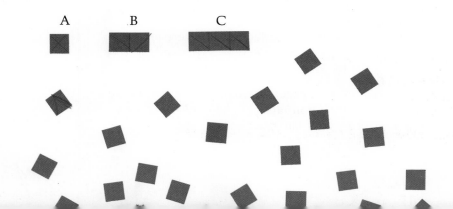

Sometimes, to simplify an expression, you need to subtract. Valerie and Yvonne thought of using algebra tiles to simplify $(2m + 4) - (3m - 2)$. Remember: To subtract $3m - 2$, you need to interpret $2m + 4$ in a different way as shown.

Step 1
Represent $2m + 4$. How?

Step 2
Show $2m + 4$ in a different way. Why?

Step 3
Remove three black x-tiles and two red unit tiles. What remains?

Step 4
Interpret the result. How?

There is one red x-tile and six black unit tiles.

Think:
How many x-tiles and red unit tiles do you need to remove?

Thus,
$(2m + 4) - (3m - 2)$
$= -m + 6$.

You can create a problem using your skills with substitution.

Did you know that the world's largest herds of wood bison are protected in Elk Island National Park, Alberta? You can find the size of Elk Island, in square kilometres, by substituting $m = 16$ and $n = 33$ into the expression $5m + 6n - m + 4m - 4n$. What is the size of Elk Island National Park?

To find the value of an expression, it is often more efficient to simplify the expression first.

$5m + 6n - m + 4m - 4n$
$= 5m - m + 4m + 6n - 4n$
$= 8m + 2n$

Now substitute. Use $m = 16$, $n = 33$.

$8m + 2n = 8(16) + 2(33)$
$= 128 + 66$
$= 194$

Thus, the size of Elk Island National Park is 194 km^2.

A Use algebra tiles to help you.

1. (a) Describe how you can use tiles to represent the expression $(2x + 5) - x$.
   (b) Use tiles to find the answer.

2. Interpret your answer in Question 1. What simple procedure might you use to subtract polynomials? Use your procedure to simplify each of the following.
   (a) $2a + (3a - 1)$ (b) $6x + (2x + 9)$ (c) $9m + (9 - 2m)$
   (d) $10p + (-3p - 4)$ (e) $(6r + 4) + 7r$ (f) $15w + (3 - 2w)$

3. (a) Describe how you can use tiles to represent the expression $(4x + 7) - (2x - 3)$.
   (b) Use tiles to find the answer.

4. Interpret your answer in Question 3. What simple procedure might you use to subtract polynomials? Use your procedure to simplify each of the following.
   (a) $(4d + 3) - (2d - 1)$ (b) $(2w - 3) - (w - 2)$ (c) $(3q - 9) - (5q + 9)$
   (d) $(3u - 4) - (2u - 5)$ (e) $(3x - 4) - (7x - 2)$ (f) $(5k + 7) - (11 - 2k)$

5. (a) To evaluate $3a + 2b + 5a - 3b$, suggest your first step.
   (b) Use $a = 3$ and $b = 5$ to evaluate the expression.

6. (a) To evaluate $(2n - 5) - (4n + 2)$, suggest your first step.
   (b) Use $n = -2$ to evaluate the expression.

B Think how you can simplify expressions without tiles.

7. Simplify.
   (a) $(3x + 8) + 4$ (b) $(3x + 8) - 4x$ (c) $5 + (2a - 6)$
   (d) $5 - (2a - 6)$ (e) $3m + (2m - 2)$ (f) $3m - (2m - 2)$
   (g) $3k + (2k + 2)$ (h) $(4k - 6) - 5k$ (i) $(5k - 2) - 9k$

8. Use tiles to help you simplify each of the following. What is the first step?
   (a) $(3x + 7) - (2x - 4)$ (b) $(3x + 2) - (4x + 1)$ (c) $(2x - 5) - (3x + 2)$
   (d) $(2x + 6) - (4x - 5)$ (e) $(5x - 8) - (6x + 10)$ (f) $(x - 3) + (4x + 1)$
   (g) $(5x - 4) - (2x + 3)$ (h) $(2x + 7) - (3x - 9)$ (i) $(3x + 6) - (4x - 8)$

9. Write each expression without brackets. Simplify.
   (a) $(2x - 3) - (-11x - 6)$ (b) $(3n - 6) - (2n - 5)$ (c) $(x - 4) - (x - 4)$
   (d) $(2x + 3) - (2x - 3)$ (e) $(3n + 6) - (-4n + 2)$ (f) $(-2n - 6) - (-5n + 6)$

10. Simplify. Watch your signs.
    (a) $(2x - 3y) + (4x + 5y)$ (b) $(2a - b) + (-a + 5b)$
    (c) $(3m - 2n) - (5m + 5n)$ (d) $(3x - 2y + z) - (-2x + y - z)$
    (e) $(3b - 2a + b) - (-3a + 2b)$ (f) $(2x + 4y - 5z) + (4x - y - z)$
    (g) $(4f + 2g + h) + (3f - 2g + h)$ (h) $(4k + 2n - 3m) - (5k - 4n - 2m)$

11. Simplify and then evaluate each expression for $x = 3$ and $y = 2$.
    (a) $5x + 2y + 3x + 4y$ (b) $2y - 5x + x + 4y$ (c) $3x + 4y - 3 + y - 1 - x$

12. (a) To evaluate $(5m - 4) - (7m + 2)$, suggest your first step.
    (b) Use $m = -2$ to evaluate the expression.

13. Evaluate each expression.
    (a) $(10m - 3) - (7m - 3)$ for $m = -4$ (b) $(2k + 4) - (3k - 2)$ for $k = -7$

14. Evaluate each expression for $x = 3$ and $y = 2$.
    (a) $(5x + 3y) - (2x + y)$ (b) $(3x + 2y) + (4x + 5y)$
    (c) $(3x + 4y) - (x + y)$ (d) $(5x - y) + (y - 3x)$

15. For each expression, use $x = 3$ and $y = -2$.
    • Estimate which has the greatest value.
    • Then evaluate the expressions.
    (a) $3x - 2y - (2x - 5y) + 3x + 2y$
    (b) $-(x^2 - y) + x^2 + y - (x^2 - 3y)$
    (c) $(x + 2y) - (x - 7y) + (x + 5y)$

16. Work with a partner.
    (a) In your journal, describe how you can use $a = 1$ to check your simplification for
        $3a + 6 + 3a - 2a + 8$.
    (b) Use your suggestion in (a) and check your simplifications in the questions on this
        page. What did you find?

17. Work with a partner and refer to your work in Question 16. Simplify each of the
    following and check your work.
    (a) $3m - 4n - (2m - 5n) + (6n + 3n)$ (b) $5a - 2b - (4a - 3b) + 6a - 2b$
    (c) $4x + 2y + (5x - 3y) - (4x - 2y)$ (d) $2p + 2q - (3q + 2p) + (5q - 3p)$

18. A design like the one shown is created
    using disks.
    (a) How is the pattern created?
    (b) How many disks would be used in
        all if 10 "rings" were constructed?
    (c) How many disks would be used in
        all if 200 "rings" were constructed?
    (d) What assumptions have you made
        in (c)?

MAKING CONNECTIONS

Refer to page 279. The amount of cable used for the movie stunt, in metres, is given
by $3m + 2n - 4m + 6n + 4n$.
(a) Suppose $m = 2$ and $n = 3$. How many metres of cable is used for the stunt?
(b) In your journal, describe a stunt that could use cable. What steps would you take
    to ensure the stunt is safe?

Algebra can be used to simplify calculations in geometry. This is often done in engineering.

For example, suppose the triangle represents a section of an aircraft fusilage.

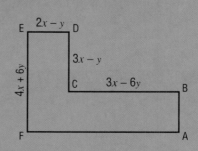

The perimeter, P, is given by $P = 16x - 12$. Find the expression for side BC.

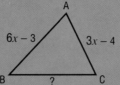

Step 1   Find the sum of the two variable sides.
$(3x - 4) + (6x - 3) = 3x - 4 + 6x - 3$
$= 9x - 7$

Step 2   To find the expression for BC, use
BC = Perimeter – sum of two sides
$= 16x - 12 - (9x - 7)$
$= 16x - 12 - 9x + 7$
$= 7x - 5$

The expression for side BC is $7x - 5$.

1. The perimeter of the figure to the right is given by $11x + 6$.
   (a) Find the perimeter when $x = 8$.
   (b) Find the expression for side LN.
   (c) Find each of the sides when $x = 8$.
   (d) Suggest another strategy to find the perimeter of $\triangle$LMN.

2. (a) Use the results in the previous question. Find the perimeter when
   (i) $x = 6$ (ii) $x = 11$ (iii) $x = 20$
   (b) For which of the values is the perimeter the greatest (a maximum)?
   (c) Explain how you could check your answers in (a).

3. The expressions for the dimensions of a field used in a movie stunt are given in the diagram.
   (a) Write an expression for the length of side FA.
   (b) Write an expression for the length of side AB.
   (c) Write an expression for the perimeter.
   (d) Find the perimeter of the field if $x = 2$ and $y = 3$.

In a previous section, you explored the product of powers. You noticed the following relationship.

Think: Think:

$$2^4 \times 2^3 = \underbrace{(2 \times 2 \times 2 \times 2)}_{4 \text{ factors}} \times \underbrace{(2 \times 2 \times 2)}_{3 \text{ factors}} = 2^7$$

Thus, it seems that $2^4 \times 2^3 = 2^{4+3} = 2^7$.

From the above relationship, it appears that to multiply powers with the same base, you add the exponents.

To simplify the product of monomials, you then use this relationship for exponents.

$$p^3 \times p^2 \qquad k \times k^3$$
$$= p^{3+2} \qquad = k^{1+3}$$
$$= p^5 \qquad = k^4$$

Sometimes, when you multiply monomials, the variables are different. To interpret the product $(3m)(2n)$, you can use the area of the figure shown to the right.

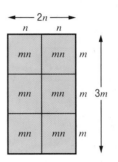

Step 1   From the diagram,
Area = length × width
     = $(3m)(2n)$

Step 2   The area can also be found as
Area = $mn + mn + mn + mn + mn + mn$
     = $6mn$

Thus, the diagram suggests that $(3m)(2n) = 6mn$.

ACTIVITY

1. Use a diagram to help you interpret each product. What do you notice?
   (a) $(4a)(3b)$ (b) $(2x)(3y)$ (c) $(5p)(3q)$

2. Think of your relationships above to suggest how to find these products.
   (a) $(2m^2)(3m^3)$ (b) $(-a^3)(-2a)$ (c) $(-y^4)(-3a^2)$

EXERCISE

A   Review your skills with powers.

1. Write each as a single power.
   (a) $2^3 \times 2^4$ (b) $5^3 \times 5^4$ (c) $3^2 \times 3^3$ (d) $10^2 \times 10^3$

2. Simplify. Use a single base.
   (a) $x^3 \times x^2$ (b) $a^5 \times a$ (c) $m^3 \times m^4$ (d) $p \times p \times p$

   (e) $b^3 \times b^4 \times b$ (f) $p \times p^3$ (g) $y^3 \times y^8$ (h) $a^4 \times a^4$

3. Find each product.
   (a) $(m^3)(m^5)$ (b) $(x^3)(x^4)$ (c) $(p^2)(p^4)$ (d) $(y^6)(y^3)$

4. Simplify.
   (a) $2(-3m)$ (b) $3(-5b)$ (c) $-2(-3k)$ (d) $-3(-3n)$ (e) $-5(-2r)$

5. (a) To find the product of $(2a^3)(3a^2)$, suggest a first step.
   (b) Find the product in (a).

6. (a) To find the product of $(5b^3)(-2b^2)$, suggest a first step.
   (b) Find the product in (a).

7. Use the diagram to find each product.
   (a) $(2x)(2y)$ (b) $(4a)(2b)$

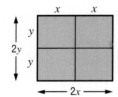
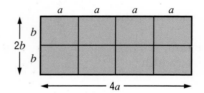

B   Use diagrams to help you.

8. Find each product.
   (a) $(3x)(-2y)$ (b) $(-3y)(5z)$ (c) $(3b)(-2a)$ (d) $(-6m)(-2n)$

   (e) $(-4x)(2y)$ (f) $(6m)(5n)$ (g) $(2a)(5b)$ (h) $(-m)(3n)$

9. Simplify.
   (a) $(2xy)(3xy^3)$ (b) $(3mn^2)(-2m^2n)$ (c) $(-8ab^2)(-3a^2b)$

10. Simplify.
    (a) $-2x(6x)$ (b) $-4p(-2p^3)$ (c) $-3y(-3y^5)$ (d) $-5a(2a)$

    (e) $-5x(2x)$ (f) $4x^2(-2x^3)$ (g) $8p^4(-4p^6)$ (h) $4w^4(-2w^3)$

11. Simplify. Remember: $(3a)^2$ means $(3a)(3a)$.
    (a) $(5a)^2$ (b) $(-2xy)^2$ (c) $(4ab^2)^2$ (d) $(-3m^2n^3)^2$

12. Write each of the following with a single exponent. Remember: $(3^2)^3$ means $(3^2)(3^2)(3^2)$.
    (a) $(2^5)^2$ (b) $(2^6)^3$ (c) $(3^2)^3$ (d) $(4^3)^3$

    (e) $(x^3)^3$ (f) $(x^4)^6$ (g) $(w^2)^6$ (h) $(p^2)^7$

13. Find each product.
   (a) $(3x)(-2y)$ (b) $(-3y)(3y)$ (c) $(-6m)(-2n)$ (d) $(3ab)(-2a)$
   (e) $(2x^2)(3x^2)$ (f) $(-2y^3)(4y^2)$ (g) $(-4m^3)(-2m^3)$ (h) $(3a)(-2a^3)$
   (i) $(2x^2y^2)(-3x^2)$ (j) $(-6a^3)(3a^2b^2)$ (k) $(3ab^2)(-2ab)$ (l) $2a^3(-3a)^2$

14. Simplify.
   (a) $(4a)(-7a)$ (b) $-2m(-6y)$ (c) $-3x^2(-2xy)$ (d) $2a^2(-3a)$
   (e) $-3x^4y(2x^2)$ (f) $(-4x)(-3x^3)$ (g) $(-3xy)(0)$ (h) $-3(xy^3)^3$

15. Find the square of each monomial.
   (a) $3y$ (b) $2m^2$ (c) $-3ab$ (d) $4x^2y$ (e) $-3x^2y^3$

16. Find the value of the following. Use $a = -2$ and $b = 3$.
   (a) $(2a)(3b)$ (b) $(-3a)(2b)$ (c) $(3ab)(a^2)$ (d) $(2a)(-3ab^2)$ (e) $(6ab)(-2ab)$

17. Find the following products.
   (a) $(2a)(5b)(-3c)$ (b) $(-m)(5n)(-p)$ (c) $(-3s)(-t)(-v)$
   (d) $(-x^2)(2xy)(3y^2)$ (e) $(2a^3b)(-a^4)(-5b)$ (f) $(6s^4)(-2st^2)(-t^3)$

18. Simplify each of the following. Use your calculator.
   (a) $(3.2x^4)(1.5x)$ (b) $(0.9ab)(-3.7a^2b)$ (c) $(2.8mn)(-0.5m^2)$
   (d) $(4.1p^2q)(-0.3pq^2)$ (e) $(2.2xy)(-1.1x^2y^3)$ (f) $(-0.3x)(-4.8x^3)$

19. Find the value of each expression for $x = 3.6$ and $y = -1.9$. Use your calculator.
   (a) $(3x)(-2y)$ (b) $(-5x^2)(2y)$ (c) x^2y^2
   (d) $(-x^2)(3y)$ (e) $(-3.5x^2)(-4.2y)$ (f) $(0.6x)(1.2y^2)$

20. (a) Work with a partner. Write these monomials on cards and place them in a box:
   $m^1, m^2, m^3, m^4, m^5, m^6, m^7, m^8, m^9, m^{10}$.
   Make cards from n^1 to n^{10} and q^1 to q^{10} also.

   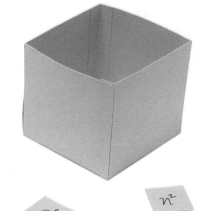

   (b) Each player takes turns selecting three monomials from the box and multiplying them. The player with the greater exponent in the expression receives one point.
   (c) The first player with ten points wins.

You can use algebra tiles to help you multiply a polynomial by a monomial. Simplify $2(x - 1)$ as shown below.

Step 1
Represent $x - 1$. How?

Step 2
Represent $x - 1$ twice. Why?

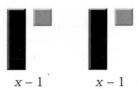

$x - 1$ $x - 1$

Step 3
Interpret your results.

Thus, $2(x - 1) = 2x - 2$.
Why?

ACTIVITY

1. Use algebra tiles to simplify the expressions.
   (a) $3(x + 1)$ (b) $4(x + 1)$ (c) $2(x + 1)$ (d) $3(x - 1)$
   (e) Use your results. What relationships do you notice?

2. Use your relationships to find the following products.
   (a) $5(x + 2)$ (b) $3(x - 2)$ (c) $2x(x + 2)$ (d) $3x(x - 1)$

The above activity illustrates the *distributive* property to help you simplify expressions.

$$5(x + 1) = 5x + 5 \qquad\qquad 3(x - 1) = 3x - 3$$

EXAMPLE
Simplify.
(a) $2(x^2 - 1)$ (b) $-3m(m^2 + 1)$ (c) $2x(x^2 - 3x + 1)$

SOLUTION
(a) $2(x^2 - 1)$
    $= 2x^2 - 2$

(b) $-3m(m^2 + 1)$
    $= -3m^3 - 3m$

(c) $2x(x^2 - 3x + 1)$
    $= 2x^3 - 6x^2 + 2x$

EXERCISE

 A   Review how to simplify an expression.

1. Write each of the following without brackets.
   (a) $2(x + 3)$ (b) $4(2x - 1)$ (c) $-6(2m - 3)$ (d) $-4(-y + 2)$

2. Expand. (Write without brackets.)
   (a) $3(x + 2)$ (b) $7(-2r - 4w)$ (c) $-7(-2m - 2)$ (d) $-9(-4d + e)$
   (e) $2a(3a + 1)$ (f) $5b(b - 4)$ (g) $-5m(6m - 2n)$ (h) $10w(3w - z)$

3. Expand each of the following.
   (a) $2(a^2 + 5a - 1)$ (b) $-2(m^2 - 3m - 4)$ (c) $-8(-p^2 - 3p + 4)$
   (d) $p(p^2 - 3p - 2)$ (e) $-r(r^2 - 6r + 9)$ (f) $-w(4 + w - 7w^2)$

B Remember: Simplify expressions before evaluating.

4. (a) Evaluate $2(3a - 4) - 3a$ for $a = 2$ without first simplifying.
   (b) Simplify the expression in (a). Then evaluate for $a = 2$.
   (c) Compare your solutions in (a) and (b). What do you notice?
   (d) In your journal, describe when you would simplify an expression before evaluating and when you would evaluate the expression directly.

5. Find the value of each expression for $a = 3$.
   (a) $6(2a + 4) - 3a$ (b) $15 + (-2)(a - 5)$ (c) $-10a - 2a(a^2 + 7)$
   (d) $a(2 - a^3) + 7a$ (e) $-3(a^2 - 8) - a^2$ (f) $2a^2 - 3a(a + 2a^2)$

6. (a) Evaluate $2(3a - b) - 3(a - 2b)$ for $a = 2$ and $b = 3$ without first simplifying.
   (b) Simplify the expression in (a). Then evaluate for $a = 2$ and $b = 3$.
   (c) Compare your solutions in (a) and (b). What do you notice?
   (d) In your journal, describe when you would simplify an expression before evaluating and when you would evaluate the expression directly.

7. (a) To evaluate $5(x^2 - 4) + 2(x^2 - 3)$ for $x = 2$, what is your first step?
   (b) Evaluate the expression in (a).

8. Evaluate each of the following for $a = -4$ and $b = 3$.
   (a) $5(a + b) + 3(a - b)$ (b) $4(2a - b) - 3(a + b)$
   (c) $-2(2a^2 + b^2) - 3(b^2 - a^2)$ (d) $4a(b - a) - 3b(2b + a)$

9. (a) Find an expression for the area of the rectangle.
   (b) Find the area when $x = 4$.
   (c) Find the area when $x = 6$.

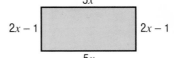

10. (a) Evaluate $2(3a - b) - 3(a - 2b)$ for $a = 2$ and $b = 3$.
    (b) Simplify the expression in (a). Then evaluate for $a = 2$ and $b = 3$.
    (c) Which solution requires fewer computations, (a) or (b)?

MAKING CONNECTIONS

Eleanor Anne Ormerod (1828–1901) was an amateur scientist. She became interested in entomology when she was 23 years old. Her research, which was printed and illustrated at her own expense, was sent free to anyone who wished a copy.
(a) Research the career of entomology. What math skills are involved in this career?
(b) In your journal, describe whether you would like to be an entomologist.

9.7 MAKING CONNECTIONS

Magicians often do amazing mind-reading tricks that leave you asking "How did they do that?" The fact is, almost all "mind-readers" use some algebra. For example, work with a partner and try the following.

MIND BENDER
Step 1 Pick a number.
Step 2 Double the number.
Step 3 Then add 10.
Step 4 Now subtract the original number.
Step 5 Add 14 to your answer.
Step 6 Subtract the original number.
Step 7 Divide by 6. What is your final answer?

ACTIVITY *Work with a Partner*

Refer to your answer in the Mind Bender activity above.

(a) Refering to the paragraph at the top of the page, count the number of words that represent your number. Do you find the word you selected "amazing"?

(b) Repeat the Mind Bender by choosing other numbers. What do you notice?

The steps above will always give you the result of 4. Thus, you will always find the word "amazing" when the steps are followed. A variable and a chart can be used to show you why.

Step	Instructions	Variable
1.	Pick a number.	n
2.	Double the number.	$2n$
3.	Add 10 to the number.	$2n + 10$
4.	Subtract the original number.	$2n + 10 - n = n + 10$
5.	Add 14 to the number.	$n + 10 + 14 = n + 24$
6.	Subtract the original number.	$n + 24 - n = 24$
7.	Divide the number by 6.	$24 \div 6 = 4$

EXERCISE

B Work with a partner.

1. (a) Choose any number and try the Mind Bender at the right.
   (b) Choose another number and repeat the steps. What do you notice?
   (c) Use a variable to show that you will always get the same number you started with.

Pick any whole number.
Add 4.
Multiply by 3.
Subtract your original number.
Divide by 2.
Subtract 6.

2. (a) Use a variable and predict the number you will get each time with the Mind Benders below.
    (b) Test your prediction using a number of your own.

    (i)
    > Pick any whole number.
    > Double your number.
    > Add 6.
    > Add your original number.
    > Divide by 3.
    > Subtract your original number.

    (ii)
    > Pick any whole number.
    > Subtract 5.
    > Double your answer.
    > Add one more than your original number.
    > Divide by 3.
    > Add 3.

3. Use the Mind Benders shown below.
    (a) Follow the instructions. Suggest what the final answer will be.
    (b) Test your suggestion in (a) using a number of your own.

    (i)

Instructions	Algebra
Pick any number.	x
Add 5.	$x + 5$
Multiply by 3.	$3x + 15$
Subtract your original number.	$2x + 15$
Subtract 15.	$2x$

    (ii)

Instructions	Algebra
Pick a number.	x
Add 10.	$x + 10$
Double the result.	$2x + 20$
Add one more than your original number.	$3x + 21$
Divide by 3.	$x + 7$

4. Refer to the procedure shown at the right.
    (a) Write the instructions that could be used for each step.
    (b) Test your instructions using a number of your own.
    (c) Try your instructions on others in your class.

    x
    $x - 4$
    $2x - 8$
    $2x - 10$
    $x - 5$
    x

5. Some of the instructions have been torn off the card to the right.
    (a) Copy and complete to suggest what the instructions might be.
    (b) Test your instructions using a number of your own.
    (c) Try your instructions on others in your class.

    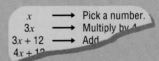

x	→	Pick a number.
$3x$	→	Multiply by 4
$3x + 12$	→	Add
$4x + 12$		

ACTIVITY

Refer to the Mind Benders on this page.
(a) Develop a similar number trick of your own. Record it in your journal.
(b) Decide how you can present the trick so that people in an audience would think you have read their minds.
(c) Try the trick on others. In your journal, describe what you liked about your performance and what you did not like.

Previously, you explored the quotient of powers. You noticed the following relationship.

Think: Think:

$$2^5 \div 2^3 = \underbrace{(2 \times 2 \times 2 \times 2 \times 2)}_{5 \text{ factors}} \div \underbrace{(2 \times 2 \times 2)}_{3 \text{ factors}} = 2^2$$

Thus, it seems that $2^5 \div 2^3 = 2^{5-3} = 2^2$.

From the above relationship, it appears that to divide powers with the same base, you subtract the exponents.

You then use this relationship for exponents to divide monomials.

$$
\begin{array}{ll}
p^5 \div p^2 & m^3 \div m \\
= p^{5-2} & = m^{3-1} \\
= p^3 & = m^2
\end{array}
$$

Dividing with monomials is similar to dividing with numbers.

ACTIVITY

Look at the examples shown.

(a) How are the examples alike? How are they different?

$$\frac{75}{25} = \frac{3 \times \overset{1}{\cancel{5}} \times \overset{1}{\cancel{5}}}{\underset{1}{\cancel{5}} \times \underset{1}{\cancel{5}}} = 3$$

(b) What patterns and relationships can help you divide monomials?

$$\frac{50xyk}{25xk} = \frac{2 \times \overset{1}{\cancel{5}} \times \overset{1}{\cancel{5}} \times \overset{1}{\cancel{x}} \times y \times \overset{1}{\cancel{k}}}{\underset{1}{\cancel{5}} \times \underset{1}{\cancel{5}} \times \underset{1}{\cancel{x}} \times \underset{1}{\cancel{k}}} = 2y$$

The activity above suggests that to divide monomials, you need to
- divide the numerical coefficients.
- divide the literal coefficients.

You will also need your work with exponents to divide monomials in the example.

EXAMPLE
Divide.

(a) $\dfrac{-12x^5}{-4x^3}$

(b) $\dfrac{18a^4b^2}{-6a^2b}$

SOLUTION

(a) $\dfrac{-12x^5}{-4x^3} = 3x^2$

(b) $\dfrac{18a^4b^2}{-6a^2b} = -3a^2b$

Think: $\dfrac{-12}{-4} = 3$, $\dfrac{x^5}{x^3} = x^2$

Think: $\dfrac{18}{-6} = -3$, $\dfrac{a^4}{a^2} = a^2$, $\dfrac{b^2}{b} = b$

A Remember: Division can be written in different ways.

1. Write each as a single power.
   (a) $2^4 \div 2^2$ (b) $5^5 \div 5^3$ (c) $3^6 \div 3^4$ (d) $10^8 \div 10^5$
   (e) $3y^3 \div y^2$ (f) $-6x^2 \div 2x$ (g) $15a^5 \div (-5a^2)$ (h) $9m^3 \div (-3m^2)$

2. (a) To simplify $15xy \div 5y$, suggest a first step.
   (b) Simplify the expression in (a).

3. Simplify each of the following.
   (a) $27mn \div 9n$ (b) $16ab \div 8b$ (c) $-8ab \div 4b$ (d) $36mn \div (-6m)$
   (e) $32bc \div (-4b)$ (f) $-16ab \div 2a$ (g) $-100mn \div 5n$ (h) $27xy \div (-9y)$

4. (a) To simplify $\dfrac{-24x^5y^2}{6x^2y}$, suggest a first step.

   (b) Simplify the expression in (a).

B Work with a partner. Discuss how you can verify each simplification.

5. Simplify.

   (a) $\dfrac{3a^2}{3}$ (b) $\dfrac{12x^2}{-6}$ (c) $\dfrac{-25a^3}{5}$ (d) $\dfrac{-27p^4}{-9}$

   (e) $\dfrac{-8c^5}{-8}$ (f) $\dfrac{36p^2}{-9}$ (g) $\dfrac{-75m^6}{-25}$ (h) $\dfrac{-18n^4}{9}$

6. Simplify each of the following.

   (a) $\dfrac{6m^3}{6m^2}$ (b) $\dfrac{8x^4}{4x^2}$ (c) $\dfrac{-12a^4}{-4a}$ (d) $\dfrac{-5p^3}{p^2}$

   (e) $\dfrac{24c^6}{-6c^2}$ (f) $\dfrac{-27n^4}{-9n^4}$ (g) $\dfrac{-100m^4}{10m}$ (h) $\dfrac{-35z^4}{-7z^2}$

7. Simplify each of the following.
   (a) $(18pq) \div (9q)$ (b) $(24rs^2) \div (-6r)$ (c) $(-12m^2n) \div (2mn)$
   (d) $(36p^3q) \div (6pq)$ (e) $(48mn^2) \div (-24m)$ (f) $(16a^2) \div (-4a)$

8. (a) Find the value of each expression for $x = -2$ and $y = 3$.

   (i) $\dfrac{12x^2y^2}{-6xy}$ (ii) $-2xy$

   (b) In your journal, explain why the answers to (i) and (ii) are equal.

9. Find the value of each expression for $a = 3$ and $b = -2$.

(a) $\dfrac{12ab}{4a}$

(b) $\dfrac{16ab^2}{-4a}$

(c) $\dfrac{-64a^2b}{-4b}$

(d) $\dfrac{-32a^2b}{16ab}$

10. (a) How is the area of a rectangle found?
    (b) Refer to your answer in (a). If the length of the figure is $5ab$, what is its width?

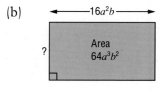

11. For each figure, find the missing dimension.

(a)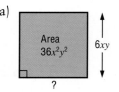

(b)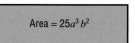

12. (a) Use a rectangle to interpret the meaning of $48mn^2 = (24m)(?)$. Draw a diagram to illustrate your answer.
    (b) Find the missing value.

13. For each of the following,
    • interpret the meaning using a diagram.
    • find the missing value.

    (a) $24x^2y = (6x)(?)$
    (b) $75a^3b^2 = (5ab)(?)$
    (c) $50m^4n^5 = (25m^2n)(?)$

C

14. (a) Use numbers to illustrate the meaning of these relationships.
    (i) $a^m \times a^n = a^{m+n}$
    (ii) $a^m \div a^n = a^{m-n}$
    (iii) $(a^m)^n = a^{mn}$
    (iv) $(ab)^n = a^n b^n$
    (b) What restrictions on the values of a, b, m, and n would you suggest? Give reasons for your answer.
    (c) Use examples of your own to illustrate each relationship.

15. (a) Place the numbers 1, 3, 9, and 27 on cards. Use the cards and the operations of + and – to create each whole number value from 1 to 40.
    (b) Suppose you wanted to represent all whole number values from 1 to 100, using a similar relationship as in (a). How would you modify the instructions in (a) to find this result?
    (c) Create a similar problem of your own. Compare your problem to others in the class.

Applying previously-developed strategies can help you develop new strategies. For example, you can use your work with monomials to help you divide polynomials.

ACTIVITY   *Work in a Small Group*

1. (a) How are the following expressions alike? How are they different?

    A $\dfrac{12 + 24}{6} = \dfrac{12}{6} + \dfrac{24}{6}$ B $\dfrac{3m^2 + 3mn}{3m} = \dfrac{3m^2}{3m} + \dfrac{3mn}{3m}$

    (b) Based on your results, summarize in your journal how you might divide a polynomial by a monomial.

2. (a) Refer to the above expressions. Suggest a next step.
    (b) Simplify each expression.

3. In your journal, describe how you could simplify the following.

    (a) $\dfrac{6ax + 9bx}{3x}$ (b) $\dfrac{5a^3 + 3a^2}{a}$

Activities such as the one above suggest that, in order to divide a polynomial by a monomial, you need to divide *each term* of the polynomial by the monomial, as shown in the following example.

EXAMPLE

Simplify.   (a) $\dfrac{4am - 8an}{4a}$ (b) $\dfrac{3a^2 - 6a^3}{3a}$

SOLUTION

(a) $\dfrac{4am - 8an}{4a} = \dfrac{4am}{4a} - \dfrac{8an}{4a}$ Why?

$= m - 2n$ Why?

(b) $\dfrac{3a^2 - 6a^3}{3a} = \dfrac{3a^2}{3a} - \dfrac{6a^3}{3a}$ Why?

$= a - 2a^2$ Why?

MATH JOURNAL

(a) For the above examples, which steps might you do mentally?
(b) As you complete the exercise on the following pages, think of steps you can do mentally. Record them in your journal.

EXERCISE

 A Review your skills with integers.

1. Simplify.

(a) $\dfrac{6y}{3} + \dfrac{18}{3}$
(b) $\dfrac{8m}{2} + \dfrac{16}{2}$
(c) $\dfrac{-6b}{-3} + \dfrac{-9a}{-3}$
(d) $\dfrac{20x}{4} + \dfrac{-16x}{4}$

2. Simplify each of the following.

(a) $\dfrac{12ab}{3a} + \dfrac{9a}{3a}$
(b) $\dfrac{-9xy}{3x} + \dfrac{-9x}{3x}$
(c) $\dfrac{8mn}{-4n} + \dfrac{8n}{-4n}$
(d) $\dfrac{-14pq}{2q} + \dfrac{-12q}{2q}$

3. Divide.

(a) $\dfrac{3y+18}{3}$
(b) $\dfrac{4y-16}{2}$
(c) $\dfrac{-16y-4}{-4}$
(d) $\dfrac{-6y+3}{-3}$

4. Divide each of the following.

(a) $\dfrac{48xy-8y}{8}$
(b) $\dfrac{6ab-12ac}{-6}$
(c) $\dfrac{16xy-8x}{8}$
(d) $\dfrac{25mn-10m}{-5}$

5. (a) Evaluate each expression for $m=6$ and $n=-2$.
   (b) Why are the answers the same?

(i) $\dfrac{4mn-6n}{2n}$
(ii) $2m-3$

B Remember: Simplify an expression before you evaluate.

6. Evaluate each of the following for $x=-2$ and $y=3$.

(a) $\dfrac{6y+12x}{3}$
(b) $\dfrac{5x+10y}{5}$
(c) $\dfrac{3ax+2ay}{a}$
(d) $\dfrac{2my+4mx}{2m}$

7. Simplify each of the following.

(a) $\dfrac{12ax+16x}{4x}$
(b) $\dfrac{-25my+10xy}{-5y}$
(c) $\dfrac{6x^2-9x^2}{-3x}$
(d) $\dfrac{-12ay^2-16ay}{-4ay}$
(e) $\dfrac{16a^2-12a^2}{-4a}$
(f) $\dfrac{25a^2b-20ab^2}{-5ab}$

8. Simplify.

(a) $\dfrac{3x+x^2-4x^3}{x}$
(b) $\dfrac{2k-k^2+8k^3}{k}$
(c) $\dfrac{9x^3+6x^2-15x}{3x}$
(d) $\dfrac{-4y^2+2y-2xy}{-2y}$
(e) $\dfrac{xy^2-x^2y^2-x^2y}{xy}$
(f) $\dfrac{a^3b-2a^2b-ab^2}{-ab}$
(g) $(6x^2y-4xy^2+10x^2y^2) \div (-2xy)$
(h) $(9a^2m^2-6am^2-18a^2m) \div (-3am)$

300

9. Evaluate each for $x = -2$, $y = -3$, and $a = -1$.

(a) $\dfrac{-12ax - 18ay}{-6a}$

(b) $\dfrac{6xy + 2x^2y^2}{-2xy}$

(c) $\dfrac{6x^2y - 3xy^2}{3xy}$

(d) $\dfrac{-6ax + 3xy}{2x}$

(e) $\dfrac{4x^2y - 2xy^2}{2xy}$

(f) $\dfrac{5ax + 15ay - 10a^2}{5a}$

10. The perimeter of an equilateral triangle is $(12x^2y + 3x)$ units.
    (a) Find an expression for the length of each side.
    (b) Find the length of each side if $x = 2$ and $y = 5$.

11. The perimeter of a square is $(16x^2y - 12xy)$ units.
    (a) Find an expression for the length of each side.
    (b) Use $x = 2$ and $y = 3$ to find the length of each side and the perimeter.
    (c) How could you check your answer in (b)?
    (d) Find the area of the square when $x = 2$ and $y = 3$.

12. Each side of an open box has the same area. The total area of five sides of the box is $15ax + 30bx$ square units.
    (a) Find an expression for the area of one side of the box.
    (b) Find the area of one side if $a = 8$, $b = 4$, and $x = 10$.
    (c) Work with a partner. Find an expression for the height of the box. What assumptions have you made?

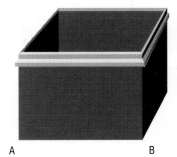

A   B

13. (a) Discuss with a partner whether it is possible to have a piece of paper with only one side.
    (b) Follow these steps.
       Step 1   Cut a strip of paper.
       Step 2   Put a half twist in it.
       Step 3   Tape the ends together as shown.
    (c) What do you notice about your strip? Does it have only one side? Give reasons for your answer.

MAKING CONNECTIONS

Inventors often have their inventions named after them. August Ferdinand Mobius invented the strip you made in Question 13. Use your strip.

(a) Start anywhere on your strip and begin to draw a line down the middle and parallel to the sides. Continue to draw the line until you are back where you started.

(b) Cut along the line you drew. How many pieces of paper do you get?

(c) Suppose you were to cut a line that started $\frac{1}{3}$ from one edge. How many pieces of paper would you get?

(d) Create a similar problem of your own. Compare your problem to others in the class.

Often, using a relationship you know can lead to discoveries of other relationships. Work with a partner to complete the activities. In your journal, record any relationships you see.

ACTIVITY 1
(a) List the relationships you know about working with exponents.
(b) Write an example of your own to illustrate each relationship.

ACTIVITY 2
(a) Refer to the examples. What do you notice about the answers in A and B?

$$\text{A} \quad \frac{4^3}{4^3} = \frac{4 \times 4 \times 4}{4 \times 4 \times 4} = 1 \qquad \text{B} \quad \frac{4^3}{4^3} = 4^{3-3} = 4^0$$

(b) Based on your results in A and B, suggest a value for 4^0.
(c) Repeat (a) using examples of your own. What conclusions can you make?

ACTIVITY 3
(a) Refer to the examples. What do you notice about the answers in A and B?

$$\text{A} \quad \frac{3^3}{3^5} = \frac{3 \times 3 \times 3}{3 \times 3 \times 3 \times 3 \times 3} = \frac{1}{3^2} \qquad \text{B} \quad \frac{3^3}{3^5} = 3^{3-5} = 3^{-2}$$

(b) Based on your results in A and B, suggest a value for 3^{-2}.
(c) Repeat (a) using examples of your own. What conclusions can you make?

To extend your work with exponents, you need to give a meaning to powers with zero or negative exponents. Your observations in the activities above suggest a meaning for the following.

$$x^0 = 1 \qquad\qquad x^{-m} = \frac{1}{x^m}$$

You can now apply your skills with exponents to simplify expressions.

EXAMPLE

Simplify. (a) $(4)^{-2}$ (b) $(2^2)^{-2} + 2^0$ (c) $x^{-2}(xy)^4$

SOLUTION

(a) $(4)^{-2} = \dfrac{1}{4^2}$

$= \dfrac{1}{16}$

(b) $(2^2)^{-2} + 2^0 = 4^{-2} + 1$

$= \dfrac{1}{16} + 1$

$= 1\dfrac{1}{16}$

(c) $x^{-2}(xy)^4 = x^{-2}x^4y^4$

$= x^{-2+4}y^4$

$= x^2y^4$

A Work with a partner. Compare your answers.

1. Evaluate.
   (a) $(2^2)(2^3)$
   (b) $(3^3)(3^{-1})$
   (c) $\dfrac{(3^2)(3^5)}{3^4}$
   (d) $\dfrac{10^6}{(10^2)(10^3)}$

2. Simplify.
   (a) 2^0
   (b) 10^0
   (c) 10^{-2}
   (d) 5^{-3}
   (e) 2^{-5}

3. (a) What is meant by $(-3)^2$ and $-(3)^2$? How are the expressions alike? How are they different?
   (b) Evaluate each expression in (a).

4. Interpret each of the following. Then evaluate.
   (a) $(2)^{-2}$
   (b) $(-2)^{-2}$
   (c) $-(2)^{-2}$
   (d) $-(-2)^{-2}$

B Use your relationships for exponents to simplify.

5. Simplify.
   (a) 3^0
   (b) $\dfrac{4}{x^0}$
   (c) $2x^0$
   (d) $(2x)^0$

6. Find the value of each of the following.
   (a) 2^{-1}
   (b) $(-2)^2 \div 4^{-2}$
   (c) 5^{-2}
   (d) $\dfrac{1}{4^{-2}}$
   (e) $\dfrac{8^0 2^3}{2}$

   (f) $(-3)^0$
   (g) $(2^4)^0$
   (h) $4^2 \div 4^{-2}$
   (i) $3^5 \div 3^2$
   (j) $\dfrac{1}{2^{-1}}$

   (k) -2^{-3}
   (l) $2^{-2} \div 2^3$
   (m) $\left(\dfrac{2}{3}\right)^{-1}$
   (n) $3^{-3} \times 3^5$
   (o) $\dfrac{-(-2)^3}{2^3}$

7. Evaluate.
   (a) $2^0 + 2^{-1}$
   (b) $2^{-1} + 2^{-1}$
   (c) $2^{-1} + \dfrac{1}{3^{-1}}$
   (d) $2^{-1} + 3^{-1}$

8. Write each of the following with the denominator 1.
   (a) $\dfrac{2}{x}$
   (b) $\dfrac{3}{x}$
   (c) $\dfrac{8}{x^2}$
   (d) $\dfrac{m}{n^3}$
   (e) $\dfrac{2t}{x^2}$
   (f) $\dfrac{ab}{n}$

9. Simplify. Write your answers so that the denominator is 1.
   (a) $\dfrac{x^3 y^2}{x^4 y}$
   (b) $\dfrac{a^4}{a^3}$
   (c) $\dfrac{xy^2}{4y^5}$
   (d) $\dfrac{y^2 x^5}{y^3}$
   (e) $\dfrac{x^3 y}{x^3 y^3}$
   (f) $\dfrac{a^4 b^2}{ab}$
   (g) $\dfrac{a^4 b^3}{a^3 b^5}$
   (h) $\dfrac{a^3 b^2}{a^3 b}$

10. (a) If $A = 6$, $B = 2$, and $C = 1$, find the value of $\dfrac{A + B^{A-6C}}{B}$.

    (b) Use the digits 1, 2, and 6 in any order to represent A, B, and C. What is the greatest value of the expression for the digits 1, 2, 6?

When you read information about the universe, you realize that measures would be difficult to express without a zero. The nearest star, other than the sun, is Proxima Centauri. It is about 40 200 000 000 000 km away. For example, the distance Proxima Centauri is from Earth would have no meaning if zeroes were not used in the measurement. Compare this number with the diameter of an electron, written as 0.000 000 000 000 435 cm. With all these zeroes, you wonder, "Is there an easier and more convenient way to write the number."

In your journal, describe how you think you can write the numbers on this page in an easier and more convenient form.

To write large numbers and small numbers in a more compact and convenient form, you can use *scientific notation*. The numbers in the article can be written in scientific notation as follows.

$$40\ 200\ 000\ 000\ 000 = 4.02 \times 10^{13}$$

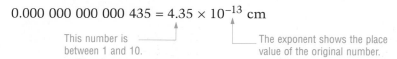

This number is between 1 and 10.

The exponent shows the place value of the original number.

To express small numbers in scientific notation, you use the same procedure. The diameter of an electron is then shown as

$$0.000\ 000\ 000\ 000\ 435 = 4.35 \times 10^{-13}\ \text{cm}$$

This number is between 1 and 10.

The exponent shows the place value of the original number.

ACTIVITY   *Work with a Partner*

Refer to the examples above.

(a) Explain to your partner how you can write a number in scientific notation. Give examples to help your explanation.

(b) Suggest how to write the following in standard decimal form.

4.5×10^2 4.5×10^3 4.5×10^4 4.5×10^5

4.5×10^{-2} 4.5×10^{-3} 4.5×10^{-4} 4.5×10^{-5}

A Check whether your answers are reasonable.

1. Find the exponent in each of the following.
   (a) $4630 = 4.63 \times 10^?$ (b) $498 = 4.98 \times 10^?$ (c) $0.003\ 45 = 3.45 \times 10^?$

2. Find the missing values of n.
   (a) $46\ 900 = n \times 10^4$ (b) $3890 = n \times 10^3$ (c) $0.000\ 896 = n \times 10^{-4}$

B Review your skills with powers.

3. Write each number as a standard decimal number.
   (a) 6.4×10^2 (b) 3.06×10^3 (c) 6.37×10^{-2} (d) 9.3×10^{-3}
   (e) 6.36×10^3 (f) 3.21×10^{-4} (g) 4.21×10^5 (h) 4.08×10^{-8}

4. Write each number in scientific notation.
   (a) 486 000   (b) 9 320 000   (c) 2 075 623   (d) 5 041 302 000 000
   (e) 0.000 453   (f) 0.001 35   (g) 0.000 000 32   (h) 0.000 000 000 421

5. Refer to the calculator display at the right.
   (a) What do you think 4.86 means?
   (b) What do you think 04 means?

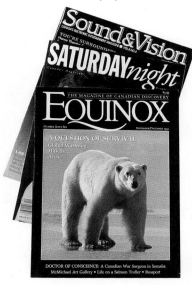

DEG

$4.86 \quad 04$

6. Write each number as it would appear in scientific notation on a calculator display.
   (a) 986 600   (b) 0.000 493   (c) 0.000 000 12   (d) 3 900 000

7. A computer uses the number 1.25 +E03 to display 1250 in scientific notation.
   (a) What do you think 1.25 means?   (b) What do you think +E03 means?
   (c) Write each number in decimal form.
       (i) 6.83 +E02   (ii) 9.25 –E03   (iii) 2.02 –E05   (iv) 4.51 +E06

MAKING CONNECTIONS

(a) Find the distance between the sun and the planets in our solar system. Write the distances in scientific notation.
(b) Find large numbers and small numbers of your own in newspapers and magazines. Write the numbers in scientific notation.
(c) Start a class collage of pictures that show distances. Write a number, in scientific notation, that can represent the distance in each picture.

Did you know that comets travel at speeds ranging from 1125 km/h to 2 000 000 km/h?

Did you know that Lexell's comet travels at a speed of 138 600 km/h? It once came within 1 200 000 km of Earth — the closest any comet has come.

Scientists often use rounded numbers when describing very large or very small distances such as 40 200 000 000 000 km. However, the accuracy of the measurements may be lost. To show the accuracy, you use the appropriate number of *significant digits*. The number above is now written as:

$$40\ 200\ 000\ 000\ 000 = 4.02 \times 10^{13} \text{ km}$$

These three digits are *significant* digits.

When zeroes are used as placeholders, they do not always indicate significant digits. The more significant digits used to express a measure, the more accurate the measure.

480 ← This zero is a placeholder.

0.004 80

These zeroes are placeholders.

This zero is not a placeholder. It is a significant digit.

Did you know that the most powerful microscope can measure 0.000 000 000 003 cm?

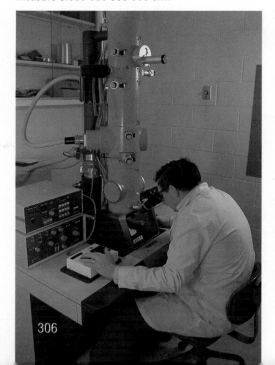

When you multiply and divide numbers resulting from measurement, you need to round the answer to the same number of significant digits as the least accurate measure as shown below.

$$\frac{4.5 \times 10^{12} \times 3.82 \times 10^{-2}}{4.8 \times 10^{3}}$$

$$= \frac{4.5 \times 3.82}{4.8} \times \frac{10^{12} \times 10^{-2}}{10^{3}} \qquad \text{Why?}$$

$$\doteq 3.581 \times 10^{12 + (-2) - 3} \qquad \text{Why?}$$

$$\doteq 3.6 \times 10^{7} \qquad \text{Why?}$$

ACTIVITY *Work Together*

(a) Write the numbers in each caption on this page in scientific notation.
(b) Record the significant digits in your numbers in (a).

A Remember: Decide on the accuracy of your answers.

1. Write each of the following in scientific notation. The number of significant digits is shown in the brackets.
   (a) 2300 (3) (b) 2300 (4) (c) 15 000 (2) (d) 0.85 (2)
   (e) 0.0085 (2) (f) 12 034 (4) (g) 48 000 (3) (h) 0.000 096 0 (3)

2. Calculate. Round your answers to the appropriate accuracy.
   (a) $(4.6 \times 10^4)(8.96 \times 10^3)$ (b) $(2.8 \times 10^4)(4.9 \times 10^{-3})$ (c) $\dfrac{4.32 \times 10^2}{2.1 \times 10^3}$

B Express the numbers in scientific notation. Then calculate.

3. Calculate a value for each.
   (a) $\dfrac{68\ 000\ 000\ 000 \times 49\ 000\ 000\ 000}{603\ 000\ 000\ 000\ 000}$ (b) $\dfrac{48\ 000 \times 0.000\ 000\ 002}{0.000\ 000\ 000\ 48}$

4. The diameter of a human red blood cell is 0.000 079 mm. How many would it take, laid end-to-end, to make a length of 1 m?

5. The mass of a hydrogen atom is 1.66×10^{-24} g. Find the mass of 1 500 000 hydrogen atoms.

6. A microsecond means 0.000 001 s. How many microseconds are there in
   (a) one minute? (b) one hour?

7. A hummingbird has a mass of about 0.0019 kg. The mass of a proton is 0.000 000 000 000 000 000 002 g. How many protons would be equivalent to the mass of a hummingbird?

C

8. A faucet drips at a rate of one drop every 5 s. One drop of water is about 0.08 mL. About 30 000 homes have a leaky faucet. Calculate the total amount of water wasted in all the homes in a year.

MAKING CONNECTIONS

(a) Make a list of situations in which you would need to write very large distances.
(b) Estimate each distance in (a). Write the distance in scientific notation.
(c) Make a list of situations in which you would need to write very small distances. For example, the distance between a proton and an electron in an atom.
(d) Estimate each distance in (c). Write the distance in scientific notation.

1. Simplify.
   (a) $3x + 5x$
   (b) $4c - 2 + c - 6$
   (c) $-2mn - 4m^2 - mn + 2m^2$
   (d) $(x^2 - 3x) + (2x^2 + 5x) + 6$

2. Simplify.
   (a) $(5x - 7) + (3x + 2)$
   (b) $(3a + 5) - (a + 8)$
   (c) $(7m - n) + (6m - 2n)$
   (d) $(a - b + 3) - (a + b - 1)$
   (e) $(p + 2q - 8) + (2p - q + 10)$

3. The perimeter of the triangle is $7x + 12$. Find an expression for the missing side.

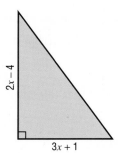

$2x - 4$

$3x + 1$

4. Write each expression as a single power.
   (a) $x^3 \times x^5$ (b) $m^4 \times m^2$ (c) $a^5 \times a^4$
   (d) $n^5 \div n^2$ (e) $k^5 \div k$ (f) $p^4 \div p^4$

5. Find each product.
   (a) $(4x)(-2y)$ (b) $(-3y)(7z)$
   (c) $(4ab)(5a^2b)$ (d) $3p^3(5p^2)$
   (e) $(-3x)(4xy)$ (f) $(5t)(-6st)$

6. Expand.
   (a) $4(a + 7)$ (b) $7(5 - 2r)$
   (c) $2m(m + 1)$ (d) $-3x(2x + 4)$
   (e) $-y(y^2 + 2y + 1)$ (f) $-k(k^3 + 3k)$

7. Simplify.
   (a) $24pq \div 6p$ (b) $(14xy) \div (-7x)$
   (c) $52ab \div 26a$ (d) $100m^2 \div 10m$
   (e) $\dfrac{25x^4}{x}$ (f) $\dfrac{-75p^3}{-5p^2}$

8. Find the missing dimension.

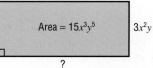

Area $= 15x^3y^5$ $3x^2y$

?

9. Write each number in scientific notation. What are the significant digits?
   (a) 850 000 (b) 3 450 000 (c) 0.000 125

THINKING ABOUT

❶ How can manipulatives help you answer the questions in this chapter?

❷ When do you think it is most appropriate to write a number in scientific notation?

❸ What are efficient ways to solve questions on this page? Compare your methods with your partner.

MAKING CONNECTIONS

Refer to the opening page of this chapter.
(a) Create a problem of your own using the picture. Solve your problem.
(b) Compare your problem with others in the class. Solve the other problems.

❹ Under what conditions would you use a calculator to help you work with numbers in scientific notation?

❺ Why do you think it is important to be aware of significant digits?

❻ Look back at the problems in this chapter. What are some strategies and skills you have learned?

SELF EVALUATION

1. Which of the following pairs of terms are like terms? unlike terms?
   (a) $4m$, $2m$ (b) $3xy$, $2x$ (c) $5a$, $-2a$
   (d) $4pq$, $-7pq$ (e) $4p$, $2pr$ (f) $8m^2$, $-4n^2$

2. Simplify.
   (a) $5x + x$ (b) $4y - 3y$
   (c) $4d + 3 - 2d$ (d) $2w - 3 + w + 2$
   (e) $3q - 9 - 5q + 9$ (f) $2x + 3y - 3x + y$

3. Simplify.
   (a) $(5p - 7) + (2p + 3)$ (b) $(4m + 6) - (2m + 3)$
   (c) $(3x - 2) - (7x - 3)$ (d) $(a - 4) + (a - 12)$

4. Evaluate each expression for $a = 3$ and $b = -2$.
   (a) $2a + 3b$ (b) $4a - b$
   (c) $3a + 4b + a$ (d) $5a + 4b - 2b$
   (e) $2a + 3b + a - b$ (f) $4a - 2b - 3a - 4b$
   (g) $(5a + b) - (2a - b)$ (h) $(7a - b) + (3a + 6b)$

5. Find the perimeter of the figure shown.

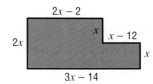

6. Find each product.
   (a) $(3x)(5y)$ (b) $(5a)(7b)$ (c) $(-m)(4m)$
   (d) $(-3k)(-4k)$ (e) $(4w^4)(-3w)$ (f) $6m^3(-3m^5)$

7. Evaluate each for $x = -1$ and $y = 3$.
   (a) $4(x + 7)$ (b) $7(y - 8)$
   (c) $5x + 7y + 11 - 2y$ (d) $6(2x + 3y) - 5$
   (e) $7(2x + y) + 3(x - y)$ (f) $(2x + y) - (3x - 2y)$

8. Find each of the following quotients.
   (a) $\dfrac{3a^2}{a^2}$ (b) $\dfrac{-6m^3}{2m^2}$ (c) $\dfrac{-6x^4}{-2x^2}$ (d) $\dfrac{-24y^5}{6y^3}$

9. Write each number in scientific notation. What are the significant digits?
   (a) 4 500 000   (b) 0.000 029
   (c) 0.000 000 000 392   (d) 400 500 300

10. Light travels at about 300 000 km/s. Write in scientific notation the distance light travels in 1 h.

Each year, different products are invented and the inventors hope that they will benefit people. The following are some actual inventions on which people have worked.

The Puddle Detector

Eight-year-old Lillian Ruth Lukas is developing the Puddle Detector. It is a small, battery-operated device that snaps on to any cane and emits a beep when the end of the cane touches water.

Moller 400

The Moller 400 is a cross between a Corvette and an Apollo rocket. It is a combination of a helicopter, a car, and an airplane. The Moller 400 can travel at 640 km/h, take off vertically, land softly, park in a garage, and is as easy to operate as a video game.

Large Capacity Smart Cards

A Large Capacity Smart Card is being designed to eventually replace the floppy disk for storing information. The card is 200 times faster at retrieving information than a conventional floppy disk and small enough to fit into your pocket. On an area the size of a credit card, you can save four million bytes (about 2000 pages) of information instead of 1.25 million bytes on a floppy disk.

ACTIVITY *Work with a Partner*

Make a name for yourself! Propose an invention of your own that you think would be helpful to people.
(a) List the benefits your invention will have for people.
(b) Describe what math skills you think might be used to develop each invention.
(c) How might you go about getting your invention on the market?

PROBLEM SOLVING WITH ALGEBRA 10

Suppose you are the architect designing these structures.

- How do you think equations can help you create your designs?
- What other math skills do you need to design buildings?
- In your journal, describe whether you would like to be an architect. What are some of the benefits of a career in architecture?

311

You have used algebra tiles to help you work with expressions. The small red and black tiles are called **unit tiles** and are used to represent numbers. The red and black strips are used to represent variables. Each strip is called an **x-tile**.

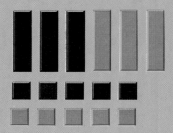

EXPLORATION ① *Work Together*

1. (a) Interpret the following steps to help you find the value of the variable in $x + 2 = 5$.

Step 1 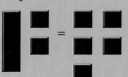 *Step 2* 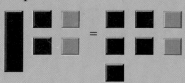 *Step 3*

(b) What is the value of the variable in $x + 2 = 5$?

2. Use tiles to represent each of the following. How are they alike? How are they different?
   (a) $x + 4 = 7$ (b) $x - 4 = 7$ (c) $x + 2 = 9$
   (d) $x - 2 = 9$ (e) $x - 3 = 5$ (f) $x + 3 = 5$
   (g) $x - 5 = 10$ (h) $x + 5 = 10$ (i) $x - 9 = 4$
   (j) $x + 9 = 4$ (k) $x + 10 = 8$ (l) $x - 10 = 8$

3. Use algebra tiles to represent each of the following equations. Then find the value of the variable.
   (a) $x + 6 = 8$ (b) $x + 4 = 9$ (c) $x + 3 = 2$
   (d) $x - 7 = 4$ (e) $x - 2 = 3$ (f) $x + 3 = -2$
   (g) $x + 2 = -4$ (h) $x - 5 = -2$ (i) $x - 3 = -6$
   (j) $x + 7 = -8$ (k) $x - 4 = -9$ (l) $x - 7 = -7$

4. Find the value of the variable in each of the following.
   (a) $x + 10 = 15$ (b) $x + 12 = 11$ (c) $x + 17 = 8$
   (d) $x - 11 = 12$ (e) $x - 10 = 15$ (f) $x - 14 = 17$
   (g) $x + 14 = -8$ (h) $x + 17 = -11$ (i) $x + 12 = -15$
   (j) $x - 16 = -12$ (k) $x - 15 = -10$ (l) $x - 19 = -14$

5. (a) In your journal, describe how you can find the value of the variable in equations using algebra tiles.
   (b) Set up similar equations of your own using algebra tiles. Find the value of the variable in each equation. Have others in your group verify your value of the variable.

6. Interpret the following steps to help you find the value of the variable in $2x = 8$.

Step 1

Step 2

7. Set up tiles to represent each of the following. How are they alike? How are they different?
   (a) $4x = 12$ (b) $-4x = -12$

8. Use algebra tiles to represent each of the following equations. Then use the tiles to suggest what the value for the variable might be.
   (a) $3x = 12$ (b) $4x = 8$ (c) $3x = -9$ (d) $2x = -10$

9. (a) In your journal, describe how you can find the value of the variable in the equations above using algebra tiles.
   (b) Set up similar equations of your own using algebra tiles. Find the value of the variable in each equation. Have others in your group verify your value of the variable.

10. Suggest how these steps can help you find the value of the variable in $2x + 3 = 1$.

Step 1

Step 2

Step 3

11. Use algebra tiles to represent each of the following equations. Then use the tiles to suggest what the value for the variable might be.
    (a) $4x + 6 = 14$ (b) $5x + 12 = 17$ (c) $2x + 6 = 10$

12. (a) In your journal, describe how you can find the value of the variable in the equations above using algebra tiles.
    (b) Set up similar equations of your own using algebra tiles. Find the value of the variable in each equation. Have others in your group verify your value of the variable.

10.2 SOLVING EQUATIONS

In the previous section, you used manipulatives to help you find the value of the variable in an equation. You used the following steps to find the value of the variable in an equation like $x + 5 = 8$. When you find the value of the equation, you **solve** the equation. The value of the variable you find is called the **root**.

Step 1
Use algebra tiles to *represent* the equation.

Step 2
To *isolate* the x-tile, use an appropriate number of red unit tiles.

Step 3
Interpret your tiles. In this case, $x = 3$.

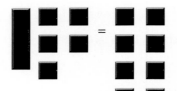

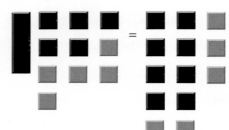

Think: $x + 5 = 8$

Think: $x + 5 - 5 = 8 - 5$

Think: $x = 3$

To learn a method, first practise with straightforward examples like the one above. Then try the same method on other examples as shown below. Use algebra tiles to represent each step. Compare the use of algebra tiles above to the solutions in the following equations. How are the solutions alike? How are they different?

EXAMPLE
Solve.   (a) $y + 5 = 8$ (b) $x - 8.4 = 23.2$

SOLUTION

(a) $y + 5 = 8$
      $y + 5 - 5 = 8 - 5$
      $y = 3$

Think: Add or subtract the same number from both sides.

(b) $x - 8.4 = 23.2$
      $x - 8.4 + 8.4 = 23.2 + 8.4$
      $x = 31.6$

Once you have discovered patterns and relationships using manipulatives, you can use these patterns to solve equations.

EXERCISE

A   Use algebra tiles.

1. For each of the following,
    • what is the first step when you solve each equation?
    • solve each equation.
    (a) $m + 8 = 12$ (b) $y - 3 = 6$ (c) $12 + x = 2$ (d) $3 = m - 6$

2. Copy and complete each of the following. (Use algebra tiles to help you interpret.)
   (a) $x + 6 = 12$
           $x + 6 - 6 = 12 - 6$
           ▬▬▬▬▬▬▬

   (b) $y - 4 = 16$
           $y - 4 + 4 = 16 + 4$
           ▬▬▬▬▬▬▬

   (c) $3 = 2m - 6$
           $3 + 6 = 2m - 6 + 6$
           ▬▬▬▬▬▬▬

3. For each equation,
   - decide which number to add or subtract from both sides.
   - then solve the equation.
   (a) $y + 6 = 9$ (b) $m + 9 = 15$ (c) $12 = p - 7$ (d) $18 = k + 7$

B   To solve an equation, estimate a value of the variable first.

4. Solve. Check your answers.
   (a) $k - 8 = 12$ (b) $3 + m = 15$ (c) $20 + p = -5$
   (d) $18 = 2 + s$ (e) $m + 2 = -12$ (f) $8 + p = 9$

5. Find each root.
   (a) $8.7 + k = 3.2$ (b) $5.4 = 12.9 + a$ (c) $p - 3.6 = 13.9$
   (d) $25.4 + m = -3.6$ (e) $5.5 = p - 8.7$ (f) $p - 4.8 = 79.2$

6. Solve.
   (a) $1.2 = m + 0.5$ (b) $1.8 = m - 0.6$ (c) $20 + s = 2.5$
   (d) $1.8 = p + 5.3$ (e) $x + 7.5 = -1.42$ (f) $3.12 = y - 1.82$

7. Which of the following equations have the same root? What is the root?

   (a) $y + \dfrac{1}{2} = \dfrac{1}{4}$ (b) $y - \dfrac{2}{3} = \dfrac{1}{5}$ (c) $y - \dfrac{1}{8} = \dfrac{3}{4}$

   (d) $\dfrac{1}{8} = y + \dfrac{1}{5}$ (e) $\dfrac{5}{8} = y - \dfrac{1}{4}$ (f) $\dfrac{2}{5} = \dfrac{4}{9} + y$

8. Work with a partner. Solve each equation.

   (a) $p - \dfrac{2}{5} = 6.3$ (b) $\dfrac{1}{5} + m = 4.5$ (c) $20 = k - \dfrac{3}{8}$

   (d) $\dfrac{3}{4} = a - 7.7$ (e) $3.1 + q = -\dfrac{2}{7}$ (f) $z - 3.3 = \dfrac{1}{4}$

PARTNER PROJECT

Work with your partner. On separate cards, write the numbers 1 through 9 and put them in a box. Then, write the operations + and – on cards and put them in another box. Finally, write different variables on cards and put them in a third box.
(a) Each player removes two number cards, one operation card, and one variable card.
(b) The player makes an equation using the cards.
(c) The opponent has 10 s to solve the equation.
(d) If the equation is solved correctly, one point is scored. The first player to reach 10 points is the winner.
(e) In your journal, describe what you feel you and your partner learned from this game.

I n the previous section, you used manipulatives to help you solve equations like $m + 9 = 2$. You can also use manipulatives to solve equations like $2x - 3 = 1$ as shown below.

Step 1

Use algebra tiles to *represent* the equation.

Step 2

To *isolate* the x-tile, use an appropriate number of black unit tiles.

Step 3

Simplify. Interpret your tiles. In this case, $x = 2$.

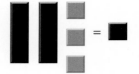

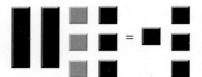

The above steps suggest that to isolate the variable, you first add or subtract the same number to both sides. You then divide both sides of the equation by the same number. Compare each step of your solution to the steps above.

$$2x - 3 = 1$$
$$2x - 3 + 3 = 1 + 3$$
$$2x = 4$$
$$\frac{2x}{2} = \frac{4}{2}$$
$$x = 2$$

To verify your work, you should check your calculations in the *original* problem. In your journal, explain why this step should be completed as part of solving any equation.

L.S. $= 2x - 3$ R.S. $= 1$
$ = 2(2) - 3$
$ = 4 - 3$
$ = 1 \checkmark$ checks

EXERCISE

A Use algebra tiles to help you.

1. For each equation,
   • represent it using algebra tiles.   • then solve the equation.
   (a) $2m = 8$ (b) $4y = 12$ (c) $6p = -12$ (d) $5k = -15$
   (e) $2n = 12$ (f) $3x = 36$ (g) $4k = 16$ (h) $8m = -64$
   (i) $5h = -35$ (j) $7m = 49$ (k) $6b = -90$ (l) $7c = -56$

2. Solve.
   (a) $2m + 1 = 9$ (b) $3p - 3 = 6$ (c) $2q + 1 = 9$ (d) $3t - 2 = 7$
   (e) $3k + 4 = 13$ (f) $5p - 9 = 31$ (g) $4a + 1 = 9$ (h) $5c - 8 = 17$
   (i) $7x - 10 = 11$ (j) $4t + 12 = 20$ (k) $5n - 14 = 31$ (l) $4z - 12 = 52$

3. To solve each equation, decide on the first step. Then solve.
   (a) $\dfrac{k}{3} = 8$ (b) $\dfrac{a}{4} = 2$ (c) $\dfrac{s}{2} = 3$ (d) $\dfrac{w}{2} = -8$

4. For each equation,
   - decide whether you need to multiply or divide.
   - then solve the equation.

   (a) $4x = 12$ (b) $\dfrac{y}{3} = 4$ (c) $3 = 3y$ (d) $\dfrac{x}{3} = -5$

   (e) $5x = -35$ (f) $\dfrac{k}{6} = 8$ (g) $55 = 11m$ (h) $9 = \dfrac{d}{5}$

B Verify your answer in the original equation.

5. Solve.
   (a) $2k + 6 = 34$ (b) $3m - 4 = 23$ (c) $5p + 2 = 22$
   (d) $11 = 2q - 3$ (e) $6m - 3 = 15$ (f) $3 + 4x = 23$
   (g) $2m - 9 = 21$ (h) $4k + 6 = 72$ (i) $2 + 6q = 56$

6. Solve.

   (a) $\dfrac{k}{3} + 1 = 4$ (b) $\dfrac{s}{2} - 3 = 11$ (c) $\dfrac{p}{3} - 1 = 9$

   (d) $\dfrac{n}{2} + 6 = 8$ (e) $\dfrac{x}{4} - 2 = 6$ (f) $\dfrac{y}{3} - 2 = 7$

7. Find the value of each variable.
   (a) $12 - 2p = 6$ (b) $18 - 6m = 12$ (c) $-3m + 2 = 8$
   (d) $-2q - 1 = 3$ (e) $20 = 8 - 2p$ (f) $13 = -2t + 3$

8. Each equation involves decimals. Solve each equation.
   (a) $2.5x + 6 = 13.5$ (b) $1.5y - 8 = 3$ (c) $3.5 = 2 + 1.5p$
   (d) $13 = 6 - 3.5k$ (e) $0.3x + 0.8 = 0.5$ (f) $11 = 4.5 - 7.5y$
   (g) $11 = 2 - 4.5z$ (h) $4.4m - 0.3 = 0.8$ (i) $16 = 7.3 + 2.4k$

9. Play a game of *Equation* with a partner or in a small group.
   (a) Use two boxes like the ones shown. Into one box, place cards with the variables x through $10x$ on them. In the other box, place cards with -10 through 10.
   (b) Follow these rules.

   Rule 1 Each player takes a turn removing a variable and a number from the boxes.

   Rule 2 An equal sign is placed between the variable card and the number card.

   Rule 3 Each player has 15 s to solve the equation mentally. A correct answer is worth 1 point.

   Rule 4 The first player with ten points is the winner.

The principal step when solving equations is to isolate the terms containing the variable. For example, you can find the value of x in $3x - 2 = x + 2$ as follows.

Using Algebra Tiles

Step 1 *Represent* the equation.

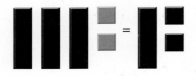

Step 2 *Isolate* the numerals on the right side.

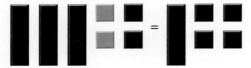

Step 3 *Isolate* the x-tiles on the left side.

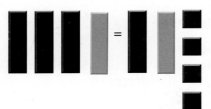

Step 4 *Simplify.* Interpret your tiles.

Using Algebra

$$3x - 2 = x + 2$$
$$3x - 2 + 2 = x + 2 + 2$$
$$3x = x + 4$$
$$3x - x = x - x + 4$$
$$2x = 4$$
$$\frac{2x}{2} = \frac{4}{2}$$
$$x = 2$$

Thus, 2 is the root of the equation.

Check:
L.S. $= 3x - 2$ R.S. $= x + 2$
     $= 3(2) - 2$ $= 2 + 2$
     $= 6 - 2$ $= 4$
     $= 4$

ACTIVITY 1

Compare the steps of the solution above with the steps using the algebra tiles. How are they alike? How are they different?

ACTIVITY 2

Use algebra tiles to solve the following. How are your solutions alike? How are they different?
(a) $4x + 7 = 3x - 4$
(b) $5x - 4 = 3x - 6$

A Work with a partner. One partner represents the solution using algebra tiles. The other writes the solution.

1. For each equation, the next step is shown. Complete each solution.
   (a) $7y = 2y + 5$ (b) $5k = 18 - 4k$ (c) $20 - 3m = m$
       $7y - 2y = 2y + 5 - 2y$ $5k + 4k = 18 - 4k + 4k$ $20 - 3m + 3m = m + 3m$

2. Which of the values shown is the root of the equation? In your journal, describe how you can find the value mentally.
   (a) $2x + 8 = x - 12$ $12, -20$ (b) $18 + 3x - 5 = 65 - x$ $13, -13$

3. To solve each equation, decide on the first step and then solve the equation.
   (a) $3y = 12 + 2y$ (b) $6y - 3 = 9$ (c) $9m = 4m - 10$
   (d) $8y + 4 = 7y$ (e) $6k = 4k - 4$ (f) $6 - 3x = 3x$

B Use algebra tiles to help you. Check your work.

4. Solve.
   (a) $6y = 36 - 3y$ (b) $8y = 36 + 7y$ (c) $2m = 6m - 20$
   (d) $7p = 6 + 5p$ (e) $2y + 1 = y + 4$ (f) $28 - y = 5y - 2$

5. Find the root of each equation. Check your work.
   (a) $5m - 2 = 2m + 4$ (b) $6t + 10 = -12 - 5t$ (c) $-7r - 1 = 2r + 26$
   (d) $6 - 8y = 2y - 44$ (e) $4m - 3m = 5m - 28$ (f) $3y + y - 7 = 2 - 2y$

6. The final number for a combination lock is given by the root of the equation $3k - 16 = 2k + 12$. What is the final number?

7. The longest Snakes and Ladders game ever played, in hours, is $5h - 230 = 3h + 70$. How long did the game take?

8. The atmosphere of Venus is n times as heavy as the atmosphere of Earth. Solve $n + 27 = 2n - 3$ to find the number of times heavier the atmosphere is on Venus.

9. A square piece of paper is folded in half. The resulting figure has a perimeter of 12 cm.
   (a) What was the area of the original piece of paper?
   (b) Create a similar problem of your own. Solve your problem. Compare your problem to others in the class.

10. (a) Start with a large piece of paper. Fold it in half as many times as you can.
    (b) Repeat (a) for other pieces of paper.
    (c) What is the greatest number of times you can fold a piece of paper in half?

The young of many animals often have unusual names. In the table, some names have been given a code number. To find the names, solve the equations given and then refer to the codes in the table.

What are young geese called?

$$3(g - 1) = 2(g - 2)$$
$$3g - 3 = 2g - 4$$
$$3g - 3 + 3 = 2g - 4 + 3$$
$$3g = 2g - 1$$
$$3g - 2g = 2g - 1 - 2g$$
$$g = -1$$

From the table above, −1 is the code number of "gosling." Thus, young geese are called goslings.

CODE	
Code number	Name of young
−4	leveret
−3	foal
−2	calf
−1	gosling
0	parr
1	squab
2	piglet
3	cygnet
4	chick
5	lamb
6	duckling

Find the root of each equation. Use the code to determine the name of each animal.

1. (a) What are young donkeys called? Solve the equation $7(d + 1) = 1 + 5d$ to help.
   (b) What are young elephants called? Solve the equation $2(e - 3) = 3(e - 5) + 11$.
   (c) What are young pigeons called? Solve the equation $3(p + 4) = 15p$ and use the table to find out.

2. (a) What are young swans called? Solve the equation $5(s - 3) = 0$.
   (b) What are young turkeys called? Solve the equation $4(t - 3) + 10 = 2(t + 3)$.

3. (a) Solve each equation in the chart.
   (b) Decide what the young animals are called. Use your library to help you to find out what the adult animals are called.
   (c) Write a problem using the code. Solve your problem and compare your solution to others in the class.

Equation	Young
$3(l + 5) = 2(l + 3) + 5$	
$2(f + 3) = f + 3$	
$4(p + 2) = 3(p + 2) + 2$	
$p - 6 = 2(p - 4)$	
$4(c + 1) = 2(c + 6)$	
$5d + 3 = 3(d + 2) + 9$	

10.6 TRANSLATING INTO MATHEMATICS

To solve some problems, you need to translate the information accurately into mathematics.

ACTIVITY 1 *Work with a Partner*

1. Copy each of the following.
   - On your copy, write a number for each blank space.
   - Follow the instructions using any number.

(a)

	Use Numbers	Use Variables
Pick a number.		n
Add 7 to the number.		$n + 7$
Double the result.		
Subtract the original number.		
Add 10 to the number.		
Subtract 24.		

(b)

	Use Numbers	Use Variables
Pick a number.		
Double the number.		
Add 10 to the number.		
Divide the result by 2.		
Subtract 5.		

2. What do you notice in each part of Question 1?

ACTIVITY 2 *Work with a Partner*

3. Refer to Activity 1.
   (a) Create a similar number pattern of your own.
   (b) Compare your pattern to those of others in the class. Solve the other number patterns.

ACTIVITY 3 *Work with a Partner*

4. In your journal, write the operation suggested by each. Give an example to help you.
   (a) decreased by (b) increased by (c) product
   (d) and (e) average (f) times the number

10.7 SOLVING PROBLEMS

Kerrin Lee-Gartner won an Olympic gold medal in the downhill skiing event of the 1992 Olympic Games.

There is another event in the Olympic Games called speed skiing. The record in this event is two times Kerrin's top speed plus 30.

If the speed-skiing record was 230 km/h, find Kerrin Lee-Gartner's top speed in the downhill event.

Did you know that Kerrin Lee-Gartner was the first Canadian to win a gold medal for downhill skiing?

Speed skiers who go downhill in a straight line can reach speeds of 230 km/h.

To find Kerrin's top speed, you need to translate the information into mathematics.

Let n be the speed she reached in kilometres per hour. Thus, two times her speed plus 30 is $2n + 30$. The speed record is 230 km/h. Thus, you write $2n + 30 = 230$.

Solve.
$$2n + 30 = 230$$
$$2n + 30 - 30 = 230 - 30$$
$$2n = 200$$
$$\frac{2n}{2} = \frac{200}{2}$$
$$n = 100$$

Kerrin reached a speed of 100 km/h.

The following activity will show you some of the common phrases you need to be able to translate.

ACTIVITY

1. Match each English expression with the corresponding mathematical expression. k represents the number.

   (a) k is decreased by 6 $2k$
   (b) the sum of 15 and k $6 - k$
   (c) the product of 3 and k $k + 12$
   (d) k is doubled $k \div 3$
   (e) 6 decreased by k $3k$
   (f) k increased by 12 $k + 15$
   (g) k divided by 3 $k - 6$

2. (a) Make a list of other English phrases that you can translate into mathematics.
   (b) Translate each phrase. Provide an example to illustrate the meaning of each phrase.

A Look for clue words in each problem.

1. Let n represent a number. Write expressions for each of the following.
   (a) 4 added to 3 times the number
   (b) 2 times the number decreased by 8
   (c) 6 subtracted from twice the number

2. A number is decreased by 8 and the result is 5. What is the number?
   (a) What letter would you use to represent the number? Why?
   (b) Write an equation. Answer the original question.

B Read each problem carefully.

3. (a) A number is decreased by 17 and 47 is obtained. What is the number?
   (b) A number is doubled and then increased by 18. The result is 66. Find the number.

4. (a) One number is 8 more than another number. If the sum of the numbers is 48, what are the numbers?
   (b) A number is doubled and the result is increased by 4. If the answer is 100, what is the number?
   (c) Three times a number decreased by 8 is equal to the number increased by 22. Find the number.

5. Bill has triskaidekaphobia (the fear of a certain number).
   (a) Predict what the number might be.
   (b) The difference between the number doubled and 7 is 19. What is the number?

6. (a) Predict how many time zones there are in Canada.
   (b) The difference between ten times the number of time zones and 30 is 30. Find the number of time zones in Canada.

7. Do you know how many eyes there are in a deck of 52 cards? The number of eyes doubled and decreased by 21 is equal to the number of eyes increased by 21. How many eyes are there?

C

8. The difference between two numbers is 12. Four times the larger number decreased by 25 equals 48 increased by three times the smaller number. Find the numbers.

9. Use a scrap piece of paper.
   (a) Cut the largest possible square from the piece of paper.
   (b) Cut the largest possible circle from the square in (a).
   (c) Cut the largest possible square from the circle in (b).
   (d) How many times greater is the area of the square in (a) than the area of the square in (c)?

...VING: USING DIAGRAMS

...with algebra to solve a word problem. An architect wants the length ...'s foyer to be twice as long as its width. Its perimeter is 90 m. Find ...yer.

... Problem.

...nat you must find.
 - ...ne dimensions of the foyer.
(b) Think of what you are given.
 - The foyer is rectangular.
 - The perimeter is 90 m.
 - The length is twice the width.

2. Think About a Strategy.

(a) Think of a strategy you could use.
 - Draw a diagram and record the given information.
 - Use your skills with rectangles to solve the problem.
(b) Think of a reason for your strategy.
 - Recording information on a diagram can help you visualize the problem.

3. Work it Out.

Let the width, in metres, be represented by w.
Then the length is $2w$.
Use the diagram to help you write the solution.

$$2w + w + 2w + w = 90$$
$$6w = 90$$
$$\frac{6w}{6} = \frac{90}{6}$$
$$w = 15$$

The width is 15 m.
The length is 30 m.
Interpret the answer.

Think: The length is twice the width.

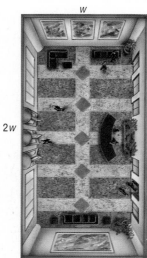

4. Think About Your Solution.

Thus, the foyer is 30 m long and 15 m wide.
 - Did you verify your solution?
 - Is there another solution?

EXERCISE

B Use your *Problem Solving Plan.*

1. (a) Write an expression for the perimeter of the triangle.
   (b) Find the value of k if the perimeter of the triangle is 133 cm.
   (c) Find the length of each side of the triangle.

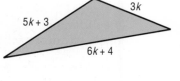

2. The perimeter of each rectangle is given. Find the dimensions.

   (a)

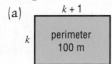

   (b)

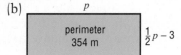

   (c)

3. The sides of a triangle, in centimetres, are given by $3n - 4$, $3n + 9$, and $4n + 5$.
   (a) Draw a diagram to show the information.
   (b) If the perimeter of the triangle is 114 cm, find the length of each side.

4. The length and width, in metres, of a rectangular parking lot are given by $8w + 5$ and $6w - 2$ respectively. If the perimeter of the lot is 972 m, find its dimensions.

5. Lori is 8 cm taller than Chris, and Mike is 16 cm taller than Chris.
   (a) Draw a diagram to show the information.
   (b) If their total height is 465 cm, find each height.

6. The difference between the width and height of an office building's garage is 3 m. The perimeter of the door is 42 m.
   (a) Find the dimensions of the door.
   (b) Find the area of the door.

7. The length of a rectangle decreased by 6 cm is equal to the width. The perimeter is 68 cm. Find its dimensions.

8. (a) The largest flag ever made had a perimeter of 378 m. Twice the width of the flag is 3 m more than the length. Find the dimensions of the flag.
   (b) Create a problem of your own that will give you the dimensions of a football field. Have others in the class solve your problem.

9. The world's largest swimming pool is the Orthlieb Pool in Casablanca, Morocco. Its length is 30 m more than 6 times its width. The perimeter is 1110 m. Find the pool's dimensions.

PARTNER PROJECT

(a) Create the models shown below.
(b) By cutting along the dotted lines, one of the models will form a square and the other will fall apart. Predict which will form a square. Give reasons for your prediction.

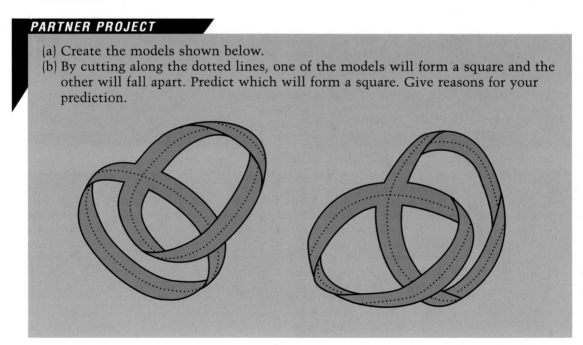

SCIENCE

Uncover the science facts in the exercise by solving problems like the following.

EXAMPLE

A condor has reached a record age of $2a - 50$ years. A cat has reached a record age of $a - 31$. If the sum of their ages is 108, what age has each reached?

SOLUTION

$$(2a - 50) + (a - 31) = 108$$
$$2a + a - 50 - 31 = 108$$
$$3a - 81 = 108$$
$$3a - 81 + 81 = 108 + 81$$
$$3a = 189$$
$$a = 63$$

Condor: $2a - 50 = 2(63) - 50$
$$= 76$$
Cat: $a - 31 = 63 - 31$
$$= 32$$

Thus, a cat has reached 32 years and a condor 76 years.

EXERCISE

B As you answer each question, list in your journal any information about science that you did not know.

1. In your hand, there are $(3h + 2)$ bones in the wrist, $(2h + 1)$ bones in the palm, and $7h$ bones in the fingers. The total number of bones is 27.
   (a) Write an expression for the total number of bones in your hand.
   (b) Find the number of bones in each part.

2. The tiger shark can grow to a length of $(3k - 0.6)$ m. The great blue shark can grow to a length of $(2k - 0.2)$ m.
   (a) Write an expression for the difference in length.
   (b) Suppose the difference in length is 1.6 m. Find the length of the tiger shark.

3. A snapping turtle has a mass of $(3x + 1.7)$ kg. An alligator snapping turtle has a mass of $(13x - 0.1)$ kg. Each turtle is shipped separately to an aquarium in a case with a mass of $(x + 5.2)$ kg.
   (a) Write an expression for the total mass to be charged for shipping.
   (b) Suppose the total mass is 138 kg. Find the mass of each turtle.

4. A fertilizer for fruits and vegetables is made up of $(2k - 4)$ kg of nitrogen, $(4k)$ kg of phosphorous, and $(5k - 1)$ kg of potash.
   (a) Write an expression for the total mass of the fertilizer.
   (b) Find the mass of each substance in a 50-kg bag.

5. A lawn fertilizer is made up of p kg of potassium, $(2p + 3)$ kg of potash, and $(3p + 1)$ kg of nitrogen.
   (a) Write an expression for the total mass of the fertilizer.
   (b) Find the mass of each substance in a 40-kg bag.

6. Brass is made from copper and zinc. In a piece of brass with a mass of $(33c - 25)$ g, there is about $(28c - 20)$ g of copper.
    (a) Write an expression to determine the amount of zinc.
    (b) After the copper was removed from the piece of brass, the mass of zinc remaining was 120 g. Find the mass of the copper and the brass.

7. The amount of air inhaled into your lungs each time you breathe is about $(4a + 1)$ cm^3 of oxygen and $(16a - 1)$ cm^3 of nitrogen.
    (a) Write an expression for the total amount of air you inhale in one breath.
    (b) How much oxygen and nitrogen would be inhaled in 240 cm^3 of air?

8. Herbert's collection of coloured gems consists of 40% amethysts and 15% moonstones. If he has 33 amethysts and moonstones in total, how many moonstones are in his collection?

9. Yakona's hobby is woodcarving. Of a number of carvings he has completed, 20% are songbirds and 15% are ducks. If there are 14 carvings of songbirds and ducks in all, how many carvings are there altogether?

10. Frieda's hobby is working with computer programs. Fifty-eight percent of her programs were purchased and 12% were traded. These totalled 175 programs. How many programs does she have altogether?

11. One coin is rotated around another identical coin which remains motionless. The coins are constantly touching. Work together.
    (a) Estimate how many times the coin will have turned after one complete revolution.
    (b) Check your estimate by rotating a coin. How reasonable was your estimate?
    (c) Repeat (a) and (b) for other coins.

MAKING CONNECTIONS

Throughout the history of mathematics, problems have occurred that, when solved, developed new skills to solve problems. Sometimes problems are posed where a solution seems possible but one does not exist. For example, **Goldbach's Conjecture** states that every even number, except 2, can be written as a sum of two prime numbers.
(a) Write three examples to show that Goldbach's conjecture could be true.
(b) Describe how you might be able to verify the conjecture.
(c) Find out more about Goldbach. Briefly describe some of his other contributions to mathematics.

To solve problems, a chart can help you organize your work, as shown in the following example.

EXAMPLE

Dexter is nine times the age of his son. In three years he will be five times the age of his son. How old are they now?

SOLUTION

Let n represent the age of the son in years.

The chart organizes the facts given in the problem. After using the chart, one additional piece of information can be added.

	Present age	Age in 3 years
Dexter	$9n$	$9n + 3$
son	n	$n + 3$

Dexter's age in three years ——— son's age in three years

$9n + 3 = 5(n + 3)$
$9n + 3 = 5n + 15$
$4n = 12$
$n = 3$

In three years Dexter will be five times as old as his son. From this fact, an equation can be written.

Check: In three years Dexter will be 30 and his son will be six. Dexter will be five times his son's age. ✔

Thus, Dexter's age is 27 years and his son's age is three years.

EXERCISE

B Use a chart to organize the information to solve these problems.

1. Eight years from now Blair will be six times as old as he was two years ago. His brother is twice as old as Blair is today. Find Blair's present age.

2. Joya has $3.75 in nickels, dimes, and quarters. The number of quarters is twice the number of dimes. The number of dimes is twice the number of nickels. How many of each type of coin does Joya have?

3. The greatest age reached by a marsupial is three times the greatest age reached by an orangutan. If each had lived three years longer, the sum of their ages would have been 82 years. What is the greatest age reached by a marsupial and by an orangutan?

4. My age increased by my son's age is 48 years. In 15 years his age, increased by four times mine, will equal 234 years. How old are we now?

5. If I had a quarter, I would have $4.00. However, I have only nickels and dimes. The number of dimes is one less than three times the number of nickels. How many of each coin do I have?

6. Three years ago Elaine was five times as old as Jerry. Today she is three times as old as Jerry. Jerry is one year older than Samantha was four years ago. How old are Jerry and Elaine today?

Any triangle that contains a right angle is called a **right triangle**.

Work together to complete the explorations that follow to study the properties of right triangles. In your journal, record all patterns and relationships you find.

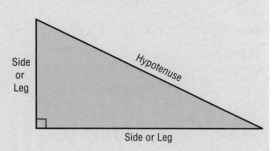

EXPLORATION ① Work Together

1. (a) Cut out paper strips with these lengths:
       3 cm, 4 cm, 5 cm, 6 cm, 8 cm, 10 cm, 12 cm, 13 cm, 15 cm, 17 cm.
    (b) Create as many triangles as you can using the strips of paper. Trace each triangle.
    (c) Draw a square on each side of the triangles. Calculate the area of each square. Copy and complete the chart using your areas. What do you notice?
    (d) In particular, how does the area of the square drawn on a hypotenuse seem to relate to the squares drawn on the sides?

Area Side 1	Area Side 2	Area Side 3
?	?	?
?	?	?
?	?	?

2. The side lengths of various right triangles are shown in the chart. Also include some of your own.
    (a) For each triangle, draw a square on each side.
    (b) How does the area of the square drawn on the hypotenuse seem to relate to the areas of the squares drawn on the sides?

Side 1	Side 2	Hypotenuse
4.0 cm	3.0 cm	?
8.0 cm	6.0 cm	?
6.0 cm	3.0 cm	?
3.5 cm	2.6 cm	?
4.8 cm	5.6 cm	?

3. (a) Repeat Questions 1 and 2 for your own triangles. What do you notice?
    (b) Make a summary of all observations and relationships you found in these explorations. Use an example to help you show any relationships.

EXPLORATION ② Work Together

4. Right triangles occur in many situations involving construction. Refer to the pictures below.
    (a) Identify the right triangles in each picture.
    (b) In your journal, explain why you think right triangles are used so often in construction.

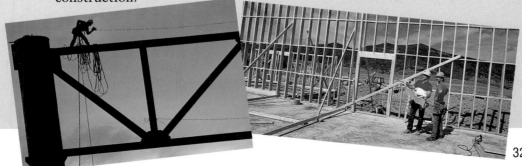

329

In the previous section, you found the following relationship.

$$\underset{a^2}{\underbrace{\text{area of}\atop\text{square A}}} + \underset{b^2}{\underbrace{\text{area of}\atop\text{square B}}} = \underset{c^2}{\underbrace{\text{area of}\atop\text{square C}}}$$

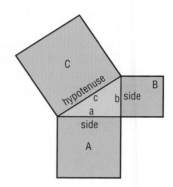

The relationship is called the **Pythagorean Relation**. It is read as, "In a right triangle, the square of the hypotenuse is equal to the sum of the squares of the other two sides." It can be used to solve problems like the following.

EXAMPLE

(a) A ladder reaches 5.6 m up a wall. If the base of the ladder is 2.5 m from the wall, how long is the ladder?

(b) A tower is 20 m in height. A guy wire 25 m in length is secured a distance from its base. Find the distance from the base.

SOLUTION

(a) Use $c^2 = a^2 + b^2$.

$$c^2 = 5.6^2 + 2.5^2$$
$$= 31.36 + 6.25$$
$$= 37.61$$
$$c = \sqrt{37.61}$$
$$= 6.13$$

$$\boxed{C}\ \boxed{5.6}\ \boxed{x^2}\ \boxed{+}\ \boxed{2.5}\ \boxed{x^2}\ \boxed{=}\ \boxed{37.61}\ \boxed{\sqrt{}}\ \boxed{6.13}$$

The ladder is about 6.1 m long.

(b) If d represents the distance from the base in metres, then

$$25^2 = 20^2 + d^2$$
$$625 = 400 + d^2$$
$$625 - 400 = 400 - 400 + d^2$$
$$225 = d^2$$
$$\sqrt{225} = d$$
$$15 = d$$

Thus, the distance from the base is 15 m.

EXERCISE

A Round your answers to one decimal place.

1. Find the missing measure in each triangle.

(a)

(b)

(c)

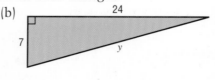

(d)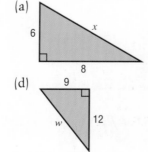

(e)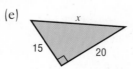

(f)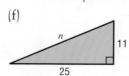

2. Find the value of each variable.
   (a) $x^2 = 12^2 + 5^2$ (b) $y^2 = 9^2 + 4^2$ (c) $k^2 = 3^2 + 6^2$
   (d) $14^2 = x^2 + 4^2$ (e) $20^2 = y^2 + 12^2$ (f) $31^2 = 20^2 + m^2$
   (g) $14^2 + 12^2 = x^2$ (h) $13^2 + 15^2 = y^2$ (i) $p^2 + 6^2 = 15^2$

3. Find the missing measure in each triangle.

   (a)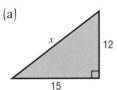
   (b)
   (c)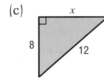
   (d)

B Use a calculator.

4. (a) Calculate the length of each ramp.

   A 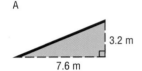 3.2 m
   7.6 m

   B   3.5 m
   3.5 m

   C 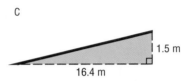 1.5 m
   16.4 m

   (b) Describe in what circumstances each ramp might be used.

5. Six hills are shown. Calculate the height of each hill.

   (a)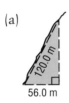
   120.0 m
   56.0 m

   (b)
   228.0 m
   125.0 m

   (c)
   325.0 m
   160.0 m

   (d)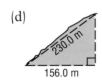
   230.0 m
   156.0 m

   (e)
   215.0 m
   108.0 m

   (f)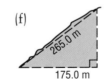
   265.0 m
   175.0 m

6. Calculate the length of the guy wire for each sign.

   (a)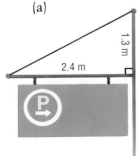
   1.3 m
   2.4 m

   (b)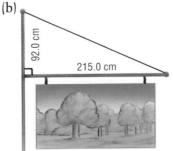
   92.0 cm
   215.0 cm

   (c)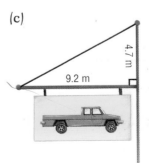
   4.7 m
   9.2 m

331

7. Find other examples of right triangles. Make two measurements and then calculate the missing measure. Estimate where necessary.

8. A ladder leans against a wall as shown. Use the information in the picture to calculate the length of the ladder.

9. A ladder 7.0 m long is placed against a wall. The foot of the ladder is 2.0 m from the wall. Calculate how far up the wall the ladder reaches.

10. Find the length of each diagonal to two decimal places.

(a)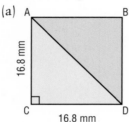

(b)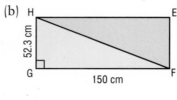

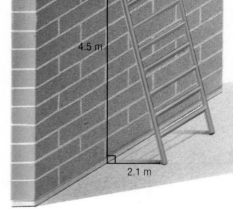

11. As a shortcut to school, Joelle cuts across a rectangular field along the diagonal. If the sides of the field are 120.0 m by 160.0 m, how much walking does Joelle save?

12. A baseball diamond is a square. The distance between bases is 27.4 m. Find the direct distance from home plate to second base.

13. Use a piece of cardboard 12 cm × 8 cm and a roll of tape.
    (a) Construct a box, with a top, that has a volume of 24 cm³. How much cardboard will you have left over?
    (b) Is it possible to construct a box with a larger volume than the box in (a)? Justify your answer.
    (c) Is it possible to construct a box with a smaller volume than the box in (a)? Justify your answer.
    (d) What are the dimensions of a box with the maximum volume using all the cardboard?

$\mathbf{A}$s you work on the following activity, summarize any skills you can use to help you solve an inequality.

ACTIVITY 1   *Work in a Small Group*

You already know that 12 < 24. Use the inequality 12 < 24 and work in your group to apply the instructions in A and B to it. Compare your group's answers to those of others. What do you notice?

A	B
(a) Add 3 to both sides.	(a) Add (–3) to both sides.
(b) Subtract 3 from both sides.	(b) Subtract (–3) from both sides.
(c) Multiply both sides by 3.	(c) Multiply both sides by (–3).
(d) Divide both sides by 3.	(d) Divide both sides by (–3).

- Repeat A and B for inequalities of your own.
- What do you notice about the inequality after each calculation?
- What conclusions can you make about inequalities?

Once you have solved an inequality, you can draw its graph, as shown below. To do so, you will need your earlier skills with solving equations.

EXAMPLE

—— This means x is a real number.

Solve $3x - 6 \leq x + 8$, $x \in R$. Draw a graph of your solution.

SOLUTION

$$3x - 6 \leq x + 8$$
$$3x - 6 + 6 \leq x + 8 + 6$$
$$3x \leq x + 14$$
$$3x - x \leq x + 14 - x$$
$$2x \leq 14$$
$$\frac{2x}{2} \leq \frac{14}{2}$$
$$x \leq 7$$

To show that 7 is part of the solution set, a solid dot is used.

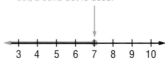

ACTIVITY 2   *Work in a Small Group*

The following graphs show the solution to different inequations. How are the graphs alike? How are they different?

(a) $x < 7$, $x \in I$ (b) $x \leq 7$, $x \in I$ (c) $x \leq 7$, $x \in R$ (d) $x < 7$, $x \in R$

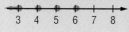

To show that 7 is not part of the solution set, an open dot is used.

A Review your skills with equations.

1. Write > or < for ? to make each sentence true.
   (a) $x + 5 > 8$ (b) $x - 3 < 4$ (c) $x > 3$
       $x + 5 - 5 \; ? \; 8 - 5$ $x - 3 + 3 \; ? \; 4 + 3$ $2x \; ? \; 2(3)$

   (d) $x > 3$ (e) $n < 2$ (f) $4n > -8$
       $-2(x) \; ? \; -2(3)$ $-2(n) \; ? \; -2(2)$ $\dfrac{4n}{4} \; ? \; \dfrac{-8}{4}$

B Remember to check whether your answer is reasonable.

2. For each inequality,
   - decide what your first step would be to write a simpler inequality.
   - find the solution.

   (a) $3m - 5 > 4$ (b) $3p + 30 < 21$ (c) $3x - 2 \leq 16$
   (d) $7x - 2 \geq 10$ (e) $3y - 8 < -14$ (f) $20 \leq 7t + 6$

3. (a) Draw a graph of $2y + 3 \leq 10$, $y \in I$.   (b) Draw a graph of $2y + 3 \leq 10$, $y \in R$.
   (c) How are your graphs in (a) and (b) alike? How are they different?

4. Draw the graph of each inequality. The variable is a real number.
   (a) $8k - 5 < 35$ (b) $6p - 4 \geq 12$ (c) $4y - 13 > 23$
   (d) $5 \geq 2k - 9$ (e) $10 < 6p - 14$ (f) $21 > 13 + 2n$

5. Solve.
   (a) $8y - 15 < 5y + 9$ (b) $5x + 8 \geq 3x + 26$ (c) $7y - 47 \leq 5y - 3$
   (d) $18 + 3x < x + 30$ (e) $5m - 9 > 9 + 4m - 2m$ (f) $3k + 2k - 5 \geq 2k + k - 7$

6. Draw the graph of all whole numbers such that 8 less than 4 times the number is greater than 12.

7. (a) A rational number is doubled and then decreased by 9. The result is less than 7 more than 3 times the rational number. What rational numbers are possible?
   (b) An integer when doubled and increased by 6 is less than the integer increased by 30. Find the possible integers.

8. A cooler will hold a maximum of 48 cans of pop. If there are 3 more cans of cola than orange and twice as many cans of ginger ale as cola, what is the maximum number of each in the cooler?

MAKING CONNECTIONS

Throughout the section, you have solved inequalities. Compare your skills with inequalities to your skills with equations.
(a) In your journal, describe how the skills are alike and how they are different.
(b) Give an example of your own to help with your description in (a).

These projects will give you an opportunity to look closely at some inventions, old and new, that put technology to good use.

PROJECT 1

The first helicopter was produced in 1907. But, did you know that Leonardo da Vinci, hundreds of years ago, designed a machine that could fly like a helicopter?

(a) In your library, find a drawing of da Vinci's "helicopter."

(b) If this machine were built, do you think it would fly? Why?

(c) Has anyone tried to build da Vinci's machine?

(d) Describe how this machine operates. Do you think that the invention would be practical in today's world? Give reasons for your answer.

PROJECT 2

Did you know that a pig can be put into a pipe? A "pig" is actually a robotic device that travels through gas pipes.

(a) What do you think the purpose of this device is?

(b) In your library, find the reason the pig was constructed. How reasonable was your prediction in (a)? What do the letters PIG represent?

(c) Write a brief report on how the machine operates. Present your report to the rest of the class.

PROJECT 3

Did you know that a computer can be made to read print or even handwriting? The computer uses an *optical scanner* to read the information.

(a) Describe how an optical scanner works.

(b) How does the computer store what the optical scanner reads?

(c) For what purposes do you think an optical scanner would be useful? Give reasons for your answer.

1. Solve.
   (a) $k - 7 = 15$ (b) $3 + m = 9$
   (c) $15 + p = -4$ (d) $18 = 2 + x$

2. For each equation,
   - decide by which number to multiply or divide.
   - solve the equation.
   (a) $2m = 8$ (b) $4y = 12$ (c) $6p = -12$
   (d) $\dfrac{k}{3} = 8$ (e) $\dfrac{a}{4} = -2$ (f) $\dfrac{s}{2} = 3$
   (g) $-2t = 6$ (h) $\dfrac{w}{-2} = -4$ (i) $-5x = 25$

3. Solve. Which have the same solution?
   (a) $2m - 3 = -7$ (b) $3 + 2m = -1$
   (c) $3 - 2m = 7$ (d) $-2m + 3 = 1$

4. Solve.
   (a) $2x + 8 = x - 12$
   (b) $18 + 3x - 5 = 65 - x$
   (c) $3 + 3x - 10 = 5x + 31$

5. (a) Solve $5(m - 2) \leq 2(m + 11)$, $m \in I$.
   (b) Draw a graph of the solution set in (a).

6. Find each number.
   (a) A number decreased by 12 is 28.
   (b) 10 divided by a number is 5.
   (c) A number diminished by 24 is 16.
   (d) A number increased by 53 is 76.
   (e) A number subtracted from 100 is 72.

7. Find the missing measure in each triangle.
   (a)   (b)   (c)

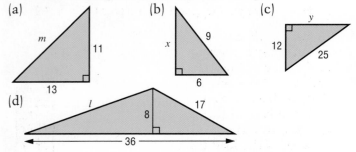

   (d)

8. A ladder 7 m long is placed against a wall so that the foot of the ladder is 2.5 m from the wall. Calculate how high up the wall the ladder reaches.

THINKING ABOUT

❶ Have you updated your *Problem Solving Plan* with skills like the following?
   - using manipulatives
   - using a diagram

❷ Are the solutions in your notebook clearly organized?

❸ Choose a question on this page. Describe to your partner how you can solve it. Have your partner suggest how your description can be improved.

MAKING CONNECTIONS

Refer to the opening page of this chapter.
(a) Create a problem of your own using the picture.
(b) Compare your problem with others in your class. Solve the other problems.

❹ Write two examples of how you might use the skills in this chapter in your daily life.

❺ What can you do to improve your Problem Solving skills?

❻ Which problems in this chapter did you find difficult? How did you try to make them less difficult?

SELF EVALUATION

1. Find each root.
   (a) $2x + 5 = 9$ (b) $3x - 6 = 6$ (c) $2x + 8 = 2$
   (d) $11 = 3x - 1$ (e) $3(2x + 8) = 6$ (f) $-25 = 5x - 10$

2. Find the root. Verify your answers.
   (a) $3x + 7 = 22$ (b) $4x - 6 = 3x - 2$
   (c) $2m = 3m - 9$ (d) $5k - 4 = 3k + 12$

3. The perimeter of the triangle is 37 m. Find the length of each side.

   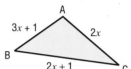

4. One number is three more than another. If the sum of the numbers is 13, find the numbers.

5. Calculate the length of the hypotenuse in each right triangle.

   (a) (b) (c)

6. Solve each of the following. The variable is a real number.
   (a) $3t - 12 \geq -18$ (b) $2r + 6 < 22$
   (c) $8t < 35 + 3t$ (d) $8x - 10 < 3x - 4$
   (e) $3m + 2 \geq 2m - 4$ (f) $4y < 2y - 8$

7. (a) Solve $2x + 8 > 10$, $x \in I$.
   (b) Draw a graph of your solution set in (a).
   (c) How would your graph be different if $x \in R$?

MATH JOURNAL

In this chapter, you have used symbols and skills to help you communicate mathematics.
(a) List all the symbols and skills you have learned.
(b) Write an example to show how to communicate your ideas with each.

8. A crane with a 19-m rotating lever lowers a load of cement on the end of a 12-m cable so that the load is level with the base of the rotating arm as shown. How far is the load from the edge of the building?

   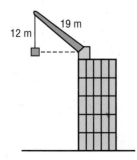

1. (a) Tom has three plums 3 cm in radius. Tanya has one plum 5 cm in diameter.
   Who has the greatest volume of plums? What assumptions have you made?
   (b) In your journal, describe how you can solve the problem in (a) mentally.

2. The circumference of the circle at the right is
   5π cm. The triangle inscribed in the circle has
   sides that are all represented by whole numbers.
   (a) Find the length of each side of the triangle.
   (b) How many times greater is the area of the
   circle than the area of the triangle?

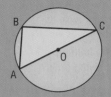

3. Ten straws are placed in a hat. The straws are 2 cm, 4 cm, 6 cm, ..., 20 cm. You are
   to reach into the hat and select three straws. What is the probability that you can
   form a right triangle with the straws you selected? List any assumptions you have
   made.

4. The area of square ABCD is 200 cm². Find the area
   of figure WXYZ.

5. Dimitri was stuffing envelopes as a volunteer
   during the election. For the first eight envelopes
   he stuffed, he also had to address them. Which of
   the following statements is reasonable? Give
   reasons for your answer.
   (a) Dimitri got exactly 7 addresses correct.
   (b) Dimitri got exactly 6 addresses correct.
   (c) Dimitri got exactly 1 address wrong.

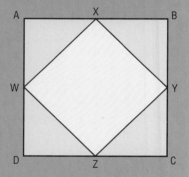

6. What numeral is represented by each letter?
   (a) O D D   (b)   S E N D
        O D D   + M O R E
      + O L D   ─────────
      ─────────   M O N E Y
        C L E O
   (c) Create and solve a similar problem. Compare your answer to others in the class.

7. Complete and verify each pattern for three more rows.

   (a) $1^3 = 1^2 - 0^2$ (b) $1 \times \dfrac{1}{2} = 1 - \dfrac{1}{2}$

   $2^3 = 3^2 - 1^2$ $2 \times \dfrac{2}{3} = 2 - \dfrac{2}{3}$

   $3^3 = 6^2 - 3^2$ $3 \times \dfrac{3}{4} = 3 - \dfrac{3}{4}$

   $4^3 = 10^2 - 6^2$ $4 \times \dfrac{4}{5} = 4 - \dfrac{4}{5}$

   (c) Create and solve a similar problem. Compare your answer to others in the class.

Have you ever read a mystery novel where the detective retraced the suspect's movements to solve the crime? This is known as working backwards towards a possible solution.

In your journal:

- Describe how retracing your movements can help you remember something or find a lost object.
- Describe how working backwards has helped you solve problems in your previous work in mathematics.

You have used algebra tiles to help you work with expressions and solve equations. They can also help you explore how to multiply a binomial by a binomial.

In the exploration, algebra tiles are used to help you find the product of expressions like $(x + 3)(x + 2)$. Summarize any patterns and relationships that can help you find the product.

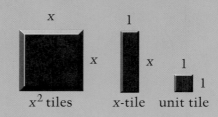

x^2 tiles   x-tile   unit tile

EXPLORATION

1. (a) Interpret the diagram. How can you use these tiles to find the product of $(x + 3)(x + 2)$?
   (b) What is the product in (a)?

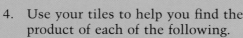

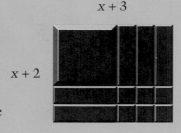

2. Construct a rectangle with the following lengths and widths. Which algebra tiles do you need to use to cover the area?
   (a) $x + 3$, $x + 5$ (b) $x + 6$, $x + 1$
   (c) $x + 2$, $x + 4$ (d) $x + 5$, $x + 2$
   (e) $x + 1$, $x + 7$ (f) $x + 2$, $x + 8$

3. (a) Interpret the diagram. How can you use these tiles to find the product of $(x + 3)(2x + 1)$?
   (b) What is the product in (a)?

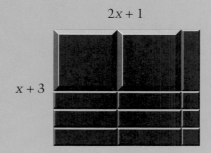

4. Use your tiles to help you find the product of each of the following.
   (a) $(2x + 1)(x + 2)$ (b) $(3x + 5)(x + 2)$
   (c) $(4x + 3)(2x + 1)$ (d) $(5x + 4)(x + 1)$
   (e) $(2x + 1)(2x + 7)$ (f) $(3x + 3)(4x + 3)$

5. (a) Interpret the diagram. How can you use these tiles to find the product of $(x + 2)(x - 1)$?
   (b) What is the product in (a)?

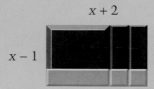

6. Use your tiles to help you find the product of each of the following.
   (a) $(x - 1)(x + 2)$ (b) $(x - 5)(x + 2)$
   (c) $(x + 3)(x - 1)$ (d) $(x + 4)(x - 1)$
   (e) $(x + 5)(x - 7)$

To help you find the product of $(x + 3)(x + 2)$, you can use your algebra tiles. You can also work backwards from your knowledge of the distributive property to find the product. $a(b + c) = ab + ac$

Use the Distributive Property

$(x + 3)(x + 2) = (x + 3)x + (x + 3)2$

factors

$= x^2 + 3x + 2x + 6$

$= x^2 + 5x + 6$

terms

Use Algebra Tiles

$x + 3$

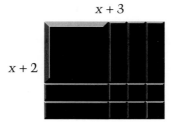

$x + 2$

Think:
Interpret the diagram. How might it help you find the product?

You can extend your skills with the distributive property to find the product of other binomials as shown below.

EXAMPLE

Expand and simplify.

$(2y + 3)(3y + 2)$

SOLUTION

$(2y + 3)(3y + 2)$

$= (2y + 3)3y + (2y + 3)2$

$= 6y^2 + 9y + 4y + 6$

$= 6y^2 + 13y + 6$

$3y + 2$

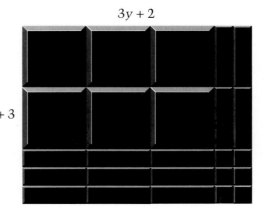

$2y + 3$

Think:
How might the diagram help you find the product?

EXERCISE

A Use algebra tiles to help you.

1. A diagram is shown. How might you use algebra tiles to complete it? Find each product.

(a)

	x	7
x	?	?
6	?	?

$(x + 6)(x + 7) = ?$

(b)

	x	3
$2x$	?	?
1	?	?

$(2x + 1)(x + 3) = ?$

2. (a) To find the product $(x + 4)(x + 5)$, Carol wrote
   $(x + 4)(x + 5) = x(x + 5) + 4(x + 5)$.
   Complete her solution to find the product.
   (b) To find the product, Andy wrote $(x + 4)(x + 5) = (x + 4)x + (x + 4)5$.
   Complete his solution to find the product.
   (c) What do you notice about the answers in (a) and (b)?

3. Find each of the following products.
   (a) $(x + 3)(x + 6)$ (b) $(y + 5)(y + 7)$ (c) $(a + 4)(a + 4)$
   (d) $(k + 6)(k + 8)$ (e) $(m + 5)(m + 6)$ (f) $(n + 5)(n + 5)$

B   Think of how you can check your answers.

4. Find each product.
   (a) $(x + 1)(x + 5)$ (b) $(a - 4)(a + 3)$ (c) $(m + 5)(m - 8)$
   (d) $(x - 2y)(x - 3y)$ (e) $(k + 5)(k - 1)$ (f) $(6 + x)(8 + x)$

5. Find each product. What do you notice about your answers?
   (a) $(a - 3)(a + 3)$ (b) $(x + 5)(x - 5)$ (c) $(2y + 3)(2y - 3)$
   (d) $(3m + 6)(3m - 6)$ (e) $(6 - 2m)(6 + 2m)$ (f) $(8 - 3x)(8 + 3x)$

6. Find each product.
   (a) $(x + 6)(x + 3)$ (b) $(y + 7)(y - 9)$ (c) $(2t - 3)(2t - 3)$
   (d) $(k - 6)(k + 6)$ (e) $(y^2 + 6)(y^2 - 6)$ (f) $(5 + x)(6 - x)$

7. Each binomial involves more than one variable. Expand and simplify.
   (a) $(x + 2y)(3x + y)$ (b) $(2c + 6d)(3c - d)$ (c) $(3a + b)(a + 2b)$
   (d) $(3y - 2x)(2y - 3x)$ (e) $(3y - x)(2y - x)$ (f) $(6k + s)(3k - 2s)$

8. Find an expression for the area of each figure.
   (a)   (b)   (c)

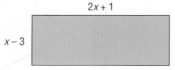

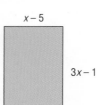

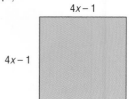

9. A machine pumps $(2x + 1)$ litres every hour. The pump works for $(x - 3)$ hours.
   (a) Find an expression for the amount pumped.   (b) Simplify the expression.

10. The cost of one delivery is $(2y - 3)$ dollars.
    (a) Find an expression for the cost of $(y + 3)$ deliveries.
    (b) Simplify the expression.

PARTNER PROJECT

Remember: $(x + 1)^2 = (x + 1)(x + 1)$
$(x + 1)^3 = (x + 1)(x + 1)(x + 1)$

(a) Find an expression for each of the following.
    A: $(x + 1)^2$ B: $(x + 1)^3$ C: $(x + 1)^4$ D: $(x + 1)^5$

(b) Use your results in (a). Predict an expression for $(x + 1)^6$. How can you check your prediction?

11.3 SQUARE OF A BINOMIAL

When the factors of a product are the same, you are able to use exponents. For example, you can write $(x + 2)(x + 2)$ as $(x + 2)^2$. To find the square of a binomial like $(x + 2)^2$, you can again use algebra tiles or work backwards from the distributive property.

Use the Distributive Property

$$(x + 2)^2 = (x + 2)(x + 2)$$
$$= x(x + 2) + 2(x + 2)$$
$$= x^2 + 2x + 2x + 4$$
$$= x^2 + 4x + 4$$

Use Algebra Tiles

Think:
How might you
interpret this diagram
to find $(x + 2)^2$?

EXERCISE

B   Remember: Think of a pattern to help you find products.

1. To find each product, how might you interpret each diagram? What is the product?

   (a)

	6	x
x	A	B
6	C	6x

   (b)

	2y	4
4	8y	A
2y	C	B

   (c)

	x	3
x	x^2	A
3	B	C

   How are the areas for A, B, and C used to find an answer for
   $(x + 6)^2$? $(2y + 4)^2$? $(x + 3)^2$?

2. Use the distributive property to expand each of the following.
   (a) $(x + y)^2$ (b) $(m - 3)^2$ (c) $(2y + 6)^2$ (d) $(3 + m)^2$
   (e) $(3y - 1)^2$ (f) $(3x - y)^2$ (g) $(3 + 2b)^2$ (h) $(3x + 2y)^2$

3. Find each product. How many can you do mentally?
   (a) $(x + 5)^2$ (b) $(y - 6)^2$ (c) $(3 - y)^2$ (d) $(5 + b)^2$
   (e) $(m - 3n)^2$ (f) $(2m + 6n)^2$ (g) $(2m - 3n)^2$ (h) $(5x - 2y)^2$

4. Square each binomial.
   (a) $(x + 3)$ (b) $(y - 4)$ (c) $(2y + 1)$ (d) $(6 + 3y)$ (e) $(8 - 2x)$

5. For each of the following, which are squares of binomials?
   (a) $a^2 + 4a + 4$ (b) $y^2 + 8y + 16$ (c) $x^2 + xy + y^2$ (d) $4x^2 + 4xy + y^2$

343

11.4 EXPLORING FACTORS

You have used algebra tiles to help you work with expressions and solve equations. Algebra tiles can also help you find the factors of an expression.

As you complete each exploration, summarize any patterns and relationships that can help you find the factors of an expression.

EXPLORATION ① *Work with a Partner*

1. (a) Review with your partner what is meant by the "factors of a *number*." Give examples to show its meaning.
   (b) How might you interpret factors of an *expression*?

2. Describe how these steps can help you write $3x - 9$ as a product of factors.

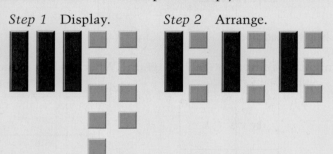

Step 1 Display.

Step 2 Arrange.

Step 3 Interpret. Thus, $3x - 9$ can be written as $3(x - 3)$.

This expression is in factored form. Thus, the factors of $3x - 9$ are 3 and $x - 3$.

3. (a) Write the expressions shown by the algebra tiles.

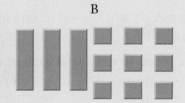

   A

   B

   (b) Factor each expression in (a).

4. Use algebra tiles to factor each expression.
   (a) $2x + 6$ (b) $4x + 8$ (c) $2x - 10$ (d) $3x - 15$
   (e) Create similar expressions of your own. Factor each expression and have others in the class factor your expressions.

5. Use algebra tiles to factor each expression.
   (a) $2m + 12$ (b) $8k - 16$ (c) $2z + 16$ (d) $4y + 20$
   (e) Create similar expressions of your own. Factor each expression and have others in the class factor your expressions.

EXPLORATION ② *Work with a Partner*

6. (a) What expression is shown by the algebra tiles?
   (b) What is the length and the width of each rectangle below?

   A

   B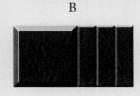

   (c) What expression represents the area of each rectangle?
   (d) Use algebra tiles and construct rectangles of your own. Repeat (a), (b), and (c) using your tiles.

EXPLORATION ③ *Work with a Partner*

7. How can the algebra tiles below help you factor $x^2 + 3x + 2$?

   Step 1

   Step 2

   Step 3

   Thus,
   $x^2 + 3x + 2 = (x + 2)(x + 1)$.

   The expression $x^2 + 3x + 2$ is written in factored form.

8. (a) Write the expression shown by the algebra tiles below.
   (b) Find the factors of each expression.

   A   B

9. For each of the following:
   • Represent the expression using algebra tiles.
   • Find the factors of the expression.
   (a) $x^2 + 4x + 4$ (b) $x^2 + 7x + 10$ (c) $x^2 + 6x + 5$

10. (a) Create similar expressions of your own.
    (b) Find the factors of your expressions.
    (c) Compare your expressions with those of your partner.

Previously you found the product $4(x + 5) = 4x + 20$. The algebra tiles below can help you work backwards to find the factors of expressions.

ACTIVITY 1 *Work with a Partner*

1. Discuss how these steps can be used to find the factors of $3x + 6$.

Step 1 Display.
Represent the
expression using
algebra tiles.

Step 2 Arrange.
Use the tiles to form
a rectangle.

|← —— $x + 2$ —— →|

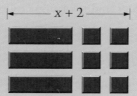

Step 3 Interpret.
Write the expression as the
product of the length and
width. Thus, $3x + 6 = 3(x + 2)$.

From the steps above, $3x + 6$
has factors of 3 and $x + 2$.

The *factors* of $3x + 6$ are 3 and $(x + 2)$. 3 is called the *common factor* of $3x$ and 6.

2. Use the steps above to factor each expression.
   (a) $4x + 8$ (b) $5x - 10$ (c) $-3x + 9$ (d) $-2x - 8$

ACTIVITY 2 *Work with a Partner*

3. Use the above steps to find the common factor of the expression below.

Step 1 Display.
$2x^2 + 4x$

$2x^2 + 4x = x(2x + 4)$
↑
a common factor of $2x^2 + 4x$

Step 2 Arrange.
$2x$ and 4 also have
a common factor.

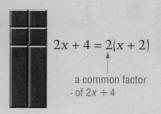

$2x + 4 = 2(x + 2)$
↑
a common factor
of $2x + 4$

Step 3 Interpret.
Thus,
$2x^2 + 4x = x(2)(x + 2)$
$= 2x(x + 2)$
↑
$2x$ is the greatest
common factor of
$2x^2$ and $4x$

To factor an expression, find the *greatest* common factor of the terms.

EXAMPLE

Factor.   (a) $25x^3 + 50x^2$ (b) $4a^2b + 12ab^2 - 16ab^3$

SOLUTION

(a) $25x^3 + 50x^2 = 25x^2(x + 2)$ (b) $4a^2b + 12ab^2 - 16ab^3 = 4ab(a + 3b - 4b^2)$

A   Use algebra tiles to help you.

1. What is the greatest common factor of each pair of terms?
   (a) $3x$, 12 (b) $5x$, 5 (c) $7x$, 14 (d) $2x$, 8
   (e) $5x$, -15 (f) $-6x$, -18 (g) $-3x$, 12 (h) $4x$, -20

2. Refer to your answers in Question 1. Factor each of the following.
   (a) $3x + 12$ (b) $5x + 5$ (c) $7x + 14$ (d) $2x + 8$
   (e) $5x - 15$ (f) $-6x - 18$ (g) $-3x + 12$ (h) $4x - 20$

B   Remember: Algebra tiles can represent any variable.

3. Write the first step to factor each of the following. Then factor.
   (a) $4m + 4p$ (b) $8r - 4k$ (c) $3m + 12n$ (d) $4q - 16p$

4. Factor each of the following.
   (a) $3x - 6y$ (b) $4x - 12y$ (c) $3n - 18m$
   (d) $4y - 10z$ (e) $6q - 4p$ (f) $-2q + 8p$
   (g) $3a + 3b + 3c$ (h) $2a - 4b - 6c$ (i) $2x - 4y + 6z$

5. Find each missing factor.
   (a) $6 + 8x = (?)(3 + 4x)$
   (b) $2\pi r + 4\pi = (?)(r + 2)$
   (c) $6y - 12y^2 = (6y)(?)$
   (d) $4y^3 - 8y^2 = (4y^2)(?)$
   (e) $6x^2y - 4xy^2 + 10x^2y^2 = (2xy)(?)$
   (f) $9a^2m^2 - 6am^2 - 18a^2m = (3am)(?)$

6. Factor each of the following.
   (a) $6 - 12x$ (b) $5x^2 - 3x$ (c) $9y - 12x$
   (d) $5xy - 3xy^2$ (e) $2x^2 - 6x$ (f) $a^2 - 2a$
   (g) $4ab - b^2$ (h) $4y^2 + 16$ (i) $28a^2 - 14ab$
   (j) $36mn - 25m^2n^2$ (k) $6x^2 - 12x + 15$ (l) $5m^3 - 25m^2 + 15$

7. Factor.
   (a) $6a - 12a^2 + 15a$ (b) $3ab^2 + 6a + 8a$ (c) $2k^2 - 3k^3 + 8k^4$
   (d) $x^3y - 2x^2y^2 - xy^3$ (e) $5b - 25b^2 + 15b$ (f) $30ab + 20a^2b^2 - 10ab$

C

8. Find a common factor of the terms and then simplify.

   (a) $\dfrac{2x^2y + 3xy^2}{xy}$ (b) $\dfrac{4xy - 24y^2}{4y}$ (c) $\dfrac{6x^3y + 12x^3y^2}{6x^3y}$

   (d) $\dfrac{5x^4y - 35xy^3}{5xy}$ (e) $\dfrac{-12x^3y^2 - 18x^2y^3}{6x^2y^2}$ (f) $\dfrac{3x^4 + 6x^3 + 9x^2}{3x^2}$

Previously, you found the products $(x + 1)(x + 3) = x^2 + 4x + 3$. Working backwards, you can also use algebra tiles to find the factors of an expression such as a trinomial. A *trinomial* is an expression with three terms.

ACTIVITY *Work with a Partner*

1. Discuss with a partner how these steps can help you factor $x^2 + 3x + 2$.

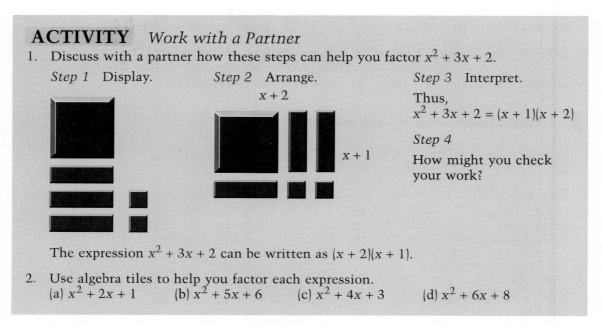

Step 1 Display.

Step 2 Arrange.

$x + 2$

$x + 1$

Step 3 Interpret.

Thus,
$x^2 + 3x + 2 = (x + 1)(x + 2)$

Step 4

How might you check your work?

The expression $x^2 + 3x + 2$ can be written as $(x + 2)(x + 1)$.

2. Use algebra tiles to help you factor each expression.
   (a) $x^2 + 2x + 1$ (b) $x^2 + 5x + 6$ (c) $x^2 + 4x + 3$ (d) $x^2 + 6x + 8$

An important method in problem solving is to summarize a strategy and ask useful questions about it. For example, you could ask yourself, "How would the method change if I subtracted terms instead of adding them?" Algebra tiles can be used to factor the expression $x^2 - 3x + 2$.

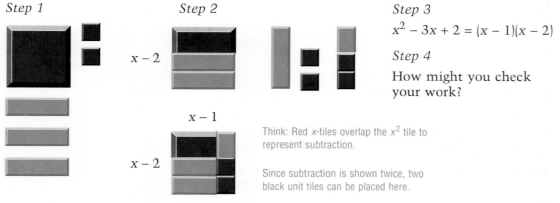

Step 1

$x - 2$

$x - 1$

$x - 2$

Step 2

Step 3

$x^2 - 3x + 2 = (x - 1)(x - 2)$

Step 4

How might you check your work?

Think: Red x-tiles overlap the x^2 tile to represent subtraction.

Since subtraction is shown twice, two black unit tiles can be placed here.

Write the expression as the product of the length and width:
$x^2 - 3x + 2 = (x - 2)(x - 1)$.

A Use algebra tiles to help you.

1. (a) What expressions are shown by the tiles?
   (b) What are the factors of each expression?

A 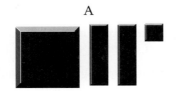   B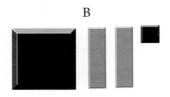

2. (a) Use algebra tiles to represent $x^2 + 6x + 5$.
   (b) Construct a rectangle using your tiles in (a).
   (c) What are the factors of $x^2 + 6x + 5$?

3. (a) Use algebra tiles to represent $x^2 - 7x + 12$.
   (b) Construct a rectangle using your tiles in (a).
   (c) What are the factors of $x^2 - 7x + 12$?

4. (a) Use algebra tiles to represent $x^2 - 2x - 15$.
   (b) Construct a rectangle using your tiles in (a).
   (c) What are the factors of $x^2 - 2x - 15$?

B Look for a common factor first.

5. (a) How are the expressions $a^2 + 5a + 6$ and $6 + 5a + a^2$ alike?
   How are they different?
   (b) Find the factors of each expression in (a). What do you notice?

6. Factor each of the following.
   (a) $x^2 - 11x + 18$
   (b) $y^2 + 6y + 8$
   (c) $m^2 + 12m + 27$
   (d) $n^2 - 11n + 30$
   (e) $25 - 10a + a^2$
   (f) $h^2 + 8h + 12$
   (g) $t^2 + 6t + 5$
   (h) $18 - 9m + m^2$
   (i) $m^2 + 9m + 14$
   (j) $t^2 - 20t + 96$
   (k) $y^2 - 10y + 9$
   (l) $d^2 + 13d + 36$
   (m) $x^2 - 3x - 10$
   (n) $y^2 + y - 6$
   (o) $m^2 - m - 2$

7. (a) To factor $2x^2 - 12x + 16$, what should be your first step?
   (b) Find the common factor of the expression in (a).
   (c) Find the other factors.

8. Factor each of the following completely.
   (a) $2x^2 - 12x + 18$
   (b) $y^3 + 14y^2 + 24y$
   (c) $2x^2 + 22x + 36$
   (d) $4m^2 + 44m - 104$
   (e) $x^3 + 8x^2 - 48x$
   (f) $a^3 - 12a^2 + 27a$
   (g) $3y^2 - 36y + 108$
   (h) $2x^2 + 2x - 84$
   (i) $b^3 + 24b^2 - 81b$
   (j) $3m^2 + 72m - 156$
   (k) $2x^2 - 36x + 112$
   (l) $x^3 - 2x^2 - 48x$

9. Factor.

(a) $k^2 + 4k - 5$ (b) $x^2 + 12x + 35$ (c) $m^2 + 10m - 11$

(d) $x^2 + x - 12$ (e) $y^2 + 10y + 9$ (f) $t^2 + 2t - 48$

(g) $m^2 - m - 42$ (h) $s^2 - 5s - 50$ (i) $t^2 - 9t + 20$

(j) $56 - 15x + x^2$ (k) $x^2 - 12x - 85$ (l) $y^2 + 8y + 15$

10. A field has an area in square metres given by the expression $x^2 + x - 6$. If the length in metres is given by $(x + 3)$, find an expression for the width.

11. The length of a trip in kilometres is given by the expression $x^2 + 8x - 20$. If the time taken in hours is given by $(x - 2)$, find an expression for the speed in kilometres per hour.

C

12. (a) The trinomial $x^2 + kx + 25$, $k \in I$, has two different binomial factors. What is the value of k? What other values can you find for k?

(b) The trinomial $x^2 + kx - 24$, $k \in I$, has two binomial factors. What is the value of k? What other values can you find for k?

(c) The trinomial $x^2 - kx - 20$, $k \in I$, has two binomial factors. What is the value of k? What other values can you find for k?

13. (a) Fold a square piece of paper into four equal sections as shown. The perimeter of the shaded shape between the folds is 25 cm.

(b) Find the area of the original square piece of paper.

(c) Create a similar problem of your own. Solve the problem and compare the solution to others in the class.

STRATEGIES TO HELP

To factor $x^2 - 12x + 27$, you can work backwards.

(a) In your journal, record the questions you should ask yourself when factoring an expression.

(b) Describe how the questions in (a) can help you factor an expression.

(c) Use your questions in (a) to factor some expressions in this section.

What two numbers have a sum of –12 and a product of 27?

$$x^2 - 12x + 27 = (x \quad ?)(x \quad ?)$$

Since the sum is negative, the numbers are both negative.
$-12 = (-3) + (-9)$

$$x^2 - 12x + 27 = (x - 3)(x - 9)$$

Since the product is positive, the two numbers are either both negative or both positive.
$27 = (3)(9)$ or $(-3)(-9)$

UNICATE

When you communicate mathematics to others, you often commu
form that is concise. The following activities will help you commun
an expression.

A

1.

2.

ACTIVITY 1 *Work with a Partner*

1. (a) Refer to the following expressions. How are they alike? How are
      different?
      A $2 \times 2 \times 2 \times 2 = 2^4$ B $y \times y \times y \times y \times y = y^5$
   (b) Refer to your results in (a). Suggest how you would write
       $(x + y)(x + y)$ in a more concise form.

2. Refer to your results in Question 1. Suppose you have just factored the
   following: $x^2 + 4x + 4 = (x + 2)(x + 2)$. How can you check your work?
   (a) How can you write the factors in a more concise form?
   (b) What math skills have you learned previously that helped you in (a)?
   (c) Repeat (a) and (b) for the following expressions.
      (i) $x^2 + 6x + 9$ (ii) $x^2 + 2x + 1$

In the activity above, you wrote $x^2 + 4x + 4$ as $(x + 2)^2$.

The expression $(x + 2)^2$ is called a *trinomial square*.

To find the factors of a trinomial square, think about the terms and work backwards, as
shown below.

$a^2 + 8a + 16 = (a + 4)^2$ Think: $a^2 = (a)^2$ Check the factors.
                               $16 = 4^2$ $(a + 4)^2 = (a + 4)(a + 4)$
                               $8a = 2(a)(4)$ $= a^2 + 8a + 16$

ACTIVITY 2 *Work with a Partner*

3. (a) To factor $x^2 - 9$, answer the questions below.

   $x^2 - 9 = x^2 + 0x - 9$ Think: What two numbers have a sum of 0
          $= (x + ?)(x + ?)$ and a product of –9?

   (b) In your journal, record why the factors of $x^2 - 9$ are as shown.
       $x^2 - 9 = (x + 3)(x - 3)$

4. (a) What do you notice about the terms in the original expression in Question 3
      and the terms in each factor?
   (b) What do you notice about the operation sign in each factor?
   (c) The original expression, $x^2 - 9$, is called the *difference of squares*. Why do
      you think it has this name?

Review your skills with factors.

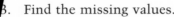

(a) What expression is shown by the tiles?
(b) What are the factors of the expression?

(a) Use algebra tiles to represent $x^2 - 16$.
(b) Construct a rectangle using your tiles in (a).
(c) What are the factors of $x^2 - 16$?

3. Find the missing values.
   (a) $(y - 6)(y + 6) = (y)^2 - (?)^2$
   (b) $(x + 5)(x - 5) = (?)^2 - (5)^2$
   (c) $(a + 1)(a - 1) = (a)^2 - (?)^2$
   (d) $(3a - 1)(3a + 1) = (?)^2 - (1)^2$
   (e) $(3a + b)(3a - b) = (?)^2 - (b)^2$
   (f) $(2x + 5)(2x - 5) = (2x)^2 - (?)^2$

4. Find the missing value required to make each a trinomial square.
   (a) $a^2 + 4a + ?$
   (b) $? - 6y + 9$
   (c) $4a^2 + ? + 1$
   (d) $? - 40y + 16y^2$
   (e) $4x^2 + 12xy + ?$
   (f) $9a^2 + ? + 4b^2$

5. Which of the following are *not* trinomial squares? Why?
   (a) $4a^2 + 4ab + b^2$
   (b) $a^2 + 20a + 36$
   (c) $a^2 + 26a + 25$
   (d) $a^2 - 6ab + ab^2$
   (e) $x^2 - 8xy + 16y^2$
   (f) $4y^2 - 12y + 9$
   (g) $x^2 - 5xy + 4y^2$
   (h) $4m^2 - 12mn + 9n^2$
   (i) $a^2 - 10ab + 9b^2$
   (j) $16 + 64y + 64y^2$
   (k) $y^2 + y + \frac{1}{4}$
   (l) $y^2 + \frac{5}{4}y + \frac{1}{4}$

B Look for a common factor.

6. Factor the trinomial squares.
   (a) $y^2 + 4y + 4$
   (b) $x^2 - 6x + 9$
   (c) $a^2 + 12a + 36$
   (d) $m^2 + 10m + 25$
   (e) $4y^2 + 8y + 4$
   (f) $1 + 4x + 4x^2$
   (g) $x^2 - 6x + 9$
   (h) $4x^2 - 4x + 1$
   (i) $9a^2 - 12a + 4$
   (j) $9 - 24y + 16y^2$
   (k) $4a^2 + 12a + 9$
   (l) $m^2 - 10m + 25$
   (m) $x^2 - 12x + 36$
   (n) $81 - 36y + 4y^2$
   (o) $a^2 + a + \frac{1}{4}$
   (p) $a^4 - 2a^2 + 1$
   (q) $1 - 4y^2 + 4y^4$
   (r) $y^2 - 3y + \frac{9}{4}$

7. Factor each of the following.
   (a) $a^2 - b^2$
   (b) $y^2 - x^2$
   (c) $a^2 - 4b^2$
   (d) $x^2 - 1$
   (e) $4m^2 - 9n^2$
   (f) $9k^2 - 16m^2$
   (g) $1 - 25y^2$
   (h) $16y^2 - 25x^2$
   (i) $2m^2 - 72$
   (j) $4t^2 - 25s^2$
   (k) $98 - 18m^2$
   (l) $36 - x^2$

8. Factor each of the following.

(a) $3m^2 - 48$ (b) $2x^2 - 128$ (c) $98 - 2y^2$ (d) $75x^2 - 3$

(e) $-8 + 18m^2$ (f) $50 - 32m^2$ (g) $50y^2 - 2$ (h) $108 - 3m^2$

(i) $72 - 98y^2$ (j) $ax^2 - 100a$ (k) $m^3 - 36m$ (l) $x^3 - 16x$

(m) $x^2 - 14x + 49$ (n) $25 - 30n + 9n^2$ (o) $y^2 - y + \dfrac{1}{4}$

(p) $4m^4 - 4m^2 + 1$ (q) $4 - 12x + 9x^2$ (r) $x^2 - 5x + \dfrac{25}{4}$

9. Factor each of the following. Check for a common factor first.

(a) $2a^2 + 12a + 18$ (b) $3y^2 - 18y + 27$ (c) $9x^2 + 12x + 4$

(d) $y^2 - 4y + 4$ (e) $4x^3 + 4x^2 + x$ (f) $y^3 - 6y^2 + 9y$

10. Factor each of the following. (Be careful! One cannot be factored.)

(a) $m^2n^2 - 25$ (b) $x^2y^2 - 4$ (c) $100 - a^2b^2$ (d) $64 - m^2n^2$

(e) $x^2y^2 - 3^2$ (f) $a^2b^2 - k^2$ (g) $x^2y^2 + 4$ (h) $1 - 25a^2b^2$

(i) $(mn)^2 - 4m^2$ (j) $(4pq)^2 - 16p^2$ (k) $100m^2 - 64n^2$ (l) $25x^2y^2 - 1$

(m) $\dfrac{x^2}{9} - 25$ (n) $x^2 - \dfrac{1}{4}$ (o) $(xy)^4 - (xy)^2$ (p) $\dfrac{4x^2}{25} - 64$

11. If $x = 3$ and $y = 4$, find the value of each expression.

(a) $x^2 + 2xy + y^2$ (b) $(x + y)^2$

Which answer, (a) or (b), was more easily obtained?

12. In finding factors, you should always check to see if the factors you obtain are factorable again. Factor each of the following.

(a) $a^4 - 1$ (b) $16m^4 - n^4$ (c) $16y^4 - 100x^4$ (d) $1 - 16b^4$

13. (a) Find four factors for $x^4 - 5x^2 + 4$.   (b) Find three factors for $x^4 - 11x^2 + 18$.

MAKING CONNECTIONS

1. To calculate 21×19, you can think of the steps shown to the right.

   (a) Give reasons for each step.

   (b) In your journal, write an example of your own to illustrate your mental calculation.

$$21 \times 19 = (20 + 1)(20 - 1)$$
$$= 20^2 - 1^2$$
$$= 400 - 1$$
$$= 399$$

2. Find the missing values. Then find the products mentally.

   (a) $22 \times 18 = (20 + ?)(20 - ?)$ (b) $34 \times 26 = (30 + ?)(? - 4)$

   (c) $32 \times 28 = (30 + ?)(? - 2)$ (d) $48 \times 52 = (? - 2)(? + 2)$

3. • Write each product in a form similar to that in Question 1.

   • Then calculate.

   (a) 57×63 (b) 27×33 (c) 24×16 (d) 68×72

11.8 PROBLEM SOLVING: SOLVE A SIMPLER PROBLEM

By applying your factoring skills to problems involving measurement, you can often reduce the amount of work you must do. For example, to calculate the area of the shaded region in the diagram to the right, you can use the following expression.

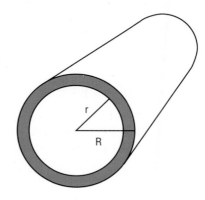

Area of shaded region
= Area of large circle – Area of small circle
$= \pi R^2 - \pi r^2$
$= \pi(R^2 - r^2)$ π is a common factor.
$= \pi(R - r)(R + r)$ difference of squares

EXAMPLE
Find the area of concrete on the cross-sectional end of the pipe above to the nearest square centimetre for $R = 52.00$ cm, $r = 48.00$ cm, and $\pi = 3.14$.

SOLUTION
Method A: Without factoring

$A = \pi R^2 - \pi r^2$
$\doteq 3.14(52.00)^2 - 3.14(48.00)^2$
$= 8490.56 - 7234.56$
$= 1256$ (to the nearest cm^2)

Method B: With factoring

$A = \pi(R + r)(R - r)$
$\doteq 3.14(52.00 + 48.00) \times (52.00 - 48.00)$
$= 3.14(100)(4)$
$= 1256$ (to the nearest cm^2)

Thus, the area of concrete on the end of the pipe is 1256 cm^2 to the nearest square centimetre.

EXERCISE

B   For each of the following questions, use your skills with factoring to reduce the number of calculations.

1. Find the area of each shaded region to one decimal place.

(a)
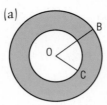

OB = 16.0 m
OC = 14.0 m

(b)
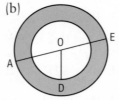

AE = 50.0 cm
OD = 21.0 cm

(c)
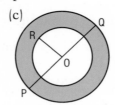

PQ = 12.5 cm
OR = 4.5 cm

2. Find the area of each shaded region.

(a)

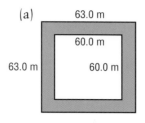

63.0 m

60.0 m

63.0 m   60.0 m

(b)

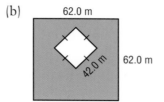

62.0 m

42.0 m

62.0 m

(c)

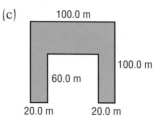

100.0 m

100.0 m

60.0 m

20.0 m   20.0 m

3. A square courtyard has a walkway 2.0 m wide. If the enclosed square garden is 42.0 m wide, find the area of the walkway.

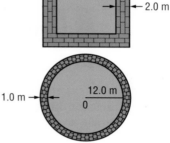

2.0 m

4. A circular sidewalk 1.0 m wide encircles a garden. Calculate the area of the sidewalk.

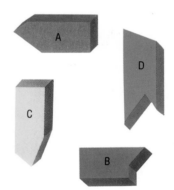

1.0 m   12.0 m

0

C

5. (a) Estimate which of the following carries the most water.

A: one pipe with a 10-cm diameter
B: ten pipes each with a 1-cm diameter
C: one square pipe with a 10-cm diagonal

(b) Calculate to determine which pipe carries the most water.

6. (a) Copy and cut out the pieces shown.
(b) Fit the pieces together to form the letter "T."
(c) Create a similar problem of your own using the pieces. Compare your problem to others in the class.

MAKING CONNECTIONS

The British mathematician, G.H. Hardy, once travelled by taxi to visit his friend, mathematician Ramanujan, in the hospital. Once there, he casually mentioned to Ramanujan that the taxi's identification number was one of the most uninteresting numbers he had ever seen. Ramanujan immediately replied that the number was actually quite interesting because it was the smallest positive integer that can be written as the sum of two cubes in two different ways.
(a) What was the taxi's identification number?
(b) Write a short dialogue to depict what the two mathematicians might have said to one another.
(c) Describe some contributions to mathematics made by each mathematician.

11.9 EXPLORING EXPRESSIONS

You have learned how to factor expressions using algebra tiles and to recognize patterns and relationships. These skills can be used to divide expressions.

Try the following explorations in a small group. Summarize any patterns and relationships that can be used to divide expressions.

EXPLORATION ① Work in a Small Group

1. (a) What expression is being shown by each of the following.

   A   B   C

   (b) Write each expression in (a) as a product of its factors.
   (c) How might you use a quotient to show your work in (b)?

2. Create similar expressions of your own.
   (a) Write each expression as a product of its factors.
   (b) How might you use a quotient to show your work in (a)?

3. Answer the following in your journal.
   (a) What relationships can help you divide expressions?
   (b) Write examples of your own to show your relationships in (a).

EXPLORATION ② Work in a Small Group

4. (a) Refer to the following relationships. How are they related?

   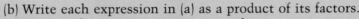

   $$15 = 5 \times 3 \qquad \frac{15}{5} = 3 \qquad \frac{15}{3} = 5$$

   (b) Show the relationship in (a) using other numbers. Compare your numbers to others in the class.

5. Refer to your results in Question 4.
   (a) For the relationships, show how the factors are related.

   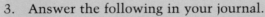

   $$3x + 9 = 3(x + 3) \qquad \frac{3x + 9}{3} = x + 3 \qquad \frac{3x + 9}{x + 3} = 3$$

   (b) Show the relationship in (a) using other expressions. Compare your expressions to others in the class.
   (c) How can the relationships in this exploration help you in Exploration 1?

EXPLORATION ③ *Work Together*

6. (a) What expression is being shown by each of the following?

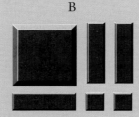

A   B

(b) Write each expression in (a) as a product of its factors.
(c) How might you use a quotient to show your work in (b)?

7. Create similar expressions of your own.
(a) Write each expression as a product of its factors.
(b) How might you use a quotient to show your work in (a)?

8. Answer the following in your journal.
(a) What relationships can help you divide expressions?
(b) Write examples of your own to show your relationships in (a).

EXPLORATION ④ *Work Together*

9. (a) For the relationships, show how they are related.

$$x^2 - 5x + 6 = (x - 3)(x - 2) \qquad \frac{x^2 - 5x + 6}{x - 3} = x - 2 \qquad \frac{x^2 - 5x + 6}{x - 2} = x - 3$$

(b) Show the relationship in (a) using other expressions. Compare your expressions to others in the class.
(c) How can the relationships in this exploration simplify your work in Exploration 3?

EXPLORATION ⑤ *Discussing in Your Group*

10. For each expression,
    • discuss the most appropriate way of dividing the expressions.
    • divide each expression to verify your method.

(a) $\dfrac{x^2 + 2x + 1}{x + 1}$ (b) $\dfrac{x^2 + 3x + 2}{x + 2}$ (c) $\dfrac{x^2 - 7x + 12}{x - 3}$

(d) $\dfrac{x^2 - x - 12}{x - 4}$ (e) $\dfrac{x^2 + 3x - 10}{x + 5}$ (f) $\dfrac{x^2 + 10x + 16}{x + 8}$

11. Answer each of the following in your journal.
(a) What relationships can help you divide a binomial by a monomial?
(b) Write examples of your own to show your relationships in (a).

357

Expressions such as $\dfrac{x+3}{x}$ and $\dfrac{x^2+6x+5}{4x}$ are called *rational expressions*. To simplify rational expressions, you can use your skills with factoring. To do so, you first need to think about the denominator.

Complete the following activity to analyze the denominator of any rational expression.

ACTIVITY   *Work with a Partner*

(a) Is it possible to divide any number by zero? Give reasons for your answer.

(b) For the rational expression $\dfrac{2x^2}{x}$, what value of x will make the denominator equal zero?

(c) For the rational expression $\dfrac{x+3}{x}$, what value of x will make the denominator equal zero?

(d) What value can the variable *never* be? Justify your answer.

The previous activity suggests that the denominator of the rational expression is *never* zero. When you work with rational expressions, you need to note the value of the variable that makes the denominator zero. This value is called the **restriction** on the variable.

Restrictions on the variable must be found *before* simplifying, as shown in the following example.

EXAMPLE
Simplify each of the following.

(a) $\dfrac{-4mn}{2m}$

(b) $\dfrac{x^2+6x+5}{x+1}$

Think: $x \neq -1$. Why is this restriction listed?
Factor any expressions.

SOLUTION

(a) In $\dfrac{-4mn}{2m}$, m cannot equal 0.

$$\dfrac{-4mn}{2m} = -2n$$

A Find the numerical coefficient.
$$\dfrac{-4}{2} = -2$$

B Find the literal coefficient.
$$\dfrac{mn}{m} = \dfrac{{}^{1}\cancel{m} \times n}{\cancel{m}_1} = n$$

(b)
$$\dfrac{x^2+6x+5}{x+1} = \dfrac{(x+1)(x+5)}{x+1}$$

$x \neq -1$

$$= \dfrac{{}^{1}\cancel{(x+1)}(x+5)}{\cancel{x+1}_1}$$

$$= x + 5, \; x \neq -1$$

Divide the numerator and the denominator by the same expression.

A   Review your skills with factoring.

1.   What is the restriction on each expression?

(a) $\dfrac{20cd}{4d}$ (b) $\dfrac{20gh}{5g}$ (c) $\dfrac{20ru}{10u}$ (d) $\dfrac{-12ab}{2a}$ (e) $\dfrac{-12pq}{3a}$ (f) $\dfrac{-12st}{4t}$

2.   List the restriction on the variable for each of the following.

(a) $\dfrac{y-5}{y-3}$ (b) $\dfrac{4x-9}{2x+6}$ (c) $\dfrac{y+8}{y^2+4y-32}$ (d) $\dfrac{y-2}{y^2-4}$

3.   (a) Find the value of $\dfrac{x^2+6x+5}{x+1}$ for $x = 8$.

(b) Find the value of $x + 5$ for $x = 8$.

(c) In your journal, explain why the answers in (a) and (b) are the same.

B   Note all restrictions on the variable before you simplify.

4.   Simplify.

(a) $\dfrac{24mn}{6n}$ (b) $\dfrac{-24pq}{4q}$ (c) $\dfrac{36rs}{-6s}$ (d) $\dfrac{-25tu}{-5t}$ (e) $\dfrac{-20pq}{4q}$ (f) $\dfrac{28st}{-7t}$

(g) $\dfrac{2a^2}{a}$ (h) $\dfrac{-4a^3}{2a^2}$ (i) $\dfrac{8m^4}{4m^2}$ (j) $\dfrac{-6m^5}{3m^3}$ (k) $\dfrac{9p^4}{-3p}$ (l) $\dfrac{-10m^5}{-2m}$

5.   Use $a = -3$, $b = -2$. Find the value of each of the following. Remember to simplify first.

(a) $\dfrac{16a^2b}{-4a}$ (b) $\dfrac{-25ab^3}{-5b}$ (c) $\dfrac{-48a^3b^2}{6a}$ (d) $\dfrac{30ab}{-6b}$ (e) $\dfrac{-30a^2b}{-5a}$

6.   Evaluate each of the following. Use $x = -1$, $y = 3$.

(a) $\dfrac{x^2-5x+6}{x-3}$ (b) $\dfrac{y^2-7y+6}{y-6}$ (c) $\dfrac{x^2-9x+20}{x-5}$ (d) $\dfrac{x^2-5x-24}{x-8}$ (e) $\dfrac{y^2-2y-15}{y^2+8y+15}$

PARTNER PROJECT

Sometimes, learning how words were developed helps you understand a topic better. In this chapter, you have been working with *algebra*. The word comes from the title of an ancient Arabic publication.

(a) What was the publication called? In what context was the word used?

(b) Write a definition of algebra as it is known today. Compare it to the meaning in (a).

(c) Suppose you could give "algebra" another name. What name would you use?

Your skills with fractions can help you multiply rational expressions. The following activity will help you to develop a plan for multiplying rational expressions.

ACTIVITY 1 *Work Together*

Refer to the examples shown to the right.
(a) How are the examples alike?
How are they different?
(b) How can you use the method above to simplify each of the following?

(i) $\dfrac{3x}{a+b} \times \dfrac{a+b}{4y}$ (ii) $\dfrac{5z}{p} \times \dfrac{p}{z}$

$$\frac{\overset{1}{\cancel{2}}}{3} \times \frac{1}{\underset{1}{\cancel{2}}} = \frac{1 \times 1}{3 \times 1}$$
$$= \frac{1}{3}$$

$$\frac{a}{\underset{1}{\cancel{x}}} \times \frac{\overset{1}{\cancel{x}}}{b} = \frac{a \times 1}{1 \times b}$$
$$= \frac{a}{b}$$

The activity above suggests that, to multiply rational expressions, you simplify the expressions first, as shown.

$$\frac{2x^2}{x+3} \times \frac{x+3}{x} = \frac{2x^2}{\underset{1}{\cancel{x+3}}} \times \frac{\overset{1}{\cancel{x+3}}}{\underset{1}{\cancel{x}}}$$
$$= \frac{2x}{1} \times \frac{1}{1}$$
$$= 2x$$

Think: $x \neq 0$ and $x \neq -3$. Why?

Sometimes, you can factor an expression before you multiply to simplify your work, as shown.

$$\frac{x-5}{2} \times \frac{x+5}{4x-20} = \frac{\overset{1}{\cancel{x-5}}}{2} \times \frac{x+5}{4(\underset{1}{\cancel{x-5}})}$$
$$= \frac{x+5}{2 \times 4}$$

Think: $x \neq 5$. Why?

ACTIVITY 2 *Work Together*

Refer to the expressions in (b) of Activity 1.
(a) Multiply each expression.
(b) Compare your answers in (a) with others in the class. What do you notice?

EXERCISE

A   Remember: Write the restrictions on the variables before you begin to simplify the expression.

1. (a) How would you factor the expression?
   (b) Write the expression in (a) in a simpler form.

$$\frac{m^2+5m}{m-4} \times \frac{2m-8}{m+5}$$

2. (a) How would you factor the expression?
   (b) Write the expression in (a) in a simpler form.

$$\frac{a^2 - 7a + 10}{2 - a} \times \frac{2 - a}{(a^2 - 25)}$$

3. (a) What would be your first step in simplifying
      the expression?
   (b) Simplify the expression in (a).

$$\frac{x^2 - x - 6}{9y^2} \times \frac{3y}{x - 3}$$

4. (a) What would be your first step in simplifying
      the expression?
   (b) Simplify the expression in (a).

$$\frac{x}{x^2 - 1} \times \frac{x - 1}{x}$$

B   Remember: Check your final answer. Is it expressed in lowest terms?

5. Simplify.

   (a) $\dfrac{36}{y^2 + 2y} \times \dfrac{y + 2}{9}$
   (b) $\dfrac{x}{2(x - 1)} \times \dfrac{2}{x}$
   (c) $\dfrac{n - 1}{3n} \times \dfrac{n}{n - 1}$

   (d) $\dfrac{x}{x + 1} \times \dfrac{x - 1}{x}$
   (e) $\dfrac{3m}{2(m - 4)} \times \dfrac{m - 3}{3}$
   (f) $\dfrac{5(m - 1)}{m + 1} \times m + 1$

6. Simplify.

   (a) $\dfrac{27}{y^2 + 3y} \times \dfrac{y + 3}{9}$
   (b) $\dfrac{x - 1}{3x} \times \dfrac{x}{x^2 - 1}$
   (c) $\dfrac{y + 2}{8} \times \dfrac{16}{y^2 - y - 6}$

   (d) $\dfrac{m^2 + 3m + 2}{m^2 + m - 2} \times \dfrac{m^2 - 4m + 3}{m^2 - 16}$
   (e) $\dfrac{6k}{3k + 6k^2 + 9k^3} \times \dfrac{5k + 10}{12}$

7. Find the missing values, then find the answers mentally.
   (a) $22^2 = (20 + ?)^2$
   (b) $32^2 = (? + 2)^2$
   (c) $43^2 = (40 + ?)^2$
   (d) $68^2 = (? - 2)^2$
   (e) $73^2 = (70 + ?)^2$
   (f) $62^2 = (? + 2)^2$

8. Find each of the following products.
   (a) 23×17
   (b) 36×44
   (c) 55×65
   (d) 42×38

9. Compute each of the following.
   (a) $36^2 - 34^2$
   (b) $48^2 - 45^2$
   (c) $96^2 - 4^2$
   (d) $75^2 - 25^2$

10. Evaluate each of the following.
   (a) 63^2
   (b) 19^2
   (c) 29^2
   (d) 97^2
   (e) 68^2
   (f) 91^2

11. Evaluate each of the following.
   (a) 88×92
   (b) $32^2 - 29^2$
   (c) 48^2
   (d) 99×101
   (e) 66×74
   (f) 38^2
   (g) $80^2 - 20^2$
   (h) 49^2

12. (a) Calculate 15×15, 25×25, and 35×35. What pattern do you see?
    (b) Predict the product of 45×45 and 55×55.

13. For each of the following,
    - simplify the expression.
    - list the restrictions that apply.

    (a) $\dfrac{a^2 - b^2}{a^2 - 16} \times \dfrac{a - 4}{a - b}$

    (b) $\dfrac{x + 1}{x^2 - 1} \times \dfrac{x - 1}{x}$

    (c) $\dfrac{3x - 12}{4x + 20} \times \dfrac{x^2 + 5x}{x^2 - 4x}$

14. (a) Simplify $\dfrac{x^2 - 9}{-(x - 3)}$.

    (b) Simplify $\dfrac{x^2 - 9}{3 - x}$.

    (c) How are the expressions in (a) and (b) alike? How are they different?

C

15. When you are simplifying expressions, remember that $-(x - y) = y - x$.
    Simplify each of the following.

    (a) $\dfrac{-(y - x)}{y - x}$

    (b) $\dfrac{x - y}{-(y - x)}$

    (c) $\dfrac{-(y - x)}{-(x - y)}$

    (d) $\dfrac{-(y - x)}{x - y}$

    (e) $\dfrac{x + y}{y + x}$

    (f) $\dfrac{m^2 - n^2}{n - m}$

    (g) $\dfrac{4a^2 - b^2}{2a - b}$

    (h) $\dfrac{x^2 + xy - 2y^2}{y^2 - x^2}$

16. (a) How can you arrange the disks shown so that each disk is the same distance from each of the other disks?
    (b) Create a similar problem of your own using the disks. Compare your problem to others in the class.

In every career, you will find problems that you need to analyze and solve. Your skills in mathematics will often help you with them. For example, refer to the shapes shown.

1. (a) What construction lines are missing?
   (b) What lines are hidden?
   (c) How are the lengths related?
   (d) How are the angles related?
   (e) Using what you have learned above, construct the shapes yourself.

2. Describe how the skills you used to solve the above problems could be useful in each of the following careers.
   (a) • Animator   • Tailor   • Fashion Designer   • Cartographer
   (b) List another problem that you might need to solve in each career.

11.12 DIVIDING RATIONAL EXPRESSIONS

Your skills with multiplying rational expressions can help you divide rational expressions. To explore how to divide rational expressions, try the following activity. In your journal, summarize any relationships you can use to help you divide rational expressions.

ACTIVITY *Work Together*

1. Refer to the examples shown below.
   (a) How are the examples alike? How are they different?
   (b) What is the first step in simplifying each expression?

$$\frac{3}{5} \div \frac{33}{15} = \frac{\overset{1}{\cancel{3}}}{\underset{1}{\cancel{5}}} \times \frac{\overset{3}{\cancel{15}}}{\underset{11}{\cancel{33}}}$$

$$= \frac{1 \times 3}{1 \times 11}$$

$$= \frac{3}{11}$$

$$\frac{2x}{3y} \div \frac{a}{3y} = \frac{2x}{\underset{1}{\cancel{3y}}} \times \frac{\overset{1}{\cancel{3y}}}{a} \qquad a \neq 0,\ y \neq 0$$

$$= \frac{2x \times 1}{1 \times a}$$

$$= \frac{2x}{a}$$

2. (a) Use your results in Question 1. What do you think is the first step when simplifying this expression?
   (b) Simplify the expression in (a).

$$\frac{x+y}{2} \div \frac{x+y}{8}$$

The activity above suggests that to divide rational expressions, you multiply by the reciprocal, as shown.

$$\frac{x^2 - 9}{x - 3} \div \frac{x + 3}{x - 3} = \frac{x^2 - 9}{x - 3} \times \frac{x - 3}{x + 3}$$

$$= \frac{(x - 3)(\cancel{x + 3})^{\,1}}{\cancel{x - 3}_{\,1}} \times \frac{\cancel{x - 3}^{\,1}}{_1\cancel{x + 3}} \qquad x \neq \pm 3.\ \text{Why?}$$

$$= \frac{x - 3}{1}$$

$$= x - 3$$

EXERCISE

A Remember: When you divide by a rational expression, invert and multiply.

1. For each expression, what is the first step? What is your final answer?

   (a) $\dfrac{3(x+2)}{5} \div \dfrac{2(x+2)}{15}$

   (b) $\dfrac{x+y}{2} \div \dfrac{x+y}{8}$

   (c) $\dfrac{a+3}{5} \div \dfrac{a+3}{4}$

2. Divide each of the following.

   (a) $\dfrac{x}{y} \div \dfrac{a}{b}$

   (b) $\dfrac{-x}{y} \div \dfrac{-a}{b}$

   (c) $\dfrac{-a}{-b} \div \left(-\dfrac{a}{y} \right)$

   (d) $\dfrac{-2}{7} \div \dfrac{3}{-x}$

   (e) $6 \div \left(\dfrac{-3}{y} \right)$

   (f) $\dfrac{-6}{y} \div \dfrac{5}{k}$

   (g) $\dfrac{-5}{m} \div \dfrac{-6}{x}$

   (h) $15 \div \left(\dfrac{-m}{n} \right)$

   (i) $\dfrac{4}{-k} \div \dfrac{16}{-k}$

3. Simplify.

   (a) $\dfrac{2(x+3)^2}{x} \div \dfrac{x+3}{x}$

   (b) $\dfrac{6(y-4)}{8} \div \dfrac{12(y-4)}{32}$

   (c) $\dfrac{3(a+7)}{a-7} \div \dfrac{a+7}{a-7}$

   (d) $\dfrac{8(x+1)}{x+1} \div \dfrac{x-2}{x-2}$

   (e) $\dfrac{2(m+4)^2}{m+4} \div \dfrac{m+4}{4}$

   (f) $\dfrac{4(x+7)}{8(x-7)} \div \dfrac{x+7}{x-7}$

B   Review your skills with factoring.

4. (a) What is the first step in simplifying the expression?

   (b) Simplify your expression in (a). What restrictions apply?

   $$\dfrac{y+1}{y^2-1} \div \dfrac{3y}{y-1}$$

5. Simplify each expression. List the restrictions that apply.

   (a) $\dfrac{36}{y^2+2y} \div \dfrac{9}{y+2}$

   (b) $\dfrac{x-1}{3x} \div \dfrac{x^2-1}{x}$

   (c) $\dfrac{a+1}{a^2-1} \div \dfrac{a}{a-1}$

   (d) $\dfrac{y+2}{8} \div \dfrac{y^2-y-6}{16}$

6. (a) What is your first step to simplify the expression?

   (b) Find the value of the expression in (a) for $k = 9$.

   $$\dfrac{k^2-6k+9}{k-3} \div \dfrac{k-6}{k+3}$$

WORKING TOGETHER

Calculators, in one form or another, have played a role in mathematics throughout the ages. From the abacus to Napier's Bones, people have developed interesting ways to help calculate expressions.
(a) Research an early calculator.
(b) Summarize how the calculator worked. Present your summary to your class.
(c) Try to duplicate the calculator you have researched. How easy was it to build? to use?
(d) Start a class booklet of these early calculators. Include the inventor and for what purpose it was originally invented.

7. Simplify each expression.

(a) $\left(\dfrac{2x}{-5}\right) \div \left(\dfrac{x^2}{-10}\right)$

(b) $\left(\dfrac{x^2}{4}\right) \div \left(\dfrac{20x^2y}{-16}\right)$

(c) $\left(\dfrac{-6x^2k}{-7xy}\right) \div \left(\dfrac{-7k}{3y}\right)$

(d) $\left(\dfrac{4x^2}{2y^2}\right) \div \left(\dfrac{-x^3}{4y}\right)$

(e) $\left(\dfrac{3a^2b}{6a}\right) \div \left(\dfrac{3ab}{-9a}\right)$

(f) $\left(\dfrac{5x}{-4a^2}\right) \div \left(\dfrac{10x^2}{2a}\right)$

8. (a) How might you apply the order of operations to do the following?

$$\dfrac{mn}{2} \times \dfrac{n}{5} \div \dfrac{-m}{15}$$

(b) Simplify. Watch the operation signs.

9. Simplify.

(a) $\dfrac{ab}{-3} \div \dfrac{a}{-9} \times \dfrac{-b}{3}$

(b) $\dfrac{3a}{-b} \div \dfrac{-a^2}{b^2} \times \dfrac{b}{-a}$

(c) $\dfrac{-5}{a} \times \dfrac{-a^3}{-ab} \div \dfrac{3a}{-2b}$

(d) $\left(\dfrac{x}{10y}\right)\left(\dfrac{-2x}{y^2}\right) \div \left(\dfrac{-1}{5y^2}\right)$

10. Simplify each of the following.

(a) $\dfrac{-4x^2}{y^2} \times \dfrac{y}{-8x} \div \dfrac{y}{2x}$

(b) $\dfrac{-10a^2}{b} \times \dfrac{-b^2}{5a} \div \left(\dfrac{b}{2a}\right)$

(c) $\dfrac{3a}{-b} \times \dfrac{b^2}{6a} \div (-a)$

(d) $\left(\dfrac{-x}{4k}\right)\left(-\dfrac{5}{3x}\right) \div \left(\dfrac{x}{12k}\right)$

(e) $\left(\dfrac{x}{10y}\right)\left(\dfrac{-2x}{y^2}\right) \div \left(\dfrac{-1}{5y^2}\right)$

(f) $-\dfrac{16m^3}{n} \times \dfrac{-1}{4m^2} \div \dfrac{-n^2}{4m}$

(g) $\left(\dfrac{3x}{5y}\right)\left(\dfrac{-4x}{8y^2}\right) \div \left(\dfrac{10x^2}{20y}\right)$

(h) $\dfrac{-25a^3}{b^2} \times \dfrac{13b^2}{a} \div \dfrac{15a^2}{-4b}$

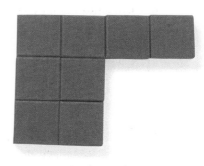

C

11. (a) Use algebra tiles to create a 4 × 4 square.
    (b) In how many ways can you fit together two identical shapes to form a 4 × 4 square? One way is shown.
    (c) To solve problems, you need to make sure you understand the meanings of all the words. Are there any words in this problem you do not understand?
    (d) Create a similar problem of your own using tiles. Solve the problem.

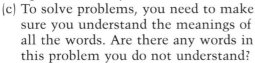

CHAPTER REVIEW

1. Find the factors of each expression. Check by multiplying the factors.
   (a) $3x - 6$
   (b) $4x - 12$
   (c) $m^2 + mn$
   (d) $m^2 - 4mn$
   (e) $4y - 10y^2$
   (f) $3k^2 - 9k$

2. Express each trinomial in factored form.
   (a) $x^2 - 9x + 20$
   (b) $m^2 - 13m + 42$
   (c) $25 - 10x + x^2$
   (d) $a^2 - 3ab - 10b^2$
   (e) $x^2 + 4x - 21$
   (f) $9x^2 - 12xy + 4y^2$
   (g) $m^2 + 8mn + 15n^2$
   (h) $50a^2 + 20ab + 2b^2$

3. Factor. Check your factors.
   (a) $x^2 - 5x - 14$
   (b) $m^2 + 5m + 4$
   (c) $y^2 + 7y - 30$
   (d) $y^2 + 2y - 15$

4. Factor.
   (a) $x^2 - 4y^2$
   (b) $25k^2 - p^2$
   (c) $100a^2 - 49b^2$
   (d) $36y^2 - 25x^2$

5. Simplify. What are the restrictions on the variable?
   (a) $\dfrac{y}{y^2 - 12y}$
   (b) $\dfrac{3x^2 + 6x}{3x}$
   (c) $\dfrac{5y - 20}{5}$
   (d) $\dfrac{2a - 8}{a^2 - 6a + 8}$

6. Simplify.
   (a) $\dfrac{-24k^2}{45} \times \dfrac{-9}{15k}$
   (b) $\dfrac{-3x^2y}{4a^2} \div \dfrac{9xy}{-5a}$
   (c) $\dfrac{3x^2}{2y} \times \dfrac{-2y}{3}$
   (d) $\dfrac{a^2}{3} \div \dfrac{a^4}{6}$

7. (a) Find an expression for the area.
   (b) Calculate the area for $x = 3$ and $y = 4$.

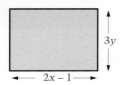

3y

2x − 1

---

❶ How can you verify that you have factored an expression correctly?

❷ Which expressions on this page can you factor mentally? What clues are in the expressions to suggest factoring mentally?

❸ Make a list of clues you can use to help you distinguish each factoring skill in the chapter.

MAKING CONNECTIONS

Refer to the opening page of this chapter.
(a) Create a problem of your own that involves the strategy of working backwards. Compare your problem to others in the class.
(b) What kind of problems can be solved using the skills in this chapter?

❹ Describe what you have learned from other members of your group. How did group work help you throughout the chapter?

❺ How often do you participate in group discussions? How can you participate more?

❻ Describe which problem solving strategy you used most often in this chapter.

MATH JOURNAL

Did you ask yourself any of the following questions when you solved problems in this chapter? Which questions were most useful to you? How would you change the questions to make them more useful? What other questions could you add?
(a) Did I check for a common factor first?
(b) What clues helped me factor the expression?
(c) Did I write my answer in its simplest form?
(d) Have I identified the restrictions on the variables at an appropriate time?

SELF EVALUATION

1. Factor the following. Check your factor.
   (a) $3x^3 - xy$
   (b) $4p^3 + p^2d$
   (c) $a^3x - 3a^2y$
   (d) $20z^2 - 12z$
   (e) $24d^4 - 8d^3$
   (f) $6x^2 - 9x$

2. Factor each of the following.
   (a) $x^2 + 8x + 15$
   (b) $y^2 - y - 30$
   (c) $3a^2 + 9a + 6$
   (d) $x^2 + 3xy + 2y^2$
   (e) $2a^2 + 8a + 8$
   (f) $2x^2 + 2x - 4$

3. Express each of the following in factored form.
   (a) $y^2 + 2y + 1$
   (b) $x^2 - x - 2$
   (c) $y^2 + y - 12$
   (d) $x^2 + 5x + 6$
   (e) $x^2 - 3x + 2$
   (f) $m^2 - 3m - 10$
   (g) $y^2 + 3y + 2$
   (h) $y^2 - 5y + 6$
   (i) $m^2 + 2m - 3$
   (j) $a^2 + 4a - 5$

4. Write each in factored form.
   (a) $9x^2 - 4$
   (b) $64y^2 - 1$
   (c) $4m^2 - 9$
   (d) $25s^2 - 36$

5. List the restrictions on the following denominators.
   (a) $\dfrac{5}{x} \div \dfrac{4}{x-4}$
   (b) $\dfrac{3}{a+1} \div \dfrac{3}{a}$
   (c) $\dfrac{3}{x+1} \div \dfrac{5}{x-2}$
   (d) $\dfrac{6}{x-y} \div \dfrac{7}{x+y}$

6. A rectangle has an area of $36ab$ square units. The width is $4b$ units. What is the length?

7. A rectangular pod has an area of $48pq$ square units. The length is $8q$ units. What is the width?

8. Simplify.
   (a) $\dfrac{2x}{4x^2 + 6x}$
   (b) $\dfrac{5a^2 - 10a}{5a}$
   (c) $\dfrac{2a - 8}{a^2 - a - 12}$
   (d) $\dfrac{4k^2 - m^2}{2k - m}$

Have you ever taken a class trip? A spreadsheet can help you plan your trip. Work in groups to complete the following project.

1. Conduct a survey within your group to determine where you will go on the trip. What type of survey should you do? Do other groups get the same results from their survey?

2. Make a list of expenses associated with your trip. Write these down in a column called expenses. Then, estimate how much money you will need for each expense.

3. Make a complete list of your sources of income. Write these down in a column called income. Then, estimate how much money you will get from each source.

4. If you have access to a spreadsheet, use it to set up a screen similar to the one below. Enter the income and expenses you listed previously. If you do not have access to a spreadsheet, you will have to do the calculations manually. How do you think the spreadsheet will save time in this project?

	A	B	C	D	E
1	**Expenses**	Amount	**Income**	Amount	**Parents**
2	Bus	1200	Student Council	300	
3	Lunch	250	School Grant	150	
4	Admission fees	80	Bake Sale	140	
5	Insurance	100	Raffle	75	
6	Souvenirs	200			
7					
8	**Totals**	1830		665	1165

Note that in this spreadsheet, cell B8 is the total of cells B2...B6. Changing any of these values will change the value in B8. Similarly, D8 is the total of D2...D5 and E8 is the difference between B8 and D8. This feature allows you to change your estimate for any expense or income and immediately see any change in the amount required from parents.

5. Use your spreadsheet or spreadsheet simulation to budget for your trip. Compare your group's budget with those of other groups. Do you think the budgets are realistic? Discuss ways in which you could minimize the amount the parents need to contribute.

RELATIONS AND FUNCTIONS 12

ACTIVITY

(a) What do you think is meant by a "relation" or "relationship"?

(b) How could you use the pictures shown here to illustrate your understanding of relationship?

(c) Find a picture of your own that demonstrates your understanding of relationship. Explain how the picture does so.

12.1 EXPLORING RELATIONS

Take a look at the photographs on this page. Use similar elastics and washers to complete the following exploration.

EXPLORATION ① *Work Together*

1. (a) Attach a paper clip to the end of an elastic as shown.
   (b) Measure the length of the elastic with no washers attached.
   (c) Put a number of washers (each the same size) onto the paper clip so that the elastic stretches. Measure the length of the elastic.
   (d) Keep adding washers and measuring the length of the elastic. Record your data in a table like the following.

Number of washers	Length of elastic
?	?
?	?
?	?

   (e) Construct a coordinate grid with axes labelled with the titles in the chart. Plot the points from (d) onto your coordinate grid. Join the points. What do you notice?

2. Based on your results above:
   (a) How long do you think the elastic would stretch if you used 44 washers? Give reasons for your answer.
   (b) How long do you think the elastic would stretch if you used $18\frac{1}{2}$ washers? Give reasons for your answer.
   (c) Refer to your answer in (b). Is it possible to verify your prediction? Why?

3. Discuss with your partner:
   Suppose that, instead of washers, you use pennies to repeat the exploration. How would you modify the experiment to collect the data?

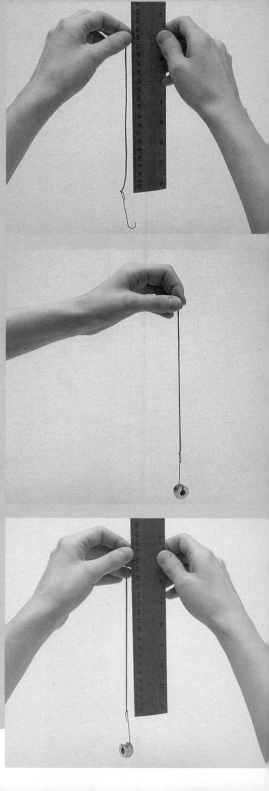

Sometimes, you need to set up your own experiment to collect data.
Refer to the steps in Exploration 1 for each of the following explorations.

EXPLORATION ② *Work with a Partner*

4. (a) Stack coins to form columns as shown. Measure the height of each stack and record your results.

   (b) Add more coins to your stacks. Measure the height of each stack and record the results.
   (c) Construct a coordinate grid and graph the results.
   (d) How high do you think a stack of 88 coins would be? Why?
   (e) How high do you think a stack of $18\frac{1}{2}$ coins would be? Why?

EXPLORATION ③

You can try this exploration at home. You will need ice cubes, each the same size and shape.

5. You are to find out how long it takes ice cubes to melt when placed into a container of hot water from a tap.
   (a) Design your experiment. Decide on the size of the container.
   (b) Record how long it takes for one ice cube, then two ice cubes, and then three ice cubes to melt, each time they are placed into the container.

6. Refer to your results in Question 5.
   (a) What do you notice about the data?
   (b) Construct a coordinate grid and graph the results.
   (c) How long do you think it would take 18 ice cubes to melt? Why?
   (d) How long do you think it would take $8\frac{1}{2}$ ice cubes to melt? Why?

EXPLORATION ④ *Work Together*

7. (a) Discuss an experiment that you can do in class where you can collect data and graph the results. Predict what you think the results of your experiment could be.
   (b) Exchange your experiment with another group. Carry out the experiment of the other group.
   (c) Once you have finished, compare the results you obtain with the original predicted results. Discuss any differences.
   (d) As a group, write a brief report, including
   (i)   the results of the experiment.
   (ii) the difference between the expected results and actual results.
   (iii) whether gathering your own data gives accurate results.

Previously, you explored the meaning of a relationship. Use your understanding of relationships to complete the following activities.

ACTIVITY 1

A meteorologist needs to study relationships to predict weather patterns.
(a) List what relationships a meteorologist might use to predict the weather.
(b) List other careers in which you might need to study relationships and solve problems.

ACTIVITY 2 *Work with a Partner*

As you develop your language in mathematics, you will see similarities between words used in English and words used in mathematics.
(a) What is meant by a relation in math? Use examples to help your explanation.
(b) How are relations in math like relations in English? How are they different? Use examples to help your explanation.

- A *table* or *chart* may be used to show how numbers are related.

  "The first number is two less than the second."

First Number	Second Number
1	3
2	4
3	5
4	6

- The relation in the chart can then be shown using *ordered pairs*.

  (1, 3)
  (2, 4)
  (3, 5)
  (4, 6)

  Think: The ordered pair (3, 5) shows that 5 is 2 more than 3.

- A *graph* of the ordered pairs can be drawn to show the relation.

  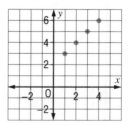

Suppose that the ordered pairs also include integers. Ordered pairs for the above relation can be shown as follows.

... (–1, 1), (0, 2), (1, 3), (2, 4), (3, 5), (4, 6), (5, 7), ...

The ordered pairs above can also be graphed to show the relation.

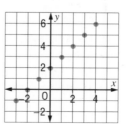

A Review your skills with coordinate grids.

1. Relations are shown in the graphs.
   (a) What are the ordered pairs of the relations?
   (b) Think of a rule that connects the coordinates.

(i)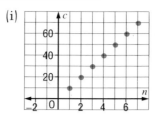

(ii)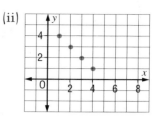

2. For each graph, find the missing coordinates in the ordered pairs.
   (a) (2, ?), (?, 5), (6, ?) (b) (0, ?), (?, 3), (5, ?) (c) (−2, ?), (−4, ?), (?, 4)

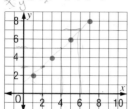 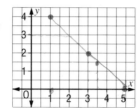 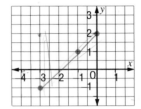

B Review your work with relations.

3. For each relation, ordered pairs are missing. What are the missing ordered pairs?

(a) 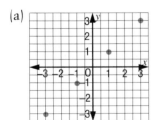 (b) 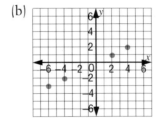 (c)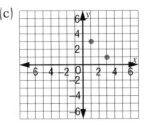

4. For each chart,
   • what are the ordered pairs?   • draw the graph of the relation.

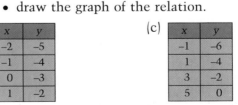

(a)

x	y
0	5
1	7
2	9
3	11

(b)

x	y
−2	−5
−1	−4
0	−3
1	−2

(c)

x	y
−1	−6
1	−4
3	−2
5	0

5. Work with a partner.
   (a) Plot ordered pairs on a grid that can be described by a rule.
   (b) Have your partner decide what the rule is. Have your partner write two more ordered pairs using the rule.

12.3 GRAPHING RELATIONS

You have seen different ways of showing a relation. After you complete the following activity, discuss with a partner how you can graph a relation.

ACTIVITY

Suppose that, in a marathon, you average a speed of 8 km/h.
(a) How could you record your distance travelled over time?
(b) How could you use your data in (a) to show the relation between distance and time on a graph?

In the above activity, the distance travelled, d, in kilometres, is related to the time, t, in hours, by the relationship $d = 8t$. You can use this relationship to find the distance travelled after time, as shown below.

Suppose $t = 1$.   Suppose $t = 2$.   Suppose $t = 3$.
Use $d = 8t$.   Use $d = 8t$.   Use $d = 8t$.
$d = 8(1)$ $d = 8(2)$ $d = 8(3)$
$\quad = 8$ $\quad = 16$ $\quad = 24$

You can summarize and display the relationship as shown below.

In a Chart   **As Ordered Pairs**   **As a Graph**

t	d
1	8
2	16
3	24

(1, 8)
(2, 16)
(3, 24)

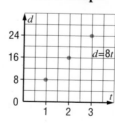

You can use these steps to help you draw the graph of a relation, such as $y = 2x - 1$.

Step 1

Obtain a table of values for selected points.

x	y
−2	−5
−1	−3
0	−1
1	1
2	3

Step 2

Plot the points.

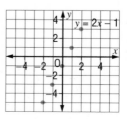

374

A Use a coordinate grid to help you.

1. Various relations are shown by the tables of values. Find the missing values.

(a)
x	$y = x + 3$
0	3
1	4
2	5
3	?
?	7

(b)
x	$y = x - 1$
2	1
3	2
4	3
?	4
6	?

(c)
x	$y = 3x$
1	3
2	6
3	9
4	?
?	15

2. (a) Copy and complete the table of values for the relation $p = 4k$.
   (b) Plot the ordered pairs.

k	p
1	?
2	?
3	?

B Review your vocabulary with relations.

3. A relation is given by the ordered pairs (t, d), where $d = 2t$ and t is a positive number. Find the missing values.
   (a) (1, ?)   (b) (?, 6)   (c) (2, ?)   (d) (?, 12)   (e) (10, ?)

4. A relation is given by (n, c), where $c = 100n$ and n is a whole number.
   (a) Construct a table of values for the relation. Plot the ordered pairs.
   (b) Find the missing values in (?, 0) and (100, ?).

5. Draw a graph of each relation.
   (a) $y = 2x$ (b) $y = x + 2$ (c) $y = 3x - 1$ (d) $y = 4x$

6. A relation is given by the ordered pair (n, c) where $c = 200n$.
   (a) Draw axes on grid paper.
   (b) Draw a graph of the relation where n is a whole number.

7. Suppose you have 1000 red disks all lined up in a row.
   - Person 1 changes all the disks to blue;
   - Person 2 changes every second disk back to red;
   - Person 3 changes every third disk back to red; and so on.
   (a) After 1000 people have changed disks, how many of them are still blue? Describe how you arrived at your solution.
   (b) Create a similar problem of your own using disks. Compare your problem with others in the class.

375

The table to the right shows a *relation* for the amount of gasoline a motorbike needs when travelling at a steady rate. The relation is shown by

$V = 0.5t$, where V is gas consumed in litres and t is the time in hours.

From the data, you can write the ordered pairs and draw a graph of the relation as shown below. To show the amount of gasoline consumed, V, at any time, you then draw a line through the ordered pairs.

Gas Consumption-Motorbikes

Time Taken, t, in hours	Gas Consumed, V, in litres	Ordered Pairs
0	0	(0, 0)
1	0.5	(1, 0.5)
2	1.0	(2, 1.0)
3	1.5	(3, 1.5)
4	2.0	(4, 2.0)

This graph shows the five ordered pairs.

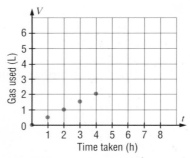

To show all the values of t, you draw a line.

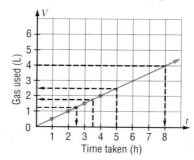

From the graph, you can make estimates and predictions of gas consumed at different times.

ACTIVITY   *Work in a Group*

1. Refer to the graphs shown above.
   (a) Estimate the time it took for 1.25 L of gasoline to be consumed.
   (b) Estimate the amount of gasoline consumed in 3.5 h.
   (c) In your journal, describe how you estimated the values in (a) and (b). What questions did you ask yourself?

2. Refer to the graphs shown above.
   (a) Estimate the time it took for 8.0 L of gasoline to be consumed.
   (b) Estimate the amount of gasoline consumed in 15 h.
   (c) In your journal, describe how you estimated the values in (a) and (b). What questions did you ask yourself?

In Question 1 of the activity, you chose two known values on a graph and estimated a value between them. This is called **interpolating**.

In Question 2 of the activity, you estimated a value which was beyond the values given. This is called **extrapolating**.

A Use a coordinate grid.

1. John and Marianne recorded measurements for stretching a spring. They recorded the mass and the length of the spring as follows.
(5, 1), (10, 2), (15, 3), (20, 4), (25, 5), (30, 6)
Suggest what the missing values might be.
(a) (35, ?)   (b) (40, ?)   (c) (45, ?)

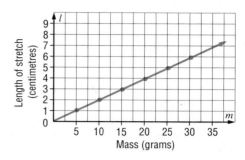

2. To find the missing values for the graph above,
• decide on the first step.
• suggest what the missing values might be.
(a) (18, ?)   (b) (28, ?)   (c) (22, ?)
(d) (50, ?)   (e) (77, ?)   (f) (65, ?)

3. John and Marianne then recorded the distance, in metres, a ball rolls over a period of time, in seconds.
(1, 3), (2, 6), (3, 9), (4, 12), (5, 15)
Suggest what the missing values might be.
(a) (?, 18)   (b) (?, 21)   (c) (?, 24)

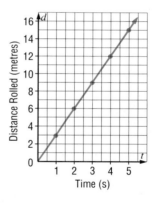

4. To find the missing values for the graph to the right,
• decide on the first step.
• suggest what the missing values might be.
(a) (6, ?)   (b) (?, 17)   (c) (?, 14)
(d) (?, 50)   (e) (?, 62)   (f) (?, 55)

5. Suppose you jog at a constant speed of 5 km/h. The distance you jog, d, in kilometres is related to the time, t, in hours by $d = 5t$.
(a) Construct a table of values for the relation.
(b) Graph the relation using your table of values in (a).
(c) Estimate how far you would jog in 2.5 h, 5.5 h, and 6.75 h.
(d) Estimate how long it would take you to jog 12 km, 36 km, and 44.5 km.

6. An experiment showed the amount of stretch resulting from adding mass to an elastic band.
(a) Plot the ordered pairs on a graph.
(b) Estimate how far the elastic band would stretch if these masses were attached: 12 g, 40 g, and 45 g.
(c) Estimate the mass attached if the elastic band were stretched 3.5 cm, 5.5 cm, and 7.8 cm.

Added Mass (g)	5	10	15	20	25	30
Stretch (cm)	1	2	3	4	5	6

377

7. Write a brief paragraph to discuss what is meant by *interpolation*. Use examples from this section to help you.
   - Decide what words to include in your paragraph.
   - Decide how to illustrate your answer.
   - Compare your paragraph to those of others in the class.

8. Write a brief paragraph to discuss what is meant by *extrapolation*. Use examples from this section to help you.
   - Decide what words to include in your paragraph.
   - Decide how to illustrate your answer.
   - Compare your paragraph to those of others in the class.

9. Radioactive material, with a mass of 100 g, is used in an experiment. As the material decays, data is recorded in the table.

After time, t, in hours	1	2	3	4	5	6	7	8	9
Amount of material, A, left in grams	65	42	27	18	11	7	5	3	2

   (a) Draw a graph of the relation shown by (t, A).

   after time in hours ——— amount of radioactive material remaining in grams

   (b) Join the points in (a) with a smooth curve.
   (c) Why is the term "decay" an appropriate word to describe the relation in (a)?

10. (a) Construct a table of values for each relation.   (i) $y = 2x$ (ii) $y = x^2$
    (b) Plot the ordered pairs for each relation in (a) and draw a smooth line through the ordered pairs. What do you notice?
    (c) What words would you use to describe the graph of each relation?
    (d) Why would "non-linear" be an appropriate way to describe the relation in (ii)? Give reasons for your answer.

GROUP PROJECT

1. Your work with relations can help you estimate values.
   (a) Use grid paper and cut out squares with sides of 1 unit, 2 units, 3 units, and so on, to 10 units.
   (b) Inside each square, write its area in square units.
   (c) Plot the ordered pairs (length of sides, area) on a graph.
   (d) Extend the graph to include real numbers by joining the points.

2. (a) Use your graph in Question 1. Estimate the square root of 24.
   (b) Use a calculator to calculate the square root of 24. How reasonable was your estimate?

3. Use your graph to estimate the value of each of the following.
   (a) $\sqrt{14}$ (b) $\sqrt{32}$ (c) $\sqrt{19}$ (d) $\sqrt{28}$ (e) $\sqrt{7}$

2.5 MAKING CONNECTIONS

GRAPHS

The skills you have learned for graphing ordered pairs with integers can be used to help you graph relationships with real numbers.

To understand and learn these connections, ask yourself two important questions:
- How are the graphs alike?
- How are they different?

The table of values to the right shows the relation $y = x + 1$. The table of values is then used to construct the following graphs. In your journal, show how these graphs are alike and how they are different.

x	y
0	1
1	2
2	3

x is a whole number

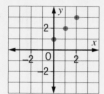

x is an integer

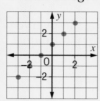

x is a real number

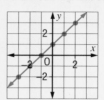

EXERCISE

B Review your skills with relations.

1. A relation is defined by $y = x - 1$.
   (a) Draw a graph of the relation if x is any whole number.
   (b) Draw a graph of the relation if x is any integer.
   (c) Draw a graph of the relation if x is any real number.
   (d) How are the graphs in (a), (b), and (c) alike? How are they different?

2. Repeat the parts of Question 1 for the following relations.
   (a) $y = 3x$ (b) $y = 3x - 1$ (c) $y = 3x + 1$ (d) $y = -3x - 1$

3. Draw a graph of each relation. (a, b)
   (a) $a = 2b$, where b is a whole number
   (b) $a = 2b$, where b is an integer   horizontal coordinate —— ⌐—— vertical coordinate
   (c) $a = 2b$, where b is a real number
   (d) How are the graphs in (a), (b), and (c) alike? How are they different?

MATH JOURNAL

(a) In your journal, describe how asking the questions "How are the skills alike?" and "How are the skills different?" helped you to learn mathematics.
(b) How have the questions in (a) helped you learn in other subjects?

12.6 COMMUNICATING WITH RELATIONS

When communicating about relations, special words are often used. Two such words are *domain* and *range*.

(3, 2)

The **domain** of a relation is all the first components of the ordered pairs.   The **range** of a relation is all the second components of the ordered pairs.

ACTIVITY

1. How are the meanings of domain and range in everyday language like the meanings of the words in mathematics? How are they different?

2. (a) What are the ordered pairs of the relation?
   (b) Make a list of the *x*-coordinates of these ordered pairs.
   (c) Make a list of the *y*-coordinates of these ordered pairs.
   (d) What is the domain and the range of the relation?
   (e) Draw a graph of a relation of your own. Record the ordered pairs, the domain, and the range.

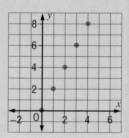

To find the domain and the range of any relation, it is often helpful to make a table of values and construct the graph of the relation as shown below.

EXAMPLE

Draw the graph of the relation given by $y = 2x - 1$, where x represents a real number. What is the domain and the range of the relation?

SOLUTION

Step 1
Construct a table of values for the relation. Then draw the graph of the relation.

x	y
-2	-5
-1	-3
0	-1
1	1
2	3

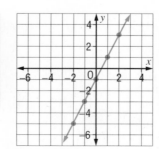

Step 2
Answer the question.
Domain: Since any real number can be chosen for *x*, the *domain* is any real number.
Range: Since the corresponding value for *y* can also be any real number, the *range* is any real number.

380

A   A graph can help you solve problems.

1. A relation is given by (0, 0), (1, 4), (2, 8), and (3, 12).
    (a) Plot the ordered pairs.
    (b) What is the domain of the relation?
    (c) What is the range of the relation?

2. (a) For each relation, write
        (i) the ordered pairs.
        (ii) the domain and range.
    (b) In your journal, describe a way to find
        the domain and range of any relation.

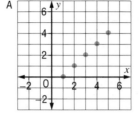
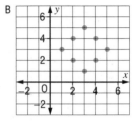

B   Review your skills with relations.

3. Write the domain and range of each relation.

(a)
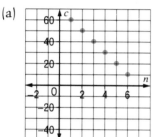

(b)
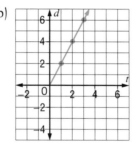

(c)
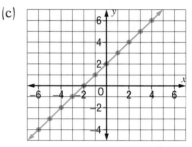

4. For each relation,
    • draw a graph.   • write the domain.   • write the range.
    (a) $y = 2x$, where x is a whole number   (b) $y = 2x + 1$, where x is an integer
    (c) $y = 2x - 1$, where x is any real number   (d) How are the graphs alike? different?

5. At a car wash, three cars are washed every minute. The number of cars washed, T, is
    given by $T = 3t$, where t is the number of minutes.
    (a) Draw a graph of the relation where the ordered pairs are (t, T).
    (b) Write the domain and the range for the relation.

PARTNER PROJECT

(a) For the counters shown
    find a path, using four line
    segments, that touches
    each counter.
(b) Create a problem of your own using
    the counters. Solve your problem.
    Compare your problem to others in
    the class.

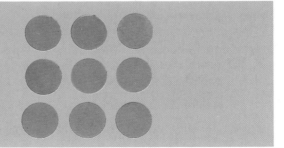

12.7 INTERSECTING GRAPHS

Suppose you are an air traffic controller. You have two planes approaching at 9000 m. One plane is travelling in a direction (heading) described by $y = -2x + 4$. The other is on a heading described by $y = x + 1$. Would you change the flight path of one of the planes? To answer the question, you need further information.

To determine if you should change the flight path of one plane, construct the graph of both flight paths.

Prepare Tables of Values

Construct the Graph

$y = x + 1$

x	y
–1	0
0	1
1	2

$y = -2x + 4$

x	y
–1	6
0	4
1	2

The same pair of coordinates show the point of intersection.

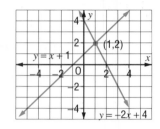

From the graph and the tables of values, you can see that the planes may collide at the point (1, 2). Thus, you may need to give instructions to change the flight path of one of the planes.

ACTIVITY   Work Together

The screen shown above is used by an air traffic controller.
(a) What do you notice about the screen?
(b) What math skills do you think an air traffic controller needs?
(c) Discuss how you think an air traffic controller actually decides whether planes are on the same heading. What is considered when deciding to change a flight plan?

EXERCISE

 Review your skills with graphing relations.

1. (a) Copy and complete the table of values for each of the following relations.
   (i) $y = x + 5$

x	0	?	13
y	?	10	?

   (ii) $y = 2x - 8$

x	0	?	–2
y	?	18	?

   (b) What is the point of intersection of the relations?

2. For the relations on each graph, identify the point of intersection.

(a)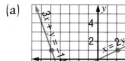

(b)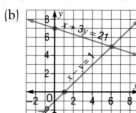

(c)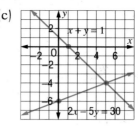

B Sketch a diagram to help you.

3. (a) Draw the graph of $y = 2x - 1$.
   (b) Draw the graph of $y = 3x - 3$.
   (c) What is the point of intersection of the relations in (a) and (b)?

4. (a) Draw the graph of each relation.
      (i) $y = x + 4$ (ii) $y = 2 - x$
   (b) At what point do the relations intersect?

5. (a) Draw the graph of each relation.

      (i) $y = x - 3$ (ii) $y = \dfrac{1}{2}x + 5$

   (b) At what point do the relations intersect?

6. For each pair of relations,
   - draw the graphs on the same coordinate grid.
   - find the point of intersection of the two relations.

   (a) $y = x$ (b) $y = x + 2$ (c) $y = -x$
       $y = -x + 2$ $y = -x + 2$ $y = x - 2$

7. The paths of two planes are given   Plane A: $y = 5x + 10$
   by the relations.   Plane B: $y = x - 2$
   (a) At what point do their paths cross?
   (b) What problem(s) might this present for the pilots?

8. The paths of two ships are given   Ship A: $y = 2x - 4$
   by the relations.   Ship B: $y = 3x - 2$
   (a) At what point do their paths cross?
   (b) What problem(s) might this present for the captains?

9. The paths of two ships are given   S.S. Quebec: $y = 2x - 27$
   by the following relations.   S.S. Alberta: $y = x + 6$
   (a) At what point do their paths cross?
   (b) Explain to your partner why you used the method you did for finding the point at
   which the paths cross.

10. The paths of two ships are given by the following relations.

Ship A: $y = 3x - 15$ Ship B: $y = x - 3$

(a) At what point do their paths cross?

(b) Describe under what conditions you would wish to change the path of one of the ships, and under what conditions you would not change the path of one of the ships.

11. Suppose you work for the coast guard. A ship sails along a path defined by $y = 2x + 4$. A motorboat travels along the path defined by $y = -x + 1$.

(a) Would you change the path taken by the boat or the ship? Give reasons for your answer.

(b) What assumptions have you made in (a)?

12. Two planes, at the same altitude, are flying along the paths defined by $y = x - 7$ and $y = x - 2$. Suppose you are an air traffic controller. Would you change the path of one of the planes? Give reasons for your answer.

13. A helicopter is flying on a path defined by $y = 1.5x + 3$. A crop duster is flying on a path defined by $y = 3x$. Both are at the same altitude.

(a) Should one of the pilots change course? Why?

(b) Which pilot do you think should change course? Why?

14. Refer to the relations shown.

(a) Create a problem of your own that can be solved using these relations.

(b) Solve your problem. Compare your problem with others in the class.

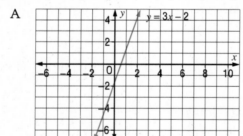

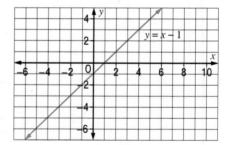

15. Work with a partner.

(a) On grid paper, make your own copy of the figure shown.

(b) For your figure, make two straight cuts to construct three congruent parts.

(c) Experiment to find a relation that can be used to describe each cut.

(d) Create a similar problem of your own. Compare your problem to others in the class.

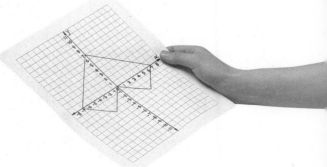

384

USINESS

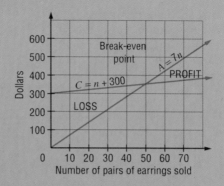

You can use graphs to analyze profit and loss. For example, suppose Naomi started her own business selling custom-made earrings. Her cost (C) in dollars for making each pair of earrings (n) can be given by the relation $C = n + 300$.

The amount (A) in dollars she receives from selling n pairs of earrings can be given by the relation $A = 7n$.

Her cost for making earrings and her profit for selling earrings are shown in the graph above. The point at which the relations cross is the point at which she **breaks even**.

1. (a) Estimate at what point Naomi breaks even.
   (b) What do you think is a reasonable profit for selling earrings?
   (c) How many pairs of earrings does Naomi need to sell in order to reach the profit you suggested in (b)?

2. Alex has a hot dog business. The graph shows her costs (C) and the amount of money she receives from sales (A).
   (a) Estimate how many hot dogs Alex needs to sell to break even.
   (b) What are her costs for the break-even point?
   (c) How much money does she receive at the break-even point?

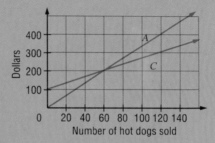

3. Katerina started a skate-sharpening business. The graph shows her costs (C) and the amount she receives from customers (A).
   (a) Estimate how many pairs of skates Katerina needs to sharpen to break even.
   (b) What are her costs for the break-even point?
   (c) How much money does she receive at the break-even point?

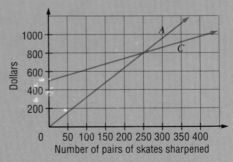

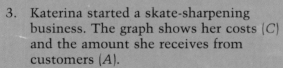

4. (a) Suppose you are the manager of a store. How might you use the break-even point in making decisions in your business?
   (b) List other situations in which the skills in this section would be useful.

DATA MANAGEMENT

Often, the value of one quantity depends upon the value of another. When you collect data, the relationship may not be seen until you graph the data.

The data in the chart show the minimum stopping distance of a car for various speeds. In its present form, you may not see the relationships.

Speed (km/h)	10	20	30	40	50	60	70	80	90	100	110	120	130	140
Reaction Time Distance (m)	2.1	4.2	6.3	8.4	10.5	12.6	14.7	16.8	18.9	21.0	23.1	25.2	27.3	29.4
Braking Distance (m)	1.6	3.4	5.7	8.7	12.4	17.2	23.2	30.7	39.7	50.6	63.4	78.3	95.5	115.3
Total Stopping Distance (m)	3.7	7.6	12.0	17.1	22.9	29.8	37.9	47.5	58.6	71.6	86.5	103.5	122.8	144.7

ACTIVITY   *Work in a Group*

1. Use the data in the chart.
    (a) Graph the data. Use the ordered pair (speed, total stopping distance).
    (b) Record your observations about the data in the graph.
    (c) How can the relationships in the chart make you a better driver?

2. Refer to your graph. What is the total stopping distance for each speed?
    (a) 50 km/h   (b) 100 km/h   (c) 75 km/h   (d) 83.5 km/h

3. At what speed are you travelling for each of the following total stopping distances?
    (a) 10 m   (b) 25 m   (c) 50 m   (d) 37.5 m

4. Suppose you are travelling at 50 km/h. By how much does the total stopping distance increase if you increase your speed by each amount?
    (a) 5 km/h   (b) 10 km/h   (c) 20 km/h   (d) 30 km/h

5. (a) Create problems of your own based on the data or the graph you constructed. Solve your problems.
    (b) Compare your problems to those of others in the class.

6. Discuss with your group what happens to your total stopping distance as you increase the speed of your car. What driving tip could you write as a result of this discussion?

2.10 EXPLORING INTERCEPTS

To help you graph relations, you can explore their properties. As you complete each exploration, summarize any relationships you discover.

EXPLORATION ① *Work with a Partner*

1. Construct a graph for each relation. How are the graphs alike? different?
   (a) $y = 2x + 3$ (b) $y = x + 3$ (c) $y = -x + 3$ (d) $y = -2x + 3$
   (e) What do you notice about the point at which each graph crosses the y-axis? What is the value of the x-coordinate at this point?

2. Construct a graph for each relation. How are the graphs alike? different?
   (a) $y = -x - 4$ (b) $y = 3x - 4$ (c) $y = 5x - 4$ (d) $y = -2x - 4$
   (e) What do you notice about the point at which each graph crosses the y-axis? What is the value of the x-coordinate at this point?

EXPLORATION ② *Work with a Partner*

3. (a) Construct a graph for each relation. How are the graphs alike? different?
   (i) $y = 2x - 2$ (ii) $y = x - 1$ (iii) $y = -x + 1$ (iv) $y = -2x + 2$
   (b) What do you notice about the point at which each graph crosses the x-axis? What is the value of the y-coordinate at this point?

4. Construct a graph for each relation. How are the graphs alike? different?
   (a) $y = -x - 2$ (b) $y = 3x + 6$ (c) $y = 5x + 10$ (d) $y = -2x - 4$
   (e) What do you notice about the point at which each graph crosses the x-axis? What is the value of the y-coordinate at this point?

EXPLORATION ③ *Work with a Partner*

You can use a graphics calculator to help you explore properties of a relation. Refer to your manual to help you.

5. (a) Use the sequence to graph $y = 2x + 2$.

   | AC | GRAPH | 2 | X, Ø, T | + | 2 | EXE |

   (b) Use a similar sequence to graph $y = x + 1$, $y = -x + 1$, and $y = -5x + 1$. How are the graphs alike? How are they different?

   (c) Press | Trace | and have the cursor follow each relation. What do you notice about the point at which each graph crosses the y-axis? What is the value of the x-coordinate at this point?

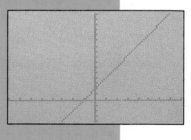

6. (a) Use an appropriate key sequence to graph each relation.
   (i) $y = x - 4$ (ii) $y = 2x - 8$ (iii) $y = -3x + 12$
   How are the graphs alike? How are they different?

   (b) Press | Trace | and have the cursor follow each relation. What do you notice about the point at which each graph crosses the x-axis? What is the value of the y-coordinate at this point?

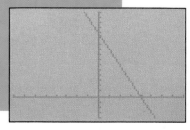

387

In the previous section, you explored graphs which cross the coordinate axes. Where they cross is called an **intercept**. A summary of the meaning of intercept is shown in the graph to the right.

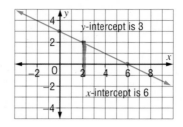

You can use your skills with algebra to find the x-intercept and the y-intercept, as shown in the following example.

EXAMPLE
Find the x-intercept and the y-intercept of the relation $y = 2x - 4$.

SOLUTION

Find the x-intercept
Use $y = 0$ in the relation.
$$0 = 2x - 4$$
$$2x = 4$$
$$x = 2$$

The x-intercept is 2.

Find the y-intercept
Use $x = 0$ in the relation.
$$y = 2(0) - 4$$
$$y = -4$$

The y-intercept is -4.

You can use intercepts to draw the graph of a relation. For example, you can use the intercepts to graph the relation $y = 2x - 4$.

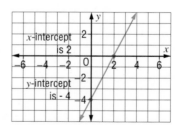

ACTIVITY   *Work with a Partner*
You could interpret the nature of mathematics using the steps shown to the right. Record these steps in your journal.

(a) How might the work you have done with intercepts illustrate the nature of mathematics as described here?

(b) Summarize what you have learned about intercepts so far.

(c) What other topics have you learned about that illustrate the nature of mathematics?

NATURE OF MATHEMATICS
1. Explore a concept.
2. Summarize relationships.
3. Apply relationships.

A The variables in each exercise represent real numbers.

1. What is the
   x-intercept and
   the y-intercept
   of each relation?

   (i)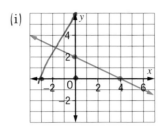

   (ii)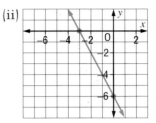

2. For the relation defined by $y = 5x - 10$,
   (a) find the x-intercept.
   (b) find the y-intercept.
   (c) Use the data in (a) and (b) to graph the relation.

B Remember: Label each graph.

3. For each relation,
   • find the x-intercept.   • find the y-intercept.   • graph the relation.
   (a) $y = x + 3$ (b) $y = 5x$ (c) $y = 2x - 3$ (d) $y = 3x + 2$

   (e) $y = 5x - 5$ (f) $y = \frac{1}{3}x - 1$ (g) $y = -\frac{1}{2}x - 4$ (h) $y = -\frac{1}{3}x + 3$

4. A grid is used to track an airplane. The airport is at the origin. A plane is travelling on a heading $y = 2x + 1$. How far is the plane from the airport when it crosses the x-axis?

5. A grid is used to track a ship. A lighthouse is at the origin. The ship is travelling on a heading $y = -3x - 6$. How far is the ship from the lighthouse when it crosses the y-axis?

6. (a) On the same axes, draw the graphs defined by the following relations.
   (i) $y = 2x$ (ii) $y = 2x + 1$ (iii) $y = 2x - 1$ (iv) $y = 2x + 2$
   (b) How are the graphs in (a) alike? How are they different?

7. (a) On the same axes, draw the graphs defined by the following relations.
   (i) $y = -2x$ (ii) $y = -2x + 1$ (iii) $y = -2x - 1$ (iv) $y = -2x + 2$
   (b) How are the graphs in (a) alike? How are they different?

SELF EVALUATION

Sometimes, it is helpful for you to explain mathematical terms in your own words.
(a) In your journal, explain what is meant by the x-intercept and the y-intercept. Use examples of your own to help your explanation.
(b) When do you think it is useful to know the x-intercept and the y-intercept? Explain your answer to your partner.

Throughout this chapter, you have worked with relations and its vocabulary. In this section, you will explore a special relation.

ACTIVITY 1

(a) List all the terms and properties you have seen for relations.
(b) Illustrate each term and property in (a) with an example of your own.
(c) Record different types of relations problems you have solved.

ACTIVITY 2

Place a ruler parallel to the *y*-axis and move it across each relation. For each relation, list
(a) how the relations are alike.   (b) how the relations are different.

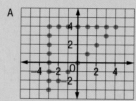
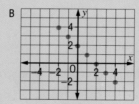
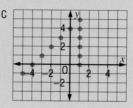
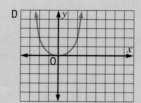
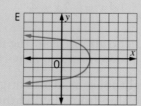
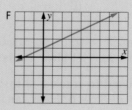

One special type of relation has the property that, when you draw a vertical line, it meets the graph at only one point. Such relations, like the one to the right, have a special name. They are called *functions*. A **function** is a relation where each *x*-coordinate has one, and only one, *y*-coordinate.

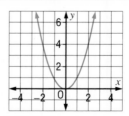

ACTIVITY 3   *Work with a Partner*

Review the graphs shown in Activity 2.
(a) Which graphs show a function? Which do not? Justify your answer.
(b) Draw graphs of your own to show functions. Justify why they are functions.

EXERCISE

B Review your skills with relations.

1. Which of the following graphs represent functions? Justify your answer.

A 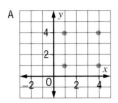 B 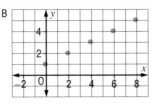 C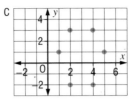

D 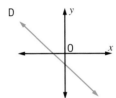 E 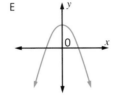 F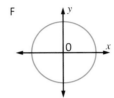

2. (a) Plot the following points.
   (0, 0), (1, 1), (2, 2), (3, 2), (4, 1), (5, 0), (6, 4), (7, 9), (8, 7)
   (b) Does the graph in (a) represent a function? Give reasons for your answer.

3. (a) Plot the following points.
   (−3, 0), (−2, 1), (−1, 2), (0, 1), (1, 0), (0, −1), (−1, −2), (−2, −1)
   (b) Does the graph in (a) represent a function? Give reasons for your answer.

4. For each of the following,
   • plot the points and draw a smooth curve through the points to show the graph.
   • decide if the graph is a function.
   (a) (1, 5), (2, 6), (3, 7), (4, 8), (5, 9), (6, 10), (7, 11), (8, 12)
   (b) (−3, 2), (−2, 7), (−1, 12), (0, 6), (2, 8), (5, 9), (4, 4), (1, −12)
   (c) (0, 0), (−1, 4), (6, 2), (0, −8), (−3, −5), (5, 5), (6, −2), (8, 3)
   (d) (−4, 5), (−2, 1), (1, −2), (6, −4), (−2, 5), (3, 3), (−3, −3), (4, −3)

5. (a) Which of the following curves created with an oscilloscope represent functions?
       Give reasons for your answer.
   (b) Suppose you are operating an oscilloscope. Create different curves of your own.
       Have your partner decide if your curves are functions.

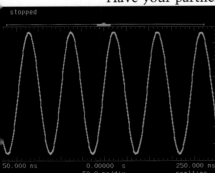

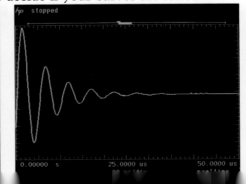

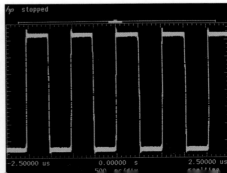

1. Which ordered pairs satisfy the relation given by
   $y = \frac{1}{2}x + 1$? Which do not satisfy the relation?
   (a) (2, 2)   (b) (3, 3)   (c) (4, 3)

2. (a) Draw a graph of the relation given by $y = 3x + 2$,
       where x is an integer. What is its domain? What is
       its range?
   (b) Draw the above graph again for x to represent any
       real number. What is its domain? What is its range?

3. (a) Find the missing value if each ordered pair satisfies
       the relation $y = 5x$.
       (i) (3, ?)   (ii) (–2, ?)   (iii) (?, 15)
   (b) Construct the graph of the relation.

4. What are the x- and y-intercepts for each graph?

   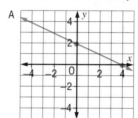
   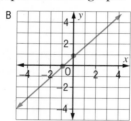

5. For each pair of relations,
   • draw the graph of each relation.
   • find their point of intersection.
   (a) $y = 2x + 1$; $y = x + 3$ (b) $y = x + 2$; $y = 2x$

6. Data are collected for Awajohn's
   running of the 100-m race.
   (a) Draw a graph of the data.
   (b) About how long will it take
       him to run 13 m?
   (c) How far will he run in 9 s?

Time in seconds	Distance in metres
0	0
1	7
4	28
7	49

7. A relation is given by the ordered pairs (t, d), where t is
   any positive number and $d = 3t$.
   (a) Find the missing value in each of the following.
       (i) (1, ?)   (ii) (?, 9)   (iii) (?, 15)   (iv) (3, ?)
   (b) How can you determine if the relation is a function?
   (c) Use your plan in (b). Is the relation a function?

❶ How can a calculator help
  you to draw the graph of a
  relation?

❷ Evaluate your progress.
  What skills did you find
  difficult at the beginning of
  the year? What did you do to
  improve them?

❸ What skills do you find
  difficult now? How can you
  improve these skills?

MAKING CONNECTIONS

Refer to the pictures on
the opening page of this
chapter.
(a) Create a problem using
    the pictures.
(b) Solve the problem
    using the skills in this
    chapter. Compare your
    problem to others in
    the class.

❹ How are a "function" and a "relation" alike? How are they different? Use examples to help your explanation.

❺ In what situations do you think you would need to find the intersection of relations?

❻ Are the solutions in your notebook clearly organized? If not, how can they be improved?

SELF EVALUATION

1. The following relations are shown by the tables of values. Find the missing values.

(a)

x	$y = x - 3$
1	−2
2	?
3	?
?	13
?	15

(b)

x	$y = 2x + 5$
2	9
?	11
4	?
?	21
6	?

2. What is the x-intercept and the y-intercept of each of the following?

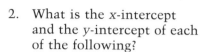

3. (a) Draw the graph of each relation.
   (i) $y = x + 1$, where x is an integer
   (ii) $y = x + 1$, where x is a real number
   (b) How are the graphs alike? How are they different?

4. A relation is given by the ordered pairs (t, d) where $d = 4t$.
   (a) Draw the axes on grid paper.
   (b) Draw a graph of the relation where t is a whole number.
   (c) What is the domain and range of the relation?

5. Find the missing values for the relation shown.
   (a) $(-3, ?), (-1, ?), (1, ?)$
   (b) $(6, ?), (?, 10), (-8, ?)$

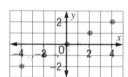

6. For each pair of equations,
   • draw the graph of the relation.
   • find the point of intersection.
   (a) $y = x + 4$ (b) $y = x - 2$
       $y = 3x$ $y = 3x + 2$

7. Which of the following graphs represent functions? Give reasons for your answer.

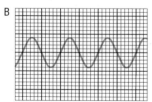

MATH JOURNAL

In this chapter, you have used many math symbols and skills to help you work with relations.
(a) List all the symbols and skills you have learned.
(b) Write an example of each.

1. Sanjay works part-time as a salesperson and gets paid each month. Last month, Sanjay spent $\frac{1}{3}$ of his income on car repairs, $\frac{1}{4}$ on groceries, and $\frac{1}{5}$ on entertainment. He put $\frac{1}{2}$ of what was left into the bank and then spent the remaining $100 on car insurance. How much did Sanjay earn last month?

2. (a) Three playing cards are arranged as shown. Predict what the three cards are, using the following clues.
   - A 9 is just below a 9.
   - A 10 is just above a 9.
   - A spade is just above a spade.
   - A heart is just below a spade.

   (b) Create a similar problem of your own. Compare your problem to others in the class.

3. Suppose you have a scale that can measure the exact mass of an object. You also have ten bags, each containing ten coins. One of the bags contains coins that are fake and are 1 g less than the mass of a regular coin.
   (a) How can you use the scale exactly once to find the bag that has the fake coins?
   (b) Compare your solution to those of others in the class. How are your solutions alike? How are they different?

4. Suppose there are 100 animals on a farm. Of the animals, 99% are chickens and 1% are dogs. How many chickens must be sold so that 98% of the animals on the farm are chickens?

5. A transportation department finds that it takes five employees exactly five days to machine-sweep 180 km of road. Suppose the department needs to have 250 km of road swept in six days.
   (a) Will the five employees be enough to machine-sweep 250 km of road? Give reasons for your answer.
   (b) List any assumptions you have made in (a).

6. (a) Arrange the stir sticks shown below to form three rectangles with equal areas.
   (b) Create a problem of your own based on the arrangement in (a). Solve your problem and compare your problem to others in the class.

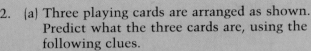

Gymnasts are marked on the way they perform certain moves. In your journal:

- Describe how geometry is involved in gymnastic moves.
- List any ways you have used geometry in your favourite sport or hobby.
- List any other mathematics skills you have used in your favourite sport or hobby.

This gymnast will score more marks when his arms are parallel to the ground.

This gymnast will score more marks when her body and legs form a 90° angle.

395

For each exploration:
- List the discoveries you make. Write them in your journal.
- Think of other experiments you can perform with geometry. Make a list in your journal.

Scientists Discover Possible Cause

Scientists have been researching the earth's ozone layer for years. Through repeated experiments, they have found that certain substances have caused a 'hole'.

(a) What substances do you think caused the hole?

(b) Describe a possible experiment scientists could have used.

EXPLORATION ① *Work with a Partner*

1. (a) Draw three different triangles. Cut them out.
   (b) Tear off the corners of one and fit them together as shown. Do this also with the second and third triangles.
   (c) What do you notice about the sum of the angles of your triangles?

2. Four different triangles are shown below.
   (a) Measure the angles.
   (b) Copy and complete the table.

Triangle	Measure			Sum
	∠A	∠B	∠C	
1				
2				
3				
4				

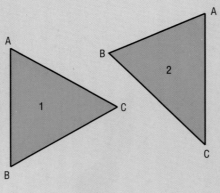

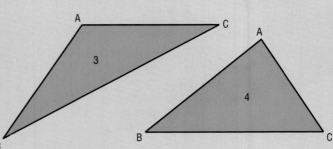

3. Use your results from the previous questions.
   (a) Write a conclusion about the sum of the angles in a triangle.
   (b) Describe to your partner another way that you can verify the sum of the angles in a triangle. Have your partner perform the exploration you describe.
   (c) Create problems of your own based on the results of the exploration. Compare your problems to those of your partner. Solve each other's problems.

You can experiment and explore the angle properties of a quadrilateral. List your observations in your journal.

4. (a) Draw any three quadrilaterals of your own. Cut them out.
   (b) Tear off the corners. Fit the corners of each together as shown.
   (c) What do you notice about the sum of the angles in a quadrilateral?

5. Draw a quadrilateral.
   (a) Find the measures of the angles of your quadrilateral.
   (b) Find the sum of the measures in (a). Round your answer to the nearest 10°.
   (c) Draw two other quadrilaterals of your own. Repeat (a) and (b). What do you notice about your answers?
   (d) Based on the above results, write a probable conclusion.

6. Use your results from the previous questions.
   (a) Write a conclusion about the sum of the angles in a quadrilateral.
   (b) Describe to your partner another way that you might verify the sum of the angles in a quadrilateral. Have your partner perform the experiment you describe.

7. Two parallel lines and a *transversal* are used to form the angles shown below.
   (a) Estimate which angles appear to be equal to angle 1.
   (b) Measure the angles. Were your choices correct?

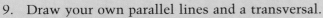

8. (a) Estimate which angles appear to be equal to angle 2.
   (b) Measure the angles. Were your choices correct?

9. Draw your own parallel lines and a transversal.
   (a) Identify all angles that are equal.
   (b) In your journal, list the relationships you see. Compare your relationships to those found by others in the class.

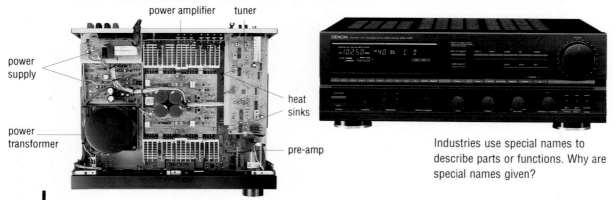

power amplifier   tuner

power supply

heat sinks

power transformer

pre-amp

Industries use special names to describe parts or functions. Why are special names given?

In geometry, special words are used to describe figures or special features of the figures. Work in groups to complete the following activities.

ACTIVITY 1

1. Triangles are named according to their special properties. Refer to the triangles shown below.
   (a) Classify each triangle using the appropriate name from the chart.
   (b) For each name in the chart, draw a triangle that has the same property.

Type of triangle	Special property (sides)
Scalene	No sides are equal.
Isosceles	Two sides are equal.
Equilateral	Three sides are equal.

2. Triangles can also be classified according to other properties. Refer to the triangles shown below.
   (a) Classify each triangle using the appropriate name from the chart.
   (b) For each name in the chart, draw a triangle of your own that has the same property.

Type of triangle	Special property (angles)
Acute	All angles less than 90°.
Right	One angle is 90°.
Obtuse	One angle greater than 90°.
Equilateral	All angles are equal.

3. Some triangles may have more than one name. For example, triangle D could be classified as *isosceles* and *right*.
   (a) Find other triangles that have more than one name.
   (b) Start a class collage of triangles found in magazines and newspapers. Classify each triangle.

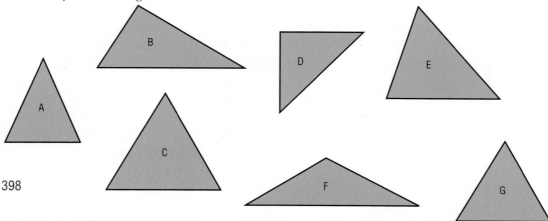

ACTIVITY 2

4. Quadrilaterals can also be named according to their special properties. For each quadrilateral described on the cards shown:
   (a) Sketch the quadrilateral described.
   (b) Compare your sketch with others in the group. How are the quadrilaterals alike? How are they different?

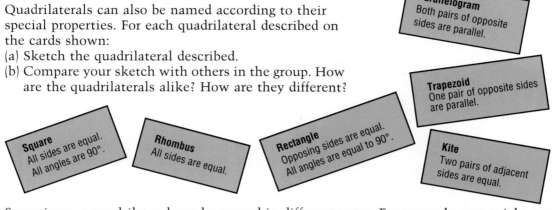

Parallelogram
Both pairs of opposite sides are parallel.

Trapezoid
One pair of opposite sides are parallel.

Square
All sides are equal.
All angles are 90°.

Rhombus
All sides are equal.

Rectangle
Opposing sides are equal.
All angles are equal to 90°.

Kite
Two pairs of adjacent sides are equal.

5. Sometimes, a quadrilateral can be named in different ways. For example, you might say that "A square is also a kite."
   (a) Is the statement true?
   (b) How else can you classify a square?
   (c) Create statements of your own about other quadrilaterals. Have others in the class decide if they are true.

ACTIVITY 3

6. To communicate mathematics clearly, you need to know some special words.
   (a) What do you think is meant by the word "conjecture"?
   (b) Find the meaning of the word in a dictionary. In your own words, write what you think is meant by the word "conjecture."

Try the computer program Geometric Supposer to help you verify results in this activity.

7. (a) Do you think the following conjecture is true? "The diagonals of a square are the same length."
   (b) Draw a square to check your conjecture in (a).
   (c) Repeat (b) for another square. What is your conclusion?

8. (a) Do you think the following conjecture is true? "The diagonals of a rectangle intersect at right angles."
   (b) Draw a rectangle to check whether the statement is true.
   (c) Repeat (b) for a rhombus. What is your conclusion?

9. Each of the following statements is a conjecture. Draw figures to check whether the statement is true. Place any new words in your journal.
   (a) "The diagonals of a rhombus intersect at right angles."
   (b) "The diagonals of a rhombus are equal in length."
   (c) "The sum of the opposite angles of a parallelogram is 180°."
   (d) "The diagonals of a kite are perpendicular to each other."

Did you know that stunts are set up in advance to ensure they are safe? Suppose you are a stunt performer. You need to set up a stunt using skateboards. The skateboards are on wires that are attached to form a triangle as shown below. This gives the appearance that the skateboards are floating in air.

Two of the angles formed by the wires are shown. What is the measure of the third angle?

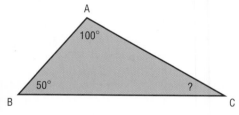

$$\angle A + \angle B + \angle C = 180°$$
$$100° + 50° + \angle C = 180°$$
$$\angle C = 180° - 150°$$
$$\angle C = 30°$$

You have found that the sum of the angles in a triangle is 180°.

Thus, the third angle is 30°.

ACTIVITY *Work with a Partner*
List what math skills you think are needed when setting up the stunt shown in the photograph.

EXERCISE

A Give reasons for your answer.

1. Refer to △RST.
   (a) How can you use the equation $x + 57 + 43 = 180$ to find the measure of ∠R?
   (b) Solve the equation in (a). What is the measure of ∠R?

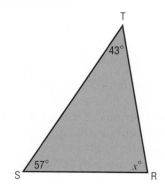

2. Work with a partner.
   (a) Find the missing angle measures.
   (b) Classify each triangle.

(i)
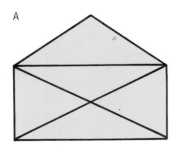

(ii)

(iii)
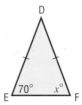

(iv)
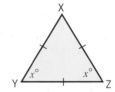

B To help you solve problems, you can sketch a diagram.

3. Refer to △ABC, △DEF, and △XYZ.
   (a) What type of triangle is each?
   (b) Write an equation for the sum of the angles in each triangle.
   (c) What is the missing angle measure in each?

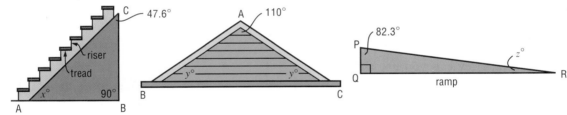

4. Each drawing shows a type of construction. Find the missing measures.

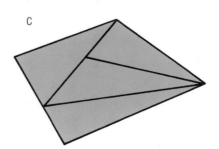

5. (a) Which of the designs below can you trace without lifting your pencil or going over any line segment twice?
   (b) Create similar designs of your own. Have others determine which designs can be copied without lifting up your pencil and without going over any line segment twice.

A

B

C

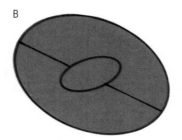

401

13.4 MAKING CONNECTIONS

You can combine your skills with algebra and geometry to help you solve problems.

YOU ALREADY KNOW...

- How to solve equations.
- The sum of the angles in a triangle is 180°.
- How to classify triangles.

You can find the measure of ∠A as shown below.

The sum of the angles is 180°.
Thus, $x + x + 50 = 180$
                $2x + 50 = 180$
                        $2x = 130$
                          $x = 65$

Therefore, ∠A measures 65°.

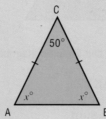

Think: In an isosceles triangle, the angles opposite the equal sides are equal.

To help you complete the following exercise, refer to your journal and review how to classify triangles.

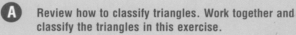
EXERCISE

A Review how to classify triangles. Work together and classify the triangles in this exercise.

1. (a) How can you use the equation
      $2x + 2x + x = 180$ to find the measure of each angle?
   (b) Solve the equation in (a). What is the measure of each angle in △ABC?

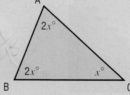

2. Estimate the missing measures in each triangle. Then decide on an equation to find the missing measures. Find the missing measures.
   (a)   (b)   (c)

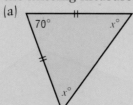   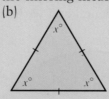   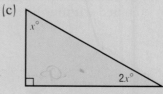

3. In △DEF, ∠E is 30° greater than ∠D as shown. Use the diagram to find the measure of each angle.

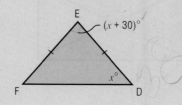

4. (a) Two angles of a triangle are 72° and 30°. Find the remaining angle.
    (b) What type of angle have you found in (a)?

5. In △ABC, ∠B is three times the size of ∠A and ∠C is four times the size of ∠A. Find the measure of each angle.

6. In △ABC, ∠A is 15° more than twice ∠B, and ∠C is equal to the sum of ∠A and ∠B. Find the measure of each angle.

7. (a) Based on your earlier work, what is the sum of the angles in a quadrilateral?
    (b) Use your answer from (a) to find the missing measure in each.

(i)

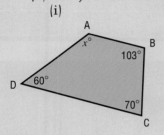

(ii)

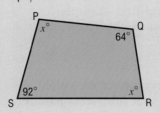

(iii)

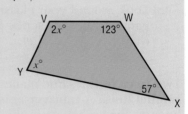

C

8. Find each missing measure. Give reasons for your answer.

(a)

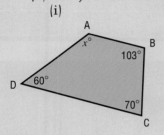

(b)

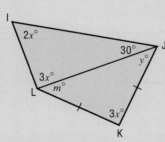

(c)

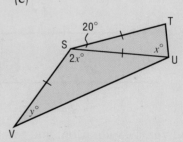

(d) Create similar figures of your own and include some angle measures. Have others in the class find the missing measures.

SELF EVALUATION

Look back to other chapters you have completed in this book.
(a) What skills have you learned that are used in this section?
(b) Are you confident that you can use the skills accurately?
(c) Describe the skills to your partner. Does your partner feel you have left anything out of your description?

Previously, you investigated relationships among the angles in parallel lines. Review any relationships you found and try the following activity in a small group. One member of the group could present the group's findings to the rest of the class.

ACTIVITY

Refer to the pictures at the right.
(a) What would you do to determine whether the lines shown are parallel?
(b) Look around your classroom and find examples of parallel lines. Describe how you might check that the lines are parallel.

Two lines in the same plane that never meet are called **parallel lines**. A **transversal** is a line that intersects parallel lines as shown below. In the diagram, EF is the transversal.

In the diagram, AB and CD are parallel. Thus, you can write AB ∥ CD to show parallel lines.

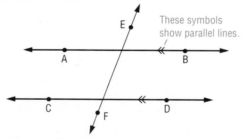

These symbols show parallel lines.

In a previous exploration, you found relationships among different angles in parallel lines. Special names are given to the angles created by parallel lines and a transversal as shown below. Identify the angles on the parallel lines shown above.

Interior Angles **Corresponding Angles** **Alternate Angles**

A This exercise investigates properties of special pairs of angles which are related to parallel lines. Work together.

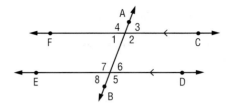

1. What type of angle is shown by each pair of angles?
   (a) 1, 8   (b) 1, 6   (c) 1, 7   (d) 2, 5
   (e) 3, 6   (f) 4, 7   (g) 2, 6   (h) 2, 7

2. In the diagram, name special pairs of angles. Justify your answer.

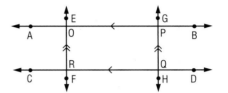

B Questions 3 to 5 are based on the diagram to the right.

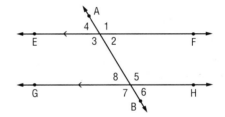

3. (a) Choose a pair of alternate angles and measure them. What do you notice about their measures?
   (b) Choose a different pair of alternate angles and measure them. What do you notice this time?
   (c) Write a probable conclusion for your findings about alternate angles.

4. (a) Choose pairs of corresponding angles and measure them. What do you notice?
   (b) Write a probable conclusion for your findings about corresponding angles.

5. (a) Choose pairs of interior angles on the same side of the transversal AB. Measure them and find the sum of the angles. What do you notice?
   (b) Write a probable conclusion for your findings about interior angles on the same side of the transversal.

6. (a) On a geoboard, use elastics to show quadrilaterals with parallel lines.
   (b) Make conjectures about relationships in the quadrilaterals.
   (c) Test your conjectures. Compare your relationships with others in the class.

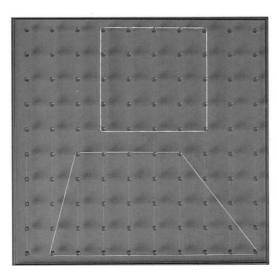

In the previous section, you explored relationships when two parallel lines and a transversal form angles. You can make connections between the properties of parallel lines and the angles of a triangle to solve problems like the following.

EXAMPLE 1

Find the measures of $\angle AGH$ and $\angle CHG$. Justify your answers by giving a reason for each step in the solution.

SOLUTION

From the diagram:

$$x + 2x = 180 \qquad \text{Why?}$$
$$3x = 180 \qquad \text{Why?}$$
$$x = 60 \qquad \text{Why?}$$

Thus, $\angle AGH = 60°$ and $\angle CHG = 120°$.

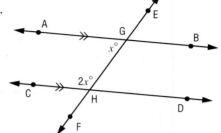

EXAMPLE 2

Find the measure of $\angle BFE$. Justify your answer by giving a reason for each step in the solution.

SOLUTION

Refer to the diagram.

$$\angle ABE = \angle BEF = 80° \qquad \text{Why?}$$
$$\angle EBF = \angle BFE \qquad \text{Why?}$$
$$80 + x + x = 180 \qquad \text{Why?}$$
$$80 + 2x = 180 \qquad \text{Why?}$$
$$2x = 180 - 80 \qquad \text{Why?}$$
$$2x = 100 \qquad \text{Why?}$$
$$x = 50 \qquad \text{Why?}$$

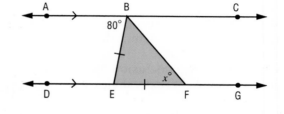

Thus, $\angle BFE = 50°$.

Always make a concluding statement.

ACTIVITY

In your journal, describe why writing reasons can help you when you review your solutions for further study or writing tests.

EXERCISE

A Give a reason for each step in your solution.

1. Find the value of x in each diagram.

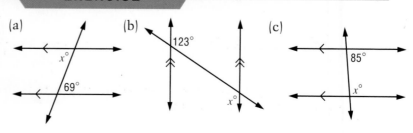

(a) $x°$ $69°$

(b) $123°$ $x°$

(c) $85°$ $x°$

2. Work with a partner. Find the measure of as many angles as you can. Justify your answers.

(a)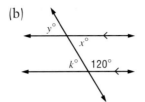

(b)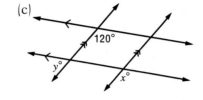

B Remember: Always justify each step of your solution.

3. Find the value of each variable. Estimate first.

(a)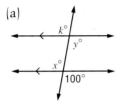

(b)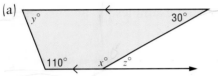

(c)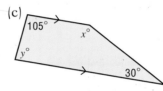

4. Find the value of each variable. Give reasons for each step of your solution.

(a) (b) (c)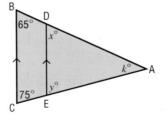

5. (a) Which lines are parallel?
   (b) List angles that are equal.
   (c) Use your results in (a) and (b). Find the values of x, y, and k. Give reasons for your answer.

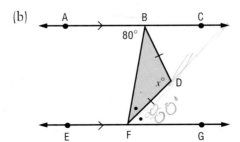

6. Find the value of each variable. Estimate first.

(a)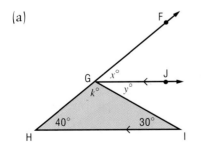

(b)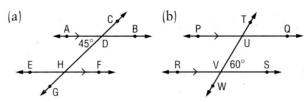

(c) Work with a partner. Create a question similar to those above. Write a solution and provide reasons for each step.

407

When you see a pattern evolving, you can make a *probable conclusion*. For example, using manipulatives, what probable conclusion can you make about the number pattern shown?

1, 4, 9, 16, 25, 36, 49, ...

Based on the manipulatives, you might make the probable conclusion "It appears that each number is the sum of consecutive odd numbers."

$$1 = 1$$
$$4 = 1 + 3$$
$$9 = 1 + 3 + 5$$
$$16 = 1 + 3 + 5 + 7$$

When you see the pattern, you then make a probable conclusion. To test your probable conclusion, you often collect more data by exploring further examples.

EXERCISE

B   Use your *Problem Solving Plan* to help you organize your work.

1. For the following number patterns, use manipulatives to make any probable conclusions. Use further examples to test your probable conclusions.
   (a) 1, 5, 9, 13, ...   (b) 1, 3, 6, 10, ...   (c) 1, 1, 2, 5, 8, 13, ...

2. (a) Draw any triangle. Find the midpoint of two sides of the triangle.
   (b) Connect the points in (a).
   (c) Compare the line in (b) with the third side of your triangle. What do you notice?
   (d) Repeat parts (a) to (c) for other triangles. Based on your results, write a probable conclusion.

3. Copy the right triangle shown.
   (a) Measure the length of the hypotenuse.
   (b) Find the midpoint of the hypotenuse.
   (c) Join the midpoint of the hypotenuse to the vertex of the right angle.
   (d) Measure the length of the line segment you have drawn. What do you notice?
   (e) Repeat parts (a) to (d) for other right triangles that you draw.
   (f) Based on your results, write a probable conclusion.

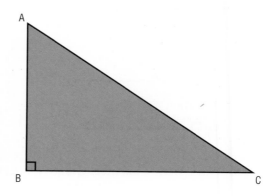

4. (a) Refer to your triangles in Question 3. Use each line segment you constructed in Question 3 as a radius. Use the midpoint of the hypotenuse as the centre. Draw a circle.
   (b) What do you notice about your circles in (a)?
   (c) Based on your observations, write a probable conclusion. Test your probable conclusion.

5. Work with a partner and draw any triangle.
   (a) Draw the perpendicular bisectors of all sides of the triangle.
   (b) Extend your perpendicular bisectors in (a) so that they intersect. What do you notice?
   (c) Repeat (a) and (b) for other triangles that you and your partner draw.
   (d) Based on your observations, write a probable conclusion. Test your probable conclusion.

6. (a) Refer to your triangles in Question 5. Use the point of intersection as the centre of a circle and the distance from the point to a vertex as the radius. Draw the circle.
   (b) What do you notice about your circles in (a)?
   (c) Based on your observations, write a probable conclusion. Test your probable conclusion.

7. ΔDEF is a special triangle constructed inside ΔABC. It is called a **pedal** triangle.
   (a) Based on the following steps, construct a pedal triangle.
       (i) Construct the altitudes of ΔABC.
       (ii) Bisect the angles of ΔDEF.
       (iii) What do you notice about your line segments in (i) and (ii)?
   (b) Choose a triangle of your own. Use the steps above to construct a pedal triangle.

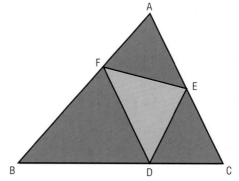

WORKING TOGETHER: PROJECT

This aerial photograph, covering an area of 500 km², shows a monkey carved in the ground in Peru. The carving is huge and was done over 1000 years ago. Work together to write a paragraph to answer the following.
(a) How do you think the ancient Peruvians created the carving and made it so accurate?
(b) What mathematics do you think they used?
(c) Find out more about this carving. Report what you find to the rest of the class.

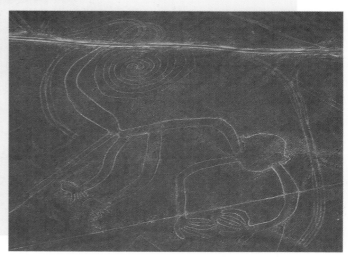

Book Review: *What's What*

Recently, we had the opportunity to read *What's What* by Reginald Bragonier, Jr. and David Fisher. The book shows the parts of many everyday objects.

What's What provides a practical alternative to using a dictionary or an encyclopedia. You can locate words that you are seeking by finding the detailed illustrations and reading the labels included.

Some of the above book's illustrations are shown on these two pages. Each of the pictures shows how parallel lines are used. For each picture:

1. Describe how you can determine whether the working parts that appear to be parallel are really parallel.
2. Describe why you think the working parts need to be parallel.
3. The descriptions are from the book. Do you think the descriptions are thorough? Why?

Frame

Any diagonally placed piece of timber in a frame is a *brace*. A *cat* is a small piece of lumber nailed between studs for reinforcement. *Beams* are squared-off pieces of timber, such as *joists*, used to support *floor* or *ceiling*, or *lintels*, horizontal *members* designed to carry loads above openings such as doors and windows.

▼

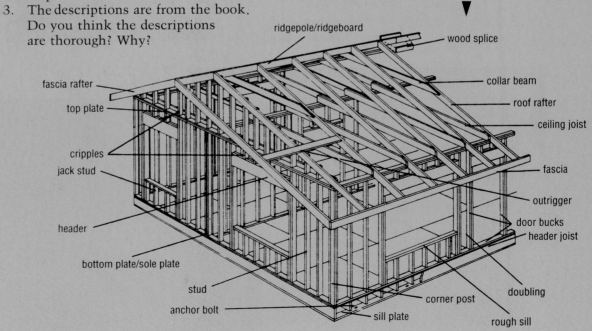

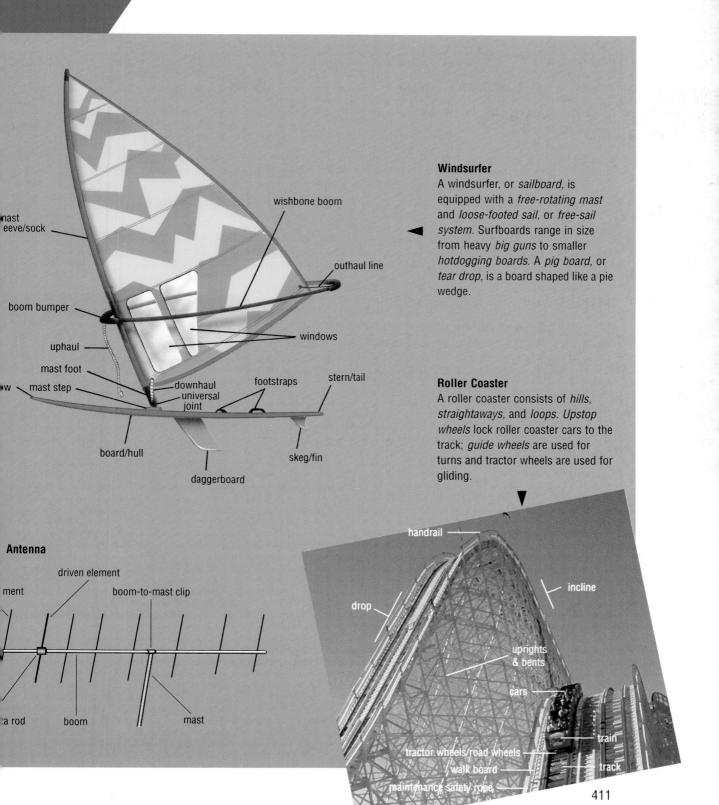

mast
sleeve/sock

wishbone boom

outhaul line

boom bumper

windows

uphaul

mast foot

mast step

downhaul
universal
joint

footstraps

stern/tail

board/hull

skeg/fin

daggerboard

Windsurfer

A windsurfer, or *sailboard*, is equipped with a *free-rotating mast* and *loose-footed sail*, or *free-sail system*. Surfboards range in size from heavy *big guns* to smaller *hotdogging boards*. A *pig board*, or *tear drop*, is a board shaped like a pie wedge.

Roller Coaster

A roller coaster consists of *hills, straightaways*, and *loops*. Upstop wheels lock roller coaster cars to the track; *guide wheels* are used for turns and tractor wheels are used for gliding.

Antenna

driven element

ment

boom-to-mast clip

rod

boom

mast

handrail

incline

drop

uprights & bents

cars

train

tractor wheels/road wheels

track

walk board

maintenance safety rope

411

To solve a problem or follow the steps for a construction, first ask yourself:

- What am I asked to find?
- What am I given?

YOU ALREADY KNOW...

- How to bisect a line.
- How to bisect an angle.
- How to construct a perpendicular bisector.
- How to construct a perpendicular from a point to a line.
- How to copy an angle.

A useful step is also to sketch a rough diagram. A diagram can help you think about your work and plan your solutions. For each exploration, use a pair of compasses, protractor, or a ruler.

For example, follow the steps shown in the explorations. They will show you how to construct copies of triangles. Before you begin the explorations, in your groups predict the least amount of information you need about a triangle to construct an exact copy.

EXPLORATION ① **Work Together**

1. Use only a pair of compasses and a ruler. Follow these steps to construct △ABC, with ∠B = 45°, BC = 4 cm, and ∠C = 45°.

   A Sketch the triangle and record the known information.

   B Draw BC = 4 cm.

   C To obtain a 45° angle, you can bisect a right angle. Thus, construct BX perpendicular to BC at point B. Then construct BY, the bisector of ∠XBC.

   D Repeat *Step C* to construct another 45° angle at C. The point of intersection of the two lines is vertex A.

   E Measure the remaining parts of the triangle. Compare your measures to those of others. What do you notice? Write your observations in your journal.

EXPLORATION ② **Work Together**

2. (a) Construct △SDF so that SD = 4 cm, DF = 3 cm, and SF = 2 cm.

   (b) Measure the remaining parts. Compare your measures with others in the class. Is your triangle unique?

   (c) Repeat (a) and (b) for each of the following triangles.
   △QWG: QW = 3 cm, WG = 4 cm, GQ = 3 cm
   △TYH: TY = 5 cm, YH = 4 cm, TH = 3 cm

   (d) Based on your results, is the following true or false? "If sides of a triangle are known, the triangle when constructed is **unique**."

EXPLORATION ③ *Work Together*

3. (a) In △ABC, ∠A = 45°, AC = 8 cm, and AB = 6 cm. Use the triangle shown to construct your own triangle.
   (b) Measure the remaining parts. Compare your measures with others in the class. Is the triangle unique?
   (c) Sketch and construct each triangle. Repeat (b).
   △ABC: AB = 3 cm, ∠B = 55°, BC = 5 cm
   △VWX: VW = 4 cm, ∠W = 35°, WX = 4 cm
   (d) Based on your results, is the following true or false? "If the measures of two sides and the contained angle are known, then the triangle is unique."

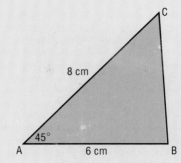

∠A is called the contained angle.

EXPLORATION ④ *Work Together*

4. (a) In △ABC, ∠A = 45°, ∠B = 30°, and AB = 6 cm. Use the triangle shown to construct your own triangle.
   (b) Measure the remaining parts. Compare your measures with others in the class. Is the triangle unique?
   (c) Sketch and construct each. Repeat (b).
   △GLF: ∠G = 60°, ∠L = 55°, GL = 4 cm
   △BDR: ∠B = 95°, ∠D = 35°, DB = 6 cm
   (d) Based on your results, is the following true or false? "If the measures of two angles and the contained side are known, then the triangle is unique."

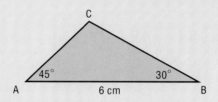

AB is called the contained side.

EXPLORATION ⑤ *Work with a Partner*

5. Copy the lines and angles shown below.
   (a) Which parts can be used to construct a unique triangle?
   (b) Decide on the least amount of information you need so that your partner can construct each unique triangle.

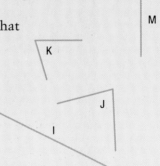

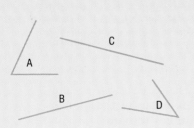

13.10 TAKING SIDES: SSS

Formation flying has entertained crowds for many years. One popular formation is shown. The six planes form a triangle that never varies.

ACTIVITY
(a) How do you think the pilots maintain the formation? Why is it necessary?
(b) What mathematics do you think is involved?

In the previous section, you saw that when you were given information about the parts of a triangle, you were able to construct only one unique triangle. All triangles you constructed had the same shape and size and the corresponding parts were equal. Such triangles are called **congruent** triangles.

CONGRUENCE RELATION: SSS

If all three pairs of corresponding sides of two triangles are equal, then the two triangles are congruent. To show that the two triangles below are congruent, you write the vertices in a special order.

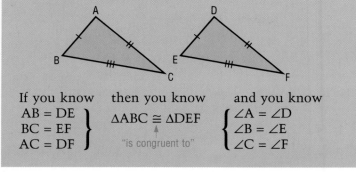

If you know	then you know	and you know
AB = DE BC = EF AC = DF }	ΔABC ≅ ΔDEF "is congruent to"	{ ∠A = ∠D ∠B = ∠E ∠C = ∠F

So that the pilots can maintain a "safe" triangle, they measure the distance, using radar, from the nose of one plane to the nose of the others. The noses of the planes will form a triangle. Since all distances remain constant, the pilots can construct a congruent formation each time.

A Review the relationships you know about triangles.

1. For each of the following congruence relations, name the sides and the angles that correspond.
   (a) $\triangle DEF \cong \triangle MNP$ (b) $\triangle STP \cong \triangle UVM$ (c) $\triangle ABC \cong \triangle PQR$

2. (a) Write the congruence relation to show the triangles are congruent.

   (i) 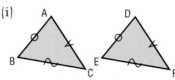   (ii)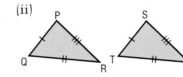

   (b) What new information can be obtained because the triangles are congruent?

B Use your *Problem Solving Plan*. Write what you are given.

3. Find the missing measures in each pair of congruent triangles. Justify your answers.

   (a) 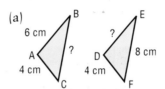   (b)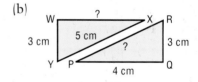

4. (a) Figure ABCD is a rhombus. Copy and complete the steps to show why $\angle B = \angle D$. Give reasons for each step.
   (b) What other corresponding parts are equal?

AD = AB	Why?
DC = BC	Why?
AC = AC	Why?
Thus, $\triangle ADC \cong \triangle ABC$.	Why?
Therefore, $\angle D = \angle B$.	Why?

   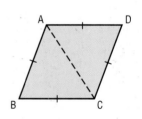

5. (a) Give reasons for each step to show why $\angle M = \angle Q$.
   (b) What other corresponding parts are equal?

MN = QN	Why?
MP = QP	Why?
NP = NP	Why?
$\triangle MNP \cong \triangle QNP$	Why?
Thus, $\angle M = \angle Q$.	Why?

   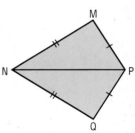

6. Refer to the diagram shown. Work with a partner.
   (a) Create a probable conclusion about the diagram.
   (b) Verify your probable conclusion.

   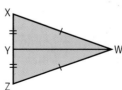

13.11 THE CONTAINED ANGLE

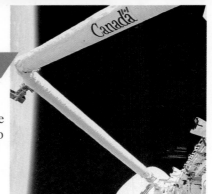

Did you know that congruent triangles are involved when the Canadarm is operated? The length of the two sides of the Canadarm remains the same and the angle between the two arms changes.

CONGRUENCE RELATION: SAS

If two pairs of corresponding sides and the corresponding contained angles of two triangles are equal, the triangles are congruent.

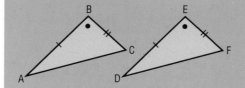

If you know
$$AB = DE$$
$$\angle B = \angle E$$
$$BC = EF$$

then you know
$$\triangle ABC \cong \triangle DEF$$

and you know
$$AC = DF$$
$$\angle A = \angle D$$
$$\angle C = \angle F$$

EXERCISE

A To solve problems, you need to understand the symbols used.

1. If $\triangle PQR \cong \triangle STV$, name the angles and sides that are equal.

2. (a) Write the congruence relation to show that each pair of triangles is congruent.

(i)

(ii)

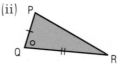

(b) What new information is obtained because the triangles are congruent?

B Give reasons for each statement you make.

3. Find the missing measures.

(a)

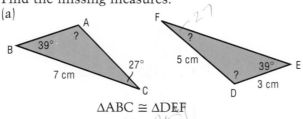

$$\triangle ABC \cong \triangle DEF$$

(b)

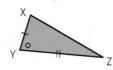

$$\triangle GHI \cong \triangle LKJ$$

4. Match pairs of congruent triangles. Write the congruence relation. Give reasons why the triangles are congruent.

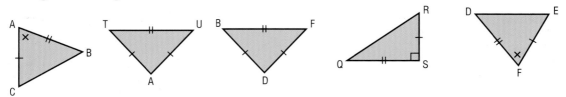

5. Give reasons for each step to show why AC = DF.

∠B = ∠E	Why?
AB = DE	Why?
BC = EF	Why?
ΔABC ≅ ΔDEF	Why?
Thus, AC = DF.	Why?

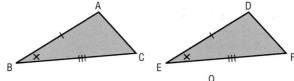

6. Give reasons for each step to show why QR = SR.

PQ = PS	Why?
∠QPR = ∠SPR	Why?
PR = PR	Why?
ΔPQR ≅ ΔPSR	Why?
Thus, QR = SR.	Why?

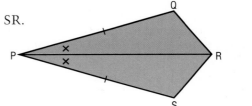

7. A robot, like Canadarm, was used to retrieve a malfunctioning satellite. The two sections were 30 m long and 25 m long. They formed an angle of 15°.
   (a) Draw a model of the robot and the satellite.
   (b) In your journal, write a short paragraph to describe how the satellite was retrieved. In your paragraph, describe how congruent triangles could be used.

8. Use scrap paper.
   (a) Fold one piece of paper in half as many times as you can.
   (b) Take another piece of paper that is a different size. Fold it in half as many times as you can.
   (c) Compare the number of times you can fold your paper to others in the class. What do you notice?
   (d) What hypothesis can you make about the number of times you can fold any piece of paper? How can folding paper verify your hypothesis?

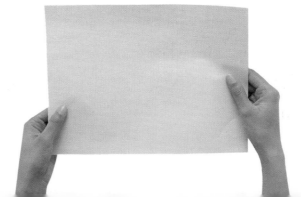

To help you learn, you look for patterns. For example, to construct congruent triangles, you need at least three pieces of information.

Three Sides

Two Sides and a Contained Angle

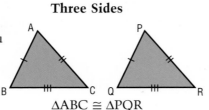

$\triangle ABC \cong \triangle PQR$

$\triangle DEF \cong \triangle MNO$

The pattern suggests that you can also construct congruent triangles if you know one side and two angles as shown below.

CONGRUENCE RELATION: ASA

If two angles and a contained side of one triangle are equal to two angles and a contained side of another triangle, the two triangles are congruent.

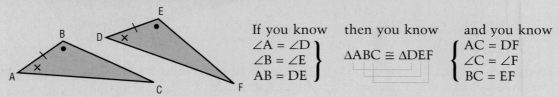

If you know
$\angle A = \angle D$
$\angle B = \angle E$
$AB = DE$

then you know
$\triangle ABC \cong \triangle DEF$

and you know
$AC = DF$
$\angle C = \angle F$
$BC = EF$

EXERCISE

A To show that triangles are congruent, carefully match the vertices that correspond.

1. For each pair of triangles, what other information is needed to prove they are congruent?
   (a)

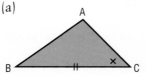

   (b)

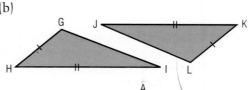

2. (a) From the diagram, what other corresponding parts are equal?
   (b) Which triangles are congruent? Why?

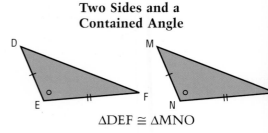

3. (a) Write the congruence relation to show that the triangles are congruent.
   (b) What new information is obtained because the triangles are congruent?

4. (a) Write the congruence relation to show that the triangles are congruent.
   (b) What new information is obtained because the triangles are congruent?

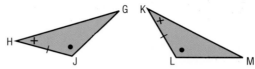

5. Decide which triangles could be congruent. What one piece of information is needed to prove they are congruent?

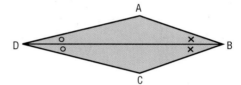

B Review how to determine if two triangles are congruent.

6. Give reasons for each step to show why ∠A = ∠C.

∠ADB = ∠CDB	Why?
BD = BD	Why?
∠ABD = ∠CBD	Why?
△ABD ≅ △CBD.	Why?
Thus, ∠A = ∠C.	Why?

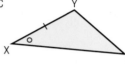

7. Find the missing measures in each of the following.

(a)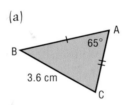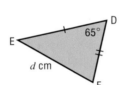

(b)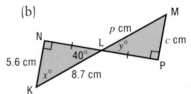

8. (a) What corresponding parts are equal?
   (b) Why does ∠DFE = ∠DFG?
   (c) Why is △DEF ≅ △DGF?

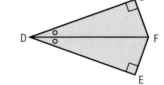

C

9. Refer to the diagram. Justify each step.
   (a) List the given information. What corresponding parts are equal?
   (b) Show why △EAB ≅ △EDC.
   (c) Show why AB = DC.
   (d) Show why AB ∥ CD.

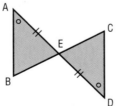

10. (a) How many triangles are in the diagram?
    (b) How many pairs of congruent triangles are in the diagram?
    (c) Create a problem of your own using the diagram. Solve the problem and then have others in the class solve it.

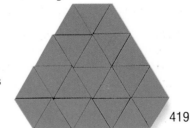

419

Suppose you are a cyclist raising money for charity by riding between cities.

ACTIVITY 1

You mark your routes on the map above connecting three cities at a time. You decide to use tracing paper and construct the following triangles. Locate the three cities that represent the vertices of each triangle.

(a) 1.9 cm, 3.4 cm, 4.3 cm

(b) 3.7 cm, 8.7 cm, 5.7 cm

(c) 4.7 cm, 7.2 cm, 3.3 cm

(d) 3.7 cm, 4.3 cm, 7.3 cm

(e) 3.8 cm, 0.8 cm, 4.1 cm

(f) 1.9 cm, 0.8 cm, 2.4 cm

ACTIVITY 2

(a) On tracing paper, draw a triangle of your own connecting three cities.

(b) Measure the sides and give the measurements to others in the class. Can they find the three cities that are at the vertices of your triangle?

ACTIVITY 3

In your journal:

(a) Describe a career that requires a knowledge of congruent triangles. Give reasons for your choice.

(b) Describe a situation when you might need to use congruent triangles or figures.

GAMES

Play the game of "Congruence" with a partner or in a group.

1. Construct a spinner like the one shown.
2. Decide who spins first. Spin the spinner. Find pairs of triangles below that match what you spin.
3. You receive one point for each correct answer. You lose one point for each incorrect answer.
4. Once a triangle has been named, it cannot be named again. If you do, you lose one point.
5. The player with the most points when all the triangles have been eliminated is the winner.

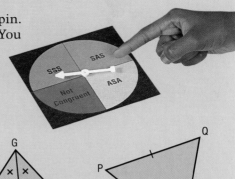

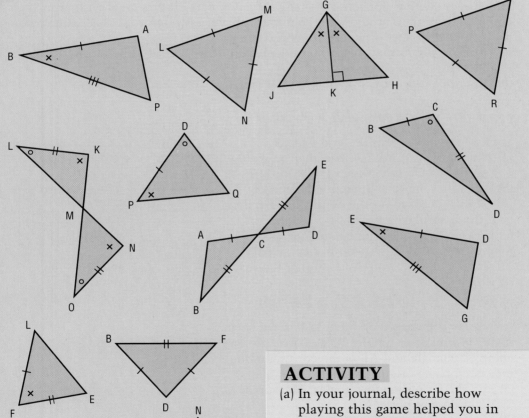

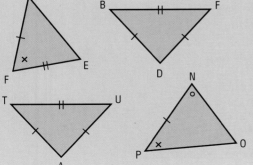

ACTIVITY

(a) In your journal, describe how playing this game helped you in your understanding of congruent triangles.

(b) Work with a partner. Create a game based on congruent triangles.

EXPLORATION ① Discuss with a Partner

1. Did you know that, for some movies, special effects experts create miniature sets and models in their studios? In the picture above, a miniature set is created before the similar life-sized versions are constructed.
   (a) How are the miniature set and the similar life-sized set alike? How are they different?
   (b) Describe situations in which similar constructions could be helpful.

EXPLORATION ② Work with a Partner

2. Look at the crosses on the grid paper.
   (a) What do you think is meant by the word "similar"? Do the crosses look similar?
   (b) Use a dictionary to find a definition of "similar." Based on the definition, are the crosses similar?
   (c) Measure the side lengths and angles of the crosses. What do you notice? What relationships do you think similar figures have?

EXPLORATION ③ Work with a Partner

3. A triangle is enlarged on a grid as shown so that $\triangle ABC$ is similar to $\triangle PQR$. PQ is a measure on the enlarged triangle and AB is the corresponding measure on the original triangle.
   (a) List the corresponding angles. Measure them. What do you notice?
   (b) Measure the side of each triangle. Calculate each of the following. What do you notice?

   $$\frac{PQ}{AB} \qquad \frac{PR}{AC} \qquad \frac{QR}{BC}$$

   (c) Draw figures that are similar on grid paper. Measure the corresponding sides. What do you notice?

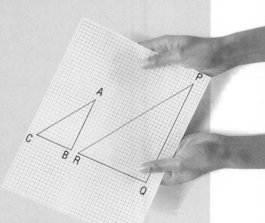

In your study of mathematics, you learn a new concept or skill, you practise the skill, and then you apply the skill to solve problems.

For example, in the previous exploration, you found that two similar triangles have the following properties.

1. The corresponding angles are equal.
2. The ratios of the measures of corresponding sides are equal.

You can use these properties to find lengths in similar triangles.

For example, ΔABC ~ ΔDEF.
The symbol "~" means "is similar to."
Find the length of AB.

Since the triangles are similar,

$$\frac{AB}{DE} = \frac{AC}{DF}$$

$$\frac{AB}{4.5} = \frac{4}{6}$$

$$AB = 3$$

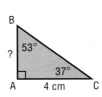

Thus, AB = 3 cm.

Similar triangles can be used to solve problems with measurement. For example, how can you find the height of the crane shown below?

In the diagram, AC = 60 m and EC = 4 m.
Thus, from the diagram, ∠E = ∠E
∠DCE = ∠BAE   (Both are 90°.)
Thus, ∠EDC = ∠EBA   (Angle sum of any triangle is 180°.)

All corresponding angles are equal.

Thus,   ΔEBA ~ ΔEDC

$$\frac{BA}{DC} = \frac{EA}{EC}$$

$$\frac{BA}{1.5} = \frac{64}{4}$$

$$BA = 24$$

The height of the crane is 24 m.

A Check whether your answers are reasonable.

1. Each equation is written to find the measures of the missing sides. Solve for x.

(a) $\dfrac{x}{3} = \dfrac{20}{6}$ (b) $\dfrac{x}{8} = \dfrac{35}{40}$ (c) $\dfrac{x}{4} = \dfrac{18}{12}$ (d) $\dfrac{x}{52} = \dfrac{5}{26}$ (e) $\dfrac{x}{4} = \dfrac{35}{20}$

2. Triangles ABC and DEF are similar.
   (a) List the information you know about the triangles.
   (b) How can you find the missing lengths in each triangle?
   (c) Find the lengths in (b).

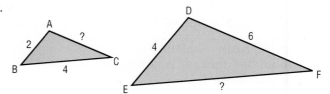

3. Triangles PQR and VWT are similar. Find the missing lengths by solving these proportions.

   (a) $\dfrac{y}{8} = \dfrac{12}{4}$ (b) $\dfrac{x}{5} = \dfrac{12}{4}$

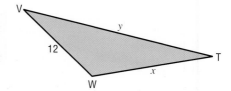

4. For each pair of similar triangles, find the values of the missing measures.

   (a)   (b)   (c)

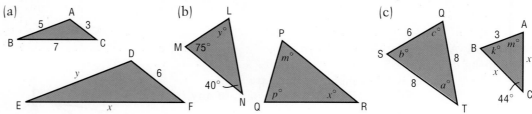

5. To show similar triangles clearly, the triangles can be drawn separately as shown.
   (a) Which angles are equal?   (b) Find the missing measure of the side.

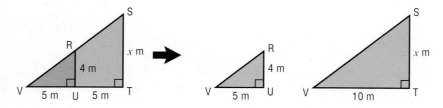

(c) Use $\dfrac{x}{4} = \dfrac{10}{5}$ to solve for x.   (d) What is the measure of ST?

6. (a) Draw the similar triangles separately.
   (b) Find the measure of AD.
   (c) Write an equation to find AC.
   (d) What is the measure of AC?

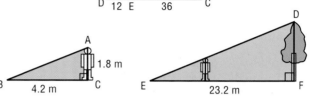

7. Shadows were used to calculate the height of a tree.
   (a) Why is ∠ABC = ∠DEF?
   (b) Find the height of the tree.

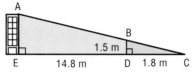

8. To calculate the height of a building, AE, the measurements shown at the right were made. How tall is the building?

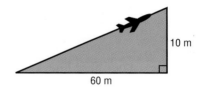

9. During a takeoff, a jet climbs (rises) 10 m for every horizontal distance of 60 m.
   (a) Calculate the height of the jet after it has travelled 1 km horizontally.
   (b) What assumptions did you make in (a)?

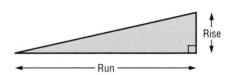

10. Refer to the diagram.
    (a) If a road rises 2.6 m for every 8.5 m of run, calculate the rise for 100.0 m of run.
    (b) A ramp rises 12.6 cm for every 65.3 cm travelled horizontally. If the end of the ramp is 2.3 m high, find the run of the ramp.

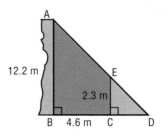

11. A ladder, AD, is placed against a wall, AB, as shown. A fence, EC, is 2.3 m high. Calculate the distance of the foot of the ladder from the fence if the fence is 4.6 m from the wall.

12. (a) Cut out six equal strips of paper as shown below.
    (b) Use the strips to form six congruent triangles.
    (c) Identify pairs of similar triangles. How many pairs of similar triangles are there?
    (d) Use strips of paper to create a problem of your own. Solve your problem. Compare your problem to others in the class.

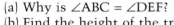
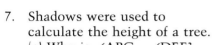

425

You can use your knowledge of congruent and similar triangles to find the measure of inaccessible distances. To do so, you need to:

- Make a plan.
- Combine your skills in geometry with your skills in equations.

On June 30, 1859, Jean Francois Gravelet (Blondin) walked across the Niagara Gorge on a tightrope. To construct the tightrope, he had to calculate the distance he would walk.

Use the diagram to find the length of tightrope, AB.

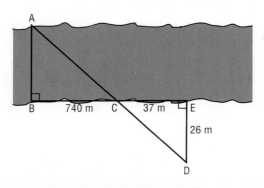

Blondin Does It Again

Well-known tightrope walker, Blondin, has just carried his manager across the Niagara Gorge, piggyback. The spectators cheered wildly as Blondin emerged triumphant from his crossing. Previously, Blondin had offered to place the Prince of Wales in a wheelbarrow and wheel him across the gorge. Now, after this incredible feat, witnesses feel that maybe it is not beyond the realm of possibility.

ACTIVITY   *Work with a Partner*

(a) Use the diagram. Find the distance, AB. How long was the tightrope?
(b) In what other situations could your process in (a) be used to find a distance? Why?
(c) Find out more about Blondin. How did he secure both ends of the tightrope? How did he get the tightrope across the gorge? Was the "tightrope" really a tightrope?

EXERCISE

B   Sketch a diagram to help you organize your solution.

1. (a) To find the length of a pond, these measurements are used. Which triangles are similar? Why?

   (b) Complete the equation $\dfrac{CA}{CB} = \dfrac{\blacksquare}{\blacksquare}$ for finding the length.

   (c) Let *l*, in metres, represent the length, and solve for *l*.

   (d) What is the length of the pond?

426

2. To measure the width of a river, the measurements given in the diagram were made. Find the width of the river.

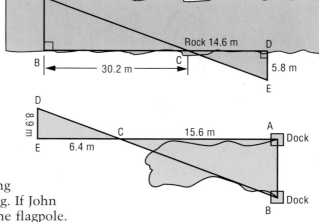

3. To find the distance from one dock to another, the measurements shown were made. Find the distance from Dock A to Dock B.

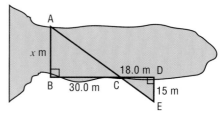

4. A flagpole's shadow is 15.5 m long when John's shadow is 3.6 m long. If John is 1.8 m tall, find the height of the flagpole.

5. The length of the shadow of a monument is 26.8 m when the length of Marie's shadow is 6.8 m. If Marie is 1.6 m tall, calculate the height of the monument.

6. The length of the shadow of a metre stick is 3.6 m. Find the height of a tree if its shadow length at the same time of day is 26.3 m.

7. How long will the shadow of a pole, 15.6 m high, be if Jean–Luc is 1.7 m tall and casts a shadow 3.8 m long?

8. The width of a bay was found by making the measurements shown at the right. How wide is the bay?

9. Use indirect measurements to calculate the width of a
   (a) street or road.   (b) building.

10. Use the width of a geoboard as the base of a triangle.
    (a) How many different triangles can you make?
    (b) Which triangles have an equal area? Are these triangles congruent? Are these triangles similar?
    (c) What can you conclude about triangles with the same area?
    (d) Create a similar problem of your own. Solve it and compare your solution with others in the class.

PARTNER PROJECT

Use indirect measurement to calculate the
(a) width of your street.
(b) height of your school.
(c) height of any monument or tower in your area.

427

Pictures can be enlarged and reduced in size. The logos shown to the left are those for Adidas. The actual logo is shown in the middle and the image of the logo is shown above and below.

ACTIVITY

In your journal, describe what is meant when you say something is twice as big as something else. Do you mean length? width? area? Give examples of your own to help your description.

1. Use grid paper to construct the images of the figures for the scale factors shown. A scale factor of $k = 2$ means a figure is enlarged by doubling each part.

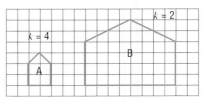

2. Use grid paper to construct the image of the cross for these scale factors.

   (a) $k = \dfrac{1}{2}$ (b) $k = 0.75$

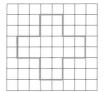

3. Find the image of each logo below for the following scale factors.
   (a) $k = 0.25$ (b) $k = 3.5$ (c) $k = 2.75$

4. Some logos are shown below.
   (a) Sketch them using scale factors of 3 and 0.25.
   (b) Find other logos of your own in the Yellow Pages. Select scale factors and draw the images of the logos.

Often, you encounter difficulties when you try to solve a problem directly. For example, the student council at Victor Blair School wanted to create a new banner, in a large V-shape, for their gymnasium. To order material for the banner, they needed to calculate its area.

By thinking of the figure on a grid, the students were able to calculate the area more easily.

They enclosed the banner in a rectangular figure. The area of ABCD is 30 sq. units

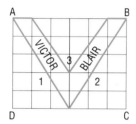

Calculate the Areas

Triangle 1	7.5 sq. units	
Triangle 2	7.5 sq. units	
Triangle 3	6 sq. units	
Total	21 sq. units	

Area of ABCD	30 sq. units
Areas of triangles in chart	21 sq. units
Area of banner	9 sq. units

EXERCISE

B Refer to the strategy above.

1. Use the above strategy to estimate the area of each of the following figures.

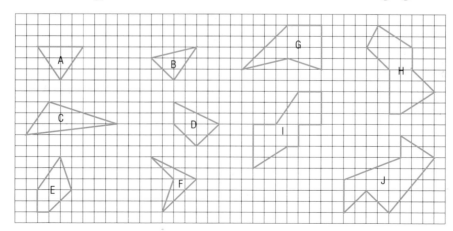

2. Use your own grid. Draw figures on the grid. Find the area of each figure. Compare your method to others in the class.

1. (a) Write the congruence relation to show that the triangles are congruent.
   (b) What new information can be obtained because the triangles are congruent?

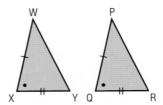

2. Refer to the diagram.
   (a) Name the alternate and the corresponding angles.
   (b) Which angles are equal?
   (c) Which angles are interior angles on the same side of the transversal?
   (d) Which angles sum to 180°?

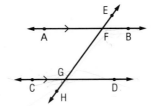

3. Find the value of the variables in the following.

   (a)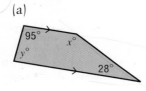

   (b)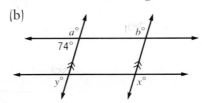

4. In a triangle, one angle is 55° more than a second angle. A third angle is 20° less than the first angle. Find the measure of each angle.

5. Refer to the diagrams below. Find the value of each variable.

   (a)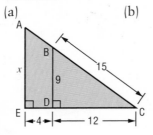

   (b)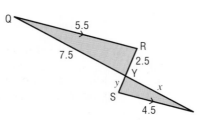

6. Draw an example of
   (a) an acute triangle that is isosceles.
   (b) a quadrilateral with two right angles and an obtuse angle.
   (c) your own triangle. Classify it in as many ways as you can. Have others classify your triangle.

❶ What have you learned about triangles that you did not know before?

❷ How do you think you will use these skills in other subjects?

❸ When reviewing your skills, how easy is it to use your notebook? How can you make it easier?

MAKING CONNECTIONS

Refer to the opening page of this chapter.
(a) Create a problem of your own using the pictures. Solve your problem.
(b) Compare your problem with others in the class. Solve the other problems.

❹ Look at the problems in the chapter. How are they like problems you have solved before? How are they different?

❺ Refer to Question 4 in the Self Evaluation on this page. Suppose AB = 10 cm. How would the question change?

❻ What do you know about the measure of corresponding angles?

SELF EVALUATION

1. Find the measures indicated by the variables.
   (a)   (b)   (c)

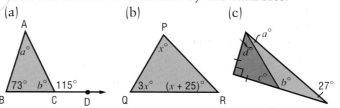

2. Illustrate each of the following with an example of your own. Compare with others in the class.
   (a) SAS   (b) ASA   (c) SSS

3. Find the missing angle measures. Estimate first.
   (a)   (b)   (c)

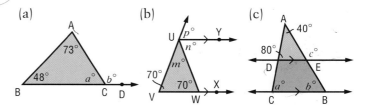

4. Triangle ABC has measures AB = 8 cm, BC = 6 cm, and AC = 10 cm. Triangle DEF has measures DE = 4 cm, EF = 3 cm, and DF = 5 cm.
   (a) Sketch each triangle. Why are they similar?
   (b) Write the ratio of corresponding sides.

5. Find the height of Mario's clothesline pole using the measures shown in the diagram.

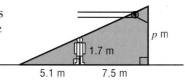

MATH JOURNAL

What types of problems are still difficult for you to solve
(a) in this chapter?
(b) in previous chapters?

What can you do to overcome these problems? How can the Self Evaluation features throughout this book help you?

6. Jana wanted to start a ferry service across the bay. To find the distance from one dock to the other, he took the measurements given in the diagram. Find the distance between Dock A and Dock B.

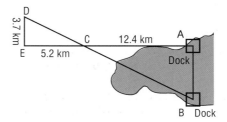

1. Evaluate.
   (a) 2^5 (b) $2^3 + 3^2$ (c) $3^3 - 3^2$ (d) $2^3 \times 3^2$

   (e) $\dfrac{4 + 6 - 2}{2^2}$ (f) $\dfrac{8^2 \times 4 - 8 \times 2}{16 \div 4 + 8}$ (g) $\dfrac{12^2 - 3 \times 12}{2 + 4 \div 2}$

   (h) $158 \div 2 + 3[6(8 - 5)]$ (i) $3(8 - 2) \div 9$

2. Suppose that you are to close your eyes and touch the diagram shown to the right. What is the probability that you will touch the shaded part? Give reasons for your answer.

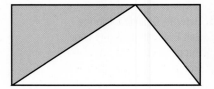

3. Simplify.
   (a) $(4x)(3x^3y)$ (b) $(-2x)(3xy^2)$ (c) $3y(x + xy - y)$ (d) $-4x(x^2 - 7)$

   (e) $\dfrac{48x^3y}{6xy^2}$ (f) $\dfrac{-18x^2y}{-2x^3y}$ (g) $\dfrac{3x^2 - 6x}{-3x}$ (h) $\dfrac{2y^2 - 6y}{-2y}$

4. If $x = 3$ and $y = -2$, find the value of each of the following.
   (a) $x^2y + xy^2$ (b) $x^2y \div xy^2$ (c) $x^3 \div x^2$ (d) $(xy)^3 \div x^2y$

5. What is the probability that two people on Earth have the same number of hairs on their head? Give reasons for your answer.

6. Solve.
   (a) $3m + 4m - 5 = 9$ (b) $8k - 3 = 6k - 8$ (c) $(2k - 9) - (k + 7) = 4$

   (d) $0.6x - 1 = 10$ (e) $p = \dfrac{2}{3}p + 7$ (f) $\dfrac{3}{4}x - 2 = \dfrac{1}{2}x + 5$

7. Find the missing terms.
   (a) $18 : 8 = 36 : y$ (b) $k : 10 = 24 : 60$ (c) $p : 8 = 6 : 4$
   (d) $18 : 14 = 9 : b$ (e) $8 : x = 12 : 18$ (f) $m : 2 = 10 : 1$

8. A 3.5 m ladder is leaning against a house. To be safe, the base of the ladder should be 1.75 m from the house. If the ladder needs to reach 2 m up the wall, can the ladder be leaned safely against the wall?

9. Brass is made of copper and zinc mixed in the ratio $17 : 3$. How much zinc is in a 100 kg brass sculpture?

10. Suppose you invested $750.00. How long will it take to earn $123.75 in interest, at $9\dfrac{1}{2}\%$ interest, if
    (a) interest is calculated as simple interest?
    (b) interest is compounded annually?

How would you collect data to develop effective ways of preventing accidents?

How would you collect data to decide which product would sell the best?

How would you collect data to decide on the most appropriate tires for the race?

14.1 EXPLORING DATA

Making sense of data is important in many fields like sports, medicine, business, and entertainment. Everyday decisions are made based on data that have been gathered. For example:

- Which television show should be placed in prime time?
- At which intersections should lights be placed?
- Which pitches will be most effective against a particular batter?

When you work with data, you are involved in the branch of mathematics called **statistics**. Statistics involves:

A Collecting the data.
B Organizing and analyzing the data collected.
C Interpreting the data.

EXPLORATION ① Work with a Partner

1. Refer to the careers shown in the pictures.
   (a) Which career appeals to you the most?
   (b) Which career do you think your class will choose most often?
   (c) How can you check your answer in (b)?
   (d) Use your answer in (c). Predict which career will be chosen most often in your school. Give reasons why you made this prediction.

2. Make a list of several Canadian recording artists.
   (a) Which artist do you like best?
   (b) Which artist do you think your class will like the most?
   (c) How can you check your answer in (b)?
   (d) Use your answer in (c). Predict which recording artist will be the most popular at your school. Give reasons why you made this prediction.

Have you ever heard the claim, "Four out of five dentists surveyed recommend sugarless gum for their patients who chew gum"?

3. (a) How do you think the data were collected: in person, over the phone, or by questionnaire?
   (b) How many dentists do you think were surveyed? Why?
   (c) List questions the dentists might have been asked.
   (d) Do you think the claim is valid? Give reasons for your answer.

4. Suppose you were in charge of determining whether sugarless gum is the most recommended gum.
   (a) What questions would you ask? Do they differ from the questions listed above?
   (b) How many people would you survey? How would you select them?
   (c) How would you collect the data?
   (d) How would you present the data that you collected?
   (e) Collect some data of your own. Organize the data that you collect. What conclusions can you draw from your data?

5. Suppose you have just developed a new gum that you believe is "tastier" than any other gum on the market. However, the gum has sugar. You are in charge of gathering data and developing an advertising campaign for the gum.
   (a) Whom do you feel it is best to survey?
   (b) List the questions you might ask.
   (c) Describe how you will collect your data — in questionnaires, personal interviews, or by telephone.
   (d) Use the data. Set up an advertising campaign of your own for the gum. Present your campaign to the rest of the class. What math skills were involved in developing your campaign? Write the skills in your journal.

6. Put the topics shown below onto cards and place the cards in a box. Choose one of the cards.
   (a) Write a question about the topic that needs data to answer it.
   (b) Collect and display the data that answers the question.
   (c) Present your data and your conclusions to the rest of the class. Answer any questions that may be posed by the class, such as how your group collected its data and whether your conclusions are logical.

Television   Radio   Movies   Advertising

Newspapers   Magazines   Video Games

Suppose you are a manufacturer of baseball cards. You could use the following steps to collect and analyze data to test the quality of your products.

1. Since each card cannot be checked individually, a practical alternative is to choose a sample. So that you can make an accurate assessment of your products, the sample must be representative of all the cards. You can use a *random* sample which ensures that all cards have an equal chance of being tested.

2. After the sample is obtained, you can then conduct tests for quality, collect data, and record the information.

3. Finally, you can analyze the information you collected in *Steps 1* and *2* so that you can estimate the total number of cards that are defective.

Manufacturers regularly check the quality of their products. What are the advantages of doing this?

ACTIVITY

1. Suppose, as the manufacturer, you decide you have too many defective cards. What would you do? Give reasons for your answer.

2. Sometimes, a particular model of car is recalled because of defects in some of its working parts.
    (a) What kinds of defects have caused cars to be recalled in the past?
    (b) In your opinion, were they good reasons?
    (c) In your journal, describe the steps you think the car manufacturer would take to decide whether or not a particular model of car should be recalled.

EXERCISE

 A Review ways to organize data.

1. Use your journal.
    (a) Make a list of different methods you can think of to collect data.
    (b) List sources for obtaining information that has already been collected.
    (c) List the advantages and disadvantages of each source in (b).

2. (a) What do you think is meant by a sample that is random? one that is not random?
   (b) Give examples to illustrate each sample in (a).

3. Describe how you would collect data to determine the following.
   (a) your class's favourite novel   (b) the quality of a cassette tape

B Work together.

4. (a) Pick three comic strips from the newspaper.
   (b) How can you collect data to find out which comic strip is most popular?
   (c) Collect the data using your method in (b). Which comic strip is most popular?

5. (a) Create a list of the different ways students travel to school.
   (b) How can you collect data to determine the most frequent means of student travel?
   (c) Collect the data using your answer in (b). What is the most frequent means of travel to school?

6. To decide on what movies to show, theatre managers often preview them at screenings. In your journal, list the criteria that the manager of your neighbourhood theatre might use to select movies. Refer to examples.

7. Experiments were conducted to collect information about the effectiveness of air valves in tires. List the advantages and the disadvantages of using experiments (observations and measurements in this instance).

8. (a) List the methods of collecting information first-hand that have been considered in this section.
   (b) List sources of obtaining information that has already been collected.
   (c) List the advantages and the disadvantages of each source in (b).

9. Which method would you use to collect data on the following? Give reasons.
   (a) the school's favourite movie star
   (b) the quality of a brand of running shoes
   (c) the attitude towards building an expressway
   (d) the most popular flavour of soft drink

GROUP PROJECT: FAST FOOD SURVEY

(a) Make a list of the most popular fast foods.
(b) Choose a method of collecting information to answer the question "Which fast food is most popular?" Then, gather the data.
(c) What percent of the sample chose the most popular food? the least popular food?
(d) Suppose you are going to invest in a fast food outlet near your school. Which foods should you sell?
(e) Based on the success of your outlet in (d), you decide to build another outlet. What might be your first step in determining where the outlet should be built? Where would you build it?

Suppose you wanted to collect data on the best-selling computer in Canada. You could survey the entire **population**, that is, all the computer stores in Canada. This is called a **census**. However, this would be time-consuming and expensive. To make collecting data easier and more economical, you may decide to sample only part of the population.

- When you take a sample from a particular part of the population, you are taking a **clustered sample**. For example, to get advice on hockey sticks, you could survey people who use them.
- When you take a sample of an entire population so that all different groups that make up a population are represented proportionally, you are taking a **stratified sample**.
- To test a quantity of steaks for flavour and tenderness, you might take a steak, barbecue it, and taste it. Since the steak cannot be used again, you have taken a **destructive sample**.

Work together to explore different ways of sampling data.

ACTIVITY   *Work with a Partner*

Which type of sample is involved in each of the following? Discuss your choices with your partner. Now create a sample of your own similar to the ones listed.
(a) selecting the best repair kit for a 15-speed bicycle
(b) determining the easiest lawn mower engine to repair
(c) determining the best clothing outlet in the country, by taking samples from Prince Edward Island
(d) testing the taste of an apple by eating the apple
(e) deciding on the most popular baseball player in the world
(f) testing the life of a light bulb by leaving it on until it burns out
(g) deciding whether Canadians feel Canada should host the next Olympic games, by surveying people from each province proportionally

Suppose you wanted to collect data from a clustered sample of 1000 people across the country.

To poll 1000 people, you could select the sample in proportion to the number of people in each province.

percent of people	Saskatchewan has 4.1% of the total Canadian population.
number of people from Saskatchewan in sample	4.1% of 1000 or 41 people

What skills did you use to help you construct the sample?

A In your journal, describe how you choose a method for collecting data.

1. To find the most popular type of tennis racket, you might use a questionnaire and mail it to a sample of tennis players. What word best describes the sample — random, clustered, stratified, or destructive?

2. To test the quality of a cola, samples are taken from the production line. What words best describe the type of sampling — random, clustered, stratified, or destructive?

3. To collect ideas on how arena facilities might be improved, the hockey organizations that use the arena were each given a questionnaire for their members.
   What type of sample was obtained — random, stratified, clustered, or destructive?

   > Bluehawks: 60 members
   > Nats: 80 members
   > Bandos: 50 members

B Review your methods of collecting data.

4. Would you use a census, a random sample, a clustered sample, a destructive sample, or a stratified sample for the following? Give reasons.
   (a) Evaluate the facilities at the local gym.
   (b) Decide who will be the next prime minister.
   (c) Check the compression tanks used for scuba diving.
   (d) Test the quality of this year's corn crop.

5. (a) A sample of 10 000 people is taken from across Canada to decide on the date of a new national holiday. The chart shows the percent of people in each province. How many people should be selected from each province?
   (b) Create a problem of your own using the chart. Solve your problem and compare it to others in the class.

British Columbia	10.2%
Alberta	8.6%
Saskatchewan	4.1%
Manitoba	4.3%
Ontario	36.0%
Quebec	26.5%
New Brunswick	3.0%
Nova Scotia	3.6%
P.E.I.	0.5%
Newfoundland	2.4%

6. At a camp, there are 115 children, 78 teenagers, and 52 adults. A survey is conducted to determine the entertainment program. If 35 persons are to be interviewed, how many should be from each group?

7. Have you heard the slogan, "When you eat your Smarties do you eat the red ones last?"
   (a) Describe how you can determine which colour of Smarties is made in the greatest quantities.
   (b) Use your description in (a). Which colour is made in the greatest quantities?

439

Newspapers and magazines often display information visually, using graphs. Shown here are a **pictograph** and a **bar graph**.

Presenting information in this way allows comparisons to be made visually. The pictograph and bar graph at the right show the number of nuclear reactors ordered by different countries. In your journal,

- describe what information you can see by quickly looking at each.
- describe what information you do *not* get by quickly looking at each.

To understand and interpret the information in a pictograph accurately, a legend must be shown. From the pictograph, you can see that:

- The greatest number of nuclear reactors was ordered by Germany.
- The least number of nuclear reactors was ordered by the U.K., Finland, and Spain.

In your journal, describe what other information you can interpret from the two graphs.

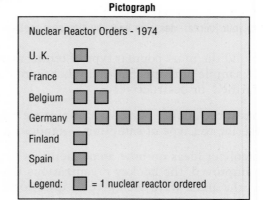

Pictograph

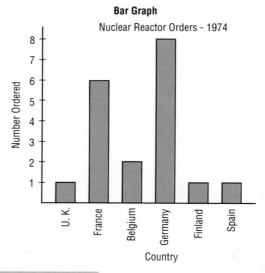

Bar Graph

A   Questions 1 and 2 are based on the pictograph.

1. A touchdown is worth six points.
   (a) How many points did each player score?
   (b) What percent of the total number of touchdowns did each score?

2. In the next three games, Lofthouse scored two touchdowns, Turnbull scored one touchdown, and Lane scored three touchdowns.
   (a) Revise the pictograph to include this information.
   (b) Create and solve a problem of your own based on the pictograph.

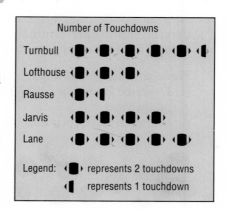

440

Questions 3 to 6 are based on the bar graph.

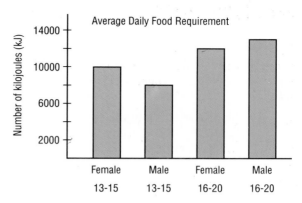

Average Daily Food Requirement

3. Which age group requires the
   (a) greatest number of kilojoules?
   (b) least number of kilojoules?

4. Carla is 14 years old. So far today she has consumed 6500 kJ.
   (a) How many more kilojoules does she require today?
   (b) What percent of her total for today has she consumed?

5. Mike is 15 years old and consumed 3000 kJ at breakfast.
   (a) How many more kilojoules are needed to obtain his average daily requirement?
   (b) What percentage of his daily requirement of kilojoules did he consume at breakfast?

6. Use the bar graph.
   (a) Create a problem of your own. Solve your problem.
   (b) Compare your problem to others in the class.

7. Use strips of paper like those shown.
   (a) Construct a bar graph of your own using the strips. Invent labels for the graph.
   (b) Create a problem of your own whose solution can be the bar graph.

PROJECT

1. (a) Make a list of the types of energy people use in their homes.
   (b) Find pictures of the sources of energy in (a) and create a class collage.

2. Refer to the class collage made in Question 1.
   (a) Compare the advantages and disadvantages of each type of energy.
   (b) Use your list in (a). Write a short paragraph about how you think homes will be heated in the year 2050. Give reasons for your prediction.

Did you know that most of the earth is covered by water? The oceans cover the greatest area, but even the earth's rivers can stretch for many kilometres. In the following, you will learn more about the water that covers the earth's surface.

1. Compare the lengths of the following rivers. Which is longer?
   (a) Nile and Congo
   (b) Rio Grande and St. Lawrence
   (c) Yangtze and Amazon
   (d) Mississippi and Congo

2. Refer to the bar graph. At a rate of 8 km/h, how long will it take a raft to float the length of each river?

3. (a) Suppose 30% of the lengths of the rivers listed are covered with debris. What is the total length of water that is debris-laden?
   (b) Suppose it takes two months to clean up the debris along 1 km of river. How long will it take to clean up all the rivers?
   (c) Create a problem of your own using the information. Compare your problem to others in the class.

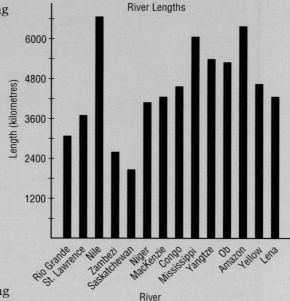

4. (a) Construct a bar graph for the information to the right.
   (b) The average depth of the Caribbean Sea is 2575 m. What percent of the bodies of water in (a) are shallower?
   (c) The average depth of the Red Sea is 540 m. What percent of the bodies of water are deeper?
   (d) Create and solve a problem of your own based on your graphs.

Body of Water	Average Depth (metres)
Hudson Bay	90
Mediterranean Sea	1500
Arctic Ocean	1330
Atlantic Ocean	3740
Pacific Ocean	4190
Black Sea	1190

ACTIVITY *Work with a Partner*

In your library, find information about other bodies of water.
(a) Use a bar graph to display the information.
(b) Create problems of your own based on the information. Compare your problems to those of others in the class.

A broken-line graph can be used to present data. For example, the number of cars in use worldwide is shown in the table below. To show the change in data year by year, the line graph shown to the right is used.

Year	Number of Cars
1960	98 000 000
1965	148 000 000
1970	194 000 000
1975	260 000 000
1980	326 000 000
1985	374 000 000
1990	416 000 000
1995	?
2000	?

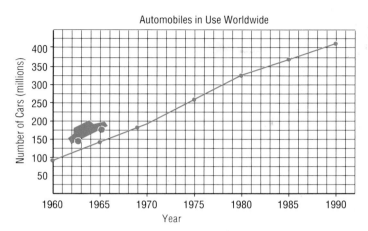

Automobiles in Use Worldwide

In your journal, describe why you think the above is called a broken-line graph. Give reasons for your answer.

EXERCISE

A Work with a partner.

1. Refer to the graph shown above.
   (a) In your journal, describe how the table has been used to construct the broken-line graph.
   (b) How many cars were in use in 1960, 1970, and 1985?
   (c) Predict how many cars will be in use by the year 2000 and the year 2050.
   (d) What other information can you find from the graph?

2. Refer to the graph to the right. How much gasoline would you expect to use to travel
   (a) 40 km?   (b) 60 km?   (c) 85 km?

3. Refer to the graph to the right. About how many kilometres would you have travelled if you had used
   (a) 7 L of gas?   (b) 8.5 L of gas?
   (c) 18.5 L of gas?   (d) 25 L of gas?

4. In your journal, explain how your methods for finding your answers in Questions 2 and 3 are alike. How are they different?

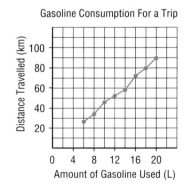

Gasoline Consumption For a Trip

443

5. On Saturday, a survey was made to determine how many people watch the Community TV Channel XKR. Programming begins at 07:00 and ends at 01:00. The findings were plotted.

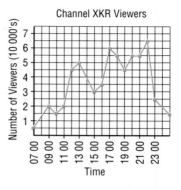

Channel XKR Viewers

(a) How many people watch Channel XKR at
   (i) 09:00?   (ii) noon?   (iii) 15:00?   (iv) 22:30?
(b) What times of day are the popular viewing times?
(c) At what time of day does the number of viewers peak? How might you interpret your answer? Give reasons for your interpretation.
(d) At what time(s) were the following number of people watching the channel?
   (i) 15 000   (ii) 35 000

6. Suppose the population in a city is currently 5 000 000 people. The graph shows the results of the population growing at the rate of 1% per year, 2% per year, 3% per year, and 4% per year. Use your journal to answer the following.

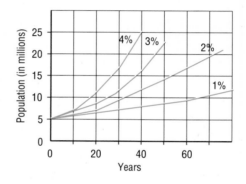

(a) How long will it take the population to double at each rate?
(b) Find the population of your province for each of the last ten years. At what rate is the population increasing?
(c) Estimate how long it will take the population to double.
(d) In what year do you think your province may be overpopulated? Give reasons for your prediction.

7. Draw broken-line graphs to show the following sets of data. The data are the average monthly temperatures.

(a) For Victoria, British Columbia

Month	J	F	M	A	M	J	J	A	S	O	N	D
Temp (°C)	4.1	4.3	6.2	9.5	13.7	15.6	17.4	17.1	14.3	10.2	7.7	4.8

(b) For Victoria, Australia

Month	J	F	M	A	M	J	J	A	S	O	N	D
Temp (°C)	19.8	18.9	17.6	15.3	14.4	12.6	12.8	13.7	24.9	15.3	16.9	20.4

(c) How are the graphs in (a) and (b) alike? How are they different? Give reasons why you think the graphs are shaped as they are.

8. Gasoline consumption depends on a number of factors, such as the type of car, size of engine, speed, and so on. One car maker recorded the following gasoline consumptions at certain speeds for their new model.

Speed (km/h)	20	30	40	50	60	70	80	90	100
Gasoline (L/100 km)	8.4	9.6	9.9	10.4	10.6	10.8	11.3	11.9	12.4

(a) Draw a broken-line graph for the above data.
(b) You drive at 40 km/h. How much gasoline will you use for a 500-km trip?
(c) You drive at 80 km/h. How much gasoline will you use for a 500-km trip?
(d) Create a problem of your own using the graph. Compare your problem to others in the class.

9. The chart shows the population of the earth at different times in the last 300 years.

Year	1650	1700	1750	1800	1850	1900	1950
Population in billions	0.60	0.62	0.80	0.95	1.20	1.70	2.55

(a) Construct a broken-line graph for the data shown.
(b) Use the graph. By what percentage did the population increase from
   (i) 1800 to 1850?   (ii) 1850 to 1900?
(c) Estimate what the population of the earth was in
   (i) 1875.   (ii) 1925.
(d) Estimate what the population of the earth will be in the year 2000. What assumptions did you make to obtain your answer?

10. (a) Attach an elastic to a cup as shown.
(b) Measure the length of the elastic.
(c) Set up a table of values for the length of the elastic and the number of bottle caps.
(d) Add a few bottle caps to the cup. Measure the length of the elastic. Add more bottle caps and measure the length of the elastic. Repeat until the cup is full.
(e) Plot the values from (d). Join them to form a broken-line graph. How much will the elastic stretch for $4\frac{1}{2}$ bottle caps? $8\frac{1}{2}$ bottle caps?
(f) Predict how long the elastic will stretch if there are (i) 44 bottle caps, and (ii) 64 bottle caps. What assumptions have you made?

Graphs display information in a variety of ways. A graph provides information visually and in a more organized way than a list or a table. For instance, the data in a *frequency table* can be displayed using a special type of bar graph called a **histogram**.

The data shows scores on a driver-education test taken by a group of students. The students are grouped into classes of 20.

The histogram shows the data obtained in each class. Each class has the same width. There is no space between the bars. From the histogram, you can see that the majority of students scored between 60 and 100.

Frequency Table

Class	Tally	Frequency
0–20	ЖН ЖН	10
20–40	ЖН ЖН ЖН I	16
40–60	ЖН ЖН ЖН II	17
60–80	ЖН ЖН ЖН ЖН ЖН III	28
80–100	ЖН ЖН ЖН ЖН ЖН	25

0–20 means data up to, but not including, 20.

Histogram

ACTIVITY

Refer to the frequency table and the histogram above.
(a) What information can be found by looking at each quickly?
(b) Create a problem of your own based on the histogram or the frequency table. Compare your problem to others in the class.

EXAMPLE

A battery manufacturer is interested in the lifetime of its product. Thirty batteries are tested until they fail and the time to failure (in hours) is recorded in the table.

41.3	21.1	35.6	13.5	4.2	15.8	5.5	5.8
33.6	18.6	24.3	18.1	23.5	8.4	42.1	9.4
10.6	8.9	13.7	19.6	9.2	5.9	19.4	
24.2	27.3	30.6	29.4	18.0	32.8	15.6	

(a) Make a frequency table using classes 0–10, 10–20, 20–30, and so on.
(b) Construct a histogram to show the data.
(c) What percentage of the batteries last less than 20 h?

SOLUTION

(a)

Class	Frequency
0–10	8
10–20	10
20–30	6
30–40	4
40–50	2

(b)

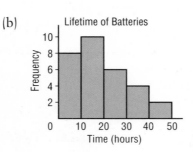

(c) Eight + ten batteries last less than 20 h.

Thirty batteries were tested.

Percentage lasting less than 20 h is

$$\frac{18}{30} \times 100\% \text{ or } 60\%.$$

446

A Check whether your answers are reasonable.

1. The information in the graph shows the
    mass of players on the volleyball team.
    (a) How many players have masses
        between
        (i) 55 and 60 kg?   (ii) 70 and 75 kg?
    (b) How many players have a mass less
        than 70 kg?
    (c) How many players have a mass 70 kg
        or more?
    (d) How many players are on the volleyball
        team?
    (e) Create a problem of your own using
        the histogram. Compare your problem
        to others in the class.

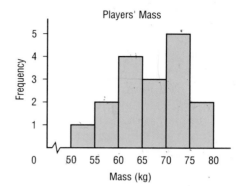

Players' Mass

2. The results of a survey of distances
    travelled (in kilometres) by students
    during the summer vacation are shown
    by the histogram.
    (a) What information is missing from the
        histogram? Provide it.
    (b) In what ways are histograms and bar
        graphs alike? In what ways are they
        different?

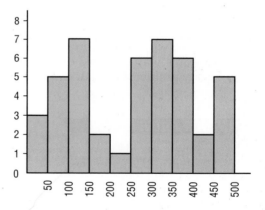

B Histograms display data involving classes.

3. The table gives data on the distribution of the life span of electric light bulbs.
    (a) Draw a histogram to show the data.
    (b) Create a problem based on the histogram. Solve the problem.

Life of Light Bulbs (in hours)	900– 1000	1000– 1100	1100– 1200	1200– 1300	1300– 1400	1400– 1500	1500– 1600	1600– 1700	1700– 1800	1800– 1900	1900– 2000
Number of Bulbs	10	14	19	26	35	43	49	54	39	18	12

4. The data show the height in centimetres
    of a group of students.
    (a) Organize the data into a frequency
        table using the class intervals
        155–160, 160–165, 165–170, and so on.
    (b) Display the data in a histogram.

158	169	156	174	180	163	162	159
177	167	179	181	172	167	170	164
175	161	174	176	182	173	168	160
183	157	165	174	169	180	176	168

447

5. A survey was conducted to determine the number of major appliances the average household in Canada contains. The data to the right were obtained.
   (a) What classes would you use for the data?
   (b) Complete a frequency distribution for the data.
   (c) Construct a histogram for the data.
   (d) Create a problem based on your histogram. Solve the problem.

5	4	2	3
5	5	4	5
3	7	6	5
2	6	2	5
2	5	3	3
6	3	1	5
4	1	2	7
6	4	3	2

6. A study of air pollution in a large Canadian city yielded the daily readings, shown to the right, of the volume of sulphur dioxide (in parts per million).
   (a) What classes would you use for the data?
   (b) Complete a frequency distribution for the data.
   (c) Construct a histogram for the data.
   (d) Create a problem based on your histogram. Solve the problem.

0.14	0.06	0.12	0.10
0.18	0.09	0.09	0.17
0.08	0.16	0.10	0.06
0.07	0.09	0.09	0.08
0.15	0.14	0.05	0.09
0.11	0.08	0.11	0.27
0.13	0.04	0.06	0.15

C

7. (a) Choose five different current popular TV programs. Conduct a survey of students to find out which program most prefer. Organize the data in a frequency table.
   (b) Choose a way to display the data.
   (c) Create problems of your own using your graph in (b). Compare your problems to others in the class.

PARTNER PROJECT

Checking your pulse as you exercise gives you useful information.
(a) Determine different ways of taking your pulse.
(b) Take your pulse, in beats per minute, as you are sitting.
(c) Complete some activities such as those shown below for about five minutes. Find your pulse rate in beats per minute.
(d) Sit down for three minutes. Find your pulse rate in beats per minute. Compare your pulse rate to others in the class during exercise and at rest. Draw an appropriate graph to compare the pulse rate of those in your class.
(e) Interpret the graph you have drawn. What conclusions can you make?

This chart shows the chemical elements that form the gas from a volcano.

Volcanic Gas	Percent	Central Angle
Potassium	0.85%	3°
Magnesium	2.7%	10°
Calcium	1.35%	5°
Sulfate	8.3%	30°
Sodium	30%	108°
Chlorine	56.8%	204°
TOTAL	100%	360°

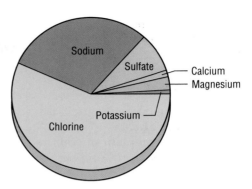

Think: $\frac{108}{360} \times 100\% = 30\%$

A circle graph is often used to show data expressed as part of the whole population. Each piece of data is expressed as a percent of the total. The percents are used to calculate the central angle for each sector of the circle graph.

ACTIVITY

(a) Find information and pictures about volcanoes that are currently active.

(b) Some scientists state that volcanoes affect the weather on the earth. How do they think this happens?

EXERCISE

A Review your skills with percent.

1. For each shaded region,
   - estimate and then measure the central angle.
   - calculate the percent of the circle that is shaded.

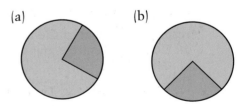

(a)   (b)

2. The central angle for the washers and dryers in the circle graph shown is 72°. Give reasons why the washers and dryers account for 20% of the total sales.

3. (a) Measure the central angle for the refrigerators.
   (b) For what percent of the total sales did the refrigerators account?
   (c) The total sales last month were $125 060. Calculate the sales for refrigerators.

Home Appliance Monthly Sales

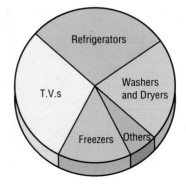

Use a calculator.

People's Favourite Winter Sports

Sport	Percent of people	Calculation of central angle	Measure of central angle
Skiing	25%		
Hockey		0.40 × 360°	
Snowshoeing			54°
Curling	20%		
Total			

4. (a) Copy and complete the chart.
   (b) Construct a circle graph for the data shown.

5. (a) Construct a circle graph for each set of data.
   (b) Create a problem of your own using the data. Compare your problem to others in the class.

Composition of the Human Body

Elements	Percent
Carbon	19%
Oxygen	67%
Other	14%

Causes of Air Pollution

Cause	Percent
Industry	15%
Transportation	44%
People	9%
Fuel	20%
Other	12%

6. Refer to the chart to the right.
   (a) Construct a circle graph for the data.
   (b) Discuss with your partner what "other" might represent. Check your prediction for a landfill site in your area.

Garbage in Landfill Sites

Type of garbage	Percent
Diapers	2%
Newspapers	14%
Yard Waste	20%
Other	64%

7. City Council conducted a survey to obtain an answer to the question, "When was your home built?" The survey's results are shown in the table.

Date home built	Responses
before 1945	252
1945–1970	540
since 1970	408

   (a) Construct a circle graph to show the data.
   (b) If you did a similar survey in your area, would you expect the responses to be similar or different? Give reasons for your answer.

8. A research group recorded the blood types of a random sample of people.

Blood type	O	A	AB	B
Number of people	661	616	53	121

   (a) Construct a circle graph.
   (b) Based on the data, how many people would you expect to have type AB blood at a football game with 14 000 in attendance?
   (c) Research what is meant by blood type. How many types are there? What percent of people have each type? Which type is rarest? most common?
   (d) Calculate the percent of people in each group. Construct a circle graph to display your data. Compare your circle graph with the circle graph in (a).

Circle graphs can be used to show the nutritional content of various foods. The circle graph shows the nutritional content of white bread. Remember: To find the percentage of the elements in white bread, measure each central angle.

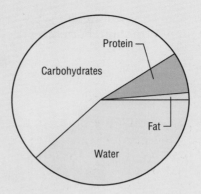

1. Refer to the circle graph. What percent of the bread is
   (a) protein?   (b) carbohydrates?   (c) fat?

2. Several loaves of white bread were bought and put in the freezer. The bread cost $12.50 in all.
   (a) How much was paid for water?
   (b) In your journal, describe whether the amount paid for water is reasonable. Why?

3. A common fast-food lunch consists of a cheeseburger, french fries, and a chocolate milk shake. This lunch provides 13% protein, 44% carbohydrates, and 43% fat.
   (a) Construct a circle graph for the data.
   (b) Research what a well-balanced lunch should give you with respect to protein, carbohydrates, and fat. Construct a circle graph for the data.
   (c) Compare your circle graphs in (a) and (b). What conclusions can you draw?

4. For each of the following:
   • Construct a circle graph to show the data.
   • Create a problem of your own based on the circle graph.
   • Solve the problem and compare your problem to others in the class.
   (a) Beef steak is 20.4% protein and 20.4% fat. The rest is water.
   (b) A wedge of cheese consists of 78.4 g of protein, 188.1 g of fat, and 83.7 g of water.

5. Refer to the photo of the three different types of cereal.
   (a) Draw a circle graph to show the percent of oats, wheat, and corn shown.
   (b) Create problems of your own based on the circle graph you constructed in (a). Compare your problem with others in the class.
   (c) Obtain a box of cereal like Triples and find the percentage of rice, wheat, and corn in a handful. Repeat (a) and (b) for your favourite cereal.

You can choose different types of graphs to display data. Each of the graphs displays the same information, but each provides a different visual impression.

Circle Graph

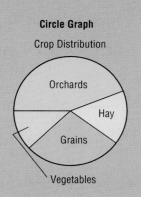

Pictograph

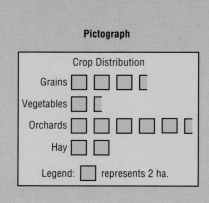

Bar Graph

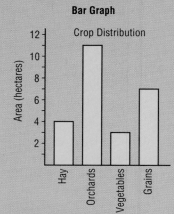

ACTIVITY   *Work with a Partner*

(a) What impressions do you get from each of the graphs above?
(b) Which appears to be most effective in conveying information?
(c) Describe when you might use each type of graph to display data. Give an example of each.

EXERCISE

A   Review ways to display data. Work with a partner.

1. Refer to the chart.
   (a) Pulse rates vary with age as shown in the chart. Which type of graph would be most suitable to display this data?
   (b) Construct the graph you chose in (a). Explain your choice of graph to your partner.

Age (years)	Pulse Rate (beats/min)
Newborn	135
1–10	87
10–20	71
20–60	72
60–70	73
70 plus	75

2. An apple consists of 0.3% protein and 12.2% carbohydrate. The rest is water.
   (a) Which type of graph would be most suitable to display the data?
   (b) Construct the graph in (a). Explain your choice of graph to your partner.

For each set of data in Questions 3 to 8:
- Decide on the most effective type of graph for displaying the data. Draw the graph.
- Create two questions based on the graph. Then answer the questions.

3.

Year	Amount of Garbage Produced per Person
1960	450 kg
1970	540 kg
1980	600 kg
1990	700 kg

4.

Distance (in kilometres) Cycled by Bike-a-thon Participants										
17	20	53	27	29	33	36	19	61	13	28
27	16	54	19	42	56	45	8	15	36	25
47	44	32	12	10	65	31	53	35	30	

5.

Total Monthly Precipitation (in millimetres)												
	J	F	M	A	M	J	J	A	S	O	N	D
Prince George	59	42	32	30	42	58	58	73	56	61	55	54
Saint John	126	114	98	100	103	94	90	100	100	105	145	132
Calgary	17	20	20	30	50	92	68	56	35	19	16	15

6.

Average Monthly Sunshine (in hours) in September		
Kamloops, B.C. 194	St. John's, Nfld 145	Prince Rupert, B.C. 95
Schefferville, Que. 101	Sydney, N.S 168	Coppermine, N.W.T. 69

7.

Methods of Getting to Work in Newfoundland	
Driving alone	45%
Driving with passenger	10%
Riding as passenger	20%
Shared driving	5%
Public transportation	4%
Walking	16%

8.

Total Airline Passengers Arriving or Departing Each Year	
Sydney, N.S.	198 954
Moncton, N.B.	242 158
Victoria, B.C.	569 748
Gander, Nfld.	196 617
Charlottetown, P.E.I.	195 538
Sept Iles, Que.	232 308
Windsor, Ont.	242 158

SMALL GROUP PROJECT: WHICH GRAPH?

To answer the questions below you may need to do research or conduct a survey.
- Choose one of the questions below.
- Collect data to answer the questions. Research the information.
- Draw a suitable graph to display the data.
- Use your graph to answer the original question.
- Create problems of your own that can be solved using the data.

A How much time do people spend sleeping as teenagers? as adults?

B In the weekend comics section, what percent of the cartoon strips are about animals? about people?

C How does your rate of breathing change when you perform different activities such as jogging, doing pushups, climbing stairs, reading?

14.11 BIAS IN STATISTICS

To obtain a sample that is representative of an entire population, the sample must be chosen at random. Each member of the sample must have an equal chance of being selected. If this is not so, then the sample is said to be **biased**.

EXAMPLE

Fred and his group wanted to survey 25 out of 512 people in the school to determine if the cafeteria should alter its menu. The group developed the following three plans. Which plan should they use?

Plan 1
Select 25 students from those students in the cafeteria at lunch time.

Plan 2
Choose a class in the school that has 25 students and survey them.

Plan 3
Assign each student in the school a number from 1 to 512. Have a computer select 25 numbers and then interview those students.

SOLUTION

Plan 1 is *biased* because any students that do not eat lunch in the cafeteria cannot be selected.

Plan 2 is *biased* because students whose class contains more than 25 students are eliminated.

Plan 3 is *non-biased* because each student has an equal chance of being selected randomly by a computer.

You will find a table of random digits on page 554 of this book. These random digits can be used to obtain a random sample as shown in the activity.

ACTIVITY   *Work with a Partner*

Suppose you want to select half of your class to fill out a questionnaire.
(a) Make a list of all students in the class. Assign each a three-digit number.
(b) Refer to the table of random digits at the back of the book.
(c) Choose a column. When a three-digit number found in the column matches one in your class, that student is one of the random sample.
(d) In your journal, describe why the above steps obtain a random sample of students.

B   Work in a group.

1. From a group of 100 persons, a sample of 10 are to be interviewed.
    (a) How can the table of random digits be used to obtain the 10 people?
    (b) Use your process in (a). List the digits of the 10 people who will be interviewed.
    (c) In your journal, describe how the table of random digits helped you to avoid a biased sample.

2. To obtain a sample of 50 persons from a group of 1000, you can also use the spinner shown.
    (a) Describe how you can use the spinner to select 50 persons from 1000.
    (b) Use your process in (a). List the digits of the 50 people in the sample.
    (c) In your journal, describe how a spinner helped you to avoid a biased sample.

3. From your class, you are to choose a person at random to organize the next school dance.
    (a) How would you use a table to select the person at random?
    (b) Use your process in (a). Whom did you select?

4. For each of the following, decide how the sample, in order to be unbiased, should be taken.
    (a) One member of the Olympic team is to be chosen to carry the country's flag.
    (b) A player is to be selected for the Most Improved Player trophy.
    (c) A bank teller is to be selected as employee of the month.
    (d) A captain is to be chosen for the volleyball team.

5. (a) Play this game with a partner.

    Rule 1 Randomly create three piles of disks like the ones shown.
    Rule 2 Each player takes turns removing disks. Any number of disks can be removed from any one pile. Keep a record of the number of disks removed during each turn.
    Rule 3 The winner is the player who removes the last disk.

    (b) Play the game in (a) a number of times. Based on the data, create a strategy so that one player always wins the game.

455

To determine when a crop of cherries is ready to be picked, a farmer takes a sample from each tree. Suppose 100 cherries are picked from each of 10 trees. The number of unripe cherries, out of 100 cherries from each tree, is shown:

15   3   17   23   12   18   24   15   8   28

The farmer can then make the following calculations.

Mean

$$\text{Mean} = \frac{\text{sum of the unripe cherry samples}}{\text{number of samples}}$$

$$= \frac{163}{10}$$

$$= 16.3 \qquad \text{The mean is about 16.}$$

Mode

The mode is the result that occurs most often.
The mode is 15.

Median

The median is the middle number when the data are arranged in order.

→ Think: Find the average.

3   8   12   15   15   17   18   23   24   28

The average of 15 and 17 is 16. Thus, the median is 16.

From experience, if the mean is over 19, the farmer will not pick the cherries. Since the mean is less than 19, she will probably pick the cherries.

ACTIVITY *Work with a Partner*

Suppose the same farmer selected 11 samples instead of 10, and in the eleventh sample tree she found that 50 cherries were not ripe.
(a) Calculate the mean, median, and mode using this new piece of information.
(b) If you were the farmer, would you pick the cherries now? Give reasons for your answer.

A Use a calculator when necessary.

1. Find the mean, median, and mode for each of the following.
   (a) 4, 7, 9, 9, 11
   (b) 17, 29, 17, 12, 50, 17, 17, 25
   (c) 6, 7, 9, 19, 35, 19, 8, 25, 19
   (d) 150, 123, 128, 150, 149, 132, 11
   (e) 4.9, 4.0, 3.9, 5.6, 2.1, 5.6, 3.4, 0.7
   (f) 19.86, 22.34, 21.98, 19.11, 19.86

2. (a) Refer to your results in Question 1. In which sets of data is the mean a member of the set? In which is the median a member of the set? In which is the mode a member of the set?
   (b) Which of the mean, median, or mode is always a member of the set of data you are exploring? Give reasons for your answer.

3. The mean water depth is 16 m. What effect will each of the following additional measures have on the mean depth? Give reasons for your answer.
   (a) 16 m   (b) 20 m   (c) 6 m

4. Answer each of the following in your journal.
   (a) Refer to a dictionary. What is meant by "average?"
   (b) How can each of the mean, the median, and the mode measure average?
   (c) Under what conditions is the mean the best indicator of average?
   (d) Under what conditions is the median the best indicator of average?
   (e) Under what conditions is the mode the best indicator of average?

B Work in a small group. Justify your answers to others in the class.

5. The heights of a group of students are given in centimetres as follows.

   160, 158, 180, 180, 171, 168, 166, 160, 169, 173, 172, 181, 174, 160, 179, 160, 176, 157, 165, 159, 183, 162, 177, 167, 163, 170, 178, 161, 175

   (a) Find the mean, the median, and the mode of the group.
   (b) Which of your results in (a) best represents the data? Give reasons.

6. The number of injuries in the past year at a sports complex is shown.

J	F	M	A	M	J	J	A	S	O	N	D
4	3	3	2	4	6	7	8	2	0	3	0

   Of the mean, median, or mode, which best represents the data? Give reasons.

Did you know that Canadian rower, Silken Laumann, broke her leg just six weeks before the Olympic Games? She recovered in time to win a bronze medal.

7. The points won by a school swim team during the past eight competitions are: 210, 186, 170, 73, 175, 180, 73, 196.
   (a) Find the mean, the median, and the mode.
   (b) Which of the measures in (a) best represents the data?
   (c) Predict the number of points you would expect the team to obtain in the next swimming competition.
   (d) Predict the total number of points you would expect the team to obtain in the next four swimming competitions.
   (e) Which answer, (c) or (d), would you expect to be more reliable? Why?

8. Refer to the histogram. Give reasons for each answer.
   (a) In which class do the most data occur?
   (b) In which class do the least data occur?
   (c) Predict in which class the mean might occur.
   (d) Predict in which class the median might occur.
   (e) Which answer, (c) or (d), is more likely to be reliable?

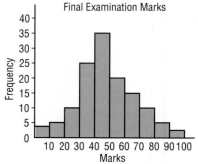

Final Examination Marks

9. (a) Describe how the histogram can be used to determine in which class the median might occur.
   (b) Can the histogram be used to determine in which class the mode occurs? Give reasons for your answer.

10. You can use elastics to form squares on a geoboard.
    (a) How many squares, with unique areas, can you form on a geoboard?
    (b) How many squares can you place on the geoboard with each area?
    (c) What is the "average" area of a square? Describe to your partner how you found this "average."

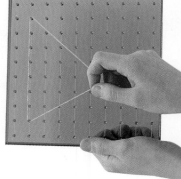

11. The mean of two numbers is 11. When a third number is included, the mean is 15. What is the third number?

12. Lorimer High's wrestling team has six wrestlers with a mean mass of 96 kg. If the masses of five of the wrestlers are 100 kg, 93 kg, 89 kg, 98 kg, and 95 kg, then what is the mass of the sixth wrestler?

PROJECT

The following words are ones you have met so far in this chapter.

destructive sample	population	sample	median	mode
broken-line graph	circle graph	histogram	bias	average
stratified sample	pictograph	bar graph	census	class
clustered sample	random sample	statistics	mean	

Illustrate the meaning of each word using an example of your own. Continue to build a vocabulary list throughout the year. It will be a useful reference.

14.13 PREDICTIONS FROM DATA

To make predictions, look for a *trend* in the data you collect.

EXAMPLE

Suppose residents in your area collected and organized data to show a potential traffic problem.

	Week 1	Week 2	Week 3	Week 4
Number of vehicles counted	395	281	484	386
Number of vehicles turning left onto Elm St.	110	65	131	97

(a) What percent of the vehicles turned left onto Elm Street each week?

(b) Predict how many vehicles, out of 400, will turn left onto Elm Street next week.

SOLUTION

Refer to the chart.

(a) The data shows that about 25% of the vehicles turn left onto Elm Street.

(b) 25% of 400 = 0.25 × 400
         = 100

Thus, the residents predict about 100 vehicles out of 400 will turn left onto Elm Street next week.

Number of vehicles turning left onto Elm St.	Total number of vehicles	Calculation
110	395	$\frac{110}{395} = 0.28$ or 28%
65	281	$\frac{65}{281} = 0.23$ or 23%
131	484	$\frac{131}{484} = 0.27$ or 27%
97	386	$\frac{97}{386} = 0.25$ or 25%

ACTIVITY   *Work with a Partner*

Suppose you are to show that an advanced green light is needed for this corner on Elm Street to help motorists turn left.

(a) What further data, if any, is needed to help you make your presentation? Give reasons for your answer.

(b) Once you have gathered the data, describe the presentation you would use.

(c) In your journal, describe some effective ways to collect data about traffic.

(d) You might gather similar data for an intersection in your area. Determine whether you think there is a potential traffic problem at this corner. Present your data and your conclusions to the rest of the class.

A Use the data in Question 1.

1. For a school project, Sonya recorded the number of sandwiches ordered for lunch in the school cafeteria. Calculate the percent of all meals that were sandwiches.

Day	Total number of lunches	Number of sandwiches
Mon.	124	49
Tues.	108	43
Wed.	115	47
Thurs.	132	52

2. Refer to your results in Question 1. Predict what percent of the students are likely to order sandwiches for lunch on Friday.

3. Suppose 1250 lunches were ordered. How many lunches would you expect to be sandwiches?

4. Besides Sonya, who else might be interested in the data? For what use?

B Remember: You analyze data you obtain in order to make reliable predictions.

5. The catalogue department of a store kept a record of orders placed and items returned each day for one week.

	Mon.	Tues.	Wed.	Thurs.	Fri.	Sat.
Orders	125	132	156	147	172	205
Returns	19	17	20	18	22	38

(a) On which day of the week is the percent of items returned the greatest?
(b) On which day is the percent of items returned the least?
(c) How can this data be used by the manager in the catalogue department? Give reasons.

6. Refer to the chart in the previous question. Predict the number of returns next week for the following number of orders.
(a) Monday 165   (b) Wednesday 186   (c) Friday 123
(d) In your journal, describe whether there is enough information given in the chart to make the predictions above confidently. Give reasons for your answer.

7. For two years, the manager of the catalogue department has recorded the percent of returns each day.

Mon.	Tues.	Wed.	Thurs.	Fri.	Sat.
13.5%	12.5%	12.3%	12.1%	13.2%	16.9%

(a) Use the chart to answer Questions 5 and 6. How do your answers compare?
(b) In your journal, describe which answers you would expect to be more reliable. Give reasons.

4.14 EXPLORING PROBABILITY

You have probably heard statements such as the following:
- The chance of rain today is 15%.
- The police predict that 25 accidents will occur this weekend.
- Edmonton will probably win the Stanley Cup.

Probability is the branch of mathematics that helps you measure the chance of an event occurring.

EXPLORATION ① Work in a Small Group

1. Copy the frequency table. Use two coins and toss them at the same time. Complete the table by tossing the coins 50 times. Write the number of times you get two heads (HH), two tails (TT), and a tail and a head (TH or HT).

Experiment: Tossing Coins		
Event	Tally	Frequency
HH	?	?
HT	?	?
TH	?	?
TT	?	?

2. (a) Obtain the results of the coin toss from four other groups. Place their results in your frequency table. Write the number of times you get two heads, two tails, and a tail and a head.
   (b) Write the number of times you get two heads, two tails, and a tail and a head, as a fraction of 250.

3. Refer to your previous results.
   (a) How many times would you expect to get two heads in 1000 tosses?
   (b) How many times would you expect to get two tails in 1000 tosses?
   (c) How many times would you expect to get a head and a tail in 1000 tosses?
   (d) Is it more likely that tossing two coins will give you either two heads or two tails, or is it more likely that tossing two coins will give a head and a tail? Give reasons for your prediction.

EXPLORATION ② Work with a Partner

4. (a) Have your partner flip the pages of this book. Without looking at the pages, say "STOP" to your partner.
   (b) Record the last digit of the page number at which your partner stops.
   (c) Repeat (a) and (b) 20 times.

5. Refer to your results in the previous question.
   (a) Suppose you flipped the pages 400 times. How many nines would you expect?
   (b) How many of each other number would you expect?
   (c) What do you notice about your answers?

EXPLORATION ③

6. Refer to the information in the opening paragraph.
   (a) For each statement, how do you think the data might be collected?
   (b) Collect similar statements of your own. How do you think the data might be collected?

14.15 WORKING WITH PROBABILITY

If you attend any games such as soccer or football, you will see a referee toss a coin to decide which end each team takes. Each captain knows the chances of winning the toss are equal. The coin, when tossed, will either land heads or tails. You write this probability as follows:

The probability of heads is $\dfrac{1}{2}$. $\dfrac{\text{number of favourable outcomes (heads)}}{\text{total number of possible outcomes (tosses)}}$

The probability, P, of an event is usually written as a proper fraction. For example, suppose you have a bag containing three dimes, six nickels, and a penny. If you have one chance to pick at random, is it more likely you will select a dime (D) or a nickel (N)?

Probability (D) = P(D)   Probability (N) = P(N)

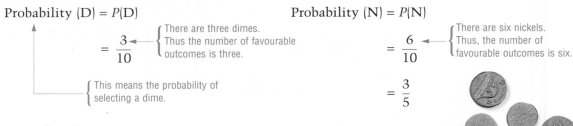

$= \dfrac{3}{10}$ ⟵ { There are three dimes. Thus the number of favourable outcomes is three.

{ This means the probability of selecting a dime.

$= \dfrac{6}{10}$ ⟵ { There are six nickels. Thus, the number of favourable outcomes is six.

$= \dfrac{3}{5}$

Since $\dfrac{3}{5} > \dfrac{3}{10}$, it is more likely you will select a nickel.

EXERCISE

A   Review your skills with fractions and decimal numbers.

1.   Assign an approximate value, 0 to 1, to show the probability of each event.
    (a) A bottle of soda is dropped on concrete. What is the probability of the bottle remaining intact?
    (b) What is the probability of snow in July in Winnipeg, Manitoba?
    (c) Work with a partner. List different events. Describe the probability of each event happening.

2.   What is the probability of rolling each number on a die?
    (a) 2   (b) 6   (c) an odd number   (d) 12

3.   A bag contains 6 green balls, 9 white balls, and 12 blue balls. You are asked to pick a ball from the bag. What is the probability that you will pick the following?
    (a) a white ball   (b) a blue ball   (c) a green ball

4.   A game show spinner is divided into different sectors as shown. Find the probability of the pointer selecting the following.
    (a) a black sector   (b) a red sector

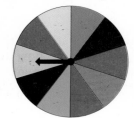

5. Suppose you tossed a thumbtack 50 times and it landed point up 34 times. What is the probability that, on the next toss, the thumbtack will land point up?

6. In an old movie, six prisoners of war choose straws. The one who picks the short straw has the first chance to escape.
   (a) What is the probability of picking the short straw?
   (b) What assumptions did you make in (a)?

7. In a bag, there are 12 cubes numbered from 1 to 12. You choose one from the bag. Calculate the probability of each of the following.
   (a) P(a cube marked 1)   (b) P(a cube marked 12)
   (c) P(a cube with an even number)   (d) P(a cube with an odd number)

8. Write the name of each province in Canada on separate cards. Place the cards in a box and mix them. What is the probability of selecting
   (a) the province that begins with a Q?
   (b) the province that borders on the Pacific Ocean?
   (c) a province that borders on the Atlantic Ocean?
   (d) a province that does not begin with x?
   (e) a province that does not begin with a vowel?

9. A deck of cards has 52 cards with 13 spades, 13 diamonds, 13 clubs, and 13 hearts. What is the probability of selecting
   (a) an ace?   (b) a king?   (c) a 10 of clubs?
   (d) a red king?   (e) not a 2?   (f) not a red card?

10. A box contains 25 dimes, 10 pennies, and 15 nickels. If you have one chance to pick a coin, what would be the probability that you would pick the following?
    (a) a dime   (b) a nickel   (c) a penny

11. If you were to conduct an experiment based on the previous question, how many times would you expect to pick a penny for each number of attempts?
    (a) 50   (b) 500   (c) 200   (d) 150

12. A jar of jelly beans is spilled over the bottom of the page.
    (a) Close your eyes and touch a jelly bean. What is the probability that you will touch a red jelly bean? a black jelly bean?
    (b) Create a probability problem of your own using the jelly beans. Compare your problem to others in the class.

Earlier you completed an experiment in which you tossed two coins at the same time. The probability of tossing a head with the second coin was not affected by the outcome of the toss of the first coin. In such cases, the two events are said to be **independent**.

YOU ALREADY KNOW...

The probability of an event, E, is found using the following:

$$P(E) = \frac{\text{number of favourable outcomes}}{\text{number of possible outcomes}}$$

Complete the following activity. Summarize any relationships you see to help you find the probability of two independent events.

ACTIVITY *Work with a Partner*

(a) What is the probability of tossing a head with one coin? a tail?

(b) If the coins are tossed one at a time, what is the probability of tossing a head followed by a head? a head followed by a tail? a tail followed by a head? a tail followed by a tail?

(c) How are your answers in (a) and (b) alike? How are they different?

The above activity suggests the following results for tossing two heads in a row.

$$P(\text{two heads}) = P(\text{head}) \times P(\text{head}).$$

This relationship can be used to solve problems like the following.

EXAMPLE

To win on a game show, you need to select from a bag two "yesses" in a row. The bag contains five "yesses" and seven "no's." What is the probability of winning?

SOLUTION

The probability of selecting a "yes" is $\frac{5}{12}$.

Thus, the probability of selecting a "yes" and then a "yes", if the first "yes" is replaced, is found at the right:

$$P(Y \text{ and } Y) = P(Y) \times P(Y)$$
$$= \frac{5}{12} \times \frac{5}{12}$$
$$= \frac{25}{144}$$

Thus, the probability of winning is $\frac{25}{144}$.

EXERCISE

A Review your skills with probability.

1. Two cola bottle caps and three orange bottle caps are placed in a bag.
   (a) What is the probability of selecting a cola cap? an orange cap?
   (b) What is the probability of selecting a cola cap, putting it back in the bag and then selecting another cola cap?

2. (a) What is the probability of tossing one coin and getting a head?
   (b) What is the probability of getting two heads in a row?
   (c) What is the probability of getting three heads in a row?
   (d) What is the probability of getting ten heads in a row?

3. Refer to your work in Question 2. In your journal, describe how you can find the probability of tossing any number of heads in a row.

B Use a calculator.

4. A bag contains four red gum balls and seven green gum balls.
   (a) Find the probability of drawing two red gum balls in a row if the first gum ball is put back in the bag.
   (b) Find the probability of selecting two green gum balls in a row if the first gum ball is put back in the bag.
   (c) Repeat (a) and (b) for bags containing gum balls of your own.

5. A deck of 52 cards is shuffled. In the following, each card is drawn from the deck and returned to the deck before the next draw. Find the probability of
   (a) drawing an ace and then a king.
   (b) drawing a two and then another two.
   (c) drawing a king and not drawing another king.
   (d) drawing a red card followed by another red card.

6. Work with a partner.
   (a) Both of you enter a one-digit number on your calculator.
   (b) What is the probability that your partner's number is the same as yours?
   (c) Repeat (b) by having both of you enter a two-digit number.
   (d) Create a similar problem of your own. Solve your problem by working with your partner.

7. Suppose you are part of a TV studio audience with 100 people. At the end of the show, four prizes are selected and given to members of the audience. You can win more than one prize.
   (a) What is the probability of your winning all four prizes?
   (b) What assumptions have you made in (a)?

MAKING CONNECTIONS: THE WEATHER

The weather bureau has claimed that there is a 70% chance that it will rain today and an 80% chance that it will rain tomorrow.
(a) Write each percent as a fraction.
(b) What is the probability that it will rain today and tomorrow? Justify your answer.
(c) A weather forecaster uses this information and says "There is greater than a 50% chance that it will rain both today and tomorrow." Do you agree with this claim?

14.17 DEPENDENT EVENTS

Previously, you selected items from a bag and then replaced them. Thus, the events were said to be independent. However, if you do not replace the items, the events are **dependent** because selecting one item affects the probability of the selection of the next item.

Complete the following activity. Summarize any relationships you see to help you find the probability of two dependent events.

ACTIVITY 1 *Work with a Partner*

(a) Put two orange disks and two yellow disks into a bag.
(b) Select one disk and put it to one side. Then select another disk. Repeat the process 25 times.
(c) Record the number of times that you select two orange disks in a row.
(d) Use your results. Predict the probability that, in a bag containing two orange disks and two yellow disks, you will select two orange disks in a row.

The relationships found in the activity can be used to help Susan in the following activity.

Step 1

Susan put four orange disks and five yellow disks into a bag. She selected one of the disks.

The probability of selecting an orange disk is $\frac{4}{9}$.

Step 2

Susan then selected another disk from those remaining.

The probability of selecting an orange disk is $\frac{3}{8}$.

Notice how the total number of disks has changed.

Step 3

Susan then calculated the probability of selecting two orange disks in a row as follows:

$$\frac{4}{9} \times \frac{3}{8} = \frac{12}{72}$$

$$= \frac{1}{6}$$

ACTIVITY 2

Refer to the calculations you have made for independent events and dependent events.
(a) How are the calculations alike? How are they different?
(b) Write examples of your own to help explain your answers in (a).

466

EXERCISE

A Use disks to help you.

1. (a) Show the steps to calculate the probability of selecting an orange disk and then a green disk from the disks shown.
   (b) Show the steps to calculate the probability of selecting two green disks in a row from the disks shown.

B Review your skills with dependent and independent events.

2. A box contains four hockey cards and seven baseball cards.
   (a) What is the probability of selecting a hockey card?
   (b) What is the probability of selecting a baseball card?
   (c) What is the probability of selecting a hockey card, keeping it out of the box, and then selecting another hockey card?
   (d) What is the probability of selecting a hockey card, keeping it out of the box, and then selecting a baseball card?

3. Seven regular quarters and four "Mountie" quarters are placed in a bag.
   (a) What is the probability of selecting a regular quarter? a Mountie quarter?
   (b) What is the probability of selecting a regular quarter followed by a Mountie quarter?
   (c) What is the probability of selecting two Mountie quarters in a row?
   (d) What is the probability of selecting two regular quarters in a row?

4. All the hearts and all the diamonds from a deck of cards are placed into a bag. What is the probability of selecting two aces in a row
   (a) if the first card is replaced before selecting the second?
   (b) if the first card is not replaced before selecting the second?

5. Two cards are selected from a well-shuffled deck. A card is selected, kept, and another card is selected.
   (a) What is the probability that the first card is a two?
   (b) What is the probability that the second card is a five?
   (c) What is the probability that the second card has a value greater than a two? than a five?
   (d) What assumptions have you made in (c)?

C

6. Two dice are rolled separately. The sum of both needs to be seven for a win. The first die is rolled and is a five.
   (a) What is the probability that the roll of the second die will be a number that gives a winning sum?
   (b) Are the events described in (a) dependent events or independent events? Give reasons for your answer.

In the previous section, you explored events where only two outcomes were possible. Work with a partner to complete the following activity.

ACTIVITY *Work with a Partner*

(a) Put two orange disks, two yellow disks, and two green disks into a bag.
(b) Select one disk and put it to one side. Select another disk and put it to one side. Then select a third disk and put it to one side. Repeat the process 25 times.
(c) Record the number of times you select an orange disk, a yellow disk, and a green disk in that order.
(d) Use your results. Predict the probability that, in a bag containing two orange disks, two yellow disks, and two green disks, you will select an orange disk, followed by a yellow disk, followed by a green disk.

In the activity above, you found the probability of dependent events, where there are more than two outcomes, in the same way as you did in the previous section. Suppose Susan was given five orange, four yellow, and three green disks. She was asked to find the probability of selecting an orange disk, followed by a yellow disk, followed by a green disk.

Step 1

Susan put five orange disks, four yellow disks, and three green disks into a bag. She selected one disk.

The probability that Susan selected an orange disk is $\frac{5}{12}$.

Step 2

Susan then selected another disk from those remaining.

The probability that Susan selected a yellow disk is $\frac{4}{11}$.

Step 3

Finally, Susan selected a third disk from those remaining.

The probability that Susan selected a green disk is $\frac{3}{10}$.

Step 4

Susan then calculated the probability.

$$\frac{5}{12} \times \frac{4}{11} \times \frac{3}{10} = \frac{60}{1320}$$
$$= \frac{1}{22}$$

Thus, the probability is $\frac{1}{22}$.

A Use disks to help you.

1. (a) Show the steps needed to calculate the probability of selecting an orange disk, followed by a yellow disk, followed by a green disk. What is the probability?
   (b) Show the steps needed to calculate the probability of selecting three orange disks in a row. What is the probability?

B In your journal, write any observations you have.

2. In a box of 1000 spark plugs, 10 of them are defective.
   (a) What is the probability of choosing a defective plug?
   (b) What is the probability of not choosing a defective plug?
   (c) A defective plug is chosen and not placed back in the box. Why is the probability of choosing a defective plug again $\frac{9}{999}$?
   (d) Explain why the probability of choosing two defective plugs is $\frac{10}{1000} \times \frac{9}{999}$.
   (e) What is the probability of choosing three defective plugs in a row?

3. Suppose all the letters in the title of this book were put into a bag and then selected one at a time.
   (a) What is the probability of selecting an A and then selecting an E if no letters are replaced?
   (b) What is the probability of selecting a T, followed by a T, followed by a T, if no letters are replaced?
   (c) Create a probability problem of your own using the letters. Compare your problem with others in the class.

4. A quarter, nickel, dime, and penny are placed in a bag.
   (a) What is the probability of selecting each coin?
   (b) What is the probability of selecting a quarter, then a nickel, then a dime, and then a penny if none of the coins are replaced? What assumptions have you made?
   (c) What is the probability of selecting a penny, a nickel, a dime, and then a quarter if none of the coins are replaced?
   (d) What do you notice about your answers in (b) and (c)?

5. Use a deck of cards.
   (a) What is the probability of being dealt the king of hearts followed by the king of spades?
   (b) What is the probability of receiving four aces from the top of a deck of cards if the cards are dealt to you one at a time?
   (c) Create a problem of your own using playing cards. Solve your problem and compare your solution to others in the class.

Bad-weather sometimes causes an event to be cancelled. If you are responsible for making the decision to cancel an event, you need to have as much information as possible. To make a decision, you need to consider the weather forecast for the day of the event. The more data you have, the more reliable your prediction.

Work with a partner to complete each of the following exercises. In your journal, describe why you made each prediction based on the data given.

EXERCISE

B Express your answers in lowest terms.

1. A die was rolled 10 times and the results were recorded in the table.

Number	1	2	3	4	5	6
Occurrence	1	1	4	2	1	1

(a) In the next 10 rolls, how many times would you expect to roll a three?
(b) Roll a die 10 times and record the results.
(c) Was your prediction in (a) reliable? Why or why not?
(d) How could you improve your prediction in (a)?

2. After 500 rolls of the die, the data in the table were obtained.

Number	1	2	3	4	5	6
Occurrence	76	78	83	81	86	96

Based on the sample, if the die was rolled 1000 times, estimate how many times you would roll
(a) a three.   (b) a two.   (c) a six.

3. The results shown, were obtained by drawing one card from a deck of regular playing cards 100 times. The card drawn was replaced and the deck shuffled after each draw.

Ace	Face Card	2 to 10
8	22	70

Based on the results shown, if a card is drawn 300 times, estimate how many times you would expect each of the following outcomes.
(a) an ace   (b) a face card

4. Three sets of trials of 500 rolls of a die are shown in the table.

   (a) Total each number based on the three trials and find the average per trial.
   (b) Use the results of (a) to predict the number of threes in another trial of 500 rolls.

Number	1	2	3	4	5	6
Trial 1	93	93	82	80	93	59
Trial 2	87	81	92	73	74	93
Trial 3	88	77	74	93	90	78
Total	268					
Average per trial						

5. Data are given in the table to the right for the range of marks on a quiz. You select an exam paper at random. What is the probability of each of the following?
   (a) The student passed.
   (b) The student received over 80.
   (c) The student did not have a mark in the 60–70 limit.

Class	Class Limits	Frequency
1	1–10	0
2	10–20	0
3	20–30	3
4	30–40	4
5	40–50	5
6	50–60	18
7	60–70	20
8	70–80	15
9	80–90	9
10	90–100	2

6. A histogram shows the frequency distribution of the normal pulse rates of students. If you select a student at random, what is the probability of each of the following pulse rates?
   (a) less than 60
   (b) more than 80
   (c) between 60 and 80

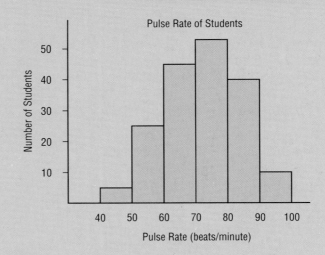

7. Suppose you are a concert promoter and want to schedule a major outdoor event for July 1.
   (a) What are some of the questions you would ask to determine if this is an appropriate date?
   (b) What skills from this chapter would you use to help you interpret the answers to your questions in (a)?
   (c) What other math skills would you use?

In order to prepare for landing an aircraft, pilots practise in a flight simulator. In your journal:
- Explain what you think a flight simulator is.
- Describe what other actions you think a pilot might simulate, other than landing.
- Write what you think "simulate" means in mathematics.

It would be difficult to calculate precisely the probability of some events, such as those in the following explorations. Thus, an experiment is planned to collect suitable data. Such an experiment is called a **simulation**.

EXPLORATION ① Work with a Partner

1. Suppose you want to explore the question "Out of five people, what is the probability that two were born in December?"
   (a) The spinner is used to collect data for this simulation. In each trial, the spinner is spun five times and the number of times it lands on D is recorded in the chart.
   (b) Copy the chart and record the data.

Trial	1	2	3	4	5	6	7	8	9	10	11	12	13	14	15	16	17	18	19	20
Number of times spinner points to D																				

   (c) Use the data in (b) to find the answer.
   (d) Plan another simulation to obtain the data to answer the question. Compare your answer to your answer in (c).

EXPLORATION ② Work with a Partner

2. Suppose you are to complete a true/false quiz of ten questions.

Trial	1	2	3	4	5	6	7	8	9	10
Number of Heads										

   (a) What is the probability of guessing all the answers or obtaining exactly five correct answers?
   (b) To obtain the data, use ten coins. The head on each coin represents a correct guess.
   (c) For each trial, toss ten coins. Record the number of heads (correct guesses). Copy and complete the table for four trials.
   (d) Use the data in (c) to find the probability of getting five correct answers.
   (e) Refer to the manipulatives below. How might you use them to obtain data in this exploration? Obtain the data and find the answer.

14.21 SIMULATIONS

A survey showed that about one half of all car drivers listen to the radio. An advertising consultant wanted to estimate the probability, P, that, when three cars are chosen at random, all three drivers are listening to the radio. To obtain data to calculate the probability, she simulated the event by using three coins. A toss of a head represents a driver listening to the radio. The first trial is shown below. The chart below gives the results of 15 trials.

Trial	1	2	3	4	5	6	7	8	9	10	11	12	13	14	15
Number of heads	1	1	3	2	0	2	2	1	3	0	1	2	1	2	0

Based on the data collected, she calculated the probability as follows.

$$P = \frac{\text{number of times three heads occur}}{\text{number of trials}}$$

$$= \frac{2}{15}$$

The probability that all three drivers are listening to the radio is $\frac{2}{15}$.

Think: In your journal, list any assumptions the consultant would make when collecting data.

EXERCISE

B   Work in a small group.

1. (a) Predict the probability that, out of ten people, five were born in the summer.
   (b) To obtain an answer in (a), use a spinner with one sector for each of the four seasons. Use 20 trials with ten spins in each trial. Set up a chart to record your data.
   (c) Use your data in (b). Calculate the probability.
   (d) Repeat the above experiment using a table of random digits to simulate the method of collecting data. Use this data to answer the question. Compare your answers.

2. Plan a simulation to obtain data to answer the following question: "An ice cream shop serves five flavours of milk shakes. How many milk shakes must be served before one of each flavour is served?"

3. Refer to the advertising consultant's experiment above.
   (a) Create a similar experiment of your own.
   (b) Plan a simulation to collect data to answer the question. Find the answer.

4. For the following, discuss with your partner what the question means, select a suitable simulation to estimate the probability, and find the answer.
   (a) What is the probability that, in a group of four people, all of them were born between July 1 and December 31?
   (b) Each box of a cereal has one of ten models of an endangered species. Suppose you already have seven models. How many boxes of cereal do you think need to be opened to obtain a complete set? List any assumptions.

473

1. (a) Make a list of all the sampling techniques you have learned in this chapter.
   (b) List the advantages and the disadvantages of each technique you listed in (a).

2. A survey of 50 people provided data on their preferred types of television program. The following data were obtained.

   Drama 12   Sports 15   Comedy 18   Other 5

   (a) What is the most suitable type of graph to display this data? Give reasons for your choice.
   (b) Construct the graph in (a).
   (c) What conclusions can you draw from your graph?

3. A farmer measured the masses of 30 eggs in grams and recorded the results as follows.

49.8	62.3	47.3	55.9	61.3	52.8	50.7	65.5
52.4	50.8	63.4	49.9	53.6	57.4	51.2	41.6
57.9	56.3	49.3	53.5	58.0	61.4	60.4	55.1
59.2	67.1	61.5	47.7	50.8	54.7

   (a) Organize the data above in a frequency table.
   (b) Display the data in a histogram.
   (c) Do you think that a histogram is the most appropriate way to display the data? Give reasons for your answer.

4. The number of people visiting the zoo is given for a one-week period.
   Mon. 475   Tues. 823   Wed. 765   Thurs. 648
   Fri. 1289   Sat. 1425   Sun. 2648
   (a) Draw a suitable graph to display the data.
   (b) Find the mean, median, and mode for the data.
   (c) Suppose an average of 700 people each day is needed for the zoo to be profitable. Write an argument to show that the zoo is profitable.

5. You are rolling two dice. What is the probability of getting each of the following?
   (a) an even number
   (b) a prime number

6. Lila wears her blue sweater twice as often as she wears any of her other four sweaters. What is the probability that Lila will wear her blue sweater the next time she wears a sweater?

THINKING ABOUT

❶ Compare the graphs you drew on this page with others. How are the graphs alike? How are they different?

❷ Suppose you were buying eggs from the farmer in Question 3. What average mass would you expect the whole shipment to have?

❸ In what situations do you think you would need to calculate probability? Give examples.

MAKING CONNECTIONS

Refer to the pictures and captions on the first page of this chapter.
(a) How might your answers to the questions be different, now that you have completed the chapter?
(b) Write examples of when you might need to collect data in the future.

❹ In this chapter, under what conditions is a calculator helpful? a hindrance?

❺ How do you think data are collected for Question 2 on this page?

❻ Using the skills in this chapter, how might you better understand data provided to you in newspapers and magazines?

1. The number of strikeouts by a pitcher is shown. Rena has 12 strikeouts.
   (a) What information is missing from the graph?
   (b) How many strikeouts does each pitcher have?

Rena	⚾⚾⚾⚾⚾⚾
Hank	⚾⚾⚾⚾⚾⚾⚾⚾⚾
Jane	⚾⚾⚾
Greg	⚾⚾⚾⚾⚾

2. A survey was conducted to obtain an answer to "How is your home heated?"
   (a) Construct a circle graph to show the data.
   (b) If you did a similar survey in your area, would you expect the responses to be the same? Why?

Heat Source	Responses
Oil	252
Gas	540
Electricity	408

3. For each of the following, find the
   (a) mean.   (b) median.   (c) mode.

A	15	10	17	11	20	9	16	14	22
B	44	36	40	35	41	43	35		
C	24	29	20	22	21	18	32	15	19	25
D	7.3	8.2	5.5	9.8	10.3	8.7	3.9	7.1	8.5

4. In a shipment of 1000 field hockey sticks, ten of them are cracked.
   (a) What is the probability of choosing a defective stick?
   (b) What is the probability of choosing three defective sticks in a row? (The sticks are not returned to the shipment each time.)

MATH JOURNAL

Refer to Question 5 on this page.
(a) What pattern do you notice in the data?
(b) Do you think all drivers should be familiar with this data? Why?

5. The faster a car is moving, the greater the distance required to come to a safe stop. The graph shows the safe stopping distance at various speeds.
   (a) What is a safe stopping distance for each of the following speeds?
      (i) 30 km/h   (ii) 40 km/h
   (b) Find the safe speed to drive if the stopping distance is
      (i) 20 m   (ii) 40 m

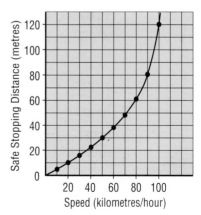

PROJECTS

You have seen that larger samples enable you to make better predictions. Choose one of the following projects. Work with a partner. Before you begin the project, answer the following.

- What type of sample do you need to collect data?
- How can you ensure your sample is random?
- How can you collect the data for the project?
- What skills should you review before you collect the data?

Project 1

An optical illusion is shown

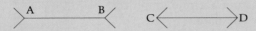

(a) Which of the following responses do you think most people would choose?
  1. AB is equal to CD.
  2. AB is longer.
  3. CD is longer.
(b) Design a questionnaire based on the above information and have different people complete it.
(c) Use the data in (b) to make a prediction. Which statement is most likely to be chosen? least likely to be chosen?
(d) Out of 100 people, predict the percentage that will choose each statement.

Project 4

A thumbtack can land two ways, as shown below.

Devise an experiment to establish whether the following statement is more likely to be true or false.

"When a thumbtack is dropped it will most likely land with its point down."

Project 2

(a) Predict what you think is the favourite colour in your class.
(b) Collect data to verify your prediction.
(c) In a group of 100 people, what percentage will choose the same colour?
(d) What assumption did you make in finding the answer in (c)?

Project 3

(a) Decide on what you think are the five most popular songs played on the radio.
(b) Design a questionnaire to collect data on what other people think are the five most popular songs. Use the data from the questionnaire to establish the five most popular songs.
(c) Use another method such as a telephone survey to collect data on what other people think are the five most popular songs. Use this data to establish the five most popular songs.
(d) How do your answers in (a), (b), and (c) compare? Which of the above methods would you use to predict the five most popular songs played on the radio across Canada?

ACTIVITY

Star Trek's Captain Kirk is well known for the expression, "Beam me up, Scotty."

(a) What is meant by this expression? In what way does it involve a "transformation"?

(b) The word "transformation" also has a special mathematical meaning. What do you think the meaning is? (Flipping through this chapter may help you.)

(c) Think back on the math that you have studied this past year. What skills do you think will be useful in the future?

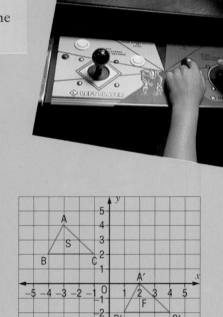

Most electronic games involve a specific movement or series of movements.

ACTIVITY

(a) Think of a video game that involves movement. Describe the movements.

(b) How does movement affect the outcome of the game?

Geometry can also involve movement, as you will see in these explorations.

EXPLORATION ① **Work with a Partner**

1. A triangle is shown at position S and shown at position F. Make a copy of the diagram.
   (a) How are the triangles ABC and A′B′C′ alike? How are they different?
   (b) How would you describe the triangle in position F in relation to the triangle in position S?

2. (a) List pairs of angles that correspond at S and F. Compare their measures. What do you notice?
   (b) List pairs of segments at S and F that correspond. What do you notice?
   (c) Draw segments to connect the corresponding vertices. Measure the segments. What do you notice?
   (d) Find the slope of the segments that connect corresponding vertices in (c). What do you notice about the slopes of the segments?

3. In the above diagram, the triangle at position S is *translated* to position F.
   (a) Draw a coordinate grid and place a triangle on the grid. Call it S.
   (b) Show the triangle in another position after a translation. Repeat Questions 1 and 2 for your translation.
   (c) In your own words, describe to your partner how to draw triangle S. Then describe the translation needed so that your partner can draw triangle F.

478

4. A triangle is shown at position S and shown at position F. Make a copy.
   (a) How are the triangles alike? How are they different?
   (b) How would you describe the triangle in position F in relation to the triangle in position S?

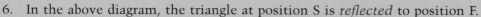

5. (a) List pairs of angles that correspond at S and F. Compare their measures. What do you notice?
   (b) List pairs of segments at S and F that correspond. What do you notice?
   (c) Draw a segment to connect the corresponding vertices. Measure the distance from each vertex to the *y*-axis. What do you notice?
   (d) Construct the perpendicular bisector of each segment joining corresponding vertices. What do you notice?

6. In the above diagram, the triangle at position S is *reflected* to position F.
   (a) Draw a triangle on a coordinate grid. Call it S.
   (b) Show the triangle in another position after a reflection. Repeat Questions 4 and 5 for your reflection.
   (c) Describe to your partner how to draw triangle S. Then describe the reflection needed so that your partner can draw triangle F.

7. A triangle is shown at position S and shown at position F. Make a copy.
   (a) How are the triangles alike? How are they different?
   (b) How would you describe the triangle in position F in relation to the triangle in position S?

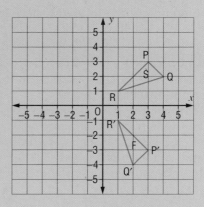

8. (a) List pairs of angles at S and F that correspond. Compare their measures. What do you notice?
   (b) List pairs of sides at S and F that correspond. Compare their measures. What do you notice?
   (c) Draw a line from each vertex in S and F to O. Measure the distance from corresponding vertices to O. What do you notice?

9. In the above diagram, the triangle at position S is *rotated* to position F.
   (a) Draw a triangle on a coordinate grid. Call it S.
   (b) Show the triangle in another position after a rotation. Repeat Questions 7 and 8 for your rotation.

In the previous exploration, you explored these relationships about translations:

1. The distance between corresponding vertices is the same. In the diagram, AA' = BB' = CC'.
2. The measure of the corresponding angles and sides remains the same.
3. The segments AA', BB', and CC' are parallel.

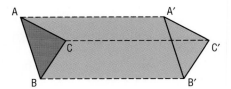

A translation is applied to △ABC to obtain △A'B'C'.

There are different ways you can communicate translations, as shown below. (The figure drawn before any translation has occurred is the **object**. The figure you draw after a translation is called the **image**.)

Using Words
Right 3, Down 2

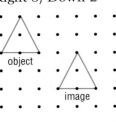

object

image

Using an Arrow

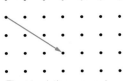

The translation arrow shows:
• how far left or right.
• how far up or down.

Using Symbols
[+3, −2] means 3 units right and then 2 units down.

As you complete the following activity, record any patterns and relationships you find.

ACTIVITY *Work with a Partner*

You will see translations used in many different places. For example, translations are often used to create designs.

(a) How are the designs shown below alike? How are they different?
(b) How are translations used to create these designs?
(c) Create similar designs of your own using translations. Have your partner answer (a) and (b) for your designs.
(d) In your journal, describe other examples of the uses of translations.

A   Use a diagram to help you. Use a grid or dot paper.

1. A figure is translated in each. Describe each translation.

(a)   (b)   (c)

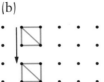
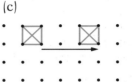

2. Copy each figure shown.
   (a) Translate each figure
   - 5 units to the right.
   - 3 units down.
   (b) Translate each figure
   - 6 units to the left.
   - 3 units up.

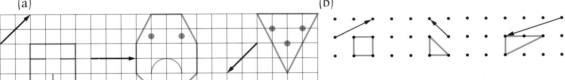

B   Review different ways to communicate translations.

3. Copy each figure. Use the translation arrow and the properties of translations to draw an image of each.

(a)   (b)

4. Make a copy of each object. Describe a translation that can be used to find each image.

(a)   (b)   (c)

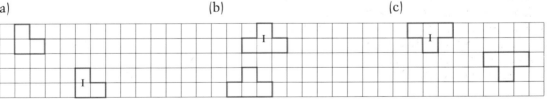

5. △ABC and its image △A′B′C′ are shown. Why is △A′B′C′ the translation image of △ABC?

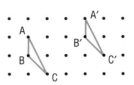

6. Suppose you needed to communicate information about the translations on this page to someone who speaks a different language.
   (a) In your journal, describe how you might communicate these translations.
   (b) Give reasons why you would use the method of communication you chose in (a).

15.3 TRANSLATIONS AND COORDINATES

In the previous section, you saw that symbols like [+4, +1] can be used to show a translation. In the diagram, ∆ABC is translated to form ∆A'B'C'.

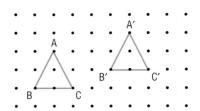

You can also use your skills with coordinates to represent translations and to explore the properties of translations.

ACTIVITY

Triangle XYZ and its image, ∆X'Y'Z', are shown.
(a) Write the coordinates of ∆XYZ and ∆X'Y'Z'. How are the corresponding coordinates related?
(b) Use the following to communicate the translation used: [■, ■]

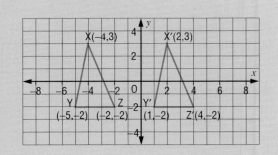

In the previous activity, you saw that the notation [+6, 0] can be used to communicate the translation. The following mapping can also be used to communicate the translation:
$(x, y) \rightarrow (x + 6, y)$.

The mapping above is read as "The coordinates of point (x, y) are mapped to the point $(x + 6, y)$." How are the two methods of communication alike? How are they different?

EXERCISE

B Use your skills with coordinates to explore the properties of translations.

1. A translation is applied to obtain the image of figure ABCDE.
   (a) Write the coordinates of corresponding points.
   (b) How are the x-coordinates related?
   (c) How are the y-coordinates related?
   (d) Complete the following mapping for the translation.
      $(x, y) \rightarrow (?, ?)$

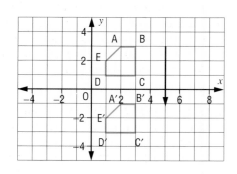

2. A translation is applied to obtain the image of figure PQRST. Repeat (a) to (d) in Question 1.

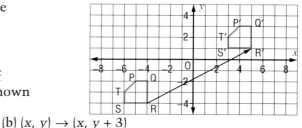

3. Find the coordinates of the image of each figure. Why do the mappings shown describe translations?
(a) $(x, y) \rightarrow (x - 2, y)$

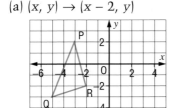

(b) $(x, y) \rightarrow (x, y + 3)$

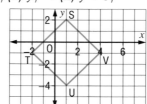

4. The mapping for a translation is given by $(x, y) \rightarrow (x + 1, y - 2)$. Find the coordinates of the image of each figure.

(a) (b)

5. Copy and complete the chart for each translation.

	Original point	Image point	Mapping
(a)	(2, 3)	(4, ?)	$(x, y) \rightarrow (x + ?, y - 3)$
(b)	(5, ?)	(?, 0)	$(x, y) \rightarrow (x - 2, y + 1)$
(c)	(3, 4)	(-6, ?)	$(x, y) \rightarrow (x - ?, y - 1)$
(d)	(-7, -8)	(?, -5)	$(x, y) \rightarrow (x + 1, y + ?)$

6. (a) Plot the points A(-3, 3), B(2, -2), and C(-6, -3). The *sense* of the points A, B, C written in order is *clockwise* (cw) and of A, C, B written in order is *counterclockwise* (ccw).
(b) Find the coordinates of A', B', and C' for the translation $(x, y) \rightarrow (x - 3, y + 2)$.
(c) Are the points A', B', and C' clockwise or counterclockwise?
(d) Choose a polygon of your own. Record the coordinates and repeat (a), (b), and (c).
(e) Write a probable conclusion about the sense of the vertices in a figure and its image under a translation.

7. Use the disks shown to the right.
(a) How can you arrange the disks so that all disks touch each other?
(b) Create a problem of your own that uses the five disks. Solve your problem. Compare your problem to those of others in the class.

483

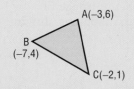

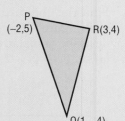

You have explored some of the relationships of translations. In this section, you will explore more relationships of translations on a coordinate grid.

EXPLORATION

For each question, refer to the diagrams shown at the right.

1. A translation given by
$(x, y) \rightarrow (x + 1, y - 2)$ is applied to $\triangle ABC$.
(a) Find the coordinates of A′, B′, and C′.
(b) Find the slopes of AA′, BB′, and CC′. What do you notice?

2. A translation given by $(x, y) \rightarrow (x - 2, y + 3)$ is applied to $\triangle PQR$.
(a) Find the coordinates of P′, Q′, and R′.
(b) Find the slopes of PP′, QQ′, and RR′. What do you notice?

3. Use your results in Questions 1 and 2. Write a probable conclusion.

4. Calculate each of the following distances. What do you notice?
(a) AA′, BB′, and CC′   (b) PP′, QQ′, and RR′
(c) What probable conclusion can you make?

5. Find the slopes of each pair of sides. What do you notice?
(a) AC and A′C′, AB and A′B′, BC and B′C′
(b) PQ and P′Q′, PR and P′R′, QR and Q′R′
(c) Write a probable conclusion about the slope of corresponding sides of a figure and its image under a translation.

6. Calculate the lengths of each pair of sides. What do you notice?
(a) AC and A′C′, AB and A′B′, BC and B′C′
(b) PQ and P′Q′, PR and P′R′, QR and Q′R′
(c) Write a probable conclusion about the length of corresponding sides of a figure and its image under a translation.

7. Compare the measures of each pair of angles. What do you notice?
(a) ∠BAC and ∠B′A′C′, ∠ABC and ∠A′B′C′, ∠BCA and ∠B′C′A′
(b) ∠PQR and ∠P′Q′R′, ∠PRQ and ∠P′R′Q′, ∠RPQ and ∠R′P′Q′
(c) Write a probable conclusion about the corresponding angles of a figure and its image under a translation.

8. (a) Draw $\triangle ABC$ and an image $\triangle A′B′C′$ so that AA′ is the same length as BB′ and also has the same length as CC′. What translation can you use to communicate how $\triangle ABC$ is moved to $\triangle A′B′C′$?
(b) Draw $\triangle PQR$ and an image $\triangle P′Q′R′$ so that PP′ ∥ QQ′, PP′ ∥ RR′, and QQ′ ∥ RR′. What translation can you use to communicate how $\triangle PQR$ is moved to $\triangle P′Q′R′$?
(c) Suppose you have two triangles that look as if they are translated images. What is the least number of measurements you need to make to ensure a translation was used? What are they?

A steady wind pushes a boat from its original position A to position B. The boat is *displaced* from A to B. A translation arrow is used to show the displacement.

At B, the wind changes and pushes the boat as shown.

The diagram shows the ship's original position, A, and its final position, C.

The translation arrow shows the displacement of the boat

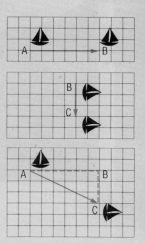

from A to C. The translation arrow represented by the arrow AC is called the **resultant displacement** of the arrow AB and the arrow BC.

1. Make a copy of each diagram. Find the resultant displacement for each of the following.

(a)  (b)  (c)  (d)

2. For each vessel, the original position is given and the translation arrows for each trip are shown.
   • Name the coordinates of the final position for each vessel.
   • Construct the resultant displacement for each.

   (a) A sailboat is at (0, 5).   (b) A tanker is at (3, 2).

       First part of trip.   Second part of trip.   First part of trip.   Second part of trip.

3. A cruise ship is at a port with coordinates (–3, –5). The translation arrows for 3 parts of the cruise are shown.

   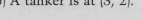

   (a) Find the coordinates of its final port.
   (b) Construct the resultant displacement for the cruise.
   (c) Rearrange the parts of the trip in different ways. Is the end result always the same?

As you have seen, a transformation involves a change in the position of an object.

ACTIVITY 1   *Work with a Partner*

Refer to the pictures above.
(a) How are the objects and the images alike? How are they different?
(b) What do you notice about the distance the object and the image appear to be from the mirror and the surface of the water?
(c) Suppose you could draw a line from the object to the image in each picture. What angle would the line make with the mirror or the water?

Earlier, you explored properties of reflections as shown below.

The reflection to the right is in the line LE. The line LE is called the **line of reflection**. A reflection in a line like LE has the following properties.

- Points P and P′ are **equidistant** (equally distant) from the line of reflection.
- The object and the image have a different sense.
- PP′ is perpendicular to the line of reflection. In other words, ∠PSE = 90°.

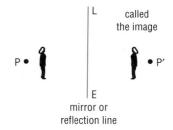

L — called the image

P •   • P′

E
mirror or reflection line

ACTIVITY 2

You can use the properties of a reflection to help you draw the image of an object after a reflection.
(a) In your journal, describe how this can be done.
(b) Use an example of your own to support your explanation in (a).

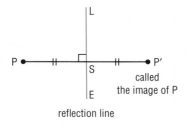

L

P •——||——□——||——• P′
              S   called
                     the image of P
E

reflection line

486

A Review your skills with transformations.

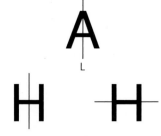

1. The letter A is a reflection of itself in RL. What other letters have this property?

2. The letter H can be reflected in two ways as shown.
   (a) What other letters have this property?
   (b) Show the letters in (a).

3. You will be able to read the following messages after they are reflected. (You may need a mirror, Mira, or a similar manipulative to help you.)

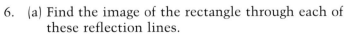

B Review the properties of transformations.

4. Make a copy of each figure and its corresponding reflection line, *l*. Use the properties of a reflection to construct each image.

(a) 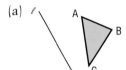 (b) 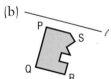 (c)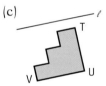

5. (a) Draw each triangle as shown. Reflect the triangles with respect to each of the reflection lines.
   (b) Draw a horizontal line through each triangle. Find the image of the triangle in the reflection line.
   (c) Draw a vertical reflection line through each triangle. Find the image of the triangle in the reflection line.

6. (a) Find the image of the rectangle through each of these reflection lines.
   (b) Draw any reflection line through your rectangle. Construct the reflection of the rectangle.

7. Reflections have been used to make each design below.
   (a) Make a copy of each design. How are reflection lines used for each?
   (b) Create a similar design of your own. Have others in the class decide how you used reflection lines to create your design.

 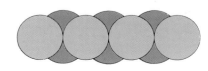

487

Points, and how they are related, are important concepts for scientists, engineers, and architects.

ACTIVITY 1

(a) What does the word "reflection" mean to you?
(b) Suppose you are an engineer. How do you think you would use reflections in your daily work?
(c) What other math skills do you think an engineer would need?

Previously, you saw that you can write a mapping to communicate a translation. You can also use a mapping to communicate a reflection, as shown in the following activity.

ACTIVITY 2   *Work with a Partner*

A triangle with vertices at P, Q, and R is reflected in the *y*-axis.
(a) Write the vertices of △PQR and △P'Q'R'.
(b) How are the vertices in (a) alike? How are they different?
(c) Describe a mapping to show how the image of △PQR is obtained.

In the activity above, △PQR was reflected in the *y*-axis. A mapping you can use to find the image of △PQR is shown $(x, y) \rightarrow (-x, y)$.

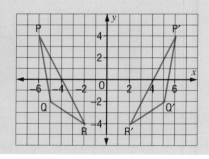

Point (x, y) is mapped onto $(-x, y)$.

ACTIVITY 3   *Work with a Partner*

(a) Draw a coordinate grid and place △ABC on the grid. What are the vertices?
(b) Draw the image of the triangle after a reflection in the *x*-axis. What are the coordinates of the vertices of △A'B'C'?
(c) Describe a mapping to show how the image of a triangle is obtained after a reflection in the *x*-axis.

B Review your skills with coordinate grids.

1. Draw a coordinate grid. Plot each of the following points and find the image of the point for the reflection line indicated.
   (a) (4, 1); x-axis (b) (−2, 5); x-axis (c) (7, −2); y-axis
   (d) (10, 5); y-axis (e) (−8, −7); x-axis (f) (5, 0); y-axis

2. Plot each figure on your own set of axes. Find the image of each figure by
   • reflecting it in the x-axis.
   • reflecting it in the y-axis.

   (a) 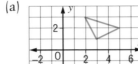   (b)

3. Find the coordinates of the image of each figure. Why do the mappings shown describe reflections?
   (a) $(x, y) \rightarrow (-x, y)$ (b) $(x, y) \rightarrow (y, -x)$ (c) $(x, y) \rightarrow (-x, -y)$

   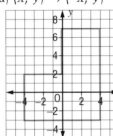   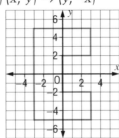   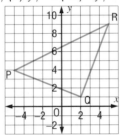

4. The mapping for a reflection is given by $(x, y) \rightarrow (-x, y)$. Find the coordinates of the image of each figure.

   (a) 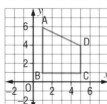   (b)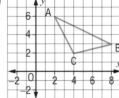

5. (a) Cut out an equilateral triangle from a piece of paper.
   (b) Fold the piece of paper so that the vertices all meet at one point inside the triangle.
   (c) What shape have you constructed by folding the paper in this way?
   (d) What transformation techniques can help you construct the figure in (c)?

   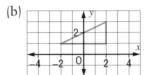

You have explored some of the relationships of reflections. In this section, you will explore more relationships of reflections on a coordinate grid.

EXPLORATION

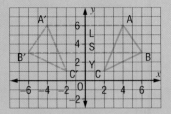

1. A triangle is reflected in the *y*-axis.
   (a) Compare the lengths of LA′ and LA, SB′ and SB, YC′ and YC. What do you notice?
   (b) Compare the measures of ∠A′LS and ∠ALS, ∠B′SY and ∠BSY, ∠C′YL and ∠CYL. What do you notice?

2. (a) Choose a figure of your own and draw it on a coordinate grid. Reflect the figure in the *x*-axis.
   (b) Based on your results, write a probable conclusion about the line of reflection and the segment joining a point and its image.

3. △ABC has coordinates A(2, 7), B(3, 1), and C(−4, 4).
   (a) Draw this triangle and reflect it in the *y*-axis.
   (b) Compare the slopes of AB and A′B′, BC and B′C′, CA and C′A′. What do you notice?
   (c) Compare the lengths of AB and A′B′, BC and B′C′, CA and C′A′. What do you notice?
   (d) Compare the measures of ∠A and ∠A′, ∠B and ∠B′, ∠C and ∠C′. What do you notice?

4. Based on your results in Question 3, write a probable conclusion about
   (a) the slopes of corresponding sides of a figure and its image.
   (b) the lengths of corresponding sides of a figure and its image.
   (c) the measures of corresponding angles of a figure and its image.

5. A quadrilateral PQRS has coordinates given by P(−6, 5), Q(−4, 8), R(−2, 2), and S(−7, −3).
   (a) Draw the figure and reflect it in the *y*-axis.
   (b) Compare the sense of the vertices of the original figure and the image. What do you notice?
   (c) Which coordinates, *x* or *y*, remain the same when reflected in the *y*-axis? Which coordinates would remain the same when reflected in the *x*-axis?

6. (a) Draw parallelogram ABCD with coordinates A(−4, 2), B(4, 1), C(2, −4), and D(−6, −3). Which sides are parallel?
   (b) Reflect parallelogram ABCD in the *y*-axis.
   (c) Compare the slopes of A′B′ and D′C′, A′D′ and B′C′. What do you notice?

7. (a) Refer to your results in the previous question. When a reflection is applied to a figure, what changes? What stays the same?
   (b) Compare your properties for reflections with your properties for translations. How are the properties alike? How are they different?

POOL

Skills with reflections can be applied to the game of pool. For example, to make the white cue ball hit the coloured ball you can deflect the white ball as shown. Obtain the image of the coloured ball by using the edge of the pool table as the reflection line.

The distance AB = AB'.

∠EAB = 90°

Then, to make the shot, shoot at the image ball.

1. For each diagram,
   - make a copy of the position of the balls.
   - draw a suitable construction so that the white ball reflects from edge PE to hit the coloured ball.

(a)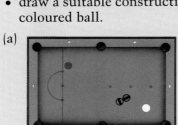

(b)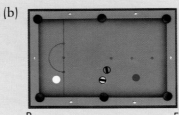

2. For each diagram,
   - make a copy of the diagram.
   - decide on the reflection edge.
   - draw a suitable construction so that the white ball hits the coloured ball.

(a)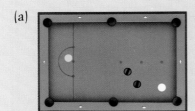

(b)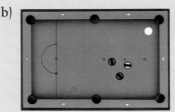

3. To make the white ball hit the coloured ball, you need to make a "two cushion" shot. (That is, you need to use 2 different reflecting edges.) For each, copy the diagram and draw a suitable construction.

(a)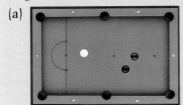

(b)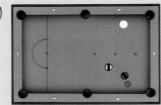

(c) What other factors are involved in deciding whether a shot will succeed?

The movement of the hands of a clock, the wheels of a bicycle, and the windshield wipers on a car are examples of rotations. In your journal, list three other examples of rotations.

ACTIVITY 1   *Work with a Partner*

(a) Describe why you might need to know about rotations to design a Ferris wheel (or a revolving restaurant).

(b) Describe what information you would need if you were to design a revolving dining room at the top of an observation tower.

When you explored rotations earlier, you used the following ideas:

1. The point about which the figure is turned is called the **centre of rotation** or the **turn centre**.
2. The amount of turn is called the **angle of rotation**.
3. The direction of the turn is either **clockwise** or **counterclockwise**.

A *turn arrow* is often used to communicate the direction of the turn and the amount of the turn, as shown below.

$\frac{1}{4}$ turn (90°)
counterclockwise

$\frac{1}{2}$ turn (180°)
clockwise

ACTIVITY 2

Once you know the information above, you can find the *image* for any *object* that has been rotated. For example, ΔPQR shown has been rotated 90° clockwise to give the image ΔP'Q'R'.

(a) In your journal, describe two other ways that you can communicate the rotation to others.

(b) Describe how you can find the image of an object after a rotation.

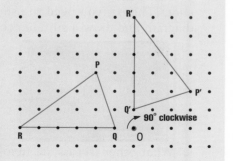

492

A Review how to communicate using transformations.

1. A figure is rotated about a turn centre T. Describe each rotation.

(a)

(b)

2. (a) Each letter of the message below has been rotated either 90° clockwise or 180° clockwise. The turn centres are indicated by a •. What is the message?

(b) Make a rotation message of your own. Have others in the class find what your message says.

B Review your skills with transformations.

3. A turn arrow is used to show each rotation. Copy each figure and use the turn arrow to find each image.

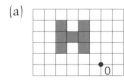 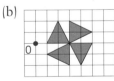 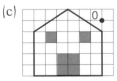

4. Find the image of each figure for a $\frac{1}{4}$ turn (90°) clockwise about the point O.

(a)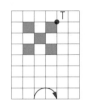

(b)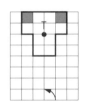

(c)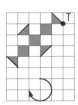

5. A rotation has been used to make the designs shown below.
   (a) Make a copy of each design.
   (b) How can you use the properties of rotations to construct each design?
   (c) Create a design of your own using rotations. Have others in the class decide how rotations were used to create your design.

A

B

C

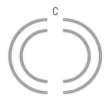

493

The following activity will extend your work with rotations to include a coordinate grid.

ACTIVITY 1   *Work with a Partner*

1. Triangle ABC has been rotated 90° about the origin to obtain △A′B′C′.
   (a) Write the coordinates for △ABC and △A′B′C′.
   (b) How are the coordinates for each triangle alike? How are they different?
   (c) Describe to your partner how you can obtain the image of △ABC after a rotation of 90°.

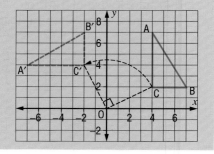

In the activity above, △ABC was rotated about the origin. A mapping you can use to find the image of △ABC is $(x, y) \rightarrow (-y, x)$.

Point (x, y) is mapped onto $(-y, x)$.

You can use the properties of rotations to show that one figure is the rotation image of another as shown in the following activity.

ACTIVITY 2   *Work with a Partner*

2. Copy the figure shown on the grid.
   (a) Rotate the figure 90° about the origin.
   (b) Join corresponding points on the object and image.
   (c) Construct the perpendicular bisector of the segments in (b). What do you notice?

3. (a) Repeat the steps of Question 2 for a rotation of 180° about the origin and a rotation of 270° about the origin.
   (b) Write a conclusion about the perpendicular bisectors of the segments joining corresponding points.

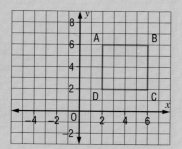

494

B Throughout this exercise, the centre of rotation is the origin.

1. The amount and direction of rotation can be expressed in three different forms. Complete the table.

90° cw (clockwise)	$\frac{1}{4}$ turn cw	−90°
90° ccw (counterclockwise)		
180° cw		
180° ccw		

2. Copy each figure. Draw its image for the given rotation about the origin.

(a) $\frac{1}{2}$ turn cw

(b) $\frac{1}{2}$ turn ccw

(c) $\frac{1}{4}$ turn ccw

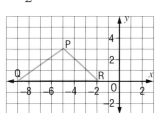
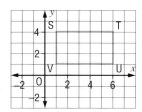
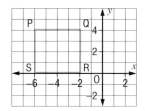

3. Copy each figure. Draw its image for the given rotation about the origin.
   (a) +90°   (b) −180°   (c) −90°

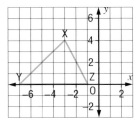
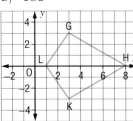
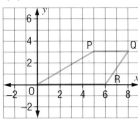

4. For each rotation in Questions 2 and 3, list the coordinates of the original figure and its image. Then write a mapping to show the rotation.

5. Use your results in Questions 2 to 4. If a figure is rotated about the origin for each angle of rotation, use a mapping to show the relation.
   (a) 90° cw   (b) 90° ccw   (c) 180° cw   (d) 180° ccw

PARTNER PROJECT

Have you ever heard that no two snowflakes are exactly alike? This may be true, but snowflakes do have a number of properties in common.
(a) Find pictures of different snowflakes.
(b) Describe how the snowflakes are alike and how they are different.
(c) Describe what properties of transformations all snowflakes have in common.
    Present your descriptions to the rest of the class.

You have explored some of the relationships of rotations. In this section, you will explore more relationships of rotations on a coordinate grid.

EXPLORATION

Questions 1 and 2 are based on the diagram to the right.

1. (a) Find the measure of ∠AOA′, ∠BOB′, and ∠COC′. What do you notice?
   (b) How do the measures in (a) compare to the measure of the angle of rotation?
   (c) Compare the lengths of OA and OA′, OB and OB′, OC and OC′. What do you notice?

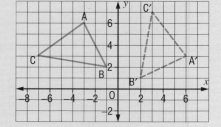

2. Compare the measures of the following. What do you notice?
   (a) corresponding angles   (b) corresponding sides

3. (a) Refer to your results in the previous questions. When △ABC is rotated to △A′B′C′, what changes? What stays the same?
   (b) Use other figures and rotate them to test your answer in (a).

4. △ABC has coordinates A(3, −2), B(7, −3), and C(4, −6). Find the coordinates of the image of △ABC for each of the following rotations.
   (a) 90° cw   (b) 90° ccw   (c) 180° cw   (d) 180° ccw
   (e) What do you notice about your answers in (c) and (d)?

5. Square ABCD has coordinates A(3, 3), B(3, −3), C(−3, −3), and D(−3, 3).
   (a) Rotate the square 90° clockwise about the origin. Plot the image points. What do you notice?
   (b) Repeat (a) for each of the following turns.
      (i) 180° cw   (ii) 270° cw   (iii) 360° cw

6. (a) Repeat the steps of the previous question using rectangle PQRS with coordinates P(4, 6), Q(4, −6), R(−4, −6), and S(−4, 6).
   (b) Compare your results in (a) with those for the square. How are your results alike? How are they different?

7. △ABC, with vertices A(−4, 1), B(−9, 2), C(−5, 6), is rotated 180° ccw about the origin.
   (a) Find the coordinates of A′, B′, and C′.
   (b) Compare the slopes of AB and A′B′, BC and B′C′, AC and A′C′. What do you notice?

SELF EVALUATION

   (a) Design a chart to summarize the relationships of transformations.
   (b) How are the relationships alike? How are they different?
   (c) What do you think is meant by a *congruence transformation*? Which of the transformations do you think is a congruence transformation?

DESIGN

A design in which one or more polygons are used to cover a plane is called a **tiling pattern.**

In this design the basic shape is an isosceles triangle. Translations and reflections are used to create the tiling pattern.

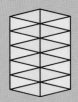

In this design a rhombus and an equilateral triangle are the basic shapes. Reflections are used to create the tiling pattern.

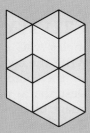

You can apply your skills with transformations to create designs. Many artists have used tiling patterns in their work. Maurits Cornelius Escher (1898–1972) used skills in geometry to create the famous design shown here.

©1967 M.C. Escher/Cordon Art–Baarn–Holland

To create a tiling pattern based on Escher's work, follow these steps.

- Start with a grid.
- Use the grid and repeat a construction
- Add some design and detail.

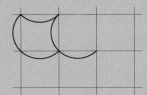
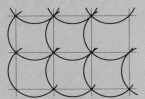

1. Use two of these shapes. Create a tiling pattern. Repeat with two other shapes.

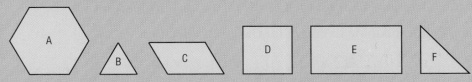

2. (a) How many different shapes can be made using four squares each sharing at least one common side?
   (b) Which of the shapes in (a) can be used to tile a plane?
   (c) Choose your own grid pattern. Create an "Escher" type tiling pattern.

15.14 DILATATIONS

Complete the following activity to explore another type of transformation.

ACTIVITY *Work with a Partner*

Triangles ABC and A′B′C′ are related.
(a) Write the coordinates for △ABC and △A′B′C′. How are the coordinates for each triangle connected?
(b) Describe to your partner how you can obtain the image of △ABC.
(c) Why do you think that this is not a *congruence transformation*?
(d) Predict what mapping has been used to map △ABC onto △A′B′C′.

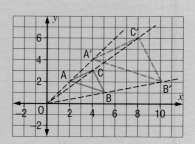

In the activity above, mapping △ABC onto △A′B′C′ in this way is a *dilatation*. A transformation that changes the size of a figure, either by making it larger or smaller, is called a **dilatation**. A mapping you can use to find the image of △ABC is $(x, y) \rightarrow (2x, 2y)$. Doubling the object coordinates shows that the *dilatation factor* above is 2.

EXERCISE

A Remember: Ask yourself: "How are the object and image alike? How are they different?"

1. Each of the following are sets of points in the original figure and the image for a dilatation. Use the pattern. Find the missing coordinates.

   (a) $(1, 3) \rightarrow (2, 6)$

   $(-2, 5) \rightarrow (-4, 10)$

   $(-2, 1) \rightarrow (?, 2)$
   $(x, y) \rightarrow (?, ?)$

   (b) $(-2, -4) \rightarrow (1, 2)$

   $(6, -2) \rightarrow (-3, ?)$

   $(?, -4) \rightarrow (1, ?)$
   $(x, y) \rightarrow (?, ?)$

   (c) $(3, 0) \rightarrow (1\frac{1}{2}, 0)$

   $(2, -1) \rightarrow (?, -\frac{1}{2})$

   $(5, 2) \rightarrow (?, ?)$
   $(x, y) \rightarrow (?, ?)$

2. What is the dilatation factor for each of the dilatations in Question 1?

3. Copy each figure and draw its image for the given dilatation.

   (a) $(x, y) \rightarrow \left(\frac{1}{2}x, \frac{1}{2}y\right)$

   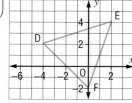

   (b) $(x, y) \rightarrow (3x, 3y)$

   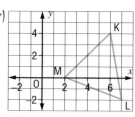

498

4. (a) Use a coordinate grid to draw an object. Give your partner a mapping to find the image.
   (b) Have your partner find the coordinates of the image and the dilatation factor.

B The questions below are based on the diagram. A dilatation $(x, y) \rightarrow (2x, 2y)$ is applied to △ABC to obtain △A′B′C′.

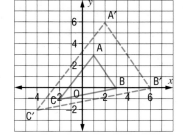

5. (a) Compare the lengths of AC and A′C′, BC and B′C′, AB and A′B′. What do you notice?
   (b) Compare the ratios $\dfrac{A'B'}{AB}$, $\dfrac{A'C'}{AC}$, and $\dfrac{B'C'}{BC}$.
   What do you notice?

6. (a) Compare the measures of corresponding angles. What do you notice?
   (b) Compare the areas of the triangles. What do you notice?

7. (a) Use your results in Questions 5 and 6. Why can you write △ABC ~ △A′B′C′ (△ABC is similar to △A′B′C′)?
   (b) Write a probable conclusion about your results.

8. (a) Compare the lengths of OA and OA′, OB and OB′, OC and OC′. What do you notice?
   (b) How is your answer in (a) related to your answer in Question 5?
   (c) Write a probable conclusion about your results.

9. (a) Compare the slopes of AC and A′C′, AB and A′B′, BC and B′C′. What do you notice?
   (b) Write a probable conclusion about your results.

10. Compare the sense of the vertices of the original and image triangle. (Are they clockwise or counterclockwise?)

11. △DEF has vertices D(2, 8), E(4, 4), and F(10, 2).
    (a) Find the coordinates of △D′E′F′ if the dilatation is given by $(x, y) \rightarrow \left(\dfrac{1}{2}x, \dfrac{1}{2}y\right)$.
    (b) Compare the lengths of corresponding sides. What do you notice?
    (c) Compare the measures of corresponding angles. What do you notice?
    (d) Compare the slopes of corresponding sides. What do you notice?
    (e) What is the dilatation factor?
    (f) What other lengths in your diagram are reduced by the dilatation factor in (e)?
    (g) Compare the sense of the vertices for the original and image triangle.
    (h) Compare the areas of the original triangle and the image triangle.

12. Refer to your results in the previous questions. When a dilatation is applied to a figure,
    (a) what changes?   (b) what stays the same?

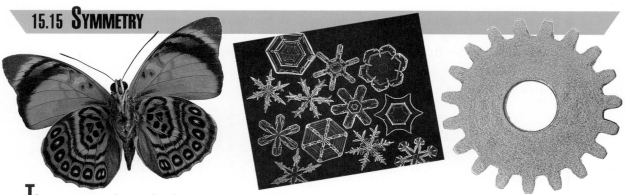

The pictures above display properties of *symmetry*. In your journal, predict what you think these properties might be. Then, complete the following activities to explore the properties of symmetry. How reasonable were your predictions?

ACTIVITY 1   *Work with a Partner*

(a) Trace the figures shown.
(b) Fold the figures as many times as you can so that one part of the figure folds exactly onto the other part.
(c) Unfold your paper and observe the folds. Each fold is a *line of symmetry*. How many lines of symmetry does each figure have?

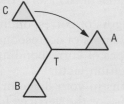

When a figure can be folded exactly onto itself, the figure has *line symmetry*.

ACTIVITY 2   *Work with a Partner*

The figures shown cannot be folded so that one part falls exactly onto the other.

(a) Trace each figure.
(b) Put the tracing on the figure in this book. Place a pin at T and turn each figure so that it is placed on top of itself. In how many different ways, in one complete turn, can the figure be placed on top of itself?
(c) When a figure can be placed on top of itself when turned, it has **rotational symmetry**. The number of times it can match its original position in one complete turn is called the **order of rotational symmetry**. What is the order of rotational symmetry of each figure?

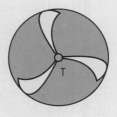

A Use tracing paper to help you.

1. How many lines of symmetry does each figure have?

   (a) 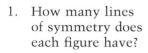 (b)  (c)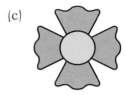

2. What is the order of rotational symmetry for each of the following figures?

   (a) 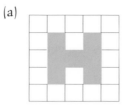 (b) 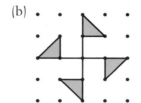 (c)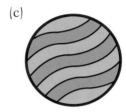

3. What type(s) of symmetry do each of the following figures have? In your journal, describe how you can determine the types of symmetry.

   (a)   (b)  (c)  (d)

B Work together.

4. Construct each figure and draw its lines of symmetry.

   (a) 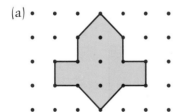 (b) 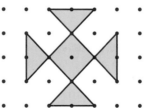 (c)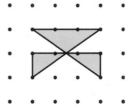

5. Construct each of the following types of figures. How many lines of symmetry does each figure have?
   (a) equilateral triangle   (b) square   (c) isosceles triangle   (d) rectangle

6. Squared paper has been used to create designs that have symmetry.
   (a) How many lines of symmetry does each design have?
   (b) Construct a design of your own. How many lines of symmetry does it have?

A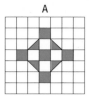

B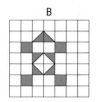

7. The figure shown on squared paper has rotational symmetry of order 4. Use squared paper to construct a figure for each.
   (a) A figure with rotational symmetry of order 3.
   (b) A figure with 2 lines of symmetry.
   (c) A figure for a description of your own.

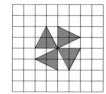

8. Figures are drawn with the following coordinates for vertices.
   • Draw each figure.
   • What type of symmetry does each figure have?
   • Indicate the order of rotational symmetry.
   • Draw all lines of symmetry.
   (a) S(–6, 4), T(–5, 1), U(–7, 1)
   (b) A(–4, 3), B(2, 3), C(2, –3), D(–4, –3)
   (c) P(4, 3), Q(1, 0), R(–3, 4), S(0, 7)

9. Refer to the logos A, B, ..., E.
   (a) Which logos have line symmetry? How many lines of symmetry are there?
   (b) Which logos have rotational symmetry? What is the order of rotational symmetry?
   (c) Which logos have both line symmetry and rotational symmetry?

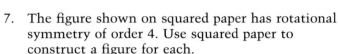

A	B	C	D	E

10. Each figure at the right fits onto itself after a half turn. Thus, each figure is said to have **point symmetry**.
    (a) Which figures in this section also have point symmetry?
    (b) Which figures in this section contain all three types of symmetry?
    (c) Design a figure of your own that has all three types of symmetry.

15.16 PUTTING IT ALL TOGETHER

The properties of transformations that you have found can be used to determine which transformation or transformations have been applied to a figure.

EXAMPLE

(a) What type of transformation maps ΔABC onto ΔA′B′C′? Be sure to give any information needed to identify the transformation.

(b) What is the mapping for the transformation?

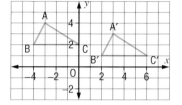

SOLUTION

(a) Think: From the diagram, it appears that the transformation is a translation. Examine the measures of the image and the original figure.

- Check whether AA′ = BB′ = CC′ sides are equal.
- Check whether the slopes of corresponding sides are equal.
- Check that AA′, BB′, and CC′ are parallel.

(b) The transformation is the translation given by the mapping $(x, y) \rightarrow (x + 6, y - 1)$.

Think: Is my answer reasonable?
Check: A(−3, 4) → A′(3, 3)
B(−4, 2) → B′(2, 1)
C(0, 2) → C′(6, 1) ✓

For translations, reflections, and rotations, the lengths of corresponding sides are congruent. Any transformation that preserves length is an **isometry**. Isometry is from Greek, *isos* meaning same, and *metria* meaning measure.

For an isometry, the original figure and the image are congruent. A dilatation is not an isometry since the original figure and the image are not congruent. The original figure and the image for a dilatation are similar in shape but not congruent.

EXERCISE

Ⓐ Summarizing properties is a useful skill for making comparisons to learn and remember properties.

1. Copy and complete the chart for translations, reflections, rotations, and dilatations. Use T (true) or F (false).

		Translations	Reflections
(a)	Corresponding sides are congruent.		
(b)	Corresponding angles are congruent.		
(c)	Slopes of corresponding sides are equal.		
(d)	The sense of the vertices is preserved.		
(e)	The image figure is congruent to the original figure.		
(f)	The transformation is related to a line of symmetry.		
(g)	The transformation is related to a centre.		

503

2. For each diagram, the original and image figures are given. Identify and describe each transformation.

(a)

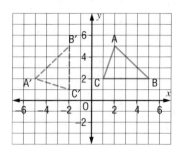

(b)

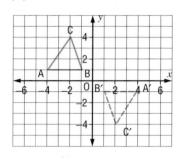

(c)

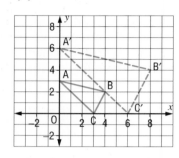

(d)

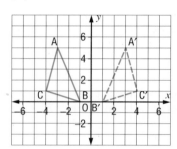

(e)

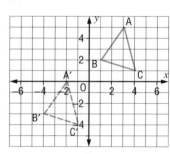

(f)

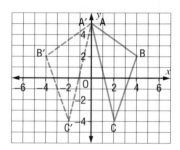

3. (a) For which transformations in Question 2 is the original triangle congruent to the image triangle?
   (b) Which of the above transformations are isometries?

4. Apply the following transformations to $\triangle ABC$ to find the image $\triangle A'B'C'$. Determine which type of transformation is represented.

   (a) $(x, y) \rightarrow (x - 2, y + 2)$ (b) $(x, y) \rightarrow (x, -y)$

   (c) $(x, y) \rightarrow \left(\frac{1}{2}x, \frac{1}{2}y\right)$ (d) $(x, y) \rightarrow (-y, x)$

   (e) $(x, y) \rightarrow (x - 3, y)$

   (f) reflected in the y-axis

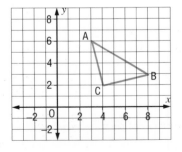

5. Refer to your results in the previous question.
   (a) For which transformations is $\triangle ABC$ congruent to its image triangle?
   (b) Which of the transformations are isometries?

6. (a) Describe each transformation related to △ABC.

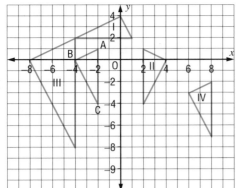

(b) Describe each transformation related to polygon PQRSTU.

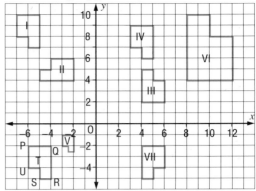

7. Which of the transformations in Question 6 are isometries?

8. Use sticks as shown.
   (a) Arrange the sticks to form exactly five equilateral triangles.
   (b) Arrange the sticks to form exactly four equilateral triangles.
   (c) Use the sticks to create a problem of your own. Solve your problem. Compare your problem to others in the class.

C

9. (a) How many different triangles are in this figure?
   (b) What properties of transformations can you describe in this figure?
   (c) Create a similar figure of your own. Have your partner answer (a) and (b) for your figure.

SELF EVALUATION

(a) Make a summary of the strategies you have learned for solving problems in this chapter.
(b) How can you use them to help organize your thoughts for solving any problem?
(c) Have you kept an updated list of all new words and terms you learned in this chapter? How can you use this list to help you review the chapter?

CHAPTER REVIEW

1. Draw a triangle as shown. Construct the image triangle with respect to each translation arrow.

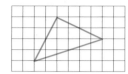

2. A translation given by $(x, y) \rightarrow (x - 3, y + 4)$ is applied to the square with coordinates A(5, –3), B(9, –1), C(7, 3), and D(3, 1). Find the coordinates of A′, B′, C′, and D′.

3. Find the image of △ABC in the reflection line ST.

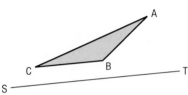

4. Make a copy of each figure. Use the turn arrow to find the image. Use the turn centre T.

(a) (b) 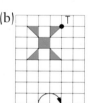 (c)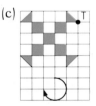

5. (a) Which logos have line symmetry? How many lines of symmetry are there?
   (b) Which logos have rotational symmetry? What is the order of the symmetry?
   (c) Which logos have both line and rotational symmetry?

A   B   C

THINKING ABOUT

❶ Is your *Problem Solving Plan* updated completely?

❷ Are your *Problem Solving Plan* and your journal organized well enough for you to use next year?

❸ Does your journal list all the skills and strategies you have learned this year?

MAKING CONNECTIONS

Refer to any picture in this chapter.
(a) Create a problem using the picture. Solve the problem.
(b) Compare your problem to others in the class. Solve the other problems.

❹ What have you learned this year to help you learn math more effectively?

❺ What have you learned this year to help you work with others more effectively?

❻ What have you learned this year to help you organize your work more effectively?

SELF EVALUATION

1. A translation has been used to make each design. How are translations used for each design? Make a copy of each design. How might you vary it effectively?

(a)   (b)

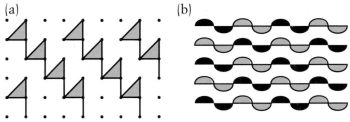

2. Square ABCD has coordinates A(−4, 3), B(3, 3), C(3, −4), and D(−4, −4).
   (a) Draw the image of square ABCD reflected in the x-axis.
   (b) Compare the sense of the vertices of the original figure and the image. (Are they clockwise or counterclockwise?)
   (c) Which coordinates, x or y, remain the same when a figure is reflected in the x-axis?
   (d) Which coordinates, x or y, remain the same when a figure is reflected in the y-axis?
   (e) Which points of the square remain fixed when you reflect it in the x-axis?
   (f) Which points of the square remain fixed when you reflect it in the y-axis?

3. A turn arrow is shown. Copy each figure. Find the image. Use the turn centre, T.

(a)   (b)

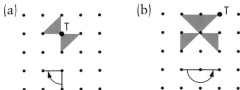

MATH JOURNAL

(a) How have your feelings towards mathematics changed this year?
(b) Which skill or strategy listed in your journal do you think is most helpful? Why?

4. The letter A is said to have a vertical line of symmetry.
   (a) Make a list of all the letters in the alphabet that have a vertical line of symmetry.
   (b) The word shown has a vertical line of symmetry. Write other words that have a vertical line of symmetry.

A
T
O
M
A
T
O

507

Extending Skills and Strategies

● ● ● ● ● ● ● ● ● ● ● ● ● ● ● ● ● ● ●

On the following pages you will find a selection of problems related to many of the sections within this book. (Solutions are provided at the end of the Answer section.)

You can use these pages in a variety of ways:
- by yourself, with a partner, or in a small group
- after each section, as confirmation that you have learned the skills in the section
- after each section, for extension and additional challenge
- after each chapter, for additional review or self evaluation
- after several chapters, as cumulative review, to help you see connections among math topics
- at the end of the year, as a year end review, to review and extend your skills

CHAPTER 1

Section 1.2

1. Karen made a series of long distance telephone calls last month. Her telephone bill showed the following charges: $1.98, $2.57, $1.83, $3.45. The bill was incorrectly totalled at $10.24.
   (a) What should the total be?
   (b) What was the amount of the overcharge?

2. Two pairs of shorts sell for $19.94. Dan bought four pairs of shorts and the total sales tax was $2.79. Dan has $45.00.
   (a) Does Dan have enough money to buy the shorts?
   (b) How much change will Dan get back?

3. A case of 48 cans of cat food costs $15.99.
   (a) Find the cost of 40 cans of cat food.
   (b) The sales tax is $1.25 on your purchase. What is the total cost?

4. Gary works at a local restaurant after school. One week his gross pay was $56.75 and he paid $9.35 in taxes. What was his take-home pay?

Section 1.3

1. A jumbo jet has 90 first class seats and 310 economy seats. There are 90 window seats in economy and 30 window seats in first class.
   (a) What is the total seating capacity of the jumbo jet?
   (b) What fraction of the seats in first class are window seats?
   (c) On a flight from Edmonton to Victoria, there were 265 passengers.
       (i) What fraction of the plane was full?
       (ii) If 72 passengers occupied window seats, what fraction of the window seats were occupied?

2. A small aircraft has a capacity of 85 passengers.
   (a) On a flight from Montreal to Fredericton, there were 34 passengers. What fraction of the plane was empty?
   (b) On a flight from Toronto to Sault Ste. Marie, there were 57 passengers. About what fraction of the plane was full?

3. A commercial airplane has a wing span of 59.2 m and a small aircraft has a wing span of 38.4 m.

   (a) How much shorter is the wing span of the small aircraft?
   (b) Write a fraction to compare the wing span of the small aircraft to that of the commercial airplane.

Section 1.4

Refer to the pizza price list shown on page 38 in Chapter 1 for the following exercises.

1. Calculate the cost of each pizza.
   (a) a medium pizza with mushrooms, bacon, and onions
   (b) a small pizza with pepperoni, green peppers, onions, and mushrooms
   (c) an extra large pizza with tomatoes, ham, anchovies, hot peppers, and green olives

2. What would be the average cost per person for each of the following pizza orders?
   (a) Four people ordered a large pizza with ham, green peppers, and tomatoes.
   (b) Nine people ordered an extra large pizza with pineapple, ham, pepperoni, and onions.
   (c) Six people split three medium pizzas with salami, green peppers, and mushrooms.

3. The 25 Student Council members ordered
   • three extra large pizzas with pepperoni, mushrooms, bacon, and onions.
   • five extra large pizzas with ham, pineapple, onions, and mushrooms.
   • four large pizzas with anchovies, onions, and tomatoes.
   • two medium pizzas with salami, hot peppers, and onions.
   Calculate the cost per person.

4. How many pizzas can you order if you use the following ingredients?
   (a) anchovies, onions, and mushrooms
   (b) green peppers, bacon, pepperoni, and green olives
   (c) pepperoni, hot peppers, onions, mushrooms, and tomatoes

Section 1.5

1. Alice, Brad, Cheryl, and David are four friends who have joined the swim team, the soccer team, the rowing team, and the chess team. Alice and Cheryl enjoy water sports. Brad is

afraid of the water. David and Alice enjoy individual challenges.
(a) Which team did each person join?
(b) List any assumptions you make in (a).

2. The area north of the Arctic Circle has periods of constant daylight during the summer. If there are 1752 h of constant daylight, how many consecutive days would this be?

3. A crate of raspberries holds 48 boxes. A shipment has 5325 crates. If 500 crates are going to Mississauga, how many boxes of raspberries are left in the shipment?

4. How many different line segments are there in the diagram?

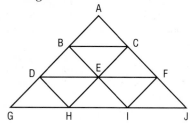

Section 1.7
1. For each of the following first estimate your answer, then calculate the actual answer. How close was your estimate?
   (a) $12.84 + $3.72 + $24.05 + $2.38
   (b) 6 tins of apple juice for $1.19 each
   (c) 9 kg of ground meat for $3.63/kg

2. The equipment manager of a hockey team purchased the following for next season.
   22 helmets $19.60 each
   15 pairs of pants $28.40 each
   28 sticks $12.20 each
   (a) Estimate the total cost of the equipment.
   (b) Calculate the exact total cost of the equipment.
   (c) How close was your estimate in (a)?

3. The local fast food restaurant has the following items on the menu.
   Hamburger $1.95
   Fries $1.45
   Hot Dog $1.65
   Milkshake $1.29

Estimate the cost of each bill. Then calculate the actual cost.
(a) 4 fries, 3 milkshakes
(b) 6 hamburgers, 4 fries
(c) 8 hot dogs, 5 milkshakes, 3 fries
(d) 5 hamburgers, 2 fries, 4 milkshakes, 2 hot dogs

Section 1.8
1. Use a calculator.
   (a) Find the decimal equivalent for $\frac{1}{99}$, $\frac{2}{99}$, and $\frac{3}{99}$.
   (b) Predict the decimal equivalent for $\frac{4}{99}$, $\frac{5}{99}$, and $\frac{6}{99}$. Verify your predictions using a calculator.

2. A calculator was used to evaluate each expression. Which of the answers are reasonable? Verify each one.
   (a) $756 + 264 + 195 = 1215$
   (b) $256 - 138 + 485 = 475$
   (c) $23.67 - 12.83 - 4.15 = 8.69$
   (d) $25.83 \times 1.45 - 16.04 = 21.4135$
   (e) $74.66 \div 3.42 + 43.29 = 68.375$
   (f) $12.45 \times 3.56 + 84.72 \div 3.57 = 68.0531$

3. For each of the following estimate an answer. Then, use a calculator to verify your answer.
   (a) Find the difference of 963.2 from 794.4.
   (b) What is the total of 486, 9832, 19 632, and 8?
   (c) By how much does the product of 932 and 4.9 exceed the quotient of 153.6 and 48?

Section 1.9
1. Convert each fraction to an equivalent decimal number.
   (a) $\frac{3}{7}$ (b) $\frac{7}{12}$ (c) $\frac{23}{36}$ (d) $\frac{35}{75}$
   (e) $\frac{54}{79}$ (f) $\frac{11}{85}$ (g) $\frac{92}{104}$ (h) $\frac{121}{154}$

2. Use a calculator to help you decide which fraction is smaller.
   (a) $\frac{34}{21}$, $\frac{22}{64}$ (b) $\frac{43}{49}$, $\frac{3}{4}$ (c) $\frac{37}{51}$, $\frac{27}{62}$
   (d) $\frac{3}{7}$, $\frac{21}{28}$ (e) $\frac{321}{122}$, $\frac{158}{734}$ (f) $\frac{163}{512}$, $\frac{254}{739}$

3. To calculate the batting average, A, for a baseball player, you use the formula

$A = \dfrac{h}{b}$ where h is the number of hits and b is the number of times at bat. Calculate the batting average for each player to three decimal places.

	Player	Number of Times at Bat, b	Number of Hits, h
(a)	Burbett	556	235
(b)	Hornsby	504	203
(c)	Musial	625	228
(d)	Mays	565	195
(e)	Rose	627	210

Arrange the players in order, from the player with the best batting average to the player with the worst batting average.

CHAPTER 2

Section 2.2

1. Use the methods described in Section 2.2 to make a copy of each angle.

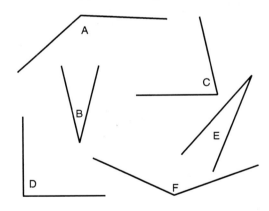

2. Use only a straight edge and a pair of compasses for the following constructions.
   (a) Draw an angle.
   (b) Make a copy of the angle.
   (c) Make an angle which is twice the size of the angle in (a).
   (d) Make an angle which is three times the size of the angle in (a).
   (e) Measure the angles in (a), (b), (c), and (d) with a protractor. How accurate are your constructions?

3. The measures of two angles are shown.

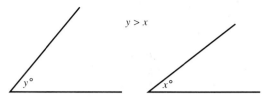

Construct angles that have the following measures.
   (a) $2x$ (b) $2y$ (c) $x + y$
   (d) $y - x$ (e) $2(x + y)$ (f) $2y - x$

Section 2.3

1. Refer to Section 2.2, Question 1.
   (a) What is the name of each angle?
   (b) Estimate the size of each angle. Then measure. How reasonable was your estimate?

2. The speedometer shown indicates that a car is travelling at 50 km/h. Find the number of degrees through which the needle has rotated.

3. Refer to the speedometer in Question 2.
   (a) The speedometer of a car registers 90 km/h. What angle is shown by the needle?
   (b) What angle is shown by each speed?
      • 30 km/h   • 65 km/h

4. Use the diagram.
   (a) Name each angle.
   (b) Estimate the measure of each angle.
   (c) Measure each angle. How reasonable is your estimate?

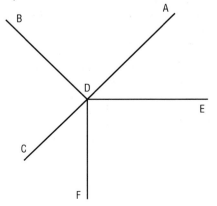

Section 2.4

1. (a) Construct ∆GEH as shown in the sketch.

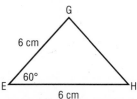

(b) Without measuring, what would you predict the measure of ∠EGH, ∠EHG, and GH to be?

(c) Measure ∠EGH, ∠EHG, and GH. How do your measures compare with your prediction in (c)?

(d) What type of triangle is ∆GEH?

2. A sketch is drawn of ∆ABC.

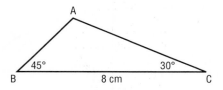

(a) Construct ∆ABC.

(b) What would you expect the measure of ∠BAC to be?

(c) Measure ∠BAC in the triangle you constructed. How does your measure compare to your answer in (b)?

(d) What type of triangle is ∆ABC?

3. (a) Construct ∆CEF so that ∠CEF = 90° and CE = EF = 8 cm.

(b) Without measuring, predict the measures of ∠ECF and ∠EFC.

(c) Measure ∠ECF and ∠EFC. How close are your measures to your prediction in (b)?

(d) What type of triangle is ∆CEF?

4. Sketch each of the following triangles.

(a) an obtuse isosceles triangle

(b) a scalene right triangle

(c) an acute scalene triangle

(d) an equilateral triangle

Section 2.5

1. Use the following steps to bisect an angle using a Mira.

(a) Draw an angle. Label it ∠ABC.

(b) Place a Mira at the vertex ∠ABC and rotate the Mira so that the arm of the angle facing you aligns with the arm behind the Mira.

(c) Draw a line along the Mira from the vertex out. Label it D.

(d) Check your work. Is ∠ABD = ∠DBC?

2. Bisect each angle by using

(a) a pair of compasses and a straight edge.

(b) tracing paper.　　　(c) a Mira.

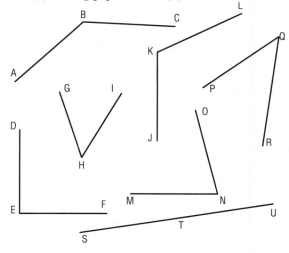

3. Construct an angle of each degree measure.

(a) 105°　　(b) 80°　　(c) 135°

(d) $22\frac{1}{2}^{\circ}$　　(e) $17\frac{1}{2}^{\circ}$　　(f) 225°

Section 2.7

1. Draw line segments similar in position to those which are shown below. Construct a perpendicular to AB passing through C.

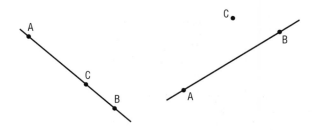

2. (a) Draw a line segment 15 cm in length.
   (b) Construct the right bisector of the line segment.
   (c) What is the measure of each segment? Check by measuring.

3. Draw any line segment. How would you find $\frac{1}{8}$ of the line segment?

4. (a) Draw a regular hexagon. Construct the right bisector of each side of the hexagon.
   (b) What do you notice about the lines?

5. (a) Draw △ABC with these dimensions.
       AB = 6 cm, BC = 6 cm, ∠B = 90°
   (b) Construct the bisector of AB. Measure how far the midpoint of AC is from the vertex B.

Section 2.11

1. Find the missing measures. All linear measures are in centimetres.

   (a)   (b)

             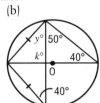

   (c)   (d)

   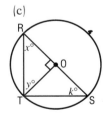   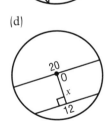

2. Study the diagram.

   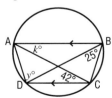

   (a) Why is ∠ACD = ∠CAB?
   (b) Why is ∠DBC = ∠DAC?
   (c) Find the missing measures.

3. The circumcircle of a triangle is the circle that passes through all the vertices of the triangle.

   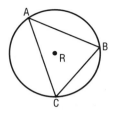

   (a) Why is R on the right bisector of AB?
   (b) Why is R on the right bisector of CB?

4. ST is a diameter of the circle with centre O. Find the following measures. All linear measures are in centimetres.

   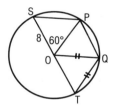

   (a) ∠SPO   (b) ∠OPQ   (c) ∠OQT
   (d) OP   (e) PQ

CHAPTER 3

Section 3.2

1. What is the sum of the following?
   (a) a rise of 18, a fall of 5
   (b) a gain of 13, a loss of 22
   (c) an increase of 19, a decrease of 4
   (d) 37 steps forward, 16 steps backward

2. Find the sums.
   (a) −4 + 6 + (−3)
   (b) 13 + (−14) + (−3)
   (c) (−4) + (−16) + (−22)
   (d) 22 + (−38) + 12 + (−21) + 17
   (e) (−64) + (−42) + 29 + 45 + (−19)

3. Find the new temperature for each of the following.
   (a) −42°C, change of −5°C
   (b) 12°C, change of 8°C
   (c) −26°C, change of −11°C
   (d) 19°C, change of 12°C
   (e) 23°C, change of −7°C

4. In hockey, players' performances are shown by their plus-minus scores, which are the sum of their plus scores and their minus scores. Copy and complete the chart to find each player's plus-minus record.

	Player	Plus	Minus	Plus-Minus Record
(a)	James	+18	−20	?
(b)	Henry	+43	−18	?
(c)	Carol	+8	−26	?
(d)	Karl	+30	−42	?
(e)	Mitzi	+76	−38	?

5. In a six-round golf tournament, the following scores were recorded. The winner of the tournament had the lowest score. List the players from lowest to highest.

Jeff	+3, +1, −2, −1, −1, +2
Joelle	−1, −1, 0, +1, −2, −1
Lesley	+2, −1, 0, −1, +1, +1
Michael	−2, +1, 0, −1, +1, 0
Lori	−1, +1, 0, −1, −1, 0

Section 3.3

1. Find the difference.
   (a) (+7) − (−5)   (b) (−8) − (−7)
   (c) (3) − (−1)   (d) (+9) − (−7)
   (e) (−14) − (+3)   (f) (−10) − (−6)
   (g) (+17) − (+10)   (h) 0 − (−12)
   (i) (+15) − 0   (j) (+7) − (−7)
   (k) (−4) − (−4)   (l) (−8) − (+8)

2. Subtract.
   (a) −3 from 13   (b) −8 from 11
   (c) 6 from −12   (d) −3 from −12
   (e) 30 from 19   (f) 25 from 31
   (g) −26 from −71   (h) −12 from 24

3. Find the value of $x − y$ for each pair of values.
   (a) $x = 34, y = 41$ (b) $x = 33, y = −54$
   (c) $x = −23, y = −51$ (d) $x = 61, y = −48$
   (e) $x = −72, y = 19$ (f) $x = 52, y = −82$

4. Replace ☐ with either < or >.
   (a) 43 − (−32) ☐ −52 − 14
   (b) 59 − (−37) ☐ −53 − (−24)
   (c) 95 − (−43) ☐ 64 − (−55)
   (d) −32 − (−73) ☐ −33 − (−29)

5. A balloon was released to record temperatures of the atmosphere. The results are shown. Find the change in temperature as the balloon rose from
   (a) S to B. (b) B to D. (c) D to E. (d) S to E.

6. Use the results from the previous question. Which is the greatest change?
   (a) S to B   (b) B to C   (c) C to D   (d) D to E

Section 3.5

1. Copy and complete the table of values.

a	−2	−7	+3	−8	+4
b	−3	+5	+8	+3	−6
$a − b$					
$b − a$					

2. Evaluate. Read carefully.
   (a) 2 − 3 + 4   (b) 3 + 7 + (−8)
   (c) −9 + 2 − (−2)   (d) 8 − 3 − (−3)
   (e) 4 − (−2) + 8   (f) −9 + (−3) − (−2)
   (g) −24 + 19 − 9   (h) −13 − (−12) + (−5)
   (i) −22 + 32 − (−21) + 5 − 12
   (j) −11 − 36 + (−18) − (−37) + 16 − (−14)
   (k) 37 − (−26) + 13 − 59 − (−56) + (−29)

3. Calculate each of the following.
   (a) Find the sum of −3, 2, −8, 5, and 4.
   (b) Which has the larger difference: −3 − 8 or 8 − (−3)?
   (c) Subtract the sum of −2 and 3 from −8.
   (d) How much more is 4 − (−3) than −8 + (−6)?
   (e) How much less is the sum of −3 and −4 than 4 − (−2)?
   (f) By how much does 2 + (−3) exceed −3?

4. The price of silver on September 1 was $16. The weekly changes in price are given as follows:

September 8	+$2
September 15	−$3
September 22	−$1
September 29	−$2

What was the price of silver on September 29?

5. A common toad has been found in a coal mine at a depth of −340 m. The plant with the deepest roots was a fig tree. Its roots were

discovered to have grown to a depth 118 m higher than where the toad was found. At what depth were the roots of the tree?

Section 3.6

1. Find each product.
   (a) $(+3) \times (-2)$
   (b) $(-5) \times (+3)$
   (c) $(-6) \times (-1)$
   (d) $(+9) \times (+4)$
   (e) $(+12) \times (-3)$
   (f) $(-25) \times (-5)$
   (g) $(-16) \times (+11)$
   (h) $(+14) \times (-21)$
   (i) $(+17) \times (+16)$
   (j) $(-20) \times 0$

2. Copy and complete the following chart.
   $(-3) \times (-1) = +3$
   ↓

×	−4	−3	−2	−1	0	+1	+2
−3				+3			
−2			+4				
−1							
0						0	
+1		−3					
+2			−4				

   ↑
   $(+2) \times (-2) = -4$

3. Use the chart from Question 2.
   (a) Which parts of the chart have negative answers? Why?
   (b) Which parts of the chart have positive answers? Why?
   (c) Which parts of the chart have zero answers? Why?

4. An object is falling at a rate of 2 km/s.
   (a) Use integers to show how to obtain the distance the object fell in 45 s.
   (b) If the object started falling from a height of 300 km, how far has it fallen in 45 s?

Section 3.7

1. Find the product.
   (a) $(-2) \times (-3)$
   (b) $0 \times (-5)$
   (c) $(+5) \times (-7)$
   (d) $(+7) \times (-1)$
   (e) $(-23) \times (+1)$
   (f) $(+37) \times (-10)$

2. Find the product.
   (a) $(-17) \times (+42) \times (-12)$
   (b) $(+21) \times (-32) \times (+25)$
   (c) $(-32) \times (+52) \times 0$
   (d) $(+45) \times 0 \times (-34)$

   (e) $0 \times (-42) \times (-34)$
   (f) $(-36) \times (-24) \times (+1)$

3. Copy and complete the charts to find the product of p and q.

p	+13	−25	0	+4	−3	−32	+16
q	−22	+31	−13	+6	−4	−9	+4
$p \times q$	?	?	?	?	?	?	?

4. You can use patterns to solve some problems. Study the pattern below.
   $(-1)^2 = +1, (-1)^3 = -1, (-1)^4 = +1, (-1)^5 = -1$
   (a) Which sign, + or −, can you use to complete each of the following?
   $(-1)^m = \square$ if m is an even number
   $(-1)^m = \square$ if m is an odd number
   (b) Evaluate each of the following.
   (i) $(-1)^{491}$ (ii) $(-1)^{1732}$ (iii) $(-1)^{3000}$

5. Use the integers shown and the signs +, −, ×, and = to make a true statement.
   (a) −4, −6, −10
   (b) −6, +3, −9
   (c) +5, +2, −3
   (d) −2, −4, +1

Section 3.8

1. Find the value of $\square$ in each of the following.
   (a) $\dfrac{+36}{+6} = \square$
   (b) $\dfrac{-36}{+6} = \square$
   (c) $\dfrac{+36}{-6} = \square$
   (d) $\dfrac{-36}{-6} = \square$
   (e) $\dfrac{-56}{+8} = \square$
   (f) $\dfrac{+56}{-8} = \square$
   (g) $\dfrac{-56}{-8} = \square$
   (h) $\dfrac{+56}{+8} = \square$

2. Refer to your results in the previous question.
   (a) When are your answers positive?
   (b) When are your answers negative?
   (c) Use your answers in (a) and (b) to help you decide whether the answer to each of the following is positive or negative.
   (i) $\dfrac{+55}{+11}$ (ii) $\dfrac{+55}{-11}$ (iii) $\dfrac{-55}{+11}$ (iv) $\dfrac{-55}{-11}$

3. Copy and complete the following chart to find $p \div q$.

p	+14	−25	0	+24	−32	−36	+16
q	−2	+5	−13	+6	−4	−9	+4
$p \div q$	?	?	?	?	?	?	?

4. Where in Canada was one of the coldest temperatures ever recorded?
To find the answer, find the values of the variables below. Then arrange your answers from least to greatest. The variables spell the place.

(a) $(-5)(+2) = E$
(b) $R \div (-2) = +2$
(c) $F \div (-2) = +9$
(d) $G \div (-4) = -2$
(e) $-8 + (-6) = L$
(f) $(-8) \div A = -2$
(g) $-12 - E = -6$
(h) $(-3)(-5) = B$
(i) $(B)(+2) = -16$
(j) $10 - (-12) = Y$
(k) $0 - (-4) = -8$

Section 3.9

1. Find the average of each of the following integers.
(a) −15, −11, 8
(b) −23, 21, −19, −18, 14
(c) −6, −4, 18, 19, 15, −12, 17, 1
(d) 21, 17, 2, 15, 3, −6, 7, 8, 14, 19

2. The temperatures of four Eastern Canada locations are recorded below:

Summerville, P.E.I.	−9°C
New Glasgow, N.S.	−12°C
Bayfield, N.B.	−6°C
Torbay, Nfld.	−5°C

(a) What is the average temperature?
(b) How much more is the average temperature than the temperature at New Glasgow?
(c) How much less is the average temperature than the temperature at Torbay?

3. The minimum average temperatures recorded for each of the following deserts are:

Mojave −14°C   Australian 21°C
Sahara 1°C   Kalahari −3°C
Mongolian −26°C

Calculate the average of these temperatures.

Section 3.12

1. Evaluate each of the following.
(a) $48 \div (-6) + 3$
(b) $43 + 12 \div (-2)$

(c) $(-8)(-5) \div 2$
(d) $(-14) \div 2 - 6$
(e) $8 \div (-4) + 4 \div (-2)$
(f) $(-12) \div (-6) + (-3)(-2)$
(g) $36 \div (-4) - 9$
(h) $(-3)(-3) + (-5)(-7)$

2. Calculate.
(a) $(-3)^2 + (-4)^2$
(b) $(-8)^2 - 3^2$
(c) $-2^2 - (-4)(-2)$
(d) $(-4)^2 + (-8) \div (-4)$
(e) $(-3)^2 + (-16) \div (+4)$
(f) $(-8 + 2) \div (-3 + 2)$

3. Find the value of each of the following expressions. Which steps can you do mentally?
(a) $-9 - 3[2(2 - 3)]$
(b) $-4[(-3)(-4) + 5]$
(c) $120 - 4[3(-5 + 4) + 5]$
(d) $160 \div (-16) + 5[3(6 - 3)]$
(e) $(26 - 18 - 4 - 10) \div (-6)$
(f) $[(-3)(-2) + (-8)(-2)] \div (-2)$
(g) $-3[(-4)^2 + (-3)^2 + (-5)^2]$
(h) $46 \div [3(2 - 4) - 2(3 - 5)]$

4. Calculate.

(a) $\dfrac{-24 - 6}{-6 - 4}$
(b) $\dfrac{(4 - 6)\,(-4)}{16 \div (-2)}$
(c) $\dfrac{-6 + (-6)\,(-6)}{(-2) + (-3)}$
(d) $\dfrac{7\,(-3)(-12)}{-16 \div (-2)}$
(e) $\dfrac{-40 \div 4 - 2}{-12 \div (6 + 6)}$
(f) $\dfrac{-2 - 3}{3 - 2}$

5. Evaluate each of the following expressions.
(a) $(9 - 3 - 12 - 6) \div (-3)$
(b) $40 \div (-4) - 2 + 2(-8 \div 2)$
(c) $-3 + 14[(-2) + (-3)] - 22$
(d) $92 \div [6(2 - 4) - 4(3 - 5)]$

Section 3.13

1. Find the value of each of the following.
(a) $|-11|$ (b) $|+12|$ (c) $|-24|$
(d) $|-87|$ (e) $|-1|$ (f) $|0|$

2. Simplify.
(a) $3|-2| + 2|-6| - 3|8 - 5|$
(b) $3|8 - 3| + 2|4 - 8| - 6|9 - 12|$
(c) $|4 - 2| + |2 - 6| + |8 - 5|$
(d) $|6 - 9| + 2|3 - 4| + |6 - 1|$

3. Use <, >, or = in place of ☐ to make each of the following true.
   (a) |–3 + 8| ☐ |–8 + –5|
   (b) |–2 + 6| ☐ |–2| + |6|
   (c) |–2 – 3| ☐ |–2| + |–3|
   (d) |–5 + 3| ☐ |–5| + |3|
   (e) |–7 + 4| ☐ |–7| + |4|
   (f) |–3 – (–2)| ☐ |(–5) – (–3)|
   (g) |(+8) – 7| ☐ |(–3) – (–5)|
   (h) 3|9 – (–2)| ☐ |(–4) + (–2)|
   (i) |9 – 6| ☐ 4|(–3) + (–5)|
   (j) 3|(–2) + (–7)| ☐ 4|(–5) + 2|

4. If $x = -1$, $y = 3$, and $z = -2$, find the value of each of the following.
   (a) $|x| - |y|$ (b) $|x - y|$
   (c) $|x| + |y|$ (d) $|x + y|$
   (e) $|x + y + z|$ (f) $|x| + |y| + |z|$
   (g) $2|x| + 3|y|$ (h) $|2x + 3y|$
   (i) $|x + y| xz$ (j) $|x + y|z$
   (k) $|x + y| + |z|$ (l) $|xy| - |yz|$

Section 3.14

1. Refer to the graph below. Name the coordinates of each point shown by a letter.

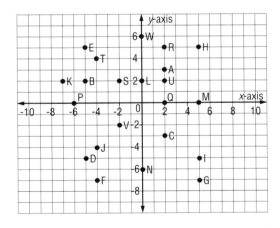

2. On a coordinate grid, mark any two points on the boundary of
   (a) the second and first quadrant.
   (b) the third and fourth quadrant.
   (c) the first and fourth quadrant.
   (d) the second and third quadrants.
   Write the coordinates of each of the points you marked.

3. The coordinates of three vertices of a square are shown below.
   A (3, –3)   B (3, 7)   C (–7, 7)
   (a) Plot the vertices on a coordinate grid.
   (b) Find the coordinates of the missing vertex.

4. The graph of ordered pairs is shown.

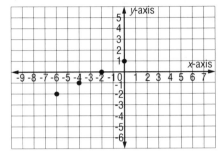

   (a) Write another ordered pair that would seem to fit the pattern.
   (b) Write an ordered pair with both coordinates negative that would seem to fit the pattern.

5. (a) Draw a graph of the following ordered pairs.
   (–1, 0)   (1, 2)   (0, 1)   (3, 4)
   (b) Use your graph in (a) to predict another ordered pair that would seem to fit the pattern.

CHAPTER 4

Section 4.3

1. (a) Use algebra tiles to represent each expression.
   (i) $7a$ and $-2a$ (ii) $-4x$ and $3x$
   (iii) $12m$ and $-9m$ (iv) $-y$ and $15y$
   (v) $-11y$ and $3y$ (vi) $6b$ and $4b$
   (b) Find the net result of each expression in (a).
   (c) Evaluate each expression using 3.2 as the value of the variable.

2. Simplify each expression.
   (a) $3x – 5x$ (b) $-4b + 6b$ (c) $-x + 5x$
   (d) $-16y – 3y$ (e) $4c – 10c$ (f) $21x + 5x$
   (g) $31x – 52x$ (h) $-3y – 83y$ (i) $48a – 12a$

3. Simplify each expression.
   (a) $3x – 4y + 2y – 7x$
   (b) $-18y + 4x – 17x + y$
   (c) $22x – 56y + 16x – 11y$
   (d) $28y – 15x – 4x + 23y – y + x$
   (e) $31x – 31y – 29y + 18x + y$

4. Evaluate each expression in Question 3 for $x = 2.5$ and $y = 1.6$.

5. Use $a = -1$, $b = 2$, and $c = 3$.
   (a) Estimate which expression, A, B, or C, has the least value.
   (b) Calculate which has the least value.
   A: $18a + 32b - 26a - 2b + 3c$
   B: $-19a - 23b + 7a - 16b + 32a - 37c + 14c$
   C: $a^2 - 6a + 2a^2 - 3a^2 - 8 + 7a + 8$

6. (a) Round the values given and estimate the value of each expression.
   (b) Find the value of each expression to one decimal place for the given values.
   (c) Use a calculator to check your answers.
   A: $3x + 2y - 4x + 5y$ $x = 3.6$, $y = 4.9$
   B: $x^2 - 3y^2 - 2x^2 + y^2$ $x = 2.5$, $y = -3.1$
   C: $4m + 6n - 7m + 5n$ $m = 4.69$, $n = -3.62$

Section 4.4

1. Identify the like terms and the unlike terms.
   (a) $2y, -3x, 5y, x, -3b$
   (b) $-4y, 3x, b, 3y, -2x$
   (c) $x^2, -3y^2, 5x, -y^2, 3x^2$
   (d) $-7y^2, 2, 6x, 4, 8y^2$

2. The cost, C, in cents, of making cards is given by $C = 125 + 2n$ where n is the number of cards. Calculate the cost of making each number of cards.
   (a) 100   (b) 150   (c) 200   (d) 1000

3. The cost of renting a car, C, in dollars is given by $C = 21t + 0.12d + 9.50$ where t is the time in days and d is the distance driven in kilometres. Find the cost for each distance and time.
   (a) 1296 km, 3 d   (b) 1375 km, 5 d
   (c) 1424 km, 4 d   (d) 2183 km, 7 d

4. In skydiving, once you leave the plane, your height, h, in metres above the earth's surface is given by $h = a - 4.9t^2$ where a is the altitude of the plane in metres and t is the time in seconds after leaving the plane.
   (a) Find Jennifer's height to the nearest metre after 6.5 s if she jumped from a height of 2500 m.
   (b) Jackson jumped 2 s after Jennifer. How far apart were they 4.5 s after Jackson jumped?

Section 4.5

1. Which value of the variable shown is the root?
   (a) $3x + 1 = 16$ 3, 4, 5
   (b) $2k - 3 = -7$ $-1, -2, -3$
   (c) $5n + 5 = 30$ 5, 6, 7
   (d) $15 - p = 9$ 4, 5, 6

2. Solve.
   (a) $2m + 5 = 21$ (b) $3y - 4 = -19$
   (c) $28 - 3r = -8$ (d) $\dfrac{p}{2} + 3 = 11$
   (e) $-3p + 5 = 17$ (f) $\dfrac{2}{3}s = 16$
   (g) $\dfrac{1}{4}t + 6 = 10$ (h) $8 - \dfrac{1}{2}g = 2$

3. Which equations have the same root?
   (a) $4k = k + 9$ (b) $3(k - 2) = 3$
   (c) $8 - 3k = -1$ (d) $\dfrac{k}{3} + 1 = 3$

4. Each equation involves decimals. Find the root.
   (a) $3m + 3.5 = 9.5$ (b) $5y - 2.5 = 22.5$
   (c) $4.5 + 2t = 2.5$ (d) $10.5 = 2.5t + 3$

Section 4.6

1. Write two equivalent fractions for each of the following.
   (a) $\dfrac{3}{5}$ (b) $\dfrac{5}{7}$ (c) $\dfrac{8}{9}$
   (d) $\dfrac{11}{20}$ (e) $\dfrac{37}{50}$ (f) $\dfrac{47}{100}$

2. Find the missing term.
   (a) $\dfrac{4}{7} = \dfrac{x}{56}$ (b) $\dfrac{y}{36} = \dfrac{24}{9}$ (c) $\dfrac{3}{5} = \dfrac{144}{x}$
   (d) $\dfrac{11}{a} = \dfrac{88}{96}$ (e) $\dfrac{7}{9} = \dfrac{161}{d}$ (f) $\dfrac{6}{15} = \dfrac{x}{105}$

3. Which pairs of fractions are equivalent?
   (a) $\dfrac{12}{18}, \dfrac{72}{108}$ (b) $\dfrac{7}{15}, \dfrac{56}{110}$ (c) $\dfrac{63}{81}, \dfrac{7}{9}$
   (d) $\dfrac{35}{100}, \dfrac{14}{40}$ (e) $\dfrac{16}{25}, \dfrac{48}{75}$ (f) $\dfrac{78}{92}, \dfrac{34}{46}$

4. The disc jockey at a local radio station plays 128 songs during a period of 4 h. For every seven rock songs, she plays nine country

songs. How many rock songs does she play during the 4 h?

(a) How can the equation $\frac{7}{16} = \frac{x}{128}$ be used to solve the problem?

(b) Solve $\frac{7}{16} = \frac{x}{128}$.

(c) Now answer the question. "How many rock songs did she play during the 4 h?"

5. A recipe calls for 75 mL of sugar for every 125 mL of flour. If 750 mL of flour are used, how much sugar is needed?

(a) How can the equation $\frac{125}{75} = \frac{750}{S}$ be used to solve the problem?

(b) Solve $\frac{125}{75} = \frac{750}{S}$.

(c) Write a concluding statement.

Section 4.9

1. For each line segment calculate its
   • rise.   • run.   • slope.

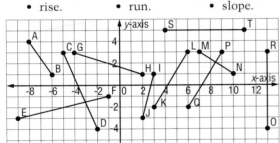

2. Calculate the slope of the line through each pair of points.
   (a) (−1, 4), (4, 2)   (b) (5, −7), (−3, 6)
   (c) (−4, 5), (−4,−3)   (d) (6, −2), (1, 0)
   (e) (7, −3), (0,5)   (f) (0, −6), (5, −6)

3. Copy and complete the chart.

Line Segment	Coordinates		Run	Rise	Slope
AB	A(1,5)	B(9, −1)	?	?	?
CD	C(1,3)	D(?,5)	−5	?	$-\frac{2}{?}$
EF	E(3,−2)	F(7,?)	?	0	?
GH	G(?,?)	H(3,1)	?	?	$\frac{3}{2}$
IJ	I(?,−6)	J(−3,2)	0	?	?

Section 4.12

1. Find the coordinates of the midpoint of each line segment.
   (a) A(1, −6), B(−3, 7)   (b) C(0, 5), D(−4, 9)
   (c) E(−5, 0), F(−3, 8)   (d) G(4, 0), H(0, −5)
   (e) P(4, −5), Q(3, 0)   (f) X(−5, 0), Y(6, −4)

2. One endpoint of a line is at (−3, 8). Find the other endpoint if the midpoint is
   (a) (3, −4).   (b) (0, 6).   (c) (−4, 7).

3. The diameter of a circle has endpoints A(−4, 5) and B(5, −8). Find the coordinates of the centre of the circle.

4. The diameter of a circle has one endpoint at P(3, 7). The centre of the circle is at O(−1, 4). Find the other endpoint of the diameter.

5. The radius of a circle has endpoints at Q(−3, 5) and R(0, 2). Find a possible endpoint of the diameter. What assumptions have you made?

CHAPTER 5

Section 5.2

1. Write two equivalent rational numbers for each of the following. (Write your answer with positive denominators.)

   (a) $\frac{-3}{5}$ (b) $\frac{5}{-8}$ (c) $-\frac{7}{10}$

   (d) $\frac{5}{12}$ (e) $-\frac{-12}{23}$ (f) $-\frac{-15}{-34}$

2. Write each of the following in mixed form.

   (a) $\frac{12}{-5}$ (b) $\frac{-27}{16}$ (c) $\frac{-74}{-19}$

   (d) $\frac{104}{42}$ (e) $-\frac{-258}{59}$ (f) $-\frac{-593}{-52}$

3. Write each set of rational numbers in order from greatest to least.

   (a) $\frac{-4}{7}, -\frac{3}{5}, \frac{5}{-8}, \frac{-2}{7}$ (b) $-\frac{4}{9}, \frac{7}{-5}, \frac{5}{2}, -\frac{-8}{3}$

   (c) $\frac{6}{-10}, \frac{4}{6}, \frac{-7}{3}, -\frac{6}{3}$ (d) $\frac{1}{6}, \frac{-3}{-2}, -\frac{6}{4}, \frac{5}{-3}$

4. Write each of the following in improper form.

   (a) $-5\frac{2}{5}$ (b) $3\frac{4}{7}$ (c) $6\frac{1}{6}$

   (d) $-7\frac{1}{10}$ (e) -12 (f) $-5\frac{9}{17}$

5. Use <, >, or = in place of ☐ to make each of the following true.

(a) $-\dfrac{3}{8}$ ☐ $\dfrac{1}{-3}$ (b) $\dfrac{-4}{7}$ ☐ $\dfrac{2}{-5}$ (c) $\dfrac{1}{5}$ ☐ $-\dfrac{7}{3}$

(d) $\dfrac{35}{-7}$ ☐ $-\dfrac{45}{9}$ (e) $\dfrac{72}{18}$ ☐ $\dfrac{-18}{4}$ (f) $-2\dfrac{3}{7}$ ☐ $1\dfrac{5}{9}$

Section 5.3

1. For each rational number determine if its decimal equivalent is terminating or non-terminating (periodic).

(a) $\dfrac{3}{5}$ (b) $-\dfrac{4}{7}$ (c) $\dfrac{2}{11}$

(d) $-\dfrac{6}{8}$ (e) $\dfrac{4}{15}$ (f) $-\dfrac{7}{10}$

2. Find the period and the length of the period of each rational number.

(a) $\dfrac{35}{99}$ (b) $\dfrac{2}{-11}$ (c) $\dfrac{1}{15}$

(d) $-\dfrac{3}{22}$ (e) $\dfrac{34}{27}$ (f) $2\dfrac{2}{3}$

(g) $-\dfrac{7}{11}$ (h) $\dfrac{49}{54}$ (i) $-\dfrac{17}{36}$

3. For each pair, which is the greater rational?

(a) $\dfrac{12}{23}, \dfrac{14}{29}$ (b) $-\dfrac{3}{17}, -\dfrac{5}{26}$

(c) $\dfrac{3}{28}, \dfrac{2}{17}$ (d) $-\dfrac{4}{25}, -\dfrac{3}{20}$

(e) $-\dfrac{7}{30}, -\dfrac{6}{26}$ (f) $\dfrac{5}{29}, \dfrac{1}{6}$

4. For each decimal number, write appropriate fractions.
(a) 0.523 (b) 0.836 (c) 0.274

Section 5.6

1. Add each of the following.

(a) $\dfrac{3}{5} + \dfrac{-4}{7}$ (b) $\dfrac{-2}{3} + \dfrac{-1}{5}$ (c) $\dfrac{6}{17} + \dfrac{3}{7}$

(d) $\dfrac{-4}{9} + \dfrac{1}{2}$ (e) $\dfrac{-1}{5} + \dfrac{-5}{6}$ (f) $\dfrac{3}{10} + \dfrac{-2}{7}$

2. Use <, >, or = in place of ☐ to make each statement true.

(a) $\dfrac{1}{5} + \dfrac{-2}{7}$ ☐ $\dfrac{-4}{7} + \dfrac{1}{4}$

(b) $\dfrac{-2}{3} + \dfrac{1}{7}$ ☐ $\dfrac{5}{8} + \dfrac{3}{5}$

(c) $\dfrac{-3}{10} + \dfrac{4}{5}$ ☐ $\dfrac{7}{9} + \dfrac{-1}{2}$

(d) $\dfrac{12}{17} + \dfrac{-5}{9}$ ☐ $\dfrac{1}{2} + \dfrac{-5}{9}$

3. Add.
(a) $(+2.9) + (-1.8)$ (b) $(-3.6) + (+1.9)$
(c) $(-4.8) + (+2.9)$ (d) $(+2.7) + (-3.1)$
(e) $(+7.3) + (-8.2)$ (f) $(-8.3) + (-2.5)$

4. Simplify.

(a) $-1\dfrac{2}{3} + \dfrac{4}{7}$ (b) $-3\dfrac{3}{7} + 2\dfrac{4}{5}$

(c) $\dfrac{1}{3} + 3\dfrac{1}{6}$ (d) $-5 + \dfrac{7}{11}$

(e) $5\dfrac{3}{7} + 1\dfrac{5}{6}$ (f) $-7\dfrac{1}{5} + 3\dfrac{1}{4}$

5. Jerry spent $3\dfrac{1}{3}$ h at his piano lesson and $1\dfrac{2}{5}$ h writing an essay. How much time in total did he spend on the two tasks?

Section 5.8

1. Simplify each of the following.

(a) $\dfrac{-1}{2} - \dfrac{3}{5}$ (b) $\dfrac{5}{7} - \dfrac{-3}{8}$

(c) $\dfrac{5}{8} - \dfrac{-3}{7}$ (d) $\dfrac{4}{5} - \dfrac{1}{3}$

(e) $\dfrac{-6}{11} - \dfrac{5}{14}$ (f) $\dfrac{8}{15} - \dfrac{-1}{7}$

2. Find each difference. List the answers from least to greatest.
(a) $(+7.2) - (-5.9)$ (b) $(-4.8) - (+8.1)$
(c) $(-5.1) - (+7.3)$ (d) $(+9.2) - (+6.2)$
(e) $(-18.2) - (+21.5)$ (f) $(-7.6) - (-12.0)$

3. Colin spent $1\dfrac{3}{5}$ h swimming and $1\dfrac{1}{6}$ h playing tennis. At which activity did Colin spend more time? By how much?

4. Yvonne ate $\dfrac{3}{5}$ of a pizza and Ron ate $\dfrac{2}{3}$ of a pizza. Who ate the least amount of pizza and by how much?

5. Simplify each expression.

(a) $3\frac{1}{5} - \frac{-4}{7} + \frac{1}{4}$ (b) $4\frac{6}{7} - \left(-1\frac{3}{4}\right) + 2\frac{1}{5}$

(c) $-1\frac{3}{10} - 3\frac{2}{7} + \frac{1}{2}$ (d) $3\frac{5}{9} + \left(-3\frac{4}{5}\right) - \frac{7}{8}$

Section 5.11

1. Find each product. Watch the signs.

(a) $\frac{3}{4} \times \frac{-1}{3}$ (b) $\frac{1}{5} \times \frac{7}{9}$ (c) $\frac{-3}{5} \times \frac{-1}{6}$

(d) $\left(\frac{12}{7}\right)\left(\frac{-14}{6}\right)$ (e) $\left(\frac{15}{3}\right)\left(\frac{-72}{105}\right)$ (f) $\frac{-24}{81} \times \frac{3}{8}$

(g) $\left(-2\frac{3}{7}\right)\left(3\frac{5}{8}\right)$ (h) $\left(7\frac{1}{5}\right)\left(\frac{-9}{75}\right)$ (i) $\left(\frac{3}{5}\right)\left(-5\frac{12}{21}\right)$

2. Simplify each product.

(a) $-\frac{1}{2} \times \frac{1}{-5}$ (b) $\left(\frac{-1}{3}\right)\left(\frac{3}{-5}\right)$ (c) $\frac{1}{2} \times \left(-\frac{2}{5}\right)$

(d) $\frac{-1}{4} \times \frac{1}{5}$ (e) $\left(\frac{-3}{10}\right)\left(\frac{-2}{3}\right)$ (f) $\frac{-3}{4} \times \frac{-4}{3}$

(g) $\frac{-2}{5} \times \frac{4}{10}$ (h) $\frac{9}{4} \times \frac{-3}{5}$ (i) $-\frac{10}{4} \times 0$

(j) $-10 \times \frac{8}{5}$ (k) $2\frac{1}{4} \times \frac{-4}{5}$ (l) $\left(\frac{-5}{6}\right)(-24)$

3. Simplify each of the following.

(a) $\left(4\frac{1}{2}\right)\left(-3\frac{3}{5}\right)$ (b) $\left(-4\frac{1}{6}\right)\left(7\frac{3}{4}\right)$

(c) $\left(-4\frac{1}{2}\right)\left(-3\frac{1}{3}\right)$ (d) $\left(2\frac{1}{5}\right)\left(-4\frac{3}{8}\right)$

(e) $\left(\frac{2}{3}\right)\left(\frac{-1}{2}\right)\left(\frac{-3}{4}\right)$ (f) $\frac{-1}{10} \times \frac{-3}{4} \times \frac{-2}{5}$

(g) $\frac{4}{10} \times \frac{6}{-8} \times \frac{-3}{4}$ (h) $\frac{-2}{3} \times \frac{-4}{5} \times 0$

(i) $\left(-1\frac{2}{3}\right)\left(-4\frac{1}{4}\right)\left(\frac{-1}{8}\right)$ (j) $(-4)\left(4\frac{1}{4}\right) \times \frac{8}{9}$

(k) $(100)\left(\frac{-3}{10}\right)\left(1\frac{3}{5}\right)$ (l) $\left(-1\frac{3}{5}\right)(12)\left(\frac{-2}{3}\right)$

4. Simplify each of the following. The first one is done for you.

(a) $\left(-\frac{2}{3}\right)^2 = \left(-\frac{2}{3}\right)\left(-\frac{2}{3}\right) = \frac{4}{9}$

(b) $\left(\frac{1}{-3}\right)^2$ (c) $\left(\frac{-4}{5}\right)^2$ (d) $\left(-\frac{3}{2}\right)^2$

(e) $\left(\frac{-2}{5}\right)^2$ (f) $\left(-\frac{1}{3}\right)^2$ (g) $\left(\frac{-3}{2}\right)^2\left(-\frac{1}{3}\right)$

(h) $\left(-\frac{2}{3}\right)\left(\frac{1}{2}\right)^6$ (i) $\left(\frac{2}{3}\right)^3\left(\frac{1}{2}\right)^2$ (j) $\left(-\frac{2}{3}\right)^2\left(\frac{1}{-2}\right)^2$

5. On a video game, Richard scored $-3\frac{1}{4}$ points for five straight games. How many points did he score in all?

Section 5.12

1. Divide.

(a) $\frac{9}{10} \div \frac{3}{5}$ (b) $\frac{4}{3} \div \frac{2}{3}$ (c) $\frac{2}{3} \div \frac{-1}{8}$

2. Divide each of the following.

(a) $\frac{3}{-2} \div \frac{-1}{3}$ (b) $\frac{-1}{3} \div \frac{-10}{9}$

(c) $-\frac{4}{9} \div 16$ (d) $2\frac{1}{3} \div \left(-\frac{1}{2}\right)$

(e) $0 \div -\frac{3}{4}$ (f) $-\frac{1}{2} \div 1\frac{3}{4}$

(g) $2\frac{1}{3} \div \left(-3\frac{1}{2}\right)$ (h) $\frac{-3}{4} \div \frac{5}{-4}$

(i) $\frac{0}{3} \div \frac{-4}{5}$ (j) $-\frac{9}{-4} \div \frac{36}{5}$

3. Simplify each of the following.

(a) $\frac{3}{-5} \times \frac{4}{3} \times \frac{-1}{8}$ (b) $\frac{1}{3} \times \frac{3}{-4} \times \frac{1}{4}$

(c) $\frac{2}{-4} \times \frac{1}{-3} \times \frac{-4}{3}$ (d) $\left(\frac{4}{-2}\right)\left(\frac{-3}{-2}\right)\left(-\frac{9}{2}\right)$

(e) $-1\frac{1}{5} \times \frac{-2}{3} \times \frac{-12}{7}$ (f) $\left(-\frac{1}{6}\right)\left(\left(-\frac{1}{12}\right) - 2\frac{1}{3}\right)$

4. It snowed for $3\frac{1}{4}$ h on Wednesday and for $2\frac{3}{4}$ h on Thursday. How many times longer was the period of snow on Wednesday than on Thursday?

5. Suppose Brian scored the following points on a video game.

$$3\frac{1}{4}, \frac{-4}{5}, -3\frac{3}{5}, 4\frac{1}{2}, 12\frac{1}{8}, -5\frac{5}{8}$$

(a) How many total points did he score?
(b) What was his average score?

521

Section 5.13

1. Simplify each of the following.

   (a) $\dfrac{4}{3} - \left(\dfrac{2}{3} - \dfrac{-3}{4}\right)$

   (b) $\dfrac{4}{5} + \dfrac{-1}{4} \times \dfrac{-1}{2}$

   (c) $\left(\dfrac{-1}{4} + \dfrac{7}{-8}\right)$

   (d) $-\dfrac{3}{4}\left(\dfrac{-2}{3} + \dfrac{1}{5}\right)$

   (e) $\dfrac{-1}{2} - \left(\dfrac{2}{3} + \dfrac{3}{-4}\right)$

   (f) $\dfrac{1}{2} \div \left(\dfrac{2}{3} - \dfrac{1}{-2}\right)$

   (g) $\dfrac{1}{-8} - \dfrac{-3}{4} \div \dfrac{5}{8}$

   (h) $\dfrac{2}{-3} \div \dfrac{1}{2} + \dfrac{-2}{3}$

   (i) $\dfrac{3}{5} - \left(\dfrac{-3}{5} - \dfrac{-2}{3}\right)$

   (j) $-\dfrac{3}{2} + \dfrac{-1}{-2} - \dfrac{-3}{5}$

2. Simplify each of the following.

   (a) $\left(\dfrac{2}{3} - \dfrac{-1}{3}\right) \div \left(\dfrac{-3}{4} - \dfrac{-2}{3}\right)$

   (b) $\left(\dfrac{-1}{8} + \dfrac{1}{-4}\right)\left(\dfrac{-1}{-2} + \dfrac{1}{-6}\right)$

   (c) $\left(\dfrac{2}{-3} - \dfrac{-1}{2}\right) \div \left(\dfrac{-3}{2} - \dfrac{3}{2}\right)$

   (d) $\left(1\dfrac{3}{4} - \dfrac{3}{-4}\right)\left(\dfrac{-1}{3} - \dfrac{1}{4}\right)$

   (e) $\left(\dfrac{-2}{5} + \dfrac{1}{-2}\right) \div \left(\dfrac{5}{-8} - \dfrac{-1}{2}\right)$

   (f) $\left(1\dfrac{3}{4} + \dfrac{-1}{8}\right) \div \left(\dfrac{-3}{4} - \dfrac{1}{4}\right)$

3. Evaluate.

   (a) $\dfrac{\dfrac{-4}{5} - \dfrac{-3}{5}}{\dfrac{1}{3} - \dfrac{-1}{8}}$

   (b) $\dfrac{\dfrac{3}{5} - \dfrac{-1}{10}}{\dfrac{-3}{4} - 1\dfrac{2}{3}}$

   (c) $\dfrac{\dfrac{1}{-4} + \dfrac{1}{-3}}{\dfrac{5}{-12} + 1\dfrac{3}{4}}$

   (d) $\dfrac{1\dfrac{3}{5} - \dfrac{-2}{3}}{\dfrac{1}{-8} - \dfrac{-3}{4}}$

4. In Marie's experiment, the temperature in a container dropped every 3 min. Initially, the temperature was $7\dfrac{1}{2}$ °C. After 3 min the temperature was −4 °C and after 6 min the temperature was $-8\dfrac{1}{4}$ °C.

   (a) Find the average temperature.

   (b) Predict what the temperature will be after 12 min. Give reasons for your prediction.

Section 5.14

1. Find a rational number for each of the following decimal numbers.

   (a) 0.2
   (b) −0.35
   (c) −0.73
   (d) 1.55
   (e) −0.33
   (f) −0.56
   (g) 0.15
   (h) 0.32
   (i) 0.125
   (j) 3.875
   (k) 0.401
   (l) −2.135

2. Find a rational number for each of the following.

   (a) $0.3\overline{5}$
   (b) $0.4\overline{9}$
   (c) $0.6\overline{8}$
   (d) $0.5\overline{9}$
   (e) $0.3\overline{15}$
   (f) $3.\overline{27}$
   (g) $0.04\overline{6}$
   (h) $2.\overline{33}$
   (i) $0.4\overline{13}$

3. Find a rational number for each of the following.

   (a) $-0.4\overline{5}$
   (b) $-0.\overline{39}$
   (c) $-0.\overline{78}$
   (d) $-4.\overline{32}$
   (e) $-2.\overline{93}$
   (f) $-4.\overline{15}$
   (g) $-0.1\overline{43}$
   (h) $-3.\overline{22}$
   (i) $-4.\overline{13}$
   (j) $-2.4\overline{5}$
   (k) $-0.2\overline{23}$
   (l) $-0.1\overline{96}$

4. Copy and complete the following.

   (a) Every rational number can be written as a [   ] number.

   (b) Every periodic decimal represents a [   ] number.

Section 5.15

1. Which of the following numbers are rational? Which are irrational?

   (a) 5
   (b) −1.212 221 222 122 ...
   (c) 0.888 888...
   (d) $2\dfrac{3}{5}$
   (e) 4
   (f) $\sqrt{15}$
   (g) $-\sqrt{16}$
   (h) $\dfrac{-7}{5}$
   (i) $-\sqrt{25}$
   (j) 0.142 134 164 324 ...

2. Draw the graph of each of the following sets.

   (a) $\{x \mid x > 1, x \in I\}$
   (b) $\{x \mid x \geq 1, x \in R\}$
   (c) $\{x \mid x \leq 9, x \in I\}$
   (d) $\{x \mid 6 > x, x \in R\}$
   (e) $\{x \mid x \geq 2, x \in R\}$
   (f) $\{x \mid -2 < x, x \in R\}$
   (g) $\{x \mid 2x + 1 = 7, x \in R\}$
   (h) $\{x \mid 11 = 3x - 1, x \in R\}$
   (i) $\{x \mid x \geq 0, x \in I\}$
   (j) $\{x \mid x \leq -3, x \in R\}$
   (k) $\{x \mid x \leq 0, x \in I\}$
   (l) $\{x \mid -8 < x, x \in R\}$
   (m) $\{x \mid x < -8, x \in R\}$
   (n) $\{x \mid 8 > x, x \in R\}$
   (o) $\{x \mid x < 0, x \in I\}$
   (p) $\{x \mid 0 < x, x \in R\}$

3. Use symbols to represent each of the following.

(a)
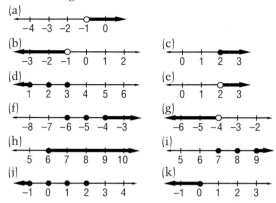

CHAPTER 6

Section 6.2

1. Calculate the perimeter for each of the following.

(a)   (b)

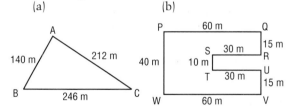

2. (a) Find the perimeter of the pool area ABCD.
   (b) Calculate the cost of enclosing the pool if fencing costs $5.25/m.

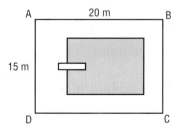

3. A rectangular Japanese garden is 27.4 m by 43.5 m.
   (a) Calculate the perimeter.
   (b) Calculate the cost of placing a low decorative fence around it if fencing costs $3.72/m.

4. The perimeter of a square is 141 m. Find the length of one side of the square.

5. The side of a rectangle measures 17.1 m. The perimeter is 45.9 m. Calculate the measures of the other three sides.

Section 6.3

1. Calculate the area of each of the following.

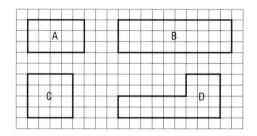

2. Jim bought a component stereo. The base of each of the two speakers is 40 cm long and 35 cm wide. His receiver measures 93 cm wide and 48 cm deep. What total area do these three pieces cover?

3. Three equal rectangular areas are to be painted on an airfield strip. The length of each is to be 27.8 m and the width 9.7 m. What total area must be painted?

4. A frozen rectangular lake, 115 m wide and 145 m long, is to be used for skating. If half of this lake will be used for pleasure skating and the other half for hockey, how big will each area be?

5. The amount of fencing needed to enclose a square field is 368 m.
   (a) Find the length of each side enclosed by the fence.
   (b) Find the area enclosed by the field.

6. One side of a rectangular field is 169.6 m. The perimeter is 486.6 m.
   (a) Find the length of each side of the field.
   (b) Calculate the area of the field.

Section 6.5
1. Calculate the area of each of the following.

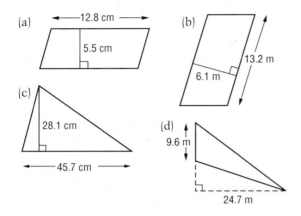

(a) 12.8 cm, 5.5 cm

(b) 13.2 m, 6.1 m

(c) 28.1 cm, 45.7 cm

(d) 9.6 m, 24.7 m

2. The measurements of a tent are shown. Calculate the area of canvas needed for the ends of the tent.

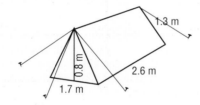

1.3 m, 0.8 m, 2.6 m, 1.7 m

3. Calculate the area of each part of the following figure.

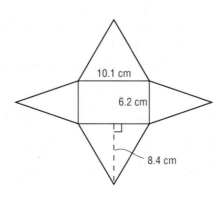

10.1 cm, 6.2 cm, 8.4 cm

4. The box lid shown is constructed from the net shown.

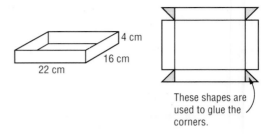

4 cm, 16 cm, 22 cm

These shapes are used to glue the corners.

(a) Calculate the total area of the triangular pieces.
(b) Calculate the total amount of material used to make the box lid.

5. A backyard has dimensions 16.3 m by 14.5 m and is to be sodded with new grass. How many strips of sod are required, if each strip has dimensions 40.0 cm by 150.0 cm?

Section 6.7
1. Calculate the area of the following shape.

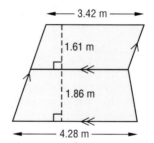

3.42 m, 1.61 m, 1.86 m, 4.28 m

2. Calculate the area of each figure.

(a)

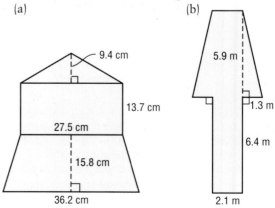

9.4 cm, 13.7 cm, 27.5 cm, 15.8 cm, 36.2 cm

(b) 5.9 m, 1.3 m, 6.4 m, 2.1 m

524

3. A walk, 65 cm wide, is placed around a rectangular flower bed measuring 14.5 m by 9.6 m. Calculate the area of the walk to the nearest square metre.

4. A sketch of the local swimming pool is shown below.

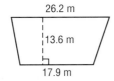

(a) Calculate the area of the floor of the pool.
(b) Tiles measuring 18.3 cm by 14.8 cm are to be used to cover the floor of the pool. How many tiles are needed?

5. A walk 72 cm wide is placed around the pool in Question 4. Calculate the area of the walk to the nearest square metre.

Section 6.8

1. Calculate the circumference of each circle. Use π = 3.14.

(a) (b) (c)

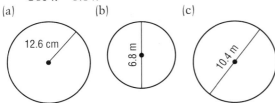

2. Copy and complete the chart.

Radius (r)	Diameter (d)	Circumference (C)
50 cm	?	?
180 cm	?	?
?	6.6 m	?
?	36.2 m	?

3. A redwood tree has grown to a diameter of 8.1 m. Calculate the circumference.

4. A satellite TV receiving dish has a radius of about 3.55 m. Find its circumference.

5. A school field has the dimensions shown.

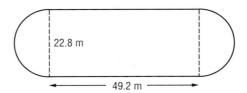

(a) Calculate the length of one lap of the track.
(b) If Amanda ran 625 m, how many laps did she run?

6. A truck tire has an outside diameter of 84.8 cm.
(a) Calculate the circumference of the tire.
(b) How many turns will the tire make to cover 1 km on a smooth highway?

7. From the top of a lighthouse, we can see about 18.6 km in all directions. Find the circumference of the region seen from the lighthouse.

Section 6.10

1. Copy and complete the chart.
(Remember: π = 3.14 to two decimal places.)

Radius	Diameter	Area
14.3 m	?	?
?	37.6 cm	?
?	?	155.26 m²
?	128.2 mm	?
?	?	276.32 cm²
73.56 m	?	?
?	183.41 km	?

2. A patrol aircraft can observe a distance of 12.1 km in all directions. Calculate the area of coverage by the plane.

3. Calculate the area of each shaded region.
(a) (b) (c)

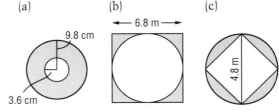

(d)

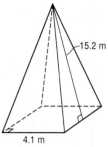

(e)

11.6 cm

12.1 cm

4.8 cm

0

4. A compact disc has a radius of 5.1 cm.
   (a) Find the area of the disc.
   (b) How many discs can be made from a sheet 2 m by 1 m?
   (c) How much material is left after making the discs in (b)?

5. The diameter of the base of a can measures 11.2 cm.
   (a) Calculate the area of the base.
   (b) How many cans can be placed on a rectangular shelf that measures 2 m by 35 cm wide?

6. A circular rug has a radius of 2.6 m.
   (a) Find the area of the rug.
   (b) Will the rug completely cover a square design on the floor that measures 4.5 m by 4.5 m? Explain why or why not.

7. The total area, A, of the shaded region is given by $A = 2\pi R^2 + 2\pi r^2$.

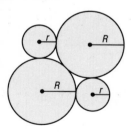

   (a) Calculate the area if $R = 4.1$ m and $r = 2.8$ m.
   (b) By how much does the area in (a) increase if each radius is increased by 1.0 m?

Section 6.12

1. The measures of a square based pyramid are shown.

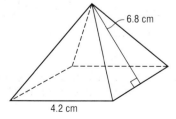

6.8 cm

4.2 cm

   (a) Draw a net.
   (b) Identify the congruent faces.
   (c) Find the area of each face.
   (d) Find the surface area of the pyramid.

2. Find the surface area of a church steeple which has the shape of the square pyramid shown.

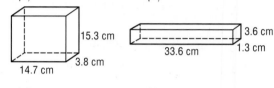

15.2 m

4.1 m

3. Calculate the surface area of each solid.
   (a)   (b)

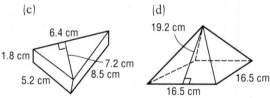

15.3 cm

14.7 cm

3.8 cm

33.6 cm

3.6 cm

1.3 cm

   (c)   (d)

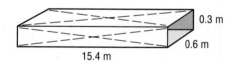

6.4 cm

1.8 cm

5.2 cm

7.2 cm

8.5 cm

19.2 cm

16.5 cm

16.5 cm

4. Find the surface area of the furnace duct. The duct is open at both ends.

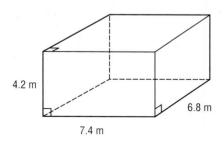

0.3 m

0.6 m

15.4 m

5. The dimensions of a room are shown below.

4.2 m

7.4 m

6.8 m

   (a) Calculate the total surface area of the room.

526

(b) The walls and the ceiling are to be painted and a 4 L can of paint covers an area of 52.2 m^2. How many cans of paint are needed?

6. A display platform is shown below.

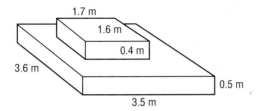

Find the area of carpeting required to completely cover the platform.

Section 6.13

1. Copy and complete the chart.

Diameter	Radius	Height	Surface Area
38.5 cm	?	11.4 cm	?
?	12.5 m	?	2273.25 m^2
?	42.7 mm	83.6 mm	?

2. A silo has a diameter of 4.3 m and a total height of 10.5 m. Find the total surface area of the silo.

3. Find the surface area of each cylinder.

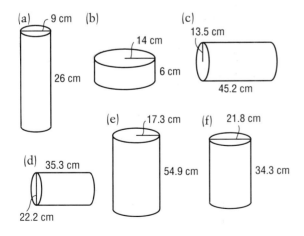

4. A company wants to paint a large gasoline storage tank, shown below, on top and all around the tank. A litre of paint covers 8.8 m^2 and costs $6.95. How much will it cost to paint the tank?

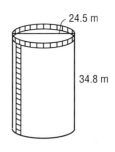

5. A piece of pipe, open at both ends, is shown below.

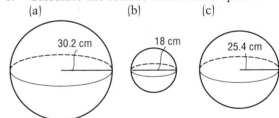

(a) Calculate the outer surface area.
(b) Calculate the inner surface area.

Section 6.15

1. Calculate the surface area of each sphere.
   (a)   (b)   (c)

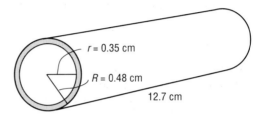

2. Find the surface area of each cone.
   (a)   (b)   (c)

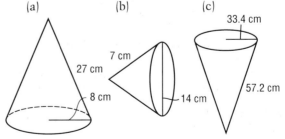

3. A soccer ball has a circumference of 65.5 cm. What is its surface area?

4. A cone-shaped paper cup had a radius of 21.6 mm and a slant height of 62.4 mm. About 81.12 mm² are used to make the seam.
   (a) Calculate the total area of paper needed to make the paper cup.
   (b) How many paper cups can be made from a sheet of paper measuring 72.4 cm by 51.8 cm?

5. Plastic tree ornaments with a radius of 4 cm are made from sheets of plastic. How many ornaments can be made from a sheet of plastic 60 cm by 60 cm? (There is no wastage.)

6. A diagram shows a sphere inside a cube with edges 20 cm in length.
   (a) Find the surface area of the cube.
   (b) Find the surface area of the sphere.
   (c) Which solid has the greater surface area? By how much?

7. A funnel has the shape of a cone. Its diameter is 90 cm and has a height of 160 cm. Find the surface areas of the funnel. (Hint: Use the Pythagorean Property to find the slant height.)

2. Copy and complete the chart.

Height	Area of Base	Volume
17.4 cm	94.6 cm²	?
21.8 mm	?	198.32 mm³
?	157.1 m²	634.89 m³

3. Copy and complete the chart.

Radius	Height	Volume
?	65.1 m	232.9 m³
21.5 mm	26.9 mm	?
128.6 cm	?	718.38 cm³

4. A cylindrical storage tank with a radius of 3.4 m and a height of 7.3 m is filled with wheat.
   (a) Find the volume of wheat in the tank.
   (b) Find the mass of wheat in the tank if wheat has a mass of 120 kg/m³.

5. Which cylinder, A or B, holds more?
   Cylinder A: diameter 9.4 cm, height 8.2 cm
   Cylinder B: radius 54 cm, height 7.9 cm

6. A trench is dug as shown below.

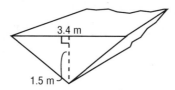

Calculate the the amount of earth removed if the trench is 12.5 m in length.

7. Find the volume of material used to make the concrete pipe.

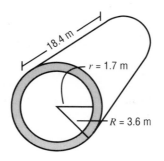

Section 6.18
1. Calculate the volume of each solid.
   (a)

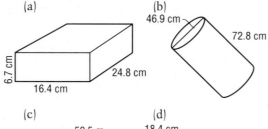

   (b)
   46.9 cm
   72.8 cm

   (c)

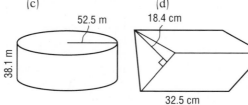

   (d)
   18.4 cm
   18.9 cm
   32.5 cm

8. (a) Find the amount of steel used to make a pipe 7.39 cm long, if the outside radius is 1.04 cm and the inside radius is 0.72 cm.

(b) If 1.35 cm³ of steel has a mass of 0.17 kg, find the mass of the pipe.

Section 6.19

1. Find the the volume of each solid.

(a)

(b)

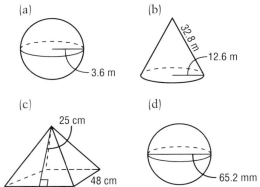

(c)

(d)

2. Find the missing measures for each cone.

Radius	Height	Volume
?	35.7 cm	172.8 cm³
183.2 mm	59.3	?
174.92 m	?	836.92 m³

3. Calculate the volume of gas in a balloon if the radius is 2.6 m.

4. The thickness of an orange peel is 0.6 cm. If the diameter of an orange is 7.4 cm, calculate how much of the orange consists of actual fruit.

5. The radius of the earth is 6376.8 km. If the thickness of the crust of the earth is 35 km, then
   (a) how much of the earth is crust?
   (b) what percent of the earth is crust?

6. A conical tank has an altitude of 14.8 m and a radius of 4.2 m. Calculate the number of oil drums that can be filled from the tank if each oil drum is 0.8 m high and has a radius of 0.3 m.

7. A large cubical tank, whose sides measure 5.6 m, is filled with liquid. How much will be left in the tank if the liquid is used to fill a cylindrical tank with a radius of 3.2 m and a height of 3.6 m?

8. How much more does a hemispherical tank hold than a conical tank?

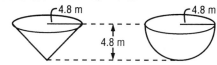

CHAPTER 7

Section 7.2

1. For each rectangle, write the ratio AB:AD.

(a)

(b)

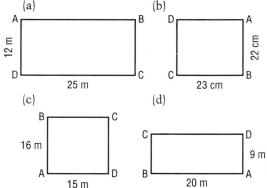

(c)

(d)

2. Use the recipe for white bread. Write the ratio for each of the following.

(a) warm water to cold water
(b) milk to flour
(c) shortening to sugar
(d) sugar to milk

White Bread
25 mL sugar
125 mL warm water
125 mL cold water
1 package dry yeast
625 mL flour
125 mL milk
10 mL shortening

3. There is a village on the island of Anglesey in Wales called *Llanfairpwllgwyngyllgogerychwyrndrobwyllllantsiliogogogooch*.
   Write the ratios of
   (a) a's to w's.   (b) y's to o's.
   (c) h's to d's.   (d) y's to l's.
   (e) i's to w's.   (f) n's to l's.
   (g) l's to all letters. (h) d's to all letters.

Questions 4 to 6 are based on the following table. The data for the N.H.L. scoring and penalties are shown in the table.

Player	GP	G	A	PIM
Boldirev	80	24	38	40
Jensen	78	22	23	62
Lafleur	80	56	80	20
MacAdam	80	22	41	68
McKechnie	80	25	34	50
Monaham	76	18	26	78
Sargent	80	14	40	85
Trottier	76	30	42	34

4. Write a ratio to compare the goals scored to games played for each player.
   - (a) Boldirev
   - (b) MacAdam
   - (c) Sargent
   - (d) Trottier

5. Write a ratio to compare games played to penalty minutes for each of the following players.
   - (a) Lafleur
   - (b) Monaham
   - (c) Jensen
   - (d) McKechnie

6. Write a ratio to compare goals scored to assists for each player.
   - (a) Trottier
   - (b) Boldirev
   - (c) Lafleur
   - (d) MacAdam

Section 7.4

1. Write an equivalent ratio for each of the following.
   - (a) 3:4
   - (b) 3:8
   - (c) 5:9
   - (d) 2:3
   - (e) 4:7
   - (f) 1:2
   - (g) 3:10
   - (h) 5:3
   - (i) 1:5

2. Find the missing terms in each proportion.
   - (a) $3:2 = x:6$
   - (b) $15:y = 3:2$
   - (c) $3:13 = 6:d$
   - (d) $10:3 = t:15$
   - (e) $12:15 = 4:w$
   - (f) $25:b = 5:3$
   - (g) $q:10 = 2:5$
   - (h) $2:3 = m:45$

3. Find the missing terms in each of the following.
   - (a) $\dfrac{x}{8} = \dfrac{15}{6}$
   - (b) $y:15 = 2:6$
   - (c) $\dfrac{9}{k} = \dfrac{7}{21}$
   - (d) $\dfrac{14}{7} = \dfrac{20}{t}$
   - (e) $\dfrac{10}{15} = \dfrac{z}{9}$
   - (f) $\dfrac{12}{a} = \dfrac{16}{12}$

4. The cost of a trailer and the cost of a boat are in the ratio 2:5. The total cost of the boat and the trailer is $21 000.
   - (a) What is the cost of the boat?
   - (b) What is the cost of the trailer?

5. Using a pulley arrangement, a person can lift 225 kg with a pull of 10 kg.
   - (a) How many kilograms can be lifted with a pull of 1 kg?
   - (b) If 270 kg were lifted, how much was the pull?

6. The record amount of snow that fell in a 24 h period was 1.83 m at Silver Lake, Colorado.
   - (a) How much snow do you think fell in one week?
   - (b) What assumptions did you make in (a)?

7. In a poll, 366 out of 488 drivers were in favour of stricter seat belt legislation.
   - (a) If 200 more drivers were polled, how many more drivers would you expect to be in favour of stricter seat belt legislation than those against?
   - (b) What assumptions did you make in (a)?

Section 7.8

1. The scale on a map is 1 cm represents 15 km. Find the actual distance for each distance measured on the map.
   - (a) 8 cm
   - (b) 6.5 cm
   - (c) 18.2 cm

2. The scale on a map is 1:10 000. Find the distance, in centimetres, on a map for each distance.
   - (a) 150 m
   - (b) 500 m
   - (c) 1.5 km

3. On a map of Canada, the scale used is 1 cm represents 37.4 km. The distance measured between two cities is shown. Copy and complete the table.

City	City	Actual Distance	Distance on Map
Edmonton	Sudbury	?	82.4 cm
London	Regina	2853 km	?
St. John	Montreal	?	25.1 cm
Victoria	Winnipeg	2337 km	?

Section 7.9

1. The scale on a map of Canada is 1:13 000 000.
   (a) The distance on the map between North Bay and Sudbury is 1 cm. What is the actual distance?
   (b) The distance between Edmonton and Vancouver is 820 km. What will be the distance between these places on a map?

2. The record wing span of the Wandering Albatross is 3.6 m. What scale would you use to fit the bird horizontally on this page?

3. The height of the North African ostrich is about 2.7 m. What scale would you use to fit the bird vertically on this page?

4. A miniature railway is constructed to a scale of 1:85. If the model of the caboose is 15 cm long, then what is the length in metres of the real caboose?

5. The television image of the height of a horse is 31 cm and its jockey is 19 cm. If the actual height of the horse is 164 cm, find the actual height of the jockey.

Section 7.13

1. A water fountain uses water at the rate of 20 L/min.
   (a) How many litres are used in 1 min?
   (b) How many litres are used in 1 h?
   (c) How many litres are used in 1 h 30 min?
   (d) A bathtub holds 180 L. How long will it take to fill it?

2. A jet climbs at a rate of 12 m/s. How far would the jet climb in 1 min?

3. Larry earns $6.25/h washing cars. How much will Larry earn in an 8 h day?

4. Maureen scored a total of 34 points in two basketball games.
   (a) How many points did she average per game?
   (b) How many points would you expect her to score in ten games? Give reasons for your answer.

5. At the driving range, 20 golf balls are hit every 10 s. If the range is open for 14 h each day, then how many balls are hit each day?

6. Use the ads below. Will you make more money working 10 h at the bowling alley or 12 h at the Place of Pizza?

Section 7.14

1. Calculate the unit cost for the following.
   (a) 4 L of milk cost $3.99
   (b) $42 for 4.5 m of fabric
   (c) 500 mL of juice for $1.39

2. (a) The cost of six grapefruit is 89¢. Find the cost of 10 grapefruit.
   (b) How much would 12 glasses cost if five glasses cost $4.00?
   (c) How much would a 24-can case of pop cost if five cans cost 95¢?

3. Marty can pick four baskets of Delicious apples in 30 min. At this rate, how many baskets can Marty pick in 5 h?

4. A rock group travelled 1980 km in 4 d. At this rate, how far would they travel in 9 d?

5. If 48 L of gasoline cost $23.50, then how many litres of gasoline can you buy for $10.00?

6. Suppose gasoline sells for 48.9¢/L. What is the cost of
   (a) 10.5 L?   (b) 30.8 L?
   (c) Harriet paid $21.97 for gas. How many litres were bought?
   (d) Anna paid $18.00 for gas. How many litres were bought?

7. Which is the better buy?
   A Kodachrome 110 film, 20 exposures for $2.29.
   B Kodachrome 110 film, 12 exposures for $1.69.

Section 7.16

1. Calculate.
   (a) 15% of 500   (b) 6.2% of 36

   (c) 125% of 360   (d) $12\frac{1}{2}$% of 150

2. Write a percent to show how much of each figure is shaded. What percent is not shaded?

A   B

3. Write a percent to show how much of each figure is shaded. What percent is not shaded?
   (a)   (b)   (c)

4. Do you know why ice floats? When water freezes, its volume increases by about 11%. Find the volume of ice when these amounts of water freeze.
   (a) 100 mL   (b) 150 mL   (c) 600 mL
   (d) 10.2 L   (e) 49.2 L   (f) 5.8 L

5. For a human being, 43% of the body mass is muscle.
   (a) The mass of muscle John has is 25.8 kg. What is his body mass?
   (b) The mass of muscle that Sandra has is 21.5 kg. What is her body mass?

Section 7.17

1. Suppose 1% of a number is 48.
   (a) What is 10% of the number?
   (b) What is 100% of the number?

2. Suppose 1% of a number is 1.2.
   (a) What is 10% of the number?
   (b) What is 100% of the number?

3. Find the value of each of the following.
   (a) 40% of 12 is ☐.
   (b) 200 is ☐% of 1000.
   (c) 10% of ☐ is 22.

4. Find the value of ☐ in each of the following.
   (a) 12% of 250 is ☐.
   (b) 36 is ☐% of 144.
   (c) 25% of ☐ is 24.

5. Out of a total of 48 points, Debra scored 21. What percent did she score?

6. A banana is about 76% water. If the amount of water in a banana is 114 g, what is the total mass of the banana?

Section 7.18

1. Calculate each of the following.
   (a) 126% of 305   (b) 157% of 692
   (c) 255% of 830   (d) 280% of 569
   (e) 301% of 730   (f) 375% of 375

2. Evaluate.
   (a) 142% of 362.5 km   (b) 197% of 417.2 g
   (c) 328% of 163.7 mL   (d) 168% of $35.73
   (e) 419% of 519.2 kg   (f) 205% of $195.94

3. The dough for a loaf of bread was left to rise for 2 h. The dough rose to 185% of its original mass. If the original mass was 85 g, calculate the new volume.

4. (a) Estimate which is greater.
       A: 175% of $740.00
       B: 130% of $875.00
   (b) Calculate which is greater. How close was your estimate?

5. By his first birthday, Richard's mass increased by 364%. If Richard's original mass was 1595 g, what was his mass on his first birthday?

6. The traffic in downtown Vancouver during the holiday season is 170% of the regular traffic. If there are 68 000 cars on the road during regular traffic, how many cars are there on the road during the holiday season?

CHAPTER 8

Section 8.2

For each question in this section, use the provincial sales taxes shown in Chapter 8, Section 8.2 for each province. The Goods and Services Tax is 7%.

1. Copy and complete the chart.

Item	Province	Selling Price	Total Price
Helmet	B.C.	$74.60	?
Snow Mobile Drive Track	Nova Scotia	$93.50	?
Insulated Boots	Quebec	$49.65	?

2. (a) Calculate the total cost of a colour television in British Columbia if the list price for the television is $385.95.
   (b) Would you pay more for the television in Ontario? Give reasons for your answer.

3. During a recent trip, Betty bought the following souvenirs.

   Flag $3.69   Postcards $6.25
   Slides $16.25   Carvings $36.95

   (a) If she paid $72.61 in all, in which province did she purchase the souvenirs?
   (b) How much would she pay in all for the souvenirs in your province?

Section 8.4 and 8.5

1. Find the missing values.

List Price	Rate of Discount	Amount of Discount	Selling Price
$24.50	10%	?	?
$18.75	?	$2.25	?
$29.99	15%	?	?
?	12%	$9.00	?
?	10%	$12.25	?
?	18%	?	$123.00

2. The list price of a chair is $175.00.
   (a) Calculate the discount if the rate of discount is 18%.
   (b) Calculate the cost to the consumer if the sales tax is 8%.

3. To buy golf clubs as a gift, Chuck paid $444.95, which included all taxes. The rate of discount was 25%.
   (a) Find the original selling price of the clubs.
   (b) If the retailer still made a profit of 10%, calculate the amount of profit.

(c) Calculate the retailer's profit if the clubs were sold at the original selling price.
(d) Write the profit from (c) as a percent.

4. To sell a tent, the price was reduced by 10%. Since it did not sell, it was further reduced by 25%. If the final selling price was $485.75, find the original selling price.

5. An outdoor trampoline was reduced in price by 15% in August. By the end of September, it was further reduced in price by $20.00. If John paid a total of $142.31 (which included all taxes), find the original selling price.

6. Adam bought two oil paintings as an investment. He later sold them at $1000 each. On one painting, he made a 20% profit. On the other painting, he had a loss of 20%.
   (a) Estimate whether Adam broke even, made money, or lost money.
   (b) Solve the problem from (a). How reasonable was your estimate?

Section 8.7

1. The rate of interest paid on a bank account is 13% per year simple interest. Find the interest paid after one year if the amount in the account is $1630.50.

2. Jason borrowed $4000 from a bank to buy a motorcycle. He agreed to repay the loan plus interest in one year. At the rate of 16% interest per year, how much money would Jason pay back to the bank?

3. The rate of interest paid by a bank is 12% per year. Find the interest on $1800 paid after
   (a) one year.   (b) six months.
   (c) three months.   (d) five months.

4. The rate of interest at a bank is 10% per year. The bank also states that interest is calculated monthly.
   (a) Calculate the interest earned on a deposit of $520 after 1 month.
   (b) What is the total amount in the bank account at the end of 1 month?
   (c) Calculate the total interest earned in the second month.

5. Copy and complete. Interest is paid at the end of each month.

Amount Deposited	Rate of Interest	Interest Paid	Length of Time
$2000	14%/a	?	1 month
$3550	10.5%/a	?	2 months
$4500	$12\frac{1}{2}$%/a	?	3 months

Section 8.9

1. Calculate the interest payable on each loan.
   (a) $9000 at 11% per annum for 1 year calculated annually
   (b) $10 000 at 12% per annum for 1 year compounded semi-annually
   (c) $2500 at 8% per annum for 3 months compounded monthly

2. Mike borrowed $1118.50 at 11% per annum to buy a racing bicycle and accessories.
   (a) Calculate the interest payable at the end of the year.
   (b) Calculate the interest payable if he paid off the loan in 16 months.

3. Refer to the information in Question 2. How much money would be saved if Mike paid the money back one month earlier than in part (b)?

4. Interest is paid on a loan at the rate of 8.5% per annum, compounded annually.
   (a) What is the rate per month?
   (b) Calculate the amount owed if $4500 is borrowed for three months.
   (c) What assumptions did you make in finding your answer in (b)?

5. Jean received the monthly statement for her charge account and saw that she owed $350. The interest being charged was 17.5% per annum, calculated monthly.
   (a) How much interest would Jean pay if she paid off the money at the end of three months?
   (b) How much interest would Jean pay if she paid $50 each month and the balance at the end of seven months?

6. Do you know how a banking system works?
   (a) Why is a bank able to pay you interest?
   (b) Suppose one customer of the bank had borrowed about 2% of the money in the bank. Then that customer went bankrupt. How do you think that might affect your account?

Section 8.11

1. Copy and complete the chart.

Amount of Sales	Rate of Commission	Amount of Commission
$250.00	6%	?
?	22%	$18.48
$128.50	11%	?
?	2%	$68.00
$4540	?	$136.20
?	$1\frac{1}{2}$%	$187.50

2. Each week a sales representative receives a salary of $225.00, a 2% commission on sales between $850 and $1000, and a 3% commission on sales above $1000. Suppose this representative received $290.70 last week. Calculate the amount of his sales last week.

3. Refer to the information in Question 2. What career do you think the sales representative has? Give reasons for your choice.

4. Suppose Ron has the option of two methods of payment.
   - $800 per month plus 1% of sales
   - straight commission of $2\frac{1}{2}$% of sales
   (a) Last month Ron had $60 000 in sales. Which method would pay Ron the most money?
   (b) Suppose this month Ron has $115 000 in sales. Which method would pay Ron the most money?

5. Refer to the information in Question 4. When Ron was offered the job, he researched the sales the previous representative had made in ten months. The data is shown below.

   1. $65 000
   2. $75 000
   3. $90 000
   4. $75 000
   5. $95 000
   6. $85 000
   7. $90 000
   8. $60 000
   9. $120 000
   10. $90 000

(a) Based on the information, which method should Ron choose?

(b) Suppose you were offered the job instead of Ron. Which method would you choose? Give reasons for your answer.

CHAPTER 9

Section 9.2

1. What is the numerical coefficient of each of the following? the literal coefficient?

   (a) $2x$ (b) $\frac{2}{3}y$ (c) $6x^2$

   (d) $-4xyz$ (e) $\frac{4}{5}z^2$ (f) $1523b$

   (g) $\frac{1}{3}x$ (h) a^2 (i) $-m$

2. Pairs of terms are shown below.
   - $4y^2$, $4y$
   - $-6x^2$, $-6x^3$
   - $4ab$, $4ac$
   - $8x$, 8

   (a) How is each pair of terms alike? How is each pair different?

   (b) Why can each pair of terms be called "unlike" terms?

3. Simplify each of the following expressions.
   (a) $2a + 6a - 3 + 5$
   (b) $(6y - 2y) + (3x - 8x)$
   (c) $(8k - 3m) + (2k - m)$
   (d) $(x^2 - 3x^2) + (2x^2 + x)$
   (e) $2y^2 + 3y^2 - 6y^2 + 8$
   (f) $y^2 + 8y + 2y^2 - 6y$
   (g) $3x + 8 - 3x + 9$
   (h) $4a - 5a - 6a + 7a - 8$
   (i) $4 - 3b + 5b + 11b - 6$
   (j) $15x^2 - 5x + 8x^2 - 3x$

4. Simplify each of the following expressions.
   (a) $a + 3a - a - b$ (b) $6x - 8 + 3x$
   (c) $x^2 - y^2 + 2y^2 - x^2$ (d) $3x - 2x + 4y - 3y$
   (e) $2x^2 + 3x - 2x^2$ (f) $a + a - 3b - 2b$
   (g) $3x - y + x + 2y$ (h) $2xy - y^2 - 2xy + y^2$
   (i) $3a - a + b - 3b$ (j) $4x + 2y - x - 2y$
   (k) $-3y + 3x + 4y - 2x$ (l) $x^2 + x - x^2 + 2x$

Section 9.3

1. Simplify each of the following.
   (a) $(3x - 4y) - (2x + 2y)$
   (b) $(2a + 3b) - (-2a + b)$
   (c) $(6 - x) - (3 - x)$
   (d) $3x - (2x - y)$
   (e) $x - 2 - (x - 4)$
   (f) $6y - 12 - (y - 16)$
   (g) $9m - 3n - (-5m - 2n)$

2. Subtract.
   (a) $(2x - 3y) - (-3x + 2y)$
   (b) $(-3x + 2y) - (-3x + 2y)$
   (c) $(-3a + 4b) - (-3a - 4b)$
   (d) $(-4m - 8n) - (6m + 8n)$
   (e) $(3k - 2a) - (-6k - 2a)$
   (f) $(3k - 4m) - (-3k - 4m)$

3. Simplify.
   (a) $3x - 2y - (2x - 5y) + 3x + 2y$
   (b) $-(n^2 - 1) + n^2 + 5 - (n^2 - 3n)$
   (c) $x + 2 - (x - 7) + (x + 2)$
   (d) $x^2 - 3x + x^2 - (3x - x^2) - 2x$
   (e) $(x - 2y + z) - (x + 2y - 2z)$
   (f) $6x - y - (7x + y) + (3x - 2y)$

4. Find the sum of $3x - 2y$, $x - y$, and $x - 3y$.

5. Read each of the following carefully. Then simplify.
   (a) Subtract $2x - 3y$ from $x - 5y$.
   (b) How much less is $-3x + 2y$ than $4x - 2y$?
   (c) Subtract the sum of $2a$ and $-3a + 4b$ from $-6a - 2b$.
   (d) Find the sum of $a + 2b$, $6a - 3b$, and $-4a + 6b$.
   (e) Subtract $4a - 2b$ from $-6a + 4b$.
   (f) How much more is $2x - 3y$ than $6x - 6y$?
   (g) Find the sum of $2a$, $3a + 4b$, and $6a - 2b$.

Section 9.4

1. Find the value of each of the following expressions for $a = -3$, $b = 5$, and $c = -2$.
   (a) $2a + 3a + 7a$ (b) $3a - 2a + c$
   (c) $2a - 3b + 4b$ (d) $-2a + 3c + 6c$
   (e) $3a + 2b - a + c - 2b$
   (f) $2a - 6b + 4a - 3b - 6a$
   (g) $-3c + 2a + 3c - 3b + 4a$
   (h) $8a + 2b - 6a - 2b + 3c$

2. If $x = -8$, then find the value of each expression.
   (a) $3x + 2x - 8x$ (b) $x^2 - 6x + 2x$
   (c) $3x^2 - 2x^2 + x$ (d) $9x^2 - x - 8x^2$
   (e) $3x + x^2 - 5x$ (f) $9x + 7x - 6x + 2x$
   (g) $3x^2 - x + x^2 - x$ (h) $3x + 8 + 2x$
   (i) $-9x - 8 + 8x - 6$ (j) $x^2 - 4 + 2x^2 + 6$

(k) $3x^2 - 2x + x - 6 - x^2 + 8$
(l) $3x - 2x + x - 6 - x$

3. Find an expression for the perimeter of each of the following figures. Then, find the perimeter of each figure for $x = 6.5$ cm.

(a)

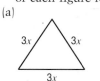

(b)

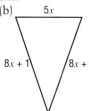

(c)

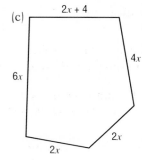

(d)

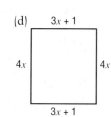

4. (a) Find an expression for the perimeter of this figure.

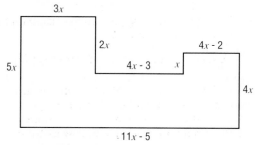

(b) Find the perimeter of the figure in (a) for $x = 3.65$ cm.

Section 9.5

1. Multiply each of the following.
   (a) $(2a)(3b)$
   (b) $(-3x)(2y)$
   (c) $(-3m)(5n)$
   (d) $(4xy)(2h)$
   (e) $(-3ab)(-2c)$
   (f) $(6mn)(-2mn)$
   (g) $(-5kr)(-2r)$
   (h) $(-2x)(-5x)$
   (i) $(-4a)(-2a^2)$
   (j) $(3z^2)(2z^2)$

2. Find the product of each of the following pairs of monomials.
   (a) $2a, -a$
   (b) $6x, x$
   (c) $-4y, y^2$

(d) $-x^2, -4$ (e) n^2, n^3 (f) $-2x^2, -3x^2$
(g) $-2x, -3x^3$ (h) $0, -2x^2$ (i) $3y^2, -3$
(j) $-4y, -6y^4$ (k) $2xy, 3x$ (l) $4a, -3ab$
(m) $-3y^2, 0$ (n) ab, ab (o) $-3ab, 2ab$
(p) $6ab, -4ab$ (q) $-2a^2b, 3a^2b$ (r) $4x^2y, 0$

3. Simplify each of the following.
   (a) $(4a)(-7a)$
   (b) $(-3x)(4y)$
   (c) $-2m(-6y)$
   (d) $-3x(-2xy)$
   (e) $-4(-2xy)$
   (f) $-6y(-3y^2)$
   (g) $2a^2(-3a)$
   (h) $-3xy(2x^2)$
   (i) $(-4x)(-3x^2)$
   (j) $(-3xy)(0)$

4. Find the following products.
   (a) $(2a)(5b)(-3c)$
   (b) $(-m)(5n)(-p)$
   (c) $(-3s)(-f)(-v)$
   (d) $(-x)(2xy)(3y)$
   (e) $(2ab)(-a)(-5b)$
   (f) $(6s)(-2sf)(-f)$
   (g) $(-5xy)(-x^2)(3y^2)$
   (h) $(-a^2)(-4ab)(-6b^2)$
   (i) $(a^2b)(-2ab)(ab^2)$
   (j) $(-2a^2b)(a^2b^2)(4b^2)$

Section 9.6

1. Find the product of 7 and $(x - 4)$.

2. Find the product of -5 and $(2x + 3)$.

3. Write each expression without brackets.
   (a) $5(-5x - 4)$
   (b) $-3(x + 8)$
   (c) $0(-3a + 10)$
   (d) $12(-5a + 42)$
   (e) $(4x - 26)(-15)$
   (f) $(-x - 12)(34)$
   (g) $(-x - 19)(-1)$
   (h) $-(15x + 4)$

4. Expand.
   (a) $-2a(7a + 3)$
   (b) $6x(-4x + 5)$
   (c) $-s(25s + 73)$
   (d) $a(-83a - 52)$
   (e) $9y(12y - 84)$
   (f) $(-5c - 36)(-17c)$
   (g) $(83v + 1)(83v)$
   (h) $(-32r)(6r + 38)$

5. Simplify each expression.
   (a) $29(-x^2 + 4x - 26)$
   (b) $-52(3x^2 - 6x + 10)$
   (c) $39(12x^2 - 86)$
   (d) $(5x^2 + 28x - 347)(-26)$
   (e) $(42y^2 - 83x + 24)(4)$

6. Simplify each of the following.
   (a) $3x(x^2 - 5x + 2)$
   (b) $-4a(6a^2 - 5a + 1)$
   (c) $-21x(-7x^2 + 16x - 24)$
   (d) $14y(9y^2 + 13y - 53)$
   (e) $(-51a^2 + 27a - 74)(-7a)$

(f) $(72y^2 - 83y + 100)(28y)$

(g) $(-5x^2 - 9)(-72x)$

(h) $(4x^2 + 13)(-ax)$

(i) $(xy)(5y^2 - 82)$

7. (a) Multiply $(3x^2 - 47x + 18)$ by $(-12x^2)$

(b) Multiply $(-5ax^2 - 19ax + 39)$ by $(7ax^2)$

(c) Find the product of $(-15a^2y^2)$ and $(3ay - 4y + 7a - 6x^2)$.

8. Evaluate the expressions in Question 7 for $a = 3$, $x = -1$, and $y = 5$.

9. Find the value of each expression for $x = -2$.

(a) $2(x + 1) - (x + 1)(-4)$

(b) $-3x(2x - 1) + x(-4x + 1)$

(c) $2(5x^2 + 2x - 3) - (x + 4)$

(d) $-(4x^2 + 3x - 1) + 2(3x^2 + 4)$

(e) $4x(x^2 - 5x + 7) - 3x(x + 14)$

10. Find the area of the shaded region if $x = 5$ m.

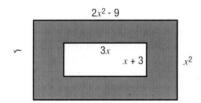

Section 9.8

1. Divide.

(a) $12x \div 4$ (b) $38y^2 \div -16y$

(c) $-54a^3 \div 24a^2$ (d) $-186z^7 \div -23z^4$

(e) $39a^2b^6 \div -3ab^3$ (f) $-195x^9y^5 \div 80x^4y^2$

2. Simplify.

(a) $\dfrac{54mn}{6n}$ (b) $\dfrac{-36x^5}{9x^2}$ (c) $\dfrac{-y^3}{-5y^2}$

(d) $\dfrac{-96m^2n^3}{-45mn}$ (e) $-\dfrac{36x^5y^2}{78x^3y^2}$ (f) $\dfrac{90a^3b^5}{-15a^2b^4}$

3. Find the value of each expression if $x = -2$ and $y = 1$.

(a) $\dfrac{136x^6y^2}{-45x^3y}$ (b) $\dfrac{-49x^2y}{28x}$ (c) $\dfrac{315x^6y^4}{105x^3y^2}$

(d) $\dfrac{-195x^5y^2}{78x^3y^2}$ (e) $\dfrac{-32x^6y^2}{56x^3y}$ (f) $\dfrac{385xy^2}{-35y}$

4. A manufacturer programs a machine to create boxes. The area of the base is $64x^5$ square units.

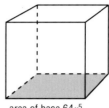

area of base $64x^5$

(a) One box is ordered which has a width of $4x^3$ units. Write an expression for the length.

(b) Find the length and width in (a) if $x = 3$.

(c) For what value of x will the base of the box be a square?

5. The area of a square is $49x^4y^3$ square units.

(a) If the length is $21x^2y$, find an expression for the width.

(b) If $x = 1$ and $y = 4$, find the
   • width.   • length.

(c) How could you use your answer from (b) to check your accuracy?

6. The area of a rectangle is $136a^5b^3c^2$ square units.

(a) If the width is $17a^2b^2c$, find the length.

(b) If $a = 1$, $b = 3$, and $c = 2$, find the
   • length.   • width.   • area.

(c) How can you check your answers from (b)?

Section 9.9

1. Find the value of ? in each of the following.

(a) $(3x + 6) \div 3 = \dfrac{? + 6}{3}$

(b) $(3y + 12) \div 3 = \dfrac{3y + 12}{?}$

(c) $(-6km + 6kn) \div (-3k) = \dfrac{? + 6kn}{-3k}$

(d) $(-6kx + 12ky) \div (-6k) = \dfrac{-6kx + 12ky}{?}$

(e) $\dfrac{-3mx - 6nx}{-3x} = \dfrac{?}{-3x} + \dfrac{-6nx}{-3x}$

(f) $\dfrac{2xy - 3py}{2y} = \dfrac{2xy}{2y} + \dfrac{?}{2y}$

(g) $\dfrac{-3xy + 6my}{-3y} = \dfrac{-3xy}{-3y} + \dfrac{6my}{?}$

2. Evaluate each of the following for the value of the variable given.

(a) $\dfrac{6x - 9x^2}{3x}$ for $x = -2$

(b) $\dfrac{18x^2 - 12x}{-6x}$ for $x = -6$

(c) $\dfrac{4a^2 - 4a}{-4a}$ for $a = -3$

(d) $\dfrac{6xy + 2x^2y^2}{-2xy}$ for $x = -2$ and $y = 3$

(e) $\dfrac{6x^2y - 3xy^2}{3xy}$ for $x = 4$ and $y = -1$

3. Each side of an open box has the same area. The total area of four sides of the box is $(12ax + 24bx)$ square units.
   (a) Sketch and label a diagram of the box.
   (b) Find an expression for the area of one side of the box.
   (c) Find the area of one side if $a = 8$, $b = 4$, and $x = 10$.
   (d) Use your results in (c). Find the surface area of the box.

4. The perimeter of a square is given by $(4x^2 + 8a)$ units.
   (a) Find an expression for the length of one side.
   (b) Find the length of one side if $x = 6$ and $a = 4$.
   (c) Find an expression for the area of the square.

Section 9.10

1. Find the value of each of the following.

(a) 2^0

(b) $(2^2)(2^3)$

(c) $\dfrac{3^3 \times 3^2}{3^4}$

(d) 2^{-1}

(e) $\dfrac{5^0 3^3}{3}$

(f) $\left(\dfrac{1}{5}\right) - 1$

(g) $3^{-3} \times 3^5$

(h) $6^{-2} \times 6^2$

(i) $(-8)^0$

(j) $(3^{-1})^0$

(k) $(5^4)^0$

(l) $7^2 \div 7^{-2}$

2. Evaluate each of the following.

(a) $2^0 + 3^0$

(b) $2^{-1} + 3^{-1}$

(c) $3 + 2^{-1}$

(d) $\left(\dfrac{1}{2}\right)^{-1}\left(\dfrac{2}{3}\right)^{-1}$

(e) $(-3)^{-2}$

(f) $3^0 + 3^{-1}$

(g) $2^3 \times 2^{-3}$

(h) $2^2 \times 3^{-2}$

(i) $\left(-\dfrac{4}{3}\right)^{-1}$

(j) $(-2)^3$

(k) $4^0 \times 4^{-1} \div 3^{-1}$

(l) $3^{-2} + 3^{-1}$

(m) $2^{-2} + 2^{-2}$

(n) -2^{-3}

(o) $(-2)^{-3}$

(p) $3(2^{-1} + 3^{-1})$

(q) $\dfrac{1}{2^{-1}} + \dfrac{1}{3^{-1}}$

(r) $2^{-1} + \dfrac{3}{2^{-1}}$

(s) $\left(\dfrac{3}{4}\right)^2$

(t) $\left(\dfrac{2}{3}\right)^{-2}$

(u) $\dfrac{2}{3^{-1}} + \dfrac{3}{2^{-1}}$

Section 9.11 and 9.12

1. Write each of the following in scientific notation.
   (a) 3400
   (b) 5609
   (c) 15 967
   (d) 0.0074
   (e) 0.007 98
   (f) 15 093
   (g) 78 000
   (h) 912 000 708
   (i) 0.000 002
   (j) 0.000 234 098
   (k) 0.016 078 912

2. Write each number in scientific notation.
   (a) There are 8 400 000 pollen grains.
   (b) In one year, the earth travels 9 400 000 000 km about the sun.
   (c) The diameter of the human red blood cell is 0.000 079 mm.
   (d) The thickness of this page is 0.000 080 m.
   (e) The farthest distance the earth is from the sun is 152 000 000 km.
   (f) The closest distance the earth is from the sun is 147 000 000 km.
   (g) The mass of a hydrogen atom is 0.000 000 000 000 000 000 000 000 66 g.

3. Calculate each of the following.
   (a) $(5.6 \times 10^3)(8.96 \times 10^6)$
   (b) $(7.83 \times 10^6)(4.78 \times 10^{-4})$
   (c) $(4.86 \times 10^{-3})(1.9 \times 10^2)$
   (d) $(2.8 \times 10^4)(5.9 \times 10^{-3})$
   (e) $(2.8 \times 10^5) \div (4.5 \times 10^6)$
   (f) $(9.31 \times 10^{20}) \div (4.2 \times 10^{15})$

4. A faucet drips at a rate of one drop every 5 s. One drop of water is about 0.08 mL. About 30 000 homes have a leaky faucet.
   (a) Calculate the total amount of water wasted in all homes in one year.

(b) A container has a circular base 1.1 m in diameter. What would be the height of the container needed to hold all the water in (a)?

CHAPTER 10

Section 10.2

1. Solve. Check your answers.
   (a) $x + 3 = 6$ (b) $14 = y - 2$ (c) $k - 4 = 32$
   (d) $m + 3 = 9$ (e) $-3 - k = 6$ (f) $k - 2 = 12$
   (g) $p - 1 = 3$ (h) $m - 2 = 12$ (i) $m - 8 = -4$

2. Find the value of the variable.
   (a) $k - 3.2 = 27.8$ (b) $m + 12.7 = -22.8$
   (c) $15.3 + m = 17.9$ (d) $-x + 14.6 = -19.5$
   (e) $m + 4.4 = 1.6$ (f) $13.25 - n = 16.78$
   (g) $1.43 - a = 12.43$ (h) $15.25 = f - 12.6$
   (i) $5.87 = m - 8.12$ (j) $12.4 - b = -3.87$

3. Solve. Verify your solution.
   (a) $\dfrac{2}{3} + p = \dfrac{3}{4}$ (b) $\dfrac{4}{5} - m = \dfrac{5}{8}$
   (c) $m + \dfrac{1}{3} = \dfrac{2}{7}$ (d) $\dfrac{1}{4} + b = \dfrac{4}{5}$
   (e) $\dfrac{3}{4} = x - \dfrac{1}{5}$ (f) $\dfrac{1}{8} = \dfrac{1}{4} - z$
   (g) $\dfrac{2}{3} = b - \dfrac{2}{5}$ (h) $\dfrac{1}{8} - n = \dfrac{2}{3}$

Section 10.3

1. Find the root for each of the following.
   (a) $6p + 8.1 = 32.1$ (b) $3q - 2.1 = 12.9$
   (c) $9.6 + 2p = 21.6$ (d) $12.8 - 3q = -11.2$
   (e) $2p + 3.1 = 8.7$ (f) $3r - 8.9 = -12.3$

2. Solve.
   (a) $3a - 2 = -17$ (b) $40 + m = -8.7$
   (c) $7 = 1 + \dfrac{2}{3}x$ (d) $\dfrac{4}{5}x = -5$
   (e) $4 - 3m = 10$ (f) $5 + 2a = 15$

3. Solve each equation. Check whether your answer is reasonable.
   (a) $2m + 6.1 = 16.1$ (b) $4x - 2.8 = 4.8$
   (c) $15.8 - 6m = 5$ (d) $8y - 16.5 = -23.9$
   (e) $7y - 3.6 = 2.9$ (f) $12.8 - 2m = 15.6$

4. Use your calculator to help you find the value of the variable in each of the following.
   (a) $k + 3.8 = 7.1$ (b) $9.5 - p = 1.8$
   (c) $7.8 \div y = 2.4$ (d) $-6.5m = 22.1$

(e) $2.1 + q = -8.7$ (f) $-3.5 = x - 9.4$
(g) $a \div 1.5 = 2.2$ (h) $5.5n = -68.2$

Section 10.4

1. The instructions for each of the following are basically the same.
   (a) Solve. $-2(2x - 3) + 6x = 36$
   (b) Find the root of $2x - 6 = 3x - 6$.
   (c) What is the solution to $6(y - 2) = 3y + 3$?

2. Find the solution set for each of the following equations.
   (a) $3(n + 4) = 5n$
   (b) $3y - 10 = 2(y - 3)$
   (c) $2(x - 2) = 2(3 - x)$
   (d) $4(x - 2) = 3(x + 1)$
   (e) $8(n - 1) = 4(n + 4)$
   (f) $2(x + 3) = 3(x - 3)$
   (g) $4(3 - m) = 5(2m + 1)$
   (h) $12(2m - 3) = 2(m + 4)$

3. Find the root of each equation.
   (a) $0.3y + 1.1 = 0.4(2y - 1)$
   (b) $2(0.2m - 0.1) - 0.8 = -3.9 - 0.3(m - 5)$
   (c) $0.3(4 - 5x) + 0.7 = 1.1 + 0.5x$
   (d) $0.2(n - 3) + 0.3 = 1.5 - n$
   (e) $0.3(y - 2) + 0.1y = 0.2(y + 1)$
   (f) $0.5(m + 2) = 0.1m + 0.6(m - 3)$
   (g) $1.4 + 0.5(x - 20) = 0.3(x - 2)$

4. Solve.
   (a) $2y + \dfrac{1}{3} = \dfrac{2}{3}$ (b) $\dfrac{3m}{2} = 15$
   (c) $\dfrac{3}{5}n - 4 = 12$ (d) $\dfrac{7}{6}x - 2 = \dfrac{1}{3}$

5. Solve.
   (a) $\dfrac{n}{4} - 1 = \dfrac{n}{5}$ (b) $3 - \dfrac{m}{2} = 5 - \dfrac{m}{3}$
   (c) $\dfrac{2}{3}y - 3 = \dfrac{4}{5}y - 5$ (d) $\dfrac{3}{5}x - 2 = \dfrac{2}{3}x + 3$
   (e) $\dfrac{60}{b} - 2 = \dfrac{20}{b} + 2$ (f) $16 = \dfrac{2}{3}k - 6$

6. Solve.
   (a) $\dfrac{1}{3}(2x - 1) = 1$ (b) $\dfrac{1}{6}(6 + 2y) = 2$
   (c) $\dfrac{1}{2}(x - 5) = \dfrac{x}{4}$ (d) $x - 1 = \dfrac{x}{2}$
   (e) $\dfrac{1}{2}(y + 2) = \dfrac{y}{3}$ (f) $\dfrac{3}{5}(2x + 15) = 3$

7. Solve. Verify your solution.

(a) $\dfrac{x}{2} = \dfrac{1}{3}(x+2)$ (b) $\dfrac{1}{2}(6+2y) = 2$

(c) $\dfrac{1}{2}(x-1) = \dfrac{1}{4}(x+1)$

(d) $\dfrac{1}{3}(y+4) = \dfrac{1}{2}(y+1)$

(e) $\dfrac{4x-1}{5} = \dfrac{2x+3}{2}$ (f) $\dfrac{y-7}{3} = \dfrac{y-2}{4}$

Section 10.7

1. (a) When six is added to a number, the sum is equal to 30. What is the number?
   (b) Five is subtracted from twice a number and the result is 45. What is the number?

2. On a biking trip from Halifax to Sydney, Jennifer cycled 30 km more on the second day than on the first day. The total distance cycled was 214 km. How far did she cycle on the first day?

3. When four is added to one quarter of a number, the result is nine. Find the number.

4. For her first parachute jump, Elsie jumped 285 m farther than twice that jumped by Jeff. If the total distance jumped is 5913 m, then find the distance each person jumped.

5. The higher of two scores is equal to 3 times the lower score. The lower score is equal to the higher score decreased by 30. Find the scores.

6. One half of a number is subtracted from the sum of one third of the number and one quarter of the number. If the result is 16, then find the number.

Section 10.8

1. The sides of a triangle, in metres, are given by $3n - 4$, $3n + 9$, $4n + 5$.
   (a) Draw a diagram to show the information.
   (b) If the perimeter is 45 m, find the length of each side.

2. The length and width, in metres, of a rectangular enclosure are given by the expression $8w + 5$ and $6w - 2$ respectively. If the perimeter is 972 m, calculate the dimensions.

3. The width of a rectangular field is 14 m and the perimeter is 86 m.
   (a) Find the measure of the length.
   (b) Find the area.

Section 10.12

1. Find the missing measure for each triangle.
   (a)   (b)   (c)

2. Find the missing value to one decimal place.
   (a)   (b)   (c)

3. Find the length of each diagonal AC.
   (a) (b)

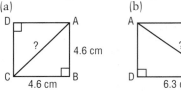

4. The span of a roof is the distance SP in the diagram.
   Calculate the span of the roof.

5. A corner lot is used as a short cut to school.

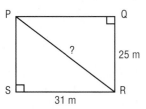

Calculate how much shorter the path PR is compared to walking along PQ and then QR.

6. (a) How long is each side of a square room that is 12.8 m between opposite corners?
   (b) What is the area of the room?

Section 10.13

1. Solve, $m \in I$.

   (a) $10 + m < 15$
   (b) $\frac{2}{3}m \leq 5$

   (c) $20 > 14 + m$
   (d) $m + 32 \geq 16$

2. Solve. Draw the graph of the solution set. The variable is an integer.

   (a) $x + 2 > 7$
   (b) $16 < m - 1$

   (c) $-12 \leq m + 5$
   (d) $3k \geq 12$

   (e) $\frac{m}{3} < 2$
   (f) $-7 \geq \frac{p}{2}$

3. Find the solution set for $x \in R$, then graph.

   (a) $2(x - 1) > 18$
   (b) $2(x + 2) \leq 26$

   (c) $2(x - 3) < -42$
   (d) $3(x - 1) \geq -27$

CHAPTER 11

Section 11.2

1. Find the missing factors.

   (a) $6 + 8x = (?)(3 + 4x)$
   (b) $2\pi r + 4\pi = (?)(r + 2)$
   (c) $6y - 12y^2 = (6y)(?)$
   (d) $4y^3 - 8y^2 = (4y^2)(?)$
   (e) $2a^2 - 8a = (?)(a - 4)$
   (f) $2\pi rh + 2\pi r^2 = (2\pi r)(?)$

2. Find the missing factors.

   (a) $-4y^2 + 2y - 2xy = (-2y)(?)$
   (b) $x^2y - x^2y^2 - xy^2 = (?)(x - xy - y)$
   (c) $2k^2 - 3k^3 + 8k^4 = (?)(2 - 3k + 8k^2)$
   (d) $x^3y - 2x^2y^2 - xy^3 = (?)(x^2 - 2xy - y^2)$
   (e) $6x^2y - 4xy^2 + 10x^2y^2 = (-2xy)(?)$
   (f) $9a^2m^2 - 6am^2 - 18a^2m = (-3am)(?)$

3. Find the common factor for each expression. Then factor the expression.

   (a) $6x^2 - 12x + 15$
   (b) $ay^2 + 6ay + 8a$
   (c) $5m^3 - 25m^2 + 15$
   (d) $5a^2 + 2ab + a$
   (e) $6a^3 - 18a^2 + 6a$
   (f) $4a^3 + 8a^2 + 6a$
   (g) $3x^2 - 12xy + 9y^2$
   (h) $4x^3 - 16x^2 + 8x$
   (i) $50a^2 + 75ab + 25b^2$
   (j) $10x^3y^3 + 20x^2y^2 - 10xy$

4. Factor each of the following. What is the common factor?

   (a) $m(a - b) + n(a - b)$
   (b) $a(x + 2y) + b(x + 2y)$
   (c) $2a(2a - b) - b(2a - b)$
   (d) $3x(x - y) - 4y(x - y)$
   (e) $2x(4x + y) + 5y(4x + y)$

Section 11.3

1. Factor.

   (a) $x^2 - 3x - 10$
   (b) $y^2 + y - 6$
   (c) $m^2 - m - 2$
   (d) $t^2 - 7t - 30$
   (e) $x^2 + 13x - 14$
   (f) $m^2 + 7m - 18$
   (g) $t^2 - 2t - 24$
   (h) $y^2 - y - 30$
   (i) $x^2 + 3x - 4$
   (j) $a^2 + 3a - 28$

2. Factor each of the following. What is the common factor?

   (a) $2m^2 - 2m - 84$
   (b) $3a^2 + 6a - 144$
   (c) $m^3 - 5m^2 - 50m$
   (d) $2x^3 + 24x^2 + 70x$

3. Factor each of the following.

   (a) $x^2 + 15x - 54$
   (b) $x^2 - 11xy + 24y^2$
   (c) $x^2 + 4x - 21$
   (d) $m^2 + 14m - 51$
   (e) $y^2 + 29y + 54$
   (f) $x^2 - 9x - 90$
   (g) $y^2 + 19y - 20$
   (h) $m^2 - 12m - 28$
   (i) $24 + 11x + x^2$
   (j) $t^2 - 4t - 12$
   (k) $a^2 - 5a - 24$
   (l) $y^2 - 2y - 8$

4. Factor completely.

   (a) $y^4 - 2y^2 - 8$
   (b) $20 - 9y + y^2$
   (c) $x^2 - 4x - 32$
   (d) $x^4 - 21x^2 + 54$
   (e) $20 + 9x + x^2$
   (f) $x^2 + 3x - 28$

Section 11.7

1. Simplify each of the following.

   (a) $\sqrt{y^2 - 4y + 4}$
   (b) $\sqrt{x^2 + 8x + 16}$
   (c) $\sqrt{4x^2 - 8x + 4}$
   (d) $\sqrt{x^2 + 6x + 9}$
   (e) $\sqrt{4a^2 + 12a + 9}$
   (f) $\sqrt{16 - 16s + 4s^2}$
   (g) $\sqrt{t^2 - t + \frac{1}{4}}$
   (h) $\sqrt{a^4 - 6a^2 + 9}$

2. Write the square root of each of the following trinomials.

   (a) $x^2 + 6x + 9$
   (b) $y^2 + 4y + 4$
   (c) $a^2 - 6a + 9$
   (d) $36 - 12b + b^2$
   (e) $1 + 4x + 4x^2$
   (f) $9y^2 - 12y + 4$

(g) $4x^2 - 12x + 9$ (h) $4m^2 - 20m + 25$

(i) $a^2 + a + \dfrac{1}{4}$ (j) $\dfrac{1}{9} - \dfrac{2}{3}a + a^2$

(k) $x^4 + 2x^2 + 1$ (l) $1 - 4y^2 + 4y^4$

3. Find an expression for the area of the following figure.

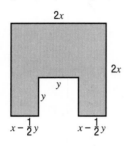

4. Write, as a product, an expression for the area.

Section 11.9

1. Find each quotient.

(a) $\dfrac{3y^3}{y^2}$ (b) $\dfrac{-6x^2}{2x}$ (c) $\dfrac{15a^5}{3a^2}$

(d) $\dfrac{9m^3}{-3m^2}$ (e) $\dfrac{9xy}{3x}$ (f) $\dfrac{12x^2y}{4x^2}$

2. Simplify each of the following. How many can you do mentally?

(a) $\dfrac{-8ab}{-4b}$ (b) $\dfrac{36mn}{-6m}$ (c) $\dfrac{-32bc}{4b}$

(d) $\dfrac{-16ab}{-2ab}$ (e) $\dfrac{100m^2n}{-10m}$ (f) $\dfrac{-27x^2y^3}{-9y^2}$

(g) $\dfrac{-24a^3b}{6a^3}$ (h) $\dfrac{-3a^2}{a^2p}$ (i) $\dfrac{-6m^3}{-2m^2}$

3. Find the value of each expression for $a = 3$ and $b = -2$.

(a) $\dfrac{12ab}{4a}$ (b) $\dfrac{16a^2b}{-4a}$ (c) $\dfrac{-64a^2b}{-4b}$

(d) $\dfrac{-32a^2b}{16ab}$ (e) $\dfrac{32b^2a}{16b}$ (f) $\dfrac{5a^2b^3}{15ab}$

4. Find an expression for the unknown side of each rectangle. The area of each rectangle is given.

(a)

(b)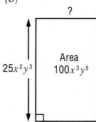

Section 11.10

For each of the exercises in Sections 11.10, 11.11, and 11.12, write the restrictions on the variables as you write the rational expressions in lowest terms.

1. Write each of the following in lowest terms.

(a) $\dfrac{3y - 15}{3}$ (b) $\dfrac{y - 4}{3y - 12}$

(c) $\dfrac{6x - 6y}{3x + 3y}$ (d) $\dfrac{x^2 - y^2}{x + y}$

(e) $\dfrac{x - y}{x^2 - y^2}$ (f) $\dfrac{6a + 6b}{3a^2 - 3b^2}$

(g) $\dfrac{n^2 + 5n + 6}{n + 3}$ (h) $\dfrac{n - 6}{n^2 - 4n - 12}$

2. Simplify each expression by writing it in lowest terms.

(a) $\dfrac{9y^2 - 16}{3y + 4}$ (b) $\dfrac{16x^2 - 25}{4x - 5}$

(c) $\dfrac{x^2 - x - 12}{x^2 + x - 20}$ (d) $\dfrac{x^2 + 5x + 6}{x^2 + 6x + 8}$

(e) $\dfrac{a^2 - 81}{2a + 18}$ (f) $\dfrac{y^2 - 25}{y^2 - 10y + 25}$

(g) $\dfrac{x^3 - x}{x^3 + 3x^2 + 2x}$ (h) $\dfrac{2 + 3x + x^2}{3 + 4x + x^2}$

3. Write each in lowest terms.

(a) $\dfrac{2y^4 - 2}{3y + 3}$ (b) $\dfrac{x^4 - y^4}{x^2 + 2xy + y^2}$

(c) $\dfrac{x^5 - x}{x^3 - x}$ (d) $\dfrac{x^4 - 9x^2}{x^3 + 3x^2}$

(e) $\dfrac{(2x^2 + 4x + 5) - (x^2 + 9x + 1)}{x^2 - 5x + 4}$

(f) $\dfrac{(x - 2y)^2 - 3(x - 2y)}{4y^2 - x^2}$

4. Find the value of each of the following for $x = 2$.

(a) $\dfrac{4x^2 - 1}{4x^2 + 4x + 4}$ (b) $\dfrac{x^2 - x - 12}{x^2 - 16}$

(c) $\dfrac{x^2 + 3x + 2}{x^2 + 4x + 3}$ (d) $\dfrac{3 - x}{x^2 - 4x + 3}$

(e) $\dfrac{x^2 - 2x - 15}{5 - x}$ (f) $\dfrac{x^2 + 7x + 10}{x^2 - x - 6}$

(g) $\dfrac{x^2 - 8x + 15}{x^2 - 2x - 15}$ (h) $\dfrac{1 - 2x^2}{2x^2 - x}$

Section 11.11

1. Simplify each of the following.

(a) $\dfrac{x^2 y}{2x - 2} \times \dfrac{2}{xy^2}$ (b) $\dfrac{x - 3}{y - 2} \times \dfrac{y - 2}{3 - x}$

(c) $\dfrac{36}{y^2 + 2y} \times \dfrac{y + 2}{9}$ (d) $\dfrac{n - 1}{3n} \times \dfrac{n}{n^2 - 1}$

(e) $\dfrac{x - y}{16} \times \dfrac{8}{x^2 - y^2}$ (f) $\dfrac{4x - 4}{8} \times \dfrac{6}{x^2 - 1}$

(g) $\dfrac{y^2 - 4}{y + 3} \times \dfrac{y^2 - 9}{y + 2}$ (h) $\dfrac{4x^2 - 1}{1 - 9x^2} \times \dfrac{1 - 3x}{2x - 1}$

2. Simplify.

(a) $\dfrac{a^2 - ab}{a^2 + ab} \times \dfrac{a + b}{a^2 - b^2}$

(b) $\dfrac{a}{a^2 - 6a + 5} \times \dfrac{a^2 - 4a - 5}{a^2 + 1}$

(c) $\dfrac{2x - 6}{4x^2 - 1} \times \dfrac{2x^2 - 7x - 4}{x^2 - 7x + 12}$

(d) $\dfrac{3x - 12}{4x + 20} \times \dfrac{x^2 + 5x}{x^2 - 4x}$

(e) $\dfrac{x^2 - y^2}{x^2 - xy} \times \dfrac{xy - y^2}{xy + x^2}$

3. Multiply.

(a) $\dfrac{x + 1}{x - 1} \times \dfrac{x + 3}{1 - x^2} \times \dfrac{1 - x}{(x + 3)^2}$

(b) $\dfrac{a^2 - a}{6a^2 + 15} \times \dfrac{4a^2 + 10}{a^2 - 7a + 12} \times \dfrac{a^2 - 4a}{2a}$

(c) $\dfrac{2x + x^2}{4 - x^2} \times \dfrac{x^2 - 2x}{x^2 - 4x} \times \dfrac{x^2 - 6x + 8}{x^2 - 16}$

Section 11.12

1. Divide.

(a) $\dfrac{x - 1}{6} \div \dfrac{1 - x}{8}$

(b) $\dfrac{a^2 - b^2}{a^2 - 16} \div \dfrac{a - b}{a - 4}$

(c) $\dfrac{y + 2}{8} \div \dfrac{y^2 - y - 6}{16}$

(d) $\dfrac{8x^3}{x - 1} \div \dfrac{2x^2}{3x - 3}$

(e) $\dfrac{8(x - 3)^2}{2x^3} \div \dfrac{2x^2}{x - 3}$

(f) $\dfrac{x^2 - y^2}{(x - y)^2} \div \dfrac{x + y}{x - y}$

(g) $\dfrac{a^2 + 6a + 9}{a^2 + 2a - 3} \div \dfrac{a^2 + 6a + 9}{a^2 - 1}$

2. Simplify.

(a) $\dfrac{x^2 - y^2}{x^2 + xy} \times \dfrac{(x + y)^2}{xy} \div \dfrac{x^2 - xy}{x^2 + xy}$

(b) $\dfrac{a^2 + a}{a^2 - 1} \times \dfrac{a^2 - 4a - 21}{a^2 - 4a} \div \dfrac{a^2 - 6a - 7}{a^2 - a - 12}$

(c) $\dfrac{a^3 + 4a^2}{a^2 - 1} \times \dfrac{a^2 - 5a + 6}{a^2 - 3a} \div \dfrac{a^2 - a - 2}{a^2 - 1}$

(d) $\dfrac{a^2 + 6a + 5}{a^2 + 7a + 12} \times \dfrac{a^2 + 2a - 8}{a^2 - 25} \div \dfrac{a^2 - a - 2}{a^2 - 2a - 15}$

543

CHAPTER 12

Section 12.3

1. Relations are shown above each table of values shown below.
   (a) Copy and complete each table of values.
   (b) Graph each relation.

$y = x - 2$

x	y
2	0
1	?
0	?
−1	−3
−2	?

$y = 2x - 1$

x	y
1	1
2	?
3	?
4	7

2. Draw a graph of each relation. For each relation, x is a real number.
   (a) $y = 4x$
   (b) $y = 2x - 3$
   (c) $y = 5 - x$
   (d) $y = 3 - 2x$
   (e) $y = \frac{1}{2}x$
   (f) $y = 3x + 1$

3. A relation is given by the ordered pairs (a, b) where $b = 2.5a$. Find each missing value.
   (a) $(6, b)$
   (b) $(a, 22.5)$
   (c) $(12.25, b)$
   (d) $(1.1, b)$
   (e) $(a, 3.75)$
   (f) $(0, b)$

4. A relation is given by (x, y) where $y = 50x$ and x is a real number.
   (a) Construct a table of values for the relation. Plot the ordered pairs.
   (b) Find the missing values in $(x, 0)$ and $(50, y)$.

5. Write an equation for each relation.

(a)

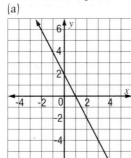

(b)

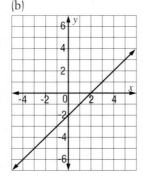

6. Barbara earns $5.50/h as a cashier at a theatre. The total amount she earns, T, per week is given by the equation $T = 5.50h$, where h is the number of hours she works.
   (a) Construct a table of values for the relation.
   (b) Use the table of values in (a) to draw the graph of the relation.

(c) For the relation, what are the missing values?
   A$(12, T)$ B$(h, \$79.75)$ C$(35, T)$

Section 12.4

1. If you walk at a constant speed of 5 km/h, then the distance walked is defined by the relation $d = 5t$, where t is the amount of time you walk. The following graph shows the relationship between d and t. Ordered pairs are plotted to find the graph of the relation.

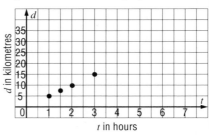

   (a) Copy and complete the graph for $0 \leqq t \leqq 7$, t is a real number.
   (b) What is the corresponding distance on the graph for
      • 2 h?   • 6 h?   • 5.5 h?   • 8.5 h ?
   (c) What is the corresponding time on the graph for
      • 10 km? • 25 km? • 7.5 km? • 14.5 km?

2. A candle burns at a rate of 0.2 cm/min. The length, L, of the candle that burns off per minute is given by the equation $L = 0.2t$, where t is the amount of time the candle has been left burning.
   (a) Use a table of values to draw a graph of the relation for $0 \leqq t \leqq 20$.
   (b) What length of candle has burned off after
      • 4 min?   • 13 min?
      • 17.5 min?   • 6.5 min?
   (c) How long has the candle been burning if the following amounts have been burned off?
      • 1 cm   • 2.4 cm
      • 1.9 cm   • 2.9 cm

3. A liquid is boiling and the amount of liquid left after each hour is shown in the table.

Amount of liquid in litres	7	5	3.8	2.5	2	1.5	1.2
After time t, in hours	0	1	2	3	4	5	6

(a) Draw a graph of the relation shown by the ordered pair (t, A).

(b) Join the points in (a) by a smooth curve.

(c) Describe the graph of the relation.

Section 12.6

1. Write the domain and range of each relation.

(a)

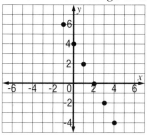

(b)

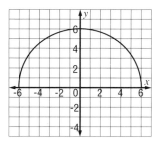

2. For each relation, write the domain and range and draw a graph.
   (a) $y = 3x$, x is a whole number
   (b) $y = 3x + 1$, x is an integer
   (c) $y = 3x - 1$, x is a real number
   (d) How are the graphs alike? different?

3. For each relation, write the domain and range and draw a graph.
   (a) $y = x + 5$, x is a whole number
   (b) $y = 4x + 5$, x is an integer
   (c) $y = -4x + 5$, x is a real number
   (d) How are the graphs alike? different?

4. The cost, C, of renting a car is given by $C = 8.5d + 20$, where d is the number of days the car is rented and 20 is the fixed cost independent of the number of days.
   (a) Use a table of values to draw a graph of the relation.
   (b) Write the domain and range of the relation.

Section 12.7

1. Identify the points of intersection for each graph.

(a)

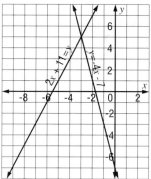

(b)

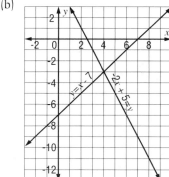

2. For each pair of relations, use a table of values to draw a graph and identify the point of intersection.
   (a) $y = 3x - 2$, $y = -x + 4$
   (b) $y = -x - 5$, $y = 2x - 1$

Section 12.11

1. (a) Draw a graph of $y = 3x + 9$. Label the point where the graph crosses the x–axis as N.
   (b) What is the value of the intercept?
   (c) What are the coordinates of N?

2. (a) Draw the graph of $2y - x = 16$. Label the point where the graph crosses the y-axis as M.
   (b) What is the value of the y-intercept?
   (c) What are the coordinates of M?

3. (a) Draw the graph of $4x - y = 12$.
   (b) What are the values of the intercepts?
   (c) What are the coordinates of the points where $4x - y = 12$ crosses each axis?

4. Find the x-intercept and the y-intercept of each line.
   (a) $3x - y = 9$
   (b) $x + y = 7$
   (c) $y = 3x - 6$
   (d) $2x + 3y = 6$
   (e) $4x - 3y = 12$
   (f) $y = \dfrac{1}{2}x + 3$

(d)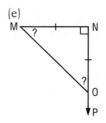

(e)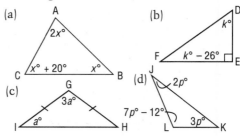

Section 12.12

1. Which of the following graphs represent functions?

   (a)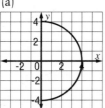
   (b)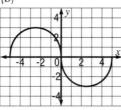

2. Refer to the graphs in Question 1.
   (a) How can you determine which of the graphs are functions?
   (b) Draw two relations of your own. Show how your method in (a) can be used to determine whether your graphs are functions.

CHAPTER 13

Section 13.3

1. Find the measure of the missing angle in each triangle.
   (a) 40°
   (b) ? 39°
   (c) 53° ?

2. (a) What type of triangle is △PQR?
   (b) What is the measure of ∠R?
   (c) What do you know about ∠P and ∠Q?
   (d) Find the measures of ∠P and ∠Q.

   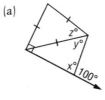

Section 13.4

1. Find the measure of each angle in the following triangles.

   (a)
   (b)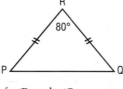
   (c)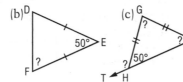

2. Find the measure of each variable in the following.

   (a)
   (b)
   (c)
   (d)

   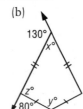

3. Find the measure of each variable.

   (a)
   (b)

   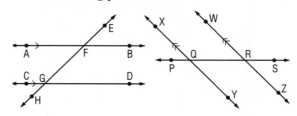

Section 13.5

1. Each diagram below shows a transversal intersecting parallel lines.

   (a) Name the alternate angles and the corresponding angles.
   (b) Which angles are equal?
   (c) Which angles are interior angles on the same side of the transversal?
   (d) Which angles have a sum of 180°?

546

2. A transversal intersects two lines as shown at the right. For which of the following statements do you think the lines will be parallel?

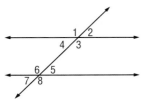

(a) $\angle 6 + \angle 4 = 180°$ (b) $\angle 8 < \angle 3$ (c) $\angle 7 = \angle 4$
(d) $\angle 1 = \angle 3$ (e) $\angle 8 = \angle 5$ (f) $\angle 3 = \angle 6$
(g) $\angle 6 + \angle 5 = 180°$ (h) $\angle 6 > \angle 3$ (i) $\angle 4 = \angle 5$

Section 13.6

1. Use the diagram shown below.

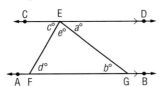

(a) Why is $a° = b°$?
(b) Why is $c° = d°$?
(c) Why are $c° + e° + a° = 180°$?
(d) How would you use the results from (a), (b), and (c) to show that $e° + d° + b° = 180°$?
(e) What property of triangles have you shown?

2. One angle of a parallelogram is three times the measure of the exterior angle adjacent to it. Find the measure of each angle.

3. In a triangle, one angle is 35° more than a second angle and 10° more than a third angle. Find the measure of each angle.

Section 13.10

1. From the diagram, why is
(a) $\triangle ADC \cong \triangle CBA$?
(b) $\angle DCA = \angle BAC$?
(c) $\angle DAB = \angle BCD$?
(d) AB ∥ DC?

2. Using the diagram, Mitch wrote:
AB = CB
AD = DC
BD = BD

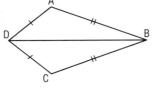

(a) What information can be seen from the above?
(b) Write other congruence relations from the above.

Section 13.11

1. Find the missing measures in each of the following.

(a)
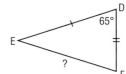

(b)
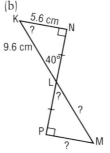

(c)
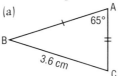

2. What information is unnecessary about each of the following pairs of congruent triangles?

(a)
(b)
(c)
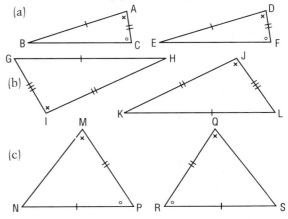

Section 13.12

1. The diagonal of a parallelogram is drawn. Why is
(a) $\triangle DEF \cong \triangle FGD$?
(b) $\angle G = \angle E$?
(c) GF = ED?
(d) DG = FE?

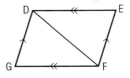

547

2. Refer to the diagram. Why is
   (a) △EAB ≅ △EDC?
   (b) AB = DC?
   (c) AB ∥ DC?

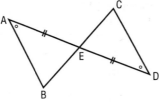

Section 13.16

1. Find the values of the variables for each diagram.

(a)

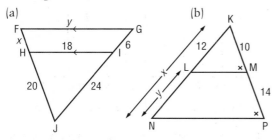

(b)

2. Find the value of y.

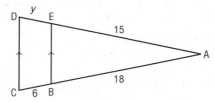

Section 13.17

1. During a take off a jet climbs 15 m for a horizontal distance of 75 m.
   (a) Calculate the height of the jet after it has travelled 1.5 km horizontally.
   (b) What assumption did you make in (a) to obtain your answer?

2. A ladder, AE, is placed against a house as shown. A fence, CD, is 3.3 m high. Find the distance of the foot of the ladder from the fence, if the fence is 3.0 m from the wall.

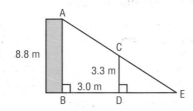

3. A ramp rises 12.6 cm for every 65.3 cm travelled. The end of the ramp is 2.3 m high. Calculate the length of the ramp.

CHAPTER 14

Section 14.4

1. The points scored by players on a team are shown below.

Player	Kelly	Green	Took	Curry	Smith	Char
Points	60	74	75	35	40	48

   (a) Construct a graph to display the information.
   (b) What percent of the total points did Smith score? Kelly score?
   (c) Who scored the greatest percent of points? What was the percent?

2. Refer to the following bar graph.

Source: Statistics Canada
Courtesy of Canadian Imperial Bank of Commerce

   (a) What was the personal savings rate in 1962? in 1966? in 1972?
   (b) If a person had an income of $12 500 in 1968, how much money would you expect the person to have saved?
   (c) Would every person with the same income save the same amount of money? Why?
   (d) What trends do you see in the graph?
   (e) What percent would you expect the personal savings rate to be in 1980? Why?

Section 14.6

1. Refer to the graph shown below.

Unemployment as a % of the Labour Force

Source: Statistics Canada
Courtesy Bank of Montreal

(a) In what year was the unemployment the lowest?
(b) If there were 7 141 000 people in the labour force in 1966, about how many persons were unemployed in 1966?
(c) Estimate which year has the fewest people unemployed?
(d) What information would you need to know to predict the number of persons unemployed any year?

2. Draw a line graph to show the following data.
    (a) Boy's Height/Mass Chart

Height (cm)	140	145	150	155	160	165	170	175	180	185
Average Mass (kg)	41	44	49	54	58	63	66	70	73	75

(b) Girl's Height/Mass Chart

Height (cm)	140	145	150	155	160	165	170	175	180	185
Average Mass (kg)	36	40	43	47	51	54	58	62	66	69

(c) How are the graphs in (a) and (b) alike?
(d) How are the graphs in (a) and (b) different?

3. Refer to the graph in Question 1.
    (a) Why is it difficult to use the graph to extrapolate information?
    (b) Why is the line graph effective in showing the information?

Section 14.7

1. The results of a survey of distances travelled in kilometres by students during the summer vacation are shown in the histogram.

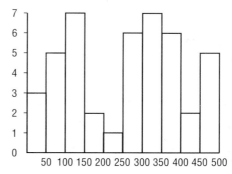

(a) What information is missing from the graph?
(b) How are bar graphs and histograms alike? How are they different?
(c) When is it most appropriate to use a histogram to show data?

2. The data below shows the height, in centimetres, of the students in a class.

    158, 169, 156, 174, 180, 163, 162, 159, 175,
    161, 174, 176, 182, 173, 168, 180, 160, 177,
    167, 179, 181, 172, 167, 170, 164, 183, 157,
    165, 174, 169, 180, 176, 168, 155, 186, 170

    (a) Organize the data into a frequency table.
    (b) Display the data in a histogram.

Section 14.8

1. (a) A concrete mix consists of 1.5 L of water, 3.8 L of sand, 1 L of cement, and 4.2 L of gravel. Construct a circle graph for the data.
    (b) For a similar concrete, how much cement is there if there are 40 L of concrete mix?

2. During one hour of radio listening, Henrietta recorded the following data.

News other than sports	6 min 36 s
Sports and sports news	4 min 42 s
Music	28 min 54 s
Commercials	8 min 18 s
Discussions	11 min 30 s

(a) Construct a circle graph.
(b) Create and solve two questions for your data.

Section 14.11

1. For each of the following:
   - Decide whether the sample taken was random.
   - If not, how would you make it random?
   (a) The most popular computer ever made was selected by 10 computer manufacturers.
   (b) The winner of the president's race for the student council was selected by one vote from each student in the school.

2. Suppose you need to select three people from your class for a trip.
   (a) How would you select the three people so that each person has an equal chance of being selected?
   (b) Use your process from (a). List the people who would take the trip.

Section 14.12

1. Which of the measures, mean, median and mode, is always a member of the data? Use an example to illustrate your answer.

2. The heights of students in centimetres are given by the following data.

   160, 158, 180, 180, 171, 168, 166, 160, 169, 173, 172, 181, 174, 160, 179, 160, 176, 157, 165, 159, 183, 162, 177, 167, 163, 170, 178

   (a) Find the mean, median, and mode.
   (b) Which of your results from (a) best represents the data? Give reasons for your answer.

3. The pulse rate in beats per minute was recorded for a group of people.

   75, 72, 91, 67, 80, 77, 73, 67, 71, 75, 72, 94, 71, 70, 69, 93, 64, 80, 54, 75, 69, 74, 73, 89, 78, 64, 81, 59, 80, 74, 76, 77, 70, 77, 70, 79, 58, 71, 82, 70, 68, 77, 81, 71, 70, 78, 63, 74, 75, 76, 56, 83, 69, 77, 53, 73, 68, 64, 59, 86

   (a) Decide on a class interval for the data and construct a histogram.
   (b) Predict, from your histogram, the average pulse. How can you check the accuracy of your answer?
   (c) What percent of the people had a pulse less than 70? more than 80?
   (d) What do you notice about your answers in (c)?

(e) What percent of the people had a pulse in the interval 70–79?

Section 14.13

1. Three sets of trials of 500 rolls of a die are listed below.

Number	1	2	3	4	5	6
Trial 1	93	93	82	80	93	59
Trial 2	87	81	92	73	74	93
Trial 3	88	77	74	93	90	78
Total	268	?	?	?	?	?
Average per trial	?	?	?	?	?	?

   (a) Total each number based on the three trials and find the average per trial.
   (b) Use the results from (a) to predict the number of threes in another trial of 500 rolls.

2. Data are given for the range of marks on an exam. You select an exam at random. What is the probability of each of the following?

Class	Class Limits	Frequency
1	1–10	0
2	11–20	0
3	21–30	3
4	31–40	4
5	41–50	5
6	51–60	18
7	61–70	20
8	71–80	15
9	81–90	9
10	91–100	2

   (a) the student passed
   (b) the student received a mark over 80
   (c) the student did not have a mark in the 61–70 class

Section 14.15

1. A die is rolled and a coin is tossed.
   (a) Record all the possible outcomes.
   (b) What is the probability of rolling an odd number and tossing a tail?
   (c) What is the probability of rolling a number greater than four and tossing a head?

2. The four aces from a deck of cards are placed face down and mixed. One card is turned up and its suit recorded. The card is turned face down and the cards are mixed up. A second and then a third card are chosen in the same way.
   (a) Find the probability that all three cards are red aces.

(b) Conduct an experiment and record the results of drawing three cards 100 times. Find the experimental probability of turning up three red aces. Compare your results with your answer in (a).

Section 14.16

1. In an experiment, a nickel and a dime are tossed and a die is rolled. Calculate the probability of obtaining
   (a) two heads and a six.
   (b) two tails and an odd number.

2. An apartment building has 10 floors with 8 apartments on each floor. One apartment is chosen at random to receive a prize. What is the probability that the apartment chosen is
   (a) on the fifth floor and has an even number?
   (b) is above the fifth floor and has an even number greater than 6?

3. A coin is tossed, a die is rolled, and one card is chosen from a deck of 52. Calculate the probability of choosing
   (a) a head, a six, and an ace.
   (b) a tail, an odd number, and a diamond.
   (c) a head, a number less than three, and an even-numbered card.

Section 14.17

1. In a box of 100 batteries, 5 are dead. If 2 batteries are chosen at random, what is the probability of choosing 2 dead batteries?

2. A drawer contains 10 black socks, 8 brown socks and 12 white socks. In the dark, what is the probability of pulling out 2 brown socks?

3. Of the 112 grade 9 students at a school, 60 are girls and 52 are boys. Three of the students are chosen by drawing names from a hat. Find the probability of drawing (a) three boys; and (b) two girls and a boy.

Section 14.18

1. If three cards are selected from a deck of 52, find the probability of choosing
   (a) 3 tens.   (b) 3 red cards.
   (c) a Jack, a Queen, and a King.

2. A bag contains 3 red marbles, 5 blue marbles, and 7 green marbles.
   (a) What is the probability of selecting 3 red marbles in a row.

(b) What is the probability of selecting a red marble, then a green marble, and then a blue marble.
(c) What is the probability of selecting a green marble, then a blue marble, and then a red marble?
(d) How are your probabilities in (b) and (c) alike? How are they different?

Section 14.20

1. Suppose one out of every six motorcycles has racing handlebars and one out of every two motorcycles has a fairing. Estimate the probability that the next three motorcycles you see will have neither racing handlebars nor a fairing.

2. The entrance tests for a military college consist of two parts. Four out of every six applicants passed the academic test. On the athletic test, one in every two passed. Estimate the probability that the next two applicants will pass both tests.

3. To field-test a new recipe, a market researcher gives ten cookies to a volunteer. Half of the cookies are the new recipe and half are the old recipe. (They look exactly the same.) Predict the probability that the first four cookies tasted are made from the new recipe.

CHAPTER 15
Section 15.2

1. A dot is enclosed by a square. Describe the translations needed for the figure to travel the corridor shown on the grid.

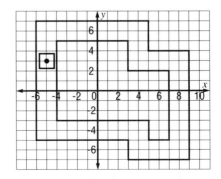

2. Describe the translations needed to move Box A through the warehouse to Box B.

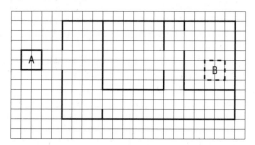

Section 15.3

1. The translation $(x, y) \rightarrow (x + 2, y - 2)$ is applied to the polygon with coordinates A(–4, 4), B(–8, 4), C(–8, 0), D(–2, –5), and E(2, –1). Find the coordinates of the image.

2. The translation $(x, y) \rightarrow (x + 1, y - 3)$ is applied to the polygon with coordinates A(–4, 5), B(–6, 4), C(–2, 0), D(–4, –4), and E(3, –1). Find the coordinates of the image.

3. The translation $(x, y) \rightarrow (x + 7, y - 3)$ is applied to the polygon with coordinates A(–5, 8), B(–3, 7), C(–6, 6), D(4, –9), E(8, 8), and F(2, –1). Find the coordinates of the image.

Section 15.6

1. Reflections have been used to make each design. How are reflections used for each design? Make a copy of each design.

   (a)   (b)

2. Copy each diagram. Construct the reflection image of each figure with respect to its reflection line.

   (a)   (b)

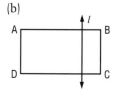

Section 15.7

1. Copy the grid shown below.

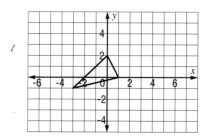

Find the image of the figure by first reflecting it in the x-axis and then reflecting it in the y-axis.

2. (a) Mark any parallelogram PQRS on a coordinate grid.
   (b) Reflect the parallelogram in the y-axis.
   (c) Compare the slopes of P'Q' and S'R', P'S', and Q'R'. What do you notice?

Section 15.10

1. Make a copy of each diagram. Use the rotation centre O. For each diagram, construct the rotation image for a half turn.
   (a) clockwise   (b) counterclockwise

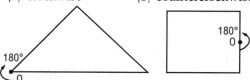

2. Make a copy of each diagram. Construct the rotation image for a quarter turn clockwise. Use the rotation centre O.

   (a)   (b)

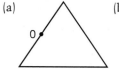

   (c)

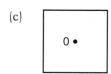

Section 15.11

1. Find the image figure under a $\frac{1}{4}$ turn (90°) counterclockwise about the origin.

(a)   (b)   (c)

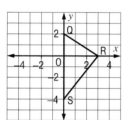 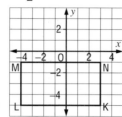

2. Predict the coordinates of the image for each figure. The centre of rotation is the origin. How can you check your predictions?

(a) +90°   (b) $\frac{1}{2}$ turn cw

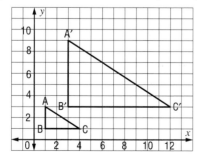

Section 15.14

1. Two triangles are related as shown.
   (a) What is the scale factor?
   (b) How are the coordinates related?
   (c) Measure corresponding angles. What do you notice about the measures?
   (d) Measure corresponding sides. What do you notice about the measures?
   (e) What is the ratio of corresponding sides?

2. A square ABCD is enlarged as shown.
   (a) Which points correspond?
   (b) Write a rule for the coordinates.
   (c) Find the ratios of corresponding sides. What do you notice?
   (d) Measure corresponding angles. What do you notice?

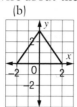 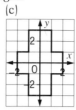

3. (a) Find the image of figure ABCD. Use the dilatation rule: Multiply both coordinates by 2.
   (b) Mark all lines that are parallel.

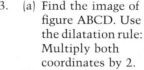 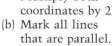 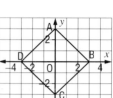

Section 15.16

1. (a) Figures with rotational symmetry that are of order 1 are not considered to have rotational symmetry. Why?
   (b) Does every figure with line symmetry have point symmetry? If your answer is no, give an example.
   (c) Does every figure with point symmetry have line symmetry? If your answer is no, give an example.

2. Use squared paper to create a design that has both reflectional symmetry and rotational symmetry. How did you decide on your design?

302	068	416	505	346	808	242	349	956	892	265	546	092	488	336	201	057	728	343	640	895	202	076	619	431
809	229	534	531	633	874	682	353	794	607	039	713	764	623	563	527	794	604	069	799	480	655	454	224	163
186	408	090	103	644	774	892	279	486	409	124	305	294	429	903	019	884	456	332	049	041	294	453	190	852
806	288	827	206	422	754	358	536	443	239	557	307	438	468	847	699	863	930	558	362	302	114	600	193	879
561	451	088	502	255	677	218	380	672	059	585	703	955	914	203	172	855	871	751	277	363	227	400	302	089
296	316	999	001	673	088	446	143	823	127	813	138	477	779	987	249	241	394	580	874	690	595	366	060	061
221	135	036	015	710	844	616	339	385	911	155	745	130	754	364	167	217	550	050	439	443	283	754	354	725
430	842	575	965	692	648	655	436	558	359	446	124	353	779	993	137	282	748	196	546	096	829	270	129	882
503	267	339	408	077	922	397	456	309	538	363	219	371	222	088	567	664	162	373	300	066	188	585	699	847
690	599	249	213	883	471	946	899	126	718	609	101	208	604	067	056	378	576	968	645	745	125	508	483	546
078	998	022	103	730	287	923	410	168	418	591	504	309	563	533	573	862	948	933	626	641	878	595	382	790
711	796	541	265	500	140	801	419	617	350	978	444	204	287	951	998	038	981	383	818	013	289	767	711	802
411	225	172	869	786	814	095	987	251	378	566	619	428	951	992	157	907	064	933	622	526	816	046	626	637
999	007	478	742	047	998	025	258	954	941	793	637	992	160	607	025	588	592	470	924	432	766	677	204	298
149	041	487	362	290	698	826	199	210	812	144	745	128	920	433	065	536	458	418	560	413	323	549	014	078
941	803	385	926	480	667	090	042	646	721	540	313	826	200	106	767	700	872	736	123	213	480	516	795	588
615	285	952	978	427	986	278	465	689	568	692	653	499	104	882	503	277	364	189	704	996	071	799	476	805
321	695	739	031	609	100	017	494	079	630	787	765	654	490	242	316	977	462	560	408	088	397	449	001	566
632	824	147	265	515	749	243	219	357	583	790	693	680	304	186	414	392	711	800	450	046	541	252	511	600
200	126	688	537	408	095	966	671	046	805	328	287	934	643	824	144	697	781	919	316	984	306	322	609	097
646	731	247	079	565	585	704	983	331	089	341	511	595	362	281	674	118	584	737	092	281	670	003	723	473
954	929	546	095	971	570	767	720	560	424	874	676	176	634	903	025	314	868	829	268	269	193	821	078	936
691	612	211	948	938	737	091	201	067	018	430	848	725	407	033	263	665	129	825	160	592	464	676	193	894
229	532	601	165	011	926	466	746	161	487	368	029	354	723	485	471	969	612	194	779	977	450	051	700	872
718	606	002	809	224	094	775	906	046	650	615	288	889	348	919	321	687	505	369	072	601	167	295	407	033

absolute value: the actual number represented by the symbol | | e.g. |−3| = 3, |2| = 2

acute angle: an angle with a measure less than 90 degrees

acute triangle: a triangle where each angle has a measure less than 90 degrees

adjacent angles: two angles which share a common side and vertex, and whose interiors do not intersect

algebra: a generalization of arithmetic where symbols represent numbers and are related by operations

altitude: the perpendicular distance between a base and the opposite vertex

angle: the figure formed by two rays with a common end point

approximate: almost exact

arc: part of the circumference of the circle

area: the number of square units needed to cover a surface

average: the sum of several numbers divided by the amount of numbers

axes: the intersecting number lines on a graph

bar graph: a diagram that uses bars to display data or information

base (of a power): the number that is the repeated factor in a power

bias: the deviation from true value or distortion of a statistic due to the neglect of a factor or factors

bisect: to divide in half

break even: the point at which relations cross

broken-line graph: a graph made up of line segments joined end to end

Cartesian plane: the grid created by the intersection of the x-axis and the y-axis; also known as the coordinate plane

central angle: an angle that has its vertex at the centre of a circle

centre (of a circle): the point that is an equal distance from any point on the circumference

centre of gravity: the point at which any object is balanced

chord: a line segment that has end points on the circumference

circle: a closed curve such that all points on the curve are the same distance from its centre

circle graph: a diagram that uses a circle to display data

circumference: the distance around a circle

clockwise: the direction in which the hands on a clock move

clustered sample: a sample from a particular part of the population

commission: an amount earned from selling a product or service

common factor: a number that is the factor of each number

common multiple: a number that is the multiple of two or more numbers

complementary angles: two angles whose degree measures add to 90 degrees

composite number: a number with three or more factors

compound interest: the interest for each time period is added to the principal before the interest is calculated for the next time period

concentric circles: circles having the same centre

congruent: having the same size and shape

contained angle: the angle between any two sides in a polygon

coordinate grid: see **Cartesian plane**

counter-clockwise: opposite of clockwise

cube: a polyhedron with six congruent square sides

data: facts or information

decimal number: a number written in the decimal system; i.e. 1.1, 2.3, …

degree: a unit for measuring angles

denominator: the bottom number in a fraction

dependent event: an event that is affected by the outcome of another event

destructive sample: a sample that cannot be used more than once

diagonal: a line segment that joins two vertices in a polygon that are not adjacent

diameter: a line segment with end points on a circle and passing through the centre of the circle

dilatation: a transformation where the original shape is increased or decreased by a common factor

dilatation factor: the common factor involved in a dilatation

domain: all the first components of the ordered pairs in a relation

equation: a mathematical sentence that shows equality

equidistant: equally distant

equilateral triangle: a triangle with sides of equal length

equivalent fractions: fractions that can be reduced to the same lowest terms

exponent: a number that shows how many times the base is used as a factor

extrapolate: to estimate a value beyond the given values

factor: any natural number that divides another number

Fibonacci sequence: a sequence of numbers where each number is the sum of the two previous numbers

fraction: a number that represents a part of a whole number

fraction form: a number written in the form a/b

geometry: the properties and relationships among lines, angles, points, surfaces, and solids

Goldbach's conjecture: every even number except two can be written as a sum of prime numbers

greatest common factor: the greatest factor common to two or more numbers

histogram: a bar graph used to illustrate data in a frequency table

incentre: centre of a circle

independent event: an event that is not affected by any other outcome

inequality: a state where one quantity is greater than or less than another quantity

inscribed angle: an angle that is inside a circle

integer: one of the set of numbers ..., $-2, -1, 0, 1, 2, ...$

interest: a percentage of principal that is multiplied by the principal

interpolate: to choose two known values on a graph and estimate a value between them

irrational number: a number that cannot be expressed as an integer

isosceles triangle: a triangle with two sides of equal length

isometry: a transformation that preserves length

kite: a quadrilateral with two pairs of adjacent sides equal in length

least common multiple: the lowest common multiple of two or more denominators

line graph: a graph that uses lines to display data or information

line of symmetry: a line that divides a figure into two congruent parts

literal coefficient: a letter

logo: a symbol designed by a company so that they can be recognized by the public

mean: the sum of several numbers divided by how many numbers there are

median: the middle number when the data is arranged in ascending or descending order

mixed number: a number consisting of a whole part and a fractional part

mode: the number that occurs most often

multiple: the product of the number and another whole number

natural number: one of the set of numbers 1, 2, 3, 4, ...

negative integer: one of the set of numbers $-1, -2, -3, -4, ...$

non-terminating decimal: a decimal that repeats itself indefinitely

numerical coefficient: a number

numerator: the top number in a fraction

obtuse angle: an angle which measures greater than 90 degrees but less than 180 degrees

obtuse triangle: a triangle with one obtuse angle

opposite angles: two angles which are formed by two intersecting lines, and share a common vertex

optical scanner: a device used by a computer to read typed or printed material

order of operations: a set of rules which govern the evaluation of expressions

ordered pair: a pair of numbers in which the first number describes horizontal displacement and the second number describes vertical displacement

origin: the point at which the horizontal and vertical axes intersect

orthocentre: point of intersection of the perpendiculars

palindrome: a number (word) that reads the same backwards and forwards

parallel lines: two lines in the same plane that never intersect

parallelogram: a quadrilateral that has both pairs of opposite sides parallel

percent: the number of parts per 100

perimeter: the distance around a closed figure

perpendicular: two lines intersecting at 90 degrees

pi: a number, symbol π, with an approximate value of 3.14, which represents the ratio of the circumference to the diameter of a circle

pictograph: a diagram that displays data using pictures

point: an object having only one position in space

point of symmetry: a point on which a figure can rotate to remain symmetrical

polygon: a closed figure made from line segments

polyhedron: a three-dimensional figure with faces that are polygons

population: the complete set of individuals or things from which samples are drawn

power: an expression using a base and an exponent

prime number: a number with factors of only one and itself

principal: an amount of money usually paid to a creditor

prism: a figure with two equal and parallel bases and whose faces are parallelograms

probability: a number that gives the likelihood of an event happening

profit: the amount of money received for a product or service less the cost of that product or service

proportion: an equation that shows the equality of two ratios

pyramid: a figure with a base that is a polygon and triangular faces that meet at a common vertex

Pythagorean Relation: theorem which relates to a right-angled triangle, where the square of the hypoteneuse is equal to the sum of the squares of the other two sides

quadrant: any of the four parts of the Cartesian plane

quadrilateral: a polygon with four sides

radius: a line segment that joins the centre of the circle to a point on the circle; half the diameter

random sample: a random survey of a section of the population

range: all the second components of the ordered pairs in a relation

rate: compare unlike quantities

ratio: a comparison of two numbers

rational number: a number which can be written as an integer or a quotient of integers

real number: any rational or irrational number

reciprocals: two numbers are reciprocals of each other if their product is one

rectangle: a quadrilateral with opposite sides equal and angle measures of 90 degrees

relation: a set of ordered pairs

reflection: a transformation where a figure is reversed on the other side of a line

rhombus: a parallelogram with all sides equal

right angle: an angle that measures 90 degrees

right-angle triangle: a triangle with a 90-degree angle

rise: distance along the y-axis

root: solution to an equation

rotation: any turn of a figure about a fixed point

rotational symmetry: symmetry around a fixed point

run: distance along the x-axis

salary: a fixed amount of income per pay period

sample: see **random sample**

scale: ratio of distance

scalene triangle: a triangle with all sides of unequal length

scientific notation: a form of writing numbers where they are expressed as a decimal product of a power of 10

significant digits: refers to scientific notation, only those numbers which are not placeholders

similar: the same shape but not necessarily the same size

simple interest: interest is not added to the principal in the following year

simulation: an experiment used to collect data

slope: rise divided by run

square: a quadrilateral with four equal sides and all angle measures of 90 degrees

square root: one of the two factors of a given number

stratified sample: a sample of an entire population where different sub-populations are all represented proportionately

supplementary angles: two angles that add to 180 degrees

surface area: the total area covered by all the faces of a polyhedron

symmetry: equality

table: an organized listing of data

terminating decimal: a decimal number with a finite number of digits

terms (of a ratio): numbers used in a ratio

transformation: a translation, reflection, or rotation

translation: a transformation where a figure slides from one position to another

transversal: a line that intersects two parallel lines

trapezoid: a quadrilateral with one pair of opposite sides parallel

triangle: a polygon with three sides

unique: leading to one and only one result

unit tile: a pictorial representation of integers

variable: a symbol used to represent a number

vertex: the common end point of two rays

volume: the amount of space occupied by a three-dimensional object

whole numbers: the numbers 0, 1, 2, 3, ...

x-axis: horizontal number line

x-tile: a strip used to represent different variables

y-axis: vertical number line

Page 11 1. a) M, 8:28; L, 8:41 **b)** 13 min **2. b)** 5040
3. a) 1881 **b)** 1881 **5. a)** Samuel, Samantha; Joe,
Jen; James, Chris **b)** Peter cycles, Steven swims,
Pitman lifts weights **6. a)** 84

Page 15 1. a) 1 fold, 2 parts **b)** 2 folds, 4 parts
2. a) 3 folds **b)** 8 parts **4. b)** 3^6, $(-2)^2$

Page 19 1. b) $\frac{4}{8}$ **c)** $\frac{5}{8}$ **2. b)** $\frac{5}{10}$ **c)** $\frac{7}{10}$ **3. b)** $\frac{4}{8}$ **c)** $\frac{3}{8}$

d) $\frac{1}{8}$ **e)** $\frac{1}{8}$ **4. b)** $\frac{4}{6}$ **c)** $\frac{3}{6}$ or $\frac{1}{2}$ **d)** $\frac{1}{6}$ **e)** $\frac{1}{6}$

Page 20 1. c) 6 **d)** $\frac{1}{6}$ **2. c)** 8 **d)** $\frac{1}{8}$ **4. c)** $\frac{1}{2} = \frac{2}{4}$

e) $\frac{1}{2} = \frac{4}{8}$ **f)** $\frac{2}{4} = \frac{4}{8}$ **6. b)** $\frac{1}{4}$ **c)** $\frac{1}{4}$ **7. b)** 5 **c)** 5 **8. b)** 2

c) 2 **9. a)** $\frac{1}{2}$ **b)** $\frac{1}{8}$ **c)** $\frac{1}{8}$ **11. b)** 6 **c)** 6 **12. b)** 8 **c)** 8

Page 22 *Adding Fractions:* **1. a)** $\frac{1}{5}$ **b)** 1 **c)** $\frac{4}{5}$

2. a) $1\frac{1}{4}$ **b)** $1\frac{1}{6}$ **c)** $\frac{7}{10}$ **3. a)** $\frac{5}{6}$ **b)** $\frac{11}{12}$ **c)** $\frac{14}{15}$ **d)** $\frac{17}{24}$ **e)** $\frac{11}{12}$

f) $\frac{23}{30}$ **4. a)** $5\frac{1}{2}$ **b)** $5\frac{4}{5}$ **c)** 6 **5. a)** $4\frac{3}{4}$ **b)** $4\frac{1}{2}$ **c)** $4\frac{5}{8}$

Subtracting Fractions: **1. a)** $\frac{3}{5}$ **b)** $\frac{1}{2}$ **c)** $\frac{3}{5}$ **2. a)** $\frac{1}{4}$

b) $\frac{7}{10}$ **c)** $\frac{1}{2}$ **3. a)** $\frac{1}{6}$ **b)** $\frac{5}{12}$ **c)** $\frac{4}{15}$ **d)** $\frac{1}{24}$ **e)** $\frac{7}{12}$ **f)** $\frac{17}{30}$

4. a) 1 **b)** $1\frac{2}{5}$ **c)** $2\frac{1}{3}$ **5. a)** $2\frac{1}{6}$ **b)** $3\frac{7}{12}$ **c)** $6\frac{2}{15}$ **d)** $1\frac{9}{10}$

e) $3\frac{13}{20}$ **f)** $1\frac{7}{12}$ *Multiplying Fractions:* **1. a)** $\frac{1}{6}$ **b)** $\frac{1}{8}$

c) $\frac{1}{10}$ **d)** $\frac{2}{9}$ **e)** $\frac{2}{15}$ **f)** $\frac{3}{16}$ **2. a)** 1 **b)** 1 **c)** 1 **d)** 1 **e)** 1 **f)** 1

3. a) $\frac{1}{6}$ **b)** $\frac{1}{8}$ **c)** $2\frac{1}{2}$ **d)** $\frac{3}{5}$ **e)** $\frac{7}{10}$ **f)** $\frac{1}{4}$ **4. a)** $1\frac{5}{9}$ **b)** $\frac{25}{32}$

c) 1 **d)** $2\frac{1}{6}$ **e)** $2\frac{4}{5}$ **f)** $4\frac{1}{6}$ **5. a)** 1 **b)** 1 **c)** 1 **d)** 1 **e)** 1 **f)** 1

Dividing Fractions: **1. a)** 3 **b)** 3 **c)** $2\frac{2}{3}$ **2. a)** $\frac{3}{4}$ **b)** $1\frac{1}{4}$

c) $\frac{16}{27}$ **d)** $\frac{1}{2}$ **e)** $1\frac{1}{3}$ **f)** $\frac{32}{49}$ **3. a)** $\frac{1}{6}$ **b)** $\frac{1}{12}$ **c)** $\frac{1}{9}$ **d)** $\frac{3}{20}$

e) 5 **f)** 12 **4. a)** 20 **b)** $6\frac{3}{4}$ **c)** 18 **d)** 32 **e)** 49 **f)** 10 **g)** 144

h) 30 **i)** 128 **5. a)** $\frac{11}{36}$ **b)** 2 **c)** $8\frac{1}{3}$ **d)** 56 **e)** 4 **f)** 2

6. a) 128 **b)** $1\frac{4}{5}$ **c)** $12\frac{4}{5}$

Page 24 1. a) 2 **b)** 3 **c)** 5 **d)** 4 **e)** 5 **f)** 2 **g)** 3 **h)** 3
2. a) 84 **b)** 27 **c)** 54 **d)** 19 683 **e)** 1040 **f)** 6 **g)** 15 600
h) 60 **3. a)** 80 **b)** 98 **c)** 56 **d)** 36 **e)** 259 **f)** 279 **g)** 55
h) 37 **4. a)** 227 **b)** 247 **c)** 106 **d)** 459 **e)** 167 **f)** 2882
g) 9 **h)** 1008 **5. a)** 243 **b)** 1024 **c)** 1024 **d)** 3125 **e)** 16
f) 36 **g)** 7 **h)** 5 **6.** Greatest value is (c), 729.
7. a) 33 + 2 **b)** 44 − 24 **c)** 11 + 15 **8.** 2048

Page 25 2. c) i) 4^5 **ii)** 5^{13} **iii)** 11^{13} **iv)** 8^{12} **4. c) i)** 5
ii) 9 **iii)** 11^5 **iv)** 8^6

Page 26 2. c) i) 5^6 **ii)** 9^{72} **iii)** 11^{126} **iv)** 8^{27}

4. c) i) $4^2 \times 7^2$ **ii)** $\frac{12^8}{5^8}$ **iii)** $11^9 \times 4^9$ **iv)** $\frac{3^3}{5^3}$ **5. a) i)** 3^4

ii) 4^5 **iii)** 6^3 **iv)** 4^7 **v)** 6^3 **vi)** 5^7 **b) i)** 3^4 **ii)** 4^5 **iii)** 6^3
iv) 7^6 **v)** 11^{17} **vi)** 8^9 **(c)** 1 **6. a) i)** 1 **ii)** 1 **iii)** 1 **iv)** 1 **v)** 1
b) i) 1 **ii)** 1 **iii)** 1 **iv)** 1 **7. a) i)** 3^3 **ii)** 4^4 **iii)** 6^{-1} **iv)** 4^6
v) 6^2 **vi)** 5^6 **b)** A power with a negative exponent is
the reciprocal of the same base with a negative

exponent, e.g., $4^{-1} = \frac{1}{4}$, $8^{-3} = \frac{1}{8^3}$. **8. a) i)** $\frac{1}{4}$ **ii)** $\frac{1}{3}$

iii) $\frac{1}{6}$ **iv)** $\frac{1}{-11}$ **v)** $\frac{1}{-6}$

Page 28 *Multiplying Powers:* **1. a)** 3^8 **b)** 4^8 **c)** 3^3
d) 12^7 **e)** 8^8 **f)** 4^8 **2. a)** 2^8 **b)** 7^8 **c)** 13^3 **d)** 12^5 **e)** 6^8 **f)** 7^8
3. a) 1024 **b)** 823 543 **c)** 1 953 125 **d)** 531 441 **e)** 1
f) 4096 **4. a)** 7^{-2} **b)** 4^2 **c)** 3^4 **d)** 12^{-1} **e)** 8^2 **f)** 5^0 **g)** 15^1

h) 6^{-2} **5. a)** $\frac{1}{2^8}$ **b)** $\frac{1}{3^7}$ **c)** $\frac{1}{11^8}$ **d)** $\frac{1}{8^6}$ **e)** $\frac{1}{7^7}$ **f)** $\frac{1}{6^9}$ **g)** $\frac{1}{11^2}$

h) $\frac{1}{4^6}$ **6. a)** 3 **b)** $\frac{1}{5}$ **c)** 1296 **d)** 1 **e)** 1 *Dividing Powers:*

1. a) 2^4 **b)** 3^3 **c)** 3^1 **d)** 11^{12} **e)** 1^{41} **f)** 10^2 **2. a)** 5^4 **b)** 9^3
c) 13^1 **d)** 7^1 **e)** 8^1 **f)** 2^2 **3. a)** 10 **b)** 729 **c)** 1 **d)** 216 **e)** 1
f) 1 **4. a)** 8^{-8} **b)** 6^{10} **c)** 3^{-9} **d)** 8^{-9} **e)** 9^{10} **f)** 5^8 **g)** 5^8 **h)** 7^7

5. a) $\frac{1}{2^1}$ **b)** 5^3 **c)** $\frac{1}{11^2}$ **d)** 7^1 **e)** 9^0 or 1 **f)** 6^3 **g)** 10^0 or 1

h) 14^0 or 1 **6. a)** 3 **b)** 282 475 249 **c)** 1 **d)** $\frac{1}{4096}$ **e)** 1
Power of a Power: **1. a)** 2^6 **b)** 3^6 **c)** 10^7 **d)** 3^8 **e)** 7^8
f) 9^4 **2. a)** 2^6 **b)** 3^8 **c)** 8^8 **d)** 5^3 **e)** 7^5 **f)** 11^4 **3. a)** $\frac{1}{2^6}$

b) $\frac{1}{3^8}$ **c)** $\frac{1}{8^8}$ **d)** $\frac{1}{5^3}$ **e)** $\frac{1}{7^5}$ **f)** $\frac{1}{11^4}$ **4.** Each part of
question 3 is the reciprocal of the corresponding
part of question 2. **5. a)** 2^{12} **b)** 3^5 **c)** 4^{12} **d)** 3^3 **e)** 1

f) 1 **g)** 2^3 **6. a)** 4^{17} **b)** 6^{54} **c)** 5 **d)** 3^4 **e)** 2^3 **f)** 5^5 *Power of a Product or Quotient:* **1. a)** $4^5 \times 3^5$ **b)** $2^5 \times 3^5$ **c)** $6^6 \times 2^6$ **d)** $5^2 \times 4^2$ **2. a)** $5^4 \times 2^4$ **b)** 7^4 **c)** $3^3 \times 3^3$ **d)** 8^5 **3. a)** $\dfrac{1}{5^4} \times \dfrac{1}{2^4}$ **b)** $\dfrac{1}{7^4}$ **c)** $\dfrac{1}{3^3} \times \dfrac{1}{3^3}$ **d)** $\dfrac{1}{8^5}$ **4.** Question 3 involves reciprocals of items in question 2.

5. a) $\dfrac{2^3}{3^3}$ **b)** $\dfrac{1}{4^4}$ **c)** $\dfrac{1}{2^6}$ **d)** $\dfrac{2^2}{5^2}$ **e)** $\dfrac{4^5}{7^5}$ **f)** $\dfrac{1}{5^2}$ **6. a)** $\dfrac{3^3}{2^3}$ **b)** 4^4 **c)** 2^6 **d)** $\dfrac{5^2}{2^2}$ **e)** $\dfrac{7^5}{4^5}$ **f)** 5^2 **7.** Each part of question 6 is the reciprocal of the corresponding part of question 5. **8. a)** $\dfrac{1}{64}$ **b)** $\dfrac{4}{9}$ **c)** $\dfrac{256}{81}$

Page 30 *Activity 1:* **a)** 1276.5 **b)** 185.46 **c)** 0.7 **d)** 69.75 **e)** 68.08 **f)** 163.68 **g)** 0.84 **h)** 3.92 **i)** 125.952 *Activity 2:* **a)** 1.2 L **b)** $17.93 **c)** $200 million **d)** 20.3 million

CHAPTER 1

Section 1.1 **3. a)** 9, 98, 987 **b)** D: $1234 \times 8 + 4 = 9876$, E: $12\ 345 \times 8 + 5 = 98\ 765$, F: $123\ 456 \times 8 + 6 = 987\ 654$ **4. a)** 111, 222, 333 **b)** $12 \times 37 = 444$, E: $15 \times 37 = 555$, F: $18 \times 37 = 666$ **5. a)** 1, 121, 12 321 **b)** D: $1111 \times 1111 = 1\ 234\ 321$, E: $11\ 111 \times 11\ 111 = 123454321$, F: $111\ 111 \times 111\ 111 = 12\ 345\ 654\ 321$ **7. a)** Carbon dioxide: 0.7°C, Methane: 0.2°C, Nitrogen: 0.1°C, CFCs: 0.4°C, others: 0.15°C **b)** 0.4°C

Section 1.2 *Activity:* **c)** GST is calculated on purchase price. In some provinces, PST is calculated on the price only, while in other provinces, PST is calculated on the price including GST. *Exercise:* **1. a)** $26.86 **b)** $345.89 **c)** $600.23 **d)** $35.93 **e)** $14.44 **f)** $17.05 **g)** $149.69 **h)** $98.90 **i)** $76.74 **2.** $35.59, $56.68, $3.10 **3.** $46.10 plus taxes **4.** $960.00 plus taxes **5.** $6.72 **6.** $50.99 **7. a)** $1.46 **8. a)** $18.90 **9.** $1.60 **10.** $3.73

Section 1.3 **1. a)** $\dfrac{5}{6}$ **b)** $\dfrac{1}{6}$ **2.** 12 **3. a)** 5.2 m **4. a)** $\dfrac{1}{2}$ **b)** $\dfrac{7}{9}$ **6. a)** 83 **7.** 28 m × 4.7 m **8. a)** 482 **b)** $\dfrac{2}{5}$ **c)** $\dfrac{3}{5}$

Section 1.4 **1. a)** $6.25 **b)** $9.50 **c)** $13.50 **2. a)** $2.67 **b)** $2.45 **c)** $2.38 **3. a)** $5.43 **b)** $4.34 **c)** $4.01 **5. a)** 12 **b)** 28 **c)** 60 **d)** 124 **6. a)** 53 cm × 53 cm **b)** 8

Section 1.5 *Activity 2:* **1. a)** 1, 3, 5, 7, 9 **b)** 3 **2. a)** white or black square **3. c)** Mitch: President, Dawna: Treasurer, Fernando: Secretary **4. b)** Nowhere – you can't bury survivors. **5. a)** 105

6. a) Bed – it has only one vowel. **7. a)** $93 + 5921 = 6014$ **b)** $30\ 578 - 6150 = 24\ 428$ **c)** $5731 + 0647 = 06378$ **d)** $956 - 802 = 154$ **8. a)** $\dfrac{14}{27}$ **b)** $\dfrac{13}{27}$ **c)** 1

Section 1.6 **3. a)** 1, 4, 9, 16 **b)** 100 **c)** 385 **4. a)** 25 **b)** 100 **c)** 1 000 000

Section 1.7 **1. a)** B **b)** D **c)** A **d)** C **2. a)** yes **b)** yes **c)** $6.40 **d)** $12.50 **e)** $63.00

Section 1.8 *Activity 1:* **a)** $0.2\overline{7}$, $0.3\overline{6}$, $0.4\overline{5}$ *Exercise:* **1. a)** $0.\overline{1}$, $0.\overline{2}$, $0.\overline{3}$ **b)** $0.\overline{4}$, $0.\overline{5}$, $0.\overline{6}$ **2.** (a), (c) **3.** (b), d)

Section 1.9 **1. a)** 0.25 **b)** 0.6 **c)** $0.\overline{6}$ **d)** 0.375 **e)** 0.3 **f)** $0.\overline{714\ 285}$ **g)** $0.\overline{4}$ **h)** $0.2\overline{36}$ **i)** 0.7719 **2. a)** $\dfrac{75}{122}$ **b)** $\dfrac{54}{74}$ **c)** $\dfrac{309}{808}$ **d)** $\dfrac{561}{1005}$ **3. b)** Harris **4.** Davise **5. a)** Moxey **6. a)** Young **b)** Young, Jarvis, Weir, Larose, Wilson, Pirus, Dupont, Irvine **c)** Jarvis, Larose

Section 1.12 *Activity 2:* **a)** Go first. *Activity 3:* **1.** Once **2. a)** No **b)** Cups were reset differently; now two cups are turned up.

Chapter Review **1. a)** $124 **b)** $1200 **c)** $4000 **d)** $2200 **2. b)** 375, 875, 1575 **c)** $45 \times 55 = 2475$, $55 \times 65 = 3575$, $65 \times 75 = 4875$, $75 \times 85 = 6375$, $85 \times 95 = 8075$ **3. a)** No **b)** $2.87 **4. a)** 26 **5. a)** 280.5 **b)** 29.82 **c)** 1.53 **6. a)** black triangle **b)** red circle

Self Evaluation **2. b)** 81, 9801, 998 001 **c)** $9999 \times 9999 = 99\ 980\ 001$, $99\ 999 \times 99\ 999 = 9\ 999\ 800\ 001$, $999\ 999 \times 999\ 999 = 999\ 998\ 000\ 001$, $9\ 999\ 999 \times 9\ 999\ 999 = 99\ 999\ 980\ 000\ 001$, $99\ 999\ 999 \times 99\ 999\ 999 = 9\ 999\ 999\ 800\ 000\ 001$ **4. a)** 1 **5.** A = 56, B = 205, C = 21 672, D = 37, E = 19; 21 989

CHAPTER 2

Section 2.2 *Activity 1:* **b)** Measure angles.

Section 2.3 *Activity:* **1. a)** 30° *Exercise:* **1. a)** A = 30°, B = 125°, C = 50°, D = 130°, E = 95°, F = 61°, G = 50°, H = 50° **4. a)** 113° **b)** 67° **c)** 55° **d)** 125° **e)** 360°

Section 2.4 **1. b)** All equal **2. a)** All sides and angles are equal. **3. b)** Two sides and two angles are equal. **4. a)** Two sides and two angles are equal. **5. b)** All sides and all angles are different. **6. a)** All sides and all angles are different. **7. b)** A: acute scalene, B: obtuse scalene, C: right scalene, D: acute isosceles, E: acute scalene, F: acute scalene, G: acute scalene, H: obtuse scalene, I: obtuse scalene

Section 2.5 **1. d)** 35° **2. d)** 22.5°

Section 2.7 **1. c)** 4 cm **2. d)** 5 cm **10.** 6.875 km

Section 2.8 **1. b)** They intersect at one point. **c)** Yes **d)** Bisectors always intersect at one point. **2. a)** Yes **b)** At the point of intersection of the angle bisectors. **3. b)** They meet. **c)** The centre is at the point of intersection of the perpendicular bisectors. **d)** Same results. **e)** Yes **4. b)** They meet. **c)** Same results.

Section 2.10 **1. b)** centre **c)** centre **2. b)** same as in Q. 1 **3. a)** The right bisector of any chord passes through the centre of the circle. **4. b)** 90° **5. b)** 90° **6. a)** The angle inscribed in a semicircle is 90°. **7. a)** $\angle$DAC, $\angle$DBC **b)** $\angle$DAC = $\angle$DBC = 40° **8. b)** The angles are equal. **9. a)** Angles inscribed on the same arc are equal. **10. a)** inscribed $\angle$BAC, central $\angle$BOC **b)** $\angle$BAC = 25°, $\angle$BOC = 50°; The inscribed angle is half the central angle. **11. a)** inscribed $\angle$BAC, central $\angle$BOC **b)** $\angle$BAC = 20°, $\angle$BOC = 40°; The inscribed angle is half the central angle. **12. b)** The inscribed angle is half the central angle. **13. a)** The measure of a central angle is twice the measure of the inscribed angle on the same arc.

Section 2.11 **1. a)** $\angle$TOS = 180°, 90° **b)** $\angle$Q = $\angle$P, $\angle$R = $\angle$S, 48° **c)** inscribed $\angle$QPR, central $\angle$QOR, **2. e)** centre **3. d)** 90° **4. e)** equal **5. d)** Inscribed angle half the central angle. **6. a)** x = 5 cm **b)** x = 4 cm, y = 6 cm **c)** y = 10 cm **7. a)** 60° **b)** 72° **c)** 50° **8. a)** 90° **b)** 40° **c)** 40°, 40° **9. a)** The paper forms a right triangle on a semicircle. **b)** Shift the paper to find another diameter. **10. c)** AB, CB are like chords on a circle; their right bisectors intersect at the centre of that circle.

Chapter Review **1. a)** 30°, acute **b)** 135°, obtuse **2. a)** obtuse, isosceles **b)** right, scalene **6. a)** $\angle$A = $\angle$B **b)** $\angle$B = 2 × $\angle$A **c)** $\angle$A = $\angle$B = 90°

Self Evaluation **1. a)** $\angle$ACB = 25°, $\angle$DEF = 140° **5. a)** 90° **b)** 60°

CHAPTER 3

Section 3.1 **1. c) i)** +4, −4 **ii)** -2, +2 **iii)** +7, −7 **iv)** −9, +9 **v)** +12, −12 **vi)** +8, −8 **2. a)** 8 black unit tiles **b)** +8 **3. a)** 8 red unit tiles **b)** −8 **4. a)** 2 red unit tiles **b)** −2 **5. a)** 2 black unit tiles **b)** +2 **c) i)** −2 **ii)** −6 **iii)** +2 **iv)** +6 **v)** +14 **vi)** +2 **vii)** −2 **viii)** −14 **7. c)** +3 **8. c)** −3 **9. a)** +3 **b)** +3 **c)** +1 **d)** +3 **e)** −4 **f)** −1 **g)** −2 **h)** −8 **11.** +7 **12. b)** −12 **13. a) i)** −12 **ii)** +15 **iii)** +18

Section 3.2 **1. a)** (+8) + (−3) **b)** +5 **2. a)** +8 **b)** +20 **c)** −9 **d)** −13 **3. a)** 4 **b)** −3 **c)** −2 **d)** 0 **4. a)** 9 **b)** 1 **c)** −9 **d)** 6 **e)** −3 **f)** −1 **g)** 0 **h)** −8 **5. a)** (−15) + (+12) = −3 **b)** (−10) + (+8) = −2 **c)** (+11) + (−2) = +9 **6. a)** 1 **b)** −1 **c)** −5 **d)** 1 **e)** −3 **7. a)** 2 **b)** −4 **c)** 6 **d)** −14 **e)** −16 **8. a)** 2

b) −1 **c)** −3 **d)** 0 **e)** −8 **f)** −15 **g)** 3 **h)** −2 **i)** −5 **j)** −50 **9. a)** 6 **b)** −9 **c)** 1 **d)** −10 **e)** 2 **f)** 0 **10. a)** 14 **b)** −40 **11. a)** 264 + (−60) + (−92) + 21 **b)** $133 **12. a)** −4 **b)** −6 **13. a)** −3 **b)** −2 **c)** 0 **d)** −3; Jennifer and José tied. **14. b)** A: −1, B: +4, C: +6; Wendel and Story qualified. **15.** Left to right: 5°C, −6°C, −16°C, −14°C, −10°C, −19°C, −29°C, 9°C, 0°C, 9°C, −4°C, −2°C, 0°C, 8°C, −3°C, 0°C, −11°C

Section 3.3 **1. a)** +2 **b)** −15 **c)** +2 **d)** +2 **e)** −7 **f)** −7 **2. a)** +15 **b)** +5 **c)** +9 **d)** +14 **e)** −4 **f)** +5 **3.** A: 3, 4, 5, 6, 7, 8, 9; B: 2, 3, 4, 5, 6, 7, 8; C: 7, 8, 9, 10, 11, 12, 13 **4. a)** 5, 6 **b)** −2, −1 **c)** −5, −6 **6. a)** +6, +5; (−2) − (−6) = +4, (−3) − (−6) = +3, (−4) − (−6) = +2, (−8) − (−5) = −3, (−8) − (−4) = −4, (−8) − (−3) = −5 **7. a)** 8 **b)** 19 **c)** 3 **d)** −6 **e)** −1 **f)** −5 **g)** 4 **h)** −9 **8. a)** 7 **b)** −11 **c)** 3 **d)** −19 **e)** 1 **f)** −16 **g)** 5 **h)** −5 **9. a)** 3 **b)** −3 **c)** −9 **d)** −4 **e)** −2 **f)** −12 **g)** −4 **h)** 0 **i)** 15 **j)** 2 **k)** 64 **l)** −10 **m)** 10 **n)** −23 **o)** −4 **p)** −9 **10. a)** 40 **b)** 10 **c)** 12 **d)** 50 **e)** 36 **f)** 113 **g)** 67 **h)** 16 **i)** 64 **j)** 38 **k)** 599 **11. a)** 18 − (−16) **b)** 34; 34°C warmer **12. a)** −16 − 18 **b)** −34; 34°C colder **13. a)** 24°C colder **14. a)** 71°C **b)** −71°C **16. a)** 5 **b)** 1 **c)** 1 **d)** 0 **e)** 37 **f)** −10 **g)** −17 **17. a)** 5 **b)** −9 **c)** −11 **d)** −3 **e)** −9 **f)** 16 *Calculation Sense:* **a)** −6 **b)** 3 **c)** −7 **d)** 1 **e)** −21 **f)** 5 **g)** −1 **h)** −8

Section 3.4 **2.** To subtract an integer, add its opposite. **3.** A: +7, +9; B: +7, +9 **4. a)** +3, +3 **b)** −7, −7 **c)** −1, −1 **6.** To subtract an integer, add its opposite. **a)** −16 **b)** 19 **c)** −2 **d)** −2

Section 3.5 **1. a)** −1 **b)** 3 **c)** −2 **d)** 1 **e)** −1 **f)** 15 **2. a)** −17 **b)** 19 **c)** 5 **d)** 16 **e)** 9 **f)** 2 **3. a)** −4 **b)** −1 **c)** 16 **d)** −23 **e)** 28 **f)** −9 **4. a)** > **b)** > **c)** > **5.** +7 **6)** −223

Section 3.6 *Activities 1 and 2:* **1. b)** −6 **2. a)** −12 **b)** −10 **c)** −12 **d)** −21 **e)** −16 **f)** −15 **4. b) i)** −10 **ii)** −21 **iii)** −12 **iv)** −56 *Exercise:* **1. a)** A: (+4) × (+2), B: (+2) × (−3) or (+3) × (−2) **b)** A: +8, B: −6 **2. a)** −12 **b)** 18 **c)** −10 **d)** 9 **e)** 10 **f)** −24 **g)** −15 **h)** 8 **3. a)** −12 **b)** 18 **c)** −10 **d)** 9 **e)** 10 **f)** −24 **g)** −15 **h)** 8 **i)** −12 **j)** −8 **k)** −4 **l)** −9 **4. a)** 30 **b)** −21 **c)** −88 **d)** −9 **e)** −24 **f)** −30 **g)** 110 **h)** −10 **i)** 44 **j)** −48 **k)** −24 **l)** −34 **m)** −45 **n)** −66 **o)** −132 **p)** −25 **5. a)** −12 **b)** −12 **c)** −24 **d)** −20 **e)** −14 **f)** −15 **g)** −32 **h)** 63 **i)** −16 **j)** −15 **k)** −22 **l)** −4 **m)** −56 **n)** −40 **o)** −156 **p)** −135 **6. a)** (+4) × (−3) **b)** −12 *Math Journal:* **a)** positive **b)** negative **c)** negative

Section 3.7 *Activity:* **2.** Product is positive. *Exercise:* **1. a)** −10, −5, 0, +5, +10; (−5) × (−3) = +15, (−5) × (−4) = +20, (−5) × (−5) = +25 **b)** −21, −14, −7, 0, +7; (−7) × (−2) = +14, (−7) × (−3) = +21, (−7) × (−4) = +28 **c)** −8, −4, 0, +4, +8; (−3) × (−4) = +12, (−4) × (−4) = +16, (−5) × (−4) = +20 **2. a)** 12 **b)** 10 **c)** 7 **d)** 20 **e)** 40 **f)** 63 **g)** 3 **h)** 36 **i)** 18 **j)** 18 **k)** 24 **l)** 1 **4. a)** −8 **b)** −4 **c)** 0 **d)** −6 **e)** −9 **f)** −12 **g)** −3 **h)** −6 **i)** −9 **j)** −15 **k)** −10 **l)** −5 **5. a)** −16 **b)** −3 **c)** 15 **d)** 0 **e)** −4 **f)** 12 **g)** −12 **h)** −18 **i)** 0 **j)** 63 **k)** 54 **l)** −36 **6. a), e)** −6 **c), g)** −12 **d), h)** 6 **7. b) i)** 12 **ii)** −35 **iii)** −72 **iv)** 42 **8. a)** −1 **b)** −12 **g)** −24

j) –60 **l)** –7 **9. a)** –6 **b)** –12 **c)** –25 **d)** –2 **e)** –9 **f)** –8 **g)** –9 **h)** 6 **i)** 16 **j)** 36 **10. a)** 5(–2) = –10 **b)** 15°C **11. a)** 6 (–12) **b)** –72 **12. a)** 5 (–15) **b)** –180°C **14. a)** 5 **b)** –5 **c)** 4 **d)** –9

Section 3.8 *Activities 1–2:* **1. a) b)** –4 **2. a)** +2 **b)** –3 **c)** +4 **d)** –2 **e)** –3 **f)** +2 **g)** –2 **h)** –3 **3. a) i)** +10 **ii)** –10 **iii)** –10 **iv)** +10 **b) i)** $\frac{+10}{+5}$ or $\frac{+10}{+2}$ **ii)** $\frac{-10}{+5}$ or $\frac{-10}{-2}$ **iii)** $\frac{-10}{-2}$ or $\frac{-10}{+5}$ **iv)** $\frac{+10}{-2}$ or $\frac{+10}{-5}$ **c) i)** +2, +5 **ii)** –2, +5 **iii)** +5, –2 **iv)** –5, –2 *Exercise:* **1. a)** A: (+8) ÷ (+2) or (+8) ÷ (+4), B: (–9) ÷ (+3) **b)** A: +4 or +2, B: –3 **3. a)** –7, –4 **b)** –4, +3 **c)** +4, –4 **d)** –6, –4 **4. a)** 6 **b)** –5 **c)** –5 **d)** 5 **e)** –6 **5.** positive, negative, negative, positive **6. a)** –6 **b)** 6 **c)** 6 **d)** –6 **e)** –6 **7. a)** 4 **b)** –4 **c)** –2 **d)** 2 **e)** –25 **f)** 45 **8. b)** –5 **d)** –2 **e)** –1 **f)** –8 **h)** –5 **9. a)** –8 **b)** 6 **c)** –8 **d)** –8 **e)** –9 **f)** 8 **g)** –21 **h)** –21 **i)** 21 **j)** –40 **k)** 40 **l)** –40 **10. a)** –750 ÷ (–5) **b)** 150 h **11. a)** (900) ÷ (4) **b)** 225 min **12.** 3 **13. a)** 9 **b)** –1, –2, –3, –4, –5, –6, –7, –8, –9

Section 3.9 *Activity 2:* **b)** Add the numbers, then divide by the number of numbers. *Exercise:* **1. a)** –5 **b)** –4 **c)** 3 **2. a)** –1 dB **b)** 0 dB **c)** –1 dB **3. a)** –1°C **b)** –1°C **c)** 4°C **4. a)** 17°C **5. a)** –15°C **7. a)** –1 dB **b)** 11 dB **c)** 8 dB

Section 3.10 **1.** –296 m **2.** –156.2 m **3.** –38 m **4. a)** –9583 m **b)** –10 123 m **5.** –7780 m **6. a)** –16 **b)** –2 **c)** negative

Section 3.11 **1. b)** +5 **2. a)** +4 **b)** –9 **c)** +6 **d)** 0 **4. b)** –6 **5. a)** –12 **b)** –15 **c)** –5 **d)** –14 **e)** –18 **f)** –2 **8. a)** +10 **b)** –3

Section 3.12 **2. a)** powers, multiply, subtract **b)** powers, divide, add **3. a)** –15 **b)** 10 **c)** –5 **d)** 1 **e)** 5 **f)** 20 **4. b)** [c] [3] [+/–] [×] [5] [+] [7] [+/–] [=] –22 **5. a)** –8 **b)** –9 **c)** 810 **d)** 93 **e)** 1.5 **f)** 4 **6. a)** –7 **b)** –7 **c)** –13 **d)** –15 **e)** –5 **f)** 1 **g)** –23 **h)** 10 **i)** –10 **j)** –13 **k)** 6 **l)** 16 **7. b) i)** 5 **ii)** 5 **8. a)** –18 **b)** 25 **c)** 55 **d)** 4 **e)** 13 **f)** 6 **9. b) i)** –4 **ii)** –180 **iii)** 1 **iv)** –29 **v)** –4 **vi)** –4 **10. b) i)** 3 **ii)** 1 **iii)** –2 **iv)** 1 **v)** –6 **vi)** 21 **11. a)** –3 **b)** –40 **c)** –16 **d)** 8 **12.** –6°C

Section 3.13 *Activity:* **a)** 3 km west: –3 km, 3 km east: +3 km **b)** no **c)** Answers include: velocity, mass of car, wind speed, direction of wind, hills, obstacles, road conditions. *Exercise:* **2. a)** 2 **b)** 3 **c)** 5 **d)** 10 **e)** 8 **3. a)** > **b)** < **c)** > **d)** < **4. a)** 6 **b)** 35 **c)** 16 **d)** 30 **e)** 20 **f)** –9 **g)** 2 **h)** 45 **5. a)** –1 **b)** 3 **c)** 5 **d)** 3 **e)** –6 **f)** 5 **g)** 5 **h)** 5 **6. a)** > **b)** < **c)** = **d)** < **7. a)** –6 **b)** –12 **c)** –9 **d)** 11 **e)** 0 **f)** –7 **g)** –18 **h)** 3 **i)** 4 **j)** 1 **k)** –1 **l)** 24 **8. a)** 9 **b)** 5 **c)** 9 **d)** 10 **9.** 41 **10. a) i)** 0, 0 **ii)** 12, 12 **iii)** 12, 12 **b) i)** 0, 0 **ii)** 16, 16 **iii)** 16,16

Section 3.15 **1. a)** (2,2) **b)** (–5,2) **c)** (2,–3) **d)** (–2,–2)

e) (5,–7) **f)** (–7,2) **g)** (–5,5) **h)** (0,–6) **2. a)** A **b)** S **c)** J **d)** I **e)** Q **f)** L **4. a)** A(–6,3), B(–3,3), C(–3,1), D(–6,1); P(3,3), Q (4,0), R(7,–1); S(–6,–3), T(–3,–2), U(–3,–4), V(–6,–5); M(2,–2), K(6,–2), T(6,–5), S(2,–5) **c)** (+,+) top right, (+,–) bottom right, (–,+) top left, (–,–) bottom left **6. a)** 0 **b)** 0 **7. b)** right scalene triangle **8. b) i)** isosceles triangle **ii)** square **iii)** rectangle **9. b)** You can draw one line through all the points. **10. b)** (2,–4) **c)** (4,–2) **11. a)** Answers include: (–2,0), (–5,–3), (3,5), (8,10) **12. b)** (7,4) **c)** Answers include: (9,4), (–1,–1) **14. b)** Four **16.** SLOW

Section 3.16 **1. a)** READ **b)** PAGE **c)** 114 **2.** BAD **3.** SET **4.** REDIVIDER

Chapter Review **1. a)** 4 **b)** –7 **c)** 17 **d)** –7 **e)** –10 **f)** 22 **2. a) i)** –12, 14 **ii)** –14, –10 **iii)** –4, –16, 19 **iv)** –7, 22, –29 **3. a)** 1 **b)** –3 **4. a)** 3 **b)** 2 **c)** 38 **d)** 0 **5. a) i)** 9 **ii)** 1089 **iii)** 110 889 **iv)** 11 108 889 **b)** 1 111 088 889 **6. b)** octagon **7.** 16°C

Self Evaluation **1. a)** 5 **b)** –9 **c)** 11 **d)** 6 **2.** oxygen: 30°C, nitrogen: 14°C, methane; 20°C, methyl alcohol: 163°C, water: 100°C, sulphur: 325°C, copper: 1512°C, iron: 1465°C **3. a)** –3 **b)** 6 **c)** 23 **d)** –10 ; –10, –3, 6, 23 **4. a)** –24 **b)** 6 **c)** 33 **d)** –14 **5. b) i)** –15 **ii)** 3; (ii) has the greater value. **6.** –10 m **7. a)** 7 **b)** –4 **c)** 13 **d)** 0 **e)** –36 **f)** 26 **8.** M

CHAPTER 4
Section 4.1 **2. a)** Deer Crossing; Falling Rocks; Curve in Road.

Section 4.2 **2. b)** x **3. a) i)** x **ii)** x **iii)** $-x$ **4. b) i)** x **ii)** $-2y$ **iii)** $-2a$

Section 4.3 *Activity:* **1. a)** $3x$ **b)** -2 **c)** $3x -2$ **2. a)** A: $x - 3$, B: $2x + 1$, C: $-3x - 2$ *Exercise:* **1. a) i)** $3x + 2$ **ii)** $-2x - 1$ **iii)** $-3x$ **b) i)** 11 **ii)** –7 **iii)** –9 **2. b) i)** –4, 2, 11, –10 **ii)** 8, –14, 3, 2 **iii)** 2, –6, 7, –4 **3. a)** A: $2x - x$, B: $-3x + x$, C: $2x$ **c)** A: x, B: $-2x$, C: $2x$ **4. b) i)** $2a$ **ii)** $7x$ **iii)** k **iv)** $3m$ **v)** $-x$ **vi)** $5y$ **c) i)** 4.4 **ii)** 15.4 **iii)** 2.2 **iv)** 6.6 **v)** –2.2 **vi)** 11 **5. a)** $2a$ **b)** $7x$ **c)** $2y$ **d)** $-6a$ **e)** $-4x$ **f)** $-9k$ **g)** $10b$ **h)** $2m$ **6. a)** $8a$ **b)** p **c)** $2n$ **d)** $-x$ **e)** p **f)** $3b$ **7. a)** Simplify each expression. **i)** $7d$ **ii)** $10d$ **iii)** $4d$ **iv)** $5d$ **v)** $6d$ **vi)** $6d$ **b) i)** 38.5 **ii)** 55 **iii)** 22 **iv)** 27.5 **v)** 33 **vi)** 33 **8. a)** $6a - 3b$ **b)** $5m - 6p$ **c)** $2p + q$ **d)** $2a + 2b$ **e)** $6b - 3a$ **f)** $5p - r$

Section 4.4 *Activity:* **a)** Same variables. **c)** Different variables. *Exercise:* **1. a)** $4x$ **b)** $4a$ **c)** $10n$ **d)** 0 **e)** $10a$ **f)** $4p$ **2. a)** $C = 7m + 3$ **b)** $V = x + 3$ **c)** $A = l - 4$ **d)** $M = 5 + x$ **e)** $K = 8y - 2$ **f)** $P = 17 - k$ **3. a) i)** like: $2x$, $3x$ **ii)** like: $5a$, $3a$, **iii)** like: $4m$, $5m$, **iv)** like: $3v$, $-4v$, **v)** like: $-4p$, $5p$, **vi)** like: $-3a$, $-2a$, **b) i)** $5x + 4y$ **ii)** $8a - 2b$ **iii)** $9m + 2n$ **iv)** $-v + 5w$ **v)** $p - 2q$ **vi)** $-5a - 4b$ **4. a)** $5m + n$ **b)** $-2a + 3b$ **c)** $6x + y$ **d)** $2p + q$ **e)** $r - 5q$ **f)** $9m + n$ **5. a)** \$325 **b)** \$425 **c)** \$525 **d)** \$795 **6. a)** 70 km/h **b)** 50 km/h

c) 30 km/h **d)** –5 km/h **e)** The car has stopped. **7. a)** 340 m/s **b)** 335 m/s **c)** 346.25 m/s **d)** 337.125 m/s **8. b)** Yes, –660°C **9.** $83.90

Section 4.5 **1. a)** 1 **b)** 4 **c)** 6 **2. a)** 5 **b)** 12 **3. a)** 6 **b)** 2 **c)** 15 **4. a)** 3 **b)** 2 **c)** –1 **d)** 2 **e)** –1 **f)** 1 **5. a)** 1 **b)** –2 **c)** 5 **d)** 4 **e)** 4 **f)** 6 **6. a)** 8 **b)** –5 **c)** 12 **d)** –4 **e)** 3 **f)** 12.5 **7. a)** 24 **b)** 8 **c)** –3 **d)** 12 **e)** 21 **f)** –6 **g)** –9 **h)** 20 **8. a)** 16 **b)** 6 **c)** –3 **d)** 27 **e)** 16 **f)** 20 **g)** 35 **h)** 18 **9.** a), d), f), g); e), h)

Section 4.6 **1. a)** $\frac{3}{4}$ **b)** 3 **c)** $\frac{3}{4}$ **2.** Possible answers given. **a)** $\frac{6}{8}, \frac{9}{12}$ **b)** $\frac{4}{6}, \frac{6}{9}$ **c)** $\frac{6}{10}, \frac{9}{15}$ **d)** $\frac{14}{20}, \frac{21}{30}$ **e)** $\frac{9}{10}, \frac{27}{30}$ **3. a)** 50 **b)** 25 **c)** 10 **d)** 20 **4. a)** 30 **b)** 30 **5. a)** 40 **b)** 10 **c)** 25 **d)** 28 **6. a)** 1 **b)** 1 **7. a)** 1 **b)** 1 **c)** 7 **d)** 3 **8. a)** 9 **b)** 10 **c)** 63 **d)** 50 **e)** 5 **f)** 15 **g)** 24 **h)** 40 **i)** 10 **j)** 25 **k)** 25 **l)** 1 **9. a)** 20 **b)** 5 **c)** 27 **d)** 5 **e)** 9 **f)** 12 **g)** 9 **h)** 5 **i)** 12 **j)** 3 **k)** 25 **l)** 49 **10. b)** 575 **c)** 575 **11. b)** 60 **12. b)** 12 **13. a)** 22.5 kg **b)** 20 kg

Section 4.7 **1. a)** 9 kg **b)** 1 kg **c)** 2 kg **2. a)** 5 kg **b)** 20 kg **c)** 22.5 kg **3.** 2 kg

Section 4.8 **1. b)** A: 0.6 cm, 3.9 cm; B: 1.5 cm, 3.5 cm; C: 1.1 cm, 4.8 cm **c)** A: 0.15, B: 0.43, C: 0.23 **e)** The greater the slope, the steeper the ramp. **2. b)** As angles increase so do slopes. **5. a)** A **b)** A: 1.2, B: 0.6, C: 0.2; steepest roof has greatest slope.

Section 4.9 *Activity:* Positive slope, line goes up to the right; Negative slope, line goes down to the right. *Exercise:* **1. a)** 4, 6, $\frac{2}{3}$ **b)** 6, –4, $-\frac{3}{2}$ **c)** 4, 2, 2 **2. a)** Rise = 0 **b)** Run = 0, and $\frac{m}{0}$ is undefined.

3. a) (4,5) **b)** (–7,8) or (3,0) **4. a)** 2 **b)** –3 **c)** $-\frac{3}{2}$ **d)** –2 **e)** 3 **f)** $-\frac{3}{2}$ **g)** same **5. a)** –2 **b)** $\frac{3}{2}$ **c)** $\frac{3}{5}$ **d)** $\frac{2}{3}$ **e)** $\frac{5}{13}$ **f)** $-\frac{5}{9}$

6. a) $\frac{1}{2}$ **b)** $\frac{1}{2}$ **c)** $\frac{1}{2}$ **d)** $\frac{1}{2}$ **e)** All equal.

Section 4.10 **1.** (c) **2.** No **3.** (b) **4.** (a), (c) **5. a)** No

Section 4.11 **1. d)** (0, 3) **3. c)** Each coordinate of midpoint is the average of corresponding coordinates of endpoints. **4. a) i)** (0,1) **ii)** (1, –2) **iii)** (1, 1.5)

Section 4.12 **1. a)** (–5, 4) **b)** (4.5, 4) **c)** (–2, 1.5) **d)** (6, 1) **e)** (–4, –1) **f)** (3, –2.5) **2. b)** (6, 4) **3. a)** (3.5, 6.5) **b)** (0, 3) **c)** (–0.5, 1.5) **4. a)** (3, 3) **b)** (1, 9) **c)** (–9, 5) **d)** (–13, –17) **5. a)** (–3.5, 5.5)

b) (–2, 2.5) **6. a)** (0, 1) **b)** (–4, 4) **7.** (1.5, 5.5) **8.** (3, –6) **9.** (0, 10)

Chapter Review **1. a)** 5x **b)** –8y **c)** 2a **d)** 3a **2.** $78 840 **3. a)** 23 **b)** 17 **c)** –56 **d)** 18 **e)** –26 **f)** –8 **4. a)** 3 **b)** 12 **c)** $\frac{1}{6}$ **5. a)** 27 **b)** 30 **c)** 12 **d)** 6 **e)** 20 **f)** 130 **6. b)** 195 **7. a) i)** $\frac{1}{2}$ **ii)** $\frac{1}{2}$; same **b)** (1, 0), (4, 1.5)

Self Evaluation **1. a)** a **b)** –2b **c)** 4m **d)** –10p **2. a)** $26.75 **b)** $41.25 **c)** $48.50 **d)** $106.50 **3. a)** 4 **b)** 5 **c)** 1 **d)** 1 **e)** 2 **f)** 1 **4. a)** 4 **b)** 10 **c)** –9 **d)** 9 **e)** 12 **f)** –8 **5. a)** 6 **b)** 2 **c)** 6 **d)** 6 **e)** 25 **f)** 15 **6. b)** 375 **7. a)** (–1, 3), $-\frac{1}{2}$ **b)** (2, 1), $\frac{3}{4}$

Cumulative Review **1. a)** 40.7 **b)** 5.818 **c)** 87.849 **2. a)** $1\frac{13}{20}$ **b)** $\frac{9}{16}$ **c)** $\frac{1}{2}$ **d)** $1\frac{1}{12}$ **3. a)** 3 **b)** 45 **c)** 134.23 **d)** 133 **e)** 2.12 **f)** 27 **4. a)** –21 **b)** 6 **c)** –17 **5. a)** –3°C **b)** 6°C **7. a)** scalene acute **b)** right scalene **c)** scalene obtuse **8. a)** May 7

CHAPTER 5
Section 5.1 **1. a)** $4\frac{1}{2}$ **b)** $2\frac{1}{2}$ **c)** $-5\frac{1}{2}$ **4. b)** $1 **6. a)** –1 **b)** 2 **c)** –2

Section 5.2 **1. a)** –2 **b)** 2 **c)** 2 **d)** 4 **e)** –4 **f)** 5

2. Sample answers given. **a)** $\frac{-8}{10}, \frac{-12}{15}$ **b)** $\frac{-4}{6}, \frac{-6}{9}$ **c)** $\frac{-2}{4}, \frac{-3}{6}$ **d)** $\frac{-6}{10}, \frac{-9}{15}$ **e)** $\frac{2}{6}, \frac{3}{9}$ **f)** $-\frac{6}{8}, -\frac{9}{12}$ **4. a)** $-\frac{4}{3}, \frac{-3}{5}, \frac{1}{-3}$ **b)** $\frac{-3}{2}, \frac{-2}{5}, \frac{1}{3}$ **c)** $\frac{-1}{2}, -\frac{2}{5}, \frac{3}{10}$ **5. a)** $-2\frac{3}{4}$ **b)** $-3\frac{1}{3}$ **c)** $-2\frac{2}{5}$ **d)** $3\frac{3}{4}$ **e)** $-2\frac{6}{7}$ **f)** $-4\frac{1}{2}$ **6. a)** $-\frac{7}{2}$ **b)** $-\frac{21}{4}$ **c)** $\frac{8}{3}$ **d)** $-\frac{17}{10}$ **e)** $\frac{6}{1}$ **f)** $-\frac{9}{1}$ **7. a)** > **b)** < **c)** < **d)** < **e)** > **f)** >

Section 5.3 *Activity 1:* **a)** $\frac{9}{12}, \frac{2}{3}$ **b)** 0.75, $0.\overline{6}$ **c) i)** 0.6 **ii)** –0.25 **iii)** 0.75 **iv)** –0.1 **v)** –0.2 **d) i)** $0.\overline{3}$ **ii)** $-0.1\overline{6}$ **iii)** $-0.\overline{2}$ **iv)** $0.\overline{27}$ **v)** $0.\overline{25}$ **e)** Part (c) answers terminate. Part (d) answers repeat. *Activity 2:* **a) i)** 0.8 **ii)** $-0.\overline{7}$ **iii)** –8.75 **iv)** $12.\overline{6}$ **v)** $-11.1\overline{6}$; $12\frac{2}{3}$

Activity 3: Sample answers given. **a)** $\frac{2}{5}, \frac{9}{20}$ **b)** $\frac{3}{8}, \frac{2}{5}$ **c)** $-\frac{7}{10}, -\frac{11}{16}$ **d)** $\frac{1}{10}, \frac{1}{8}$ **e)** $-\frac{7}{20}, -\frac{1}{3}$

Section 5.4 **1. a)** VanDer **b)** Comb Met **c)** $+\frac{7}{8}$, +2, +3, +12 **2.** Answers for "Close" column: **a)** Brunswick **b)** Bridger **c)** Bridger, Marcania, Norlex, Comb Met, C. Curtis, Ponder, C. Durham, Westfield, Merland E., C.S. Pete, VanDer, Brunswick **3. a)** 3 **b)** 6

Section 5.5 **1. c)** 4 **2. b)** –4 **3. c)** 1 **4. b)** –1

Section 5.6 **1. c)** $\frac{1}{2}$ cm **2. a)** $-\frac{1}{2}$ **b)** $-\frac{1}{2}$ **c)** $\frac{4}{5}$ **d)** –1

3. b) $-1\frac{1}{4}$ **4. a)** $\frac{-2}{4}$, $\frac{-1}{4}$ **b)** $\frac{-6}{8}$, $-\frac{5}{8}$ **c)** $\frac{-10}{15}$, $\frac{-6}{15}$ **d)** $\frac{-7}{21}$, $\frac{-6}{21}$ **5. a)** $-1\frac{3}{10}$ **b)** $\frac{1}{10}$ **c)** $-\frac{7}{10}$ **d)** $\frac{5}{8}$ **6. a)** $-\frac{1}{6}$ **b)** $-1\frac{7}{20}$

c) $\frac{5}{24}$ **d)** $-\frac{1}{12}$ **e)** $-\frac{7}{12}$ **f)** $-\frac{1}{12}$ **g)** –1 **h)** $-1\frac{1}{6}$ **7. a)** < **b)** < **c)** > **d)** < **8. a)** 11.7 **b)** –1.5 **c)** 2.5 **d)** –10.9 **e)** 1.8 **f)** 3.3 **9. a)** 11.7 **b)** –3.7 **c)** –9.7 **d)** –3.2 **e)** –0.9 **f)** –1.2 **g)** –6.5 **h)** 9.7 **i)** –26 **10. a)** $2\frac{5}{6}$ **b)** $1\frac{7}{8}$ **c)** $2\frac{3}{8}$ **d)** $\frac{7}{10}$ **e)** $\frac{3}{4}$ **f)** $-\frac{2}{3}$ **g)** $1\frac{1}{2}$ **h)** $12\frac{3}{4}$ **11.** 3 h **12.** 3.1 h **13. a)** Kim: $12\frac{3}{4}$, Dawna: $5\frac{1}{4}$ **b)** Kim **14.** $-\frac{1}{24}$ **15. b)** 1.1, 1.1, 1.1

Section 5.7 **1. b)** 1 **2. c)** 4

Section 5.8 **1. b)** $14\frac{1}{2}$ m **2. a)** –1 **b)** 1 **c)** $\frac{1}{7}$ **d)** $-\frac{2}{5}$ **3.** $-\frac{1}{6}$ **4. a)** $-\frac{9}{10}$ **b)** $-\frac{1}{8}$ **c)** $-\frac{13}{15}$ **d)** $\frac{9}{16}$ **e)** $-\frac{1}{12}$ **f)** $-1\frac{17}{40}$ **g)** $-\frac{13}{28}$ **h)** $-\frac{1}{28}$ **5. a)** $-2\frac{3}{10}$ **b)** $-17\frac{1}{4}$ **c)** –4 **d)** $-3\frac{3}{10}$

6. a) –13.7 **b)** –15 **c)** 9.4 **d)** –1.1 **e)** 11.2 **f)** 1.9 **7.** $17\frac{1}{2}$

8. –18.1°C **9. a)** $5\frac{4}{5}$ **b)** $-1\frac{5}{6}$ **c)** $-5\frac{5}{12}$

Section 5.9 *Activity 1:* **a)** –0.8 **b) i)** –0.75 **ii)** 0.8 **iii)** –0.375 **iv)** –0.7 **v)** –1.125 *Activity 2:* **c)** 0.5 **d) i)** 0 **ii)** –0.125 **iii)** 1.675 *Activity 3:* **c)** –0.15 **d) i)** 0.85 **ii)** –1.175 **iii)** $-1.4\overline{6}$

Section 5.10 **1. b)** $10\frac{1}{2}$ **2. b)** $-10\frac{1}{2}$ **3. a)** A: $(+4) \times \left(+4\frac{1}{2}\right)$, B: $(+3) \times \left(2\frac{1}{2}\right)$ **b)** A: 18, B: $-7\frac{1}{2}$

4. b) i) $16\frac{1}{2}$ **ii)** 10 **iii)** $-13\frac{1}{2}$

Section 5.11 **1. b)** 14 m **2.** $\frac{3}{10}$ **3. a)** $-\frac{1}{10}$ **b)** $\frac{2}{15}$ **c)** $-\frac{1}{5}$ **d)** $-\frac{1}{4}$ **4. a)** $-\frac{3}{8}$ **b)** 0 **c)** $1\frac{7}{15}$ **d)** $-2\frac{1}{6}$ **e)** $-\frac{8}{15}$ **f)** $-\frac{5}{16}$ **g)** $-1\frac{6}{7}$ **h)** $12\frac{3}{8}$ **5. a)** $\frac{3}{10}$ **b)** 1 **c)** $-\frac{2}{9}$ **d)** $\frac{2}{9}$ **6. a)** $-\frac{16}{25}$ **b)** $\frac{1}{2}$ **c)** $-4\frac{4}{5}$ **d)** 0 **e)** $7\frac{7}{8}$ **f)** $4\frac{3}{4}$ **g)** $-1\frac{1}{6}$ **h)** $-4\frac{31}{50}$ **7. a)** $\frac{1}{15}$ **b)** $\frac{3}{4}$ **c)** $1\frac{37}{128}$ **d)** $\frac{3}{16}$ **e)** $-\frac{1}{8}$ **f)** $\frac{25}{81}$ **8. a)** –17.1 **b)** 19.76 **c)** –12.87 **d)** 11.88 **e)** 38.19 **f)** 0 **g)** 14.31 **h)** 45.08 **i)** 27.28 **9.** $9\frac{1}{3}$ cans **10.** $\frac{11}{40}$ **11.** 10 **12.** 80 **13. a)** $-\frac{3}{4}$

14. a) $\frac{1}{10}$ **b)** $\frac{1}{50}$ **c)** $\frac{1}{8}$

Section 5.12 **1. a)** $\frac{3}{1}$ **b)** $\frac{-3}{2}$ **c)** $\frac{1}{3}$ **d)** $\frac{-3}{1}$ **e)** $\frac{2}{5}$ **f)** $-\frac{2}{9}$

2. a) $-1\frac{1}{2}$ **b)** –2 **c)** $2\frac{2}{3}$ **d)** $4\frac{1}{2}$ **3. a)** –5 **b)** $-\frac{8}{51}$ **c)** $\frac{3}{35}$ **d)** 2

4. a) –1 **b)** $4\frac{1}{2}$ **c)** $-7\frac{1}{2}$ **d)** $-\frac{2}{45}$ **e)** 14 **f)** $10\frac{11}{16}$ **g)** $-\frac{3}{14}$

h) $-\frac{11}{42}$ **5.** 2 **6.** $3\frac{3}{11}$ min **7.** 8 **8. a)** $14\frac{5}{12}$ **b)** $2\frac{5}{84}$

9. a) $2\frac{2}{3}$ **b)** 7 **c)** $-\frac{3}{64}$ **d)** –2 **e)** $-\frac{7}{15}$ **f)** $\frac{1}{4}$

Section 5.13 **1. a)** $1\frac{5}{8}$, $1\frac{5}{8}$ **2. a)** $\frac{1}{24}$, $-\frac{5}{24}$ **3. a)** $\frac{1}{2}$ **b)** $\frac{7}{12}$ **c)** $\frac{1}{8}$ **d)** $-2\frac{1}{4}$ **e)** 2 **f)** $-\frac{5}{9}$ **4. a)** $\frac{1}{2}$ **b)** $\frac{1}{5}$ **c)** $-\frac{1}{5}$ **d)** $\frac{4}{5}$ **e)** $\frac{1}{4}$ **f)** –4 **5. a)** $\frac{4}{5}$ **b)** $1\frac{1}{20}$ **c)** $-29\frac{1}{2}$; **(b) 6.** $\frac{1}{4}$ **7. a)** $-11\frac{3}{8}$ m *Making Connections:* **1. a)** –10.3°C

Section 5.14 **1. a)** $\frac{1}{5}$ **b)** $-\frac{1}{4}$ **c)** $\frac{31}{50}$ **d)** $-1\frac{3}{4}$ **e)** $\frac{3}{10}$ **f)** $-\frac{9}{25}$ **2. g)** $\frac{2}{3}$, $-\frac{332}{99}$, $\frac{1}{15}$, $\frac{16}{11}$, $\frac{5}{9}$, $\frac{1}{3}$ **3. a)** $\frac{29}{11}$ **b)** $-\frac{82}{99}$ **c)** $\frac{15}{11}$ **d)** $\frac{35}{111}$ **e)** $-\frac{1156}{999}$ **f)** $\frac{23}{495}$ **g)** $-\frac{7}{3}$ **h)** $\frac{401}{90}$ **i)** $-\frac{97}{300}$ **j)** $\frac{16}{495}$ **4. a)** $\frac{1}{2}$ **b)** $\frac{1}{2}$, same

Section 5.15 **1.** Rational: (a), (b), (c), (d), (e), (g), (j), (k), Irrational: (f), (h), (i) **4. a)** {x| x > –1, x ∈ R} **b)** {x| x < –1, x ∈ R} **c)** {x| x ≤ 3, x ∈ I} **5. a)** {x| –2 ≤ x ≤ 1, x ∈ R} **b)** {x| 7 < x ≤ 11, x ∈ R} **c)** {x| 0 ≤ x ≤ 3, x ∈ I}

Technology Insight: The Titanic **1. b)** 265 m

Chapter Review 1. a) < **b)** < **c)** > **2. a)** $\frac{1}{5}$ **b)** $-\frac{2}{3}$ **c)** $1\frac{1}{3}$

3. a) $-\frac{2}{5}$ **b)** $\frac{1}{6}$ **c)** $-\frac{7}{10}$ **d)** $\frac{2}{3}$ **4. a)** $\frac{1}{6}$ **b)** $-1\frac{1}{2}$ **c)** $1\frac{1}{2}$ **d)** $\frac{4}{9}$

5. a) $\frac{4}{15}$ **b)** -3 **7.** $2\frac{3}{20}$ **9. a)** $\frac{3}{4}$ **b)** $\frac{9}{20}$ **c)** $\frac{37}{99}$ **d)** $\frac{117}{90}$
10. 21.3 cm

Self Evaluation 1. a) > **b)** < **c)** < **2. a)** $-\frac{1}{3}$ **b)** $-1\frac{1}{2}$

c) $1\frac{5}{6}$ **d)** $-2\frac{5}{6}$ **e)** $-1\frac{1}{2}$ **f)** $2\frac{47}{60}$ **3. a)** $\frac{2}{7}$ **b)** $-8\frac{1}{6}$ **c)** $4\frac{7}{8}$

d) $-\frac{8}{9}$ **4. a)** $-1\frac{1}{3}$ **b)** $-1\frac{1}{3}$ **c)** $-\frac{1}{2}$ **d)** $-\frac{2}{5}$ **5.** 6 **7.** $37\frac{3}{4}$ °C
8. 29.7 cm

Cumulative Review: Problem Solving 1. a) 96
2. No **3. a)** 195 **5.** 90 **6. a)** 140 **b)** 0.0278

CHAPTER 6
Section 6.1 6. d) A: P = 14 units, A = 12 sq. units;
B: 24, 32; C: 26, 33; D: 28, 42; E: 42, 60; F: 32, 48
G: 64, 31 H: 24, 24; I: 50, 46

Section 6.2 *Activity:* **a)** 130 **b)** 130 m **c)** 2 × length
+ 2 × width or 2(l + w) *Exercise:* **1. a)** 26 m **b)** 12 cm
c) 15 cm **2. a)** 14 cm, 6 cm; P = 72 cm **b)** 12 cm,
14 cm; P = 124 cm **3. a)** 13 cm, P = 124 cm
b) 11 cm, P = 56 cm **c)** 6.9 cm, P = 57 cm **d)** 4.6 cm,
P = 90.3 cm **4. a)** 36.0 m **b)** 67.2 m **5. a)** 26 m
b) $163.54 **6. a)** 141.8 m **b)** $381.44 **7. a)** 12 m,
12 m, 23 m **b)** 40 m, 40 m, 42 m **c)** 42 m **8.** 4.4 m
9. 4.88 m **10.** 5.85 m, 17.1 m, 5.85 m **11. a)** 5925 m
b) 1.2 h **12. a)** 36.2 m, 48.6 m, 36.2 m **b)** 3.60 m
13. c) 89.4 units

Section 6.3 1. a) 360 cm^2 **b)** 576 cm^2 **c)** 1280 cm^2
2. a) 4156 m^2 **b)** 1142 m^2 **c)** 497 m^2 **3. a)** 888 mm^2
b) 15.5 cm^2 **c)** 13.6 cm^2 **4. a)** 24.4 m^2 **b)** 72.3 m^2
5. a) 264.6 m^2 **b)** $4741.63 **6. a)** 5344 cm^2
7. a) 98.5 m **8.** 394 **9. a)** 6

Section 6.4 1. a) 2924 cm^2 **b)** 3311 cm^2
c) 4128 cm^2 **d)** 3655 cm^2 **2.** 688 cm^2 **3. a)** 1032 cm^2
b) 688 cm^2

Section 6.5 *Activities 1 and 2:* **1. a)** A: same, 24,
B: same, 18, C: same, 24 **b)** same base and height
2. a) base × height **3. a)** A: 42 sq. units, B: 33 sq.
units **b)** triangles **c)** Each triangle is half the area of

the parellelogram. **4. a)** $\frac{1}{2}$ base × height *Exercise:*

2. a) 900 cm^2 **b)** 1.0 m^2 **c)** 8.1 m^2 **d)** 1008 cm^2
3. a) 18 **b)** 24 **c)** 20 **d)** 56 **4. a)** 450 cm^2 **b)** 12.7 cm^2
c) 8.4 cm^2 **5. a)** 10 **b)** 15 **c)** 26 **d)** 17.5 **6. a)** 102 cm^2
b) 5.0 m^2 **7. a)** 468 cm^2 **b)** 304 cm^2 **8. a)** 4.6 cm

b) 6.5 cm **c)** 6.4 m **9. a)** 28.2 cm **b)** 8.6 m **10.** 313
11. b) 3150 **12. a)** 6

Section 6.6 1. a) 18.4 m^2 **b)** 25.8 m^2 **3. a)** 821.1 m^2
b) 313.5 m^2 **c)** 106.3 m^2, 102.8 m^2 **d)** 181.5 m^2,
76.0 m^2 **e)** 119.9 m^2

Section 6.7 *Activity 2:* **b)** 3.2 cm^2 *Exercise:*
1. a) 15.5 cm^2 **b)** 42.0 cm^2 **c)** 20.5 m^2 **2. a)** 8.6 m^2
b) 12.4 cm^2 **c)** 11.9 m^2 **3. a) i)** 72 cm^2 **ii)** 12.5 cm^2
iii) 31.2 m^2 **4. a)** 181.4 cm^2 **b)** 734.4 cm^2
c) 1002.2 cm^2 **5.** 29.5 m^2

Section 6.8 1. a) 78.5 cm **b)** 113.0 cm **c)** 125.6 cm
d) 141.3 cm **2. a)** 46.5 m **b)** 74.1 cm **c)** 206.0 cm
3. a) diameter = 2 × radius **b)** C = 2πr **c) i)** 25.1 cm
ii) 18.8 m **iii)** 96.1 mm **4.** 144.4 m **5. a)** 33.9 cm
b) 5.3 m **6.** 22.3 m **7. a)** Al: 326.6 m, Ben: 301.4 m
b) i) 126 m **ii)** 252 m **iii)** 2520 m

Section 6.9 1. b) 31.4 cm **d)** parallelogram
e) 31.4 cm, 10 cm **f)** 314 cm^2 **3. a)** A = πr^2
b) A: 9.1 cm^2, B: 6.2 cm^2, C: 4.9 cm^2, D: 2.0 cm^2

Section 6.10 1. A: 4.9 cm^2, B: 2.5 cm^2,
C: 3.8 cm^2, D: 1.8 cm^2 **2. a)** 28.3 m^2 **b)** 4.5 cm^2
c) 59.42 mm^2 **3.** 389 cm^2 **4. a)** 538.9 cm^2 **b)** 70.8 m^2
5. 3.5 m^2 **6.** 12 **7.** 26 **8. a)** 491 cm^2 **b)** 1256 cm^2
9. 481 cm^2 **10. a)** $8.60 **b)** 1.8¢/cm^2 **11. a)** 64 **b)** 256
Making Connections: **b)** Each radius must be
measured. For the largest circle,
C = 25.13 cm, A = 50.27 cm^2. For the smallest
circle, C = 4.40 cm, A = 2.24 cm^2

Section 6.11 1. c) Add areas of the different parts.
4. b) square-based pyramid **c)** height, base of
triangle **d)** 8.9 cm^2

Section 6.12 *Activity 2:* **2. a)** A = C = 25.42 cm^2,
B = D = 21.7 cm^2, E = F = 14.35 cm^2 **b)** 122.9 cm^2
3. a) A = B = C = D = 14.28 cm^2 **b)** 74.8 cm^2
Exercise: **1. c)** 3.68 m^2, 9.43 m^2, 6.56 m^2 **d)** 39.3 m^2
2. c) 2 cm^2, 1.6 cm^2, 1.2 cm^2, 1.5 cm^2 **d)** 7.8 cm^2
3. b) 4 **c)** 30.66 cm^2 **d)** 122.6 cm^2 **4. a)** 2400 cm^2
b) 62.7 m^2 **c)** 10.8 m^2 **5. a)** 11.3 m^2 **6.** 217.9 cm^2

Section 6.13 1. a) 55.4 cm^2 **b)** 105.5 cm^2
c) 216.3 cm^2 **2. a)** 432.6 cm^2 **b)** 397.8 cm^2
c) 2002.6 m^2 **d)** 33.9 m^2 **3.** 233.5 cm^2 **4.** 515.4 cm^2
5. 314 cm^2 **6. a)** 2.8 m^2 **b)** 7 L **7. b)** 1004.8 cm^2
c) 12.0 cm × 50.2 cm **8. b)** Cube: 9.1 cm × 9.1 cm ×
9.1 cm. Cylinder: Suggested answer, r = 5.4 cm,
h = 9.3 cm. *Making Connections:* **a)** 5.7 km^2
b) 1512.9 km^2

Section 6.15 1. a) 314 cm^2 **b)** 221.6 cm^2
c) 366.2 cm^2 **2. a)** 113.04 cm^2 **b)** 301.44 cm^2
c) 414.5 cm^2 **3. a)** 678.2 cm^2 **b)** 57.3 cm^2
c) 266.9 cm^2 **4.** 597.8 cm^2 **5. a)** 514 457 600 km^2
b) Earth is a sphere. **6. a)** 459 727 400 km^2

b) 145 193 600 km^2 **7.** 813.9 cm^2 **8. a)** 55.2 km^2

Section 6.16   1. a) 7.5 m **b)** 86 turns, assuming straight path **2. a)** 300.8 cm **b)** 88 **3. a)** 68.5 cm **b)** 373.1 cm^2 **c)** 1492.3 cm^2 **4. a)** 76.0 cm **b)** 1838.9 cm^2 **5. a)** 21.4 cm, 145.2 cm^2 **b)** 23.2 cm 171.9 cm^2 **c)** baseball, 26.7 cm^2

Section 6.17   1. b) 24 **c)** 24 cubes **d)** 3, 2, 4; length × width × height **2. a)** 6 **b)** base area × height **3. b)** 30 **c)** 30 cubes **d)** 4, 4, 3 **4. a)** 10 **b)** base area × height **5. e)** base area × height

Section 6.18   1. a) 11.6 m^3 **b)** 14.5 m^3 **c)** 9.8 m^3 **d)** 7.7 m^3 **2. a)** 2016 cm^3 **b)** 305.9 cm^3 **3. a)** 371.3 cm^3 **4. a)** 151.8 m^3 **5. a)** 80.4 m^3 **6. a)** 9.7 m^3 **b)** 49 243 kg **7.** 27.4 m^3 **8. a)** 11.8 L **b)** 9.2 L **9. c)** Volume would remain the same.

Section 6.19   1. b) D **c)** the change in side lengths **d)** Find V for A, B, C, D: A, 64; B, 25.5; C, 23.4; D, 22.3. Volume of D about $\frac{1}{3}$ volume of corresponding prism **2. b)** D **c)** the number of layers, the difference in diameters **d)** $\frac{1}{3}$ volume of corresponding pyramid; area of base × height **3. b)** 3 **4. b)** 3

Section 6.20   1. a) 60.5 m^3 **b)** 48.4 m^3 **c)** 1296.3 cm^3 **d)** 215.0 m^3 **e)** 721.2 cm^3 **f)** 330.6 cm^3 **g)** 44.6 m^3 **2. a)** 10.77 cm^3 **b)** 29.1 m^3 **c)** 75.4 m^3 **3. a)** 229.7 m^3 **b)** 229 731 L **4.** 4397.0 m^3 **5.** 5.54 cm^3 **6.** 4.7 m^3 **7.** hemisphere **8. a)** 75.73 cm^3 **b)** 160.95 cm^3 **c)** tennis ball, 14.1 cm^3 *Making Connections:* **a)** A: rectangular prisms, B: cone, hemisphere, C: rectangular prisms, D: cylinder, hemisphere **c)** A: 68 881.9 m^3, B: 250.0 m^3, C: 2713.6 cm^3, D: 412.6 m^3

Chapter Review   1. A: 22 m, B: 47.4 m **2. a)** A: 48 cm^2, B: 20.5 m^2 **b)** A: 265 m^2, B: 242.9 cm^2 **3. a) i)** 1.3 m^3 **ii)** 1239 cm^3 **b)** A: 967.0 cm^3, B: 332 cm^3 **4.** A: 62.8 cm, 314 cm^2; B: 30.1 cm, 72.3 cm^2; C: 38.6 m, 118.8 m^2 **5.** A: 2512 cm^2, 7234.6 cm^3; B: 494.0 cm^2, 830.5 cm^3

Self Evaluation   1. a) A: 108 cm^2, B: 64.3 cm^2 **b)** 98.8 m^2 **2. a)** A: 17.8 m^3, B: 72 cm^3 **b)** 4032 m^3 **3. a)** A: 376.8 cm, B: 452.2 cm; 60 288 cm **b)** 101 736 m **4.** A: 211.1 cm^2, B: 21.9 m^2, C: 140.3 cm^2 **5.** A: 26.6 cm^3, B: 463.0 cm^3, C: 13.5 cm^3

CHAPTER 7

Section 7.1   1. a) 5:24, 2:1 **2. a)** 3:4 **b)** 2:1 **c)** 7:5 **3.** Each term increases by same factor from (a). **5. a)** 7:12, 5:12, 451:939 **b)** 10 **c)** 25 **d)** 60

Section 7.2   *Activity:* a) 1: 1 **b)** $\frac{1}{2}$ *Exercise:* **1. a)** $\frac{5}{9}$, 5:9 **b)** $\frac{9}{5}$, 9:5 **c)** same numbers, different order **2. a)** $\frac{7}{2}$, 7:2 **b)** $\frac{7}{5}$, 7:5 **3. a)** $\frac{1}{5}$, 1:5 **b)** $\frac{10}{1}$, 10:1 **c)** $\frac{10}{5}$, 10:5 **d)** $\frac{25}{10}$, 25:10 **e)** $\frac{100}{10}$, 100:10 **f)** $\frac{5}{25}$, 5:25

4. a) 3:4 **b)** 8:9 **c)** 2:19 **d)** 250:5000 **e)** 40:2500 **f)** 400:2000 **g)** 500:35 000 **h)** 250:2000 **5. a)** 8:3 **b)** 3:5 **c)** 3:3 **d)** 5:3 **6. a)** 40:40 **b)** 160:10 **c)** 10:160 **d)** 40:160 **7. a)** cashews to filberts or Brazil nuts to filberts **b)** peanuts to cashews or peanuts to Brazil nuts **c)** cashews to Brazil nuts or Brazil nuts to cashews **d)** filberts to peanuts **8. a) i)** 28:20 **ii)** 8:6 **9. a)** 24:48 **10.** False

Section 7.3   3. a) Count. **5. a)** Count.

Section 7.4   2. a) 2 **b)** 6 **c)** 3 **d)** 7 **e)** 4 **f)** 5 **3. a)** 6 **b)** 8 **c)** 4 **d)** 2 **e)** 1 **f)** 3 **g)** 4 **h)** 25 **4. b)** 3 m **5. b)** 10 **6. a)** angelfish to goldfish **b)** goldfish to angelfish **c)** angelfish to total **d)** total to angelfish **e)** goldfish to total **f)** total to goldfish **7. a)** 27 **b)** 12 **c)** 40 **d)** 26 **8. a)** The number of times the drive shaft turns to the number of times the rear wheels turn. **b)** 1000 **9.** 150 **10.** 30 **11.** 210 **12. a)** 300 **b)** 400 **13. a)** 4 **b)** 16:7, 16:12, 16:15, 16:16

Section 7.6   *Activity:* Equal numbers of blemished, unblemished apples. *Exercise:* 1. a) 765:225, $\frac{765}{225}$ **b)** 3:1 **2. a)** 332:765, $\frac{332}{765}$ **b)** 1:2

3. a) Toronto 334:358, $\frac{334}{358}$; Saskatchewan 291:469, $\frac{291}{469}$ **b)** Toronto 1:1, Saskatchewan 3:5, $\frac{3}{5}$ **4. a)** 11:4, $\frac{11}{4}$; 3:12, $\frac{3}{12}$

Section 7.7   1. a) 5 **b)** 6 **c)** 9 **d)** 15 **2. a)** 108 **b)** 195 **3.** 20.9 m **4.** 10 017 kg **5.** 180 t **6.** 56 t **7. a)** 216 000 t **b)** 24 000 t **8. a)** 14.1 g **b)** 1.6 g **9.** 38 **10.** 96

Section 7.8   1. a) 1 cm represents 8 cm **b)** 1 cm represents 20 cm **c)** 1 cm represents 25 cm **d)** 1 cm represents 100 cm **e)** 1 cm represents 50 cm **f)** 7 cm represents 30 cm **2. a)** 8 cm **b)** 10 cm **c)** 20 cm **d)** 50 cm **e)** 100 cm **f)** 200 cm **3. a)** 4 cm **b)** 16 cm **c)** 10 cm **4. a)** 1:4 **b)** 1:5 **c)** 1:4 **d)** 1 cm represents 15 m **e)** 5 m represent 1 cm **f)** 1 cm represents 9 km **g)** 20 m represent 1 cm **5. a)** 8 m **b)** 32 m **c)** 48 m **d)** 50 m **e)** 5.8 m **f)** 1.6 m **g)** 73 m **h)** 202 m **i)** 94.8 m **6.** 45 m **7. a)** 8.8 m **b)** 17.6 m

Section 7.9 *Activity:* **a)** 3.4 cm, 40.8 cm
Exercise: **1.** 8.85 cm **2. a)** 8.75 cm **b)** 1.25 cm
c) 4.375 cm **3.** 3.6 cm **4.** 3 m **5.** 750 m **6.** 4 cm:3 m
7. 13.5 m **8.** 148 cm

Section 7.10 **1. a)** 350 **b)** 350 kg **c)** 200 kg of
oxygen **2. a)** 440 g **b)** 2117.5 g **3. a)** 18 000 g

b) hydrogen $\dfrac{1}{16} = \dfrac{x}{1200}$, carbon $\dfrac{15}{16} = \dfrac{x}{1200}$ **c)** 75 g
hydrogen, 1125 g oxygen **4.** 500 kg **5.** 75 kg
6. a) 91 g **b)** 39%

Section 7.11 **1. a)** 22 m **b)** 3.0 m **c)** 4.4 m
d) 20.4 m **2.** 11 m **3. a)** 6.4 m **b)** 8.4 m **c)** 5.4 m
d) 6.4 m **4.** 3.4 m **5.** 6.4 m **6.** 8 m **8.** A: 17.6 m,
B: 18.2 m, C: 12.4 m, D: 14 m, E: 13.4 m, V: 7.6 m,
W: 17.8 m, X: 11.6 m, Y: 7.6 m, Z: 11.2 m

Section 7.13 **1. a)** 2 m/s **b)** 40 sheets/s
2. Brenda: 1 lap/min, Nancy: 1.2 laps/min,
Bernice: 1.25 laps/min **3. a)** 90 km **b)** 20 h
4. 108 000 **5.** 8 **6.** 25 words/min **7.** $50/m^2
8. 8 L/100 km **11.** 13 600 min

Section 7:14 **1. a)** $0.595/tin
b) $1.138/package **c)** $1.49375/can **d)** $0.4225/roll
e) $0.29125/can **2.** 9.17¢/nectarine, 0.98¢/cup,
5.0¢/cookie **3. a)** regular 56.5¢/L, super 61.5¢/L
b) regular **4. a)** $0.2917/package
b) $0.2975/package **c)** A **d)** $0.28125/package; yes
5. (b); Calculate the unit price.

Section 7.15 **1. a)** 155 mm **b)** 1860 mm **2.** 0.8 m
3. a) 22.99 m **b)** 1.9 m **4. a)** 0.6 g **b)** 1.1 g **5. a)** 140
b) cat **6. a)** cat 13.9 m/s, cheetah 30.6 m/s, elk
19.4 m/s, elephant 11.1 m/s, lion 13.9 m/s, pig
4.2 m/s, rabbit 15.3 m/s, squirrel 5.6 m/s **b)** 40 km
c) 25 km

Section 7.16 **1. a)** 2:100 **b)** 12:100 **c)** 25:100
d) 2.5:100 **e)** 12.1:100 **f)** 13.5:100 **2. a)** 0.25 **b)** 0.37
c) 0.08 **d)** 0.635 **e)** 0.755 **f)** 0.037 **3. a)** 39% **b)** 75%
c) 47% **d)** 80% **e)** 31% **f)** 1% **4. a)** 70% **b)** 29%
c) 80% **d)** 24% **e)** 24% **f)** 20% **5. a)** 6.4 **b)** 3 **c)** 7.2
d) 1276.5 **6. a)** 1% **b)** 0.1% **c)** 0.1% **d)** 1% **7. a)** 5%
b) 95% **8. a)** 20% **9.** 21 560 000 **10. a)** 5% **b)** 11%
11. a) 454.2 km **b)** 653.3 km **12.** 20 904 000
13. 21 150 **14.** 380 000 **15.** 175 830 **16. a)** 13%
b) 64% **c)** 81% **d)** 4% **17. a)** 33% *Making
Connections:* **b)** fresh vegetables: 1.35 kg, whole
milk: 1.305 kg, fresh fruits: 1.275 kg, cooked
oatmeal: 1.275 kg, eggs: 1.11 kg, medium lean
beef: 0.9 kg, white bread: 0.54 kg, uncooked
oatmeal: 0.12 kg

Section 7.17 *Activity:* **a)** 75% **b)** 294 **c)** 200
Exercise: **1. a)** 20% **b)** 33% **c)** 50% **2. a)** 60 **b)** 2.232
c) 450 **d)** 18.75 **e)** 35.1 **f)** 82.04 **3. a)** 5250 **b)** 96 000
c) 450 **d)** 360 **4. b) i)** 150 g **ii)** 4% **5.** 51% **6.** $24.50

7. 180 **8.** 120 **9.** 65 **10.** 72% **11. a)** 112 mL
b) 168 mL **c)** 672 mL **d)** 11.4 L **e)** 55.1 L **f)** 6.5 L

Section 7.18 **1. a)** 540 **b)** 170.8 **c)** 259.6 **d)** 523.2
2. a) $310.50 **b)** 506.9 m **c)** 682.5 kg **d)** 1012.5 mg
3. (b) (ii) is greater. **4. a)** both equal **b)** both equal
5. 5.1 m **6.** 156 L **7.** $33 376 **8.** $77.19 **9.** $1118
10. 5233% **11.** 8365% **12.** 749 900% **13. a)** sewing
machine 1218%, picture frame 746%, jug 650%,
lantern 2062%, bell 757%, clock 1665%

Section 7.19 **1.** 0.8 kg **2. a)** 0.9 kg **b)** 0.8 kg
3. a) 1500 **b)** 36 000 **c)** 13 140 000 **4.** 1230 cm^3
5. a) 45 000 cm^3 **b)** 1 080 000 cm^3
c) 394 200 000 cm^3 **6. a)** 0.925 m **7. a)** 6.5 kg
b) 7.9 kg **8.** 78 **9.** 52 **10. a)** 7.35 mm **b)** about 138
days **11.** 245 000 **12. a)** 1200 h **b)** 50 **13.** Grace
16.9 kg, Michelle 15.3 kg, Alicja 10.9 kg, Yuval
18.1 kg **14. a)** 60 kg **b)** 50 kg

15. a) ⟐ **b)** bottom right

Chapter Review **1. a)** 75% **b)** $\dfrac{7}{10}$ **c)** 0.49 **d)** 80%

2. a) 4 L/3 min **b)** 9/5 min **3. a)** 1:10 **b)** 4:1 **c)** 1:4
4. a) 50% **b)** 9 **5.** 20 kg **6.** 3.3 h/day, 23.1 h/week,
100 h/month **7.** No **8.** $1 141 700

Self Evaluation **1. a)** 20 **b)** 4 **c)** 20 **2. a)** 2.5 m/s
b) 4 pizzas/h **3. a)** 75% **b)** 56% **4. a)** 120 **b)** 6
5. a) 33.04 m **b)** 7.9 cm **6.** 2 min **7.** $188 +
applicable taxes for each province. For example,
in British Columbia, $212.44. **8.** 217% **9.** $558.04

Technology Insight: Electric Cars
1. 42.5 L **2.** 1.1 h

CHAPTER 8
Section 8.1 **b)** $187.49, $552.50 **2. a)** Answers
will vary depending on province. **b)** 7%

Section 8.2 **1. a)** A **b)** A **c)** B **2. a)** $3.92 **b)** $2.07
3. a) GST is 7% of the cost, generally listed first
b) Saskatchewan, Manitoba, Ontario, British
Columbia **c)** Newfoundland, New Brunswick,
Nova Scotia, Québec, Prince Edward Island **d)** on
purchase price **4. a)** GST $0.56, PST $0.56 **b)** $9.07
5. $42.70 **6. a)** $156.21 **b)** $43.79 **7.** $19.49
8. a) Nova Scotia, British Columbia, Alberta
b) $100.05, $297.19, $53.49 **9. a)** 11% **c)** $24.71
10. a) Answers will vary. For example, in Ontario
$570.38 **b)** Alberta **c)** $29.76 **12. a)** Ontario
b) British Columbia **c)** Prince Edward Island, Nova
Scotia **d)** Manitoba, Saskatchewan

Section 8.3 Answers will vary depending on
province. Answers given for Ontario. **1. a)** $0.75
b) $0.12 **c)** $7.80 **d)** $13.50 **e)** $0.34 **f)** $6.43
2. a) $3.75 **b)** $28.75 **3.** $2.11 **4.** $6.83

5. a) telephone $113.71, 5-disc carousel $275.98, watch $114.99, keyboard $68.16

Section 8.4 1. a) $7.36 **b)** $10.79 **c)** $3.39
2. a) $4.79 , $19.16 **b)** $47.92 , $88.98 **3. a)** $42.98
b) $34.19 **4. a)** $28.33 **b)** $56.67 **5.** $192.07
6. a) 18%

Section 8.5 1. Batteries: $73.52, $23.52, 47%;
Tires: $46.11, $6.11, 15%; Telephone: $103.84,
$23.84, 30%; Tape Deck: $130.36, $25.36, 24%
2. a) $97.12 **b)** $22.12 **c)** 29% **3. a)** $195.50
b) $30.50 **4. a)** 25% **b)** $89.85 **c)** $17.97 **d)** 25%
5. a) $11.99 **b)** $38.75

Section 8.6 1. 77% **2. a)** 80% **3.** 15% **4. a)** 950
000 **b)** 47.5% **c)** Number of farmers decreased by
47.5%. **5. a)** 23 000 000 **b)** 767% **c)** Population
projected to be 767% of 1953 population.
6. a) 38%

Section 8.7 1. a) $30.00 **b)** $12.72 **c)** $72.45
2. a) $10.00 **b)** $24.00 **c)** $12.00 **d)** $2.28
3. a) $72.00 **b)** $90.00 **c)** $62.50 **d)** $48.13
4. a) $745.50 **b)** $725.09 **5. a)** $980.01, $712.13,
$949.59 **6.** $587.38 **7.** $966.88 **8. a)** $37.50
9. a) (ii) **10. a)** $1076.25 **11. a)** $750.00 **b)** $1087.50
c) $1312.50 **d)** $1425.00 **12. a)** 5 **b)** 20% **c)** 12, 0%

Section 8.8 *Activity 1:* **a)** 110 **b)** 121 **c)** 161
Activity 2: **a)** $110.00 **b)** $121.00 **c)** $133.10

Section 8.9 *Activity:* **a)** $160.00 **b)** compound
Exercise: **1. a)** $649.28 **b)** $316.80 **c)** $1501.78
2. a) $5940.50 **b)** $2702.17 **c)** $14 615.38 **3.** A
4. a) $5073.38 **b)** $6534.44 **c)** $7815.90
d) $4373.22 **5.** $2500 at 6 3/4%, $94.35
6. a) i) $60.00 **ii)** $123.60 **iii)** $338.23 **iv)** $790.85
v) $1396.56 **c)** 2 **d)** 4 **e)** 12 **7. a)** $480.23 **b)** $1026.74
c) No *Making Connections:* **2. a)** $147.51
b) $6564.66

Section 8.10 1. a) $62.30 **b)** $46.50 **c)** $92.30
2. a) $7.80 **b)** $5.85 **c)** $350 **3. a)** $13.95 **b)** $34.51
c) $1836 **d)** $3090 **4.** $35.80 **5.** $3870 **6.** $172
7. $5400 **8.** $312.29 **9.** $626.81 **10.** $5202

Section 8.11 1. 26 **2.** 55 **3. a)** 54 **b)** 36 **c)** 27 **d)** 8
e) 0

Chapter Review 1. a) $286.87 **b)** $35.25, $270.25
c) $625.00 **2. a)** PST $5.60, GST $4.90, total cost
$80.45 **b)** $110.33; for example, in Alberta,
$118.05 **c)** 12%, $373.90 **3. a)** $32.81 **b)** $29.10
c) 7.7% **4. a)** $1.73 **b)** $521.73 **c)** $1.74 **d)** $523.47
e) $563.23 **5.** $44.94

Self Evaluation 1. a) $2.95 **b)** $11.80 **2.** $18.12
3. a) $81.97 **b)** $13.95 **4. a) i)** $15.63 **ii)** $200.00
iii) 44% **b)** $37.82 **5. a)** A: Ont. $110.98, Qué.,
$111.52; B: Ont. $75.78, Qué. $76.15 **b)** $129.43

6. $7125.00

Practice: Cumulative Review

1. a) 12 **b)** $\frac{1}{96}$ **c)** $\frac{8}{35}$ **d)** $\frac{3}{20}$ **2. a)** $\frac{1}{6}$ **b)** $\frac{112}{15}$ **d)** 1.6 **e)** $1\frac{13}{210}$
3. a) 4 **b)** 6 **c)** 4 **4.** 1115 **5. a)** –3 **b)** 17 **c)** 71 **d)** –20 **e)** –3
f) 9 **6.** B: 5.4 m^3 **7. a)** 540 L **b)** 60% **c)** 2 h **8. a)** $5.60,
$80.45 **b)** $103.33, $116.76 **c)** 7%, $355.68

CHAPTER 9

Section 9.1 1. a) A: +4, B: $4x$, C: –3, D: $-4x$
2. b) A: $3x$, B: $-x + 2$, C: $-2x + 4$ **4.** $2x - 10$
5. a) $3x - 6$ **b)** $4x + 4$ **c)** $5x + 15$ **d)** $2x - 12$ **6. a)** $x^2 + x + 1$ **b)** $x^2 - 2x$ **c)** $2x^2 - x - 4$ **d)** $-2x^2 - 3$ **e)** $-x^2 - x$
f) $x^2 - 3x$

Section 9.2 1. a) like **b)** unlike **c)** unlike **d)** like
e) like **f)** unlike **g)** like **h)** unlike **2. b) i)** $5x$ **ii)** $-8y$
iii) $2a$ **iv)** $-6x^2$ **3. a)** $5a$ **b)** $14b$ **c)** $8m$ **d)** $2p$ **e)** $-a$ **f)** $3q$
g) a **h)** $-2y$ **4. b)** $6x^2$ **5. a)** $10x^2$ **b)** $10x^2$ **c)** $3x^2$ **d)** $-2x^2$
6. a) $-5x$ **b)** $7m$ **c)** $4ab$ **d)** $12mp$ **e)** xy **f)** $21pq$
7. a) $10x$ **b)** $5a$ **c)** $4n$ **d)** $7pq$ **e)** $16m^2$ **f)** $14rq^2$ **8. a)** $6a - 3b$ **b)** $5m - 6p$ **c)** pq **d)** $2a + 2b$ **e)** $4a - ab$ **f)** $5p - r$
9. a) $5m + n$ **b)** $6a + 3b$ **c)** $9x - 2y$ **d)** $7k + 2m$ **e)** $p + 3q$ **f)** $-4g - 3t$ **10. a)** $5a + b$ **b)** $5x + 2y$ **c)** $3y - x$ **d)** $13a - 5b$ **e)** $2y + 3x$ **f)** $2m - n$ **12. a)** A: x^2, B: $x^2 - x - 6$
b) $2x^2 - x - 6$ **13. a)** $7x^2 + 9x + 4$ **b)** $7a^2 - 2a + 3$
c) $-2y^2 + 3y + 6$ **d)** $9m^2 + m + 4$ **14. a)** $4x^2 - 6$
b) $-2ab + 6b$ **c)** $5g^2 + g + 4$ **d)** $m^2 - 4m + 1$ **e)** $3p^2 + p + 8$ **f)** $-x^2y - 2xy + 5$ **15. a)** $3a - b$ **b)** $9x - 8$ **c)** $x + y$
d) $3x$ **e)** $2a - b$ **f)** $2a - b$ **g)** $3x$ **h)** $y + x$ **i)** $3x$ **j)** $x + y$
k) $4y - 5x$ **l)** $10k - 8m$; c) h), j); d), g), i); e), f)
16. a) 2, 3 **b)** –7, 4 **17. a)** A:1, B: 3, C: 6 **b)** 10; 15
c) triangular numbers

Section 9.3 1. b) $x + 5$ **2. a)** $5a - 1$ **b)** $8x + 9$
c) $7m + 9$ **d)** $7p - 4$ **e)** $13r + 4$ **f)** $13w + 3$ **3. b)** $2x + 10$
4. a) $2d + 4$ **b)** $w - 1$ **c)** $-2q - 18$ **d)** $u + 1$ **e)** $-4x - 2$
f) $7k - 4$ **5. a)** Simplify, $8a - b$ **b)** 19 **6. a)** Simplify,
$-2n - 7$ **b)** –3 **7. a)** $3x + 12$ **b)** $-x + 8$ **c)** $2a - 1$
d) $11 - 2a$ **e)** $5m - 2$ **f)** $m + 2$ **g)** $5k + 2$ **h)** $-k - 6$
i) $-4k - 2$ **8. a)** $x + 11$ **b)** $-x + 1$ **c)** $-x - 7$ **d)** $-2x + 11$
e) $-x - 18$ **f)** $-3x - 4$ **g)** $3x - 7$ **h)** $-x + 16$ **i)** $-x + 14$
9. a) $13x + 3$ **b)** $n - 1$ **c)** 0 **d)** 6 **e)** $7n + 4$ **f)** $3n - 12$
10. a) $6x + 2y$ **b)** $a + 4b$ **c)** $-2m - 7n$ **d)** $5x - 3y + 2z$
e) $2b + a$ **f)** $6x + 3y - 6z$ **g)** $7f + 2h$ **h)** $-k + 6n - m$
11. a) $8x + 6y$; 36 **b)** $6y - 4x$; 0 **c)** $2x + 5y - 4$; 12
12. a) Remove brackets and simplify; $-2m - 6$
b) –2 **13. a)** –12 **b)** 13 **14. a)** 13 **b)** 35 **c)** 12 **d)** 6
15. a) 2 **b)** –19 **c)** –25; (a) greatest **17. a)** $m + 10n$
b) $7a - b$ **c)** $5x + y$ **d)** $-3p + 4q$ **18. b)** 331 **c)** 120 601
d) Centre disk is not a ring. *Making Connections:*
a) 34 m

Section 9.4 1. a) 94 units **b)** $4x + 14$ **c)** LM = 22
units, LN = 46 units, NM = 26 units
2. a) i) 72 units **ii)** 127 units **iii)** 226 units **b)** $x = 20$

3. a) $5x - 7y$ **b)** $x + 7y$ **c)** $18x - 2y$ **d)** 30 units

Section 9.5 *Activity:* **1. a)** $12ab$ **b)** $6xy$ **c)** $15pq$
2. a) $6m^5$ **b)** $2a^4$ **c)** $3a^2y^4$ *Exercise:* **1. a)** 2^7 **b)** 5^7
c) 3^5 **d)** 10^5 **2. a)** x^5 **b)** a^6 **c)** m^7 **d)** p^3 **e)** b^8 **f)** p^4 **g)** y^{11}
h) a^8 **3. a)** m^8 **b)** x^7 **c)** p^6 **d)** y^9 **4. a)** $-6m$ **b)** $-15b$
c) $6k$ **d)** $9n$ **e)** $10r$ **5. b)** $6a^5$ **6. b)** $-10b^5$ **7. a)** $4xy$
b) $8ab$ **8. a)** $-6xy$ **b)** $-15yz$ **c)** $-6ab$ **d)** $12mn$ **e)** $-8xy$
f) $30mn$ **g)** $10ab$ **h)** $-3mn$ **9. a)** $6x^2y^4$ **b)** $-6m^3n^3$
c) $24a^3b^3$ **10. a)** $-12x^2$ **b)** $8p^4$ **c)** $9y^6$ **d)** $-10a^2$
e) $-10x^2$ **f)** $-8x^5$ **g)** $-32p^{10}$ **h)** $-8w^7$ **11. a)** $25a^2$
b) $4x^2y^2$ **c)** $16a^2b^4$ **d)** $9m^4n^6$ **12. a)** 2^{10} **b)** 2^{18} **c)** 3^6
d) 4^9 **e)** x^9 **f)** w^{12} **h)** p^{14} **13. a)** $-6xy$ **b)** $-9y^2$
c) $12mn$ **d)** $-6a^2b$ **e)** $6x^4$ **f)** $-8y^5$ **g)** $8m^6$ **h)** $-6a^4$
i) $-6x^4y^2$ **j)** $-18a^5b^2$ **k)** $-6a^2b^3$ **l)** $18a^5$ **14. a)** $-28a^2$
b) $12my$ **c)** $6x^3y$ **d)** $-6a^3$ **e)** $-6x^6y$ **f)** $12x^4$ **g)** 0
h) $-3x^3y^9$ **15. a)** $9y^2$ **b)** $4m^4$ **c)** $9a^2b^2$ **d)** $16x^4y^2$
e) $9x^4y^6$ **16. a)** -36 **b)** 36 **c)** -72 **d)** -216 **e)** -432
17. a) $-30abc$ **b)** $5mnp$ **c)** $-3stv$ **d)** $-6x^3y^3$ **e)** $10a^7b^2$
f) $12s^5t^5$ **18. a)** $4.8x^5$ **b)** $-3.33a^3b^2$ **c)** $-1.4m^3n$
d) $-1.23p^3q^3$ **e)** $-2.42x^3y^4$ **f)** $1.44x^4$ **19. a)** 41.04
b) 246.24 **c)** 46.7856 **d)** 73.872 **e)** -361.9728
f) $9.357\ 12$

Section 9.6 *Activity:* **1. a)** $3x + 3$ **b)** $4x + 4$
c) $2x + 2$ **d)** $3x - 3$ **2. a)** $5x + 10$ **b)** $3x - 6$ **c)** $2x^2 + 4x$
d) $3x^2 - 3x$ *Exercise:* **1. a)** $2x + 6$ **b)** $8x - 4$ **c)** $-12m$
$+ 18$ **d)** $4y - 8$ **2. a)** $3x + 6$ **b)** $-14r - 28w$ **c)** $14m + 14$
d) $36d - 9e$ **e)** $6a^2 + 2a$ **f)** $5b^2 - 20b$ **g)** $-30m^2 +$
$10mn$ **h)** $30w^2 - 10wz$ **3. a)** $2a^2 + 10a - 2$ **b)** $-2m^2 +$
$6m + 8$ **c)** $8p^2 + 24p - 32$ **d)** $p^3 - 3p^2 - 2p$ **e)** $-r^3 + 6r^2$
$- 9r$ **f)** $-4w - w^2 + 7w^3$ **4. a)** -2 **b)** $3a - 8$; -2
c) same **5. a)** 51 **b)** 19 **c)** -126 **d)** -54 **e)** -12 **f)** -171
6. a) 18 **b)** $3a + 4b$; 18 **c)** same **7. a)** Simplify. **b)** 2
8. a) -26 **b)** -41 **c)** -61 **d)** -130 **9. a)** $10x^2 - 5x$ **b)** 140
c) 330 **10. a)** 18 **b)** $3a + 4b$; 18 **c)** (b)

Section 9.8 **1. a)** 2^2 **b)** 5^2 **c)** 3^2 **d)** 10^3 **e)** $3y$ **f)** $-3x$
g) $-3a^3$ **h)** $-3m$ **2. b)** $3x$ **3. a)** $3m$ **b)** $2a$ **c)** $-2a$ **d)** $-6n$
e) $-8c$ **f)** $-8b$ **g)** $-20m$ **h)** $-3x$ **4. a)** $-4x^3y$ **b)** $-3x$ **5. a)** a^2
b) $-2x^2$ **c)** $-5a^3$ **d)** $3p^4$ **e)** c^5 **f)** $-4p^2$ **g)** $3m^6$ **h)** $-2n^4$
6. a) m **b)** $2x^2$ **c)** $3a^3$ **d)** $-5p$ **e)** $-4c^4$ **f)** 3 **g)** $-10m^3$
h) $5z^2$ **7. a)** $2p$ **b)** $-4s^2$ **c)** $-6m$ **d)** $6p^2$ **e)** $-2n^2$ **f)** $-4a$
8. a) i) 12 **ii)** 12 **b)** (ii) is (i) simplified. **9. a)** -6
b) -16 **c)** 144 **d)** -6 **10. a)** $l \times w$ **b)** $5a^2b$ **11. a)** $6xy$
b) $4ab$ **12. b)** $2n^2$ **13. a)** $4xy$ **b)** $15a^2b$ **c)** $2m^2n^4$

Section 9.9 *Activity:* **2. b)** A: 6, B: $m + n$
3. a) $2a + 3b$ **b)** $5a^2 + 3a$ *Exercise:* **1. a)** $2y + 6$
b) $4m + 8$ **c)** $2b + 3a$ **d)** x **2. a)** $4b + 3$ **b)** $-3y - 3$
c) $-2m - 2$ **d)** $-7p - 6$ **3. a)** $y + 6$ **b)** $2y - 8$ **c)** $4y + 1$
d) $2y - 1$ **4. a)** $6xy - y$ **b)** $-ab + 2ac$ **c)** $2xy - x$
d) $-5mn + 2m$ **5. a) i)** 9 **ii)** 9 **b)** (ii) is (i) simplified.
6. a) -2 **b)** 4 **c)** 0 **d)** -1 **7. a)** $3a + 4$ **b)** $5m - 2x$ **c)** x
d) $3y + 4$ **e)** $-a$ **f)** $-5a + 4b$ **8. a)** $3 + x - 4x^2$ **b)** $2 - k +$
$8k^2$ **c)** $3x^2 + 2x - 5$ **d)** $2y - 1 + x$ **e)** $y - xy - x$ **f)** $-a^2 +$
$2a + b$ **g)** $-3x + 2y - 5xy$ **h)** $-3am + 2m + 6a$

9. a) -13 **b)** -9 **c)** -1 **d)** $-\dfrac{3}{2}$ **e)** -1 **f)** -9 **10. a)** $4x^2y + x$

b) 82 units **11. a)** $4x^2y - 3xy$ **b)** side: 30 units,
perimeter: 120 units **d)** 900 square units

12. a) $3ax + 6bx$ **b)** 480 square units **c)** $\sqrt{3ax + 6bx}$
units *Making Connections:* **b)** 1 **c)** 2

Section 9.10 **1. a)** 2^5 **b)** 3^2 **c)** 3^3 **d)** 10 **2. a)** 1 **b)** 1
c) $\dfrac{1}{100}$ **d)** $\dfrac{1}{125}$ **e)** $\dfrac{1}{32}$ **3. b)** 9; -9 **4. a)** $\dfrac{1}{4}$ **b)** $\dfrac{1}{4}$ **c)** $-\dfrac{1}{4}$ **d)** $-\dfrac{1}{4}$

5. a) 1 **b)** 4 **c)** 2 **d)** 1 **6. a)** $\dfrac{1}{2}$ **b)** 64 **c)** $\dfrac{1}{25}$ **d)** 16 **e)** 4 **f)** 1

g) 1 **h)** 256 **i)** 27 **j)** 2 **k)** $-\dfrac{1}{8}$ **l)** $\dfrac{1}{32}$ **m)** $\dfrac{3}{2}$ **n)** 9 **o)** 1 **7. a)** $1\dfrac{1}{2}$

b) 1 **c)** $3\dfrac{1}{2}$ **d)** $\dfrac{5}{6}$ **8. a)** $2x^{-1}$ **b)** $3x^{-1}$ **c)** $8x^{-2}$ **d)** mn^{-3}

e) $2tx^{-2}$ **f)** abn^{-1} **9. a)** $x^{-1}y$ **b)** a **c)** $4^{-1}xy^{-3}$ **d)** x^5y^{-1}

e) y^{-2} **f)** a^3b **g)** ab^{-2} **h)** b **10. a)** $\dfrac{7}{2}$ **b)** 7

Section 9.11 *Activity:* **b)** 450, 4500, 45 000,
450 000, 0.045, 0.0045, 0.000 45, 0.000 045
Exercise: **1. a)** 3 **b)** 2 **c)** -3 **2. a)** 4.69 **b)** 3.89 **c)** 8.96
3. a) 640 **b)** 3060 **c)** 0.0637 **d)** 0.0093 **e)** 6360
f) 0.000 321 **g)** 421 000 **h)** 0.000 000 040 8
4. a) 4.86×10^5 **b)** 9.32×10^6 **c)** $2.075\ 623 \times 10^6$
d) $5.041\ 302 \times 10^{12}$ **e)** 4.53×10^{-4} **f)** 1.35×10^{-3}
g) 3.2×10^{-7} **h)** 4.21×10^{-10} **5.** 4.86×10^4
6. a) 9.866 05 **b)** 4.93 –04 **c)** 1.2 –07 **d)** 3.9 06
7. c) i) 683 **ii)** 0.009 25 **iii)** 0.000 020 2 **iv)** 4 510 000

Section 9.12 *Activity:* **a)** 1.125×10^3, 2×10^6,
1.386×10^5, 1.2×10^6, 3×10^{-12} *Exercise:* **1. a)** 2.30
$\times 10^3$ **b)** 2.300×10^3 **c)** 1.5×10^4 **d)** 8.5×10^{-1} **e)** 8.5
$\times 10^{-3}$ **f)** 1.203×10^4 **g)** 4.80×10^4 **h)** 9.60×10^{-5}
2. a) 4.1×10^8 **b)** 1.4×10^2 **c)** 2.1×10^{-1} **3. a)** $5.5 \times$
10^6 **b)** 2×10^5 **4.** 1.3×10^7 **5.** 2.49×10^{-18} **6. a)** $6 \times$
10^7 **b)** 3.6×10^9 **7.** 9.5×10^{20} **8.** 1.5×10^{10} mL

Chapter Review **1. a)** $8x$ **b)** $5c - 8$
c) $-3mn - 2m^2$ **d)** $3x^2 + 2x + 6$ **2. a)** $8x - 5$ **b)** $2a - 3$
c) $13m - 3n$ **d)** $-2b + 4$ **e)** $3p + q + 2$ **3.** $2x + 15$
4. a) x^8 **b)** m^6 **c)** a^9 **d)** n^3 **e)** k^4 **f)** 1 **5. a)** $-8xy$
b) $-21yz$ **c)** $20a^3b^2$ **d)** $15p^5$ **e)** $-12x^2y$ **f)** $-30st^2$
6. a) $4a + 28$ **b)** $35 - 14r$ **c)** $2m^2 + 2m$ **d)** $-6x^2 - 12x$
e) $-y^3 - 2y^2 - y$ **f)** $-k^4 - 3k^2$ **7. a)** $4q$ **b)** $-2y$ **c)** $2b$
d) $10m$ **e)** $25x^3$ **f)** $15p$ **8.** $5xy^4$ **9. a)** 8.5×10^5, 85
b) 3.45×10^6, 345 **c)** 1.25×10^{-4}, 125

Self Evaluation **1. a)** like **b)** unlike **c)** like
d) like **e)** unlike **f)** unlike **2. a)** $6x$ **b)** y **c)** $2d + 3$
d) $3w - 1$ **e)** $-2q$ **f)** $-x + 4y$ **3. a)** $7p - 4$ **b)** $2m + 3$
c) $-4x + 1$ **d)** $2a - 16$ **4. a)** 0 **b)** 14 **c)** 4 **d)** 11 **e)** 5
f) 15 **g)** 5 **h)** 20 **5.** $10x - 28$ **6. a)** $15xy$ **b)** $35ab$
c) $-4m^2$ **d)** $12k^2$ **e)** $-12w^5$ **f)** $-18m^8$ **7. a)** 24 **b)** -35

c) 21 d) 37 e) –5 f) 10 8. a) 3 b) –3m c) 3x^2 d) –4y^2
9. a) 4.5 × 10^6, 45 b) 2.9 × 10^{-5}, 29 c) 3.92 × 10^{-10},
392 d) 4.005 003 × 10^8, 4 005 003 10. 1 × 10^9 km

CHAPTER 10

Section 10.1   1. b) 3 **2. a)** 3 **b)** 11 **c)** 7 **d)** 11 **e)** 8 **f)** 2
g) 15 **h)** 5 **i)** 13 **j)** –5 **k)** –2 **l)** 18 **3. a)** 2 **b)** 5 **c)** –1 **d)** 11
e) 5 **f)** –5 **g)** –6 **h)** 3 **i)** –3 **j)** –15 **k)** –5 **l)** 0 **4. a)** 5 **b)** –1
c) –9 **d)** 23 **e)** 25 **f)** 31 **g)** –22 **h)** –28 **i)** –27 **j)** 4 **k)** 5
l) 5 **5. a)** Isolate one x-tile by adding appropriate
number of tiles to both sides of the equation. **6.** 4
7. a) 3 **b)** 3 **8. a)** 4 **b)** 2 **c)** –3 **d)** –5 **9. a)** Isolate one
x-tile by forming equal groups. **10.** –1 **11. a)** 2 **b)** 1
c) 2

Section 10.2   1. a) $m = 4$ **b)** $y = 9$ **c)** $x = -10$
d) $m = 9$ **2. a)** $x = 6$ **b)** $y = 20$ **c)** $m = \frac{9}{2}$ **3. a)** $y = 3$
b) $m = 6$ **c)** $p = 19$ **d)** $k = 11$ **4. a)** $k = 20$ **b)** $m = 12$
c) $p = -25$ **d)** $s = 16$ **e)** $m = -14$ **f)** $p = 1$ **5. a)** –5.5
b) –7.5 **c)** 17.5 **d)** –29 **e)** 14.2 **f)** 84 **6. a)** $m = 0.7$
b) $m = 2.4$ **c)** $s = -17.5$ **d)** $p = -3.5$ **e)** $x = -8.92$
f) $y = 4.94$ **7. c)** $\frac{7}{8}$ **e)** $\frac{7}{8}$ **8. a)** $p = 6.7$ **b)** $m = 4.3$
c) $k = 20.375$ **d)** $a = 8.45$ **e)** $q = -3.386$ **f)** $z = 3.55$

Section 10.3   1. a) $m = 4$ **b)** $y = 3$ **c)** $p = -2$ **d)** $k = -3$
e) $n = 6$ **f)** $x = 12$ **g)** $k = 4$ **h)** $m = -8$ **i)** $h = -7$ **j)** $m = 7$
k) $b = -15$ **l)** $c = -8$ **2. a)** $m = 4$ **b)** $p = 3$ **c)** $q = 4$
d) $t = 3$ **e)** $k = 3$ **f)** $p = 8$ **g)** $a = 2$ **h)** $c = 5$ **i)** $x = 3$
j) $t = 2$ **k)** $n = 9$ **l)** $z = 16$ **3. a)** $k = 24$ **b)** $a = 8$ **c)** $s = 6$
d) $w = -16$ **4. a)** $x = 3$ **b)** $y = 12$ **c)** $y = 1$ **d)** $x = -15$
e) $x = -7$ **f)** $k = 48$ **g)** $m = 5$ **h)** $d = 45$ **5. a)** $k = 14$
b) $m = 9$ **c)** $p = 4$ **d)** $q = 7$ **e)** $m = 3$ **f)** $x = 5$ **g)** $m = 15$
h) $k = 16.5$ **i)** $q = 9$ **6. a)** $k = 9$ **b)** $s = 28$ **c)** $p = 30$
d) $n = 4$ **e)** $x = 32$ **f)** $y = 27$ **7. a)** 3 **b)** 1 **c)** –2 **d)** –2
e) –6 **f)** –5 **8. a)** $x = 3$ **b)** $y = 7.3$ **c)** $p = 1$ **d)** $k = -2$
e) $x = -1$ **f)** $y = -\frac{13}{15}$ **g)** $z = -2$ **h)** $m = 0.25$ **i)** $k = 3.625$

Section 10.4   *Activity 2:* a) $x = -11$ **b)** $x = -1$
Exercise: **1. a)** $y = 1$ **b)** $k = 2$ **c)** $m = 5$ **2. a)** –20 **b)** 13
3. a) $y = 12$ **b)** $y = 2$ **c)** $m = -2$ **d)** $y = -4$ **e)** $k = -2$
f) $x = 1$ **4. a)** $y = 4$ **b)** $y = 36$ **c)** $m = 5$ **d)** $p = 3$ **e)** $y = 3$
f) $y = 5$ **5. a)** 2 **b)** –2 **c)** –3 **d)** 5 **e)** 7 **f)** 1.5 **6.** 28
7. 150 h **8.** 30 **9. a)** 16 cm^2

Section 10.5   1. a) –3, foal **b)** –2, calf **c)** 1, squab
2. a) 3, cygnet **b)** 4, chick **3. a), b)** –4, leveret; –3,
foal; 0, parr; 2, piglet; 4, chick; 6, duckling

Section 10.6   1. a) $2(n + 7)$; $n + 14$; $n + 24$; n
b) n;$2n$; $2n + 10$; $n + 5$; n **2.** The result is the same
as the original number. **4. a)** – **b)** + **c)** × **d)** + **e)** ÷ **f)** ×

Section 10.7   *Activity:* 1. a) $k - 6$ **b)** $k + 15$ **c)** $3k$
d) $2k$ **e)** $6 - k$ **f)** $k + 12$ **g)** $k ÷ 3$ *Exercise:* **1. a)** $3n + 4$

b) $2n - 8$ **c)** $2n - 6$ **2. b)** $n - 8 = 5$; 13 **3. a)** 64 **b)** 24
4. a) 20, 28 **b)** 48 **c)** 15 **5. b)** 13 **6. b)** 6 **7.** 42 **8.** 25, 37
9. d) 2

Section 10.8   1. a) $P = 14k + 7$ **b)** $k = 9$ **c)** 48 cm,
27 cm, 58 cm **2. a)** 25.5 m × 24.5 m **b)** 120 m ×
57 m **c)** 225 m × 150 m **3. b)** 27.2 cm, 40.2 cm,
46.6 cm **4.** 281 m × 205 m **5. b)** Lori: 155 cm, Chris:
147 cm, Mike: 163 cm **6. a)** $w = 9$ m, $l = 12$ m
b) 108 m^2 **7.** $w = 14$ cm, $l = 20$ cm **8. a)** $w = 64$ m,
$l = 125$ m **9.** $w = 75$ m, $l = 480$ m *Making
Connections:* The second one will form a square.

Section 10.9   1. a) $(3h + 2) + (2h + 1) + 7h = 27$
b) wrist: 8 bones, palm: 5 bones, fingers: 14 bones
2. a) $(3k - 0.6) - (2k - 0.2) = k - 0.4$ **b)** 5.4 m
3. a) $(3x + 1.7) + (13x - 0.1) + 2(x + 5.2)$ **b)** snapping
turtle: 22.7 kg, alligator snapping turtle: 90.9 kg
4. a) $(2k - 4) + 4k + (5k - 1)$ **b)** Nitrogen: 6 kg,
Phosphorous: 20 kg, Potash: 24 kg **5. a)** $p + (2p + 3)$
$+ (3p + 1)$ **b)** Potassium: 6 kg, Potash: 15 kg,
Nitrogen: 19 kg **6. a)** $(33c - 25) - (28c - 20)$
b) Copper: 680 g, Brass: 800 g **7. a)** $(4a + 1) +$
$(16a - 1)$ **b)** Oxygen: 49 cm^3, Nitrogen: 191 cm^3
8. 9 **9.** 40 **10.** 250 **11. b)** 2

Section 10.10   1. 4 **2.** nickels: 3, dimes:
6, quarters: 12 **3.** marsupial: 57, orangutan: 19
4. 37, 11 **5.** nickels: 11, dimes: 32 **6.** Jerry: 6 years,
Elaine: 18 years

Section 10.11   2. b) The area of the square on the
hypotenuse equals the sum of the areas of the
squares on the two other sides.

Section 10.12   1. a) 10 **b)** 25 **c)** 11.3 **d)** 15 **e)** 25
f) 27.3 **2. a)** 13 **b)** 9.8 **c)** 6.7 **d)** 13.4 **e)** 16 **f)** 23.7
g) 18.4 **h)** 19.8 **i)** 13.7 **3. a)** 19.2 **b)** 11.4 **c)** 8.9 **d)** 12
4. a) A: 8.2 m, B: 4.95 m, C: 16.5 m **5. a)** 106.1 m
b) 190.7 m **c)** 282.9 m **d)** 169.0 m **e)** 185.9 m
f) 199.0 m **6. a)** 2.7 m **b)** 233.9 cm **c)** 10.3 m
8. 5.0 m **9.** 6.7 m **10. a)** 23.76 mm **b)** 158.86 cm
11. 80 m **12)** 38.7 m **13. b)** Yes **c)** Yes, 1 cm^3
d) 4 cm × 4 cm × 4 cm

Section 10.13   *Activity 1:* A: a) 15 < 27
b) 9 < 21 **c)** 36 < 72 **d)** 4 < 8 **B: a)** 9 < 21
b) 15 < 27 **c)** –36 > –72 **d)** –4 < –8 Multiply, divide
by negative reverses inequality. *Exercise:* **1. a)** >
b) < **c)** > **d)** < **e)** > **f)** > **2. a)** $m > 3$ **b)** $p < -3$ **c)** $x \leq 6$
d) $x > \frac{12}{7}$ **e)** $y < -2$ **f)** $t \geq 2$ **4. a)** $k < 5$ **b)** $p \geq \frac{8}{3}$ **c)** $y > 9$
d) $k \leq 7$ **e)** $p > 4$ **f)** $n < 4$ **5. a)** $y < 8$ **b)** $x \geq 9$ **c)** $y \leq 22$
d) $x < 6$ **e)** $m > 6$ **f)** $k \geq -1$ **6.** $x > 5$ **7. a)** $x > -16$, $x \in R$
b) $x < 24$, $x \in I$ **8.** 12 colas, 9 oranges, 24 ginger ale

Chapter Review   1. a) $k = 22$ **b)** $m = 6$ **c)** $p = -19$
d) $x = 16$ **2. a)** $m = 4$ **b)** $y = 3$ **c)** $p = -2$ **d)** $k = 24$
e) $a = -8$ **f)** $s = 6$ **g)** $t = -3$ **h)** $w = 8$ **i)** $x = -5$

3. a) $m = -2$ **b)** $m = -2$ **c)** $m = -2$ **d)** $m = +1$; (a), (b), (c) **4. a)** $x = -20$ **b)** $x = 13$ **c)** $x = -19$ **5. a)** $m \leqq \dfrac{32}{3}$, $m \in I$ **6. a)** 40 **b)** 2 **c)** 40 **d)** 23 **e)** 28 **7. a)** 17.0 **b)** 6.7 **c)** 21.9 **d)** 22.5 **8.** 6.5 m

Self Evaluation 1. a) 2 **b)** 4 **c)** –3 **d)** 4 **e)** –3 **f)** –3 **2. a)** 5 **b)** 4 **c)** 9 **d)** 8 **3.** 16 m, 10 m, 11m **4.** 8, 5 **5. a)** 13 **b)** 10 **c)** 20 **6. a)** $t \geqq -2$ **b)** $r < 8$ **c)** $t < 7$ **d)** $x < \dfrac{6}{5}$ **e)** $m \geqq -6$ **f)** $y < -4$ **7. a)** $x > 1$ **8.** 14.7 m

Problem Solving: Cumulative Review
1. a) Tommy **2. a)** AC = 5 cm, AB = 3 cm, BC = 4 cm **b)** 3.3 **3.** $\dfrac{1}{60}$ **4.** 100 cm² **5.** (b) **6. a)** O = 6, D = 2, L = 9, C = 1, E = 3 **b)** S = E = N = Y = 9, M = 1, D = O = R = 0 **7. a)** $5^3 = 15^2 - 10^2$, $6^3 = 21^2 - 15^2$, $7^3 = 28^2 - 21^2$ **b)** $5 \times \dfrac{5}{6} = 5 - \dfrac{5}{6}$, $6 \times \dfrac{6}{7} = 6 - \dfrac{6}{7}$, $7 \times \dfrac{7}{8} = 7 - \dfrac{7}{8}$

CHAPTER 11
Section 11.1 1. b) $x^2 + 5x + 6$ **3. b)** $2x^2 + 7x + 3$ **4. a)** $2x^2 + 5x + 2$ **b)** $3x^2 + 11x + 10$ **c)** $8x^2 + 10x + 3$ **d)** $5x^2 + 9x + 4$ **e)** $4x^2 + 16x + 7$ **f)** $12x^2 + 21x + 9$ **5. b)** $x^2 + x - 2$ **6. a)** $x^2 + x - 2$ **b)** $x^2 - 3x - 10$ **c)** $x^2 + 2x - 3$ **d)** $x^2 + 3x - 4$ **e)** $x^2 - 2x - 35$

Section 11.2 1. a) $x^2 + 13x + 42$ **b)** $2x^2 + 7x + 3$ **2. a)** $x^2 + 9x + 20$ **b)** $x^2 + 9x + 20$ **c)** same **3. a)** $x^2 + 9x + 18$ **b)** $y^2 + 12y + 35$ **c)** $a^2 + 8a + 16$ **d)** $k^2 + 14k + 48$ **e)** $m^2 + 11m + 30$ **f)** $n^2 + 10n + 25$ **4. a)** $x^2 + 6x + 5$ **b)** $a^2 - a - 12$ **c)** $m^2 - 3m - 40$ **d)** $x^2 - 5xy + 6y^2$ **e)** $k^2 + 4k - 5$ **f)** $48 + 14x + x^2$ **5. a)** $a^2 - 9$ **b)** $x^2 - 25$ **c)** $4y^2 - 9$ **d)** $9m^2 - 36$ **e)** $36 - 4m^2$ **f)** $64 - 9x^2$ Products have two terms only, both of them perfect squares. **6. a)** $x^2 + 9x + 18$ **b)** $y^2 - 2y - 63$ **c)** $4t^2 - 12t + 9$ **d)** $k^2 - 36$ **e)** $y^4 - 36$ **f)** $30 + x - x^2$ **7. a)** $3x^2 + 7xy + 2y^2$ **b)** $6c^2 + 16cd - 6d^2$ **c)** $3a^2 + 7ab + 2b^2$ **d)** $6y^2 - 13xy + 6x^2$ **e)** $6y^2 - 5xy + x^2$ **f)** $18k^2 - 9ks - 2s^2$ **8. a)** $2x^2 - 5x - 3$ **b)** $3x^2 - 16x + 5$ **c)** $16x^2 - 8x + 1$ **9. a)** $(x - 3)(2x + 1)$ **b)** $2x^2 - 5x - 3$ **10. a)** $(2y - 3)(y + 3)$ **b)** $2y^2 + 3y - 9$ *Partner Project:* **a)** A: $x^2 + 2x + 1$, B: $x^3 + 3x^2 + 3x + 1$, C: $x^4 + 4x^3 + 6x^2 + 4x + 1$, D: $x^5 + 5x^4 + 10x^3 + 10x^2 + 5x + 1$ **b)** $x^6 + 6x^5 + 15x^4 + 20x^3 + 15x^2 + 6x + 1$

Section 11.3 1. a) A = 6x, B = x^2, C = 36; $x^2 + 12x + 36$ **b)** A = 16, B = 8y, C = $4y^2$; $4y^2 + 16y + 16$ **c)** A = 3x, B = 3x, C = 9; $x^2 + 6x + 9$ **2. a)** $x^2 + 2xy + y^2$ **b)** $m^2 - 6m + 9$ **c)** $4y^2 + 24y + 36$ **d)** $9 + 6m + m^2$ **e)** $9y^2 - 6y + 1$ **f)** $9x^2 - 6xy + y^2$ **g)** $9 + 12b + 4b^2$ **h)** $9x^2 + 12xy + 4y^2$ **3. a)** $x^2 + 10x + 25$ **b)** $y^2 - 12y + 36$ **c)** $9 - 6y + y^2$ **d)** $25 + 10b + b^2$ **e)** $m^2 - 6mn + 9n^2$ **f)** $4m^2 + 24mn + 36n^2$ **g)** $4m^2 - 12mn + 9n^2$ **h)** $25x^2$

$- 20xy + 4y^2$ **4. a)** $x^2 + 6x + 9$ **b)** $y^2 - 8y + 16$ **c)** $4y^2 + 4y + 1$ **d)** $36 + 36y + 9y^2$ **e)** $64 - 32x + 4x^2$ **5.** (a) $(a + 2)^2$, (b) $(y + 4)^2$, (d) $(2x + y)^2$

Section 11.4 3. a) A: $2x + 6$, B: $-3x - 9$ **b)** A: $2(x + 3)$, B: $3(-x - 3)$ or $-3(x + 3)$ **4. a)** $2(x + 3)$ **b)** $4(x + 2)$ **c)** $2(x - 5)$ **d)** $3(x - 5)$ **5. a)** $2(m + 6)$ **b)** $8(k - 2)$ **c)** $2(z + 8)$ **d)** $4(y + 5)$ **6. a)** A: $x^2 + 3x + 2$, B: $x^2 + 3x$ **b)** A: $(x + 1)$, $(x + 2)$, B: x, $(x + 3)$ **c)** A: $x^2 + 3x + 2$, B: $x^2 + 3x$ **8. a)** A: $x^2 + 2x + 1$, B: $x^2 + 5x + 4$ **b)** A: $(x + 1)(x + 1)$, B: $(x + 4)(x + 1)$ **9. a)** $(x + 2)^2$ **b)** $(x + 5)(x + 2)$ **c)** $(x + 5)(x + 1)$

Section 11.5 *Activities 1–2:* 2. a) $4(x + 2)$ **b)** $5(x - 2)$ **c)** $3(-x + 3)$ **d)** $2(-x - 4)$ or $-2(x + 4)$ *Exercise:* **1. a)** 3 **b)** 5 **c)** 7 **d)** 2 **e)** 5 **f)** –6 **g)** 3 **h)** 4 **2. a)** $3(x + 4)$ **b)** $5(x + 1)$ **c)** $7(x + 2)$ **d)** $2(x + 4)$ **e)** $5(x - 3)$ **f)** $-6(x + 3)$ **g)** $3(-x + 4)$ **h)** $4(x - 5)$ **3.** Find the greatest common factor. **a)** $4(m + p)$ **b)** $4(2r - k)$ **c)** $3(m + 4n)$ **d)** $4(q - 4p)$ **4. a)** $3(x - 2y)$ **b)** $4(x - 3y)$ **c)** $3(n - 6m)$ **d)** $2(2y - 5z)$ **e)** $2(3q - 2p)$ **f)** $2(-q + 4p)$ **g)** $3(a + b + c)$ **h)** $2(a - 2b - 3c)$ **i)** $2(x - 2y + 3z)$ **5. a)** 2 **b)** 2π **c)** $(1 - 2y)$ **d)** $(y - 2)$ **e)** $(3x - 2y + 5xy)$ **f)** $(3am - 2m - 6a)$ **6. a)** $6(1 - 2x)$ **b)** $x(5x - 3)$ **c)** $3(3y - 4x)$ **d)** $xy(5 - 3y)$ **e)** $2x(x - 3)$ **f)** $a(a - 2)$ **g)** $b(4a - b)$ **h)** $4(y^2 + 4)$ **i)** $14a(2a - b)$ **j)** $mn(36 - 25mn)$ **k)** $3(2x^2 - 4x + 5)$ **l)** $5(m^3 - 5m^2 + 3)$ **7. a)** $3a(7 - 4a)$ **b)** $a(3b^2 + 14)$ **c)** $k^2(2 - 3k + 8k^2)$ **d)** $xy(x^2 - 2xy - y^2)$ **e)** $5b(4 - 5b)$ **f)** $20ab(1 + ab)$ **8. a)** $2x + 3y$ **b)** $x - 6y$ **c)** $1 + 2y$ **d)** $x^3 - 7y^2$ **e)** $-2x - 3y$ **f)** $x^2 + 2x + 3$

Section 11.6 *Activity:* 2. a) $(x + 1)^2$ **b)** $(x + 3)(x + 2)$ **c)** $(x + 1)(x + 3)$ **d)** $(x + 4)(x + 2)$ *Exercise:* **1. a)** A: $x^2 + 2x + 1$, B: $x^2 - 2x + 1$ **b)** A: $(x + 1)(x + 1)$, B: $(x - 1)(x - 1)$ **2. c)** $(x + 5)(x + 1)$ **3. c)** $(x - 4)(x - 3)$ **4. c)** $(x + 3)(x - 5)$ **5. b)** $(a + 3)(a + 2)$, $(3 + a)(2 + a)$ **6. a)** $(x - 9)(x - 2)$ **b)** $(y + 4)(y + 2)$ **c)** $(m + 9)(m + 3)$ **d)** $(n - 6)(n - 5)$ **e)** $(5 - a)^2$ **f)** $(h + 6)(h + 2)$ **g)** $(t + 5)(t + 1)$ **h)** $(6 - m)(3 - m)$ **i)** $(m + 7)(m + 2)$ **j)** $(t - 8)(t - 12)$ **k)** $(y - 1)(y - 9)$ **l)** $(d + 4)(d + 9)$ **m)** $(x + 2)(x - 5)$ **n)** $(y + 3)(y - 2)$ **o)** $(m - 2)(m + 1)$ **7. a)** Find the common factor. **b)** 2 **c)** $2(x - 4)(x - 2)$ **8. a)** $2(x - 3)^2$ **b)** $y(y + 2)(y + 12)$ **c)** $2(x + 2)(x + 9)$ **d)** $4(m + 13)(m - 2)$ **e)** $x(x + 12)(x - 4)$ **f)** $a(a - 9)(a - 3)$ **g)** $3(y - 6)^2$ **h)** $2(x + 7)(x - 6)$ **i)** $b(b + 27)(b - 3)$ **j)** $3(m + 26)(m - 2)$ **k)** $2(x - 4)(x - 14)$ **l)** $x(x + 6)(x - 8)$ **9. a)** $(k + 5)(k - 1)$ **b)** $(x + 7)(x + 5)$ **c)** $(m + 11)(m - 1)$ **d)** $(x + 4)(x - 3)$ **e)** $(y + 9)(y + 1)$ **f)** $(t + 8)(t - 6)$ **g)** $(m - 7)(m + 6)$ **h)** $(s - 10)(s + 5)$ **i)** $(t - 4)(t - 5)$ **j)** $(8 - x)(7 - x)$ **k)** $(x - 17)(x + 5)$ **l)** $(y + 3)(y + 5)$ **10.** $(x - 2)$ **11.** $(x + 10)$ **12. a)** 26, –26 **b)** 2, –2, 5, –5, 10, –10, 23, –23 **c)** 1, –1, 8, –8, 19, –19 **13. b)** 100 cm²

Section 11.7 *Activities 1–2:* 1. b) $(x + y)^2$ **2. a)** $(x + 2)^2$ **c) i)** $(x + 3)^2$ **ii)** $(x + 1)^2$ *Exercise:*

1. a) $x^2 + 4x + 4$ **b)** $(x + 2)^2$ **2. c)** $(x + 4)(x - 4)$ **3. a)** 6
b) x **c)** 1 **d)** $3a$ **e)** $3a$ **f)** 5 **4. a)** 4 **b)** y^2 **c)** $4a$ **d)** 25 **e)** $9y^2$
f) $12ab$ **5.** (b), (c), (d), (g), (i), (l) **6. a)** $(y + 2)^2$ **b)** $(x - 3)^2$ **c)** $(a + 6)^2$ **d)** $(m + 5)^2$ **e)** $(2y + 2)^2$ **f)** $(1 + 2x)^2$
g) $(x - 3)^2$ **h)** $(2x - 1)^2$ **i)** $(3a - 2)^2$ **j)** $(3 - 4y)^2$
k) $(2a + 3)^2$ **l)** $(m - 5)^2$ **m)** $(x - 6)^2$ **n)** $(9 - 2y)^2$
o) $\left(a + \dfrac{1}{2}\right)^2$ **p)** $(a^2 - 1)^2$ **q)** $(1 - 2y^2)^2$ **r)** $\left(y - \dfrac{3}{2}\right)^2$

7. a) $(a + b)(a - b)$ **b)** $(y + x)(y - x)$ **c)** $(a + 2b)(a - 2b)$
d) $(x + 1)(x - 1)$ **e)** $(2m + 3n)(2m - 3n)$ **f)** $(3k + 4m)(3k - 4m)$ **g)** $(1 + 5y)(1 - 5y)$ **h)** $(4y + 5x)(4y - 5x)$
i) $2(m + 6)(m - 6)$ **j)** $(2t + 5s)(2t - 5s)$ **k)** $2(7 + 3m)(7 - 3m)$ **l)** $(6 + x)(6 - x)$ **8. a)** $3(m + 4)(m - 4)$
b) $2(x + 8)(x - 8)$ **c)** $2(7 + y)(7 - y)$ **d)** $3(5x + 1)(5x - 1)$
e) $-2(2 + 3m)(2 - 3m)$ **f)** $2(5 + 4m)(5 - 4m)$
g) $2(5y + 1)(5y - 1)$ **h)** $3(6 + m)(6 - m)$ **i)** $2(6 + 7y)(6 - 7y)$ **j)** $a(x + 10)(x - 10)$ **k)** $m(m + 6)(m - 6)$
l) $x(x + 4)(x - 4)$ **m)** $(x - 7)^2$ **n)** $(5 - 3n)^2$ **o)** $(y - \dfrac{1}{2})^2$
p) $(2m^2 - 1)^2$ **q)** $(2 - 3x)^2$ **r)** $(x - \dfrac{5}{2})^2$ **9. a)** $2(a + 3)^2$
b) $3(y - 3)^2$ **c)** $(3x + 2)^2$ **d)** $(y - 2)^2$ **e)** $x(2x + 1)^2$
f) $y(y - 3)^2$ **10. a)** $(mn + 5)(mn - 5)$ **b)** $(xy + 2)(xy - 2)$ **c)** $(10 + ab)(10 - ab)$ **d)** $(8 + mn)(8 - mn)$
e) $(xy + 3)(xy - 3)$ **f)** $(ab + k)(ab - k)$ **g)** cannot be factored **h)** $(1 + 5ab)(1 - 5ab)$ **i)** $(mn + 2m)(mn - 2m)$ **j)** $16p^2(q + 1)(q - 1)$ **k)** $(10m + 8n)(10m - 8n)$ **l)** $(5xy + 1)(5xy - 1)$ **m)** $\left(\dfrac{x}{3} + 5\right)\left(\dfrac{x}{3} - 5\right)$
n) $\left(x + \dfrac{1}{2}\right)\left(x - \dfrac{1}{2}\right)$ **o)** $x^2y^2(xy + 1)(xy - 1)$
p) $\left(\dfrac{2x}{5} + 8\right)\left(\dfrac{2x}{5} - 8\right)$ **11. a)** 49 **b)** 49; (b)

12. a) $(a^2 + 1)(a + 1)(a - 1)$ **b)** $(4m^2 + n^2)(2m + n)(2m - n)$ **c)** $4(2y^2 + 5x^2)(2y^2 - 5x^2)$ **d)** $(1 + 4b^2)(1 + 2b)(1 - 2b)$ **13. a)** $(x + 2)(x - 2)(x + 1)(x - 1)$
b) $(x^2 - 2)(x + 3)(x - 3)$ *Making Connections:*
2. a) $(20 + 2)(20 - 2)$, 396 **b)** $(30 + 4)(30 - 4)$, 884
c) $(30 + 2)(30 - 2)$, 896 **d)** $(50 - 2)(50 + 2)$, 2496
3. a) $(60 - 3)(60 + 3) = 3591$ **b)** $(30 - 3)(30 + 3) = 891$
c) $(20 + 4)(20 - 4) = 384$ **d)** $(70 - 2)(70 + 2) = 4896$

Section 11.8 1. a) $188.4\ m^2$ **b)** $577.8\ cm^2$
c) $59.1\ cm^2$ **2. a)** $369\ m^2$ **b)** $2080\ m^2$ **c)** $6400\ m^2$
3. $352\ m^2$ **4.** $78.5\ m^2$ **5. b)** A

Section 11.9 1. a) A: $2x - 4$, B: $3x - 3$, C: $2x + 8$
b) A: $2(x - 2)$, B: $3(x - 1)$, C: $2(x + 4)$ **c)** A: $\dfrac{2x - 4}{2}$,

B: $\dfrac{3x - 3}{3}$, C: $\dfrac{2x + 8}{2}$ **6. a)** A: $x^2 - 4x - 5$, B: $x^2 + 3x + 2$

b) A: $(x - 5)(x + 1)$, B: $(x + 1)(x + 2)$ **c)** A: $\dfrac{x^2 - 4x - 5}{x - 5}$ or

$\dfrac{x^2 - 4x - 5}{x + 1}$, B: $\dfrac{x^2 + 3x + 2}{x + 2}$ or $\dfrac{x^2 + 3x + 2}{x + 1}$ **10. a)** $x + 1$
b) $x + 1$ **c)** $x - 4$ **d)** $x + 3$ **e)** $x - 2$ **f)** $x + 2$

Section 11.10 *Activity:* **a)** No **b)** 0 **c)** 0 **d)** 0
Exercise: **1. a)** $d \neq 0$ **b)** $g \neq 0$ **c)** $u \neq 0$ **d)** $a \neq 0$
e) $a \neq 0$ **f)** $t \neq 0$ **2. a)** $y \neq 3$ **b)** $x \neq -3$ **c)** $y \neq 4$, $y \neq -8$
d) $y \neq 2$, $y \neq -2$ **3. a)** 13 **b)** 13 **c)** b) is a) simplified.
4. a) $4m$, $n \neq 0$ **b)** $-6p$, $q \neq 0$ **c)** $-6r$, $s \neq 0$ **d)** $5u$, $t \neq 0$
e) $-5p$, $q \neq 0$ **f)** $-4s$, $t \neq 0$ **g)** $2a$, $a \neq 0$ **h)** $-2a$, $a \neq 0$
i) $2m^2$, $m \neq 0$ **j)** $-2m^2$, $m \neq 0$ **k)** $-3p^3$, $p \neq 0$
l) $5m^4$, $m \neq 0$ **5. a)** -24 **b)** -60 **c)** -288 **d)** 15 **e)** 36
6. a) -3 **b)** 2 **c)** -5 **d)** 2 **e)** $-\dfrac{1}{4}$

Section 11.11 *Activity 2:* **a) i)** $\dfrac{3x}{4y}$ **ii)** 5
Exercise: **1. a)** $\dfrac{m(m + 5)}{m - 4} \times \dfrac{2(m - 4)}{m + 5}$ **b)** $2m$, $m \neq 4$,
$m \neq -5$ **2. a)** $\dfrac{(a - 5)(a - 2)}{2 - a} \times \dfrac{2 - a}{(a + 5)(a - 5)}$
b) $\dfrac{a - 2}{a + 5}$, $a \neq 2$, $a \neq 5$, $a \neq -5$ **3. a)** factor **b)** $\dfrac{x + 2}{3y}$,
$y \neq 0$, $x \neq 3$ **4. a)** factor **b)** $\dfrac{1}{x + 1}$, $x \neq 0$, $x \neq 1$, $x \neq -1$
5. a) $\dfrac{4}{y}$, $y \neq 0$, $y \neq -2$ **b)** $\dfrac{1}{x - 1}$, $x \neq 1$, $x \neq 0$ **c)** $\dfrac{1}{3}$,
$n \neq 0$, $n \neq 1$ **d)** $\dfrac{x - 1}{x + 1}$, $x \neq -1$, $x \neq 0$ **e)** $\dfrac{m(m - 3)}{2(m - 4)}$,
$m \neq 4$ **f)** $5(m - 1)$, $m \neq -1$ **6. a)** $\dfrac{3}{y}$, $y \neq 0$, $y \neq -3$
b) $\dfrac{1}{3(x + 1)}$, $x \neq 0$, $x \neq -1$, $x \neq 1$ **c)** $\dfrac{2}{y - 3}$, $y \neq 3$,
$y \neq -2$ **d)** $\dfrac{(m + 1)(m - 3)}{(m + 4)(m - 4)}$, $m \neq -2$, $m \neq 1$, $m \neq -4$,
$m \neq 4$ **e)** $\dfrac{5(k + 2)}{6(1 + 2k + 3k^2)}$, $k \neq -2$ **7. a)** $(20 + 2)^2$, 484
b) $(30 + 2)^2$, 1024 **c)** $(40 + 3)^2$, 1849 **d)** $(70 - 2)^2$, 4624
e) $(70 + 3)^2$, 5329 **f)** $(60 + 2)^2$, 3844 **8. a)** 391
b) 1584 **c)** 3575 **d)** 1596 **9. a)** 140 **b)** 279 **c)** 9200
d) 5000 **10. a)** 3969 **b)** 361 **c)** 841 **d)** 9409 **e)** 4624
f) 8281 **11. a)** 8096 **b)** 183 **c)** 2304 **d)** 9999 **e)** 4884
f) 1444 **g)** 6000 **h)** 2401 **12. a)** 225, 625, 1225

b) 2025, 3025 **13. a)** $\dfrac{a+b}{a+4}$, $a \neq -4$, $a \neq 4$, $a \neq b$ **b)** $\dfrac{1}{x}$, $x \neq -1$, $x \neq 1$, $x \neq 0$ **c)** $\dfrac{3}{4}$, $x \neq -5$, $x \neq 4$, $x \neq 0$

14. a) $-(x+3)$, $x \neq 3$ **b)** $-(x+3)$, $x \neq 3$ **15. a)** -1, $y \neq x$ **b)** 1, $x \neq y$ **c)** -1, $x \neq y$ **d)** 1, $x \neq y$ **e)** 1, $x \neq -y$ **f)** $-(m+n)$, $m \neq n$ **g)** $2a+b$, $a \neq \dfrac{b}{2}$ **h)** $-\dfrac{(x+2y)}{(y+x)}$, $x \neq y$, $x \neq -y$

Section 11.12 *Activity:* **2. a)** Write as a multiplication. **b)** 4 *Exercise:* **1.** Multiply by reciprocal. **a)** $\dfrac{9}{2}$, $x \neq -2$ **b)** 4, $x \neq -y$ **c)** $\dfrac{4}{5}$, $a \neq -3$

2. a) $\dfrac{xb}{ya}$, $a \neq 0$, $b \neq 0$, $y \neq 0$ **b)** $\dfrac{xb}{ya}$, $a \neq 0$, $b \neq 0$, $y \neq 0$ **c)** $-\dfrac{y}{b}$, $a \neq 0$, $b \neq 0$, $y \neq 0$ **d)** $\dfrac{2x}{21}$ $x \neq 0$ **e)** $-2y$, $y \neq 0$ **f)** $-\dfrac{6k}{5y}$, $y \neq 0$, $k \neq 0$ **g)** $\dfrac{5x}{6m}$, $m \neq 0$, $x \neq 0$ **h)** $-\dfrac{15n}{m}$, $m \neq 0$, $n \neq 0$ **i)** $\dfrac{1}{4}$, $k \neq 0$ **3. a)** $2(x+3)$, $x \neq 0$, $x \neq -3$ **b)** 2, $y \neq 4$ **c)** 3, $a \neq 7$, -7 **d)** 8, $x \neq -1$, $x \neq 2$ **e)** 8, $m \neq -4$ **f)** $\dfrac{1}{2}$, $x \neq 7$, -7 **4. a)** Multiply by reciprocal. **b)** $\dfrac{1}{3y}$, $y \neq 1$, -1, 0 **5. a)** $\dfrac{4}{y}$, $y \neq 0$, $y \neq -2$ **b)** $\dfrac{1}{3(x+1)}$, $x \neq 0$, 1, -1 **c)** $\dfrac{1}{a}$, $a \neq 0$, 1, -1, **d)** $\dfrac{2}{y-3}$, $y \neq 3$, $y \neq -2$ **6. a)** Multiply by reciprocal. **b)** 24, $k \neq 3$, -3, 6 **7. a)** $\dfrac{4}{x}$, $x \neq 0$ **b)** $\dfrac{1}{-5y}$, $x \neq 0$, $y \neq 0$ **c)** $-\dfrac{18x}{49}$, $x \neq 0$, $y \neq 0$, $k \neq 0$ **d)** $-\dfrac{8}{xy}$, $x \neq 0$, $y \neq 0$ **e)** $\dfrac{-3a}{2}$, $a \neq 0$, $b \neq 0$ **f)** $\dfrac{1}{-4ax}$, $a \neq 0$, $x \neq 0$ **8. b)** $\dfrac{-3n^2}{2}$, $m \neq 0$ **9. a)** $-b^2$, $a \neq 0$ **b)** $\dfrac{3b^2}{-a^2}$, $a \neq 0$, $b \neq 0$ **c)** $\dfrac{10}{3}$, $a \neq 0$, $b \neq 0$ **d)** $\dfrac{x^2}{y}$, $y \neq 0$ **10. a)** $\dfrac{x^2}{y^2}$, $x \neq 0$, $y \neq 0$ **b)** $4a^2$, $a \neq 0$, $b \neq 0$ **c)** $\dfrac{b}{2a}$, $a \neq 0$, $b \neq 0$ **d)** $\dfrac{5}{x}$, $x \neq 0$, $k \neq 0$ **e)** $\dfrac{x^2}{y}$, $y \neq 0$ **f)** $-\dfrac{16m^2}{n^3}$, $m \neq 0$, $n \neq 0$ **g)** $-\dfrac{3}{5y^2}$,

$x \neq 0$, $y \neq 0$ **h)** $\dfrac{260b}{3}$, $a \neq 0$, $b \neq 0$ **11. b)** 6

Chapter Review   1. a) $3(x-2)$ **b)** $4(x-3)$ **c)** $m(m+n)$ **d)** $m(m-4n)$ **e)** $2y(2-5y)$ **f)** $3k(k-3)$ **2. a)** $(x-4)(x-5)$ **b)** $(m-6)(m-7)$ **c)** $(5-x)(5-x)$ **d)** $(a-5b)(a+2b)$ **e)** $(x+7)(x-3)$ **f)** $(3x-2y)^2$ **g)** $(m+3n)(m+5n)$ **h)** $2(5a+b)^2$ **3. a)** $(x+2)(x-7)$ **b)** $(m+1)(m+4)$ **c)** $(y+10)(y-3)$ **d)** $(y+5)(y-3)$ **4. a)** $(x+2y)(x-2y)$ **b)** $(5k+p)(5k-p)$ **c)** $(10a+7b)(10a-7b)$ **d)** $(6y+5x)(6y-5x)$ **5. a)** $\dfrac{1}{y-12}$, $y \neq 0$, $y \neq 12$ **b)** $x+2$, $x \neq 0$ **c)** $y-4$ **d)** $\dfrac{2}{a-2}$, $a \neq 4$, $a \neq 2$ **6. a)** $\dfrac{8k}{25}$, $k \neq 0$ **b)** $\dfrac{5x}{12a}$, $a \neq 0$, $x \neq 0$, $y \neq 0$ **c)** $-x^2$, $y \neq 0$ **d)** $\dfrac{2}{a^2}$, $a \neq 0$ **7. a)** $3y(2x-1)$ **b)** 60

Self Evaluation   1. a) $x(3x^2-y)$ **b)** $p^2(4p+d)$ **c)** $a^2(ax-3y)$ **d)** $4z(5z-3)$ **e)** $8d^3(3d-1)$ **f)** $3x(2x-3)$ **2. a)** $(x+5)(x+3)$ **b)** $(y-6)(y+5)$ **c)** $3(a+2)(a+1)$ **d)** $(x+2y)(x+y)$ **e)** $2(a+2)^2$ **f)** $2(x+2)(x-1)$ **3. a)** $(y+1)(y+1)$ **b)** $(x+1)(x-2)$ **c)** $(y-3)(y+4)$ **d)** $(x+3)(x+2)$ **e)** $(x-1)(x-2)$ **f)** $(m-5)(m+2)$ **g)** $(y+1)(y+2)$ **h)** $(y-3)(y-2)$ **i)** $(m+3)(m-1)$ **j)** $(a-1)(a+5)$ **4. a)** $(3x+2)(3x-2)$ **b)** $(8y+1)(8y-1)$ **c)** $(2m+3)(2m-3)$ **d)** $(5s+6)(5s-6)$ **5. a)** $x \neq 0$, 4 **b)** $a \neq -1$, 0 **c)** $x \neq -1$, 2 **d)** $x \neq y$, $-y$ **6.** $9a$ units **7.** $6p$ units **8. a)** $\dfrac{1}{2x+3}$, $x \neq 0$, $\dfrac{-3}{2}$ **b)** $a-2$, $a \neq 0$ **c)** $\dfrac{2}{a+3}$, $a \neq 4$, -3 **d)** $2k+m$, $k \neq \dfrac{m}{2}$

CHAPTER 12

Section 12.2   1. a) i) $(1, 10)$, $(2, 20)$, $(3, 30)$, $(4, 40)$, $(5, 50)$, $(6, 60)$, $(7, 70)$ **ii)** $(1, 4)$, $(2, 3)$, $(3, 2)$, $(4, 1)$ **b) i)** $10x = y$ **ii)** $x = 5 - y$ **2. a)** 3, 4, 7 **b)** 5, 2, 0 **c)** 0, -2, 2 **3. a)** $(-2, -2)$, $(0, 0)$, $(2, 2)$ **b)** $(-2, -1)$, $(0, 0)$, $(6, 3)$ **c)** $(0, 4)$, $(2, 2)$, $(4, 0)$ **4. a)** $(0, 5)$, $(1, 7)$, $(2, 9)$, $(3, 11)$ **b)** $(-2, -5)$, $(-1, -4)$, $(0, -3)$, $(1, -2)$ **c)** $(-1, -6)$, $(1, -4)$, $(3, -2)$, $(5, 0)$

Section 12.3   1. a) 6, 4 **b)** 5, 5 **c)** 12, 5 **2. a)** 4, 8, 12 **b)** $(1, 4)$, $(2, 8)$, $(3, 12)$ **3. a)** 2 **b)** 3 **c)** 4 **d)** 6 **e)** 20 **4. b)** 0, 10 000 **7. a)** 1

Section 12.4 *Activity:* **1. a)** 2.5 h **b)** 1.75 L **2. a)** 16 h **b)** 7.5 L *Exercise:* **1. a)** 7 **b)** 8 **c)** 9 **2. a)** 3.6 **b)** 5.6 **c)** 4.4 **d)** 10 **e)** 15.4 **f)** 13 **3. a)** 6 **b)** 7 **c)** 8

4. a) 18 **b)** 5.7 **c)** 4.7 **d)** 16.7 **e)** 20.7 **f)** 18.3 **5.**
c) 12.5 km, 27.5 km, 33.75 km **d)** 2.4 h, 7.2 h,
8.9 h **6. a)** 2.4 cm, 8 cm, 9 cm **c)** 17.5 g, 27.5 g, 39 g
10. b) Graph (i) is a straight line; graph (ii) a curve.
They cross at (0, 0) and (2, 4). *Group Project:*
2. b) 4.9 **3. a)** 3.7 **b)** 5.7 **c)** 4.4 **d)** 5.3 **e)** 2.6

Section 12.6 *Activity:* **2. a)** (0, 0), (1, 2), (2, 4),
(3, 6), (4, 8) **b)** 0, 1, 2, 3, 4 **c)** 0, 2, 4, 6, 8 **d)** D: 0, 1,
2, 3, 4; R: 0, 2, 4, 6, 8 *Exercise:* **1. b)** 0, 1, 2, 3 **c)** 0,
4, 8, 12 **2. a)** A **i)** (1, 0), (2, 1), (3, 2), (4, 3), (5, 4)
ii) D: 1, 2, 3, 4, 5; R: 0, 1, 2, 3, 4 B **i)** (1, 3), (2, 2),
(2, 4), (3, 1), (3, 5), (4, 2), (4, 4) (5, 3) **ii)** D: 1, 2, 3, 4,
5; R: 1, 2, 3, 4, 5 **3. a)** D: 1, 2, 3, 4, 5, 6; R: 10, 20,
30, 40, 50, 60 **b)** D: positive reals; R: positive reals
c) Domain: *R*; Range: *R* **4. a)** Domain: *W*; Range:
even whole numbers **b)** Domain: *I*; Range: odd
integers **c)** Domain: *R*; Range: *R* **5. b)** Domain: *W*;
Range: positive multiples of 3

Section 12.7 **1. a) i)** 5, 5, 18 **ii)** –8, 13, –12
b) (13, 18) **2. a)** (–4, –2) **b)** (6, 5) **c)** (5, –4) **3. c)** (2, 3)
4. b) (–1, 3) **5. b)** (16, 13) **6. a)** (1, 1) **b)** (0, 2) **c)** (1, –1)
7. a) (–3, –5) **b)** collision **8. a)** (–2, –8) **b)** collision
9. a) (33, 39) **10. a)** (6, 3) **11. a)** Answers will vary.
They would meet at (–1, 2). **12.** No. They don't
meet. **13. a)** Yes. They will collide at (2, 6).
b) Helicopter; it can change altitude easily.
15. c) $y = x$, $y = -x$

Section 12.8 **1. a)** (50, 350) **2. a)** 60 **b)** $200.00
c) $200.00 **3. a)** 250 **b)** $800.00 **c)** $800.00

Section 12.9 **2. a)** 22.9 m **b)** 71.6 m **c)** 42.7 m
d) 51 m **3. a)** 25 km/h **b)** 53 km/h **c)** 84 km/h
d) 69 km/h **4. a)** 3.5 m **b)** 6.9 m **c)** 15 m **d)** 24.6 m

Section 12.10 **1. e)** $y = 3$; $x = 0$ **2. e)** $y = -4$;
$x = 0$ **3. b)** $x = 1$; $y = 0$ **4. e)** $x = -2$; $y = 0$ **5. c)** In
each case $y = 1$, $x = 0$ **6. b)** In each case $x = 4$, $y = 0$.

Section 12.11 **1. i)** $x = 4$, $y = 2$ **ii)** $x = -3$, $y = -6$
2. a) 2 **b)** –10 **3. a)** $x = -3$, $y = 3$ **b)** $x = 0$, $y = 0$
c) $x = \frac{3}{2}$, $y = -3$ **d)** $x = -\frac{2}{3}$, $y = 2$ **e)** $x = 1$, $y = -5$
f) $x = 3$, $y = -1$ **g)** $x = -8$, $y = -4$ **h)** $x = 9$, $y = 3$
4. 0.5 units **5.** 6 units **6. b)** parallel, different
intercepts **7. b)** parallel, different intercepts

Section 12.12 *Activity 3:* **a)** B, D, F are
functions since each *x*-coordinate has only one
y-coordinate. A, C, E are not functions since each
x-coordinate has more than one *y*-coordinate.
Exercise: **1.** B, D, E **2. b)** Yes. Each *x*-coordinate
has only one *y*-coordinate. **3. b)** No **4. a)** Yes
b) Yes **c)** No **d)** No **5. a)** A, B

Chapter Review **1. a)** Yes **b)** No **c)** Yes
2. a) Domain: *I*; Range; {...–4, –1, 2, 5, 8, ...}

b) Domain: *R*; Range: *R* **3. a)** 15 **b)** –10 **c)** 3 **4. a)** 4, 2
b) –1, 1 **5. a)** (2, 5) **b)** (2, 4) **6. b)** 1.9 s **c)** 63 m
7. a) i) 3 **ii)** 3 **iii)** 5 **iv)** 9 **b)** Plot it. **c)** Yes

Self Evaluation **1. a)** –1, 0, 16, 18 **b)** 3, 13, 8, 17
2. a) $x = -4$, $y = 3$ **b)** $x = 5$, $y = -3$ **4. c)** Domain: *W*;
Range: positive multiples of 4 **5. a)** (–3, –1.5),
(–1, –0.5), (1, 0.5) **b)** (6, 3), (20, 10), (–8, –4)
6. a) (2, 6) **b)** (–2, –4) **7.** A, B

Cumulative Review: Problem Solving
1. $923.08 **2. a)** 10 of spades, 9 of spades, 9 of hearts
4. 50 **5. a)** No. They would only do 216 km at
36 km/day.

CHAPTER 13

Section 13.1 **2.** Δ1: ∠A = 60°, ∠B = 60°,
∠C = 60°, Sum = 180°; Δ2: ∠A = 67°, ∠B = 68°,
∠C = 45°, Sum = 180°; Δ3: ∠A = 124°, ∠B = 27°,
∠C = 29°, Sum = 180°; Δ4: ∠A = 83°, ∠B = 40°, ∠C
= 57°, Sum = 180° **3. a)** Sum of the angles is 180°.
4. c) Sum of the angles is 360° **5. a)** Answers will
vary. **b)** 360° **d)** Sum of the angles is always 360°
6. Sum of the angles is 360°. **7. a)** ∠3, ∠5, ∠7
b) 130° **8. a)** ∠4, ∠6, ∠8 **b)** 50°

Section 13.2 **1. a)** A: Isosceles, B: Scalene,
C: Equilateral, D: Isosceles, E: Scalene, F: Scalene,
G: Equilateral **2. a)** A: Acute, B: Obtuse, C:
Equilateral, D: Right, E: Acute, F: Obtuse,
G: Equilateral **3. a)** A: Isosceles, Acute, B: Scalene,
Obtuse, E: Scalene, Acute, F: Scalene, Obtuse
5. a) Yes **b)** a rhombus, a rectangle, a parallelogram
7. c) Diagonals of a square are equal in length.
8. c) Conjecture not true for all rectangles, but true
for rhombus. **9. a)** True **b)** False **c)** False **d)** True

Section 13.3 **1. b)** 80° **2. a) i)** 70° **ii)** 70° **iii)** 30°
iv) 49° **b) i)** Scalene, Acute, **ii)** Scalene, Acute
iii) Isosceles, Obtuse **iv)** Scalene, Acute
3. a) ΔABC: Right, ΔDEF: Isosceles, ΔXYZ:
Equilateral **b)** ΔABC: $x° + 42° + 90° = 180°$, ΔDEF:
$x° + 70° + 40° = 180°$, ΔXYZ: $2x° + 60° = 180°$
c) ∠A = 48°, ∠F = 70°, ∠Y = 60°, ∠Z = 60°
4. $x = 42.4°$, $y = 35°$, $z = 7.7°$ **5. a)** A and C

Section 13.4 **1. b)** ∠A = ∠B = 72°, ∠C = 36°
2. a) 55° **b)** 60° **c)** 30°, 60° **3.** ∠D = ∠F = 50°,
∠E = 80° **4. a)** 78° **b)** acute **5.** ∠A = 22.5°,
∠B = 67.5°, ∠C = 90° **6.** ∠A = 65°, ∠B = 25°,
∠C = 90° **7. a)** 360° **b) i)** 127° **ii)** 102° **iii)** 60°, 120°
8. a) ∠ADB = 36°, ∠BDC = 18°, ∠C = 82°
b) ∠I = 60°, ∠JLI = 90°, ∠K = 90°, ∠KJL = ∠JLK
= 45° **c)** ∠TUS = 80°, ∠USV = 160°, ∠SVU = 10°

Section 13.5 **1. a)** corresponding **b)** alternate
c) interior **d)** corresponding **e)** corresponding
f) corresponding **g)** interior **h)** alternate
2. Sample answers given. Corresponding: ∠EOA,

∠ORC; ∠AOR, ∠CRF; ∠EOP, ∠ORQ; ∠POR, ∠QRF; ∠GPO, ∠PQR; ∠OPQ, ∠RQH; ∠GPB, ∠PQD; ∠BPQ, ∠DQH; ∠CRF, ∠RQH; ∠FRQ, ∠HQD; ∠CRO, ∠RQP; ∠ORQ, ∠PQD; ∠AOR, ∠OPQ; ∠ROP, ∠QPB; ∠AOE, ∠OPG; ∠EOP, ∠GPB **Alternate:** ∠POR, ∠CRO; ∠AOR, ∠QRO; ∠BPQ, ∠RQP; ∠OPQ, ∠DQP; ∠ERQ, ∠HQR; ∠FRQ, ∠PQR; ∠ROP, ∠OPG; ∠EOP, ∠OPQ **Interior:** ∠AOR, ∠CRO; ∠POR, ∠QRO; ∠OPQ, ∠RQP; ∠BPQ, ∠DQP; ∠FRQ, ∠HQR; ∠ORQ, ∠PQR; ∠ROP, ∠QPO; ∠EOP, ∠GPO **3. a)** equal **b)** equal **c)** Alternate angles are equal. **4. a)** equal **b)** Corresponding angles are equal. **5. a)** sum to 180° **b)** Sum of interior angles is 180°.

Section 13.6   1. a) 69°; alternate **b)** 123°; alternate **c)** 95°; interior **2. a)** ∠EHG = ∠CDB = ∠DHF = 45°, ∠EHD = ∠CDA = ∠BDH = ∠FHG = 135° **b)** ∠TUQ = ∠PUV = RVW = 60°, ∠QUV = ∠SVW = ∠RVU = ∠PUT = 120° **3. a)** x = y = k = 100° **b)** x = y = k = 60° **c)** x = 120°, y = 60° **4. a)** x = 150°, y = 70°, z = 30° **b)** x = 30° **c)** x = 150°, y = 75° **5. a)** BC ∥ DE **b)** ∠CBA = ∠EDA, ∠BCA = ∠DEA **c)** x = 65°, y = 75°, k = 40° **6. a)** x = 40°, y = 30°, k = 110° **b)** x = 100°

Section 13.7   2. c) New line parallel to third side. **d)** Line formed by connecting midpoints of two sides will always be parallel to third side. **3. a)** 7.3 cm **d)** Line segment equal to half distance of hypotenuse. **f)** All three vertices are equidistant from the midpoint of the hypotenuse. **4. b)** All three points on same circle. **c)** Midpoint of hypotenuse forms centre of circle that passes through the three points of triangle. **5. b)** Intersect at same point. **d)** Perpendicular bisectors always intersect at one point. **6. b)** Vertices of each triangle lie on the circumference of the circle. **c)** Point of intersection is equidistant from the three vertices of the triangle. **7. a) iii)** Intersect and coincide.

Section 13.9   1. AB = AC = 2.8 cm **2. b)** ∠S = 46°, ∠D = 30°, ∠F = 104°; Yes **c)** ΔQWG: ∠G = 48°, ∠W = 48°, ∠Q = 84°; ΔTYH: ∠H = 90°, ∠Y = 37°, ∠T = 53° **d)** True **3. b)** ∠B = 87°, ∠C = 48°, BC = 5.7 cm; Yes **c)** ΔABC: AC = 4.1 cm, ∠A = 87°, ∠C = 38°, Yes; ΔVWX: XV = 2.4 cm, ∠X = 72.5°, ∠V = 72.5°, Yes **d)** True **4. b)** ∠C = 105°, AC = 3.1 cm, BC = 4.4 cm; Yes **c)** ΔGLF: ∠F = 65°, FG = 3.6 cm, FL = 3.8 cm, Yes; ΔBDR: ∠R = 50°, BR = 4.5 cm, RD = 7.8 cm, Yes **d)** True

Section 13.10   1. a) DE = MN, EF = NP, DF = MP, ∠D = ∠M, ∠E = ∠N, ∠F = ∠P **b)** ST = UV, TP = VM, SP = UM, ∠S = ∠U, ∠T = ∠V, ∠P = ∠M **c)** AB = PQ, BC = QR, AC = PR, ∠A = ∠P, ∠B = ∠Q, ∠C = ∠R **2. a) i)** ΔABC ≅ ΔDEF, SSS **ii)** ΔPQR

≅ ΔSTU, SSS **b) i)** ∠A = ∠D, ∠B = ∠E, ∠C = ∠F **ii)** ∠P = ∠S, ∠Q = ∠T, ∠R = ∠U **3. a)** BC = 8 cm, DE = 6 cm **b)** WX = 4 cm, PR = 5 cm **4. a)** given, given, common side, SSS, congruency **b)** ∠DCA = ∠BAC, ∠DAC = ∠BCA **5. a)** given, given, common side, SSS, congruency **b)** ∠MNP = ∠QNP, ∠NPM = ∠NPQ **6. a)** ΔXYW ≅ ΔZYW, SSS **b)** XW = ZW, XY = ZY, YW = YW

Section 13.11   1. ∠P = ∠S, ∠Q = ∠T, ∠R = ∠V, PQ = ST, QR = TV, PR = SV **2. a) i)** ΔGHJ ≅ Δ MKL, SAS **ii)** Δ PQR ≅ ΔXYZ, SAS **b) i)** GH = MK, ∠G = ∠M, ∠H = ∠K **ii)** PR = XZ, ∠P = ∠X, ∠R = ∠Z **3. a)** ∠A = 114°, ∠D = 114°, ∠F = 27° **b)** ∠I = 73°, ∠J = 73°, ∠K = 63° **4.** ΔABC ≅ ΔFDE (SAS), ΔATU ≅ Δ DBF (SSS) **5.** given, given, given, SAS, congruency **6.** given, given, common side, SAS, congruency

Section 13.12   1. a) ∠B = ∠E or AC = DF **b)** ∠H = ∠K or GI = LJ **2. a)** AD = AD, ∠ADB = ∠ADC **b)** ΔABD ≅ ΔACD, SAS **3. a)** ΔDEF ≅ ΔTSR, ASA **b)** ∠F = ∠R, DF = TR, EF = SR **4. a)** ΔGHJ ≅ ΔMKL, ASA **b)** GH = MK, GJ = ML, ∠G = ∠M **5.** ΔABC and ΔFDE, AB = FD or ∠C = ∠E **6.** given, common side, given, ASA, congruency **7. a)** EF = 3.6 cm **b)** LM = 8.7 cm, MP = 5.6 cm, x = 50°, y = 40° **8. a)** ∠G = ∠E, ∠GDF = ∠EDF, DF = DF **b)** angle sum of a triangle **c)** ASA **9. a)** ∠A = ∠D, AE = DE, ∠AEB = ∠DEC **b)** ASA **c)** congruency **d)** ∠A = ∠D, Alternate angles of transversal AD **10. a)** 35 **b)** 290

Section 13.13   Activity 1: a) Vancouver, Calgary, Juneau **b)** Toronto, Halifax, Regina **c)** Whitehorse, Calgary, Winnipeg **d)** Winnipeg, Toronto, Halifax **e)** Whitehorse, Juneau, Edmonton **f)** Quebec, Halifax, Montreal

Section 13.15   1. a) same features; different measurements **3. a)** ∠A = ∠P, ∠B = ∠Q, ∠C = ∠R; corresponding angles are equal. **b)** $\frac{PQ}{AB} = \frac{PR}{AC} = \frac{QR}{BC}$ **c)** The ratios of the measures of corresponding sides are equal.

Section 13.16   1. a) 10 **b)** 7 **c)** 6 **d)** 10 **e)** 7 **2. a)** AB = 2, BC = 4, DE = 4, DF = 6 **b)** $\frac{AB}{DE} = \frac{BC}{EF}$, $\frac{AB}{DE} = \frac{AC}{DF}$ **c)** EF = 8, AC = 3 **3. a)** y = 24 **b)** x = 15 **4. a)** x = 14, y = 10 **b)** x = 40°, y = 65°, m = 65°, p = 75° **c)** x = 4, a = 44°, b = c = k = m = 68° **5. a)** ∠RVU = ∠SVT, ∠RUV = ∠STV, ∠VRU = ∠VST **b)** ST = 8 m **c)** x = 8 **d)** 8 m **6. b)** AD = 36 **c)** $\frac{AC}{45} = \frac{48}{36}$ **d)** AC = 60 **7. a)** common angle

b) 9.9 m **8.** 13.8 m **9. a)** 167 m **b)** The jet climbs steadily in a straight line. **10. a)** 30.6 m **b)** 11.9 m **11.** 1.1 m

Section 13.17 *Activity:* **a)** 520 m *Exercise:*
1. a) ΔBCD ~ ΔACE **b)** AE, BD **c)** 31.9 **d)** 31.9 m
2. 12.0 m **3.** 21.7 m **4.** 7.8 m **5.** 6.3 m **6.** 7.3 m
7. 34.9 m **8.** 25 m **10. a)** 90 **c)** Triangles with the same area have equal base lengths and heights.

Section 13.19 **1.** A: 6 sq. units, B: 5 sq. units, C: 11 sq. units, D: 8 sq. units, E: 8.5 sq. units, F: 5 sq. units, G: 16.5 sq. units, H: 21 sq. units, I: 20 sq. units, J: 24 sq. units

Chapter Review **1. a)** ΔWXY $\cong$ ΔPQR, SAS
b) $\angle$Y = $\angle$R, $\angle$W = $\angle$P, WY = PR **2. a)** Alternate: $\angle$AFG, $\angle$FGD; $\angle$BFG, $\angle$FGC, Corresponding: $\angle$EFA, $\angle$FGC; $\angle$AFG, $\angle$CGH; $\angle$EFB, $\angle$FGD; $\angle$BFG, $\angle$DGH **b)** $\angle$EFA = $\angle$BFG = $\angle$FGC = $\angle$DGH, $\angle$EFB = $\angle$AFG = $\angle$FGD = $\angle$CGH **c)** $\angle$AFG, $\angle$FGC; $\angle$BFG, $\angle$FGD **d)** $\angle$EFA, $\angle$EFB; $\angle$AFG, $\angle$BFG, $\angle$FGC, $\angle$FGD; $\angle$CGH, $\angle$DGH; $\angle$AFG, $\angle$FGC; $\angle$BFG, $\angle$FGD; $\angle$AFE, $\angle$AFG; $\angle$EFB, $\angle$BFG; $\angle$FGC, $\angle$HGC; $\angle$FGD, $\angle$HGD
3. a) x = 152°, y = 85° **b)** a = 106°, b = 106°, x = 106°, y = 74° **4.** Angle 1 = 85°, Angle 2 = 30°, Angle 3 = 65° **5. a)** x = 12 **b)** x = 6.1, y = 2.0

Self Evaluation **1. a)** a = 42°, b = 65° **b)** $\angle$P = 31°, $\angle$Q = 93°, $\angle$R = 56° **c)** a = 18°, b = 135°, c = 45°, d = 45° **3. a)** a = 59°, b = 121° **b)** m = 40°, n = 70°, p = 70° **c)** a = 80°, b = 60°, c = 120° **4. a)** Ratios of corresponding sides are equal. **b)** AB:DE = BC:EF = AC:DF = 2:1 **5.** 4.2 m **6.** 8.8 m

Cumulative Review **1. a)** 32 **b)** 17 **c)** 18 **d)** 72 **e)** 2 **f)** 20 **g)** 27 **h)** 133 **i)** 2 **2.** $\frac{1}{2}$ **3. a)** $12x^4y$ **b)** $-6x^2y^2$
c) $3xy + 3xy^2 - 3y^2$ **d)** $-4x^3 + 28x$ **e)** $\frac{8x^2}{y}$ **f)** $\frac{9}{x}$
g) $-x + 2$ **h)** $-y + 3$ **4. a)** -6 **b)** $-\frac{3}{2}$ **c)** 3 **d)** 12 **5.** 1
6. a) m = 2 **b)** k = -2.5 **c)** k = 20 **d)** x = 18.3 **e)** p = 21 **f)** x = 28 **7. a)** y = 16 **b)** k = 4 **c)** p = 12 **d)** b = 3.1 **e)** x = 12 **f)** m = 20 **8.** No **9.** 15 kg **10. a)** 1.74 years **b)** 1.68 years

CHAPTER 14
Section 14.2 **3. a)** Ask each student. **b)** Play some of the tapes. **5. a)** bus, car, bike, walk, subway **8. a)** telephone, in person, questionnaire, measurement, experiment

Section 14.3 *Activity:* **a)** clustered **b)** stratified **c)** clustered **d)** destructive **e)** stratified **f)** destructive **g)** stratified *Exercise:* **1.** clustered

2. random, destructive **3.** clustered **4. a)** clustered **b)** stratified **c)** destructive **d)** random **5. a)** B.C. 1020, Alta. 860, Sask. 410, Man. 430, Ont. 3600, Que. 2650, N.B. 300, N.S. 360, P.E.I. 50, Nfld. 240 **6.** 16 children, 11 teens, 8 adults

Section 14.4 **1. a)** Turnbull 66, Lofthouse 36, Rausse 18, Jarvis 48, Lane 60 **b)** Turnbull 28.95%, Lofthouse 15.79%, Rausse 7.89% Jarvis 21.05%, Lane 26.32% **3. a)** Male 16–20 **b)** Male13–15 **4. a)** 3500 kJ **b)** 65% **5. a)** 5000 kJ **b)** 37.5%

Section 14.5 **1. a)** Nile **b)** St. Lawrence **c)** Amazon **d)** Mississippi **2.** Rio Grande: 387.5 h, St. Lawrence: 462.5 h, Nile: about 825 h, Zambezi: 325 h, Saskatchewan: about 250 h, Niger: 512.5 h, MacKenzie: about 525 h, Congo: about 575 h, Mississippi: 750 h, Yangtze: 675 h, Ob: 662.5 h, Amazon: about 800 h, Yellow: 575 h, Lena: 525 h **3. a)** about 18 840 km **b)** about 3140 years **4. b)** 67% **c)** 83%

Section 14.6 **1. b)** 98 million, 194 million, 374 million **2. a)** about 9 L **b)** about 14 L **c)** 19 L **3. a)** 30 km **b)** 35 km **c)** 85 km **d)** 110 km **5. a) i)** 20 000 **ii)** 45 000 **iii)** 30 000 **iv)** 45 000 **b)** 13:00, 17:00, 22:00 **c)** 22:00 **d) i)** 10:00, 01:00 **ii)** 11:30, 14:30, 16:00, 22:30 **6. a)** 4%: 18 years, 3%: 25 years, 2%: 33 years, 1%: 65 years **8. b)** 49.5 L **c)** 56.5 L **9. b) i)** 26.3% **ii)** 41.7% **c) i)** 1.5 billion **ii)** 2.1 billion **d)** suggested answer, 4 billion

Section 14.7 *Activity:* **a)** Most and least frequent scores. *Exercise:* **1. a) i)** 2 **ii)** 5 **b)** 10 **c)** 7 **d)** 17 **2. a)** Titles **4. b)** 155–160: 5, 161–165: 5, 166–170: 7, 171–175: 6, 176–180: 6, 181–185: 3 **5.** 2 or 3 **6.** 0.05

Section 14.8 **1. a)** 90° (25%) **b)** 90° (25%) **2.** 72° = 20% of 360° **3. a)** 102° **b)** 28% **c)** $35 016.80 **4. a)** Skiing: 0.25 × 360°; 90°; Hockey: 40%; 144°; Snowshoeing: 15%; 0.15 × 360°; Curling: 0.2 × 360°; 72°; Total 100%, 1 × 360°; 360° **5. a) i)** 68.4°, 241.2°, 50.4° **ii)** 54°, 158.4°, 32.4°, 72° 43.2° **6. a)** 7.2°, 50.4°, 72°, 230.4° **7. a)** 75.6°, 162°, 122.4° **8. a)** O: 164°, A: 152.8°, AB: 13.2°, B: 30° **b)** 511

Section 14.9 **1. a)** about 8% **b)** about 52% **c)** about 2% **2. a)** $4.69 **3. a)** 46.8°: protein, 158.4° carbohydrates, 154.8°: fat **4. a)** 73.4°; 73.4°; 213.2° **b)** 80.6°; 193.4°; 86°

Section 14.10 **1. a)** bar graph **2. a)** circle graph **3.** pictograph **4.** bar **5.** bar **6.** bar **7.** circle **8.** bar or pictograph

Section 14.12 *Activity:* **a)** mean: 19.4, median: 17, mode: 15 **b)** No; average is over 19. *Exercise:* **1. a)** 8, 9, 9 **b)** 23, 17, 17 **c)** 16.3, 19, 19 **d)** 120.4,

132, 150 **e)** 3.8, 3.95, 5.6 **f)** 20.63, 19.86, 19.86
2. a) mean: none, median: a, b, c, d, f, mode: all
b) Mode **3. a)** no effect **b)** increase **c)** decrease
5. a) 169.1, 169, 160 **b)** mean **6.** mean **7. a)** 157.9,
177.5, 73 **b)** mean **c)** about 1425 **d)** about 5700 **e)**
(d)
8. a) 40–50 **b)** 90–100 **c)** 40–50 **d)** 30–40, 40–50
e) (d) **9. a)** Find the class interval with about half
the data on each side. **b)** No. **11.** 23 **12.** 101 kg

Section 14.13 **1.** 40% **2.** 40% **3.** 500 **4.** Possibly
the cafeteria. **5. a)** Saturday **b)** Thursday **6. a)** 25
b) 24 **c)** 16 **7. a)** most: Saturday, least: Thursday
a) 22 **b)** 23 **c)** 16

Section 14.14 **3. a)** about 250 **b)** about 250
c) about 500 **d)** About the same.

Section 14.15 **1. a)** 0 **b)** 0 **2. a)** $\frac{1}{6}$ **b)** $\frac{1}{6}$ **c)** $\frac{1}{2}$ **d)** 0

3. a) $\frac{1}{3}$ **b)** $\frac{4}{9}$ **c)** $\frac{2}{9}$ **4. a)** $\frac{1}{5}$ **b)** $\frac{3}{10}$ **5.** $\frac{17}{25}$ **6. a)** $\frac{1}{6}$

7. a) $\frac{1}{12}$ **b)** $\frac{1}{12}$ **c)** $\frac{1}{2}$ **d)** $\frac{1}{2}$ **8. a)** $\frac{1}{10}$ **b)** $\frac{1}{10}$ **c)** $\frac{2}{5}$ **d)** 1

e) $\frac{4}{5}$ **9. a)** $\frac{1}{13}$ **b)** $\frac{1}{13}$ **c)** $\frac{1}{52}$ **d)** $\frac{1}{26}$ **e)** $\frac{12}{13}$ **f)** $\frac{1}{2}$ **10. a)** $\frac{1}{2}$

b) $\frac{3}{10}$ **c)** $\frac{1}{5}$ **11. a)** 10 **b)** 100 **c)** 40 **d)** 30

Section 14.16 *Activity:* **a)** $\frac{1}{2}, \frac{1}{2}$ **b)** $\frac{1}{4}, \frac{1}{4}, \frac{1}{4}, \frac{1}{4}$
c) They both sum to 1; their products are
different. *Exercise:* **1. a)** $\frac{2}{5}, \frac{3}{5}$ **b)** $\frac{4}{25}$ **2. a)** $\frac{1}{2}$ **b)** $\frac{1}{4}$

c) $\frac{1}{8}$ **d)** $\frac{1}{1024}$ **3.** $\frac{1}{2^n}$, n = number of tosses **4. a)** $\frac{16}{121}$

b) $\frac{49}{121}$ **5. a)** $\frac{1}{169}$ **b)** $\frac{1}{169}$ **c)** $\frac{12}{169}$ **d)** $\frac{1}{4}$ **6. b)** $\frac{1}{10}$ **c)** $\frac{1}{90}$

7. a) $\frac{1}{100\,000\,000}$ *Making Connections:* **a)** $\frac{7}{10}, \frac{4}{5}$

b) $\frac{56}{100}$ **c)** Yes

Section 14.17 *Activity 1:* **d)** $\frac{1}{6}$ *Exercise:*

1. a) $\frac{5}{12} \times \frac{7}{11} = \frac{35}{132}$ **b)** $\frac{7}{22}$ **2. a)** $\frac{4}{11}$ **b)** $\frac{7}{11}$ **c)** $\frac{6}{55}$

d) $\frac{14}{55}$ **3. a)** $\frac{7}{11}, \frac{4}{11}$ **b)** $\frac{14}{55}$ **c)** $\frac{6}{55}$ **d)** $\frac{21}{55}$ **4. a)** $\frac{1}{169}$

b) $\frac{1}{325}$ **5. a)** $\frac{1}{13}$ **b)** $\frac{4}{51}$ **c)** $\frac{48}{51}; \frac{36}{51}$ **6. a)** $\frac{1}{6}$

b) Independent. The probability of getting a "2" in
the second roll does not depend on the first roll of
the other die.

Section 14.18 *Activity:* **d)** $\frac{1}{15}$ *Exercise:*

1. a) $\frac{6}{15} \times \frac{5}{14} \times \frac{4}{13} = \frac{4}{91}$ **b)** $\frac{6}{15} \times \frac{5}{14} \times \frac{4}{13} = \frac{4}{91}$

2. a) $\frac{1}{100}$ **b)** $\frac{99}{100}$ **c)** 999 plugs remain and 9 of them
are defective. **d)** After one defective plug is
removed the number of plugs remaining changes.

e) $\frac{10}{1000} \times \frac{9}{999} \times \frac{8}{998} = \frac{1}{1\,384\,725}$ **3. a)** $\frac{1}{156}$ **b)** $\frac{1}{286}$

4. a) $\frac{1}{4}$ **b)** $\frac{1}{24}$ **c)** $\frac{1}{24}$ **d)** same **5. a)** $\frac{1}{2652}$ **b)** $\frac{1}{270\,725}$

Section 14.19 **1. a)** 4 **d)** Roll more often.
2. a) 166 **b)** 156 **c)** 192 **3. a)** 24 **b)** 66 **4. a)** Total
2: 251, 3: 248, 4: 246, 5: 257, 6: 230; Average per
trial 1: 89, 2: 84, 3: 83, 4: 82, 5: 86, 6: 77 **b)** 83

5. a) $\frac{64}{76}$ **b)** $\frac{11}{76}$ **c)** $\frac{56}{76}$ **6. a)** $\frac{1}{6}$ **b)** $\frac{5}{18}$ **c)** $\frac{5}{9}$

Chapter Review **2. a)** circle **b)** 86°, 108°, 130°, 36°
3. a) 40.0–44.9, 1; 45.0–49.9, 5; 50.0–54.9, 8;
55.0–59.9, 8; 60.0–64.9, 6; 65.0–69.9, 2;

4. b) 1153.3, 823, no mode **5. a)** $\frac{1}{2}$ **b)** $\frac{15}{36}$ **6.** $\frac{1}{3}$

Self Evaluation **1. a)** legend showing that 1 ball
represents 2 strikeouts **b)** 12; 16; 6; 10 **2. a)** 76°,
162°, 122° **3. a)** A: 15, B: 39, C: 23, D: 7.7 **b)** A: 15,
B: 40, C: 21.5, D: 8.2 **c)** B: 35 **4. a)** $\frac{1}{100}$

4. b) $\frac{1}{1\,384\,725}$ **5. a) i)** about 18 m **ii)** about 21 m
b) i) about 38 km/h **ii)** about 62 km/h

CHAPTER 15
Section 15.1 **1. a)** Same size and shape; different
position. **2. a)** ∠A and ∠A', ∠B and ∠B', ∠C and
∠C'; Measures are equal. **b)** AB and A'B', BC and
B'C', AC and A'C'; Measures are equal.

c) Segments are equal. **d)** $-\frac{4}{5}, -\frac{4}{5}, -\frac{4}{5}$; same

4. a) same size and shape; different orientation
5. a) ∠A and ∠A', ∠B and ∠B', ∠C and ∠C';
Measures are equal. **b)** AB and A'B', BC and B'C',
AC and A'C'; Measures are equal. **c)** For
corresponding vertices, the measures are equal.
d) Perpendicular bisectors coincide with y-axis.
7. a) same size and shape; different position
8. a) ∠P and ∠P', ∠Q and ∠Q', ∠R and ∠R';
Measures are equal. **b)** PQ and P'Q', QR and Q'R',
PR and P'R'; Measures are equal. **c)** For
corresponding vertices, the measures are equal.

Section 15.2   1. a) right 3 **b)** down 2 **c)** right 3
4. a) [+4, –3] **b)** [+1, +3] **c)** [–5, +2]

Section 15.3   1. a) A(2, 3), A'(2, –1); B(3,3),
B'(3, –1); C(3, 1), C'(3, –3); D(1, 1), D'(1, –3);
E(1, 2), E'(1, –2) **b)** $x \to x$ **c)** $y \to y - 4$ **d)** $(x, y) \to$
$(x, y - 4)$ **2 . a)** P(–5, –2), P'(4, 3); Q(–4, –2), Q'(5, 3);
R(–4, –4), R'(5, 1); S(–6, –4), S'(3, 1); T(–6, –3),
T'(3, 2) **b)** $x \to x + 9$ **c)** $y \to y + 5$ **d)** $(x, y) \to$
$(x + 9, y + 5)$ **3. a)** P'(–5, 2), Q'(–7, –3), R'(–4, –2)
b) S'(1, 5), T'(–2, 2), U'(1, –1), V'(4, 2) **4. a)** H'(3, 1),
J'(6, 1), K'(6, –1), L'(4, –1), M'(4, –4), N'(3, –4)
b) V'(–4, –7), W'(–4, –1), X'(–1, 1), Y'(2, –1),
Z'(2, –7) **5. a)** 0, 2 **b)** –1, 3 **c)** 3, 9 **d)** –6, 3
6. b) A'(–6, 5), B'(–1, 0), C'(–9, –1) **c)** clockwise
e) In a translation, the sense of the vertices in a
figure and its image are the same.

Section 15.4   1. a) A'(–2, 4), B'(–6, 2), C'(–1, –1)
b) –2, –2, –2; all are equal **2. a)** P'(–4, 8), Q'(–1, –1),
R'(1, 7) **b)** $-\frac{3}{2}, -\frac{3}{2}, -\frac{3}{2}$; all are equal **3.** The slopes
of line segments connecting corresponding
vertices are the same. **4. a)** all $\sqrt{5}$ units **b)** all $\sqrt{13}$
units **c)** The line segments connecting
corresponding vertices are the same **5. a)** –5, –5;
$\frac{1}{2}, \frac{1}{2}; -\frac{3}{5}, -\frac{3}{5}$ **b)** –3, –3; $-\frac{1}{5}, -\frac{1}{5}$; 4, 4 **c)** The slopes
of corresponding sides of a figure and its
translation image are equal. **6. a)** both $\sqrt{26}$ units;
both $\sqrt{20}$ units; both $\sqrt{34}$ **b)** both $\sqrt{90}$ units; both
$\sqrt{26}$ units; both $\sqrt{68}$ units **c)** The length of
corresponding sides of a figure and its translation
image are equal. **7. a)** ∠BAC = ∠B'A'C'; ∠ABC =
∠A'B'C'; ∠BCA = ∠B'C'A' **b)** ∠PQR = ∠P'Q'R';
∠PRQ = ∠P'R'Q', ∠RPQ = ∠R'P'Q' **c)** The
corresponding angles of a figure and its image are
equal. **8. a), b)** any translation

Section 15.5   2. a) (3, 8) **b)** (0, 0) **3. a)** (1, –8)

Section 15.6   Activity 1: b) The distances are the
same. **c)** 90° Exercise: **1.** H, I, M, O, T, U, V, W, X,
Y **2. a)** I, O, X **3. a)** Do you know any good books?
b) Don't you look silly holding a mirror to read
your book?

Section 15.7   Activity 2: a) P(–6, 4), Q(–5, –2),
R(–2, –4); P'(6, 4), Q'(5, –2), R'(2, –4)
b) y-coordinates are the same, x-coordinates are
opposite **c)** $(x, y) \to (-x, y)$ Activity 3: **c)** $(x, y) \to$
$(x, -y)$ Exercise: **1. a)** (4, –1) **b)** (–2, –5) **c)** (–7, –2)
d) (–10, 5) **e)** (–8, 7) **f)** (–5, 0) **3. a)** (0, 7), (–4, 7),
(–4, –3), (4, –3), (4, 2), (0, 2) **b)** (5, 3), (5, –3), (2, –3),
(2, 0), (–2, 0), (–2, –3), (–5, –3), (–5, 3) **c)** P'(5, –4),
Q'(–2, –1), R'(–5, –9) **4. a)** A'(–1, 6), B'(–1, 1),

C'(–5, 1), D'(–5, 4) **b)** A'(–2, 6), B'(–8, 3), C'(–4, 2)
5. c) a hexagon **d)** reflection

Section 15.8   1. a) LA' = LA, SB' = SB, YC' = YC
b) ∠A'LS = ∠ALS = ∠B'SY = ∠BSY = ∠C'YL =
∠CYL = 90° **2. b)** The line of reflection is the
perpendicular bisector of the line segment
joining a point and its image. **3. b)** –6, 6; $-\frac{3}{7}, \frac{3}{7}$;
$\frac{1}{2}, -\frac{1}{2}$; Slopes are opposite. **c)** AB = A'B', BC =
B'C', CA = C'A'; Corresponding sides are equal.
d) ∠A = ∠A', ∠B = ∠B', ∠C = ∠C'; Corresponding
angles are equal. **4. a)** Slopes are opposites.
b) Corresponding sides are equal. **c)** Corresponding
angles are equal. **5. b)** Sense of the vertices is
reversed. **c)** y-coordinates; x-coordinates
6. a) AB ∥ DC, AD ∥ BC **c)** The slopes of the
opposite sides of the image parallelogram are
equal. **7. a)** Slope and sense change, measures of
angles and sides do not. **b)** Same properties except
slope of corresponding sides and sense.

Section 15.10   1. a) $\frac{1}{4}$ turn (90°) cw **b)** $\frac{1}{2}$ turn
(180°) cw or ccw **2. a)** Hi There

Section 15.11   Activity 1: 1. a) A(4, 7), B(7, 2),
C(4, 2): A'(–7, 4), B'(–2, 7), C'(–2, 4) Activity 2:
2. c) Perpendicular bisectors intersect at the origin.
3. b) All perpendicular bisectors of segments
joining points to reflection images intersect at the
origin. Exercise: **1.** $\frac{1}{4}$ turn ccw, + 90°, $\frac{1}{2}$ turn cw,
–180°; $\frac{1}{2}$ turn ccw, +180° **2. a)** P(–5, 3), Q(–9, 0),
R(–2, 0); P'(5, –3), Q'(9, 0), R'(2, 0) **b)** S(1, 4), T(6, 4),
U(6, 1), V(1, 1); S'(–1, –4), T'(–6, –4), U'(–6, –1),
V'(–1, –1) **c)** P(–6, 4), Q(–2, 4), R(–2, 0), S(–6, 0);
P'(–4, –6), Q'(–4, –2), R'(0, –2), S'(0, –6) **3. a)** X(–3, 4),
Y(–7, 0), Z(–1, 0); X'(–4, –3), Y'(0, –7), Z'(0, –1)
b) G(3, 3), H(8, 0), K(3, –3), L(1, 0); G'(–3, –3),
H'(–8, 0), K'(–3, 3), L'(–1, 0) **c)** P(5, 3), Q(8, 3),
R(6, 0), O(0, 0); P'(3, –5), Q'(3, –8), R'(0, –6), O'(0, 0)
4. $(x, y) \to (-x, -y)$, $(x, y) \to (-x, -y)$, $(x, y) \to (-y, x)$,
$(x, y) \to (-y, x)$, $(x, y) \to (-x, -y)$, $(x, y) \to (y, -x)$
5. a) $(x, y) \to (y, -x)$ **b)** $(x, y) \to (-y, x)$ **c)** $(x, y) \to$
$(-x, -y)$ **d)** $(x, y) \to (-x, -y)$

Section 15.12   1. a) ∠AOA' = ∠BOB' = ∠COC'
= 90° **c)** OA = OA', OB = OB', OC = OC' **2. a)** equal
b) equal **3. a)** Slopes of corresponding sides
change; measures of corresponding sides do not.
4. a) A'(–2, –3), B'(–3, –7), C'(–6, –4) **b)** A'(2, 3),
B'(3, 7), C'(6, 4) **c)** A'(–3, 2), B'(–7, 3), C'(–4, 6)
d) A'(–3, 2), B'(–7, 3), C'(–4, 6) **e)** same

5. a) A'(3, –3), B'(–3, –3), C'(–3, 3), D'(3, 3); same position **b) i)** A'(–3, –3), B'(–3, 3), C'(3, 3), D'(3, –3) **ii)** A'(–3, 3), B'(3, 3), C'(3, –3), D'(–3, –3) **iii)** A'(3, 3), B'(3, –3), C'(–3, –3), D'(–3, 3) **6. a)** –90°: P'(6, –4), Q'(–6, –4), R'(–6, 4), S'(6, 4); –180°: P'(–4, –6), Q'(–4, 6), R'(4, 6), S'(4, –6); –270°: P'(–6, 4), Q'(6, 4), R'(6, –4), S'(–6, –4); –360°: P'(4, 6), Q'(4, –6), R'(–4, –6), S'(–4, 6) **7. a)** A'(4, –1), B'(9, –2), C'(5, –6) **b)** Corresponding slopes are the same.

Section 15.13   2. a) 5

Section 15.14   *Activity:* **a)** A(2, 2), B(5, 1), C(4, 3); A'(4, 4), B'(10, 2), C'(8, 6); The coordinates of the image are two times greater than the coordinates of the object. **c)** Size has changed. **d)** $(x, y) \rightarrow (2x, 2y)$ *Exercise:* **1. a)** –4; $(2x, 2y)$ **b)** 1; –2, 2; $(-\frac{1}{2}x, -\frac{1}{2}y)$ **c)** 1; $(2\frac{1}{2}, 1)$; $(\frac{1}{2}x, \frac{1}{2}y)$ **2. a)** 2 **b)** $-\frac{1}{2}$

c) $\frac{1}{2}$ **3. a)** D'(–2, 1), E'(1, 2), F'(0, 1) **b)** K'(18, 12), L'(21, –6), M'(6, 0) **5. a)** A'C' = 2AC, B'C' = 2BC, A'B' = 2AB; The sides of the image are twice as long. **b)** 2, 2, 2; Ratios are equal. **6. a)** Angles are equal. **b)** Area of image triangle is 4 times as large. **7. a)** Corresponding angles are equal and ratio of corresponding sides are equal. **8. a)** OA' = 2OA, OB' = 2OB, OC' = 2OC **b)** Same factor. **9. a)** Slopes of corresponding sides are the same. **10.** Both are clockwise. **11. a)** D'(1, 4), E'(2, 2), F'(5, 1) **b)** D'E' = $\frac{1}{2}$ DE, D'F' = $\frac{1}{2}$ DF, E'F' = $\frac{1}{2}$ EF **c)** ∠D' = ∠D, ∠E' = ∠E, ∠F' = ∠F **d)** Slopes of corresponding sides are the same. **e)** $\frac{1}{2}$ **f)** Origin to vertex. **g)** Both are counterclockwise. **h)** Area of original triangle is 4 times the area of the image triangle. **12. a)** Length of sides, distance from vertex to origin, area of figure **b)** Measures of angles, slopes of sides, sense of vertices

Section 15.15   *Activity 1:* **c)** 2, 1, 4 *Activity 2:* **b)** 3, 3 **c)** 3, 3 *Exercise:* **1. a)** 3 **b)** 4 **c)** 4 **2. a)** 2 **b)** 4 **c)** 2 **3. a)** line **b)** line, rotational **c)** rotational **d)** line, rotational **5. a)** 3 **b)** 4 **c)** 1 **d)** 2 **6. a)** A: 4, B: 1 **8. a)** line; 1 **b)** line, rotational; 4 **c)** line, rotational; 2 **9. a)** A: 2, B: 1, D: 4, E: 6 **b)** A: 2, C: 2, D: 4, E: 6 **c)** A, D, E

Section 15.16   **1. a)** T, T, T, F **b)** T, T, T, T **c)** T, F, F, T **d)** T, F, T, T **e)** T, T, T, F **f)** F, T, F, F, **g)** F, F, T, T

2. a) rotation: $\frac{1}{4}$ turn (90°) ccw **b)** rotation: $\frac{1}{2}$ turn (180°) cw or ccw **c)** dilatation: factor of 2 **d)** reflection in y-axis **e)** translation: left 5, down 5

f) reflection in y-axis **3. a)** (a), (b), (d), (e), (f) **b)** (a), (b), (d), (e), (f) **4. a)** translation: left 2, up 2

b) reflection in x-axis **c)** dilatation: factor of $\frac{1}{2}$

d) rotation: 90° ccw **e)** translation: left 3

f) reflection in y-axis **5. a)** (a), (b), (d), (e), (f) **b)** (a), (b), (d), (e), (f) **6. a)** I: rotation, $(x, y) \rightarrow (y, -x)$; II: reflection, $(x, y) \rightarrow (-x, y)$; III: dilatation, $(x, y) \rightarrow (2x, 2y)$; IV: translation, $(x, y) \rightarrow (x + 10, y - 3)$; **b)** I: translation, $(x, y) \rightarrow (x - 1, y + 12)$; II: rotation, $(x, y) \rightarrow (y, -x)$; III: rotation, $(x, y) \rightarrow (-x, -y)$; IV: translation, $(x, y) \rightarrow (x + 9, y + 11)$; V: dilatation, $(x, y) \rightarrow (\frac{1}{2}x, \frac{1}{2}y)$; VI: rotation and dilatation, $(x, y) \rightarrow (-2x, -2y)$; VII: reflection, $(x, y) \rightarrow (-x, y)$ **7. a)** I, II, IV **b)** I, II, III, IV, VII **9 a)** 36

Chapter Review   **2.** A'(2, 1), B'(6, 3), C'(4, 7), D'(0, 5) **5. a)** B: 6, C: 2 **b)** A: 2, B: 6, C: 2 **c)** B, C

Self Evaluation   **2. b)** ABCD, cw; A'B'C'D', ccw **c)** x **d)** y **e)** (3, 0), (–4, 0) **f)** (0, 3), (0, –4) **4. a)** A, H, I, M, O, T, U, V, W, X, Y

ANSWERS FOR EXTENDING SKILLS & STRATEGIES

CHAPTER 1 page 509
Section 1.2   **1. a)** $9.83 **b)** 0.41 **2. a)** Yes **b)** $2.33 **3. a)** $13.33 **b)** $14.58 **4.** $47.40

Section 1.3   **1. a)** 400 **b)** $\frac{1}{3}$ **c) i)** $\frac{53}{80}$ **ii)** $\frac{3}{5}$ **2. a)** $\frac{3}{5}$

b) $\frac{57}{85}$ **3. a)** 20.8 m **b)** $\frac{24}{37}$

Section 1.4   **1. a)** $9.50 **b)** $7.25 **c)** $16.00 **2. a)** $2.88 **b)** $1.64 **c)** $4.75 **3.** $7.32 **4. a)** 28 **b)** 60 **c)** 124

Section 1.5   **1. a)** Alice: swim; Brad: soccer; Cheryl: rowing; David: chess **2.** 73 **3.** 231 600 **4.** 30

Section 1.7   **1. a)** $42.99 **b)** $7.14 **c)** $32.67 **2. b)** $1198.80 **3. a)** $9.67 **b)** $17.50 **c)** $24.00 **d)** $21.11

Section 1.8   **1. a)** 0.0101, 0.0202, 0.0303 **b)** 0.0404, 0.0505, 0.0606 **3. a)** –168.8 **b)** 29 958 **c)** 4563.6

Section 1.9   **1. a)** 0.42857 **b)** 0.58$\overline{3}$ **c)** 0.63$\overline{8}$ **d)** 0.4$\overline{6}$ **e)** 0.68354 **f)** 0.12941 **g)** 0.88461 **h)** 0.78571 **2. a)** $\frac{22}{64}$ **b)** $\frac{3}{4}$ **c)** $\frac{27}{62}$ **d)** $\frac{3}{7}$ **e)** $\frac{158}{734}$ **f)** $\frac{163}{512}$ **3. a)** 0.423

b) 0.403 **c)** 0.365 **d)** 0.345 **e)** 0.335; Burbett, Hornsby, Musial, Mays, Rose

CHAPTER 2, page 511
Section 2.3 **1. a)** A: obtuse, B: acute, C: acute; D: right, E: acute, F: obtuse **b)** A: 135°, B: 26°, C: 78°, D: 90°, E: 19°, F: 135° **2.** 100° **3. a)** 180° **b)** 60°, 130° **4. a)** ∠BDA, ∠ADE, ∠EDF, ∠FDC, ∠CDB **c)** 90°, 45°, 90°, 45°, 90°

Section 2.4 **1. b)** 60°, 60°, 6 cm **d)** equilateral **2. b)** 105° **d)** obtuse scalene **3. b)** 45° **d)** isosceles, right

Section 2.7 **2. c)** 7.5 cm **3.** Bisect it 3 times. **4.** All 6 lines meet at one point. **5. b)** 4.2 cm

Section 2.11 **1. a)** $y = 10$ **b)** $y = 40°$, $k = 80°$ **c)** $x = 45°$, $y = 45°$, $k = 45°$ **d)** $x = 8$ **2. a)** alternate **b)** inscribed in the same arc **c)** $k = 42°$, $y = 25°$ **3.** Right bisector of any chord passes through centre. **4. a)** 60° **b)** 60° **c)** 60° **d)** 8 cm **e)** 8 cm

CHAPTER 3, page 513
Section 3.2 **1. a)** 13 **b)** –9 **c)** 15 **d)** 21 **2. a)** –1 **b)** –4 **c)** –42 **d)** –8 **e)** –51 **3. a)** –47°C **b)** 20°C **c)** –37°C **d)** 31°C **e)** 16°C **4. a)** –2 **b)** +25 **c)** –18 **d)** –12 **e)** +38 **5.** Joelle, –4; Lori, –2; Michael, –1; Lesley, +2; Jeff, +2

Section 3.3 **1. a)** 12 **b)** –1 **c)** 4 **d)** 16 **e)** –17 **f)** –4 **g)** 7 **h)** 12 **i)** 15 **j)** 14 **k)** 0 **l)** –16 **2. a)** 16 **b)** 19 **c)** –18 **d)** –9 **e)** –11 **f)** 6 **g)** –45 **h)** 36 **3. a)** –7 **b)** 87 **c)** 28 **d)** 109 **e)** –91 **f)** 134 **4. a)** > **b)** > **c)** > **d)** > **5. a)** –3°C **b)** –4°C **c)** –8°C **d)** –15°C **6.** d

Section 3.5 **1.** 1, –12, –5, –11, 10; –1, 12, 5, 11, –10 **2. a)** 3 **b)** 2 **c)** –5 **d)** 8 **e)** 14 **f)** –10 **g)** –14 **h)** –6 **i)** 24 **j)** 2 **k)** 44 **3. a)** 0 **b)** 8 – (–3), 11 **c)** –9 **d)** 21 **e)** 13 **f)** 2 **4.** $12 **5.** –222 m

Section 3.6 **1. a)** –6 **b)** –15 **c)** 6 **d)** 36 **e)** –36 **f)** 125 **g)** –176 **h)** –294 **i)** 272 **j)** 0 **2.** 12, 9, 6, 0, –3, –6; 8, 6, 2, 0, –2, –4; 4, 3, 2, 1, 0, –1, –2; 0, 0, 0, 0, 0, 0; –4, –2, –1, 0, 1, 2; –8, –6, –2, 0, 2, 4 **4. a)** (–2) × (45) **b)** –90 km (to 210 km)

Section 3.7 **1. a)** 6 **b)** 0 **c)** –35 **d)** –7 **e)** –23 **f)** –370 **2. a)** 8568 **b)** –16 800 **c)** 0 **d)** 0 **e)** 0 **f)** 864 **3.** –286, –775, 0, 24, 12, 288, 64 **4. a)** + , – **b)** –1, 1, 1

Section 3.8 **1. a)** 6 **b)** –6 **c)** –6 **d)** 6 **e)** –7 **f)** –7 **g)** 7 **h)** 7 **2. b) i)** +5 **ii)** –5 **iii)** –5 **iv)** +5 **3.** –7, –5, 0, 4, 8, 4, 4 **4. a)** –10 **b)** –4 **c)** –18 **d)** 8 **e)** –14 **f)** 16 **g)** –6 **h)** 15 **i)** –8 **j)** 22 **k)** –12; FLOEBERG BAY

Section 3.9 **1. a)** –6 **b)** –5 **c)** 6 **d)** 10 **2. a)** –8°C **b)** 4°C **c)** 3°C **3.** –4.2°C

Section 3.12 **1. a)** –5 **b)** 37 **c)** 20 **d)** –13 **e)** –4 **f)** 8 **g)** –18 **h)** 44 **2. a)** 25 **b)** 55 **c)** –12 **d)** 18 **e)** 5 **f)** 6

3. a) –3 **b)** –68 **c)** 112 **d)** 35 **e)** 1 **f)** –11 **g)** –150 **h)** –23 **4. a)** 3 **b)** –1 **c)** –6 **d)** 31.5 **e)** 12 **f)** –5 **5. a)** 4 **b)** –20 **c)** –95 **d)** –23

Section 3.13 **1. a)** 11 **b)** 12 **c)** 24 **d)** 87 **e)** 1 **f)** 0 **2. a)** 9 **b)** 5 **c)** 9 **d)** 10 **3. a)** < **b)** < **c)** = **d)** < **e)** < **f)** < **g)** < **h)** > **i)** < **j)** > **4. a)** –2 **b)** 4 **c)** 4 **d)** 2 **e)** 0 **f)** 6 **g)** 11 **h)** 7 **i)** 4 **j)** –4 **k)** 4 **l)** –3

Section 3.14 **1.** A(2, 3) B(–5, 2) C(2, –3) D(–5, –5) E(–5, 5) F(–4, –7) G(5, –7) H(5, 5) I(5, –5) J(–4, –4) K(–7, 2) L(0, 2) M(5, 0) N(0, –6) P(–6, 0) Q(2, 0) R(2, 5) S(–2, 2) T(–4, 4) U(2, 2) V(–2, –2) W(0, 6) **3. b)** (–7, –3) **4. a)** For example, (2, 2) **b)** For example, (–8, –3) **5. b)** For example, (4, 5)

CHAPTER 4, page 517
Section 4.3 **1. b) i)** $5a$ **ii)** $-1x$ **iii)** $3m$ **iv)** $14y$ **v)** $-8y$ **vi)** $10b$ **c) i)** 16 **ii)** –3.2 **iii)** 9.6 **iv)** 44.8 **v)** –25.6 **vi)** 32 **2. a)** $-2x$ **b)** $2b$ **c)** $4x$ **d)** $-19y$ **e)** $-6c$ **f)** $26x$ **g)** $-21x$ **h)** $-86y$ **i)** $36a$ **3. a)** $-4x - 2y$ **b)** $-17y - 13x$ **c)** $38x - 67y$ **d)** $50y - 18x$ **e)** $49x - 59y$ **4. a)** –13.2 **b)** –59.7 **c)** –12.2 **d)** 35 **e)** 28.1 **5. b)** B: –167 **6. b)** A: 30.7, B: –25.47, C: –53.9

Section 4.4 **1. a)** $-3x, x$; $2y, 5y$ **b)** $-4y, 3y$; $3x, -2x$ **c)** $-3y^2, -y^2$; $x^2, 3x^2$ **d)** $-7y^2, 8y^2$; 2, 4 **2. a)** $3.25 **b)** $4.25 **c)** $5.25 **d)** $21.25 **3. a)** $228.02 **b)** $279.50 **c)** $264.38 **d)** $418.46 **4. a)** 2293 m **b)** 107 m

Section 4.5 **1. a)** 5 **b)** –2 **c)** 5 **d)** 6 **2. a)** 8 **b)** –5 **c)** 12 **d)** 16 **e)** –4 **f)** 24 **g)** 16 **h)** 12 **3. a), b), and c)** have the same root: 3 **4. a)** 2 **b)** 5 **c)** –1 **d)** 3

Section 4.6 **1.** Sample answers given. **a)** $\dfrac{6}{10}, \dfrac{9}{15}$ **b)** $\dfrac{10}{14}, \dfrac{15}{21}$ **c)** $\dfrac{16}{18}, \dfrac{24}{27}$ **d)** $\dfrac{22}{40}, \dfrac{33}{60}$ **e)** $\dfrac{74}{100}, \dfrac{111}{150}$ **f)** $\dfrac{94}{200}, \dfrac{141}{300}$ **2. a)** 32 **b)** 96 **c)** 240 **d)** 12 **e)** 207 **f)** 42 **3. a)** Yes **b)** No **c)** Yes **d)** Yes **e)** Yes **f)** No **4. b)** $x = 56$ **c)** 56 rock records **5. b)** 450 **c)** 450 mL

Section 4.9 **1.** Slopes given. AB, $-\dfrac{3}{2}$; CD, $-\dfrac{7}{3}$; EF, $\dfrac{1}{4}$; GH, $-\dfrac{1}{3}$; IJ, 4; KL, $\dfrac{5}{3}$; MN, $-\dfrac{2}{3}$; PQ, $\dfrac{5}{3}$; OR, undefined; ST, 0 **2. a)** $-\dfrac{2}{5}$ **b)** $-\dfrac{13}{8}$ **c)** undefined **d)** $-\dfrac{2}{5}$ **e)** $-\dfrac{8}{7}$ **f)** 0 **3.** 8, –6, $-\dfrac{3}{4}$; D(–4, 5), 2, $-\dfrac{2}{5}$; F(7, –2), 4, 0; G(5, 4), 2, 3; I(–3, –6), 8, undefined

Section 4.12 **1. a)** $(-1, \dfrac{1}{2})$ **b)** (–2, 7) **c)** (–4, 4) **d)** (2, –2.5) **e)** (3.5, –2.5) **f)** $(\dfrac{1}{2}, -2)$ **2. a)** (9, –16)

b) $(3, 4)$ **c)** $(-5, 6)$ **3.** $(\frac{1}{2}, -1\frac{1}{2})$ **4.** $(-5, 1)$ **5.** $(3, -1)$ or $(-6, 6)$

CHAPTER 5, page 519

Section 5.2   1. Sample answers given. **a)** $-\frac{6}{10}, -\frac{9}{15}$
b) $-\frac{10}{16}, -\frac{15}{24}$ **c)** $-\frac{14}{20}, -\frac{21}{30}$ **d)** $\frac{10}{24}, \frac{15}{36}$ **e)** $\frac{24}{46}, \frac{36}{69}$ **f)** $-\frac{30}{68}, -\frac{45}{102}$ **2. a)** $-2\frac{2}{5}$ **b)** $-1\frac{11}{16}$ **c)** $3\frac{17}{19}$ **d)** $2\frac{10}{21}$ **e)** $4\frac{22}{59}$ **f)** $-11\frac{21}{52}$
3. a) $-\frac{2}{7}, -\frac{4}{7}, -\frac{3}{5}, \frac{5}{-8}$ **b)** $-\frac{8}{3}, \frac{5}{2}, \frac{-4}{9}, \frac{7}{-5}$ **c)** $\frac{4}{6}, \frac{6}{-10}, \frac{-6}{3}, \frac{7}{-3}$ **d)** $-\frac{3}{-2}, \frac{1}{6}, \frac{-6}{4}, \frac{5}{-3}$ **4. a)** $-\frac{27}{5}$ **b)** $\frac{25}{7}$ **c)** $\frac{37}{6}$ **d)** $-\frac{71}{10}$
e) $-\frac{24}{2}$ **f)** $-\frac{94}{17}$ **5. a)** < **b)** < **c)** > **d)** = **e)** > **f)** <

Section 5.3   1. a) T **b)** NT **c)** NT **d)** T **e)** NT **f)** T
2. a) 35 (2) **b)** 18 (2) **c)** 6 (1) **d)** 36 (2) **e)** 259 (3) **f)** 6 (1)
g) 63 (2) **h)** 407 (3) **i)** 2 (1) **3. a)** $\frac{12}{23}$ **b)** $-\frac{3}{17}$ **c)** $\frac{2}{17}$
d) $-\frac{3}{20}$ **e)** $-\frac{6}{26}$ **f)** $\frac{5}{29}$ **4. a)** $\frac{523}{1000}$ **b)** $\frac{209}{250}$ **c)** $\frac{137}{500}$

Section 5.6   1. a) $\frac{1}{35}$ **b)** $-\frac{13}{15}$ **c)** $\frac{93}{119}$ **d)** $\frac{1}{18}$ **e)** $-\frac{31}{30}$
f) $\frac{1}{70}$ **2. a)** > **b)** < **c)** > **d)** > **3. a)** 1.1 **b)** –1.7 **c)** –1.9
d) –0.4 **e)** –0.9 **f)** –10.8 **4. a)** $-1\frac{2}{21}$ **b)** $\frac{-22}{35}$ **c)** $3\frac{1}{2}$
d) $-\frac{48}{11}$ **e)** $7\frac{11}{42}$ **f)** $-3\frac{19}{20}$ **5.** 4 h 44 min

Section 5.8   1. a) $-1\frac{1}{10}$ **b)** $1\frac{5}{56}$ **c)** $1\frac{3}{56}$ **d)** $\frac{7}{15}$
e) $-\frac{139}{154}$ **f)** $\frac{71}{105}$ **2. e)** –39.7 **b)** –12.9 **c)** –12.4 **d)** 3 **f)** 4.4
a) 13.1 **3.** swimming, 26 min **4.** Yvonne, $\frac{1}{15}$
5. a) $4\frac{3}{140}$ **b)** $8\frac{113}{140}$ **c)** $-4\frac{3}{35}$ **d)** $-1\frac{43}{360}$

Section 5.11   1. a) $-\frac{1}{4}$ **b)** $\frac{7}{45}$ **c)** $\frac{1}{10}$ **d)** –4 **e)** $-\frac{24}{7}$
f) $-\frac{1}{9}$ **g)** $8\frac{45}{56}$ **h)** $\frac{-108}{125}$ **i)** $-3\frac{12}{35}$ **2. a)** $\frac{1}{10}$ **b)** $\frac{1}{5}$ **c)** $-\frac{1}{5}$
d) $-\frac{1}{20}$ **e)** $\frac{1}{5}$ **f)** 1 **g)** $-\frac{4}{25}$ **h)** $-\frac{27}{20}$ **i)** 0 **j)** –16 **k)** $-1\frac{4}{5}$ **l)** 20

3. a) $-16\frac{1}{5}$ **b)** $-32\frac{7}{24}$ **c)** 15 **d)** $-9\frac{5}{8}$ **e)** $\frac{1}{4}$ **f)** $-\frac{3}{100}$ **g)** $\frac{9}{40}$
h) 0 **i)** $-\frac{85}{96}$ **j)** $-15\frac{1}{9}$ **k)** –48 **l)** $\frac{64}{5}$ **4. b)** $\frac{1}{9}$ **c)** $\frac{16}{25}$ **d)** $\frac{9}{4}$
e) $\frac{4}{25}$ **f)** $\frac{1}{9}$ **g)** $-\frac{3}{4}$ **h)** $-\frac{1}{96}$ **i)** $\frac{2}{27}$ **j)** $\frac{1}{9}$ **5.** $-16\frac{1}{4}$

Section 5.12   1. a) $\frac{3}{2}$ **b)** 2 **c)** $-\frac{16}{3}$ **2. a)** $\frac{9}{2}$ **b)** $\frac{3}{10}$
c) $-\frac{1}{36}$ **d)** $-4\frac{2}{3}$ **e)** 0 **f)** $-\frac{2}{7}$ **g)** $-\frac{2}{3}$ **h)** $\frac{3}{5}$ **i)** 0 **j)** $\frac{5}{16}$ **3. a)** $\frac{1}{10}$
b) $-\frac{1}{16}$ **c)** $-\frac{2}{9}$ **d)** $\frac{27}{2}$ **e)** $-\frac{48}{35}$ **f)** $\frac{29}{72}$ **4.** 30 min **5. a)** $9\frac{17}{20}$
b) $1\frac{77}{120}$

Section 5.13   1. a) $-\frac{1}{12}$ **b)** $\frac{37}{40}$ **c)** $-1\frac{1}{8}$ **d)** $\frac{7}{20}$ **e)** $-\frac{5}{12}$
f) $\frac{3}{7}$ **g)** $1\frac{3}{40}$ **h)** –2 **i)** $\frac{8}{15}$ **j)** $-\frac{2}{5}$ **2. a)** –12 **b)** $-\frac{1}{8}$ **c)** $\frac{1}{18}$
d) $-1\frac{11}{24}$ **e)** $7\frac{1}{5}$ **f)** $-1\frac{5}{8}$ **3. a)** $-\frac{24}{55}$ **b)** $-\frac{42}{145}$ **c)** $-\frac{7}{16}$
d) $3\frac{47}{75}$ **4. a)** $-1\frac{7}{12}$ °C **b)** –9.8°C

Section 5.14   1. a) $\frac{1}{5}$ **b)** $-\frac{7}{20}$ **c)** $-\frac{73}{100}$ **d)** $1\frac{11}{20}$ **e)** $-\frac{33}{100}$
f) $-\frac{14}{25}$ **g)** $\frac{3}{20}$ **h)** $\frac{8}{25}$ **i)** $\frac{1}{8}$ **j)** $3\frac{7}{8}$ **k)** $\frac{401}{1000}$ **l)** $-2\frac{27}{200}$ **2. a)** $\frac{35}{99}$
b) $\frac{49}{100}$ **c)** $\frac{31}{45}$ **d)** $\frac{27}{45}$ **e)** $\frac{156}{495}$ **f)** $3\frac{27}{99}$ **g)** $\frac{46}{990}$ **h)** $2\frac{1}{3}$ **i)** $\frac{413}{999}$
3. a) $-\frac{41}{90}$ **b)** $-\frac{39}{99}$ **c)** $-\frac{78}{99}$ **d)** $-4\frac{32}{99}$ **e)** $-2\frac{93}{99}$ **f)** $-4\frac{15}{99}$
g) $-\frac{143}{999}$ **h)** $-3\frac{2}{9}$ **i)** $-4\frac{13}{99}$ **j)** $-2\frac{41}{90}$ **k)** $-\frac{221}{990}$ **l)** $-\frac{196}{999}$
4. a) periodic decimal **b)** rational

Section 5.15   1. a) r **b)** irr **c)** r **d)** r **e)** r **f)** irr **g)** r
h) r **i)** r **j)** irr **3. a)** $x > -1, x \in R$ **b)** $x < -1, x \in R$
c) $x \geq 2, x \in R$ **d)** $x \leq 3, x \in I$ **e)** $x > 2, x \in R$
f) $x \geq -6, x \in I$ **g)** $x < -4, x \in R$ **h)** $x \geq 6, x \in R$
i) $x \geq 7, x \in I$ **j)** $x \leq 2, x \in I$ **k)** $x \leq 0, x \in R$

CHAPTER 6, page 523
Section 6.2   1. a) 598 m **b)** 260 m **2. a)** 70 m
b) $367.50 **3. a)** 141.8 m **b)** $527.50 **4.** 35.25 m
6. 17.1, 5.85, 5.85

Section 6.3   1. A: 15 units, B: 30 units, C: 16
units, D: 24 units **2.** 7264 cm² **3.** 809.0 m²
4. 8337.5 m² **5. a)** 92 m **b)** 8464 m² **6. a)** 169.6,
73.7, 169.6, 73.7 **b)** 12 499.5 cm²

Section 6.5 **1. a)** 70.4 cm^2 **b)** 80.5 m^2
c) 642.1 cm^2 **d)** 118.6 m^2 **2.** 0.7 m^2 per side
3. 42.4 cm^2, 26.0 cm^2, 42.4 cm^2, 26.0 cm^2,
62.6 cm^2 **4. a)** 32 cm^2 **b)** 688 cm^2 **5.** 394

Section 6.7 **1.** 12.67 m^2 **2. a)** 1009.23 cm^2
b) 33.5 m^2 **3.** 33 m^2 **4. a)** 299.9 m^2 **b)** 11 073
5. 53 m^2

Section 6.8 **1. a)** 79.1 cm **b)** 21.4 m **c)** 32.7 m
2. 100 cm, 314 cm; 360 cm, 1130.4 cm; 3.3 m,
20.7 m; 18.1 m, 113.7 m **3.** 25.4 m **4.** 22.29 m
5. a) 170.0 m **b)** 3.7 **6. a)** 266.27 cm **b)** 376
7. 116.8 km

Section 6.10 **1.** 28.6 m, 642.1 m^2; 18.8 cm,
1109.8 cm^2; 7.03 m, 14.06 m; 64.1 mm,
12 901.7 mm^2; 9.38 cm, 18.76 cm; 147.12 m,
16 990.77 m^2; 91.71 km, 26 409.67 km^2
2. 459.73 km^2 **3. a)** 260.87 cm^2 **b)** 9.94 m^2
c) 6.57 m^2 **d)** 36.17 cm^2 **e)** 57.0 cm^2 **4. a)** 81.67 cm^2
b) 171 **c)** 6034.4 cm^2 **5. a)** 98.47 cm^2 **b)** 51
6. a) 21.2 m^2 **b)** No **7. a)** 154.80 m^2 **b)** about
100 m^2

Section 6.12 **1. c)** 14.28 cm^2, 17.64 cm^2
d) 74.8 cm^2 **2.** 141 m^2 **3. a)** 677.8 cm^2 **b)** 338.6 cm^2
c) 82.3 cm^2 **d)** 905.9 cm^2 **4.** 27.7 m^2 **5. a)** 219.9 m^2
b) 4

Section 6.13 **1.** 19.25 cm, 3705.3 cm^2; 25 m,
16.5 m; 85.4 mm, 33 868.1 mm^2 **2.** 156.29 m^2
(no bottom) **3. a)** 861.9 cm^2 **b)** 1758.4 cm^2
c) 4976.6 cm^2 **d)** 3234.5 cm^2 **e)** 7844.1 cm^2
f) 3094.0 cm^2 **4.** \$2863.40 **5. a)** 38.3 cm^2
b) 27.9 cm^2

Section 6.15 **1. a)** 11 455.2 cm^2 **b)** 1017.4 cm^2
c) 8103.2 cm^2 **2. a)** 879.2 cm^2 **b)** 307.7 cm^2
c) 9501.8 cm^2 **3.** 1366.3 cm^2 **4. a)** 4313.3 mm^2
b) Estimate 55. **5.** 17 **6. a)** 2400 cm^2 **b)** 1256 cm^2
c) cube, 1144 cm^2 **7.** 23 484.1 cm^2

Section 6.18 **1. a)** 2725.0 cm^3 **b)** 125 703.3 cm^3
c) 329 741.2 cm^3 **d)** 5651.1 cm^3 **2.** 1646.0 cm^3,
9.09 mm^2, 4.04 m **3.** 1.1 m, 39 044.4 mm^3,
0.014 cm **4. a)** 264.98 m^3 **b)** 31797.4 kg **5.** B
6. 31.9 m^3 **7.** 581.8 m^3 **8. a)** 13.07 cm^3 **b)** 1.65 kg

Section 6.19 **1. a)** 195.3 m^3 **b)** 5031.6 m^3
c) 19 200 cm^3 **d)** 145 051.2 mm^3 **2.** 2.15 cm,
2 083 118.7 mm^3, 0.026 m **3.** 73.6 m^3
4. 124.7 cm^3 **5. a)** 1.78×10^{10} km^3 **b)** 1.6%
6. 1209 **7.** 59.9 m^3 **8.** 115.75 m^3

CHAPTER 7, page 529
Section 7.2 **1. a)** 25:12 **b)** 22:23 **c)** 16:15 **d)** 20:9
2. a) 1:1 **b)** 1:5 **c)** 2:5 **d)** 1:5 **3. a)** 3:4 **b)** 5:7 **c)** 2:1
d) 5:11 **e)** 3:4 **f)** 4:11 **g)** 11:59 **h)** 1:59 **4. a)** 3:10
b) 11:40 **c)** 7:40 **d)** 15:38 **5. a)** 4:1 **b)** 38:39 **c)** 39:31

d) 8:5 **6. a)** 5:7 **b)** 12:19 **c)** 7:10 **d)** 22:41

Section 7.4 **1.** Sample answers given. **a)** 6:8
b) 6:16 **c)** 10:18 **d)** 4:6 **e)** 8:14 **f)** 2:4 **g)** 6:20 **h)** 10:6
i) 2:10 **2. a)** 9 **b)** 10 **c)** 26 **d)** 50 **e)** 5 **f)** 15 **g)** 4 **h)** 30
3. a) 20 **b)** 5 **c)** 27 **d)** 10 **e)** 6 **f)** 9 **4.** \$15 000
b) \$6000 **5. a)** 22.5 kg **b)** 12 kg **6. a)** 12.81 m
b) That storm continues. **7. a)** 150

Section 7.8 **1. a)** 120 km **b)** 97.5 km **c)** 273 km
2. a) 1.5 cm **b)** 5 cm **c)** 15 cm **3.** 3081.76 km,
76.3 cm, 938.74 km, 62.5 cm

Section 7.9 **1. a)** 130 km **b)** 6.3 cm **2.** 1:20 **3.** 1:13
4. 12.75 m **5.** 100.5 cm

Section 7.13 **1. a)** 20 L **b)** 1200 L **c)** 1800 L
d) 9 min **2.** 720 m **3.** \$50 **4. a)** 17 **b)** 170 **5.** 100 800
6. Place of Pizza

Section 7.14 **1. a)** \$0.9975/L **b)** \$9.33/m
c) \$0.003/mL **2. a)** \$1.48 **b)** \$9.60 **c)** \$4.56 **3.** 40
4. 4455 km **5.** about 20 **6. a)** \$5.14 **b)** \$15.06
c) 44.9 L **d)** 36.8 L **7.** A

Section 7.16 **1. a)** 75 **b)** 2.232 **c)** 450 **d)** 18.75
2. A: 30%, 70% B: 65%, 35% **3. a)** 37.5%, 62.5%
b) 44%, 56% **c)** 62.5%, 37.5% **4. a)** 111 L **b)** 166.5 L
c) 666 L **d)** 11.32 L **e)** 54.61 L **f)** 6.44 L **5. a)** 60 kg
b) 50 kg

Section 7.17 **1. a)** 480 **b)** 4800 **2. a)** 12 **b)** 120
3. a) 4.8 **b)** 20 **c)** 220 **4. a)** 30 **b)** 25 **c)** 96 **5.** 43.75%
6. 150 g

Section 7.18 **1. a)** 384.3 **b)** 1086.44 **c)** 2116.5
d) 1593.2 **e)** 2197.3 **f)** 1406.25 **2. a)** 514.75 km
b) 821.88 g **c)** 536.94 mL **d)** \$60.03 **e)** 2175.45 kg
f) \$401.68 **3.** 157.25 g **4. b)** \$1295.00, \$1137.50
5. 5805.8 g **6.** 115 600

CHAPTER 8, page 532
Section 8.2 **1.** \$84.30, \$110.05, \$57.38
2. a) 436.13 **b)** Yes, PST = 8% **3. a)** Ontario

Section 8.4 and 8.5 **1.** \$2.45, \$22.05; 12%, \$16.50;
\$4.50, \$25.49; \$75.00, \$66.00; \$122.50, \$110.25;
\$150.00, \$27.00 **2. a)** \$31.50 **b)** \$165.03
3. Assuming 7% PST: **a)** \$520.41 **b)** \$39.03
c) \$169.13 **d)** 32.5% **4.** \$719.63 **5.** Assuming 8%
PST; \$169.12 **6. b)** lost \$83.00

Section 8.7 **1.** \$211.97 **2.** \$4640.00 **3. a)** \$216.00
b) \$108.00 **c)** \$54.00 **d)** \$90.00 **4. a)** \$4.33
b) \$524.33 **c)** \$4.37 **5.** \$23.33, \$62.13, \$140.63

Section 8.9 **1. a)** \$990.00 **b)** \$1236.00 **c)** \$534.07
2. a) \$123.04 **b)** \$164.05 **3.** \$10.26 **4. a)** 0.71%
b) \$95.85 **5. a)** \$15.32 **b)** \$21.64

Section 8.11 **1.** \$15.00, \$84.00, \$14.14, \$3400.00,

3%, \$12 500.00 **2.** \$850 + \$1623.33, or \$2473.33
4. a) B **b)** B **5. a)** B **b)** B

CHAPTER 9, page 535

Section 9.2 **1. a)** 2, x **b)** $\frac{2}{3}$, y **c)** 6, x **d)** –4, xyz

e) $\frac{4}{5}$, z **f)** 1523, b **g)** $\frac{1}{3}$, x **h)** 1, a **i)** –1, m **3. a)** $8a + 2$

b) $4y - 5x$ **c)** $10k - 4m$ **d)** x **e)** $-y^2 + 8$ **f)** $3y^2 + 2y$

g) 17 **h)** –8 **i)** $13b - 2$ **j)** $23x^2 - 8x$ **4. a)** $3a - b$

b) $9x - 8$ **c)** y^2 **d)** $x + y$ **e)** $3x$ **f)** $2a - 5b$ **g)** $4x + y$ **h)** 0

i) $2a - 2b$ **j)** $3x$ **k)** $x + y$ **l)** $3x$

Section 9.3 **1. a)** $x - 6y$ **b)** $4a + 2b$ **c)** 3 **d)** $x + y$ **e)** 2

f) $5y + 4$ **g)** $14m - n$ **2. a)** $5x - 5y$ **b)** 0 **c)** $8b$

d) $-10m - 16n$ **e)** $9k$ **f)** $6k$ **3. a)** $4x + 5y$ **b)** $-n^2 + 3n +$

6 **c)** $x + 11$ **d)** $3x^2 - 8x$ **e)** $-4y + 3z$ **f)** $2x - 4y$ **4.** $5x -$

$6y$ **5. a)** $-x - 2y$ **b)** $7x - 4y$ **c)** $-5a - 6b$ **d)** $3a + 5b$

e) $-10a + 6b$ **f)** $-4x + 3y$ **g)** $11a + 2b$

Section 9.4 **1. a)** –36 **b)** –5 **c)** –1 **d)** –12 **e)** –8 **f)** –45

g) –33 **h)** –12 **2. a)** 24 **b)** 96 **c)** 56 **d)** 72 **e)** 80 **f)** –96

g) 272 **h)** –32 **i)** –6 **j)** 194 **k)** 138 **l)** –14 **3. a)** $9x$,

58.5 cm **b)** $21x + 2$, 138.5 cm **c)** $16x + 4$, 108 cm

d) $14x + 2$, 93 cm **4. a)** $34x - 10$ **b)** 114.1 cm

Section 9.5 **1. a)** $6ab$ **b)** $-6xy$ **c)** $-15mn$ **d)** $8hxy$

e) $6abc$ **f)** $-12m^2n^2$ **g)** $10kr^2$ **h)** $10x^2$ **i)** $8a^3$ **j)** $6z^4$

2. a) $-2a^2$ **b)** $6x^2$ **c)** $-4y^3$ **d)** $4x^2$ **e)** n^5 **f)** $6x^4$ **g)** $6x^4$

h) 0 **i)** $-9y^2$ **j)** $24y^5$ **k)** $6x^2y$ **l)** $-12a^2b$ **m)** 0 **n)** a^2b^2

o) $-6a^2b^2$ **p)** $-24a^2b^2$ **q)** $-6a^4b^2$ **r)** 0 **3. a)** $-28a^2$

b) $-12xy$ **c)** $12my$ **d)** $6x^2y$ **e)** $8xy$ **f)** $18y^3$ **g)** $-6a^3$

h) $-6x^3y$ **i)** $12x^3$ **j)** 0 **4. a)** $-30abc$ **b)** $5mnp$ **c)** $-3fsv$

d) $-6x^2y^2$ **e)** $10a^2b^2$ **f)** $12f^2s^2$ **g)** $15x^3y^3$ **h)** $-24a^3b^3$

i) $-2a^4b^4$ **j)** $-8a^4b^5$

Section 9.6 **1.** $7x - 28$ **2.** $-10x - 15$ **3. a)** $-25x - 20$

b) $-3x - 24$ **c)** 0 **d)** $-60a + 504$ **e)** $-60x + 390$ **f)** $-34x$

$- 408$ **g)** $x + 19$ **h)** $-15x - 4$ **4. a)** $14a^2 - 6a$ **b)** $-24x^2 +$

$30x$ **c)** $-25s^2 - 73s$ **d)** $-83a^2 - 52a$ **e)** $108y^2 - 756y$

f) $85c^2 + 612c$ **g)** $6889v^2 + 83v$ **h)** $-192r^2 - 1216r$

5. a) $-29x^2 + 116x - 754$ **b)** $-156x^2 + 312x - 520$

c) $468x^2 - 3354$ **d)** $-130x^2 - 728x + 9022$ **e)** $168y^2 -$

$332x + 96$ **6. a)** $3x^3 - 15x^2 + 6x$ **b)** $-24a^3 + 20a^2 - 4a$

c) $147x^3 - 336x^2 + 504x$ **d)** $126y^3 + 182y^2 - 742y$

e) $357a^3 - 189a^2 + 518a$ **f)** $2016y^3 - 2324y^2 +$

$2800y$ **g)** $360x^3 + 648x$ **h)** $-4ax^3 - 13ax$ **i)** $5xy^3 -$

$82xy$ **7. a)** $-36x^4 + 564x^3 - 216x^2$ **b)** $-35a^2x^4 -$

$133a^2x^3 + 273ax^2$ **c)** $-45a^3y^3 + 60a^2y^3 - 105a^3y^2 +$

$90a^2y^2x^2$ **8.** –816, 1701, –135 000 **9. a)** –6 **b)** –48

c) 24 **d)** 23 **e)** –96 **10.** 905 m^2

Section 9.8 **1. a)** $3x$ **b)** $-\frac{19}{8}y$ **c)** $-\frac{9}{4}a$ **d)** $\frac{186}{23}z^3$

e) $-13ab^3$ **f)** $\frac{-39}{16}x^5y^3$ **2. a)** $9m$ **b)** $-4x^3$ **c)** $\frac{y}{5}$ **d)** $\frac{32}{15}mn^2$

e) $-\frac{18}{39}x^2$ **f)** $-6ab$ **3. a)** $24\frac{8}{45}$ **b)** $\frac{7}{2}$ **c)** –24 **d)** –10 **e)** $4\frac{4}{7}$

f) 22 **4. a)** $16x^2$ **b)** 144,108 **c)** 4 **5. a)** $\frac{7}{3}x^2y^2$ **b)** $\frac{112}{3}$,

84 **c)** Multiply. **6. a)** $8a^3bc$ **b)** 48, 306, 14 688

Section 9.9 **1. a)** $3x$ **b)** 3 **c)** $-6km$ **d)** $-6k$ **e)** $-3mx$

f) $-3py$ **g)** $-3y$ **2. a)** 8 **b)** 20 **c)** 4 **d)** 3 **e)** 9 **3. b)** $3ax +$

$6bx$ **c)** 480 **d)** 1920 **4. a)** $x^2 + 2a$ **b)** 44 **c)** $x^4 + 4ax^2 +$

$4a^2$

Section 9.10 **1. a)** 1 **b)** 32 **c)** 3 **d)** $\frac{1}{2}$ **e)** 9 **f)** 5 **g)** 9

h) 1 **i)** 1 **j)** 1 **k)** 1 **l)** 2401 **2. a)** 2 **b)** $\frac{5}{6}$ **c)** $3\frac{1}{2}$ **d)** 3 **e)** $\frac{1}{9}$

f) $\frac{4}{3}$ **g)** 1 **h)** $\frac{4}{9}$ **i)** $-\frac{3}{4}$ **j)** –8 **k)** $\frac{3}{4}$ **l)** $\frac{4}{9}$ **m)** $\frac{1}{2}$ **n)** $-\frac{1}{8}$ **o)** $-\frac{1}{8}$

p) $\frac{5}{2}$ **q)** 5 **r)** $\frac{13}{2}$ **s)** $\frac{9}{16}$ **t)** $\frac{9}{4}$ **u)** 12

Section 9.11 and 9.12 **1. a)** 3.4×10^3 **b)** $5.609 \times$

10^3 **c)** 1.5967×10^4 **d)** 7.4×10^{-3} **e)** 7.98×10^{-3}

f) 1.5093×10^4 **g)** 7.8×10^4 **h)** $9.120\,007\,08 \times 10^8$

i) 2×10^{-6} **j)** $2.340\,98 \times 10^{-4}$ **k)** $1.607\,8912 \times 10^{-2}$

2. a) 8.4×10^6 **b)** 9.4×10^9 **c)** 7.9×10^{-5} **d)** 8.0×10^{-5}

e) 1.52×10^8 **f)** 1.47×10^8 **g)** 6.6×10^{-25}

3. a) 5.02×10^{10} **b)** 3.74×10^3 **c)** 9.23×10^{-1}

d) 1.7×10^2 **e)** 6.2×10^{-2} **f)** 2.22×10^5

4. a) 1.5×10^{10} mL **b)** 1.6×10^4 m

CHAPTER 10, page 539

Section 10.2 **1. a)** 3 **b)** 16 **c)** 36 **d)** 6 **e)** –9 **f)** 14 **g)** 4

h) 14 **i)** 4 **2. a)** 31 **b)** –35.5 **c)** 2.6 **d)** 34.1 **e)** –2.8

f) –3.53 **g)** –11 **h)** 27.85 **i)** 13.99 **j)** 16.27 **3. a)** $\frac{1}{12}$ **b)** $\frac{7}{40}$

c) $\frac{-1}{21}$ **d)** $\frac{11}{20}$ **e)** $\frac{19}{20}$ **f)** $\frac{1}{8}$ **g)** $\frac{16}{15}$ **h)** $\frac{-13}{24}$

Section 10.3 **1. a)** 4 **b)** 5 **c)** 6 **d)** 8 **e)** 2.8 **f)** –1.133

2. a) –5 **b)** –48.7 **c)** 9 **d)** $-\frac{25}{4}$ **e)** –2 **f)** 5 **3. a)** 5 **b)** 1.9

c) 1.8 **d)** –0.925 **e)** $\frac{13}{14}$ **f)** –1.4 **4. a)** 3.3 **b)** 7.7 **c)** 3.25

d) –3.4 **e)** –10.8 **f)** 5.9 **g)** 3.3 **h)** –12.5

Section 10.4 **1. a)** 15 **b)** 0 **c)** 5 **2. a)** 6 **b)** 4 **c)** 2.5

d) 11 **e)** 6 **f)** 15 **g)** 0.5 **h)** 2 **3. a)** 3 **b)** –2 **c)** 0.4 **d)** 1.5

e) 4 **f)** 14 **g)** 40 **4. a)** $\frac{1}{6}$ **b)** 10 **c)** $\frac{80}{3}$ **d)** 2 **5. a)** 20

b) –12 **c)** 15 **d)** –75 **e)** 10 **f)** 33 **6. a)** 2 **b)** 3 **c)** 10 **d)** 2

e) –6 f) –5 7. a) 4 b) –1 c) 3 d) 5 e) –8.5 f) 22

Section 10.7 1. a) 24 b) 25 2. 92 km 3. 20 4. Jeff: 1876, Elsie: 4037 5. 15, 45 6. 192

Section 10.8 1. b) 6.5 m, 19.5 m, 19.0 m 2. 281 m × 205 m 3. a) 29 m b) 406 m²

Section 10.11 and 10.12 1. a) 5 cm b) 20 cm c) 8 cm 2. a) 10.2 b) 5.4 c) 23.8 3. a) 6.5 cm b) 8.2 cm 4. 7.7 m 5. 16 m 6. a) 9.05 m b) 81.90 m²

Section 10.13 1. a) $m < 5$ b) $m \leqq 7.5$ c) $m < 6$ d) $m \geqq -16$ 2. a) $x > 5$ b) $17 < m$ c) $-17 \leqq m$ d) $k \geqq 4$ e) $m < 6$ f) $-14 \geqq p$ 3. a) $x > 10$ b) $x \leqq 11$ c) $x < -18$ d) $x \geqq -8$

CHAPTER 11, page 541

Section 11.2 1. a) 2 b) 2π c) $1 - 2y$ d) $y - 2$ e) $2a$ f) $h + r$ 2. a) $2y - 1 + x$ b) xy c) k^2 d) xy e) $-3x + 2y - 5xy$ f) $-3am + 2m + 6a$ 3. a) $3(2x^2 - 4x + 5)$ b) $a(y^2 + 6y + 8)$ c) $5(m^3 - 5m^2 + 3)$ d) $a(5a + 2b + 1)$ e) $6a(a^2 - 3a + 1)$ f) $2a(2a^2 + 4a + 3)$ g) $3(x^2 - 4xy - 3y^2)$ h) $4x(x^2 - 4x + 2)$ i) $25(2a^2 + 3ab + b^2)$ j) $10xy(x^2y^2 + 2xy - 1)$ 4. a) $a - b$, $(m + n)(a - b)$ b) $x + 2y$, $(x + 2y)(a + b)$ c) $2a - b$, $(2a - b)^2$ d) $x - y$, $(3x - 4y)(x - y)$ e) $4x + y$, $(2x + 5y)(4x + y)$

Section 11.3 1. a) $(x - 5)(x + 2)$ b) $(y + 3)(y - 2)$ c) $(m - 2)(m + 1)$ d) $(t - 10)(t + 3)$ e) $(x + 14)(x - 1)$ f) $(m + 9)(m - 2)$ g) $(t - 6)(t + 4)$ h) $(y - 6)(y + 5)$ i) $(x + 4)(x - 1)$ j) $(a + 7)(a - 4)$ 2. a) $2(m - 7)(m + 6)$ b) $3(a + 8)(a - 6)$ c) $m(m - 10)(m + 5)$ d) $2x(x + 5)(x + 7)$ 3. a) $(x + 18)(x - 3)$ b) $(x - 8y)(x - 3y)$ c) $(x + 7)(x - 3)$ d) $(m + 17)(m - 3)$ e) $(y + 27)(y + 2)$ f) $(x + 6)(x - 15)$ g) $(y + 20)(y - 1)$ h) $(m + 2)(m - 14)$ i) $(8 + x)(3 + x)$ j) $(t - 6)(t + 2)$ k) $(a + 3)(a - 8)$ l) $(y - 4)(y + 2)$ 4. a) $(y + 2)(y - 2)(y^2 + 2)$ b) $(4 - y)(5 - y)$ c) $(x - 8)(x + 4)$ d) $(x^2 - 18)(x^2 - 3)$ e) $(5 + x)(4 + x)$ f) $(x + 7)(x - 4)$

Section 11.7 1. a) $y - 2$ b) $x + 4$ c) $2x - 2$ d) $x + 3$ e) $2a + 3$ f) $4 - 2s$ g) $t - \frac{1}{2}$ h) $a^2 - 3$ 2. a) $x + 3$ b) $y + 2$ c) $a - 3$ d) $-6 + b$ e) $1 + 2x$ f) $3y - 2$ g) $2x - 3$ h) $2m - 5$ i) $a + \frac{1}{2}$ j) $-\frac{1}{3} + a$ k) $x^2 + 1$ l) $-1 + 2y^2$ 3. $a^2 - b^2$ or $(a - b)(a + b)$ 4. $(2x - y)(2x + y)$

Section 11.9 1. a) $3y$ b) $-3x$ c) $5a^3$ d) $-3m$ e) $3y$ f) $3y$ 2. a) $2a$ b) $-6n$ c) $-8c$ d) 8 e) $-10mn$ f) $3x^2y$ g) $-4b$ h) $-\frac{3}{p}$ i) $3m$ 3. a) -6 b) 24 c) 144 d) -6 e) -12 f) 4 4. a) $6xy$ b) $4xy^2$

Section 11.10 1. a) $y - 5$ b) $\frac{1}{3}$ c) $\frac{2x - 2y}{x + y}$ d) $x - y$ e) $\frac{1}{x + y}$ f) $\frac{2}{a - b}$ g) $n + 2$ h) $\frac{1}{n + 2}$ 2. a) $3y - 4$ b) $4x + 5$ c) $\frac{x + 3}{x + 5}$ d) $\frac{x + 3}{x + 4}$ e) $\frac{a - 9}{2}$ f) $\frac{y + 5}{y - 5}$ g) $\frac{x - 1}{x + 2}$ h) $\frac{x + 2}{x + 3}$ 3. a) $\frac{2(y^2 + 1)(y - 1)}{3}$ b) $\frac{(x - y)(x^2 + y^2)}{x + y}$ c) $x^2 + 1$ d) $x - 3$ e) 1 f) $\frac{2y - x + 3}{x + 2y}$ 4. a) $\frac{15}{28}$ b) $\frac{5}{6}$ c) $\frac{4}{5}$ d) -1 e) -5 f) -7 g) $-\frac{1}{5}$ h) $-\frac{7}{6}$

Section 11.11 1. a) $\frac{x}{y(x - 1)}$ b) -1 c) $\frac{4}{y}$ d) $\frac{1}{3(n + 1)}$ e) $\frac{1}{2(x + y)}$ f) $\frac{3}{x + 1}$ g) $(y - 2)(y - 3)$ h) $\frac{2x + 1}{1 + 3x}$ 2. a) $\frac{1}{a + b}$ b) $\frac{a(a + 1)}{(a^2 + 1)(a - 1)}$ c) $\frac{2}{2x - 1}$ d) $\frac{3}{4}$ e) $\frac{y(x - y)}{x^2}$ 3. a) $\frac{1}{(x + 3)(x - 1)}$ b) $\frac{a(a - 1)}{3(a - 3)}$ c) $\frac{-x(x - 2)}{(x + 4)(x - 4)}$

Section 11.12 1. a) $-\frac{4}{3}$ b) $\frac{a + b}{a + 4}$ c) $\frac{2}{y - 3}$ d) $12x$ e) $\frac{2(x - 3)^3}{x^5}$ f) 1 g) $\frac{a + 1}{a + 3}$ 2. a) $\frac{(x + y)^3}{x^2y}$ b) $\frac{(a + 3)^2}{a^2 - 1}$ c) $\frac{a(a + 4)(a - 6)}{(a - 3)(a - 2)}$ d) 1

CHAPTER 12, page 544

Section 12.3 3. a) 15 b) 9 c) 30.625 d) 2.75 e) 1.5 f) 0 4. b) 0, 2500 5. a) $y = 2 - 2x$ b) $y = x - 2$ 6. c) $66.00, 14.5, $192.50

Section 12.4 1. b) 10 km, 30 km, 27.5 km, 42.5 km c) 2 h, 5 h, 1.5 h, 2.9 h 2. b) 0.8 cm, 2.6 cm, 3.5 cm, 1.3 cm c) 5 min, 12 min, 9.5 min, 14.5 min

Section 12.6 1. a) D: –1, 0, 1, 2, 3, 4; R: –4, –2, 0, 2, 4, 6 b) D: $-6 \leqq x \leqq 6$, $x \in R$; R: $0 \leqq y \leqq 6$, $y \in R$ 2. a) D: W; R: whole-number multiples of 3 b) D: I; R: … –5, –2, 1, 4, … c) D: R, R: R 3. a) D: W, R: $y \geqq 5$, $y \in W$ b) D: I, R: I c) D: R, R: R 4. b) D: $x \geqq 0$, $x \in R$; R: $y \geqq 20$, $y \in R$

Section 12.7 1. a) (–3, 5) b) (4, –3) 2. a) (1.5, 2.5) b) $\left(-\frac{4}{3},\ -\frac{11}{3}\right)$

Section 12.11 1. a) –3 b) (–3, 0) 2. a) 8 b) (0, 8) 3. b) 3, –12 c) (3, 0), (0, –12) 4. a) 3, –9 b) 7, 7 c) 2, –6 d) 3, 2 e) 3, –4 f) 6, 3

Section 12.12 **1. a)** No **b)** Yes

CHAPTER 13, page 546
Section 13.3 **1. a)** 50 **b)** 51 **c)** 37 **2. a)** isosceles **b)** 80 **c)** equal **d)** 50

Section 13.4 **1. a)** 60, 60, 60 **b)** 65, 65 **c)** 50, 80, 130 **d)** 54 **e)** 45, 45 **2. a)** 40 **b)** 32 **c)** 36 **d)** $p = 16$ **3. a)** $x = 80$, $y = 70$, $z = 60$ **b)** $x = 50$, $y = 110$, $z = 100$

Section 13.5 **2. a)** Yes **b)** No **c)** Yes **d)** Yes **e)** No **f)** Yes **g)** Yes **h)** No **i)** Yes

Section 13.6 **1. a)** alternate **b)** alternate **c)** straight line **2.** 135, 45 **3.** 75, 65, 40

Section 13.10 **1. a)** SSS **b)** corresponding **c)** corresponding **d)** by alternate angles **2. a)** $\Delta ADB \cong \Delta CDB$ **b)** $\angle A = \angle C$, $\angle ADB = \angle CDB$, $\angle ABD = \angle CBD$

Section 13.11 **1. a)** 3.6 cm **b)** $\angle K = 50°$, $\angle PLM = 40°$, 9.6 cm, 5.6 cm **c)** 3.2 cm, 39°, 39°, 4.6 cm **2. a)** $\angle C = \angle F$ **b)** $\angle I = \angle J$ or GH = KL **c)** NP = RS or $\angle M = \angle Q$

Section 13.12 **1. a)** ASA **b)** corresponding angles **c)** corresponding sides **d)** corresponding sides **2. a)** ASA **b)** corresponding **c)** alternate

Section 13.16 **1. a)** 5, 22.5 **b)** 16.8, 24.8 **2.** 5

Section 13.17 **1. a)** 300 m **2.** 1.8 m **3.** 11.92 m

CHAPTER 14, page 548
Section 14.4 **1. b)** 12%, 18% **c)** Took, 23% **2. a)** 5.5%, 6.25%, 8.75% **b)** $687.50 **c)** No

Section 14.6 **1. a)** 1966 **b)** 249 935 **c)** 1966 **d)** total number in labour force

Section 14.7 **1. a)** Labels and title

Section 14.8 **1. b)** 3.8 L

Section 14.11 **1. a)** No **b)** No

Section 14.12 **1.** mode **2. a)** 169.2, 169, 160

3. b) 73.03 **c)** 31.6%, 15% **e)** 50%

Section 14.13 **1. a)** 89.33; 251, 83.67; 248, 82.67; 246, 82; 257, 85.67; 230, 76.67 **b)** 248 **2. a)** 84% **b)** 14.5% **c)** 73.7%

Section 14.15 **1. a)** H1, H2, H3, H4, H5, H6, T1, T2, T3, T4, T5, T6 **b)** $\frac{1}{4}$ **c)** $\frac{1}{6}$ **2. a)** $\frac{1}{8}$

Section 14.16 **1. a)** $\frac{1}{24}$ **b)** $\frac{1}{8}$ **2. a)** $\frac{1}{20}$ **b)** $\frac{1}{16}$ **3. a)** $\frac{1}{156}$ **b)** $\frac{1}{16}$ **c)** $\frac{5}{78}$

Section 14.17 **1.** $\frac{1}{495}$ **2.** $\frac{28}{435}$ **3. a)** 0.097 **b)** 0.405

Section 14.18 **1. a)** $\frac{1}{5525}$ **b)** $\frac{2}{17}$ **c)** $\frac{16}{16\,575}$ **2. a)** $\frac{1}{455}$ **b)** $\frac{1}{26}$ **c)** $\frac{1}{26}$

CHAPTER 15, page 551
Section 15.2 **1.** (0, 3), (9, 0), (0, –3), (4, 0), (0, –9), (–4, 0), (0, 2), (–9, 0), (0, 7) **2.** slide right 5, down 4, right 9, up 6, right 4, down 3

Section 15.3 **1.** A'(–2,2), B'(–6,2), C'(–6,–2), D'(0,–7), E'(4,–3) **2.** A'(–3,2), B'(–5,1), C'(–1,–3), D'(–3,–7), E'(4,–4) **3.** A'(2,5), B'(4,4), C'(1,3), D'(11,–12), E'(15,5), F'(9,–4)

Section 15.7 **1.** Final image has vertices (0, –2), (–1, 0), (3, 1). **2. c)** Equal slopes for each pair of opposite sides.

Section 15.11 **2. a)** Q'(–2, 0), R'(0, 3), S'(4,0) **b)** K'(–3, 5), L'(4, 5), M'(4, 1), N'(–3, 1)

Section 15.14 **1. a)** 3:1 **b)** distance from the origin **c)** equal **d)** proportional **e)** 3:1 **2. a)** AA', BB', CC', DD' **b)** (x, y) becomes $(3x, 3y)$ **c)** 3:1 **d)** equal **3. a)** A'(0, 6), B'(6, 0) C'(0, –6), D'(–6, 0) **b)** A'B'∥D'C', A'D'∥B'C'

INDEX OF THEMES AND CURRICULUM AREAS

Use this index to find additional activities that can help you extend your knowledge of a theme or subject area of particular interest to you. These may help you as you complete some of your projects. Where else could you look to find additional information about each theme? What additional themes would you add to this list?

INDEX OF CREATIVE WRITING

Use this index to find creative writing activities of interest to you that you can complete throughout the year. The writing can be completed by working independently, with a partner, or within the group setting. Decide which ideas you would most like to write about.

INDEX OF WORLD RECORDS

Most world records are recorded in the *Guinness Book of World Records*. Throughout the year, you will solve problems that reveal some of these records. The following is a list of some of the records you will find. Add to the list as the year progresses.

INDEX OF TECHNOLOGY

Technology and mathematics are closely connected. The following is a list of the technology discussed in this book. What other kinds of technology involve mathematics skills?

INDEX OF CAREERS

Did you know that almost all careers use mathematics? Shown below is an index of the careers presented in the book. List other careers that involve mathematics.

INDEX OF CANADIAN FACTS

Throughout the year, you have been solving problems that use Canadian facts and figures. Shown below is a list of pages where you can find information about each province.

ACKNOWLEDGMENTS

Photo Credits

12 Tony Freeman/Photo Edit 13 Alexander Meyboom 16 Tony Freeman/Photo Edit 17 **Bottom Left** Alexander Meyboom 31 **Background** FBM Photos/ First Light **Top Left** Robert Phillips/ Image Bank **Centre** Ulli Seer/Image Bank **Bottom Right** Luis Padilla/Image Bank 32 Ontario Crafts Council 34 The Hudson Bay Company 36 Douglas J. Fisher/Image Bank 38 Pizza Pizza 48 Canadian Amateur Hockey Association 50 Courtesy Metropolitan Toronto Police 60 **Left** North York Hydro **Right** MacDonald Dettwiler 63 **Top Right** Toronto Maple Leafs, Maple Leaf Gardens Ltd. **Centre Left** Spectra Star 64 Janeart/Image Bank 73 **Centre Left** *Vertical Assemblage*, 1949, oil canvas, Hortense M. Gordon/Art Gallery of Ontario **Centre Right** National Gallery of Canada, Ottawa **Bottom Left** Alex Colville, *Study For Woman, Dog and Canoe*, March 1982, pencil and sepia ink over photocopy, 8.5 × 11 inches 74 **Top Left** Courtesy All Canadian Sports **Bottom Left** Phillip Hayson/Photo Researchers **Bottom Right** Courtesy Ontario Women's Hockey Association 82 **Centre Left** Rene Lafontaine/ First Light **Centre Right** Gregory Hiesler/Image Bank **Bottom Left** Motorola Inc. **Bottom Right** IBM Corp. 89 **Top and Centre** D.S. Henderson/Image Bank **Inset** Joe Van Os/Image Bank 94 Canadian Amateur Hockey Association 102 Jeff Smith/Image Bank 103 **Left** *The Guinness Book of World Records 1993.* Copyright © Guinness Publishing Ltd 1992. **Centre** *The Canadian World Almanac.* Used with permission of Macmillan Canada. **Right** *Junior Encyclopedia.* By Hurtig Publishers, A McClelland & Stewart Co. Used by permission of the Canadian Publishers, McClelland & Stewart, Toronto. 104 **Top Right** Morton Beebe & Associates/Image Bank **Centre Left/Right** Iron Ore Company of Canada 105 Kay Chernush/Image Bank 122 Ontario Ministry of Transportation 130 Cedarbrae Secondary School 133 Alcan Recycling 151 Bourse de Montréal 161 Ontario Ministry of Transportation 177 **Top** Ken Davies/Masterfile **Bottom** Art Stein/ Photo Researchers 183 **Top Left** Dept. of Horticultural Sciences, OMAF **Top Right** Lorraine Parov/First Light 185 **Top Right** Courtesy Toronto Blue Jays Baseball Club 189 **Bottom Left** Nova Scotia Tourism & Culture **Bottom Right** Canapress 197 Courtesy Quaker Oats Company of Canada 205 Air Canada 207 **Top Right** Imperial Oil Limited 208 Noranda 214 Courtesy Unionville High School Yearbook 217 **Top** Canadian Sport Images 218 Canapress 226 Frank Whitney/Image Bank 228 Government of Newfoundland and Labrador 232 **Bottom Right** IBM Corp. 233 William E. Townsend Jr./Photo Researchers 234 G.J. Vanco, D. Snetivy, Ontario Centre For Materials Research 237 **Centre Left** Japan Information Centre **Centre Right** Ian Burns/ Canapress **Bottom Left** Suzuki Canada **Bottom Right** National Baseball Hall of Fame 238 Air Canada 242 Pat & Tom Leeson/ Photo Researchers 246 **Bottom Left** Peter Miller/Image Bank 254 General Motors 255 **Top** Isaac Greenberg/Photo Researchers **Centre** Jay Freis/Image Bank **Bottom** Gerhard Gscheidle/Image Bank 256 Norco Products 259 **Top Left** Government of Newfoundland and Labrador **Top Centre** Joseph Slugslak, *Thanksgiving*, INAC **Top Right** Biltmore Inc. 265 **Bottom Left** John Foster/Masterfile **Bottom Centre** World Society For The Protection of Animals **Bottom Right** Ontario Ministry of the Environment 266 **Top** Courtesy Scotiabank **Centre** Adam Smith Productions/First Light **Bottom** Don Goss/First Light 272 Art Stein/Photo Researchers 279 Photofest 288 NASA 304 Dr. Jean Lorre/Science Photo Library/Photo Researchers 306 **Top** Ronald E. Royer/Photo Researchers **Bottom** Health & Welfare Canada 310 Steve Chenn/First Light 320 **Left** H. Reinhard/Photo Researchers **Right** Agriculture Canada 322 **Top** Canadian Sport Images **Centre** Gerard Vandystadt/Photo Researchers 329 **Left** Sandy King/Image Bank **Right** Larry J. Pierce/Image Bank 335 Museum of Flight Seattle 368 W. Lynch/Canadian Park Services 369 **Top** Nova Scotia Tourism and Culture **Centre Left** John Sokolowski/Toronto

Argonauts **Centre Right** Dan R. Boyd **Bottom** Ministry of Natural Resources 372 NASA 374 Derek Caron/Masterfile 382 Macdonald Dettwiler 386 Ontario Ministry of Transportation 391 Hewlett Packard 395 **Top** Canadian Sport Images **Bottom** Terje Rakke/Image Bank 398 Courtesy Denon Canada 400 British Film Institute and UNIVERSAL CITY STUDIOS, INC (1989) ALL RIGHTS RESERVED. 404 **Centre Right** George Holton/Photo Researchers 409 Gerhard Gscheidle/Image Bank 410 Hammond Inc. 411 **Bottom Right** Chuck Kuhn/Image Bank 412 Douglas E. Walker/Masterfile 414 Guy Motil/ First Light 416 NASA 422 **Top Left & Right** Photofest 433 **Top** Gerard Vandystadt/Photo Researchers **Centre** David R. Frazier/Photo Researchers **Bottom** Ontario Ministry of Transportation 434 **Top** Garry Black/Masterfile **Centre 1** Mel Degiacomo/Image Bank **Centre 2** Steve Dunwell/The Image Bank **Bottom** Courtesy CTV Television Network Ltd. 436 Major League Marketing Inc. 448 **Left** Mark Grimberg/Image Bank **Centre** Jon Feingersh/Masterfile **Right** David K. Frazier/Photo Researchers 454 Peter Arnold/Winston Churchill High School 456 **Top** U.S. Dept. of Agriculture **Bottom** Agriculture Canada 457 Canadian Sport Images 459 Bob Anderson/Masterfile 460 Peter Arnold, Winston Churchill High School 470 **Left** National Capital Commission **Right** Christine Chew/Neo-Sport Photography 477 Photofest 478 Weinberg-Clark/Image Bank 485 G.J. Images/ Image Bank 486 **Top Right** Yukon Tourism 488 IBM Corp. 492 **Left** Thomas Kitchin/First Light **Right** Joe Szkodzinsky/Image Bank 497 **Bottom** M.C. Escher, *Metamorphosis III (Boats & Fish)*, National Gallery of Canada 500 **Left** Zefa/Masterfile **Centre** Brett Froomer/ Image Bank **Right** Murray Alcosser/Image Bank

All other photographs taken by Jeremy Jones.

Other Credits

68 Chrysler logo used with permission of Chrysler Canada Ltd. Mitsubishi logo used with permission of Mitsubishi Canada Limited. Select Papers logo used with permission of Graphic Papers. Konica logo used with permission of Konica Canada Inc., Films & Cameras. 113 Vancouver Map courtesy of Allmaps Canada Ltd. Copyright Rand McNally. 188 "SOCIABLES" ® Crackers is a trademark of Nabisco Brands Ltd., Toronto, Canada © All Rights Reserved. Catelli package used with permission of Borden Catelli Consumer Products. 199 TOBLERONE ® is a registered trademark of Jacobs Suchard Ltd. Used with permission. 217 **Smarties** is a trademark used under license by Nestlé Canada Inc. 221 President's Choice bottle caps used by permission of Loblaw International Merchants. 248 Baseball card used with permission of Ray Sheppard and Topps, Copyright The Topps Company, Inc. 279 *Equinox* Magazine cover used with permission of Photo/Nats. *Saturday Night* Magazine cover used with permission of *Saturday Night* Magazine. Sound & Vision, Copyright 1985 by 846342 Ontario Ltd. Used with permission. 428 Adidas logo used with permission of Adidas Canada. Québec Nordiques logo used with permission of NHL Enterprises, Inc. Copyright Quebéc Nordiques. Volkswagen logo used with permission of Volkswagen Canada. Walking fingers logo used with permission of Tele-Direct (Publications) Inc. Recycling logo used with permission of American Forest & Paper Association. 448 **Smarties** is a trademark used under license by Nestlé Canada Inc.

*Every effort has been made to contact copyright holders of reprinted materials. Information that will enable the publishers to rectify any error or omission will be welcomed.